JOHN FORD

THE MAN AND HIS FILMS

John Ford, ca. 1930.

JOHN FORD

THE MAN AND HIS FILMS

TAG GALLAGHER

UNIVERSITY OF CALIFORNIA PRESS / BERKELEY • LOS ANGELES • LONDON

Stills courtesy of the Robert S. Birchard Collection,
Graham Greene, Richard Koszarski, Anna Lee, Hal
Roach, the Lilly Library (Indiana University), the
library of the Academy of Motion Picture Arts and
Sciences, the Wisconsin Center for Film and The-
ater Research, Columbia Pictures, Metro-Goldwyn-
Mayer, Paramount Pictures Corporation, Republic
Pictures, RKO Pictures, 20th Century–Fox Film
Corporation, United Artists, Universal Pictures,
and Warner Brothers.

University of California Press
Berkeley and Los Angeles, California

University of California Press, Ltd.
London, England

© 1986 by The Regents of the University of California

Printed in the United States of America
2 3 4 5 6 7 8 9

Library of Congress Cataloging in Publication Data

Gallagher, Tag.
   John Ford.

   Filmography: p.
   Bibliography: p.
   Includes index.
   1. Ford, John, 1894–1973. I. Title.
PN1998.A3F5698   1984   791.43'0233'0924 83-18047
ISBN 0-520-05097-5
ISBN 0-520-06334-1 (paper)

Contents

Preface

*In the annals of American film, no name shines
more brightly than that of John Ford. Director and
filmmaker for more than half a century, he stands
preeminent in his craft—not only as a creator of
individual films of surpassing excellence, but as a
master among those who transformed the early
motion pictures into a compelling new art form that
developed in America and swept the world. As an
interpreter of the Nation's heritage, he left his personal
stamp indelibly printed on the consciousness of whole
generations both here and abroad. In his life and in
his work, John Ford represents the best in American
films and the best in America.*

    *—Commendation on the presidential
    Medal of Freedom given John Ford in 1973*

John Ford's career—from 1914 to 1970—spanned almost the
entire history of the motion picture industry, and for most of that time he
was recognized as America's finest moviemaker. His movies told good stories, had vivid characters, provoked thought, kindled down-home charms;
and his own personality was apparent in them. His compositional eloquence
made dialogue virtually unnecessary—scarcely for dearth of scripted richness, but because literary structure was only a single aspect of the intricate
formal beauty and intelligence of his cinema.

It is this immense intelligence that critics have largely ignored. Ford's
apologists laud his instincts and emotions, as though he were an artist unconsciously, unintentionally. His detractors decry his sentiment and slapstick, label him racist, militarist, and reactionary, ignoring the subtleties
between extremes, the double-leveled discourses, the oeuvre's obsessive
plea for tolerance.

Fault for misapprehending Ford's intelligence lies partly with Ford himself, who hid beneath masks; partly with Hollywood, whose facility is often
deceptive; but chiefly with our culture's disinclination to take movies as
seriously as books. To propose that John Ford was as major an artist as ever
produced by America is to invite ridicule, at least today.

Perhaps I, as author of the present study, am constitutionally prejudiced in Ford's favor. I hope so. I can claim similar ethnic background, immense empathy for these movies (seen dozens of times over decades, and thus now experienced quite differently than by one viewing them for the first time), and I have wished to be useful more toward increasing appreciation and pleasure than toward revealing faults.

For assistance in obtaining prints and in research I am indebted to Joshua Bagley (United Artists), Myron Bresnick and Bea Herrmann (Audio Brandon), Kevin Brownlow, James Card, Hal Cranton (MCA-Universal), Paul Cremo, Dennis Doph (Columbia Pictures), Dan Ford, David Grossman, Joseph Judice, Kit Parker Films, Richard Koszarski, Miles Kreuger, Elaine MacDevitt (USIA), Patrick McInroy, William Murdock (U.S. Department of Defense), Bill Murphy (National Archives), Grafton Nunes, George Pratt, Adam Reilly, Patrick Sheehan and Barbara Humphries (Library of Congress), Charles Silver (Museum of Modern Art), Mort Slakoff (Viacom), Anthony Slide, John Sonneborn, John Stone, Saundra Taylor and the staff of the Lilly Library, Indiana University, and the staffs of the New York Public Library–Lincoln Center, the Free Library of Philadelphia Theater Collection, the Czechoslovak Film Archives, and the Wisconsin Center for Film and Theater Research. The American Council of Learned Societies supplied a travel grant. Olive Carey, Harry Carey, Jr., Ruth Clifford Cornelius, Cecil McLean de Prida, Gabriel Figueroa, Barbara Ford, Graham Greene, Anna Lee, George O'Brien, Leon Selditz, and John Stafford kindly shared their memories with me. I am especially grateful to the late Frank C. Baker.

Leo Braudy, John Fell, Brian Henderson, Bruce F. Kawin, William Rothman, and Michael Wood contributed invaluable editorial assistance. Gerald Mast persisted through many months of painstaking advice and encouragement; the book owes much to him. Ernest Callenbach, Mary Lamprech, and Mary Anne Stewart, at the University of California Press, have given the book a precision and beauty it would otherwise lack.

This book is dedicated to my parents and my wife, Phoebe Erb, and to William K. Everson, without whom much would be impossible.

1 Prologue:
Youth and Apprenticeship

*. . . man's unceasing search for something
he can never find.*   JOHN FORD

*I shall almost always be wrong, when
I conceive of a man's character as being
all of one piece.*   STENDHAL

Because John Ford shrouded himself in mystery, his life and personality remain inscrutable. His was a complex, perhaps multiple, individuality. Direct and devious, charismatic and sardonic, amusing and caustic, he generally dominated those around him, or at least retained his independence. He read voraciously, history especially, surrounding himself with books; his memory was virtually photographic, and he could get by in French, German, Gaelic, Italian, Spanish, Yiddish, Japanese, Hawaiian, and Navaho. But he posed as illiterate, hiding his erudition, as he hid his wealth under baggy clothes and his sensitivity under a tough crust. He was a man of many masks, a joiner who stayed an outsider, a man of action self-consciously reflective, a big man, Irish and Catholic. There will probably never be an adequate biography of John Ford, nor even an adequate character sketch, for there were as many of him as there were people who knew him.

Beginnings

"A cruel, hard place," a Ford character calls Ireland, and so it was for Ford's father, Sean, born in Spiddal, on the Galway coast, in 1854.[1]

Years of famine, typhus, mass evictions, and suppressed revolts had intensified the sufferings of a people already rendered destitute by a tiny plutocracy alien in race, religion, and language. Hope lay in escape, and Sean,
after a visit to the harbor chapel, escaped to America in 1872, sponsored by
Michael Connelly, a cousin who, after escaping enslavement by Blackfeet,
deserting the Union Army, and laying track for the Union Pacific, had established himself as a bootlegger in Portland, Maine, by marrying a widow.
Sean Americanized his name to John A. Feeney* and eventually succeeded
to Connelly's business. His dingy restaurant-saloons down near Portland's
wharves and warehouses were natural gathering places for the Irish, and
John Feeney became a ward leader. He would greet new immigrants, help
them settle and find jobs, register them as citizens and voters, and so built
himself a political base. (A nephew, Joseph Connolly, rose to be a judge on
Maine's Supreme Court.)

On July 31, 1875, Sean married Barbara "Abby" Curran, a distant cousin.
Born in Kilronan, in the Aran Islands, Abby had grown up on a mainland
farm, not far from her future husband, whom, however, she had not met
before emigrating to Portland in 1872. She was taught neither to read nor
write English (although she could write Gaelic) and her semi-illiteracy perhaps contributed to her son's ambivalence toward intellectuality.

In a season of prosperity, Feeney settled his family in Cape Elizabeth,
Maine, on 190 acres of land. And here in an old farmhouse on Charles E.
Jordan Road was born the future John Ford, youngest of six children surviv-
ing infancy. Although Ford went through his youth as John Augustine
Feeney, and later claimed even on passports that his name was Sean Aloysius O'Feeney, and although most references, including Ford himself, cite
the year as 1895, the town clerk registered him as John Martin Feeney, born
February 1, 1894, and this information appears also on his tombstone and
baptismal records. John was baptized March 13, 1894, at St. Dominic's, 163
Danforth Street; Edward and Julia Feeney were the sponsors. Aloysius was
the name John chose at Confirmation. As a boy he was called John, Johnny,
or Jack, and as he grew he acquired almost a dozen additional nicknames,
while bestowing nicknames of his own on all his friends.

"We were a comfortable, lower middle class family," John Ford recalled.
"We ate better than we do now."[2] "Father," said brother Frank, "was the
greatest actor who ever lived. When he told a story of the elves and banshees
and fairies, it was like a real experience."[3] Gaelic was often spoken in the
house, midst frequent spats over pronunciation. Ford's mother, called
Nana, ruled the home with an easy, quiet, but iron authority, undiminished
even in her sons' manhood. She held the purse, too, and when her husband
went to the races she would dole out one dollar per race—and collect the

---

*The Gaelic had various spellings: Ó Fianna, Ó Fidhne, Ó Fiannaidhe (Andrew Sinclair,
John Ford: A Biography [New York: Dial, 1979], p. 3).

Figure 1. Genealogy

EDWARD O'FIENNE m. BARBARA MORRIS   NICHOLAS CURRAN m. MARGARET O'FLAHERTY
  b. Ireland   (of Killanin barony)   b. Ireland   b. Ireland

  PATRICK O'FIENNE m. MARY CURRAN   FRANCIS CURRAN m. BRIDGET McLAUGHLIN
      b. Ireland   b. Ireland   b. Ireland   b. Ireland

          JOHN A. FEENEY = m. c. 7.3.75 = BARBARA (ABBY) CURRAN
            b. 1854 S. Galway   Portland   b. 1856 Kilronan, Aran
            d. 6.22.36 Portland   d. 3.26.33 Portland

—MARY AGNES (MAIME) = m. 4.9.00 Portland = John E. McLean b. c. 1876
  b. 6.15.76

          ┌Cecelia A. McLean (or McClain) = m. Lorenzo de Prida
          └Mary McLean

—DELIA (DELLA)
  b. 1878; d. 4.18.81 (measles)

—PATRICK H. = m.10.14.12 Portland = Katherine A. Devine
  b. 12.24.79   b. 1879 Portland

          ┌Mary Feeney
          └Francis Feeney

—FRANK T. = m. 1. = = = Della Cole
  b. 8.14.81 Portland
  d. 9.6.53 Los Angeles   └Phil b. 10.16.02 Portland. d. 1976 Los Angeles

          = m. 2 = = = Elsie Van Name

                    ┌Robert b. c. 1912
                    └Francis, Jr. ("Billy") b. c. 1921

          = m. 3. = = = Mary Armstrong

—BRIDGET
  b. 10.4.83 Portland. d. 9.2.84 Portland (cholera)

—BARBARA (ABBY)   John E. Robinson m. Delia Malia
  b. 2.4.88 d. infancy.   b. Portland   b. Portland

—EDWARD FRANCIS = m. 3.6.16 Portland = Mary T. Robinson b. 1896 Portland
  b. 2.22.89
  Cape Elizabeth   ┌Chuck
  d. 1.15.69   ├Sheila
                        └5 others

—JOSEPHINE CECILIA
  b. 12.31.91 Cape Elizabeth

—JOANNA (HANNAH)   C. E. W. Smith m. Fannie Roper
  b. 12.13.92. d. infancy   b. S. Carolina | b. N. Carolina

—JOHN MARTIN = = m. 7.3.20 Los Angeles = = Mary McBride Smith
  b. 2.1.94   b. 9.4.93 Laurinburg, N.C.
  Cape Elizabeth   d. August, 1979
  d. 8.31.73
  Palm Desert, Calif.
    (cancer)   ┌PATRICK MICHAEL ROPER = m. 1942 = Jane Mulvaney, b. 1921 Maine
                      │ b. 4.3.21 Hollywood
—DANIEL   │   ┌Timothy John. b. 2.1.44
  b. 2.17.98   │   └Daniel Sargent. b. 2.12.45
  d. infancy   │
                      │   = m. 2 = Carroal Anderson
                      │
                      └BARBARA NUGENT = m. 5.31.52 = Ken Curtis
                          b. 12.16.22   div. 7.23.64
                          Hollywood

winnings, if there were any. Her sons kissed her when they entered the house and when they left; more effective than any whipping was her refusal of their kiss when she was displeased. Jack was her sweetheart. He looked like her and held her in awe, and in later years, when the two were a continent apart, claimed a psychic bond. "She would send me messages. There were quite a few instances of that."[4] Probably from her, and as the youngest, he acquired the religious fervor of his childhood. Often he would rise before six and brave twenty-below weather to serve Mass. They also shared a love for movies. "As a kid I was fascinated by the nickelodeons of that period. Any time I got a nickel or a dime I would go to the movies."[5]

Feeney family fortunes tended to fluctuate with Maine's dry laws. Around 1898 they were obliged to sell the farm and, after a succession of residences, take a large third-floor apartment at 23 Sheridan Street, Portland. Sister Mary, eighteen years older than Jack, moved in with her two children when her husband died, and these, with the Myers and Mahoneys who shared the building, brought to sixteen the number of children. Dinner was open to anyone at the Feeneys. Harbor and bay could be glimpsed from the housetop, and Jack would spend hours at a nearby observatory tower, gazing out to sea. He loved the sea. "Ever since I was about four years old, I owned a boat. Some old wreck came up, and we caulked it with tar and everything, and I took that, and as I got old, I got a different boat."[6] Summers were spent sailing off Peak's Island, where Jack's father's sister had a house.

An attack of diphtheria at eight required a lengthy convalescence, and delayed Jack a year at Emerson Grammar School, but it gave him in return a sensitivity and love for books, such as he later depicted with young Huw Morgan in *How Green Was My Valley*. Nonetheless, he was an indifferent student, never opening his schoolbooks at home, and getting by through listening in class and a retentive memory; his 1906 report card graded him "fair" or "poor" in almost every subject. At age eleven or twelve his father took him to Ireland, and he went to school there for several months; instruction was in Gaelic and all the boys except Jack wore long red petticoats. Jack's father, or Gramps as he was called, took frequent trips to Ireland, whereas Nana, who had endured a terribly miserable crossing in steerage when she first came to America, was never willing to return.

Gramps was six feet two and vaguely resembled C. Aubrey Smith. "When the flag passes, take off your cap," he instructed his son at a Fourth of July parade. "But I don't have a cap on." "Then cross yourself, damnit!"

Gramps, despite his saloons, was a regimented drinker. He never drank during the day, only at dinner and breakfast. Jack was fond of relating the breakfast ceremony that would occur aboard ship when he took his father to Ireland in the 1930s. The crew would gather at the portholes to watch as Gramps ordered. "'I would like a glass of orange juice. I live part of the year in California and I want California orange juice. I want oatmeal, four eggs fried, and a double order of bacon and while you're at it put in a slice of ham.' The waiter would hesitate and wait, and he'd say, 'And bring me a drink of Irish whiskey. Bring the bottle.' He'd take a sip of the orange juice, then he'd pour himself a tumbler full of Irish whiskey, then another sip of the orange juice. He'd take that glass of Irish whiskey and down it in one gulp. Then he'd consume the whole meal. That's the only drink he'd have until supper time."[7]

Jack was reputed for drawing caricatures. "As a kid, I thought I was going to be an artist; I used to sketch and paint a great deal and I think, for a kid, I did pretty good work—at least I received a lot of compliments about it."[8] Toward girls he was shy; it took him days to get up nerve to ask for a date. He was tall and lanky, with terrible eyesight and thick glasses, but popular among his male companions. He engaged in track and baseball and made honorable mention on the state football team ("Bull Feeney, the human battering ram"—he broke his own nose and mangled his ear), despite finding himself frequently ejected from games for such antics as carrying a teammate across the scrimmage line. At Portland High he took two years of Latin, three of French, one of physics and biology; he did poorly in math—in fact he flunked algebra twice and never in his life did he achieve ease with numbers or possess any sense of chronology. But he drew honors in English and history, wrote a parody of the school song, and sold a story he had written for $25. His four-year average was eighty-four. While he never discovered himself in high school, he did have a reputation for brilliance and wit. Once a crowd gathered to watch the baseball team play bloomer girls, and Jack was spotted among the latter, in bloomers and wig.[9]

There was a feisty competitiveness among Portland's immigrant cultures—the Irish, Italians, Poles, and Jews—and a spirit of mutual tolerance united them in opposition to the Yankees. Jack picked up Yiddish from his friends and would occasionally attend synagogue for the music. The Ku Klux Klan at one point made an attempt to establish itself, but failed. There were only about a dozen black families among Portland's seventy thousand people. A large tent the Klan erected was blown down in a fierce storm, and Gramps, staring at it the next morning on his way home from church, huffed, "Well, *that* wasn't built on a rock!"[10] The blacks, Ford recalled decades later, "lived with us. They didn't live in barrios. Our next-door neighbors were black. There was no difference, no racial feeling, no prejudice. My sister Maime's closest friend was a Mrs. Johnson who was black. A wonderful woman."[11]

Jack worked mornings for two hours before school driving a fish wagon—the saloon was out of bounds—and later he worked as delivery boy and publicist for a shoe company. Evenings he would usher in the balcony of the Jefferson Theater or at Peak's Gem. Theater was a passion: he would come home and act out the whole play for his family, every part, every voice.

Jack graduated from high school on June 18, 1914. His ambitions to enter Annapolis were thwarted when he failed the entrance examination, so he looked into an athletic scholarship at the University of Maine, Orono. The curriculum was unattractive: he had had most of the subjects in high school and would have been required to major in agriculture. In addition he had to rise at 5:30 A.M. and wait tables at breakfast, and the third or fourth morning, jeered at with racial slurs, he slugged a student and got sent home. He sought the advice of his high school history teacher, William B. Jack (whom he later claimed was the most influential figure in his life after his father), and Nana unearthed from her green keepchest an exciting proposition from California. Jack headed west—just for the summer.* "I remember the last night on the train. I was coming tourist, and I had to go without dinner because I had no money in my pocket. So I arrived penniless, as the expression goes."[12] Perhaps he was conscious of repeating his father's emigration west to join an elder relative, for brother Frank had made a name for himself in Hollywood, and had stirred Jack's imagination. "I stole from my shoe factory the sole pair of seven-league boots there, and I crossed the Atlantic to join him."[13]

Francis Ford

Born August 14, 1881, and thus twelve and a half years older than Jack, Frank T. Feeney was always restless.[14] He had carved up desks at school, married suddenly at sixteen, run off to war (getting only as far as Tennessee, whence his father's political influence extracted him from a cholera camp), and then joined a circus—and disappeared. More than ten years passed, until the day Nana and Jack ran home all excited: they had found Frank—on the Greeley Theater's screen, in a Melies western! Through a New York agent, the prodigal was located and came home in cashmere and a Stutz Bearcat. After years of vaudeville, park benches, and film-mouthing (actors stood behind the screen and improvised dialogue), Frank had landed in the movies, had worked in hundreds of pictures for Centaur, Edison, Melies, and Ince, in New Jersey, Texas, and California, and now was a top star-director-writer with his own company at Universal.

*Various sources, among them the information in the *Motion Picture Directory* annuals from 1920 and 1921 (which Ford would have supplied himself) and also Ford's recollections of working on films shot that summer, indicate that Ford was in California in July. But other sources suggest that the days he spent at the University of Maine were in September. It has not been possible to reconcile this contradiction. It is possible—although no evidence supports it—that Ford went west in July, returned for the University of Maine in September, and then went west again. This explanation would explain why Ford at times claimed he took the train direct and at other times claimed that he worked his way west and stopped in Arizona to work as a cowboy for $13 a week. He did not go out to Frank alone but with a friend, Joe (either Joe McDonald or Joe Connolly): there is a letter to Jack from Grace Cunard, dated February 1917, in which she writes how she "promised both your mothers that I would do my best for you." (John Ford Papers, Lilly Library, Indiana University.)

Francis Ford and Anna Little, *The Outcast* (101-Bison, 1912). Typical use of a long shot with foreground figures.

Francis Ford and Grace Cunard, *Lucille Love* (Universal, 1914).

Along the way, he had changed his name to Francis Ford, inspired by the car,* to avoid stigmatizing his family.

Teamed with Grace Cunard—his red-haired, green-eyed leading lady, co-writer, and lover—the dapper, handsome Francis (five feet eleven, 160 pounds, fair skin, black hair, grey eyes[15]) was about to score his greatest mark in a virtually virgin genre: the mystery. First in a series of separate two-reelers, then in fabulously successful serials (*Lucille Love, The Broken Coin*, etc.),** detective Ford chased jewel-thief Cunard through fantastical principalities in uninhibited, peril-laden, "rattling good" melodramas ("She hates yet loves me, and everybody knows that a woman in that frame of mind is liable to do most any desperate thing."[16]).

It is not too surprising, then, that young Jack Feeney held his big brother in awe and preferred adventure in the movies to platitudes at college. So for three years Jack shadowed Frank. He could not have had a more expert teacher in every aspect of the craft; and no other major director ever got a more rigorous training. "He was a great cameraman," said John Ford in 1966. "There's nothing they're doing today—all these things that are supposed to be so new—that he hadn't done; he was really a good artist, a wonderful musician, a hell of a good actor, a good director—Johnny of all trades—and *master* of all; he just couldn't concentrate on one thing too long. But he was the only influence *I* ever had, working in pictures."[17]

Francis Ford's importance is substantial, if obscure: his most popular and personal pictures are apparently lost. Ford was greatly responsible for the westerns released beginning in 1912 under the "101 Bison" trademark (at first weekly, then twice weekly). The 101 Bisons, for their attention to minor detail, use of action to define character, exaltation of story for its own sake, epic photography, and spectacular massed battle scenes, excited the entire industry and inaugurated the great epoch of American cinema. The 101 Bisons were also the basis of the career of Ford's boss, the soon-to-be-famous Thomas Ince. But Ince, though he successfully promoted himself as a creative artist, was essentially a producer; he "invented" the production system, in which a "shooting script" details each shot and grimace prior to filming. And it was the orneriness of Francis Ford, Ince's only director besides himself until 1913, that provoked Ince to such measures. Ince, a major stockholder in his company, persistently attempted to conceal Ford's contribu-

*This is Frank's version, as given to Wilkinson. John Ford told Bogdanovich that Frank had replaced a drunk thespian named Francis Ford, then could not shake loose from the name; the original Ford supposedly showed up years later claiming to be "Frank Feeney" and in need of a job.

**Serials were tied to newspaper circulation wars, the weekly episodes being printed in novelized form. *The Adventures of Kathlyn*, debuting December 29, 1913, is considered the first serial (as opposed to "series"), with Kathlyn Williams starring for Selig and Max Annenberg. Hearst came next: *Dolly of the Dailies* (January 31, 1914, Mary Fuller, Edison), then *The Perils of Pauline* (Pearl White, Pathé-Eclectic, March 31, 1914). *Lucille Love* began April 14, 1914.

tions and even to pass them off as his own (as he was to do subsequently with William S. Hart); and he attempted to "steal" Grace Cunard from Ford's troupe. So Ford jumped to Universal.*

Contemporaries praised Ford's 101 Bisons for their vigorous action, picturesque style, and skill in showing action over vast distances— much the same remarks one finds in Jack Ford's early reviews. But surviving Bisons evince—in addition to specific shots later imitated by Jack—more significant similarities. *The Burning Brand*'s complicated flashback structures define the hero's psychology against varying truths of past and present, anticipating *Liberty Valance*. And the essentials of John Ford's acting style can be found in Francis's pictures: *relaxed relating*. Actors are, moreover, directed with minimal rehearsal, which gives freshness to characters and a degree of autonomy, promoting our belief that they possess lives independent of the screenplay or the director. It is difficult to imagine either Ford manipulating an actor the way Griffith did—for instance, Mae Marsh (in *Intolerance*'s courtroom) or Lillian Gish (in the closet in *Broken Blossoms***)—or "staring" at them with a brutality in cutting and framing that seems often to aim, like Hitchcock, for the maximum in sensationalism. And both Griffith and Hitchcock had a fondness for high angles and sudden close-ups that makes them seem rapacious alongside the Fords' low or level angles, gentler cutting, and more respectful distance.

Personal descriptions of Francis at the peak of his fame resemble later ones of John. Universal's *Weekly* described Francis as taciturn and active, "but running underneath this silence is a stream of humor that may be called distinctively Fordesquian."[18] Richard Willis, in *Motion Picture Magazine*, June 1915, wrote similarly: "Under the quiet, almost sarcastic manner, there is deep seriousness, and below the veil of indifference there is one of the warmest hearts imaginable."[19] Without much to say to strangers, but with ready smile and soft voice, "'Fordie' . . . speaks to the people who work with him as though he loved them. He never boasts; in fact, he is inclined to speak of his work with levity, and he gives a wrong impression to those who do not know him well."[20]

But this does not sound like John: "Good mixer without trying, good fellow without essaying to be particularly good—he is always natural and

*The "101 Bison" trademark went to Universal as well. The New York Motion Picture Company, Ince's employer, had agreed to merge into the new Universal combine, then pulled out. A "war" ensued, with the two staging raids on each other's facilities and Ince placing a cannon at the mouth of St. Inez canyon. But NYMPCO lost the court battle, along with the now-coveted trademark and Francis Ford, who had told Universal's Carl Laemmle that he, not Ince, deserved most of the artistic credit. Westerns, incidentally, had been issued in immense quantities (dozens per week) since 1909 and before, and were marketed in three distinct genres: Indian, Pioneer, and Civil War. In mid-1913, a year and a half before *The Birth of a Nation*, Universal announced that Civil War pictures and other westerns were stale, used-up genres and that no more would be made.

**The example is no less valid, even if Gish herself was responsible for the level of her hysteria.

always himself."[21] Indeed, in later years, the earnest John found Frank's relaxed, easygoing ways something of an irritant. Frank's superabundance of talents combined badly with streaks of impracticality. He played violin, sculpted, painted huge canvases in his garage—and would impulsively cut out sections admired by chance visitors—but lacked the stick-to-itiveness that was John's key to success. Frank's passion was variety. He enjoyed many women, through three wives and numerous affairs. And he loved makeup and disguises. Ince, writing in 1919, thought him among "the most finished of all pioneer film performers. It was nothing for him to play an Indian hero in the morning and make up as Abraham Lincoln* for the afternoon's work."[22] Often he played several roles in the same picture.

In photography, though Frank would occasionally use superimpressions to illustrate thought (as early as 1911) and generally had quietly watchful camerawork, he also (unlike John) indulged experiment for its own sake: typical, rather than exceptional, was a scene in *The Twins' Double* (1914) in which Cunard appears on screen simultaneously in three roles, in a double exposure within a triple exposure. And, again unlike John, Frank reveled in the unconventional, the shocking, macabre, and occult. The problems these caused him with producers in an era of bourgeois tastes were aggravated by carelessness with money, problems with drink, and a tendency to walk out when he could not do things his own way.

Frank flirted with success, leaving Universal to go independent, starting and failing with his own studio midst the postwar depression, returning desperately ill from the South Seas to find his wife had run off with his business manager after selling off the studio and other assets, but rebounding to form a filmmaking cooperative. That group's seven members each took turns at every job—camera, acting, directing, property—and received equal pay. They would sketch stories on postcards to suit locations, and sometimes sell for $60,000 a movie made for $2,000. "In the years we were together," said Frank Baker,** "we were just like a complete family. I don't think I ever heard a harsh word or an unkind thing said."[23]

In *Four from Nowhere*, one of thirty-some maximally cheap features Francis Ford directed in the twenties, there is a scene in which his character, awaiting revenge, sits alone in long shot in a dark-shadowed room. "Siegfried Kracauer could write a caption for it that would make it look like a collaboration between Freud and Pabst," wrote William K. Everson,[24] and perhaps the image represents one side of Francis Ford. But presently the camera cuts back, after a grim, cathartic conclusion, and one may (or

*Both Ford brothers were passionate Lincoln scholars. Francis also won note as a Lincoln impersonator, playing the role in at least seven pictures between 1912 and 1915.

**Frank Baker, an Australian anthropologist, sailor, and filmmaker, met the ill Francis Ford at Pangopango and accompanied him home. He became a bit player, quite obscure in Hollywood. But his tales, throughout this book, of his encounters with John Ford are illuminating, especially if taken as representative of Ford's impact on hundreds of others in his life.

Francis Ford, skeletons, and Grace Cunard, *The Broken Coin* (Universal, 1915).

may not) notice a secretary trying to hear what is going on inside. This sort of gag, unstressed, contrastive, and iconoclastic, became a *John* Ford signature. Both brothers brought charm to their pictures, and Frank's credo—keep the audience "glad they're seeing the picture"[25]—became John's.

Frank abandoned directing in 1927.* He aimed to emulate Wallace Beery and "get away from the dramatic and essay a comedy character."[26] Through more than a hundred small roles, this character evolved into a coonskin drunk, a child-of-nature who rarely spoke, but whose spittle could ring a spittoon clear across a room. Even under his brother's direction, Frank's routines were completely his own, and his "Brother Feeney" character's expressive gestures entrance his fans today as surely as any of Chaplin's or Keaton's.

"In some ways," said Frank Baker, Francis "was very much like John, but he and Jack didn't get on very well. That was a funny part of John Ford. Everything that John Ford did, I could see the reflection of Frank. Camera angles and different touches. He'd say, 'How do you like that?' And I'd say 'I've seen that before,' and he'd go as cold as anything. He had an amazing admiration for his brother, because Frank was about thirteen years older

---

*His last, *Call of the Heart* (January 1928), starred Dynamite, a dog; his other Dynamite movie, *Wolf's Trail*, has the odd distinction (Richard Koszarski tells me) of having the best cost-to-earnings ratio of *any* Universal feature (Frank made them *cheaply*)—and a speak-to-the-grave scene anticipating those in later John Fords.

Francis Ford as Lincoln, *On Secret Service* (Kay Bee, 1912).

than John, but he was completely jealous of him. He realized that this isn't me. I'm just walking in his footsteps, because I've always considered Frank the most picture-wise man I've ever known. Frank was not interested in making money, not in the least. He was an experimenter, always. Jack did the same thing, but he had this awful . . . I can say something that perhaps most people would give me the horse laugh for. I've studied John Ford for so long, and I realized that he was two completely different people. The real John Ford is so much different from the John Ford we know, the tough,

Francis Ford in his last role, as drummer, in *The Sun Shines Bright* (1952).

ruthless, sarcastic individual. The real John Ford was very kind, but he was afraid of that. And the John Ford we know is a legend, a living legend who was created by John Ford himself to protect the other John Ford, the sympathetic, sentimental, soft John Ford. I am quite assured now that John Ford was perhaps suffering tremendously from a very great inferiority complex, and sitting right at the foundation of that inferiority complex was his brother, Francis. He knew that this is where it all came from, and he took it out on Frank for the rest of his life.

"But John Ford, there was a man in my estimation. He had the touch of greatness. He was perhaps a great man, John Ford. There were many sides to him that people never saw . . ."[27]

Apprenticeship

When Jack Ford arrived in California in July 1914, Frank put him to work as "assistant, handyman, everything," at $12 a week, on the final episode of *Lucille Love*. His first (acting) credit came four months later, as Dopey in Frank's *The Mysterious Rose*.

Frank liked his action grit-real, so injuries, including at least one death, were frequent. But he paid bonuses for any injuries the camera could record; and as Jack would do too, Frank would goad his extras into surpassing themselves:

Now boys, remember you are not in a drawing room; don't bow to each other or apologize if you should happen to take a piece of skin away from the man you are fighting. This is to be the real thing—go to it. Who will roll down that bank? Who will fall off a horse? I don't believe one of you dare—huh! You will?—and you will? Good! I thought there might be one or two of you who did not want a cushion to fall on—no, I don't want any more. Listen, boys, a dollar for a bloody nose and two for a black eye.[28]

(This last line was echoed twenty-five years later in *How Green Was My Valley*.)

But Frank took care of Jack. He blew up a dynamite-wired desk where Jack was sitting by firing a cannonball through the tent. He had him jump seventy-five feet from a freight car rolling along a trestle; had him blown up in a car by mining the road; had him dodging shells on a Confederate battlefield before bouncing a powder grenade off his head (for a close shot)—it exploded just beneath his chin. "That was a close thing," Frank told him in the hospital. "Another second and audiences would have realized I was using a double."[29]

Two decades later, in *Judge Priest*, Jack had Frank playing a drunk resting on a wheelbarrow. But there was a rope tied to it, and, as a carriage drove off, Frank went suddenly careening down the street, swallowing his chaw at the first jolt. "That was for the grenade!" Jack scolded, just as if it had been the day before.[30]

Jack's roommate at the Virginia Apartments, 6629½ Hollywood Boulevard, was Edmund Richard "Hoot" Gibson, the future cowboy star from Nebraska, who was then a wrangler and occasional double for Harry Carey. In 1959 they met again:

Jack was worse Irish than me [Gibson recalled]. That time he wanted to play "My Wild Irish Rose" on the player piano and I wanted to play something else, I forget what, he picked up the piano stool and broke it on my head. And it was my piano!

It wasn't "My Wild Irish Rose" [retorted Ford], and there was no choice. He had exactly one roll for that piano—"Dardanella." He'd sit at that thing playing "Dardanella" morning, noon and night. Even now . . . anytime I have the black luck to hear "Dardanella," I notice my fists are clenched and I'm gritting my teeth. One night I had to get some sleep; I had a tough morning ahead. There he sat and his "Dardanella." Sure I knocked him off the piano stool and smashed it on his head. And then he came at me with a bottle.[31]

Ford was fond of telling how he played a bespectacled Klansman in *The Birth of a Nation*, fell off his horse, and woke up with Griffith bending over him. "Are you all right, son?" "I guess so." Griffith called for some whiskey, Jack objected that he did not drink, and Griffith replied, "It's for me."[32] Ford did not get to know Griffith until after the latter's retirement (and he was one of the few who attended Griffith's wake), but he was mightily impressed by Griffith's great epic: "I went to the premiere of *The Birth of a Nation* and at the end I actually strained my voice yelling. Before it, everything had been static. But then there were little things. Like when Henry Walthall comes home from the war and Mae Marsh has put cotton on her dress, pretending it is ermine, and while they talk he picks little pieces of cotton off the dress, shyly."[33] Taking time for "little things" became Ford's passion, too.

It is improbable, however, that the sensitivity in Jack's blue eyes was noticeable to many in the teens and twenties. Despites fights and firings he had graduated to Frank's chief assistant, and often his cameraman, by 1917. But toughness was his dominant characteristic. He had a long, powerful stride, with an arm swing, and even at age twenty he had impressed his bosses by the way he cursed and bullied the hardened cowhands who served as extras. His debut as director, he later claimed, occurred when he was obliged to substitute for his drunk brother and to entertain visiting dignitaries by having cowboys ride back and forth, take falls, and finally burn

Shooting the Ford-Cunard serial, *The Broken Coin* (1915). Francis and Grace, kneeling; Eddie Polo, on back, Jack Ford, hand in mouth. From the Robert S. Birchard Collection.

down a town. This was in 1916, and Carl Laemmle supposedly later said, "Give Jack Ford the job—he yells good." Ford's niece Cecil (or Cecile) McLean de Prida, says Laemmle's nephew Eddie was begging for a chance to direct, so Laemmle let Ford and Eddie direct one together.[34] No details of this picture are known. But Universal in these years was almost like a big family. Jack was close friends with Eddie and occasionally played little jokes even on Carl Laemmle himself.

Officially Jack graduated to director as Frank's star began to wane. With his brother's company Jack made a satiric action picture with a sentimental twist: the hero (Jack Ford) needs money to buy his mother a home in Ireland. Universal publicity gave *The Tornado* (two-reel 101 Bison, March 3, 1917) a good boost. His second movie, again with Frank's company, *The Trail of Hate*, was called "thrilling . . . teeming with life and color and action" by *Exhibitors' Trade Review*,[35] while Universal's *Weekly* ran a still from his *next* film, explaining, "When Jack has finished a picture his players are not fit for publication."[36] After the third, *The Scrapper*, in which he copied Francis by staging a fight in a whorehouse, the *Weekly* remarked (probably facetiously):

> For a long time people have said, as they heard the name "Ford" in connection with a picture: "Ford? Any relation to Francis?" Very soon, unless all indications of the present time fail, they will be saying: "Ford? Any relation to Jack?"[37]

The Fighting Brothers (1918). Hoot Gibson, Pete Morrison. From the Robert S. Birchard Collection.

Frank, in later years, used to say he was glad to get rid of Jack, was fed up with him. Jack was always getting into emotional arguments, would fight with everyone; he was a damn nuisance, a dunderhead that couldn't be relied on.[38] "As a prop man he 'stunk'; as an assistant director, he was worse, and as an actor . . . well, such a ham! When I would tell Jack to put a chair in the corner for a scene, Jack would turn and say, 'Joe, get a chair and put it in the corner'; Joe would turn around and holler, 'Dutch, get a chair and put it in the corner'; Dutch would turn around and holler, 'Jake, get a chair . . . .'"

Frank got his own chair; but, he added, anticipating the theme of *The Long Gray Line*, Jack was "durable," and he stressed the word. Jack's first film, "wasn't bad except for the acting," but the fourth one was "a little gem." "Jack was no good," he concluded, "until he was given something to do on his own where he could let himself go—and he proved himself then."[39]

The Soul Herder was the fourth film. "Delicious humor," said *Moving Picture World,* "an excellent picture in every way."[40] And we can note, even in its plot summary, many traits of the later Ford—oxymoronic humor, missing family members, the appeal of innocence, the reformed sinner. Gentle, sarcastic, communal, melodramatic, folksy, it is already an "ideal" Ford story— theatrical in a structure of myths and motifs developing in short scenes:

A terror Saturday night, tame by Sunday, Cheyenne Harry (Carey) has to have the sheriff remind him he shot up the town. In the desert he rescues a little girl from Indians. She makes him assume her dead daddy's parson's garb. After Harry rescues his girlfriend, he holds a funeral for her (dead) kidnapper, whose money he gives to prostitutes to leave town, and, since most of Buckhorn has missed three weeks of church, he escorts them at gunpoint to hear a four- (instead of a one-) hour sermon by him.

Harry Carey

The Soul Herder commenced a four-year, twenty-five-film association with Harry Carey—next to Francis Ford, Jack's most significant formative influence. In some ways it was a strange association. Ford was twenty-two, the son of a small-town immigrant, brash, intense, and ambitious; Carey was thirty-nine, the son of a White Plains special sessions judge, and a seasoned veteran. But they were both about six feet, 170 pounds, and they liked riding out to location on horseback, camping in bedrolls, and flushing out stories as they went along. Later they would let George Hively write up the stories and get screen credit.

Born January 16, 1878, Carey had given up thought of a legal career when, convalescing from pneumonia around 1906, he had authored *Montana*, a play in which he toured for some years. Henry B. Walthall then recruited him from a bar for Griffith's Biograph Company, where, always playing heavies, he became known as the "Biograph burglar"—except to

The Freeze Out (1921). Harry Carey on right. From the Robert S. Birchard Collection.

Unidentified Universal film of 1919: probably *Roped*. Harry Carey and Neva Gerber (?).

Griffith, who called him Gunboat.[41] In mid-1915 he joined Universal as one of their "Broadway Players" but gradually became identified as a western type. Once the studio's most hotly promoted star, his career was fading fast at the time of *The Soul Herder* (August 1917). According to Ford, "they needed somebody to direct a cheap picture of no consequence with Harry Carey, whose contract was running out. . . . There were numerous Western stars around that time—Mix and Hart and Buck Jones—and they had several actors at Universal whom they were grooming to be Western leading men; now we knew we were going to be through anyway in a couple of weeks, and so we decided to kid them a little—not kid the Western—but the leading men—and make Carey sort of a bum, a saddle tramp, instead of a great bold gun-fighting hero. All this was fifty percent Carey and fifty percent me."[42] Carey deliberately avoided giving his good-badman character any degree of epic stature (Hart), dandyism (Mix), or star quality (Bronco Billy), adopting instead a relaxed, receptive humility; he never seemed superior to his audience. Most Ford characters resemble this model. Good badmen appeared frequently in westerns, but Carey may have been the first to cling to the idea. Actually, his good-badman character antedates his association with Ford by some years, likewise his Cheyenne Harry persona.* He was in search of a director and, on Olive Carey's recommendation, got Carl Laemmle to assign Ford to do a picture with him.

Their next release was a war-bond comedy, *Cheyenne's Pal*, in which Harry regrets selling his horse for gambling debts, and so jumps ship and swims ashore. Then, for their next picture, *Straight Shooting*, Carey and Ford dis-

*The good-badman character appeared at least as early as Griffith's *The Wanderer* (Biograph: 1913); "Cheyenne Harry" appeared in *The Bad Man of Cheyenne* (Universal: December 1916)

obeyed orders, turning in *five* reels instead of two: it took Laemmle's intervention to stay the confounded cutter's hand. The result was a picture Universal advertised as "The Greatest Western Ever Made."

Straight Shooting (1917). In contrast to the agonized caricatures prevalent in later films, particularly those of today, the "professional hatchet men" portrayed by Harry Carey and Vester Pegg in 1917 seem healthy, likeable, unneurotic, and all but indistinguishable from the "goodies." Audiences today might find this "unrealistic," but, like the river serving as arbitrary barrier between *Straight Shooting*'s feuding settlers,* the division between outlaw and respected citizen is fluid; Ford's people drift freely between ranch and farm, with the saloon—a perpetual halfway house—as neutral territory. The man Carey plans to kill one day becomes his father the next day; another man, a drinking buddy now, is a mortal enemy tomorrow. Life is fragile, relationships shifting, society amorphous. *Straight Shooting* records a period of transition in the land's history and the characters' lives; like most later Fords, it stresses "passage" over "permanence."

Ford's first feature, *Straight Shooting* received critical acclaim for its graceful blend of raw action, infectious characters, compelling situations, and artful, unaffected photography. These are characteristics in which we can glimpse the mature Ford of later years. (And the Sims family bolting their food after grace will be echoed twenty-four years later in *How Green Was My Valley*.) Still, it is not easy to know how to distribute credit among Ford, Carey, and 1917. Though the western was scarcely a decade old, a decade is a century in movie history and the western had long since defined its generic conventions in marble—Universal alone had been issuing six to ten westerns a week in 1913. Agrarian, family-centered situations were among the most popular themes (which may explain something about Ford's later, populist work). And Carey, a veteran of nearly two hundred pictures, had his own notions about filmmaking. As a further difficulty, *Straight Shooting* is the sole title known to survive from Ford's Universal years (thanks to the Czechoslovak Film Archives)—one, only, of twenty-five Carey-Fords (not to mention Carey's work for other directors, including himself).

Already remarkable for Ford in 1917 is his ability to maintain an energetic narrative while pausing constantly for tangential moments of reflec-

---

*Ranchers vs. farmers. Thunder Flint (Duke Lee) sends Sam Turner (Hoot Gibson) to evict farmer Sims; but Sam loves Sims's daughter Joan (Molly Malone). So Flint hires freelance outlaw Cheyenne Harry. But Harry comes upon Sims, Joan, and Sam mourning over the grave of brother Ted, killed by Flint's man Placer (Vester Pegg). This sight, and sudden attraction to Joan, change his life; he sends word to Flint, "I'm reforming, I'm giving up killing, I'm quitting."

Planning to attack Sims, Flint sends Placer, Harry's drinking buddy, to bump off Harry; but wins the duel. Joan gallops to rally farmers; in the ensuing battle, Harry arrives in the nick of time with outlaw Mexicanos to defeat Flint, Sims asks Harry to take his son's place, but (in the 1917 issue) Harry sends Joan back to Sam and gazes toward the setting sun.

tion. At one point, he even pauses to watch the ranchers listening to a record—in a silent movie! Impressively deft are the seemingly crude reaction shots—Vester Pegg quivering in fright before the duel's final moment, or Molly Malone* gazing out her door after Harry, or the kinetic representation of terror as a static crowd suddenly flees the frame in all directions at the news of the coming duel. Filming through doorways was a standard practice in 1917, given the construction of sets, and so was the blocking of characters in triangles, but Ford (who was still doing both half a century later) makes it emotionally meaningful, as he does everything else—in this case, another instance of "passage." The famous scene of Molly fingering her dead brother's dish was probably inspired by Mae Marsh and her baby's shoe in *Intolerance* (October 1916), but Ford intercuts Molly at her pantry with Harry on the riverbank, where leaves, breeze, and flickering light mirror moods Antonioni-ishly. The exciting finale, as Molly gathers horsemen to ride to the rescue, derives directly from the gathering of the klans in *The Birth of a Nation.* Yet via Francis Ford, *Straight Shooting* owes more to the "Ince tradition" of simple lyricism than to Griffith's exalted epic. In place of Griffith's dramatic shaping, all events in *Straight Shooting* have equal value, and thus ignite a more active symbolism into land, light, water, and foliage, a plate, a donkey by a stream, a horse's tail, a glass of whiskey, a bartender's bald head.

According to contemporary accounts, the picture originally ended with tainted Harry sending Molly back to still-pure Sam, refusing her hand and a respectable life in favor of something "just over yonder" that keeps calling to him, and he is "left facing the setting sun alone."[43] The present "happy" ending—in which Harry accepts Molly—appears to have been clumsily edited into the reissue of 1925, an era less tolerant of tragedy than the heroic teens. And the earlier ending is truer to Carey—who often walked away in last scenes, an outsider—and to the Fordian hero (e.g., *The Searchers*— wherein John Wayne imitates Carey's signal arm gesture).

"Harry Carey tutored me in the early days,"[44] said Ford; "I was scared to death, but . . . Harry helped me immeasurably."[45] Carey's was a rare sort of screen personality, uncommonly charismatic, and this spirit, relaxed and communal, vivifies not only the *acting* style in Ford's work, it also epitomizes that unattainable ideal society that Ford would so often and

---

*Molly Malone, leading lady of Ford's first "stock company," was nineteen and had played western heroines for two years before being cast in *The Soul Herder.* She loved outdoors and hated cities and teamed with Carey and Ford in nine films in as many months, then in a tenth three years later. Sweet Molly Malone had a song named after her, but her career petered out in the twenties, and she died in 1952.

so wistfully invoke. Ford, in fact, lived much of the time on a ranch Carey purchased in 1917, just after Carey married actress Olive Fuller Golden.*

The "ranch," down a road going to "Happy Valley," near Newhall, California, covered barely three acres. The house had three tiny rooms and no electricity; the bathhouse stood fifty feet away; the "convenience" was the bush. There were a cow, some chickens, a couple of pigs, and the guys who made the films: Jim Corey, Pardner Jones, Hoot Gibson occasionally, Teddy Brooks. They slept outside in bedrolls. Jack had a spot in the alfalfa patch; always a hard riser, he had to be awakened by Harry's dogs. Olive, the only woman, did all the cooking. It was "a very good time," she recalls. Gilhooley McConigal, a propman with Ford for decades, had a car they called an EMF, Every-Morning-Fixit, because it would never start. Harry's $150 wage went mostly to alimony payments for two ex-wives, and they were all broke. Jack moaned he always had to pay for the butter. He was "adorable," Olive says. "He had a beautiful walk, not too argumentative, a good listener."46 Her main function was to keep them all sober.

Always basically the same, Ford was cocky, full of questions, but secretive himself, fearless, at times aggravatingly persistent. His wit, caustic, even mean, was made bearable by a terrific sense of humor. He was always wrapped up in his work, never wanting to relax, drink, and raise hell, always going full steam.47 He virtually never had a girl—Olive remembers only a single brief affair with a certain Janet, "the first girl he ever slept with."48 "He was movies, that was it, that was all his life until he met Mary."49

Probably from Carey, if not already from Francis, Ford saw the importance of characters *relating* on the screen—and this is arguably Ford's key quality. But Carey in turn gave credit for his ability to relate to Griffith: "He taught us to listen, so it would show on the screen, and he taught us to read the dialogue—despite the fact that our films were silent. I am still reading my dialogue the same way."50 It was a lesson Ford would one day pass on to John Wayne. "Duke," Ford told him, "take a look over at Harry Carey and watch him work. Stand like he does, if you can, and play your roles so that people can look upon you as a friend." ("That's what I've always done," Wayne later said.)51 Also from Carey, Wayne got his broken speech patterns: e.g., "Take your . . . [*pause*] . . . stuff and run down to the . . . [*pause*] . . . creek." At the end of *The Searchers* (1956), Wayne strikes a signal Carey pose in homage (placing his hand on his elbow) and, as Carey so often did, walks away (in fact, walks away from Ollie Carey's house). To understand this, one might recall

---

*At Universal since 1913, Olive met Harry in 1915 during *A Knight of the Range*. She, but not he, remembered an earlier meeting. In Griffith's 1913 *Sorrowful Shore*, Harry had swum out to rescue her, terrifying with big bushy eyebrows and liquor on his breath. He had not said a word to her, just put her down on the beach and walked off. Their marriage in Kingman, Arizona, in 1917, turned out to be illegal—one ex-wife was suing for divorce as late as 1919—so they were married in California again in 1921.

that the role that made Wayne a star—a role Ford had saved for him for years and fought to allow him to play—was, in *Stagecoach*, that of a good badman.*

The actors most at home in Ford's movie-worlds are, in fact, all similar to Carey: Will Rogers, J. Farrell MacDonald, Francis Ford, Ben Johnson, to name a few. Carey's son Dobe thinks Harry gave Ford the model for this basic type. Ford saw the charismatic, relaxed hero in Carey, then made him improve on that, making him "more of a Harry Carey than he really was."[52] This technique of locating an actor's eccentric traits and amplifying them into a screen personage was one Ford followed all his life.

In May 1918, Carey's salary jumped from $150 a week to $1,250, then to $2,250 in 1919. (Jack's salary went from $75 to $150 to $300, which so annoyed him that he would later claim it had dropped from $50 to $35.) During a publicity tour, Carey stated, "I wish to Jack Londonize the Western cowboy—that is, present him as he really is in life . . . a sturdy, manly fellow, totally unlike the one we see in comedies. He has his distinctive characteristics and they are amusing enough without exaggeration."[53]

But the realistic cowboy was not what audiences wanted; tastes were

*Ford also used Carey's black, triple-creased hat on future characters, notably for Henry Fonda in *My Darling Clementine*.

Desperate Trails (1921). Harry Carey, George Stone, Irene Rich. From the Robert S. Birchard Collection.

The Outcasts of Poker Flat (1919). Cullen Landis, Gloria Hope. A lost film.

switching to the flashy, dandified, fantasy types. Carey mellowed, too, into a boy-scout figure. But in the heroic teens, although sometimes the sacrificial good thief *The Soul Herder* suggests, he more often had the raw-edged meanness of Wayne in *The Searchers*, but without the namby-pamby censorship of the 1950s. Harry wreaked trails of vengeance through bars and whorehouses. *Exhibitors' Trade Review*, in November 1918, groaned that the filth and rats in prison were entirely *too* realistic: "The only wonder of it is that anyone should attempt to heroize such a type [as Carey's rough character]. There may be such men in the west, but it is best on the screen to show them up as horrible examples of what a man may be."

Carey worked for a number of studios after leaving Universal, but his career declined steadily. In 1928 a flood wiped out his ranch. Broke, he and Ollie hit the vaudeville circuit. His career resurged in 1931 when Irving Thalberg cast him in *Trader Horn*; but when Edwina Booth sued Metro for a disease she claimed she got while filming in Africa, and Carey refused Metro's request to testify against her, the studios reportedly blacklisted him, and Carey returned to B westerns on poverty row.

Building Status

In 1920, at a Hollywood Hotel St. Patrick's Day dance, Rex Ingram introduced Jack to Mary McBride Smith. She was twenty-seven, a

trained nurse from New Jersey and a former Army Medical Corps lieutenant. Her father was a New York Stock Exchange member; uncle Rupert Blue
was U.S. Surgeon General, uncle Victor Blue an admiral and Chief of Naval
Operations. She was Scotch-Irish Presbyterian. Jack's shanty-Catholic parents had a harder time accepting Mary than her upper-crust family did accepting him. Her Carolina ancestors stretched back to Thomas More, Washington, and Lee; Sherman had burned the family plantation—an incident
Ford wrote into *Rio Grande*. "He went down with me to visit my folks," said
Mary, "and to my horror told my family what a nice kindly old gentleman
Sherman was, and I had to sit there and take it!"[54] Jack was a practicing
Catholic and a member of the Knights of Columbus, but as Mary was
divorced—she had wed a soldier leaving for the war—marriage in the
Church was not possible. Accordingly, they were married July 3 at the Los
Angeles courthouse. Irving Thalberg and William K. Howard were ushers;
Allan Dwan gave them a keg of whiskey. They all went to Tijuana for the
Fourth, in Jack's blue Stutz Speedster. (In 1941, after Mary's first husband's
death, they were married before a priest, in Washington, D.C., and they

John and Mary Ford, with Patrick and Barbara, ca. 1926.

pronounced their vows again on their fiftieth anniversary.) Their first home was a rented two-bedroom stucco at 2243 Beechwood Drive. In October, for $14,000, they bought a house at 6860 Odin Street, on a hill overlooking the site of the future Hollywood Bowl, where they stayed thirty-four years. Patrick was born nine months to the day after their wedding, and Barbara on December 16, 1922. Maude Stevenson ("Steve" or "Steves") began a long tenure as governess. "He said he only married me because I didn't want to get in pictures," said Mary. "I never went on the [movie] stage the whole years I was married. Never went near. That was one of the agreements we had. He said, 'If I were a lawyer, you wouldn't sit in my office. If I were a judge, you wouldn't hear my cases.' He said, 'That's where all the trouble starts.' He'd bring scripts home, but he'd never ask me to read them. It was very funny, his work was a closed organization as far as the family was concerned." She reconciled herself. "I'd had my feelings hurt when I was first married, so I said, 'That's that!'"[55]

By 1921 Ford had been at Universal four and a half years and had made thirty-nine pictures, twenty-eight of them features. The qualities critics singled out are notable in his later work as well: "Mingling of pathos and humor . . . wealth of human touches . . . clever details . . . experimental photography . . . optic symphony . . . thrills, excitement, action, realism." But life at Universal seemed to be going downhill. Harry Carey had been dropped; the Stern brothers, in control, were always shouting at everyone; Ford's salary was still low. So in 1921 Ford signed a long-term contract with William Fox at $600 a week. Fox, like Universal, was a minor company catering to blue-collar and rural audiences. Perhaps typical (but delightful) is *Just Pals* (1920), the first of fifty Foxes Ford would make, and a simple story in which a village bum (Buck Jones) and a boy hobo thwart a robbery. The small-town detail, folksy characterizations, and elfin charm resemble less such actual Griffith as *True Heart Susie* than they do King Vidor's Griffithian *Jack Knife Man* and *Love Never Dies;* Fordian swift pacing and plentiful action replace Griffith's formally wrought presentations and lordly distance. Parallel editing in climaxes, developed by Griffith, had become endemic by 1920 (even in a modest C-budget western like Francis Ford's *The Stampede*, 1921); nonetheless Ford's finale excitingly fuses five plot lines, typically counterpointing chases, fights, and robberies with the humor of a sheriff displaying his badge to avoid a church collection. Typically Fordian too are the lynch mobs, hypocritical social strata, pompous churchgoers, busybodies, and the unobtrusive blacks (unnecessary in a story set in Wyoming, yet ignored by whites and drama). Humor is already gruff and sentimental, fighting a necessary part of friendship.

But unlike Universal, Fox's management, in the persons of Fox and Winfield Sheehan, was dynamic, and the company would shortly become a titan in the industry. As a bonus, Ford was given a trip to Europe. Mary, probably because of seven-month-old Pat, did not go along. But she did see

Unidentified person, Douglas Fairbanks, Mary Pickford, John Ford, ca. 1928.

him off from New York, and he wrote her as the boat sailed, November 19, 1921:

On Board S.S. *Balls-tic*
Dear old fruit: I am going to keep a sort of diarhea for you about happenings on board (with the provision of course that I am able). We are just leaving. I hope you are not on the wharf yet with that throng of handkerchief waving maniacs. . . .

5:30 P.M.
Darling: I am sorry to say I am slightly drunk. Yes sir!! Bummed! I also have hiccoughs. Mary, how I wish you were with me! Gosh. We would have had such a delightful trip. It's really wonderful on this boat. I have spent the entire afternoon in the "BAR" drinking Bass's Ale and feel quite wonderful. (Except for the hiccoughs.) . . .

Sunday

. . . Just as the priest lifted the host, the clouds and fog lifted & three miles away we could see the shores of our beloved fatherland, "The Emerald Isle" as green and fresh as dew on the down. Even the priest stopped, gazed and then with a gulp of joy in his throat went on with the Mass. Of course all the tads has tears running down their cheeks and when the prayer of thanksgiving came, it sounded like a hymn of heaven, so joyous these old folk were. . . .[56]

Jack hurried to Ireland from Liverpool; it had been his chief reason for making the trip. The Sinn Fein nationalists were engaged in a bloody revolution against England. Jack's father had of course contributed generously and Jack himself wanted to get involved. He wrote Mary about it in January, after his return to New York:

At Galway I got a jaunting car and rode to Spiddle and had a deuce of a time finding Dad's folks. There are so many Feeneys out there that to find our part of the family was a problem. At last I found them. Spiddle is all shot to pieces. Most of the houses have been burned down by the Black and Tans and all of the young men had been hiding in the hills. As it was during the truce that I was there I was unmolested BUT as Cousin Martin Feeney (Dad's nephew) had been hiding in the Connemara Mountains with the Thornton boys, I naturally was followed about and watched by the B & T fraternity. Tell Dad that the Thornton house is entirely burned down & old Mrs. Thornton was living with Uncle Ned's widow while her sons were away.

I went to London (which I didn't like), Paris, Marseilles, Nice, Monaco (Monte Carlo) & Italy. I had quite a wonderful trip but as I say, I missed "my family.". . . As I will be here a couple or three weeks more [shooting a picture], I will try and hick up and stand it, but it is sure tough. I hate this place. No New York for me. . . .[57]

Cousin Martin in fact had a price on his head. Years later he told Dan Ford how Jack had sought him in the hills and given him food and money, and how the British had "roughed up [Jack] pretty well" before putting him on a boat to England with the warning of imprisonment if he ever came back to Ireland.[58]

Jack Ford returned home with a much strengthened sense of identity and commitment; he channeled funds to the IRA the rest of his life. He also returned to a rather chagrined wife and a pile of debts. He was soon making good money. His salary in 1921 had amounted to $13,618, but in 1922 it came to $27,891, and in 1923 to $44,910. Moreover, at Universal he had been allowed to make only two non-westerns, whereas in his first two years at Fox, his subjects included the London theater, New York's Jewish ghetto, rural New England, Maine fishing towns, and Mississippi riverboats. And along with new prestige and bigtime money came a new name: with *Cameo Kirby* (1923), Jack Ford died as a screen name and John Ford was born.

Three Jumps Ahead (1923). A lost film with Harry Carey.

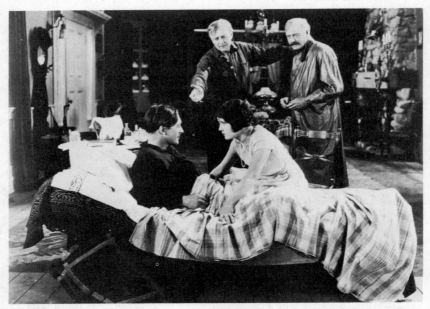

Hearts of Oak (1924). Theodore von Eltz, Hobart Bosworth, Pauline Starke. A lost film.

Ford soon found grist for his ambition. Isolated in the Sierra Nevada while filming **The Iron Horse** (1924), the story of the transcontinental railway, he commanded, it is said, 5,000 extras; construction of two whole towns; 100 cooks to feed the crew; 2,000 rail layers; a cavalry regiment; 800 Indians; 1,300 buffalo; 2,000 horses; 10,000 cattle; 50,000 properties; the original "Jupiter" and "116" locomotives that had met at Promontory Point May 10, 1869; Wild Bill Hickcock's derringer; and . . . the original stagecoach used by Horace Greeley![59] A planned four-week schedule stretched into ten as blizzard followed blizzard, shooting became impossible, and magical community grew in the troupe. "All sorts of things happened," Ford recalled, "births, deaths, marriages, and all in the icy cold. There was only one single day of sun."[60] "We nearly froze to death. We lived in a circus tent, had to dig our own latrines, build up a whole town around us. Saloons opened up; the saloon-girls moved in."[61]

"The Ford outfit was the roughest goddamdest outfit you ever saw, from the director on downward," said assistant Lefty Hough. "Ford and his brother, Eddie O'Fearna, were fighting all the time. This goes back to the days in Maine when Eddie and the others ran a saloon and they used to kick Ford out of there and wouldn't let him drink. Ford never got over this. I had to break up the fights. When we were doing some of the stuff on the tracks, they got in an argument and O'Fearna went after the old man with a pickhandle."[62]

There had never been a scenario—only a short synopsis—and Ford kept making it all up as the weeks went on. Back in Los Angeles the studio, frantic for footage, pleaded, cajoled, threatened, blasphemed, then ordered retreat. Ford tore up the wires, or held them in the air and had Pardner Jones shoot a bullet through the sender's name. Production boss Sol Wurtzel, come up to inspect, fell prey to a three-day crap game. Finally William Fox, who, on the strength of Paramount's successful *Covered Wagon* (1923) and faith in Ford, was backing the project, looked at what had been shot and said, "Let them finish it."

John Ford's career was on the line. He avoided premieres like poison—his nerves could not control his stomach—and feigned casual aloofness toward his work. Thus he played bored while those who had attended the Los Angeles opening aired their verdicts. But when Francis Ford meekly offered some suggestions, Jack jumped wildly to his feet: "Who the *hell* asked *you!*" he shouted, and stormed off, slamming doors behind him. He avoided strong language at home, but Frank awakened pathological sensitivity. (Hence it was partly to humiliate Frank that Ford cast him always as a loony or drunk, never as a Lincoln. "I want to see him *lashed*," Jack would chortle—and did, in *The Black Watch*.[63]

If *The Iron Horse* dawdles today, it is partly because we are deprived of its marvelous score; Ford rhymed rail layers' movements to songs his Uncle Mike had taught him, accelerating the tempo as the rail layers raced. And it is partly because the edition generally available is the European cut, rather

than Ford's far more dynamic version.* *The Iron Horse* uses its thousands
sparingly; Ford never allows them to detract from his simple human
story.** To add comedy, he added three soldiers (Francis Powers, J. Farrell
MacDonald, James Welch) who stole the show in the twenties. Only during
boy Davy's black-lit expressionistic poses over his father's dead body does
The Iron Horse's B-western feel turn artful. It is an epic chiefly by suggestion. As the father heads west from Springfield, a bystander remarks, "Poor
dreamer! He's chasing a rainbow." "Yes," replies a Mr. Lincoln, "and someday men like [him] will be laying tracks along that rainbow."

The Iron Horse was among the decade's top grossers; against costs of
$280,000, it returned over $2 million. It made Ford internationally famous
and put a Fox film on Broadway for the first time. As Bill Fox escorted John
and Abby Feeney to that Broadway premiere, he told them that if he had
had a son, he hoped he would have been like Jack.[64] (Fox's precepts were
also Ford's at this time: action, folksiness, uplifting sentiments, spiced with
humor.)

But two years later an attempt to repeat *The Iron Horse*'s success flopped.
Although *3 Bad Men* (1926) is a far better picture by any standard and, in fact,
was better liked by contemporaries who saw it, box-office tastes had veered
sharply away from westerns. *3 Bad Men* had to be severely cut after preview-
ing, and Ford, having made forty-three westerns in nine years, was not to
make another for thirteen years—until *Stagecoach*.

3 Bad Men mythicizes its genre. Villain Layne Hunter (Lou Tellegen), with
fancy dress and a Liberty-Valance-like whip to spur his depraved minions,
pertains to western fantasy. As does the wrath of Bull Stanley (Tom Santschi),
punching down doors, heaving varmints from balconies, or, flanked by torch-
men, descending a staircase, his dead sister outstretched in his arms. Iconically, the parson begs mercy by a flaming cross with black smoke swirling.
And the three bad men make their entrance mythically silhouetted against
the horizon, preceded by their reward posters (like Harry Carey in *Straight
Shooting*, or the Cleggs in *Wagon Master*). Below them, a wagon train
stretches across a prairie†—an early instance of Ford envisioning life as a
parade. And at the end, their ghosts, pledged even in death to watch over Lee
(Olive Borden), join hands and ride into the sunset, their memory perpetu-

Two negatives were customarily shot simultaneously, one for domestic prints, one for
foreign. Ford's version (the domestic), according to John Stone, has many more tracks and pans
during hunts and battles, closer shots of horse-falls, more emphatic cutting. Track-laying is
more rhythmic, building in one long single sequence (rather than split into two) to climax in the
meeting of the tracks. Most titles differ, are more rhymed to the beat, and sometimes change
motivation. Into both versions mismatched close-ups of Madge Bellamy were interpolated
against Ford's will. The Lincoln scene was Fox's suggestion.

**Headin' west, Davy sees his father killed by (fake) Indians. He grows up (into George
O'Brien) to scout for the railway constructors, and reencounters his childhood sweetheart engaged to his father's murderer.

†Dakota land rush, 1876: three outlaws befriend orphaned Lee, encourage romance with Dan
(George O'Brien), and give their lives to thwart Hunter stealing her gold map (but then the plot—
or cuts?—forgets the map). Tellegen partnered Bernhardt in the famous 1912 *Queen Elizabeth*

The Fighting Heart (1925). Billie Dove. A lost film.

ated (like Colonel Thursday's in *Fort Apache*) by Lee's baby's triple name. Epic themes enunciated in a prologue—immigrants on sailing ships, Dakota gold rush, ploughing oxen—are forgotten, midst informalities, plot, and comic interludes, until after the land rush. Then a broken wagon's slogan is updated ("BUSTED—BY GOD") and the wife declares, "This soil is richer than Gold." Throughout, the quaint chivalry of the good badmen punctuates Fordian themes of friendship and life's preciousness. Similar hero trios recur often in Ford (cf. *3 Godfathers*), always associated with the myth of the three kings and redemption through self-sacrifice.

Spectacle, by 1926, was no more novel than today. But who will ever forget that pan of hundreds and hundreds of Conestoga wagons waiting along a line miles long? Said Ford:

> Several of the people in the company had been in the actual rush. The incident of snatching the baby from under the wheels of a wagon actually happened. And the newspaperman who rode along with his press—printing the news all through the event —that really happened. We did a hell of a land rush—hundreds of wagons going at full tilt; it was really fast.[65]

and married Geraldine Farrar. Santschi appeared in *In the Sultan's Power,* the first story film shot entirely in California. Existent prints of *3 Bad Men* preserve none of the photographic quality whose vistas of Jackson Hole and the Mojave thrilled contemporaries.

Like *Straight Shooting* and *The Iron Horse*, *3 Bad Men* chronicles a micro-society, motley and fluid in class, and essentially in passage. Against the *chaos* of this milieu is counterpointed the *order* of individuals' initial typing (by race, nationality, class). Counterpointed also are quotidian and mythic dimensions of events. The Fordian hero, a sacrifical celibate, intervenes to preserve social harmony.

Such weighty and germinal narrative structures may, however, seem in the long run not so impressive as the inventiveness of *The Shamrock Handicap* (1926),* Ford's twenties *Quiet Man*, an Irish comedy. Here is much of his fifties compositional style, painterly, spacious and balanced, deep in field. Here a large cast and wealth of inventive incident create breezy pacing (where earlier Foxes meander). Stratifications of class (Irish, black, Wasp, Jew, doctor, etc.) function not solely as themes but as motifs to be juggled playfully. Typically for Ford, downbeat material receives comic treatment, and humor has a wacky quality uniquely his: a doctor tells laid-up Neil he's done what he could, then walks out with a golf bag on his shoulder; jockeys bring flowers "got cheap at the undertakers"; Finch shrugs off adversity by biting a banana. Contemporaries cheered the Kildare marketplace, which comes alive midst ruins, dusty roads, barefoot boys in maxi-skirts and jackets, children carrying geese and sheep, donkey carts, jigging couples, and a "corker" of a steeplechase.

Less successful was (and is) *Kentucky Pride* (1925):** narrated by a horse, the plot plods dully, but abruptly explodes into the sort of finale that became a Ford trademark in *The Quiet Man*. In seven brief vignettes:

1. Beaumont gazes greedily at his winning tickets.
2. Confederacy and Virginia's Future are reunited.
3. Donovan stands boasting with both in winner's circle.
4. Greve Carter says, "It's hard to tell you, but I've lost everything" — betting against Confederacy — and the ex-Mrs. Beaumont leaves him, word for word repeating the earlier scene when she left Beaumont.
5. Cameramen have comic difficulties taking pictures.
6. Little Mike, Jr. (the jockey) and Virginia are revealed kissing when fat Mrs. Donovan moves from in front of them.
7. Virginia's Future, who began the film admonishing, "Pride of race is everything," now concludes: "When I saw my baby flying ahead, all the aching disappointment, the bitterness of my own life [in failing to run true],

---

*Ireland: The O'Haras sell their horses for taxes, and Sheila (Janet Gaynor) bids adieu to Neil (Leslie Fenton), whom Finch takes to America to jockey. But the O'Haras mortgage everything, go to America with handyman Con (J. Farrell MacDonald) and a pet goose, enter Dark Rosaleen in the stakes, and win.

**Virginia's Future trips at the finish line, and her desperate owner Beaumont (Henry B. Walthall) disappears. Saved by groom Donovan (J. Farrell MacDonald), she foals and is sold. Donovan, now a cop, finds Beaumont selling bourbon trackside, reunites him to his daughter, rescues the mare from a junk dealer after an epic fight, and rides her in tails and tophat proudly down Main St., to see her daughter Confederacy win, 20-1.

The Shamrock Handicap (1926). Janet Gaynor, Leslie Fenton.

seemed to melt away. . . . Suddenly I knew that I had not failed, that I too had carried on. . . . My darling baby . . . had paid my debts in full."

This is the first extant appearance of the "Tradition & Duty" theme that—prominent in early Universals also—will be found important in nearly all Ford's subsequent films. And in this incipient vignette style lie seeds of Ford's greatness. Through broad playing and multitudes of tics, somewhat in the manner of the British stage or commedia dell'arte, it characterizes instantly and narrates economically. Each shot becomes a vaudevillelike "turn." Cutting isolates a character within his own "atmosphere," yet juxtaposes him between contrasting shots of others and *their* atmosphere. By rapid passage through a variety of "turns" (shots or scenes), as above, an entertaining, kaleidoscopic suite of emotions is obtained.

Always fascinated by character, Ford had drawn caricatures in school, had acted them out at home, and incessantly robbed real life to fuel his movies. His description, some forty-five years later, of a dinner at William Fox's home in 1924, has precisely the same taste for personality as his pictures:

A butler came over to Grampy [i.e., Ford's father] with a bottle of Jameson Irish Whiskey, and he lit up like the bulb on a Christmas tree when he saw it. He took his water glass, dumped the water into a potted plant, held it up for the butler, and didn't let him stop pouring until the glass was filled right up to the brim. Then he gulped the whole glass

Figure 2. Early Ford Films

Many mysteries would be clarified, were fewer early Ford films lost.

Year	Films	Survived	Westerns	With Carey	Reels			Fox	Universal
					2	3	5+		
1917	9	1	9	6	4	1	4	—	9
1918	7	0	7	7			7	—	7
1919	15	0	15	9	6		9	—	15
1920	4	1	1	0			4	1	3
1921	7	0	6	3		1	6	2	5
1922	2+	0	0	—	1?		2	2+	—
1923	5	2	3	—			5	5	—
1924	2	1	1	—			2	2	—
1925	4	2	0	—			4	4	—
1926	3	3	1	—			3	3	—
1927	1	0	0	—			1	1	—
TOTAL	59+	10	43	25				20+	39

down in a shot. He didn't bat an eye. I remember Mr. Fox staring at him in disbelief.[66]

Congeniality such as this is the outstanding characteristic of Ford's early movies. But he was valued for efficiency rather than artistic ambition. Surviving Foxes evince thrills, beauty, and invention, but little depth. Characterization abounds, but without development or complexity. Overloaded with titles, the Foxes seem more like illustrated stories than movies, their editing generally logical rather than expressive.

Oddly, *Straight Shooting*, back in 1917, did not share these failings; it alone suggests genius—along with bundles of ideas merely reworked in the subsequent ten years. And this reminds us that Ford's first three years passed as junior partner in collaboration with Harry Carey—whom, as with brother Frank, Ford ever after regarded with love and antagonism.[67]

Ford's "years of apprenticeship" would shortly come to an end. Meanwhile, he continued, as much as possible, to work with a familiar crew and company of actors (at least in bit parts), as had been the custom for many filmmakers in the teens. As assistants he employed, for forty years, his brother Edward O'Fearna* and his brother-in-law Wingate Smith. Meanwhile he was building status. In 1927 he was elected president of the Motion Picture Directors Association and sailed with Mary on a fêted voyage to Germany. The next year, his *Four Sons* would rack up spectacular earnings, and it, along with his *Mother Machree* and Murnau's *Sunrise*, would give Fox three simultaneous hits on Broadway. And meanwhile . . . .

*When Nana entered the theater lobby for *The Iron Horse*'s premiere, there were huge posters of everyone connected with the picture. She inspected them all, then queried Fox:

Upstream (1927). Earle Fox as Hamlet. A lost film.

Building a Legend

Ford was building his legend. George O'Brien,* who became a star in *The Iron Horse*, was a nobody when he auditioned for that film. But Ford's opening line, as always, was "Call me Jack," and immediately he established affection—cajoling O'Brien into exchanging a dimestore necktie for Ford's knit import—before inventing a test for O'Brien. Dozens had tested already for the part, and more weeks went by. But Ford called O'Brien back to watch him leap on a horse from the back, over and over, then snatch a glove off the ground while galloping past, over and over—until the cinch broke. O'Brien bounced painfully to the ground, but picked up the glove. Pleased, Ford got comfortable and had O'Brien wrestle for him

---

"Where's my Eddie?" And forever after Winfield Sheehan referred to him as "My Eddie." But Edward used the name O'Fearna to differentiate himself—and misled hosts of movie writers into thinking O'Fearna a Gaelic version of Feeney. Eddie directed a single film at Universal in 1920 and was erudite in history, but sometimes a dud on the set, where it was said his chief function was to echo Jack's "Quiet!" He would send people home before their roles were finished, or, more amiably, keep them on for months after they were through (according to Frank Baker). But John thought him indispensable. (Patrick, the eldest brother, stayed in Maine as a fishing captain.) Fox also gave Nana an immensely expensive black sable coat; characteristically, she returned it to the store and gave away the money.

*O'Brien, born San Francisco, 1900, son of the police chief, got into films with Tom Mix's help, played leads in six other Fords after this first big part, then in cameos as late as 1964. His career highpoint was *Sunrise*; after 1931 he starred in numerous B westerns.

with Fred Kohler. O'Brien wasn't getting paid for any of this, but he thought Ford had a great sense of humor. He, like John Wayne, always figured Ford as a coach. "Go in and do this for me," Ford would say, and whatever it was, they'd do it.[68]

John Wayne met Ford in 1926. His name then was Michael Morrison, and he was working summers as a prop boy at Fox to pay his costs at the University of Southern California. But Ford, learning he was a football player, kicked him face-first into the mud, and laughed. Morrison, in reply, challenged Ford to a scrimmage and took the opportunity to kick him in the chest. Everyone gasped. But Ford liked this: testing people's goat was his way of making friends, and Morrison was a hard sort to arouse. Later, during *Four Sons*, Morrison raked leaves into a shot Ford had sweated over all day, and Ford marched him around the set roaring like a lion, pinned an Iron Cross on him, ordered, "Assume your [football] position," and gave him a kick. But Morrison admired Ford. "[Ford] was the first person who ever made me want to be a person—who gave me a vision of a fully-rounded human being."[69] Ford took a liking, too, to Morrison's thick-hided classmate Wardell Bond. He gave them bit parts, then recommended Morrison as a new face for Raoul Walsh's epic western *The Big Trail* (1930). Walsh thought a name change was in order, Ford suggested some historical figure, Morrison said he liked General Anthony Wayne. The "John" perhaps imitated Ford. Decades later Wayne observed that many people had directed his films but that John Ford had directed his life. "I really admired him. I wanted to be like him."[70]

Part of Ford's legend came from the disciplined efficiency of his sets: since he would never tell an actor anything, they were scared at the penalties a moment's inattentiveness might bring, and hence riveted their attention totally on Ford. Fear—and fascination—were cunningly reinforced by selection of a "whipping boy," whom Ford would castigate mercilessly for days on end. Often the whipping boy was a buddy, like Bond or Wayne; but anyone expecting star privileges earned special gall: Ford would ask them for their pictures and maintain a steady current of ridicule. He could be cruel, with his cold face and sarcastic tongue: "When does your contract come up for renewal?!" he'd crack into his megaphone so everybody would hear. Big men like Victor McLaglen or Wayne would break down and cry like children, and Ford would jibe deeper, always on the megaphone: "D'ya know, McLaglen, that Fox are paying you $1,200 a week to do things that I can get any child off the street to do better?!" And he got away with it. A cult grew up around him. But if you fell from grace, if you said the wrong thing or turned down an assignment, you'd get "put on ice." For two, five, ten years you didn't exist, until one day he'd pat you on the back and ask you where you'd been all this time, why you hadn't called him.[71]

But his sets, says Dobe Carey, were not tense—rather quiet, full of reverence, like church, in part because he always had music going. This was supplied by Danny Borzage (director Frank Borzage's brother). For forty years, beginning with *The Iron Horse*, when sets were struck at production's end, Danny's accordion would play "Bringing in the Sheaves." Every mid-afternoon, there was a break for tea (Earl Grey)—and anyone who talked about movies had to pay a twenty-five-cent fine. Toward women he was generally considerate; using foul language in front of women was one way to get kicked off the picture; drink was another. Ford seldom touched a drop while making a movie. Instead he chewed handkerchiefs, big linen ones, hand-made in Ireland. His wife would stick a dozen in his pocket every morning; by day's end their four corners would be chawed to shreds. Off set, he would "bleed" people, as Frank Baker put it: "He'd get you talking and talking and suddenly you'd find half of what you said in the picture he's making."[72]

He never looked at the script or consulted his script girl, Meta Sterne; he kept everything in his head, and no one but he knew what he was doing. His concentration and memory became part of the legend. He argued once with Baker about which direction a figure on a soldier's medal was supposed to face; Ford was sure the reproduction was in error. Twenty years later, sitting with Baker and paging through a book, he suddenly stopped: "There! See! I was right!" "What're you talking about?" "The medal . . . don't you remember . . . ? *Four Sons*."

Squabbles became silently cherished traditions. Baker was playing his first bit part for Ford in *Hearts of Oak* (1924): "I thought I was wonderful. He said, 'Is that the best you can do?' And I got on my high horse right away. He said, 'A five-year-old child could show more intelligence than you did. You're the worst actor I've ever seen in my life.' I'm starting to boil. He's got me where he wants me. I said, 'Now may I reciprocate? You are the worst director that I have ever worked for.' The only other director that I'd ever worked for was his brother! Then he said, 'That is impertinent!' I said, 'I'm an older man than you, and I think your use of pertinence is altogether wrong.' 'All right,' he said, 'As long as you work for me, you're not going to get screen credit.' I didn't know what the hell screen credit was. He said, 'Your name will not be on the screen as playing a role in this picture.' I said, 'I'm very pleased to hear that. I have some friends in different parts of the world, and I'd hate to have them see my name on a John Ford production.' He said, 'You'll never ever get screen credit from me,' and I never did. And I worked on forty pictures for John Ford."[73]

Ford enjoyed playing rough. One frigid night he marooned Baker on a desert island; "You weren't cold, were you?" he asked. The Archduke Leopold of Austria, playing a bit in *Four Sons*, was kind of haughty, so Ford told Baker to knock him into a shell hole during a battle scene, "and hurt him when you do it." The hole had been filled deep with mud and Ford was there to laugh when they pulled Leopold out.* Once, at home, Jack was

---

*The impoverished archduke did not make a go of it in Hollywood, and Ford paid his way home to Austria.

drunk and pesty; Baker ran him upstairs and told him to go to bed. "He made a pass, I flopped him down the stairs right in front of Mary, who'd walked in that moment. As we stood talking, Jack came crawling up on his hands and knees, suddenly knocked me down the stairs, then ran into his room cackling." Next day, rubbing his chin, Ford caught Baker watching. "Yeh," he said, "you punch like a bloody mule."

There was a fellow called Vince Barnett who played elaborate tricks. Ford was shooting at a railroad station for *Strong Boy* (1929) when Barnett, identifying himself as the "Western Controller of Traffic," threw the film crew out. Ford spent four days back at the studio building a station set before he learned Victor McLaglen was behind the gag. He said nothing, but some weeks later the company went down on the track, where the railway ran a short distance into Mexico. Officials boarded the train, McLaglen had forgotten his I.D., Ford would not testify for him. What is more, Abdullah, McLaglen's Arab masseur, whom he had illegally imported, was found hidden in the toilet and confessed McLaglen's crime. So McLaglen was taken off the train, sobbing plaintively, locked up on bread and water, permitted no calls. "Next time you hire Vince Barnett," said Ford, "you'll think twice, won't you?"[74]

In 1934, temperatures and tempers soared as they shot *The Lost Patrol* on the Yuma Desert. One night in the commissary, Baker, his back to Ford, read a headline about a murder, "He was stabbed," and from behind came Ford's cold Maine voice: "He was shot." "He was stabbed," reiterated Baker, and back and forth it went, getting tenser as the two rose to their feet, their backs rubbing against each other. Suddenly Baker screamed, "Don't you dare call me a liar, you shanty Irish sonovabitch," and socked Ford across the table. So, Baker figured he was through on this film. He went to his tent and stretched out. Presently a voice, Ford's, came from the neighboring tent. "Are you there, Frank Baker?" "I'm here." "I want to talk to you." "You know where I am." Ford walked in, carrying a bottle and two glasses. "Will you take a drink with me?" "I'll take a drink with you, but in the commissary bar!" "You proud Australian bastard. Come on." And Ford spoke to the barman so everyone could hear: "I want you to give this stiff-necked Australian bastard a drink on me."[75]

One day during the Depression, Ford was approached outside his office by an old decrepit Southerner, an actor from the Universal days. It was pitiable. His wife was desperately in need of an operation, the hospital wouldn't admit her without a $200 deposit, and they didn't have a dime. As the old man nervously told his story the crowded room grew deathly still. Ford, staring as though terrified, kept backing away. Then, all of a sudden, he hurled himself at the actor, knocking him across the room and onto the floor. "How *dare* you come here like this?" he shouted. "Who do you think you are to talk to me this way?" And he stomped into his office.

The room seethed in indignation; the old man crawled shakingly to his feet. Frank Baker left furious. But, outside, he hid behind a bush as he saw Ford's business manager, Fred Totman, come out the door, hand the actor a $1,000 check, and have Ford's chauffeur drive him home. There, an ambulance was waiting, and a specialist was flown from San Francisco to perform the operation. Sometime later, Ford purchased a house for the couple and pensioned them for life.

"I've been trying to figure Jack since the day he was born and never could," exclaimed Francis Ford when he heard this story from Baker. "This is the key. Any moment, if that old actor had kept talking, people would have realized what a softy Jack is. He couldn't have stood through that sad story without breaking down. He's built this whole legend of toughness around himself to protect his softness."[76]

Baker acted as Ford's swallow during the Depression, sending weekly checks to twenty-two families, forwarded from various points around the country, so that Ford, who could not bear thanks, would not be connected with them.[77]

Dropping Out

Life with John Ford required forbearance—Irvin Cobb dubbed Mary "the lion tamer." When Ford was filming, the picture was never out of his mind for a minute—and one quickly learned not to disturb John Ford when he was deep in thought. After a picture he would lock himself in his room, dress in a sheet, and go on a three- or four-day binge. Objections were of no avail. "Fuck you!" he would scream defiantly, "I'm going to get drunk!"[78] Then he would repent and sign solemn pledges with his parish priest: he would never drink again.

"When we had a fight," said Mary, "it was a fight, but not very many, because Jack would go upstairs, and he'd do the worst thing a man could do. He just wouldn't speak to me for two weeks. He wouldn't answer my questions. He'd put cotton in his ears, and he just wouldn't hear me. It was the most aggravating thing."[79] Once she threatened to leave: John ran out, started the car, and held down the horn for her to come.

Drinking had been one of the things uniting Jack and Mary. During Prohibition days they made their own gin and kept it hidden in a panel over the mantel that slid back. Every Sunday cowboys and navy officers would come over to Odin Street to drink.* But as time drifted on, Jack became a lone drinker. His friends had disapproved of his marrying Mary. They thought,

---

*Among them, Tom Mix was Mary's favorite: he was always doing wildly extravagant things for her. And he sent her a Mother's Day card every year. ("You're not the type," he explained to his own wife.) No one ever made more money for a movie company than did Mix for Fox, but that Ford and Mix made only two pictures together, both in 1923, suggests Ford's discomfort with the tinsel aesthetics of Mix's personal production unit. And Mix for his part bowed out of the Ford-dominated *3 Bad Men*. Surviving fragments of their *North of Hudson Bay* hold little interest, save for a rapidly edited canoe-in-rapids chase (during which Ford, in furs, subbed for a baddy).

she said, that he was "stepping outside the fold. His gang. Ollie [Carey] wasn't nice to me at all [at first]."[80] As Jack began calling himself Sean Aloysius O'Feeney, Mary changed her middle name from McBride to McBryde and, spending fortunes on clothes, fortified her niche in Society. Religion was another thing that failed to unite them. And between Mary's socializing and drinking and Jack's filmmaking and drinking, the children were raised largely by Steve. Pat was pushed through school by Jack, at times with a razor strap, but Barbara—who never finished high school—was coddled by Mary without the slightest discipline. Whenever there was trouble at school, Mary would put her in another school—five or six schools: it was always the school's fault, never Barbara's.

Jack had become famous and wealthy—his earnings came to $279,000 in 1929 and 1930—but success made him unhappy. He loathed the panoply of position so dear to Mary—"When I became admiral she was very proud," he quipped years later, "She realized that she had achieved her mission in life"[81]—yet her aristocratic disdain for Hollywood goaded his disgruntlement with the synthetic aspect of his career. Truth to tell, he was never content unless making a movie. But he yearned for excitement; he wanted to be "one of the boys."

"Whataya doing tonight?" he asked George O'Brien the day they finished *Seas Beneath,* "Why don't you come with me to the Philippines?" "When you going?" "Tonight. Just give me $200 for the ticket."

It was the best offer O'Brien had heard all day, so that night he was standing beside Ford on the Oslo freighter *Tai Yang.* A bachelor, he was touched when a car drove up and Mary and the kids stepped out. "Gee, that's wonderful!" he thought; "Family comes down, Mary has a tear in her eye—'Don't cry, Mary!'"

"You'd cry too," she replied, "if you were me. You've got my ticket."[82]

Jack, henceforth signing himself Daddy, wrote Mary at sea in early January 1931:

We've had ten days of typhoons, hurricanes, gales, etc. The weather has been terrible. The ship was under water all the time. Mountainous waves broke over the bridge. This is the first time it's been steady enough to even write a letter. We'll probably be 10 days late. In spite of that I've had a good time. . . . O'Brien's behavior has been exemplary. I am proud of him. Never once has he been disorderly or uncouth and at all times he is a credit to the industry. . . . This trip has done me a lot of good. I've never felt better and certainly never looked better in my life. Even O'Brien looks at me admiringly. (However it will do him no good.) . . .[83]

In the Philippines, after a twenty-seven day voyage, they spent mornings on polo, swimming, tennis, and boxing, and evenings being royally fêted. On a "stinky steamer" they sailed south around the archipelago: Cebu, Illoweila, Dumagita, Jolo, Zamboanga, Mindanao. On impulse, they decided to go home, but went to Hong Kong instead, up the Yangtse to Shanghai and

George O'Brien, Lawrence Peyton (?), John Ford, ca. 1931. From the Robert S. Birchard Collection.

Peking, then to Japan, ribbing each other constantly. Three weeks surfing in Hawaii preceded their docking, artifact-laden, in San Francisco on April 11, 1931. Jack thought he should go see Mary; it had been almost four months. "Don't you think I should do that, George?" "Yes, I think you should do that, Jack."

In the years ahead, echoes often reached O'Brien of Fordian accounts of O'Brien's doings during their trip. Most frequent were tall tales of O'Brien's South Sea "orgies." According to another tale, George, eager to meet a Moro sultan with twenty-three wives, had spent days practicing court ritual; but when he walked down the palace aisle, bowing low to the ground, and lifted his eyes, there on the throne sat Jack Ford.[84] Yet despite their comradery, Ford, O'Brien confessed years later, "was the most private man I ever met. I guess I never really understood him."[85]

Mary begrudged her missed cruise, and Jack went back to being unhappy. He staged a dispute near the end of *Arrowsmith*,* walked off the picture, and holed up day after day drinking darkly mid his books.[86] Then

---

*Ford disagreed with the crowds assistant Bruce Humberstone had used to populate a lobby, wanting it empty, for a proper mood. Goldwyn backed Humberstone.

he sailed to the Philippines again on October 31, with Mary on *her* trip.* A few halcyon weeks in Hawaii, as Jack simmered his irritation with Mary's trunkloads of luggage—the very thing he had wanted to avoid— preluded a greater binge, a morbid slobbering in the dark, and ended after two weeks in hospitalization.[87]

Steve brought the children to Honolulu, they all sailed to Manila, and for awhile Jack showed Mary a good time. But the itch would not go away, and on January 22, 1932, he set out on a "man's trip," with Fox representative Larry de Prida, through Macassar, Bali (four days), Surabaya, Semarang (Java), Batavia (Jakarta), and Singapore.** His ability to share Mary's sort of fun was limited; he thrived midst dirty casualness, variety, and adventure. Mary, unwilling or unable to join in, had to resign herself to a certain aloneness.[88] In mid-February the four Fords sailed to Hong Kong, Shanghai, Kobe, Yokohama, and Honolulu, and reached San Francisco March 8.

Jack tried to make up for his shortcomings. In December, they sailed round the Panama Canal to New York and spent a month on Peak's Island. That spring, 1933, he bought her a creamy beige Rolls Royce, with a mink coat on the back seat, and a note: "This ought to shut you up for twenty years."[89] Mary wanted a chauffeur's uniform in matching colors, but that she had to pay for herself.

Ford's own car, naturally, was a filthy, littered Ford roadster. He seldom rode in the Rolls, as Mary would not permit him to smoke in it. And his personal "style" once made him miss a meeting at MGM, when a gate guard, refusing to believe he was a director, denied him admittance. In fact, when he slouched in, during the Depression, to the Rolls Royce showroom, wearing his usual scuffy sneakers, dirty baggy trousers, and grimy shirt, and began slamming doors, kicking tires, and bouncing on leather seats, they were just coming to throw the tramp out when he banged the woodwork, declared the car look solid, and announced he would take it. A certified check for $22,000 arrived ten minutes later.[90] Ford used a similar incident in *Tobacco Road.* He never carried cash; Totman kept him on a small allowance, and Ford borrowed constantly from friends.

Ford's proudest possession—the one thing he *did* lavish money on— was a two-masted 106-foot ketch he purchased in June 1934 for $30,000 (and spent another $36,235 on in repairs over the next eight years). Originally called *The Faith*, it had been built by A. D. Story in Essex, Massachusetts, in 1926, from a John G. Hanna design. Ford rechristened it *Araner*, after his

---

*Typically, Ford told an interviewer, Axel Madsen, that the Philippines were the only part of the Pacific he never got to.

**In Singapore de Prida met and married Ford's niece, Cecil McLean (with whom Ford had grown up and who appeared in several of Frank's films); she had traveled with John and Mary as far as Hawaii, as a Max Factor representative. She and her husband were interned by the Japanese in the Philippines during the war. While her husband was hospitalized, Cecil gave birth to their daughter. They were freed in February 1945. Cecil McLean de Prida has been the source of much information for all Ford biographers.

mother's birthplace. It was capable of about eight knots, flew Ford's buddies' Emerald Bay Yacht Club ensign and the house flag—orange, green, and white—and became a moviestar in *The Hurricane* and *Donovan's Reef*. Here John retreated to prepare pictures, rest after them, and every other chance he got. It had two fireplaces, two bathrooms, red carpets, a four-poster marriage bed, a dressing room for Mary, and a teakwood deckhouse Ford adopted as his hideaway and whose roof he raised so John Wayne would stop bumping his head. Here the Fords spent half their lives, cruising winters to Baja and Mexico or to Hawaii, where their children were going to high school. As the image of America in Ford's pictures grew increasingly bitter and alien, *Araner* more and more became his refuge.

2 First Period (1927-1935): The Age of Introspection

Wer den Dichter will verstehen,
muss in Dichters Lande gehen.   GOETHE

(Whoever wishes to understand a poet
must go into the poet's land.)

John Ford, by 1927, was becoming an artist. Henceforth—and progressively more so as the decades pass—understanding his pictures is the key to (and more important than) understanding the man.

His was a complex personality, and, indeed, he adored paradox. In himself, in the world, in existence itself, he searched out contradictions dear and dreadful to beggar his comprehension. Like any well-raised Irish Catholic, he strove compulsively to be a saint and to understand. Such understanding entails reconciling irreconcilables, a task easy for a simple soul, impossible for a schizoid. But to amplify irreconcilability while still suggesting a higher harmony, this is the task of the wise man, this was John Ford, and his movies, his art, are nothing less than an attempt to formulate, in aesthetic terms, this Blakean vision.

Naturally, neither his life nor profession made steady progress. There were periods of retreat, of reformulation; there were peaks and valleys. At times, particularly in the later years, the "vision" fragments, disintegrates, leaving only contradiction. It is no easy thing to find a "language," a style, a cinema capable of expressing feelings, experiences, consciousnesses that one can nowise articulate until that cinema exists. So pure must that language be, that it is identical with what it is trying to communicate; if not, we will have only description, not consciousness.

Ford's art, though, is not his autobiography; it is more a parallel existence. If his work seems to fall into general "periods," as does Beethoven's music, the rationale for the division lies more in each period's differing approaches toward certain recurrent styles and themes than in Ford's private or professional life. Certain subdivisions appear in these periods; unsettled, "transitional" stretches of experiment and strife alternate with plateau periods. The best (and poorest) movies tend to be found in plateau periods, while those from transitional periods tend to be unevenly inspired. Although the *best* work of a later period is sometimes superior to the best of an earlier period, many earlier movies are immeasurably superior to later ones.

The first period tends to be relaxed, airy, concerned with being and with contemporary social life. The second period tends to be more manipulative, closed and formal, concerned more with mood and the past. The third period is brighter and more vital, formal but open, concerned with pilgrimage and subsistence. The fourth period, following a "season in hell," is eschatological, existentially and aesthetically.

EVOLUTION OF FORM AND THEME (1927–1931)

*The camera exists in order to create a new art—to show
things on the screen that cannot be seen anywhere else,
on stage or in life; aside from that, I have no use for it;
I'm not interested in doing photography.* MAX OPHULS

Mother Machree (4/7ths lost)	1.22.28	Fox	Effects and music
Four Sons	2.13.28	"	"
Hangman's House	5.13.28	"	Silent
Napoleon's Barber (lost: a short)	11.24.28	"	All-talking
Riley the Cop	11.25.28	"	Effects and music
Strong Boy (extant only in Australia—maybe)	3.3.29	"	"
The Black Watch	5.8.29	"	All-talking
Salute	9.1.29	"	"
Men Without Women (sound version lost)	1.31.30	"	"
Born Reckless	5.11.30	"	"
Up the River	10.12.30	"	"
Seas Beneath	1.30.31	"	"
The Brat	8.23.31	"	"

In ten years John Ford had gained distinction as an efficient taskman and had made many "nice" movies. Yet suddenly in 1927 he began to make pictures on an altogether more ambitious level of artistry, the true characteristics of his mature work began to emerge, and, with smashing commercial successes, his position at Fox became preeminent. The first segment of this

Figure 3. Ford's Mature Career

1st Period		2nd Period		3rd Period		4th Period	
1927	1935	1935	1947	1948	1961	1962	1965
	1931		1939–1941		1956		

Dots indicate transitional phases; lines indicate plateau phases.

period is, nonetheless, transitional, whereas the second (1931–35) comprises a series of masterworks.

In brief, Ford's artistic leap resulted from marriage of his vignette style (see page 35) with Murnau's atmosphere-enriching expressionism. This marriage of "turn" with composition greatly intensified rapport between character and milieu, and soon blossomed into a theme that dominates Ford's work: milieu, through tradition, duty, and ritual, determines individual character. Similar themes occur in many Hollywood expressionists, and in much of the era's literature as well. What is distinctive in Ford is his juxtaposition of disparate moods, styles, and characters—suggesting a variety of possibilities, which, in turn, imply an off-setting modicum of freedom; and soon the Fordian hero emerges to moderate further the worst ravages of determinism. Ford aimed, moreover, for empathetic understanding from his audiences; satire was not an end in itself, nor the sort of identification and sensationalism one finds in, say, Hitchcock. (And it is not too much to claim that most misunderstanding of Ford results from identifying a character with oneself or with Ford.) Ford's richness thus is due to dialectical tensions at almost every level: between audience and film, between themes, emotions, compositional ideas. Not surprisingly, the "typical Ford shot" is a geometric depth in which people stare at each other across space.

Besides Ford's natural evolution, three momentous events combined to propel his sudden artistic leap: the expansion of the Fox enterprises; the advents of Murnau and *Sunrise;* and the coming of sound.

Fox

In 1925 William Fox, while retaining absolute control in his own hands, began to transform Fox Film Corporation and Fox Theatres Corporation from a New York–based enterprise with holdings in less than twenty theaters producing programs for blue-collar consumption into a $300 million giant with over a thousand theaters producing high-quality specials in the most modern studio in Hollywood. Under production boss Winfield Sheehan (but with Fox's omniscient supervision), product image was upgraded and stars created by pictures such as *What Price Glory?* (November 1926: Victor McLaglen and Dolores del Rio) and *7th Heaven* (May 1927:

Janet Gaynor and Charles Farrell)—two of the top grossers of the decade. Ford, with the success of such high-budgeted specials as *Four Sons* (possibly Fox's top grosser) and *Mother Machree*, found himself at the top of the heap of Fox directors, flanked, in company promotion, by the likes of Walsh, Hawks, Borzage, Murnau, and Blystone. Even the critics raved over his "weepies." (Besides, it was estimated that 87 percent of film audiences were women.[1])

Murnau

To gild his company's new image, Fox imported Friedrich Wilhelm Murnau from Germany, where *The Last Laugh* had made him the reigning cinema artist. And to gain the prestige a masterpiece would give, Fox gave the filmmaker carte blanche. Indeed, *Sunrise* was more prestigious than popular (and in 1958 *Cahiers du Cinéma* voted it "the most beautiful film in the world"), but, with Murnau at the Fox studios from August 1926 to March 1927, *Sunrise* had an immense and immediate stylistic effect on nearly everyone on the lot (Borzage's *7th Heaven*, for example) and thus on much of American cinema over the next two decades. Ford, after seeing a rough cut in February, told the press "that he believed [*Sunrise*] to be the

Desperate Trails (1921). Harry Carey. From the Robert S. Birchard Collection.

Desperate Trails (1921). Ed Coxen,
Barbara LaMarr. From the Robert S.
Birchard Collection.

Desperate Trails (1921). Harry Carey.
kneeling. From the Robert S.
Birchard Collection.

greatest picture that has been produced [and doubted] whether a greater
picture will be made in the next ten years."[2] He then rushed off to Germany, where Karl Freund headed Fox interests, "to shoot exteriors" (none
of which appear in the finished film) for *Four Sons,* an almost self-effacing
imitation of Murnau's style. In Berlin, he visited Murnau and was greatly
impressed by the director's sketches, designs, and production methods.

Ford was enchanted by the intense stylization of Murnau's painterly invention, in which a character's conscious rapport with his physical world
seemed suddenly palpable. Ford's movies had been relatively unstylized.
But henceforth lighting creates dramatic mood through emphatically contrasting blacks and whites, macabre shadows, shimmering shafts of light,
chiaroscuro, and other abstractions. Scenery, too, sometimes distorted
from everyday norm, becomes dramatically active — not just a passive con-
tainer. Actors, their gestures formerly natural, now often calculate the specific mood-effect of each movement. And compositions, camera movements,
and montage, previously pretty, logical, and rudimentary, now aspire to
expressive force. The camera becomes a narrating persona, activating a
compelling distance between frame and image. "Cinema", writes Erich
Rohmer of Murnau, "organizes space as music organizes time, taking that
total possession of space that music takes of time. . . . [Cinema] organizes
emotion's disorder. [So that, inserted into cinematic space, a gesture of]
man's internal tumult affirms his profound affinity with the rhythms of the
universe."[3] These ways of articulating ideas, impressions, and emotions became what, for convenience, we label Ford's "expressionism."

The term may be confusing, as it implies kinship to the brutal Expressionist (big *E*) movement that arose paroxysmally out of German anxiety
following World War I. The advent of the German artfilm had indeed been

heralded by *The Cabinet of Dr. Caligari* in 1919, but this single movie's few Expressionist roots were immediately abandoned by its successors. Nonetheless "expressionism" (small *e*) has survived to designate all in cinema that is not realist; expressionism is concerned with the subjective or poetic aspect of things, and is virtually equivalent to "style." "Subjectivity" implies meaning (or, more properly, sensibility, for artistic meaning is inseparable from emotion)—meaning imposed by form. "Reality," on the other hand, is by definition meaningless and emotionless; thus filmic realism is, in theory, styleless. For the pure realist, distrustful of man's coloring dialectic with objective reality, cinema is not an artistic experience but a means of recording reality without human interference. In practice this ideal is unachievable; the very act of framing imposes form, while disparities between human sight and cinematography produce poetic effects of intensification, particularly on sunlit air and sea. Although all so-called realist filmmakers are to some degree expressionist, the two terms are used (with confusing vagueness) to indicate antinomal tendencies.

Subjectivity may infuse a film's world through either (1) prefilmic interpretation of what is to be photographed (by story, dialogue, acting, lighting, scenery, etc.) or (2) filmic interpretation by how it is photographed (framing, camera movement and focus, cutting, etc.). Music may be either prefilmic or filmic. Composition (visual, aural, temporal) is the product of prefilmic and filmic elements, is equivalent to what we mean by "cinema," and is the artist's imposition of the judgments of his sensitivity on reality. There is no "innocent eye"; only art and lies.

Films that emphasize prefilmic qualities are usually called expressionist. Their subjectivity reflects their characters, camerawork occurs within prefilmic space and seems dictated by the action; and it is in his design of the action that the film artist may be found. *The Cabinet of Dr. Caligari* is a good example, as is most filmed theater and most sensationalist cinema.

Films that deemphasize prefilmic qualities have traditionally (and arbitrarily) been called realist. Their subjectivity reflects their director, camerawork occurs outside prefilmic space and seems imposed on the action; and it is in his arbitrage that the film artist may be found. In Rossellini's *Viaggio in Italia*, for example (although this is scarcely an essentially realist movie), when Ingrid Bergman looks out to sea, we may feel that Rossellini feels a surge of (qualified) romantic effusion, but we really do not know what Ingrid feels. Our vagueness, contradictory and ambivalent, results from certain aspects of the film—the acting— being intentionally left "not-made": Ingrid's feelings are not interpreted for us, not subjected to formalization so that they become readable.

Most major directors (including Rossellini) combine emphases of various elements, both prefilmic and filmic. These "realist-expressionists" (or "expressionist-realists," as the case may be) conjure up a genuine dialectic between their own subjectivity and that of their characters with their world.

Murnau's *Tabu* (1931) is an excellent example. *Tabu's* sets are not at all stylized as in *Sunrise* or *The Last Laugh*, and what Murnau photographs he leaves quite alone. With one exception: the acting of the three principals is intensely formalized, infused with each character's subjectivity. Filmic qualities, on the other hand, are extremely pronounced. Cutting and angles are as arbitrary as in Eisenstein, with the arbiter (Murnau) coherently exterior to the film's storyworld. Character point-of-view shots are ostentatiously avoided, with a handful of notable exceptions; cutting tends to be discordant, even jarring; and even the shadows that fall on the sleeping lovers seem, insofar as they formulate our understanding of the scene, imposed.

A camera angle should *intensify*, asserted Murnau,[4] and what Rohmer meant by calling Murnau a "cinema of presence"[5] is powerfully evident when *Tabu's* characters appear in isolated close shots. Their fluent bodies radiate their private sensibility, their feelings are palpable without the slightest vagueness, and the space they habitate is utterly infused by their subjectivity. When Murnau cuts away, we may feel their gaze infusing subsequent shots with their subjectivity; but a cut to another character is instead a conflict of private worlds. Such moments of space-dominating isolation are few, however. Characters are generally contained by a "raw," uninfused reality (their

village, the sea), and thus isolated in quite a different way. Murnau surrounds art (the characters) with the real world, rather than with a poetic world, and the characters are thus isolated ontologically. They cannot impose their will on reality, but the reality their imagination creates imposes itself on them. Yet this internal dialectic of the film between man and the physical world that contains him would be as nonexistent as it is in most films that have close shots and long shots (and how many films do not?), were it not for Murnau's throwing it into relief by his external presence all through, cutting and imposing angles and articulating his own dialectic with his characters and their world. It is, moreover, the fact that we are conscious of Murnau's gaze that accounts for our feeling we behold reality.

Contrasts between subjective and objective reality, theater and documentary, character and directorial presence become vital aspects of John Ford's cinema. But such contrasts are not equally apparent in all the dark, moody movies of twenties Germany, nor in the national cinemas influenced by the Germans. We can note, in fact, two opposing strains of expressionism, one stemming from Murnau (*realist*-expressionist: Ford, Sternberg), the second from the other major German filmmaker, Fritz Lang (*expressionist*-realist: Eisenstein, Hitchcock), and we can cursorily contrast the two strains and their imitating directors. Of course, each director mixes prefilmic and filmic elements in quite different proportions, and one might be tempted to question the placement in their respective columns of the montage-heavy Eisenstein and the decor-and-acting-heavy Sternberg. Yet there is generally a greater dialectical tension between prefilmic and filmic elements in the Murnau group, and thus a stronger tendency to meditate on consciousness and reality, whereas the Lang group tends to pursue relatively monolithic goals and to aim for sensation rather than for reflection.

Murnau—Ford—Sternberg	*Lang—Eisenstein—Hitchcock*
characterization	symbol
passion (character's consciousness of dilemma)	action (character's working out a dilemma)
gesture (motion)	shape (stasis)
angular stage (deep)	geometric picture (flat)
style for realism (realist-illusion)	reality stylized (antirealist)
people acting freely within determining milieu: organic	people as agents of determining forces: mechanical
Lumière	Méliès (French company)

So frequently does each of these six directors exhibit tendencies opposite those ascribed him (Ford's *Informer* particularly fits into the Lang column), that such pigeonholing may seem tendentious. And, in fact, Murnau is hailed as much for the "expressionism" of *The Last Laugh* as for the "realism" of *Tabu*. Nonetheless there *is* a close intermeshing of style and theme within each strain. Lang, Eisenstein, and Hitchcock are commonly praised as cerebral, calculating filmmakers, Murnau, Ford, and Sternberg as sensual, instinctual filmmakers. The former, the "stern moralists," locate their dramas intellectually— in psychology, subjectivity, or (as in early Eisenstein) in doctrinaire analysis of virtually characterless historical events; their techniques are rigorously calculated to convey the subjectivity of their subjects and to arouse the viewer; their moral viewpoint seldom admits much ambiguity—corruption may be endemic, but right and wrong are seldom in doubt. Murnau, Ford, and Sternberg, the "photographers," are as equally interested in milieu as in character, and their emphasis on determinism and passion hopelessly tangles moral issues; their techniques are calculated to involve the viewer in dialectical problems that admit of no facile solutions: they, not Eisenstein, are the true dialectical artists, aiming for a coherent cognitive experience of vastness and contradiction.

Anticipations of expressionism can be found in individual scenes of early Ford movies (and of course in many pictures of the teens). Oft-repeated citings of dark images in the 1919–21 years, descriptions of *Hoodman Blind* (1923) that suggest Murnau's *Nosferatu* (1922), and criticism of excessive amounts of characterization detail confirm, far more than isolated instances in extant movies, a predilection in Ford for what he was to find in Murnau. Yet there is an essential difference between pre- and post-Murnau Ford. Ford's cinema became totally stylized. Whereas previously his movies illustrated stories, they now tell stories, *are* stories: articulating emotions and moods and states of the soul and tactile impressions of being alive. Ford found cinema could be completely poeticized; he discovered movies might be art.

Sound

Ironically, although Ford was to retain a silent-film style (i.e., visual articulation) throughout his career, such a style only really becomes manifest in his work with the coming of sound.

Fox was a good studio for sound, having pioneered a sound-on-film process simultaneously with Warner Brothers' development of the Vitaphone disc system. The turn-around year for sound was 1928; some eighty-five features were issued that year with synch-score or some talk, in contrast to five or six in 1927. Ford directed Fox's first dramatic talkie, a lost three-reeler called *Napoleon's Barber*, and shot their first song sung on screen in *Mother Machree*.

Some critics have theorized that sound made movies more theatrical and less cinematic. The opposite was true for Ford. Sound freed his characters from enslavement to intertitles, allowing them to communicate directly to the audience. And it allowed the filmmaker to dictate precisely the music and sound effects he wished. He thus had more control over an audience's total experience during their time in the dark, and that experience became immeasurably more intense. Ford wrote at the time about exploring "sound as well as sight images,"[6] and it is clear that he thought of sound not merely for convenience but for poetic effect. Perhaps had Ford been able to use sound in early 1926 he would have used it in natural ways, but now, influenced by Murnau, he employed it expressionistically to contribute to mood.

Thus both sound and Murnau prompted Ford toward creating cinema that would itself be an experience rather than a mere means to an end (i.e., to illustrating stories or to treating a script). Suddenly his work evinces consciousness of the dynamically expressive potentials of movement within the frame and of cutting, which, when wedded to predetermined music, Ford develops into his particular sort of "music-drama" cinema. Combined with vaudevillian cameos, Ford's cinema can, without too much exaggeration, at times be likened to a trailer for a musical.

Evolution of Expressionism and Sound . . .

We can follow in four films certain developments of sound and of Murnau's influence, and see them come to fruition, along with John Ford, in *The Black Watch* and *Salute*. Millions wept over *Four Sons* (1928), while Fox cheered the "Biggest Success in Last Ten Years" and I. A. R. Wylie, struck by the "restraint" with which her story had been filmed, praised the "simple, half-completed gestures and the commendable absence of tears."[7] *Photoplay* voted it best film of the year. The plot concerns a Bavarian mother who loses three sons in World War I, then goes to America to join the fourth, but has to sneak through immigration when she forgets the alphabet the U.S. requires she know.

Strangely, the extravagantly mobile camera, which Ford aped from *Sunrise* and other German movies and which tracks ceaselessly with characters, in front or behind, the longer the better, was not singled out for mention by reviewers. Rather they were fascinated that he kept actors still for long moments. Indeed, however atypical the mobile camera for Ford, ponderous pacing was, at this date, even more so. Each muscle movement is parsed with elaborate detail, as in Murnau's *Last Laugh;* framings are high, as in Murnau; the script derives from a stream-of-consciousness treatment by Herman Bing, a Murnau assistant; and even the sets of the Bavarian village and New York are reused from *Sunrise*—as in many other Fox films of the day (not surprisingly, considering the city street alone cost $200,000 to construct).

So alien to Ford are these aspects of *Four Sons*'s style, and so singular this instance of blatant imitation, that one wonders whether his declared fondness for it does not stem solely from the technical tour de force of his homage to Murnau. Fordian melodrama often inspires tears without appreciable effort, but Margaret Mann's studied eloquence, so lauded in 1928, seems now surprisingly unempathetic for a Ford mother.

It was remarked (and imitated) at the time that Ford had reversed the usual rule and photographed intimate moments in long shot rather than close-up, thus achieving greater intimacy.* When, for example, the mother

---

*Good filmmakers, of course, had always used long shots for intimacy, notably Griffith in *Intolerance* (1916).

Mother Machree (1928).

learns two sons are dead, she sits in still dejection, the room dark except for
a single stream of light. Extending the poetry, pigeons fly from a belfry, and
in the river water the clock tower is reflected upside down; the postman
throws a coin into the water, and it makes rings. *Four Sons* is filled with such
sustained meditation, sometimes dynamically, but too often overly studied.

In contrast, Murnau's influence is well digested in ***Mother Machree*** (1928)
and the score (with sound effects), unlike the insipid thing plastered onto
Four Sons, is wholly sympathetic to nuances of action.* Oddly, the movie
got put *back* into production after sound (and Murnau) came along, having
originally been shot in September 1926. Instructively, pre-Murnau Ford—
pretty and picturesque, just like *The Shamrock Handicap*—contrasts with
post-Murnau expressionism: light and perspective. Angled shots of a tenement staircase express hardship's struggles (as in *The Crowd*). Scenes are
center-lit, with darkened top and bottom (much like thirties Fords). During a
night storm, a mother and child shiver anxiously in their hut, viewed from a
theatrically expanded perspective—i.e., the distance from the camera to

*An Irish fishing village, 1899: Ellen McHugh's husband is lost in a storm. Later, in difficulty
in America, three Irish sideshow folk find her work as a "half-woman" on the midway. Forced to
surrender her son to a school principal, she becomes housekeeper for a wealthy Fifth Avenue
family. Years later, the son falls in love with their daughter, and rediscovers his mother.

Alas, only reels 1, 2, and 5 of the original seven are extant, and the only available copy of
Ford's best (?) silent resides in the Library of Congress.

them is more than twice the length of the hut itself. All is total darkness, except for a rotating beam of light that shines intermittently through the windows from a lighthouse. The mother's later hysteria is the most expressionistic acting in Ford, coupled to unusually trenchant cutting and framing. Most importantly, for the first time in extant Ford work, tensions are created in the spaces *between* characters, and their motions in relation to one another are fluidly choreographed. Generally expeditious on set, Ford all his career virtually exhausted himself over such choreography. It remains today virtually unimitated (except in actual musical numbers) by any other filmmaker, and is thus perhaps the signal peculiarity of Ford's *mise en scène*.

The Murnau influence, no longer imitative, pervades **Hangman's House** (1928), a darkly moody studio-Ireland created from colorful mist, expressive acting, cutting, and decor; but pacing is swift, camera movements few, and framings, though not yet at slanted angles, have recognizably Fordian balance and tension.* Expressionism blends with Ford's nineteenth-century romanticism. Glenmalure Castle's echoing halls and stony gargoyles reflect its owner, who looms menacingly over his daughter's Gothic-chapel marriage and her wedding-gown encounter with Hogan just after, and who dies midst fireplace visions of scaffolds, decapitated heads, and crying widows spinning vertiginously toward him. As in *Four Men and a Prayer* (1938) and *The Long Gray Line* (1955), death is signaled by a dropped hand. Use of such *signifying gesture* is another expressionist trait that became a Ford hallmark.

Misty forest love scenes and a festive-village steeplechase provide some contrast to the gloom. And toward the end of the castle holocaust, the camera tilts down to the castle's reflection in a lake: already Ford puts emphasis on memory and legend.

Hogan's motivation for returning from Algeria remains tacit until the final scene, near a grass-thatched seacoast cottage; now he emerges as a romantic self-sacrificer, a Fordian hero in the Carey tradition. Having bidden farewell to the girl and her lover ("I'm going back to the brown desert, but I'm taking a green place with me in my heart"), he is left alone on the shore. Ford cuts closer, and swiftly Hogan's smile fades and a lump forms in his throat; we realize it is not just Ireland he loves. Hogan is the first Ford character to possess incipient qualities of alienated consciousness. Such a development was perhaps inevitable in Ford, given expressionism's obsession with psychological moods (German Expressionism having originated in articulation of *Angst*).

---

*Ireland: Dying, a hanging judge compels his daughter (June Collyer) to forsake Dermott and wed scoundrel D'Arcy (Earle Foxe), who kills her horse and steals her estate. Fighting Hogan (Victor McLaglen), an exiled patriot whose sister he killed, D'Arcy is consumed in the burning castle.

John Wayne debuts as a spectator so excited he busts fence pickets unawares; he appears earlier, in silhouette in the judge's fireplace, as a man being hanged.

Hangman's House was announced in May 1927, filmed in seven weeks starting in January, but not released until May. Though Fox was heavily promoting Victor McLaglen* and Ford, it let the picture die, providing neither Movietone score nor mention in publicity. But Wilfred Beaton, editor of the trade review *Film Spectator* and an incipient auteurist, praised it as "the finest program picture ever turned out by a studio, [its] merit due [not to any] sure-fire hokum," like *Mother Machree* and *Four Sons,* but to Ford's direction: "There could have been no more of him in [it] than if he had played the leading part." Beaton called it

an Irish poem . . . spread [up] on the screen. . . . The photography almost outdoes for sheer beauty the amazing shots in *Street Angel* and *Sunrise.* . . . As [Ford's] humans move through the gorgeous settings we keep our eyes on them and are concerned with what they are doing, but all the time the beauty of the scenes and the wistful quality of the atmosphere play upon our senses as an alluring and soothing obligato.

And Beaton noted how Ford, to achieve such (expressionist) context for his characters, is "one of the few directors competent enough to avoid sticking in close-ups at each opportunity."[8]

Rediscovered after half a century of oblivion, *Hangman's House* justifies Beaton's claims; as does *Riley the Cop* (1928):**

[*Riley the Cop*] is composed of the darnedest lot of rot ever assembled in one picture, but so deftly is it handled, so intelligently directed, that it is the funniest thing that has been brought to the screen this year. . . . When Jack Ford made his other pictures, he had stories, and all he had to do was to tell them. When he tackled *Riley* he had nothing except a cameraman. At least I imagine that there was no script. Every excruciatingly funny bit in the picture gives you the impression that it was shot the moment someone thought of it. . . . The beauty of the job from a craftsman's standpoint is that there is not a single broad stroke in the whole thing, not a caricature, not an extravagant costume or make-up. It's just funny because it is downright brilliant. . . . Farrell MacDonald[†] [Riley] gives the finest performance of his career . . . but it's a director's picture and my hat is off to Jack Ford.[9]

*McLaglen, born 1885, South Africa, son of an Anglican bishop, ran away at sixteen; as prizefighter became British Empire champ; served as deputy provost in Bagdad during World War I; made twenty films in England before coming to America in 1924 and leaping to stardom in *What Price Glory?* (1926). He played romantic leads (e.g., *Dishonored,* 1931), not assuming slapstick until later.

**When Davy leaves to visit his girl vacationing in Germany, lovable Officer Riley is sent in pursuit of a missing $5,000. He takes Davy from a Munich jail to a beergarden, has to be hauled by Davy onto a plane to Paris and, drunk again and pursued by a beermaid, has to be handcuffed onto a taxi. On ship Davy finds his girl; a cable exonerates.

†John Farrell MacDonald (1875–1952) graced twenty-four Fords. Born in Waterbury, Conn., schooled in Toronto, he held a B.A. and LL.B. from Yale and an LL.D. from Stewarton University, had worked as a civil engineer, a mining engineer, on geologic surveys and newspapers, till joining the Comstock Minstrels and touring light opera. He composed music and once sang

Indeed, the very aspect that hampered development of deep, complex characters in Ford perfectly suited comedy: the vignette technique, with its successions of representative "types" and their "turns," yielded surface variety. And Ford's invention of such variety is almost profligate. Most gags in *Riley* are visual. The broader ones, such as the running joke about Riley's big feet, counterpoint the more abundant "invisible" humor. While principal action occurs centerframe in a Paris nightclub, a foreframe dandy sniffs a rose all the while, which goes unnoticed through the long scene, till Riley unaffectedly takes, sniffs, and returns it without comment. Although *Riley's* topic, tone, and treatment derive somewhat from a Francis Ford series about a comic cop, this Fordian comedy benefits, thanks to Murnau, from a heightened visual style. Players and milieu seem more physical, the camera more contemplative, editing something more than mere pacing. (There are even multiply exposed half-naked chorus girls and spinning trumpeters to show Riley is drunk—imitative of Lubitsch's 1926 *So This Is Paris* and the city scenes of *Sunrise.*) With a buoyant Movietone score, *Riley* is the one Ford silent that does not give the impression it is illustrating the titles and would rather be a talkie. This is a *movie*.

. . . and Evolution of Character and Theme

Expressionism had originated as a means to externalize psychology. And Murnau found that, just as detail and atmosphere could intensify "thereness" and give "soul" to water and trees, so too they could deepen the personality and realism of characters. That his characters, like virtually all twenties expressionist ones, were fairly simple souls, and that his "cinema of presence" stayed on their exterior, suited interwar popularist doctrine, which tended to view exteriority as determinant of man's ethnic (and even personal) identity, and which lauded representation of common-man group consciousness ("social realism") as art's highest representation. Two-dimensionality was less important than elucidation of determining social mechanisms.

These attitudes influenced a generation of moviemakers, for all of whom drama lay in the relation between society and the alienated (separated) individual. For "Jansenists," like Eisenstein, Lang, Hitchcock, and Vidor, bad political, social, or economic systems have been imposed on basically innocent humanity and cause individuals to become alienated—divorced from the community—which is bad. In Eisenstein, such systems encourage people's worst traits and punish their good ones, but in the long run virtuous

---

baritone in Lillian Russell's *Princess Nicotine;* he loved football and golf, and exhibited eighteen paintings in Los Angeles in 1924. His film career started with Selig and Biograph (Griffith), then, after stage work, continued with Imp, Pathé, Universal (where he joined the Oz Company, had his own production unit as director, and probably knew Francis Ford), Tiffany, and, in 1915, Biograph (as feature play director).

ideas will win out. In Lang and Hitchcock, alienation leads people into greater misery and lunacy, away from community, where alone there is hope for security and happiness. In Vidor, alienation incites a search for individual answers to universal questions, but what is learned is that answers can only be realized within the family fold. Of course, there are many exceptions to these broad thematic tendencies; Ford's *Informer*, for example, belongs to the "Jansenist" school. But generally, for "Franciscans" like Ford, Murnau, and Sternberg, hope (and fault) lies in the individual rather than in the community. Alienation refers not to the malicious pettiness of everyday life but rather to a critical dialectic of consciousness whereby the individual may rise above his culture; group consciousness and conventional wisdom enslave society to neurosis, intolerance, and war. The alienating dialectic may take the form of love, power, or wisdom. In Murnau, love sets individuals apart, but in *Tabu* their culture destroys the lovers, and without malice. In Sternberg, love makes people saints, power makes them monsters; his Dietrich characters (somewhat like the Ford hero) perceive more truly the nature of things—for better or worse.

Symptomatically, Lang and Eisenstein heroes—Siegfried, Freder, Jr., Nefsky—and even Hitchcock ones (although Vidor rejects heroism entirely) tend to be paragons of simplicity personifying common-man purity, whereas their villains and victims tend to be complex. Only the most symbolic villains are simple in Ford, Murnau, and Sternberg; their heroes tend to be paragons of anguished complexity—*Tabu*'s lovers, Shanghai Lily, X-27, Blonde Venus. In Ford, Cheyenne Harry (*Straight Shooting*) undergoes such traumas of alienation on his way toward moral responsibility that he turns completely against everything he formerly stood for and ends by exiling himself even from the love that initially ignited his alienation.

But between *Straight Shooting* (1917) and *Arrowsmith* (1931), as far as surviving films allow one to judge, Ford's characters are simpler sorts. Not until *Hangman's House* (1928) do we know of someone evincing incipient alienation. But Hogan's anguish, like that of subsequent principals in *The Black Watch*, *Salute*, *Men Without Women*, and *Seas Beneath*, is not critical self-awareness, but only fear that failure in duty will result in ostracism from the group.

Truth to tell, Ford characters, after the youthful fluidity of the Harry Carey years, rarely change. As their subjectivity affects their space, so their space affects them. It is because the worlds they inhabit are so drenched with their own sensibility that changes become violently difficult for them. Ironically, change is everywhere around them. But this is all the more reason to resist change, even if imagination and culture did not already imprison them in static definitions. How can we define our beliefs, duties, morals, goals, loves, even our selves, if everything is in constant flux? Culture—communal subjectivity—provides surety midst chaos.

In full maturity, the Ford movie abounds with tensions between individuals, cultures, change, and subsistence. But in this 1927–31 transitional phase, it is social mechanisms, intensified in presence and detail, that interest Ford: any progress in characterization is coincidental, for the individual's morality merely represents class consciousness (King emerges out of, and returns into, the chorus; Paul Randall yearns to fit in; *Up the River's* cons sneak *back* into prison for a ball game). *The Black Watch* and *Salute* exemplify the Ford formula at this date.

Ford's first talking feature, ***The Black Watch*** (1929), is virtually a neo-Wagnerian music-drama, exploiting aural-visual storybook pageantry in order to intensify milieu—the social structures (ethnic customs, values, rituals, myths) by which an individual is formed and of which he becomes a perpetuating instrument, and which, by their insularity, breed intolerance, greatest of evils.

The underlying plot structure is simple: a Scottish regiment's war rally is juxtaposed with a Pashtu liberation movement's war rally; then the suicidal bravery of the Scots during World War I is juxtaposed with the suicidal bravery of the Pashtus. Both groups die for duty, a duty necessary for their societies. In the triumph of this duty, some spectators may find satisfying celebrations of accepted social values; others may find a lament that such familiar duty is unquestioned by those who die, and that the very structures that maintain society also destroy its heroes. Duty leads people astray.

Midst ritual in the Black Watch officers' mess—parading regalia, the colonel's World War I entry speech ("Your forefathers rest their honor in your keeping"), a toast (to "Bonnie Laddie"), Davey's song ("Annie Laurie")—it is disturbing that Captain Donald King is summoned away. Notably, he is signaled out of the chorus. We have glimpsed him before, in brief cut-aways, but as one of the regiment rather than a man apart. As King, Victor McLaglen has the stature and simplicity to support this character, for whom self-identity is indistinguishable from chivalric pledge; only within the closed society of his regiment, with its rites and mystiques, will he be the story's hero. But he is told to skip out on his brethren, to "slink away" from the war, to transfer to the Khyber Rifles, then to desert and to seduce a white-goddess stirring up an Afghan hill tribe! To his protests of horror comes the reminder: "Your father was a soldier and he obeyed orders."

So now he stands reluctant in the foyer, taking an eternity to put on his greatcoat, unfold his cap, and light his pipe, until the savored song ends. It is typical of Ford to prolong such an incident, realizing in its sentimentality the psychic milieu out of which King's —and the regiment's—motivation will flow. Now King stands apart, the regiment visible in the room behind him; but protracted parallel editing marks his split, King walking into fog while his "pals," hands entwined, sway to "Auld lang syne," then again, at the train station, where King from the crowd watches their departure.

The regiment marches in, piping "Bonnie Laddie" (a seventy-second take); a sergeant's wife lectures, "Poul doun yer kilt. Dounna ferget yeh're a member of the kirk, an' hide yer shame!"; a woman mounts a box and sings

"Loch Lomond"; like most, she holds heather (the sort of detail only Ford would find); a little girl begs, "Tat' mi wi yeh, pay-tr!" The Colonel thrusts a bitter "Cheerio" at King, whose feelings the singing crowd echoes:

> You'll take the high road, and I'll take the low road . . . For me and my
> true love will never meet again . . .

To this polyphonic orchestration of incident and sound (ritual demonstrative of cultural bonds), Ford adds spatial representation (demonstrative of cultural depth and power). A shot through the gate displays five distinct layers of field: background, train, policemen, triangle of sailors, gate. Typically, having established a composition quickly, Ford sets it into choreographic motion. One movement balances another: the train rightward, the crowd upward, more entering from below (to reinforce the motion). Bagpipes cede to a hymnal "Annie Laurie," train bells chime, a woman cries, "O Angus! Angus!" and some elderly parents make their way in halting contrapuntal motion out the gate.

Wonderfully uneconomic, at seven and a half minutes, the sequence is an ultimate Fordian mixture of pathos, comedy, and romantic spectacle, its hokum redeemed as it takes on the profound aura of documentary truth about a sentimental era.

The contrasting warrior society in Peshawa receives equally modal, if briefer, treatment: golden sunlight to contrast Scottish fog, Moslem songs, mysticism, rituals, and beliefs that bind. Yasmani is bathed in translucent veils, shimmering jewelry, and shifting chiaroscuros; Myrna Loy's awkward, stilted performance is not inconsistent with goddesshood. Steeped in storyland dew, she dwells "beyond British rule—in the Cave of the Echoes": outside, mist, howling wind, tinkling bells, squawking blackbirds; inside, midst gusts of smoke, ragged prisoners are chained to a mammoth wrench beneath a cracking bullwhip (among them, King's "chum"—Francis Ford). In the cave below, huge, chiaroscuroed, long-echoing, a hundred tribesmen howl curses on unbelievers. King, to prove himself, wrestles a Pashtu above a flaming cauldron, while Yasmani gazes excitedly from a rocky precipice (cf. 7 *Women*, when Anne Bancroft distastefully watches two Mongols fight over her). A boiling fire billows smoky flame, prisoners crouch in tiny cages hung from the cavern ceiling, and Yasmani, in white transparent robe, bestows a herd of virgins for her followers' "desire." Fantastic? Yes. But Scotland was almost equally exotic, equally emotional.

Yet, is their juxtaposition contrast or metaphor? Perhaps both. The Pashtu are anonymous and almost "campy" beside the Scots' sincerity; and they seem pure fantasy, while the "opera" in Scotland had at least theatrical realism. But exaggeration in degree is only the metaphor's poetic license, the better to hold a mirror to our own (Western) society—and there is certainly no exaggeration in the similar results obtained by the two societies.

The truth—the war in Europe—is revealed to King in Yasmani's crystal ball. High-angle forward tracking shot: the regiment marching through woods into battle, pipes playing; the men have trouble keeping up with the Colonel, who trots along brusquely ahead, smoking his pipe and carrying a walking stick, oblivious to enemy fire. Dissolve, low-angle: men leap logs. Dissolve: a piper, MacDarvish, falls wounded. Dissolve: another falls in fog, and a hymn, piano and male chorus, appears briefly. Dissolve: another falls, and we hear the little girl, "Tat' mi wi yeh, pay-tr." Dissolve: the men line up, along a tree-bordered road, vertical on the screen. Dissolve: the Colonel, wounded against a tree, rebuffs solicitations, "Carry on!" Dissolve: over a hundred mass along the road; the pipes play "Bonnie Laddie" and their sound blots out the battle for the remainder of the sequence. The men charge across the screen, and, as they do so, Ford dissolves (typically) into the receding angle of the road for a closer shot. Dissolve: they rush by the Colonel. A bomb explodes, bathing the screen white, and a "white" dissolve into the fog shows Malcolm (King's brother) falling. Dissolve: his face lies in the mud, eyes still, wide, staring open; men pass over him. King's face appears in superimpression, watching, calling; and we return to Pashtustan.

The sequence is among Ford's best: swift, muscular, lucid spectacle in picture and sound. How can men watch friends die and then rush eagerly themselves toward certain death? But King's men have mounted machine guns atop a colossal staircase, and the tribesmen, with swords, shields, and Islamic banners, charge up to the guns' mouths and die. Yasmani expires in King's arms, as Ford pans laterally along the British line, staring at the faces of the killing colonial soldiers.

Duplicity, betrayal of love, mass suicide, all in the name of Duty. King, drawn to Yasmani (who loves him), had moaned, "Dirtiest job I ever tackled"; but it was necessary, because this "native Joan of Arc" threatened to "turn these wild tribesmen loose to ravage a peaceful country." He had not reflected, earlier, on the wisdom of opposing "Joan of Arc," and he did not get a chance, later, to reflect on the "ravage" in Europe before his command perpetrated its own ravage on the Pashtus. The irony of citing right and wrong to justify slaughter is caricatured in Mohammed Khan (Mitchell Lewis), who, like many Ford "fool" characters,* reveals social values by exaggerating and theatricalizing them in comic skits. The big bearded Pakistani's skit is thrice repeated: he swats a beggar, slits a prisoner's throat, slaps another off a precipice, and each time intones, "For all the violence I have displayed toward my fellow men, Allah, forgive me!" But Khan's caricature is not of Moslem society: his initial skit is prefaced by his introduction by a British general, who describes him as holding "the highest rank possible in His Majesty's Service, a gallant soldier, and a gentleman!" Thus Khan's colonial chauvinism parodies King's own native chauvinism.

Slow fade to the regiment in another dining hall, framed by a bunkered doorway where two sentries stand in battle dress: only half as many men at

---

*Such as Mose Harper (*The Searchers*), many Francis Ford characters, and the feisty cavalry sergeants sometimes played by McLaglen himself—in his later career as a comedian.

table; the Colonel speaks, the pipers march round, the hands toast, the drummer twirls his sticks. Then King appears, in a stunning high-angle reverse shot, his back to us, overlooking the table. "I'm reporting for *duty*, sir."

Davey's arm is in a sling, a blanket hangs over his chair, but the Black Watch is never unable to sing; individuals may die, but the parade goes on. He starts weakly "Auld lang syne"; others join for the chorus, those on the right rising, to heighten rhythms toward climax. The left side rises, hands interlock, and all sway. Outside, three common soldiers stand cold in overcoats, caps, mittens, and foggy breath; they also sing with joined hands; we recognize the two sergeants. Within and without, everyone starts simultaneously to wish a "Happy New Year," and the most operatic of all Ford movies fades out Renoiresquely to the buzz of muffled conversation. The soundtrack continues over the black screen for a few seconds. It is the sound of the group.

In order to elucidate the social mechanisms that lead to war, *Salute** (1929) assumes, as did *The Black Watch,* a formidable myopia by which it is true to the subjectivity of its microsociety, if not to that society's objective situation in the greater world. Nothing could be more typical of expressionist-realism, and *Salute*'s comedy of manners documents establishment gentility in twenties America. Our impression that Paul Randall is heir to wealth beyond care is supported by the ancestral portraits, ancestral colored servants, and ancestral estates overlooking Chesapeake Bay, but nowhere does the film suggest there is anything extraordinary in this (unless it is the intensity of open-air atmosphere, or the way wind and sun flicker tree leaves). Rather than overtly criticize Paul's myopia, his lack of consciousness that life could hold problems greater than his schoolboy sense of dynastic duty, Ford represents Paul's class consciousness as an onerous actuality:

> *Grandfather:* (indicating the ancestral portrait gallery) These are the men of our family—all Navy men.
> *Paul:* I'll try to be worthy of these men, grandfather. Well, most of all, I want to be worthy of you.

At Annapolis, Paul finds in ceremonies, uniforms, exercises, hazing, and music ("Anchors Aweigh" at every occasion) equivalents of Black Watch regalia. But Duty and Tradition prove enticingly pretty, too, in the person of Nancy Wayne. Little surpasses, for lovely ingenuousness, Paul on her windowsill being taught "*Anchors Aweigh*"; their gentle voices blend sweetly, and explain in one magic moment all the wars ever fought. For wars

---

*Setting out for Annapolis, raised by his admiral grandfather, Paul does not notice girlfriend Marion flirting with his big brother John, who, raised by the *general* grandfather, is a West Point football star. At Annapolis, Paul meets Nancy Wayne; but too light for football and accused of ratting on upperclassmen, he nearly quits. At the Spring Weekend ball, Marion ignores Paul, and brother John devours Nancy. But next fall, Paul beats John in the army-navy game, and realizes Nancy loves him.

are not caused, says Ford, by "bad" people, but by "innocent" ones, for whom war becomes an extension of every fine impulse. Witness this incredibly "cute" dialogue, whose attitudes seem to our heroes all the more legitimate in virtue of their being enunciated midst the bright air of a campus walk* (filmed by Ford in a single frontal tracking shot):

Nancy: What's amatter? Bad news? Trouble?

Paul: No, I'm alright. Nothing wrong. Nothing at all.

N: Oh. I see. It's a lovely morning, isn't it?

P: Is it?

N: Yes, it is. Come on, let's walk and see. Now, tell me, what is the trouble?

P: No trouble, I told you, Nancy. No trouble at all.

N: I suppose that's why you're absent from formation without pass, looking as though you'd spent the night sleeping in a gutter.

P: I didn't sleep. I just walked, walked all night.

N: No trouble?

P: Oh, well, I might as well tell you. I quit the Academy.

N: Oh!

P: Hmm. You're disgusted with me, aren't you?

N: Well, no, but I'm disappointed. Why, you see, I'm a naval officer's daughter, Paul. Dad's a . . . invalid at home from the North Sea Patrol and the Navy means a lot to me. Well, it should to you too, Paul, with your grandfather.

P: Oh, granddad will understand. He'll know I'm doing the right thing.

N: Well of course he will, but he'll be disappointed too. Why, he's part of the tradition of the fleet. And he expected you to carry on that tradition. And now it dies with him.

P: Oh, I've tried, Nancy, I've thought of that and I've tried, but, well, I just can't seem to live up to it. It's too big for me.

N: I see. Do you suppose everyone will understand that? This girl, Marion?

P: Marion?!

N: Girls are funny, Paul.

P: Do you think Marion would be disappointed if I quit?

N: Terribly disappointed. 'Course she'll never let you know how disappointed she really is, if she cares for you. She'll just go on fighting the whole world for you, shielding it from everyone as much as she can, even from yourself. 'Course, sometimes she'll wish she didn't have to fight, she could just sit back secure and be proud of you.

P: You think Marion would want me to stick it out?

---

*Fox Movietone News first shot sound outdoors in 1927, and Walsh's *In Old Arizona*, a talking outdoor western, had been released nine months before *Salute*. Still, the sequence, filmed on location, is noteworthy for 1929.

As Paul, William Janney is bland, likeable, and (unlike the rest of the cast) anxious in diction. An early instance of many a guileless young brave in Ford, his abashed sensitivity does not essentially distinguish him among the naval officer caste (more aristocratic and Southern than Ford's army). As Nancy Wayne, Helen Chandler* makes a difficult (because so admirable) character credible and intriguing. Ford had a miraculous knack for milking fascination from ingenues in trite situations, their subtle turns of intonation and gesture due probably to deliberate underrehearsal and the resulting cloying mixture of uncertainty and sincerity.** It is the surreal quality of the performances, the patent artifice of James Kevin McGuinness's dialogue,[†] and Joseph August's realistic photography that lift much of *Salute* into realms of fond whimsy and poetic prosaism.

Ford will increasingly indict indoctrinated, ingenuous dutifulness, such as Nancy and Paul's, as cause of most social evils. In *Salute*, "evil" is latent, at worst, and even attractive (although too aristocratic to attract recruits), and no connection is made between cultural values and war, when beauty pays its dues to duty. Did postwar audiences require explicit reminders? Perhaps. But it is not primarily important to question how much Ford finds Nancy and Paul admirable, how much lamentable, how much objects of praise or satire. What *is* important is that *Salute* holds up a mirror to its age, and shows clearly enough the social dynamics that produce myopic naval officers.

When satire does appear, Ford does not, like Mel Brooks or Stanley Kubrick, announce it with flashing neon lights. Yet, short of thinking Ford a mindless racist jingoist even more ingenuous than Paul, how else, than as satire, can one interpret the scene immediately following Nancy's pep talk?: Stepin Fetchit (as Smoke Screen [?!], an old Randall servant) shows up at Annapolis, and proclaims to Paul, "I's yer Mammy!" Surely among the more redolent symbols in twenties movies, Smoke Screen has snuck away from the Randall household in the admiral's dress uniform (sword, tails, mammoth hat) to take care of Paul. For it appears that this navy world of manly tradition is a matriarchy, and despite a paragon of navy wifehood like Nancy (especially in comparison to Minne Wead in *The Wings of Eagles*, 1957), Paul, and the navy, still need a Mammy. Fetchit, in keeping with the theatrical traditions of the "original Negro,"[††] is acting as a mirror, satirically reflecting establishment values—like many Ford "fool" characters.

*Janney debuted in Mary Pickford's *Coquette* and had a small role in *Dawn Patrol* the following year. Chandler (1909–68) retired her unusual personality in 1935; cf. *Dracula, Outward Bound, Christopher Strong*.

**Claire Luce (*Up the River*), Karen Morley (*Flesh*), Rochelle Hudson (*Doctor Bull*), Anne Shirley (*Steamboat Round the Bend*), and Grace Kelly (*Mogambo*) easily surpass their screenwork elsewhere. *Riley the Cop* has another lovely open-air (park) scene between ingenuous young lovers; this sort of purity is lacking after World War II, when Ford's youths are naive, but awkward.

[†]McGuinness (1893–), Catholic publicist, drinking buddy ("Shaun" dubbed him "Seamus"), later a production chief at MGM. Credits include *Rio Grande, Tarzan and His Mate, China Seas*.

[††]Stepin Fetchit (né Lincoln Theodore Monroe Andrew Perry, 1892– , his stage name a

Satire of big brother John is more ambivalent, with some suggestion in his "American credo" lecture to Paul that, in flirting with Nancy, John had wished to arouse therapeutic anger in the callow youth:

> *John (to Paul):* If you want anything, you've got to grab it. After you grab it, hold onto it. No one in this world is going to give you anything, not even your own brother. So make up your mind to what you want, and then go and take it.

But George O'Brien cannot portray so vainglorious a character without slightly alienating us—and Ford's purpose is to reflect, not to nauseate— so, whatever the soundness of his advice, there is no reason for not supposing John the paragon of grabbiness he seems. Thus the staging—an expressionistically lit depth-of-field confrontation—seems less a "moment of truth" for Paul than a "study in contrast" for us. A second confrontation, after Paul beats John in the game, is similarly ambiguous:

> *John:* I had a spill coming to me, Paul. I've been a big shot here too long. In fact, it was good to learn I could be spilled, 'cause, Paul, when I get that ole commission and go out to the army, I'll only be a punk shavetail. Some grizzled ole sergeant probably knows more about soldiering than I'll ever know, 'have to take me in hand and play nurse to me. Huh? I'm not sore, Paul, I'm thankful to you. I'm proud of you.
>
> *Paul:* Gee, John, you're sure regular!

---

racehorse's, but also suggesting "step and fetch it") entered Fox films from vaudeville (*In Old Kentucky*, 1927) and became the studio's house darkie and the only really successful black moviestar of the era. He flaunted his wealth among blacks—a pink Rolls Royce with his name in neon lights—who adored his success while regretting his roles (the only sort available to blacks), but he hid his intelligence from whites, touting himself in trade ads as "a convincing, unexaggerated original or modern negro . . . that will meet the approval of the Board of Censorship and the patrons of North and South." His stereotype was not all his humor (and he is funny aside from it), but was an exaggeration by which to satirize Uncle Tomism. His skits and dialogues were of his own invention. "He played for two audiences," wrote Thomas Cripps, "giving to one a reassuring vision of Southern nostalgia, and to the other a covert, unstated metaphor for insurrection." John Wayne (who, with Ward Bond, had a substantial part as an upperclassman hazing Paul) was Fetchit's personal dresser on *Salute*. In later years, however, Fetchit found it almost impossible to find work; he hoped to film Satchel Paige's life, but was desperate for *any* work, and wrote Ford often. To Ford's suggestion that he be cast in *My Darling Clementine* in 1946, Darryl Zanuck replied: "No one has laughed longer and louder at Stepin Fetchit than I have, but to put him on the screen at this time would I am afraid raise terrible objections from the colored people. Walter White, when he addressed us on the problem of colored people, singled out Stepin Fetchit, as I recall, as an example of the humiliation of the colored race. Stepin Fetchit always portrays the lazy, stupid half-wit, and this is the thing that the colored people are furious about." (Memo, February 5; in the John Ford Papers, Lilly Library, Indiana University). It was an act of fierce independence for Ford to cast Fetchit in *The Sun Shines Bright* six years later—and he paid for it with that film's commercial failure. But Ford believed in Fetchit who, for his own part, was still defending himself as a liberator who paved the road that others tread. See: Joseph McBride, "Stepin Fetchit Talks Back," *Film Quarterly*, Summer 1971, pp. 20–26; Thomas Cripps, *Slow Fade to Black* (New York: Oxford University Press, 1977), p. 286.

What is "regular" about John is his hubris, a hubris perhaps ultimately equivalent in myopia to the naiveté that infests Paul.

Tradition and Duty, growing out of ethnic origins and with generally gloomy consequences, will be a major theme in virtually every subsequent Ford movie. Sensibly, in most of his early talkies (as in most of his post-1945 pictures), he sets his theme within highly structured societies in which social mechanisms motivating duty manifest themselves clearly. Even when Duty is not indicted, as in *The Black Watch* and *Salute*, it nonetheless precipitates noble tragedy. In *Men Without Women*, a disgraced officer redeems himself by staying behind in a sunken submarine so that others can escape. In a third navy movie, *Seas Beneath*, the conflicting duties of Americans and Germans, treated with remarkable equanimity, lead to sacrifices in love, liberty, or life for all the principals.

Despite *Salute*—Fox's biggest grosser of 1929—Ford was obliged, as with *The Black Watch*, to share credit on his next three pictures with dialogue directors.* Perhaps he was inflicted with an uncredited one on *Salute*, also. Some technical problems were inevitable: since rerecording had not yet been developed, *actual* army-navy-game footage *with* crowd noise alternates awkwardly with *staged* field action *minus* crowd noise. Yet how could Ford have been responsible both for the technically difficult but graceful outdoor dialogue scenes (often with traveling camera) and also for the technically simple but woodenly staged indoor ones (with mikes ill-disguised as lampcords)?

Interference had been disastrous for *The Black Watch*. It had been planned as a part-talkie, with only a couple of dialogue scenes, but Ford's train-station farewell, with its astonishingly virtuosic sound, had so bowled over Fox executives that production was shut down in order to replan the project as a full-talkie. Even so, Ford was not allowed to direct dialogue, which was entrusted instead to Lumsden Hare (a British stage actor who also plays King's colonel). Thus King and the Field Marshall speak with pompous slowness, stand stiff, project two nuances per minute: here where drama ought to peak—as King is ordered to desert—narrative halts. Hare also added love scenes ("I wanted to vomit when I saw them," said Ford, still bitter thirty-five years later) and seems to have taken over whenever there was extended talk. Perhaps it was as much to evade Hare as to try out his expressionist sound theories that Ford's portions (85 percent?) avoid dialogue in favor of operalike spectacle. And, of course, Ford's endless digressions never disrupt suspense. King, for example, arrives at the Field Marshall's midst a long foggy skit with tweedy streetsingers ("'Ome Sweet 'Ome"), then traverses one of filmdom's first offices of clapping typewriters.

Up the River does not suffer from whatever William Collier, Jr., contributed. Andrew Bennison may have added to *Born Reckless*'s woodenness, but *Men Without Women* is unassessable, the only extant copy lacking a soundtrack.

It was, in any case, a period of experimentation for Ford. For his first talkie, he used a single microphone (as he would always do!), and enjoyed underlaying foreground conversations with background talk, or the decrescendo effect of people walking away from the mike, or having characters perform with their backs to the camera. Insofar as they enhance *presence*, such techniques concur with Ford's expressionism. Foreign accents also provide fun, pipes and drums play at every opportunity, there is more singing than in most musicals, and as many sounds as possible are deliberately included.*

In *Men Without Women* (1930), Ford used a real submarine, dove his camera in a glass box, and took "impossible" dolly shots down bars and streets, with men carrying microphones on fish poles overhead. In *Up the River*, to accentuate Claire Luce's charisma and helplessness, he abandoned for once his eye-or-lower camera angle to frame her from above in three-quarter profile. The final shoot-out in ***Born Reckless*** (1930), mimicking a Ford western, complete with beloved bartender, is realized within a single long take—as are many action scenes in *Seas Beneath*. Such pyrotechnics are exceptions, rather than the rule; but in *The Brat*, the camera is unusually fluid throughout—Ford even mounts it on a garden swing.

Experiment—and comic invention—outside the plotline were Ford's invariable approaches to unsympathetic or inferior material. *Salute*'s platitudinous plot is redeemed by sheer quantity of invention, and building up tangential incidents in *Born Reckless* nearly diverts us from its pointless story.

The Brat (1931), a trivial Maud Fulton drawingroom comedy of manners, becomes thoroughly enchanting because of rapid pacing and a light, pointed touch. Piquant Sally O'Neil's fascination is heightened by her huge intense eyes, Yankee-Cockney accent, and friendly youthfulness wedded to sophisticated theatrical manners. Rather than try to lessen the "typing" of the "stock" roles (which would only have further dehumanized them—one might as well discard the whole play!), Ford has his actors play them for all their worth— with constant confirmatory "business," often in Ford's "wacky" manner: Mac-Millan's self-proclaimed genius is mocked by his confusion when handed an olive away from table, and his affectation by his habit of writing in a Russian shirt at a monk's desk. When June Collyer dismisses "Cyril," we see a Viking helmet and spear turn round to reveal a Brooklyn goon in pants who, seeing her cubist portrait of him, begins punching his head. Also added by Ford is a night-court prologue, whose half-dozen docket cases are a sideshow of freaks, while in a back room some cops (Ward Bond among them) "destroy" (Prohibition) champagne, wishing for beer and pretzels.

---

*Various drums, bagpipes, accordion, piano, honking and backfiring car, train bells and whistles, locomotive steam, squeaking brakes, tomtoms, wrench-wheel, whip lashes, tiny tinkling bells, squawking birds, bubbling oil, gunfire, machine guns, bombs, horses, howling wind, swords and shields, disembodied voices, a soda dispenser, a phonograph, dog barks, clapping typewriters.

In **Up the River** (1930), Ford again accentuates types to mock-epic proportions, drawing out caricature to suit the personalities of three fresh new actors—befuddled Warren Hymer, anxious Humphrey Bogart, and roguish Spencer Tracy—then sets them to trading lines in a spontaneous, quasi-vaudevillian style. *Up the River* had been planned as a grim prison drama, was nearly canceled when MGM released one first (*The Big House*), and then was rewritten delightedly by Ford and William Collier into a comedy.* Tracy, for example, arrives for prison by limousine, and poses for photos while the band plays "Stars and Stripes Forever." Commented Mordaunt Hall in *The New York Times*:

> Whatever may be one's opinions of depicting levity in a penitentiary, this screen offering often proved to be violently funny for the thousands who filled the seats of the [Roxy].[10]

In fact, the bizarreness of the project was especially fortuitous for Ford. Throughout this period, some sequences in *The Black Watch* aside, Ford impresses far more in comedy than in drama. And *Up the River* has lots of his wacky humor: dowagers touring prison, a pixilated mother (Edythe Chapman), a show, the unstressed presence of the ball team's mascot—a zebra—another instance of Ford's "invisible humor." But, in *Up the River* this humor counterpoints tragedy: marching files of prisoners, cellblocks, Claire Luce's depression, lovers' shame, the horror of a youth whose arrest killed his mother. And the result of this counterpointing was to throw both drama and comedy into relief and to create numerous "magic moments" that moved audiences. In a way, it was proof of expressionism—the movie once again creating its own reality.

Ford's comedies had always used vignette techniques, presenting characters initially as stock types in poses and situations supporting their basic definitions. The vignetting made them memorable, and made them fun to contrast. Each such character study constituted a world; their juxtaposition accentuated the bizarre qualities of each. Ford's expressionist techniques, meanwhile, came to be employed in drama for purpose of, essentially, "typing" atmosphere, milieu, and psychic vibrations of entire sequences. Basi-

---

*St. Louis (Tracy) deserts Dan (Hymer) during a prison escape, then shows up looking opulent in K.C., where Dan, street-singing for a gospel group, slugs him, and, as the band plays, both are hauled back to Bensonatta Penitentiary. There, Judy (Claire Luce), who plans to marry parolee Steve (Bogart), hears ex-boyfriend Frosby is blackmailing Steve to help cheat their wealthy New England neighbors. So St. Louis and Dan break out during a variety show, hop a freight, set things right for Steve—and return to prison for the big ball game with Upstate.

Up the River was Tracy's first film. Ford had seen him on Broadway in *The Last Mile*, talked baseball with him afterwards until 4 A.M. at the Lambs Club, and persuaded Fox to sign him despite an earlier rejection. Tracy, as ever, is quietly impressive, but even more quietly so than in later career, and, compared to the older, more affected actor, fresher and more natural at thirty. Bogart was also signed on Ford's advice (it was his second film), but Fox soon dropped both actors.

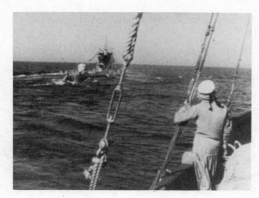

The Seas Beneath (1931).

On set, *The Seas Beneath* (1931). William Collier, Sr., in chair; John Ford with elbow on knee. From the Robert S. Birchard Collection.

cally methods of "weighting," expressionist techniques can have only limited (though vital) applications to comedy. But by applying comedy to expressionism, kaleidoscopic results were obtained. Not only would Ford contrast emotional *moods,* juxtaposing tragic and happy moments, but also *style* (slapstick with impressionism, expressionism with naturalness, theatricality with realism), and also *cinematic elements* (shapes, motions, light and dark, color, sound, music, cutting, camera movement) as autonomous "lines" of polyphonic formal inventiveness. This triple level of contrast is the route that all Ford's best movies follow. Like his penchant for choreographing movement, it is a signal quality.

There are few incidents anticipating such contrast prior to *Up the River*, and they tend to be unartful, or else to lack the pointing of comedy.* Whether or not serendipitously discovered in *Up the River*, these polymodal techniques were applied quite deliberately by Ford to his next picture, **Seas Beneath** (1931), and for the first time to a dramatic subject, rendering it, despite dreadful acting** and splendid photography, an instructive failure for its three distinctly incompatible modes of "realism":

1. Documentary Realism. The camera stares watchfully at immense varieties of natural lighting (Joseph August, again) and at water. The gaze from hundreds of yards' distance is steady as sailors board a lifeboat, row away, and the trawler sinks—nearly a minute, but seeming much longer. Another long take accentuates bizarre humor, as a girl wistfully watches her lover's departure on a funnily contrived submarine. A half-hour battle sequence almost follows real time, with little "action" but with weighty concentration on waiting, communication, and events between gunshots.

2. Comedic Vignettes. Despite a fat, braggart, McLaglen-like bo's'n, all the characters are low-keyed and humdrum, with George O'Brien average to the point of banality; thus both corn and naiveté have flavors of authenticity.

3. Operatic Mannerism. The Latin music accompanying siren Lolita's every appearance is matched by the white lace draping her and the exotica of her gesture and language (like Myrna Loy in *The Black Watch*). Though overdone, such atmosphere aims at least for inner realism.

DEPRESSION (1931–1935)

Arrowsmith	12.1.31	Goldwyn–United Artists
Air Mail	11.3.32	Universal
Flesh	12.9.32	Metro-Goldwyn-Mayer
Pilgrimage	7.12.33	Fox
Doctor Bull	9.22.33	Fox
The Lost Patrol	2.16.34	RKO
The World Moves On	6.27.34	Fox
Judge Priest	10.5.34	Fox
The Whole Town's Talking	2.22.35	Columbia

*The bizarrely mismatched prologues to *Men Without Women* (boisterous bar scenes) and *The Brat* (police cars screaming down Broadway midst black expressionist night and alternating high/low-angles) seem contradictions of all that follows them, rather than contrasts.

**Canary Island, 1918: Commanding a Q-boat—a German-hunting schooner with hidden cannon, reservist crew, and trailing U.S. sub—Capt. Bob (George O'Brien) romances Anna Marie, who, unknown to him, is German U-172's commander's sister. Ens. Cabot, drugged by Lolita, later dies sinking a German trawler; Anna, rescued by Bob, fails to warn off U-172, which is sunk. She, her brother, and fiancé go off to prison, leaving Bob hoping she'll return at

John Ford in the Dutch East Indies, 1932.

In contrast to the uneven experiments of this period's first half, its second half contains a series of mature and major masterpieces. No longer tentative, "polyphony" in mood, style, and element, whether subdued in moody tragedy or ebullient within depressed comedy, is fully adequate to thematic material. Contemporary America, in eight of nine films, is insular, static, misanthropic, and oppressive, every individual victim to determinist forces. Cultural values alone no longer provide surety. The Duty that formerly propelled bold heroes to get things done now seems full of contradictions; heroes find themselves ridiculous and destructive, and turn introspective. Their alienation symbolizes the common woe, serves to mature and reintegrate them, but only gradually becomes a positive force for altering social rot. Arrowsmith and Hannah Jessop are the first Fordian characters to attain critical consciousness and, with Jones (*Whole Town*), DeLaage (*Hurricane*), and some postwar instances, are the only ones who achieve *change*—but with what violence! Only with Hannah, then more fully with Will Rogers, in *Doctor Bull* and *Judge Priest*, does the Fordian hero appear,

war's end. (Marion Lessing (Anna) turns the ambivalence of her parting into total confusion; Ford was obliged to use her.)

There is even more atmosphere in the German edition's reedited music track: Wagner, Wagner, Wagner. Their sub sinks to the "Liebestod." But it contains a scene, missing from the U.S. edition, in which the Germans bury Cabot at sea—to "Taps." (Ford was unhappy with Fox's editing.)

as one capable of containing the contradictions that in earlier heroes threatened sanity and demanded resolution. The hero, of whom Abraham Lincoln will be typical, has a priestly quality: both of and above the people, he is a mediator, a lonely soul, continent but tragic. He alone brings light to an otherwise intolerably bleak existence: *Tabu*'s was a world lacking a hero. He is a Christ figure in the Augustinian scheme, a hero in the Hegelian—one whose knowledge of right and wrong transcends ordinary human limits and who single-handedly elevates his community out of its sloughs of intolerance and onto a higher moral plane. Outside normal human history, he is generally celibate.

These thematic developments were implicit in earlier pictures. Still, one can see here a commentary on the social catastrophe of the Depression years. But while there are attacks on business and government, Ford defines the horror not by 33 percent unemployment (12 million out of work) but by the moral meanness corrupting social bonds at every level—including, especially, the common man.

Although Ford wrote off $76,000 of stock losses between 1930 and 1932 (a lot of it in Fox subsidiaries), his earnings in those years came to $268,000 and exceeded $1.4 million between 1933 and 1941. His personal depression was not financial but moral, externalized in two wandering voyages to the South Seas and, in contrast to his ten steady years at Fox, in wandering visits to Goldwyn, Universal, MGM, RKO, and Columbia. A new contract negotiated by a newly acquired agent, Harry Wurtzel (brother of Fox production chief Sol Wurtzel), kept Ford under salary as a Fox contract director, but permitted him to work elsewhere as well. The advantages of this nonexclusive clause were less artistic than financial. Ford's Foxes are better and more personal than his movies at other studios, but production was long stagnant at Fox, following William Fox's ouster and the bankruptcy into which the new owners milked the company.

Arrowsmith (1931). Ford's first picture* away from Fox was a prestigious and ambitious undertaking for Ford, and it scored a box-office and critical triumph (with four Oscar nominations).

*Dr. Martin Arrowsmith (Ronald Colman) declines research under Prof. Gottlieb at famed McGurk Institute, choosing to practice medicine with Leora (Helen Hayes) in yokel-ful Wheatsylvania, S.D., where his cure for Blackleg wins him his own invitation to McGurk. There, a crazed burst of research is deflated, first by supercilious director Tubbs announcing it as "A Cure for All Disease," then by similar findings published in France. A year later Martin accompanies eccentric doctor-soldier Sondelius to the plague-ridden West Indies, where indignation greets Gottlieb's insistence on testing Martin's serum by treating only half the islanders, until a black doctor offers his people. Leora is left behind, Martin contemplates adultery with Joyce (Myrna Loy), Sondelius dies, then Leora, alone. "To hell with science!" screams Martin, releasing serum to everyone. In New York, a hero, he confesses his failure as scientist to Gottlieb, but Gottlieb has gone insane. Martin rejects Tubbs, refuses Joyce's hand, and rushes madly after a departing colleague to be a "true" scientist.

There is more than a fleeting similarity between Sinclair Lewis and John Ford in this period. Lewis wanted to expose the barrenness of American life, its hypocrisies, its insipidities, its myopia, and this, together with such gestures as refusing the Pulitzer Prize because of its advocacy of novels that would represent "the wholesome atmosphere of American life and the highest standard of American manners and manhood," gave Lewis a reputation as an angry, engaged writer. Where Ford differed was not so much in his low estimation of America, as in satiric sense. For him the dumbest bumpkin had a soul, and ugly personalities might have some charm. Lewis's satire concentrates on a character's defects, Ford's on his likeable qualities (e.g., Arrowsmith's purposefulness, Leora's agreeableness). Ford's less condescending satire increases empathy while simultaneously increasing distance. When you are amused with someone you like, you may also view him with some objectivity, and his defects, if clearer, seem less alienating. It may be argued that Ford's approach is better suited for films than Lewis's, since a more palatable movie may (ultimately) be more seditious.

Arrowsmith had appeared in 1925 and won Lewis the Pulitzer the following year. In 1930, again for *Arrowsmith*, he became the first American to be awarded the Nobel Prize for Literature. It was apparently assumed that the public was familiar with the book when the movie was made, for the adaptation by Ford and Sidney Howard (himself a Pulitzer winner in drama), attempting and failing to telescope the novel into a dramatic structure, has a shorthand quality to it, which today may leave an unprepared viewer somewhat mystified. And the confusion begins with the opening legend: "The story of a man who dedicated his life to science and his heart to the love of one woman"—which, while hinting at the antinomies, is not quite true.

Lewis's Arrowsmith is a stuffed shirt, lacking the bedside manner, unable to get along with the laity, hopelessly misplaced outside the laboratory. The movie sought a more sympathetic character, and with Ronald Colman playing the part, Arrowsmith becomes more empathetic, less satiric, and frailer. Howard-Ford even invented a scene in which Arrowsmith pulls a young boy's tooth with a painless trick, thus demonstrating character traits quite contrary to the novel's Arrowsmith. Two qualities, however, do set Colman-Arrowsmith apart. One, ironically, is Colman's suavity and assurance, which, when combined with his neglect of Leora for the glory-road,

---

Commentators claim McGurk refers to the Rockefeller Institute, and that Gottlieb and Arrowsmith are loosely based on Drs. F. G. Novy and Paul de Kruif. In the novel, Martin marries Joyce, who tries to train him into a society figure, until he leaves her to join Terry in a rustic Vermont lab. But when the movie was reissued under the more rigorous Production Code of 1934, nearly all Joyce's scenes were omitted; even the thought of adultery—Martin and Joyce going to bed in separate rooms—was unpalatable. Thus, glimpsing Joyce only once or twice in the background in St. Hubert, we are puzzled in the reissue when she pops up proposing in New York. Martin's lines over his dead wife ("I loved you Lee, didn't you know that? Didn't you know I couldn't love anyone else?") are deleted—the silence makes the scene more moving—and also his rush into her closet where he strokes and kisses her clothes.

makes him subtly pompous and silly; his theatrical manner suits a character so abstracted from reality. The second distancing quality is a peculiarly cinematic device: speed, his impatient drive. Thus, for example, a scene not in the book: on their date, Martin and Leora decide to get married, and she puts a coin in the jukebox, wanting to hear soft music. Instead she gets the "Lone Ranger" portion of the William Tell Overture, a prophecy of the galloping vigor of the man to whom she is tying herself. (The "tying" quality is expressed in another interpolated scene, when the county clerk gives the marriage certificate to Leora, insisting, "The lady gets it.")

Lewis's Leora was a much admired character at the time, although today so self-effacing a woman would not inspire plaudits. Ford beefs her up a bit, and the casting of Helen Hayes doubtless had that intention; but Hayes's screen-presence is not quite charismatic enough to permit her to compete with Colman and give the requisite force to Leora's side of the drama. She is still wholly Martin's and although in the book he is never forcibly accused of neglect, in the movie's telescoped sequencing implications become more explicit: the miscarriage Martin discovers she has suffered when he returns home having proved his Blackleg serum anticipates the dead woman he will discover when he returns having proved his plague serum. Thus the film becomes virtually the story of their *non*relationship. Martin's quest for glory kills Leora.

The implied antinomy between science and humanity is echoed in the use of the serum. While Lewis is at pains to indicate the need for scientific knowledge, as opposed to traditional "cures," mostly worthless yet widely accepted and whose value has never been ascertained, the movie, in the severest defect of its shorthand method, declines to make a case for the scientific method— i.e., for having a "control group" from which medication given to another group is withheld. We are left, like John Qualen's quaint Swedish farmer, feeling that it was a trifle silly not to have inoculated all the cows.

When Martin wants to follow the same procedure with human beings, and threatens to withhold the serum unless they "come to heel," the whites of St. Hubert's declare they will "die like men" instead. But a black doctor named Marchand (Clarence Brooks) offers the blacks on a small plague-stricken island: "It will be a privilege for my people to have served the world." Subsequently, we see Arrowsmith inoculating half the natives, sending away the other half with nothing, deciding to withhold the serum from a baby but giving it to the mother. The movie's morality seems slightly confused, for we seem expected to respond to the Negro doctor as a noble example of his race, whereas, if we hold that people are not cattle, he is instead a pitiable example of indoctrinated values and the mechanics of racism.* The latter interpretation is somewhat farfetched, given the film's am-

---

*In the novel, the black doctor did not make this offer, and Lewis's subsequent comment avoids the issue: "The negro doctor [in the film], I think, is the first one of his kind on the screen who has failed to come out as a quaint and obvious character. . . . I presented him honestly in my book . . . and the movie has miraculously [sic] presented him in the same honesty." (*The New York Times,* December 9, 1931, p. 23.)

bivalence on the issue of using humans as control groups (and its unwillingness ever to juxtapose starkly its implied antinomies), yet some credibility is given it by the unusually pyrotechnic camera movement with which Ford begins the St. Hubert's meeting: first we see a group of blacks; then the camera pulls back to show they are on a balcony loge with some whites seated in front; then the camera, on a crane, descends and pulls straight back across the hall's length and a long table where the meeting of whites is taking place. This indicates the power structure and the fate of the blacks, but the implications of moving camera linkage are too subtle, particularly coming at the very beginning of the sequence.

Other critics have not been bothered by the screenplay's inconsistencies. Lewis himself wrote to Colman, "I want to thank you for *Arrowsmith*; it completely carried out everything I tried to do in the novel."[11] And Richard Griffith, writing in 1956, saw the script as exemplifying "the 'Goldwyn touch': in its elusion of the incidental and highlighting of the genuinely thematic elements of the plot." He declared it a "forerunner of 'message pictures.' . . . To make such a conflict of ideas and levels of knowledge the heart of a film drama was unheard of in 1931."[12]

Compared with the relative naturalism of Ford's four preceding Fox assignments, *Arrowsmith* has elaborate demonstrations of depth of field and shows strongly Murnau's influence. But as the Black Death sequences begin, expressionistic stylization intensifies greatly, and elements of frenzy invade a hitherto sedate development. Leora's and Martin's aberrant motivations hereafter belong more properly to Ford's familiar "Duty Gone Astray" theme than to anything in Lewis. Five times Leora repeats, "I have no life without you," but Martin pays no attention as he sets out for Marchand's island: "I'm off to glory, Lee. If I pull this off I'll be a great man!" This key scene is shot from a low angle far back in the large room. Foreground chairs provide a proscenium arch, distancing and judging Leora and Martin, who appear isolated and small in the middle of the room. We may recall Leora's tremors of fear on the night of Martin's great discovery a year before. Outside her door now, overexposed in contrast to the dark menacing shadows inside, black natives pass carting their dead, chanting, "Lord help us!"

The picture's great accomplishment, and its definite advantage over the book is the mood it creates of paranoiac helplessness in confrontation with disease.* Set off against this central mood is the spectacle of the scientist who is at once the doctor-soldier and the dehumanized glory-hunter. On Martin's orders, native villages are burned, warehouses raided, a whiteman's plantation commandeered, selective inoculations begun. Sondelius dies midst a gradual crescendo of the sound of rain and the incessant sobbing of a woman off-camera (expressionistic sound). Intercut with these scenes, Leora struggles alone in that dark-shadowed room, a bell tolling, blacks chanting, and dies, crawling on the floor calling for Martin. He later kneels

---

*Cf. the plague sequence in *The Prisoner of Shark Island* (1936).

beside her dead body in a mannerist-like composition; streams of racing natives express his craze as he screams, "To hell with science! To hell with Gottlieb!" and runs to stroke and kiss Leora's clothes.

Somewhat less comprehensible is Martin's similar exit from McGurk. Again, on paper, where conflicts are tidily stated, it is clear he desires to return to innocence. But in the movie's crescendo dynamics the ending is abrupt and crazed: Gottlieb found insane, Tubbs and Joyce quickly rejected, Martin racing madly down the hall, "Hey Terry, wait! Lee and I are coming too, we're both coming with you!" Close-up freeze-frame, fade out. Has Martin really found wisdom? Or has his galloping idealism merely shifted tracks? He still feels he betrayed Science by hysterically releasing serum to everyone after Leora's death.

What, furthermore, is the connection between the body of the film and its prologue—a line of covered wagons, in one of which a girl stares ahead determinedly, dissolving to the drunk town doctor telling young Arrowsmith (engrossed in Gray's *Anatomy*), "That was your grandmother, Martin, fine stock, pioneer stock, stubborn stock"—unless the conjunction of a drunk doctor and stubbornness intends to prefigure the fable's moral—whatever that moral is?

Considering, though, that Martin Arrowsmith is Ford's first real attempt at a profound character, and a confusedly complex one at that, it is not surprising that the personage is not entirely satisfying—especially given Colman's polished superficiality. What is surprising is that, a few scenes excepted, the picture has little period mood; Howard's telescoping has not been filled out with the normal, heavy dose of Fordian density. Perhaps there is too much plot, too much speed. Eight characters are developed to some degree, but some are left unfinished and others disappear, like John Qualen, as soon as their chapter concludes. And eight was a small number for Ford; even in 1931 his narrative technique was capable of developing far more tangential, cameo roles than this script's compression permits. Instead, opportunities walk on and off without even putting in their two cents. For example, when Sondelius and Martin get drunk in a Minneapolis beerhall, the eccentric Swedish Communist who (in the book) joins them is replaced (in the film) by a fellow who waltzes in with a chicken leg and a beer mug—and waltzes out again. One misses, too, Lewis's McGurk, the nefarious capitalist who has founded the Institute for his public image and entrusted its care to his wife Capitola.

Gustav Sondelius, on the other hand, is a triumph of Richard Bennett's burly flesh and gesture humanizing Lewis's sketch (which typically tries to grasp characters' essences in chronicling their deeds and words). No words could capture the grandiloquent and funny humanitarianism with which his thick accent and emphatic arm-raise announce, "And I will go wit' you! [to fight the plague]." Even, or especially, in this instance, however, it is apparent that the cinematic and the literary are rarely, if ever, synonymous in *Arrowsmith*.

Arrowsmith begins like a sad dream and concludes like a nightmare; moments of ebullience along the way seem in retrospect to have been so many alternatives that died prematurely. *Arrowsmith*'s incredible modal intensity grows in richness and artifice, until its multiple thematic contradictions (personified in Dr. Arrowsmith) burst into crazed rejection. But this madcap rejection, resolving none of life's contradictions, seems more a continuation under new guise of Dr. Arrowsmith's galloping glory-quest than a correction of prior wrongness.

      ***Air Mail* (1932).** In ensuing Ford pictures—*Air Mail, Flesh, Pilgrimage, Doctor Bull*—the very air is suffused with palpable weight of lonely, God-bereft existence. In *Air Mail*, the modal experiments of the past five years reach another culmination of sorts, and, with Murnau's frequent collaborator Karl Freund as photographer, no movie better illustrates Murnau's realist-expressionist influence on Ford. Pictorial subtleties abound: a brutalized young wife gazes desperately out rainy windows, whose gently dappling chiaroscuro midst contrasting stillness mirrors her mood with Antonioni-like expressivity; elsewhere, the psychic emptiness of "Desert Airport" is filled by glistening fog and darkness. But more important than lovely graytones is the neorealist intensity of space, the camera's meditative stare, the fact that every shot is already a world drenched by the personage inhabiting its space—whence the extraordinary dynamics of the contemplative two-shots: an intersection of "worlds." Surprisingly, such artiness

occurs without strain in this supposedly tough male pic; in this we recognize, for the first time strongly, a most Fordian trait. And, indeed, *Air Mail*, both in 1932 and today, seems too much a depressed little commercial programmer to attract the critical attention it merits. But its characters, story, and milieu are handled with a complementary duplicity by Ford.

Air Mail's would-be mythic men ostensibly attract us as a movie's stars usually do; but, if we pay them closer attention, we may see that really they are unlikeable antiheroes, unwittingly subverting accepted values. It is easy to connect, in this respect, the screenwriter Frank "Spig" Wead biographied in *The Wings of Eagles* (1957, q.v.) with Frank W. Wead, scenarist of *Air Mail*. *Air Mail's* pilots are dominated by professionalism *in duty* (even as a wrecked flyer burns alive, we shift to saving his mail pouches); *in honor* (self-hate by a pilot who bailed out as his passengers crashed is heavier penance than the deafness of his ostracizing peers to his pleas for a chance to "save my soul"); *in machismo* (daredevil stunts by Duke [Pat O'Brien] are mere stage-setters to the articulate "Nuts!" he humphs when unanimous verdicts of "Impossible!" goad him into rescuing downed Mike [Ralph Bellamy] from a narrow canyon). But such dedication toward manly mannequinhood leaves gaping vacuities elsewhere in their lives. Woman may be the warrior's repose, but not for these misogynists. Husband Dizzy so tyrannizes Irene (Lillian Bond), and Mike is so righteous, it is difficult to disapprove her opportunism, as soon as Dizzy is killed, in running off with Duke. Duke, however, discards her to rescue Mike, thus redeeming himself while acknowledging her perfidy. Such conventional justice chimes ambiguously; we sense a story working on two levels of morality. Indeed, Ruth (Gloria Stuart), the "good" woman, provides a satisfying emotional focus for audiences unadventurous in their sympathies; but the true empathetic center (as often in this period) is the brash, alienated, victimized woman. But neither as victim nor as discarded refuse does Irene, the first such character in Ford, arouse our empathy without our conscious decision; ostensibly, she repulses us, symbolizing society's rot, and fixated solely on her own wants. Duke, moreover, will probably return to Irene; he has not rescued Mike out of humaneness but to prove he can do anything. Thus he survives a fatal crash not so much to provide a "happy ending" as because death would be inconsistent. "Say, how many of the stories you hear about that guy are true?" asks Slim. "All of 'em!" exclaims Mike, whereupon Duke zooms in out of nowhere. (One story: hired to bomb by revolutionaries, the princess fell in love with him, and so the government expelled him.) As in Murnau's *Last Laugh*, the impossible distances gloomy reality.

Isolation of professional caste binds the flyers together in a pseudo- and acerbic community and excludes the world. Gloom and desert serve not merely as props to express this isolation, as they would in pure expressionism, but extend and compound it in a realist dialectic. For, like the disgruntled, eccentric passengers stranded one foggy night in the terminal, the flyers are just passing through and refuse alliance with land or one another.

A subtext of racism, in form of local Indians lurking unobtrusively in back-grounds, contrasts this alienation; but they come stage center only once, to hold a *Donovan's-Reef*-like Christmas service (the children sing "Silent Night") and, as often in Ford, to point up the discordant impoverishment of white community. Slim Summerville plays the classic simpleman who, alone among the whites, does not war with life (anticipating later Francis Ford roles in this and in spitting across a room and making a can ring). Into this misanthropic murk intrudes Duke, scornful of propriety or danger, a figure of liberation, chaos, and nature, frolicking recklessly in his plane be-neath a (for once) sunny sky—a typically Fordian disruption of which Tunga Khan in *7 Women* will be the ultimate representation.

Little of this "subversion" may be apparent to the casual viewer, who will like Duke and deplore Irene, and probably not bother to probe the discom-fort of conventional moral attitudes. Similarly, special effects (by John P. Fulton, later of *Invisible Man* fame) so well integrate models and rear pro-jection with actual stunts by flyer Paul Mantz (plus footage from *Pitz Palu*) that one never suspects the artifice. When Duke sees Mike from the air, he really sees a three-inch dummy with mechanical waving arm surrounded by six-foot mountains in a two-hundred-foot-long miniature canyon set.[13]

John Ford and Howard Hawks are frequently confused in the public mind. Ford himself often acknowledged plaudits for (Hawks's!) *Red River*. Yet, although *Air Mail* has some resemblances to Hawks's *Only Angels Have Wings* (1939), comparing Ford and Hawks is usually like comparing fruits and fishes: points of similitude are as few as points of difference. Hawks might be classed with Chaplin, Lubitsch, Wilder, and Cukor, all of whom appeal strongly to those who conceive cinema as an extension of theater, while Ford may be classed among the expressionists or even certain realists (Rossellini, Flaherty, Straub). The distinction is less that of "theater" versus "cinema" than of emphasis on body and dialogue versus emphasis on compo-sition. Where expressionist Eisenstein will elaborate a point through a se-ries of cuts, Chaplin will do a solo ballet, and Hawks will stage a long ab-surdist "duet," such as Jean Arthur's "Do you think I should?" dialogue with Dutch toward the end of *Only Angels*. Ford's dialogue normally is sparingly expressionist (as in *How Green Was My Valley*), but he too will use run-on talk-for-talk's-sake, particularly in his Irish pictures; the "Will you be wan-tin' the car, inspector?" exchange between Cyril Cusack and a gateguard at the start of *The Rising of the Moon* is typical. But such dialogues are rarely the rhythmic *pièces de résistance* they are for Hawks, and we tend to re-member Ford's words within his total composition, while we remember Hawks's words with his actors and their (often frantic) gestures rather than with his compositions.

These facile distinctions correspond to deeper ones. Both Ford and Hawks movies can be described as series of skits by character actors. But whereas Ford's actors become fictional beings, Hawks's star personalities *are* his characters. Cary Grant, on paper, plays radically different people in *His Girl Friday, Only Angels,* and *Bringing Up Baby,* but in practice he seems a single identity, "Cary Grant," in three different moods. Artifice, in the best sense, is Hawks's aim; his art's realism is based on our delight at Cary Grant being "Cary Grant." In contrast, John Wayne in *Stagecoach, The Quiet Man, The Searchers, The Wings of Eagles,* and *Liberty Valance* is less "John Wayne" than five autonomous personages. True, no amount of auteur criticism will convince some people that *The Searchers* is not "a John Wayne movie." But Ford wants us to experience Ethan Edwards (John Wayne) and to believe as firmly in the "reality" of that character and that filmic world as we do in the characters and worlds of Balzac. He uses stars less for their personalities than for their presence, their ability to make a storybook character vivid.

Accordingly, Ford's characters have different cultural identities, Hawks's only have different jobs. Indeed, Hawks's people tend to be deracinated (no families in Hawks!) and their stories' locales—specific culture, atmosphere, and thereness—are relatively inconsequential. *Rio Bravo,* a western, and *The Big Sleep,* a gangster film, could exchange sets and costumes with little adjustment in scripting. Atmosphere in Hawks is mostly backdrop (the darkness in *Only Angels* has the unvarying constancy of a stage set), and his action typically involves the prolonged *development* of a few main characters (often just two or three) within a few situations and extremely long sequences. In contrast, Ford's intense pictorialness serves to create worlds both spatially and in cultural consciousness. Thus his atmosphere has variety, vim, and vigor, and is drenched with the sort of documentary details of daily life that Hawks reserves for feats of engineering, and his action, generally complex with many characters, involves constant cameo *exposition* of novel situations; a character is developed through constant insertion into short, contrasting sequences.

In sum, Ford movies are dialectics between world and sensibility; Hawks movies are between people. Hawks's people are bound together because they want to be: getting the mail through in *Only Angels* is a pretext for community. Ford's people are bound by ideology and purpose rather than affection: getting the mail through in *Air Mail is* the community's *raison d'être.* Accordingly, the mailbags play an infinitely greater part in *Air Mail* than in *Only Angels,* but often with heavy irony: tradition, almost nonexistent in Hawks, is always opprobrious in Ford. Correspondingly, while *Air Mail's* pilots shun the pilot who bailed out and deserted his *passengers,* Hawks's shun the pilot who abandoned his *mechanic.* For Ford, it is duty and pride that are at stake; for Hawks it is the team. Thus the Hawks man can be redeemed and accepted back onto the team, but the Ford man, having offended God, is held by his colleagues to be damned beyond human forgiveness.

Hawks characters are almost chameleons. But character is fate in Ford; people do not change; they undergo fortune and awake to destiny. His cinema is a tapestry of excommunications—in these years alone: blacks, half-castes, fallen women, illegitimate children, impolitic doctors, sons, and blacksmiths—and the ostracized can be saved only by the lonely hero (lacking in *Air Mail*). Hawks opposes Ford's notions of the lonely man who is great. His movies are about how people change each other and create community. The entire gargantuan structure of transcendental idealism that powers the Catholic Ford's worlds is reduced in Protestant Hawks's worlds to the immediate structures of personal loyalty, desire, and biology. It is not so much that Ford's people are undersexed or idealized (although his cameos *are* sometimes excessively iconic); indeed, Ford's people are scarcely less *physical* than the people of Renoir, Rossellini, Sirk, Walsh, Bresson, Hitchcock, Cukor, Minnelli, Ophuls, Sternberg, Capra, or Godard. It is that Hawks's people are hyperbolically physical, with sex as their motive force and animals or herds as their frequent metaphor (cattle, horses, leopards, minions who build pyramids). Personality, or physical emotion, stands atop Hawks's materialism, like a transcendent; in Ford, it is caught in the meshes of the cultural world ancestors have begotten, struggling to emerge, as in *Tabu*, from the masses that are nature.

Curiously, nature is more metaphorical in Hawks than in Ford, just as Hawks is verbal where Ford is visual. In treating a pilot's fatal attempt to land in fog, Hawks emphasizes dialogue between those on land and the (essentially) unseen pilot's voice; Ford alternates visual shots. The "moral" for Hawks, who dislikes dissension, lies in the attempted stoicism afterward by which death knits his community closer. But Ford emphasizes what Hawks elides: people's immediate anguish juxtaposed with the burning pilot, and his "moral" is a set of diffuse, multiple conflicts excited by the crash: the irony of the mailbags, the rapport between Mike and Ruth in contrast to the hatred between Irene and Dizzy (four cameos), and the pedantic, almost Brechtian observation to a teenager, "Still want to be a flyer, stupid?" Similarly, Ford's film is precisely about all the mundane realities Hawks's leaves out: what happens to Jean Arthurs and Cary Grants once they settle down.

Flesh (1932). Whereas *Arrowsmith* dealt with insanity and *Air Mail* with boredom, and gloom pervaded both, *Flesh* deals with a melodramatic conflict—alienation vs. simplicity—and offsets gloom with Fordian comedy. It thus marks an important step for Ford in the adaptation of his comic, vignette style to tragic material. But the step was probably made inadvertently. It is evident that Ford was not involved in *Flesh*'s initial planning and was subsequently prohibited from editing its script—dialogue is verbose, characters talk on and on without saying much—and it may be that he did not direct large chunks of it—scene after scene is filmed shallow focus in interminable three-quarter poses, with a dozen shots lasting almost ninety seconds and another dozen exceeding thirty (versus less than ten seconds for the average Ford shot). But most of *Flesh* feels like pure Fordian invention—sparse dialogue, lively action, articulate angles and cutting—

and with all its unevenness *Flesh* still is a serious study of America and creates in Lora Nash Ford's most profound character to date.*

Horrifying scenes begin *Flesh*: from high above a chimneyed rooftop, a circle of women tramping in a prison courtyard, then Lora, brash and alienated, in the self-righteous warden's office. Visually, these are Germanically expressionistic, but mood switches totally for the beergarden scenes. Polokai gaily takes his ritual postfight bath in a mammoth barrel, quaffs a gallon of beer, and submerges. Then the band plays, people sing, and he carries around a huge keg, filling mugs.

Another contrast sets off Germany, her officialdom grim but her people idyllic, from New York, a labyrinth of corruption. "You're not in Germany now; you're in America," says the wrestling-czar. And the meaning is ironic: the Germans were simple folk, all of a piece; they liked to sing, eat, and drink, but propriety was propriety. The Americans, consistent with Ford's depressing views in these years, are neurotic, conniving, and power hungry. Between the two there is no mutual language.

Contrast also sets off the three principal characters—Polokai: naive, oafish, good; Lora: alienated, pretty, amoral; Nicky: opportunistic, debonair, evil. Their qualities, and their isolation, are emphasized by Ford's vignette method through an abundance of portraitlike medium close-ups— Lora backed by translucent drapes or by dark water rippling in surreal serenity, like Monet's water lilies—that drench the character in her or his own mood. This technique reaches a high point when Nick reappears and discovers Lora has borne Polokai's child. After a three-shot and the baby's entry—Polokai hands him to Nicky—Ford cuts to portraitlike close shots of /Nicky, confused with the baby, glancing toward /Lora, implacable, then /Nicky turning toward /Polokai, beaming fraternally, then /Nicky, still confused with the baby.** The sequence needs no dialogue, and each little shot isolates each character in his own private world. Such cutting becomes typical of Ford—as in *Stagecoach*'s coach scenes.

But this isolation, this alienation, is, like our own initial impressions of the characters, something to be got beyond. Wallace Beery, although slightly more restrained than usual, with a bit more tenderness and hint of

---

*Just released from German prison (and awaiting Nicky's release), American Lora (Karen Morley) contemptuously accepts oafish Polokai's hospitality (Wallace Beery), and gets his money for her "brother" (boyfriend) Nicky (Ricardo Cortez). Nicky skips for America and Lora, bereft, marries Polokai, bearing a child the night he becomes Germany's champ wrestler. She makes him move to New York, where Nicky compels her to make him sign with Nicky's crooked syndicate. But learning German friends have all bet on a fight he is supposed to throw, Polokai gets drunk. Lora finds him in bed, Nicky enters, beats her, she tells Polokai the truth, he strangles Nicky, and, encouraged by Lora, breaks out of his stupor to win the match. In jail, he forgives Lora, who will await his release. Metro doubtless saw *Flesh* as a follow-up to Vidor's *The Champ* (1931), in which Beery played a boxer. (Compared to the post-1935 Metro of God, motherhood, and patria, Metro before 1935 was raw and earthy: compare Judy Garland chasing her dog around Oz in 1939 with Garbo playing phallus with her bedpost in 1934 in *Queen Christina*.)

** / = cut.

hidden depths, is typecast as a stupid but kind-hearted buffoon; we must come to accept the personage, forgetting the actor, and then must come to admire the man rather than the "big hunk of flesh." Ricardo Cortez's Nicky disengages our sympathies by his actions rather than by his body or manner; only from a benign distance can we summon compassion for him. ·Lora's heartless manipulation of Polokai all but destroys our nascent sympathy. She acts streetwise but she is a complete fool for Nicky (trembling sexually: "Love me . . . kiss me") and has none of the sweet appeal of, say, *Stage-coach*'s Claire Trevor. Yet her terrible realism, thrust into Polokai's compassion, in time enables us to feel her suffering, dread her isolation, and admire her guts; she seems to typify the Depression era.*

An easy ability to slip into deep feeling lifts these performances beyond the commonplace. The stock, stereotypical characters take on a certain independence as we, in line with the movie's moral, see beyond the flesh. Nicky himself never succeeds in this. Menacingly lit in close silhouette, he confronts Lora, hits her, and watches her fall back out of the frame as though she were just a thing he swats—and to him she *is* just a thing. A matching shot of Nick follows immediately, but now, as he gives his orders, his menace becomes frightening through blurred focus. Similarly, when Polokai kills Nick, it is Nick who, silhouetted with his back to the camera, dies like a thing. Thus do camera angles become moral statements. Lora's final rebellion against Nick is iterated by: /An empty frame: Lora jumps into frame, close-up, from *right*. /Medium shot of Lora: Nick jumps into frame, close-up, from *left*. The two shots with their two motions complement each other, convey kinetically the frenzy of the moment and the moral revolution in Lora's personality.

Lora is a development of the Irene character in *Air Mail*, but such an explored study of alienation is new to Ford. Early Ford characters embody their native culture without complexity or neuroses; even when an Irish family comes to America (*Shamrock Handicap*, 1926), no culture shocks prompt anyone to remeasure his existential awareness. Indeed, it probably is Murnau's chief contribution to Ford that he taught him that people live and breathe and feel within decor, and that consciousness is a continuously renewing dialectic between inner self and outer world. Hence in *Hangman's House* a Ford character finally falls into deep introspection over his life's failure to be what it yearns to be, and Ford sets the scene looking out to sea. In *The Black Watch*, the displacement is far more extreme: a Scotsman is transported to Pakistan and (to his guilt-ridden credit) begins to feel guilt and self-questioning. Similar displacements occur in *Arrowsmith* and *Air Mail*, and in *Flesh* Lora's dilemma is initially characterized by her being an

---

*Period evocations in films today have every prop accurate but ignore period atmosphere for "realism," and impose, as demythicization, revisionist mythologies upon bygone eras' feelings and beings.

American in Germany. But whereas such displacement was the *cause* of misery in earlier films, in *Flesh* it is merely the symbol. Lora's displacement extends to everywhere and everyone, even to her child, and the fact that in Nicky alone does she feel at home only emphasizes her displacement the more ironically. Her "dialectic" with reality is immeasurably more active and intense than that of any prior Ford character— precisely because her notions of reality are so blurred by alienation and delusion. Somewhat like Hannah (*Pilgrimage*), whom she anticipates, Lora's story is a passage toward consciousness of herself as an actor in life (rather than as a mere brunt of others' abuse or as an abuser of others herself), toward a realization not so much of her sinfulness as of her value.

The world Lora rises out of is suffused from its opening prison scenes with languid depression, loneliness, helplessness. The world that, through Polokai, beckons her is suffused by joviality. The pace is swift, the mood bubbles, *Flesh* becomes a comedy, and Ford adds amusing touches at every opportunity: the giant Polokai comes to the hospital to see his newborn with a three-foot elephant, and passes a little man walking proudly behind two nurses carrying three new babies. In a newspaper we read Polokai will fight "Zbyszko," and during the match, our attention on the fight, we may not notice some of Ford's "invisible humor," the hysterical gestures of Polokai's silhouetted trainer. Earlier, a shot of Ed Brophy in an office twiddling a toothpick in his mouth dissolves into a matching shot of Brophy still twiddling while bobbingly refereeing.

Lora confronts Polokai with an intensifying series of outrages: stealing his money, making him fight dishonestly, confessing Nicky is her boyfriend, causing him to murder Nicky; she drags him down into dishonor, drink, and finally prison, like herself. But at each confrontation Polokai replies with love and trust that, if at first they seem imbecilic, eventually seem redemptory. At times one half suspects that Polokai's simplicity may be a guise for guile—as when he breaks down a door that supposedly will not open (then does), or as when he breaks an egg after demonstrating that even the strongest man in the world could not break it. But it is the nature of the Fordian "fool"—a character developed in a number of directions in subsequent films—that he "sees true," or that (one is never sure) he refuses to see what he does not want to see, and therefore makes the world conform. At any rate, happiness in Ford will belong only to the determinedly simple. In *Flesh* it is the intertwining and eventual union of these two "stories" so mutually contradictory— the persistently simple man, the evolvingly alienated woman—that provides the catharsis.

Pilgrimage (1933). Yet Ford was searching in this period for a polyphony more sober than *Flesh*'s boisterous melodramatics; two melancholic comedies—by far his finest films to date—marked his return to Fox. *Pilgrimage*, like *Four Sons*, is drawn from a simple, sentimental I. A. R.

Wylie story, and such it doubtless remains for the unexploring viewer. But *Pilgrimage*, like *Doctor Bull*, portrays the insipid mundanity of a culture; its dreary comedy stresses hard-souled individuals, intolerant communities, repressive ideologies, and idiosyncratic subcultures.

Three Cedars, Arkansas, 1918: Widow Hannah Jessop is a jealous, possessive mother; blind to her son Jim as an individual person, she mistakes her intolerance for love. "For his own good" she has Jim sent to war: "I'd rather see him dead than married to that girl!" And Jim dies, buried alive, but ten years later Hannah, unrepentant, shuns his posthumous son by Mary as proof that Jim was "no good." Hannah (Henrietta Crosman) is an old farmer woman, mean and nasty. Far from liking her despite herself (as we do Katharine Hepburn's obnoxious old ladies), our empathy for Hannah is unpleasant. Ford wants us to be empathetic, even sympathetic, but from the outside, where we can feel Hannah's "good reasons" without succumbing to them, and where we can understand her evilness as the eternally repeated tragedy of everyman. To show Hannah in such depth, Ford's direction becomes a distancing dialectic, rather like Murnau's in *Tabu*.

Through Ford's direction, objects become testimonials casting into perspective people enshrouded in private myopia and self-deception. Old Dad Saunders slumbers while Mary and Jim discuss him in the background, but a whiskey jug foreground tells the tale (frame 1). Gazing down a road, the pointed tops of a zig-zaggy fence tell us the sleigh is bringing Hannah news of Jim's death (2). Subtler roles for objects are prepared by the picture's initially deliberate pacing: we feel time heavily as we feel the dark, misty, palpable atmosphere of the farm. Mist, forest, pools, and barn doors enclose the lovers' *Sunrise*-like tryst (3); fiery blackness, a lamp, and a jutting bannister enclose a violent quarrel between mother and son (4). Thus, when mother and son debate while sawing a log and Ford watches through a proscenium-like gateway, the witnessing fence distances their drama into an "arena" or "court," encouraging a perspective of moral sympathy (5, 6). Similarly, a foreground table and lamp witness the long-shot scene when Hannah learns Jim is dead (7); their steadfast presence reminds us that time can neither be turned back nor halted: Hannah has to live every second. Comparable procedures distance many scenes in *Pilgrimage*—and throughout Ford's career. The tendency of distance to encourage reflection is additionally exploited during sharp altercations: frontal shots of Hannah's victims (Mary; later, Jimmy) are exceptionally close, projecting direct sensations of agonized appeal, but the answering frontal shots of Hannah are roomier head-to-chest, less projecting, less sensation-laden, and require us to "go in" toward Hannah, to reflect on her.

Sequencing, in linking one scene to another via ellipsis and thus implying cause-and-effect, also prompts the distance of reflection. A snowy window vista reinforces the ironic dimensioning of Ford's long single take as Hannah signs Jim into the army ("You are the first person to walk in here and offer up her own son. You have to love your country a lot to do that.") Whereupon a

1 2
3 4
5 6
7 8

9

10

11

12

13

14

15

16

black locomotive hurtles toward us out of a black night—Hannah's love. (And we see the effect of the locomotive, which takes Jim away, during a remarkable sustained study of Mary, watching [8].) A similar instance, years later, pivots on a fencepost knob. The foreground, oversized knob "judges" a close-up of Hannah's piercing stare (9), then, in a matching long shot, with its fence stabbing diagonally into the frame (10), the knob "judges" tiny Jimmy fleeing Hannah's stare; after the ellipsis, Jimmy battles malicious gossip in a schoolyard fight, witnessed by a wide, prosceniumlike circle of children (11). A third ellipsis links Hannah's adamant refusal to join fifty Gold Star mothers on a pilgrimage to their sons' graves in France ("after spending ten years remembering to forget") to her standing on the station platform, going; and she is tiny, distanced a long perspective from the station entrance (12). The witnessing entranceway subsequently becomes personable when Mary and Jimmy enter frame bottom and stand in trepidation before petitioning Hannah to carry *their* flowers to Jim's grave (13).

This last ellipsis delicately demonstrates Hannah's inability to acknowledge her heart, which is confirmed when her hand, reaching down from the train window, accepts Mary and Jimmy's flowers without her face acknowledging their presence.

Pilgrimage, like many Fords, pleads for harmony between myth and human needs. Hannah's disharmony, however, reflects noxious distortions of reality by her culture. Her myopia is shared by the draftboard clerk who praises her love, by the farmhand who smokes on the haywagon, by the mayor (Francis Ford) who tries to stop the train with his cane, by the Wac who treats Hannah with amusement and undue respect, by the general's daughter who pompously declaims, "Think of how wonderful and reconciling it would be to really stand beside the graves of one's heroic dead!" The mayor of Three Cedars urges Hannah to take the pilgrimage because her "goin' will help put our town on the map," and his New York counterpart tells a reporter, as they watch the mothers board ship, that "that's the most eloquent speech this country ever made"; but Ford's foreground placement of the reporter (14) (who rushes off to quote the mayor) reinforces the irony between the motives of mothers visiting graves and the motives of a government that, having sent boys to die in a disastrously silly war, makes political capital ten years later by sending forth their mothers. (An ethnic cross-sample of mothers, too: Mrs. Goldstein, Mrs. Carluzzi, Mrs. MacGregor, Mrs. Quincannon, Mrs. Hammerschmidt.) The mothers do not question their culture's doctrines; patriotic sacrifice and maternal love coexist without protest. At the Arc de Triomphe they are told that "the altar of freedom is wet with your tears"; but it is hard not to wonder why Ford's French general strikes us as such an outrageous caricature during so sincere a ceremony (15). In fact, the ceremony precipitates an orgy of grief that evening in the mothers' commonroom. First (16), a foreground mother, all heart, dissolves into hysteric tears on hearing "Then You'll Remember Me" on the piano. Second, she is "comforted" by hillbilly Tally Hatfield,* who tells her, "I'd rather my [three] boys died as they did, than feuding with the McCallisters, 'cause they was all *good* boys"—which is not quite played for comic relief, making the Chekhovian absurdity all the more provocative. Are such memorial services worth their paroxysmal grief? Hannah's reaction, the third effect, is even worse: she publicly denounces her son as "no good," as an affront to "decent god-fearing people," and declares she will not join their pilgrimage to the graves. The all-heart mother in the foreground places Hannah's middle-ground hysteria into relief (17).

An altogether different sequence of events will indeed lead Hannah to Jim's grave. But then there is no talk of "heroic dead," and she does not "stand": she collapses. For Hannah herself was the war that killed her son, just as comparable intolerance in rival patriotic communities killed so many others.

Hannah's "bridge" scene is also the loveliest of George Schneiderman's varied photographic beauties. She walks across a Seine bridge at night, framed of course from afar, so as to include the arches below and the dark sky above (18). Street noise is blocked out by the soundtrack music. Fog mists drift thinly, and a few period automobiles and bicycles glide silently across. Now Hannah, just after having denounced her son, meets Gary, contemplating suicide. Her motherhood, in this dreamworld, responds to him, and morning shows life in a new context. Atmosphere in Three Cedars was glumly expressionist, the light always chrome-dark and the wheat fields studio-shot interiors. In the French country village Hannah visits with Gary and his friend Suzy, the atmosphere changes to heightened naturalism, light, freedom, real countryside. Hannah's intolerance of drink befitted Three Cedars as the plump, jolly curate with wine bottle befits France. Wealthy, bossy Mayor Elmer Briggs contrasts with the genial French mayor, whose wealth is his manure pile, and Hannah's tyrannical insistence on unending work (she even yells at her hens, "Come on! Lay some eggs! Earn your keep!") contrasts with French merrymaking. And in this new context Hannah responds differently to a doubled situation. From behind a distancing tree (19) she watches Gary tell Suzy he must leave her because of his mother's opposition, she watches Suzy's heart break, and abruptly Hannah slaps a palm to her forehead. This picture is frozen and over it is superimposed a series of flashbacks of Mary and Jim at the railroad station and the ominous black train roaring into the night taking Jim away. Three Cedars is imposed upon France, the old lovers upon the new, and Hannah recognizes the truth. She confesses to Gary's mother, stops her from hurting Gary as she did Jim (20), throws herself on Jim's grave and lays the flowers there, then goes home to embrace Mary and Jimmy (21).

---

*The outrageous hillbilly Tally Hatfield is played by Lucille La Verne, Griffith's Madame Frochard in *Orphans of the Storm* and the voice of the witch in Disney's *Snow White*.

17 18

19 20

21

Almost alone among Ford characters, Hannah changes—from virulent, raging intolerance to the sowing of tolerance. If she can surpass her myopia, suggests Ford, there is an alternative to wars and to worlds like *Tabu's*, where lovers are sacrificed to ideas (20). Hannah epitomizes her world, yet her hyperbolic qualities lead her to a wisdom from which her interference can save others from moralistic hypocrisies similar to those that led her to murder her own son. Hannah reunites a family, then walks away. Perhaps she is only a *deus ex machina* wrenched out of the necessities of Ford's fiction. Whatever, with this little old lady is born the first "Fordian hero," whom we will encounter in most subsequent Ford pictures in the guise of Will Rogers, Henry Fonda, and John Wayne, among others, and whose judging, priesting, Christ-like interventions will momentarily but repeatedly redeem mankind from its myopic intolerance. Flowers mark Hannah's passage. Ford's most constant symbol, they mark most heroes' loves— Lincoln, from and to Ann Rutledge; Nathan Brittles and Frank Skeffington, to their dead wives; Tom Doniphon, to and from Hallie; and so on. Hannah's flowers signify not only conscious intention (to honor the dead) and reversal (Hannah's initial refusal to honor her dead), but also their ultimate power: Hannah succumbs. Objects may do more than witness and judge. We so infuse the world with our feelings and thoughts, that eventually the world infuses us in return.

Doctor Bull (1933). As do dozens of Ford pictures, *Doctor Bull* begins and ends with a linking vehicle (a train here and in *Liberty Valance*, a steamboat in *The Sun Shines Bright*, a stagecoach in *Fort Apache*, etc.), which suggests the community's self-containment and isolation from the outer world. That Ford begins *Doctor Bull* with dead time—a long Bressonian stare at the New Winton station—before panning slowly toward the tracks and distant approaching train establishes both Ford's distancing consciousness and time's heavy presence. In contrast to the Odyssean *Pilgrimage*, the Iliadic *Doctor Bull* endures one Connecticut town through winter. Drama is placid and earthy, but the yearning desolation and labyrinthian prison of the social milieu impregnate light and air.

The train porter (a black man who shows no signs of racial oppression) hops off, calling "New Winton!" and greets the postmistress.

— "Why, good morning, Miss Helen. Did you have a good
  Christmas?"
— "Don't be silly! In this dull place, how could ya?"
— "Yes, it is dull, isn't it. All aboard! Next stop, New Haven!"

Inside the post-telephone office (where we frequently return for New Winton gossip), the mood for the rest of the picture is announced as May Tripping (Marian Nixon) reads to Helen from a book:

— "So he said: 'Death, where is thy victory?' So he passed over it,
  and all the trumpets blazed for him on the other side."

May was married only a week when her husband Joe became paralyzed from a fall. His legs, he later tells Doc Bull, are "like two slabs of stone."

Individual solitude is relieved (or, as often, exacerbated) by George Bull (Will Rogers), who, always tired, continues his rounds from one patient to the next. His aged aunt sits at home reading murder mysteries and ignoring the telephone. She persists in calling him "Kenneth," though her son Kenneth has been dead fifty years. Such oblivion is denied Bull. He is a sad man, yet cannot resist Abraham-Lincoln-like witticisms or inviting contempt by calling himself "a cow doctor." He passes a night without sleep, as usual, delivering an Italian family's seventh baby, then watches another patient die. "I've seen a hundred people die," he says, in a gauche attempt to console, "and none of them seemed to mind it. They was all too sick to care." Some women begin arguing whether the dead girl was seventeen or eighteen. "Hey, wait a minute!" he interrupts irascibly, "It doesn't make any difference, now does it?" (a sentiment echoed in *The Grapes of Wrath*'s funeral scene).

Bull has as clear an attitude toward death as toward life, in contrast to New Winton's myriad gossipy hypocrites and most especially to his counterpart, the hypochondriac Larry Ward (Andy Devine), a strident Fordian fool summing up a *doctor's* afflictions: Larry even wakes up Bull to recount his nightmares.

Bull is not a Capraesque hero. On the contrary, he is a strong man, authoritative and confident. The whole town has been his patient for twenty years and he has a weary sense of its lack of gratitude. He unloads himself during his visits with the widow Janet Cardmaker (Vera Allen, whose theatrical poise suits her role). Stretched out on her couch by the fire, dreaming of sleeping a month, he states the picture's theme when he tells her, "I kinda relax when I get up here on these wind-swept hills—with *thee*. . . . You know, some old early settler had the thing about right when he said that most of life is a storm and without a harbor a man is lost." "And a woman?" "Oh, a woman don't need refuge like a man." "I wonder . . . ."

> When that I was and a little tiny boy,
> With hey, ho, the wind and the rain,

sing George and Janet, in spontaneous reflection over approaching old age (both are nearing fifty). Janet keeps a jog of apple cider for Bull, and it too becomes a metaphor. "Guess I'm getting old," he muses, "or maybe your cider was younger in those days."

In the town below there is nothing but vicious gossip about the two friends. One old lady whispers into another's ear, "*I'll* tell you what they're doing up there . . . ." and Ford cuts to George lying on the couch while Janet reads from *Alice's Adventures in Wonderland* about the cat disappearing and leaving its smile behind. (Thirty years later, in *Donovan's Reef*, Lewis Carroll verses are again exchanged as code for understanding.)

"Another dividend check for Mr. Banning," says Helen in the post office, just as Ford cuts to the magnate and his wife making their ceremonious entrance (last) into the church and their front pew, where Herbert Banning (Berton Churchill, who plays obnoxious magnates also in *Judge Priest, Four Men and a Prayer*, and *Stagecoach*) magisterially removes his overcoat. As the choir starts "Hark the Herald Angels Sing," Doc Bull rushes in late and adds his bright, unmodest tenor. Outside, a beautifully desolate snowy scene, he joins them standing at a family grave and quips, "What're you all gathered here for? What's amatter? Somebody get out?" Ford often depicts the rich nastily (and New Englanders especially so), whereas Bull is as likeable as can be. But the resentment Bull builds against himself by a hundred insignificant things is, despite his compassion, charisma, and self-sacrifice, not unmerited. A common occurrence in real life, this sort of interpersonal friction is a rare topic in movies. Occasionally oblivious to the effects he produces, Bull takes delight in irritating the Bannings. Their nice daughter Virginia (Rochelle Hudson*) fights with her mother, gets drunk, then nearly kills herself in her spiffy sports car. Winning her confidence, Bull learns she is pregnant by a boy her parents will not accept and has her phone him for a rendezvous. The timid temerity with which she tells him, "Of course I like you . . . I mean . . . I love you," is among Ford's more sensitive moments. The Bannings read of Virginia's marriage in the paper; Mrs. Banning rises, addresses the maid, "Mary, will you leave the room, please," then announces the horror: "Virginia has married a German! O the disgrace of it!" Echo the others, as the scene fades, "O the disgrace of it!"

They soon find a weapon against Bull. Despite his warnings, their profitable power plant's pollution has caused a typhoid epidemic, and they manipulate a town meeting to hold Bull, as health officer, responsible. Mrs. Banning, sweet with amiable gentility, rises to call the vote and, with only five dissents, Bull is fired as town physician.

He tells them off (anticipating Judge Priest's more diplomatic acknowledgment of everyone's sinfulness in *The Sun Shines Bright*), then spends the night by Joe Tripping's bed. Despite an expected diagnosis of permanent paralysis and advice that Joe be consigned to a nursing home, Bull has injected Joe with "a little serum I brewed up at home." It worked on a cow and it works on Joe, and Bull and Janet ride honking and shouting through town.

Bull marries Janet and they leave New Winton. As before, the train pulls in and the porter calls out, "New Winton! . . . Why, good morning, Miss Helen. Did you have a good Easter?" "In this dull place!?" He shows her the New York paper headlining Bull's "Miracle Cure." "Why, medical circles are agog!" As Bull and Janet board, May and Joe (walking now) watch sadly (and step forward, as watching characters will do during the finales of *The Quiet Man*, *A Minute's Wait*, and *The Long Gray Line*). Larry Ward boards too, with his new shotgun wife, and her brother swats him with a big stick, breaking (a frequent Ford gag) his hip flask. Thus cadential slapstick concludes and brightens a typically depressed but varied series of vignettes, and the train pulls off.

Doctor Bull's 1933 New Winton seems at least as much a portrait of a bygone age as *Judge Priest*'s 1890s Kentucky. It exemplifies a depressed sub-

---

*An ingenue in *Laugh and Get Rich* (1930), *She Done Him Wrong* (1933), *Les Miserables* (1935), Natalie Wood's mother in *Rebel Without a Cause* (1955)—but never so interesting as here.

ject vivified by Ford's pacing (each scene leisurely, but fifty scenes in seventy-six minutes), constant whiffs of humor, and detailed characterization (everyone plays to the hilt, as in *Donovan's Reef*'s Boston scenes). "*Doctor Bull* was a downbeat story," said Ford, "but Bill [Will Rogers] managed to get a lot of humor into it — and it became a hell of a good picture. It was one of Bill's favorites."[14] Rogers must have reminded Ford of Harry Carey. Congenial, relaxed, conspirational with characters and audience, Rogers gives Bull a pudgy weariness dissimilar to his other roles with Ford. His Bull can even tell his aunt that he wouldn't know anything without her reading the papers and not have the line remind us of Rogers's famous vaudeville line ("All I know is what I read in the papers"). His Bull is so dependent on Janet, like a small child that bares its every moan; this sort of lovers' relationship, though reminiscent of *Flesh*'s, is rarely encountered in films, where love is either just about to bloom or drifting into memory. And in many ways Bull as a Fordian hero contains contradictions that earlier heroes had either to resolve or burst. In *Pilgrimage*, a hero (Hannah Jessop) is born; in *Air Mail*, the hero (Duke) is a crass superman; in *Judge Priest*, he (Rogers again) is perhaps the compleat Fordian hero. But in *Doctor Bull*, the hero, both glorying in his alienation and accepting his priestly role, ultimately flees his community, escaping rather than just walking away. Yet as the picture's prologue states,

— Doctor Bull brings his neighbors into the world and postpones their departure as long as possible. He prescribes common sense and accepts his small rewards gratefully. His patients call him Doc.

The Lost Patrol (1934). Ford's next movie, about eleven British soldiers stranded midst sand dunes and being picked off one by one by unseen Arabs, has little relation to the themes and characters whose development we have been tracing. And it may seem unattractive today. But in 1934, while Ford's most personal work was passing unnoticed or being dismissed as commercial yuk, *The Lost Patrol*'s gutsy "realism" aroused critical raves. The National Board of Review placed it in the year's Top Ten, *The New York Times* sixth, and an Oscar went to Max Steiner for his (turgid) score. Had Ford correctly estimated contemporary tastes, or was success a fluke? Or did he make it just for the fun of "a character study — you got to know the life story of each of the men"?[15]

The critics were attracted partly by its claustrophobic, mechanical staginess, a quality usually attributed to scenarist Dudley Nichols's influence on Ford: a small group of isolated people, theatrically revealing their character under stress, within classical unities of space and time — as in *Men Without Women*, *The Informer*, *The Hurricane*, *Stagecoach*, and *The Long Voyage Home*. Yet, in the case of *The Lost Patrol*, the novel, already containing these features, had been purchased by Ford prior to RKO's or Nichols's involvement (and had already been filmed by Victor McLaglen's brother

Cyril). And while the "isolated group under stress" formula had been exploited in the first Nichols-Ford, *Men Without Women* (1930, also a prestigious critical success), it had equally been used in the Wead-Ford *Air Mail*
(1932). Probably Ford engaged Nichols because *The Lost Patrol*, like their
Men Without Women, *Seas Beneath*, and *Born Reckless*, was a drama about
men in war, and Nichols had served in the navy during the war. Frank Baker
was similarly employed as an expert in military ordnance.

Ford's practice of preparing each character's biography, with tastes,
opinions, and eccentricities, and then slipping in such tidbits mid the principal drama, is first noticeable here (albeit the situation left little alternative), and again in subsequent Nichols scripts. But strangely it is in the do-
main of character that the movie fails. The biographies are blatantly
present, but interest-arousing details invariably get announced just before
the character gets killed. A young soldier, for one example, talks about
home and mother and the future, and in the next scene he is dead. The
result, dramatically, is zero, repetitiously; and it is all the contrary to *Men
Without Women,* where a character's life conditions his actions and is not
merely a footnote to his death, and where Nichols's O'Neill-like drama of
reactions had been able to reap results. The distinction is one of plot leading
characters as opposed to characters producing plot. Nothing happens in *The
Lost Patrol* beyond the encroachment of aloneness and insanity (personified
by a variation on the Fordian fool, a Boris Karloff character who, like a
Nichols character in *Men Without Women*, goes berserk, tries to kill everyone, and shouts, "Vengeance is mine, saith the Lord!"), and no sooner is
Victor McLaglen alone, finally, than he kills the Arabs and is rescued by a
second patrol. Yet only at this penultimate moment does McLaglen com-
mence to engage us.

The movie might be called a study in the lack of leadership. The patrol is
lost because a young lieutenant dies without confiding anything in his sergeant. A man is killed when McLaglen lets him climb an exposed palm tree.
The Arabs are able to sneak up, kill two sentries, and steal horses. Most of
our men eventually die because they panic and run into the desert. In short,
McLaglen, an excellent top soldier, lacks the foresight and leadership an
officer is supposed to have. McLaglen is just "one of the men." The men are
not of lower class, or at least do not act or talk as though they were. Instead
they behave as a relatively educated next-door neighbor might have behaved in bourgeois America 1934, and not at all like British privates in 1916.
Their truncated roles increase their anonymity, and thus render them into
fashionable populist heroes—another Nichols trait. Ford repeated this idea
in *December 7th* (1943) when the same voice, speaking from the grave, together with scenes of various parents at home, describes itself in turn as the
voice of seven different dead GIs.

Max Steiner's style of scoring, in which each emotion is mimicked in the
music ("Mickey Mousing"), was less in fashion in 1934 than limited music

from on-set sources. And *The Lost Patrol*, according to Steiner, was at first "not intended to have any music, but after [it] was finished the producer decided that, because of the long silent scenes, it was necessary to underscore the entire production."[16] Steiner's subsequent Oscar brought "Mickey Mousing" back into vogue and led Ford to collaborate more intimately with him for *The Informer*.

The Lost Patrol was filmed with some hardship in the Yuma Desert. Tempers would flare and violent fights were not infrequent. Wallace Ford is reputed to have chased a cook over many a sand dune when the latter refused to serve a blackman. A more typical Ford-set incident occurred during a scene when McLaglen machine-guns an Arab. McLaglen was drunk to oblivion at the time, as Frank Baker, playing the Arab, knew. Thus Baker was vitally concerned when the bullets—Ford *always* used live ammunition—started grazing his feet. Charging furiously on the blubbering McLaglen, Baker might well have killed him, had he not noticed the second machine gun, manned by a sober marksman, which Ford had placed behind McLaglen, without, of course, mentioning the fact to Baker.

The World Moves On (1934). His next picture was even more incidental to Ford's career: "really a lousy picture—I fought like hell against doing it."[17] Yet these scenes of a family's hundred-year history are at least as entertaining and far more interesting than Winfield Sheehan's

creaky *Cavalcade*, the smash-hit it mimics expensively. Ford went beyond himself for every other scene, but the invention never coheres. Midst talky nothings, magic moments occur: the way Mary drops back her head faintly when Richard goes to war; the way water mounts over struggling men inside a submarine, filling the screen till all is black and still; a vivaciously stylized dance, a glittering Prussian wedding, a romantic ship scene, the parade of life outside windows. The family's avarice and pernicious irresponsibility contribute to all woes, but its members too are mindlessly determined. To contrast them and mock the war, Ford inserts Stepin Fetchit within a mad five-minute battle montage (far surpassing *Cavalcade*'s): slightly wounded midst trench cacophony, he squawks, "You mean . . . ? I can *go*?!"

Judge Priest (1934). One of 1934's top grossing movies, *Judge Priest* is also one of Ford's finest and most convivial works. Its 1890 Kentucky town is treated with a leisurely pacing and relaxed entrancement with the subtleties of diction, bearing, and facial expression that place it in another age entirely from the chic sophistication of other good movies of 1932–34. *Judge Priest* today has not aged; a storyland of myth and symbol, it looks just as fresh and old-fashioned as it did half a century ago (though, alas, extant prints are poor!). Based, like *The Sun Shines Bright* (1953), on Irvin S. Cobb stories, *Judge Priest*, in Cobb's words heading the picture, seeks to evoke "familiar ghosts of my own boyhood" and "the tolerance of the day and the wisdom of that almost vanished generation," as typified by "one man *down yonder*" in a "reasonably fair likeness" called Judge Priest.*

Will Rogers combines a laid-back Harry-Carey-like charisma with rich vocal characterization of each of his lines to make Bill Priest into possibly the most personable character in Ford, and a prototypical Fordian hero. "First thing I learned in politics," he tells Reverend Brand, "was when to say 'ain't'." The patrician Priest, cannier and less irascible than Dr. Bull, embodies the Southerner's political craftiness; but his ambitions are community centered. Ford often punctuates the tickling flow of Priest's high humor by cutting back from a close-up before a punchline's last word. A gag's effect is thus dispersed amid the community rather than employed to illuminate Priest's "star" quality. For, as with Rogers's other roles for Ford, the Priest character's tender humanity seems the fruit of secretive melancholy and loneliness. For this reason, his meetings with others—and most of the movie is a series of "duets"—seem engagements met with resourceful

*Kentucky, 1890. Judge Priest's court's folksy informalities irk prosecutor Maydew (who is running for Priest's seat), but Priest goes fishing with Jeff, a young black charged with loitering. Nephew Rome returns from law school and Priest encourages romance with Ellie May despite Rome's mother's disapproval of the girl's unknown parentage. When blacksmith Bob Gillis gets into a fight defending Ellie May's honor, Rome gets his first case, but when Gillis refuses to introduce Ellie May's name into the trial, Rev. Brand reveals Gillis's past life as a condemned prisoner pardoned for war heroism and as father and secret provider for Ellie May. All join in a Memorial Day parade.

This production still is possibly all that remains of a controversial lynch-mob sequence removed from *Judge Priest* before release. Paul McAllister, Will Rogers, Charley Grapewin, Hy Meyer, Tom Brown.

tact and delicacy. We know his encouraging remark to Rome, that no one ought live alone, refers to himself (see still). And we understand his reply, that he'd not gone to live with Rome's mother because he didn't care for her cooking, for we have just watched his desire to be charming overcome distaste for her haughty meanness. Later, his going to talk to his wife beside her and their children's tombstones is in itself almost less significant than his eagerness to get there; the words on the gravestone, "Margaret Beckenridge Priest, April 24, 1871," suggest how long he has been coming to visit her. Priest he is by celibacy and by a consciously transitory attitude toward his life; and by the moral superiority of those who, claiming knowledge of higher good and right of higher judgment, invade others' privacy: note that Billy Priest, judge and minister, refuses to return Gillis's accusing gaze as he proceeds to violate him. Priest's purpose is the Fordian hero's usual task—to reunite a family (Gillis's)—but does a good purpose justify moral arrogance? For good or ill, such types frequent Ford's ·vorlds, constituting a major theme; but whether their arrogance stems from duty appointed or duty assumed, Ford is always critically concerned about their moral humility—or lack thereof.

The richness in Priest's characterization is complemented in Ford's cameo portraits of the other townspeople. During the trial, there is a se-

"No one ought live alone." Priest dominates
the frame as he advises his nephew Rome.
The enclosing porch rail suggests Priest's
celibate aloneness. Then, across the
backyard, Ellie May, Rome's love, comes
out onto her porch. (Her frame-within-
the-frame is illuminated, so that the
composition anticipates *Citizen Kane*'s
shot of boy Kane frolicking in the snow
outside a window while, foreground, his
parents decide his future.) Off-camera
right, sounds of a rival suitor's arrival
counterpoint Ellie May's entrance, causing
Priest to gaze in the opposite direction.

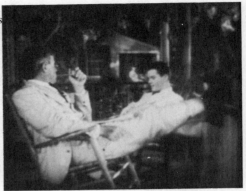

quence that ought to astound us in its virtuosity: Francis Ford, a juror, does
one of his famous spittoon-ringing spits. /Maydew (Berton Churchill)
orates. /The first witness against Gillis testifies. /The second bad witness. /
The judge speaks. /Ellie May (Anita Louise) reacts, concerned. These six
shots of six characters are not edited in a fragmentary way. As with a similar
sequence in *Flesh* (see page 84), each shot—each with formally articulated

beginning, middle, and end—constitutes an autonomous scene in itself. Each character, in doing his "turn" (to borrow a vaudeville term apt here), expands on a basic archetype by a half-dozen inventive variations. Ford's ingeniously simple cutting places the six shots in linelike blocks, and the movie's real subject becomes not just our concern at diabolic developments in the trial, but rather the contrasts and interreactions of character.

As with most good Fords, our sense of experiencing a people's culture and values powerfully transports us into Ford's storybook world. Today's jargon on racism, for example, is not adequate to describe the intimate interactions of whites and blacks in *Judge Priest*. Just as the singing of "Anchors Aweigh" in *Salute* (1929) defines an era, a class, and an ideology, so too here does Priest's joining the blacks in "Old Kentucky Home." The blacks (roly-poly Hattie McDaniel and sloe-eyed Stepin Fetchit among them) relate readily to racial types, but so too do Ford's whites, and no values of existential individuality suffer on that account (indeed, the values become more complex in individuals derived from types). Priest, in his mediative role, bridges racial barriers not only in song, but in assuming—without condescension—comparable diction and crooked-neck pose when palling with Fetchit. No doubt that Ford captures the spirit of a racist community— Priest uses Jeff to fetch croquet balls, blacks sit in gutters, are called "boy," and treated like pets—but Ford also suggests that seeing, as Priest does, the attractive aspects in censorable individuals and societies is more promotive of true tolerance than seeing only the censorable. (Uglier sides of racism, however, were more apparent in Ford's original cut, which included a lynching scene and an antilynching plea by Priest ["one of the most scorching things you ever heard," said Ford]. These were excised by the studio, to Ford's chagrin, for lynchings were frequent during the thirties, but Ford used similar scenes in *The Sun Shines Bright*, 1953.)

For charisma, Rogers has his equal in Henry B. Walthall:* "a personality that just leaped from the screen," said Ford, "one of the greatest actors of all

*Walthall played a famous role as Griffith's "Little Colonel" in the Civil War sequence in *The Birth of a Nation* (1915).

time."[18] Walthall's Ashby Brand seems alone to appreciate the effort and intelligence behind Priest's personality. We can catch a gleam of playful recognition in his eye at Priest's trial ploy—giving Brand chance to correct reference to the "war of rebellion" to "The War for the Southern Confederacy" and thus attach the jury's sympathies, which the preacher in a long monologue immediately warms by recalling the shared deprivations of the war's last months. Grizzled veterans nod tearfully in empathetic recollection. "As many of you know, I am a Virginian," he begins, and relates how he recruited life-prisoners from a chain gang to fight "for what we thought was right." Ford superimposes scenes during Brand's chronicle, but keeps Brand's face in a corner of the screen.* As the camera tracks along prisoners' chains, Brand tells how they became known as "The Battalion from Hell" and Priest (who has directed this whole affair) signals out the window. Jeff, sitting on the curb in Priest's raccoon coat, starts "Dixie" on his banjo; other blacks join in. Meanwhile Brand, spiritualized by a halo, holds the courtroom entranced. He tells how one of those ex-convicts rescued a wounded Union officer, how he rode out ahead to recapture a flag, how he stood alone with a ramrod to face a cavalry charge (we see it all), and how

*Ford used similar tricks in *Lightnin'* (1925).

this man lives now in this town "watching over his daughter, providing for her education, through me, all unknown to Ellie May." Cut to Ellie May for her reaction at discovering her father; then back to Brand, who stands: "Gentlemen, you know him today as Robert Gillis."

The pandemonium of communal conviviality mustered by Brand is comically set off by Francis Ford shouting, "Hooray for Jeff Davis, the Southern Confederacy, and Bob Gillis!!!" And congeniality is orchestrated to "Dixie" in the parade coda: the blacks strut happily into the camera, Gillis is embraced into the veterans' ranks, Francis Ford spits into Maydew's tophat, and *Quiet-Man*-like curtain calls for the principals conclude, rather as in *The Black Watch*, with passing memorial wreaths and the sound of voices— one of Ford's finest finales.

Of course, the Reverend Brand's testimony is irrelevant: it is never brought out that Gillis was defending Ellie May. A comparable irrelevance occurred in the film's opening trial: the question of Jeff's guilt for stealing chickens got lost midst heated debate over what *kind* of chickens Priest's cronies stole during the war, and the next scene showed Jeff going fishing with Priest. These two anomalies explain a third: Priest's lachrymose lament at having to step down as judge for Gillis's trial, which, so clearly is he prejudiced in Gillis's behalf, seems absurd to modern sensibilities. But in all three instances the point is "higher knowledge"—the irrelevance of "facts" in face of the relevance of character. Priest *knows* Gillis, knows the man's craftsmanship, just as he *knows* barber Flem Tally (Gillis's accuser), and knows Tally's lousy shaves. Such knowledge would not be prejudice, even in a judge, but would serve justice—justice that would indeed have miscarried without Brand's last-minute revelations. Facts without character are almost always delusory. And Judge Priest's town concurs: Gillis, having shown his character during the war, would certainly have acted properly in his dealings with Flem Tally; further justification would be superfluous.

Does it strike us as odd, this notion that character does not change? R. G.

Collingwood, a philosopher of history, lambastes this notion in Tacitus enlighteningly:

> Furneaux pointed out long ago [*The Annals of Tacitus* (Oxford, 1896), vol. i, p. 158] that when Tacitus describes the way in which the character of a man like Tiberius broke down beneath the strain of empire, he represents the process not as a change in the structure or conformation of a personality but as the revelation of features in it which had hitherto been hypocritically concealed. Why does Tacitus so misrepresent facts? . . . It is because the idea of development in a character, an idea so familiar to ourselves, is to him a metaphysical impossibility. A "character" is an agent, not an action; actions come and go, but the "characters" (as we call them), the agents from whom they proceed, are substances, and therefore eternal and unchanging. Features in the character of a Tiberius or a Nero which only appeared comparatively late in life must have been there all the time. A good man cannot become bad. A man who shows himself bad when old must have been equally bad when young, and his vices concealed by hypocrisy. As the Greeks put it, *archē andra deixei*. Power does not alter a man's character; it only shows what kind of man he already was.[19]

If change in Ford, in most movies, in Dickens and Balzac and Greek tragedy, is essentially a stripping bare of character always there in the first place, perhaps it is because in all of them concern to express ideal "truths" surpasses the temptation to record the shifting surfaces of reality. Collingwood again quotes Furneaux:

> [Tacitus's] professed purpose in writing is to hold up signal examples of political vice and virtue for posterity to execrate or to admire, and to teach his readers, even through a narrative which he fears may weary them by its monotonous horrors, that good citizens may live under bad rulers; and that it is not mere destiny or the chapter of accidents, but personal character and discretion, dignified moderation and reserve, that best guard a senator of rank unharmed though time of peril.[20]

Ford's central characters—people like Priest, Lincoln, Ethan Edwards, Ransom Stoddard, Dr. Cartwright—are infinitely more complex morally than either the foils surrounding them (Maydew, Ellie May) or the normal protagonists of Manichaean melodrama. And destiny plays its own separate but important role in Ford, for like Augustine he feels history as a surging passage through time and as governed by God, rather than as the eternal and senseless cycle of repetition perceived by the Ancients. Still, there is something of Tacitus in Ford. It is not that his characters do not stare into Sartrian voids of freedom: Judge Priest does so constantly. It is that freedom is meaningless save as means to fulfillment of their nature—which is not a meaningless message for a film made in the middle of the Great Depression, or for a film (*Sergeant Rutledge*, 1960) made in the middle of the black struggle for freedom.

The notion that character is more trustworthy than logic or statistics is, of course, an axiom of popular wisdom as prevalent today as in 1890. Yet we are, if anything, more aware of a corollary danger: character is hard to distinguish from feeling; and where, as in the mass, demagogic politics of today, character can be manipulated to market consumer goods, presidents, and wars, we may place even *less* trust in our feelings than we do in logic or statistics. We can trust neither ourselves nor the information given us. And our virtuous leaders employ the same tactics of manipulation as history's arch villains. Judge Priest, like young Mr. Lincoln and like Lieutenant Cantrell (*Sergeant Rutledge*), recognizes that theatrics will reveal intuited truth better than mere facts or logic: he *stages* Brand's testimony, accompanies it with Jeff playing "Dixie," and has in Brand (as we have in Henry B. Walthall) one of the age's greatest orators. In real life, we seek, when we can, to know someone thoroughly before crediting the feelings his character projects. Still, all human knowledge is ultimately built upon feeling, and it is art's task in the scheme of things not only to heighten our sensibilities but also to educate them, so that our consciousness is no longer easily corruptible. Movies like Judge Priest do not simply move and manipulate us; they compel a subtle and critical analysis of the interplay of feeling, character, and the real world.

The Whole Town's Talking (1935). As medicine for the Depression, or even as homily, Ford's messages may appear excessively traditional. But the identical message transposed from the stable 1890s of *Judge Priest* into the corrupt 1930s of *The Whole Town's Talking* becomes the lava of rebellion.* Critics, however, have tended to overlook one as much as the other, for both belong to despised genres—*Judge Priest* to sentimental, folksy melodrama, *The Whole Town's Talking* to low-budget comedy. Jean Mitry has described the latter in terms that might never occur to an American:

> Of all John Ford's films, *The Whole Town's Talking* is the most dynamic, brilliant and funny. . . . Not a work of genius, no, but dazzling and surpassingly virtuosic. . . . Edward Robinson's performance in the double role of Jones and Mannion is not just a brilliant tour de force. Along with memorable creations by Wallace Beery, Raimu, McLaglen, Spencer Tracy, Michel Simon or Fresnay, it is one of the summits of film acting. . . . The film's density is achieved by the greatest amount of action in

---

*After eight years' punctuality, Jones is late for work and discovers he looks like "Killer" Mannion. At lunch he is arrested, with his secret love, Miss Clark. After confusion, the D. A. gives him a passport and his boss asks him to write on Mannion for the papers. But at home he finds Mannion, who declares he will use Jones's passport at night and dictates his life story himself. To get Jones out of the way, the D. A. sends him to prison; but Mannion goes instead, to rub out an informer, then escapes. He sends Jones on an errand to the bank and informs police Mannion is coming, but Jones, having forgotten something, misses the ambush. When Mannion's mob suggest killing Jones, Jones lets them kill Mannion, then overpowers them with a tommy gun, rescues his kidnapped aunt, Clark, and Seaver, and wins an award and Miss Clark.

the least amount of time. . . . The situations jostle each other in a bewildering rhythm, in a species of chaos which mixes logic and illogic, truth and improbableness and, as Alexandre Arnoux said, "the peak of the natural at the very heart of artifice." Rapid, alert, wonderfully cut and mounted, supercharged, taut like a spring, it is a work of total perfection in its genre.

It is a minor genre, to be sure, merely a dexterous and witty game. And yet it is a game of a virtuoso who transforms drama into comedy and, juggling the resemblance of two characters, masterfully renews a stock situation treated hundreds of times on stage and screen. Is it not possible that genius, in a creator, *also* consists in gathering together all the commonplaces, all the clichés, all the things most used up and worn out everywhere else, in mixing them all together, and producing from them something absolutely new, original and personal?[21]

Swiftness and dynamism are accentuated in Ford's cutting of Robert Riskin's rapid-fire, newspaper-style script. The cuts break into action, not only just as dialogue lines begin, but often with the characters spinning around to speak. Amid the rapid crosscutting between rooms and characters, the same composition is rarely repeated. We return to Miss Clark being questioned by Boyle and Howe four or five times, and each time the camera setup is different. But cuts are never without logic. Boyle and Howe muse about collecting the $25,000 reward for Mannion while waiting outside Jones's apartment; a change of angle comes with a change of topic and tone, when they begin to wonder why Jones is taking so long.

We know that Ford's people are almost always conditioned by their society and beliefs and that, unless they are heroes, they are seldom able to see themselves outside of their situation. Still, we must time and again be struck by Jones's failure to complain—of the tyranny of the office, of the police, of Mannion. Yet some free will and self-determination remain. When Jones is able to have Mannion killed, it is true the occasion is handed him and he is desperately motivated by the plight of his great romantic love, Miss Clark (Jean Arthur); nonetheless he takes the initiative. Earlier, too, finding himself suddenly in a position of power, he can cry out to his office mates, "So long, slaves!"

As *Steamboat Round the Bend* will be, *The Whole Town's Talking* is structured around confusions of reality vs. appearance. The theme is suggested by the confusing resemblance of Jones and Mannion—at one point even *Jones* screams out, "My name's not Jones, it's Mannion, I mean, it's not Jannion, it's Mones . . . "—and is echoed by mirrors, by newspaper headlines that distort truth, by the bank doorman who thinks "Mannion" forgot his gun, by the verbal pun of "Boyle . . . and Howe!" But more important echoes center around the twin antinomies of (1) whether the real "killer" is Mannion or the system, and of (2) Jones's dreams vs. the real world, drab, oppressive, tyrannical. Jones's pets summarize the dilemma—his cat Abelard and his canary Heloïse. The monk Peter Abelard (1079–1142) is legend-

ary for his tragic love affair with the nun Heloïse: Jones and Clark. The lovers' correspondence contained seditious conspiracies against the prevailing realism and wisdom of the age, and Abelard was condemned as a heretic. Abelard opposed the notion that freedom was simply unquestioning acceptance of God's plan and our nature. He suspected that each person is unique, that appearances may be deceiving, that individuals are not necessarily subsumable under universal concepts. He held we must also employ our intellect freely, not just our hearts, in order to discern the true nature of things. These are the movie's themes.

Ford's opening lateral track of Jones's office and its forty desks does not have the crushing, antlike feel of King Vidor's *The Crowd* (1928), with its progression from city, to skyscraper, to a particular outside floor and window, and into a particular desk; but the sense of oppression is at least as palpable, while Jones is more palpable an individual than Vidor's everyman John (James Murray). The monklike Jones typifies the Fordian character whose "virtue" consists in myopic reconciliation with poverty and hopelessness. He is fundamentally unrebellious, polite even to mobsters. But his dreams are of faraway places, of Egypt, Shanghai, and of Miss Clark. He sings myopically, "Oh, the world owes me a living . . . ," but four different clock faces contradict him: he is late for work; duty calls. Even in prison, where Seaver brings him "the McIntyre account" to work on, Jones is obsessed by his menial duties. There is a bookkeeperish compulsive quality to Jones, evident in the careful absorption he gives to putting on his glasses, that is comparable to Mannion's willfulness and that eventually breaks out in Jones's violence too. But for the moment Jones seems a symbol of the exploited working class and an illustration, along with the forces of crime, government, and business, of aberration in "duty and tradition." Duty has become meaningless role-playing. But perhaps habitual duty alone keeps the system functioning. And if this is the case, are we not serving a system, rather than being served by it, and ought we not to destroy this system?

Gangster films often give covert expression to such ideas as these, just as westerns often proffer escape to virgin land. But in treating gangster-film conventions parodically, Ford does not undermine the conventions' purposes; he satirizes arrogance of power simultaneously. Police always arrive in masses of forty or fifty, and shove everyone around brutally. After terrorizing poor Jones, when his true identity is discovered the D.A. sneers, "You're free to go. Get out!" And Jones, meekly holding his hat, replies typically: "Oh, thank you, sir. Oh! gentlemen, I'm sorry I caused you all this trouble!" "That's alright," snaps the D.A., brusquely. The prison warden is similarly rude a few scenes later. Even boss J. G. Carpenter complains of being "dragged down here without a word of explanation." And when the police take over the bank, they roughly grab employees' coats and herd everyone down to the basement.

One would expect this litany of misanthropes to climax in Killer Mannion. But though much is told of his dastardly deeds, nothing is shown. His disposals of Slugs Martin and the prison chauffeur both occur off-camera.

Although never sympathetic, Mannion embodies typical gangster symbolism: on one hand he is the rebellious little man, the populist hero who delights in making fools of bigshots and seeing his name in print; on the other hand, he personifies the unbridled aggrandizement of the reputable powers—government, police, wealth. Jones at first reacts to him as to established order: with fear and without antipathy. He does not inform on him, he does not shoot him when he gets the chance ("You don't shoot somebody who's asleep"), he goes to the bank for him, and even comes back when he thinks he has lost the money for Mannion's "mother." (Virtue then brings its own reward, for had Jones not returned, what would have happened to Miss Clark, Aunt Agatha, Seaver, and the $25,000?)

The Mannion story, until the fateful moment when his crimes touch at Jones's heart, is slightly comical. The real evil, as Joseph August's brooding photography reminds us continually, is the system. The cruelest scenes and actual climax of misanthropy are those of the columns of hundreds of prisoners marching in a claustrophobic prison yard, all dressed alike, all in conformity—just like "free" people. Naturally, a guard complains to the warden that Slugs Martin (hiding there from Mannion, and not a prisoner) is giving them a lot of trouble: he refuses to wear the prison uniform! Pointedly, the guard's attitude does not differ from that of the Seavers, Hoyts, and Carpenters.

Miss Clark (the "canary") is the antithesis of all this. She does not care when she is fired. She even thinks it might do Jones good to get fired. Imagine such insouciance in the heart of the Depression, with twelve million unemployed! She counsels courage and perseverance in one's dreams. And when Jones, the romantic dreamer, grabs the machine gun and starts it spurting, he acts not only for Miss Clark, but also in rebellion against all the tyranny of his life. Then, they all go to Shanghai, Abelard and Heloïse, too.

Seven of Ford's pre-1935 talkies are cynical portraits of somber oppression and tight-fisted misanthropy. The Depression itself is never mentioned directly; but the wealthy and powerful are the villains, while the populist classes abet their own exploitation. *The Whole Town's Talking*, despite its witty *allegretto* pacing, closes this series of pictures. Only once again, twenty-three years later, will Ford venture a portrayal of contemporary American city life, in *The Last Hurrah*.* Why? In part, perhaps, because the grimness of the urban present encouraged him to turn, like Jones, to the past and to faraway places to continue, allegorically, his themes of social

---

*The Grapes of Wrath and *Tobacco Road* (1940–41) are contemporary Americana, but depressing as they are, their *rural* settings are less suffocating, and offer wider possibilities, than the city films. *When Willie Comes Marching Home* (1950) is small-town America, and though the action misses being contemporary by only six years, the point of view (on World War II) is retrospective rather than modern, albeit cynical and deterministic. *The Long Gray Line* (1955) takes only a critical peek at contemporary life. *Gideon's Day* (1958), a police tragicomedy with London as its locale, offers a contrast with *The Whole Town's Talking*.

interaction. But, more practically, stricter enforcement of the Production
Code (i.e., industry self-censorship) made topical subjects tabu. Hollywood
retreated to adaptations of the classics, family pictures, or anything uncon-
troversial. Upon *The Whole Town's Talking*, the Code imposed deletion of
the kidnapping scene (we see Jones's aunt captive, but not her capture) and
an on-screen prison murder (now more interestingly rendered by shadows).
But, ironically, Ford, by treating a crime movie as comedy, finessed the
Code's effective prohibition of the crime genre, in force for about a year,
and the picture's box-office success inspired a general resuscitation of crime
movies from several years' doldrums.[22]

The Established Rebel

With *Araner* to retire to, John Ford found it easier to accom-
modate to life as an establishment figure. Perhaps he found it too easy. He
played occasional, high-strung games of golf and abusive games of bridge
(and cheated at both); he got drunk periodically at home, caught hell from
Mary, and then escaped down the back alley to seek solace in the parish
priest; and he passed his afternoons usually naked in the Hollywood Athletic Club's steamroom. His drinking buddies there formed an inner social
club, the "Young Men's Purity, Total Abstinence, and Snooker Pool Association" (the latter part soon changed to "Yachting Association"), whose members included Emmett Flynn, Liam O'Flaherty, Dudley Nichols, Tay Garnett, Wingate Smith, Preston Foster, Harry Wurtzel, Gene Markey,
Merian Cooper, Johnny Weismuller, Frank Morgan, John Wayne, and Ward
Bond. To spoof establishment pomposity, the club renamed itself "The Emerald Bay Yacht Club" and chose "Jews But No Dues" as a motto.* The members all had elaborate uniforms and titles. But they continued to meet in
steamroom or bar.

Ford was frequently considered cruel in these years, and he seems to
have encouraged his reputation for masticating actors and getting drunk.

---

*Dan Ford (p. 114) quotes the slogan this way. Andrew Sinclair (p. 56) quotes it as "No Jews
and No Dues"—Ford's riposte to his exclusion as a gentile from Jewish yacht clubs. Scenarist
Henry Ephron has claimed Ford was prejudiced, but the claim seems based on miscompre-
hension of Ford's temperament and bitterness over Ford's cavalier rewriting of Ephron's script.
Ephron's evidence is (1) that Ford pronounced his friend Daniel Fuchs's name as though ending
in a K sound and (2) that when Phoebe Ephron remarked on an apparent overabundance of
churches in the French village set of *What Price Glory* (a Ford regular would know such a remark
was courting trouble), Ford replied, "Don't you think there are a lot of synagogues in a Jewish
village?" The Ephrons stalked off, mortally offended. Sinclair, however, quotes Leon Selditz
that Ford was not at all anti-Semitic (p. 56). Ford, of course, had a good many Jewish friends and
even spoke some Yiddish; he once resigned from a club when it blackballed a Jewish army officer,
and he donated a menorah to a Temple through his friend Jack Fier. His agent Harry Wurtzel was
Jewish, and was something of a friend as well, having looked after Ford's family during the war.
Nonetheless, Ford's nickname for Wurtzel was "Herschel," and in their correspondence he typically would advise him to hire a "smart hebe lawyer." (Ephron's allegations are in his *We Thought
We Could Do Anything* [New York: Norton, 1977], pp. 117–20.)

The Emerald Bay Yacht Club, 1938, on board the *Araner*. Front row at right, John Ford and Preston Foster. Second row at left, John Wayne. Back row, center and right, Ward Bond and Frank Morgan.

Philip Dunne contends that "Jack's courtesy to any individual was always in inverse proportion to his affection. I knew Jack liked me, because in all the years I knew him intimately he never said a polite word to me, not one."[23]

His relations with women, in contrast, could bring out a markedly different, kinder person in him. When he made *Mary of Scotland* his attraction toward Katharine Hepburn was immediate, and was reciprocated. On the first day of shooting, he found her seated in his chair mimicking him with a clay pipe and a hat pulled over her eyes—and, to her frustration, he typically ignored the gag. But her brassy ways eventually got to him. "You're a hell of a fine girl," he told her. "If you'd just learn to shut up and knuckle under you'd probably make somebody a nice wife."[24] She did not, of course, shut up. And when she found fault with Ford's lack of interest in her tower scene with Fredric March—its long expository speech for Queen Mary was the sort of thing Ford hated in scripts—he yelled for McNulty, told him to give Hepburn the megaphone and script, and walked out. She directed the scene herself—for her first and only time—and it is perhaps the most moving scene in the film.[25] What fascinated her in Ford was his peculiar combination of qualities—"enormously rough, terribly arrogant, enormously tender . . . never smug, never phoney, and enormously, truly sensitive. . . . Spencer and Sean [Tracy and Ford] were very different, but they were similar in being able to be devastated by the world."[26] For his part, Ford found a kind of gumption in her he rarely met in women. Once, playing golf, she so irked him by insisting he shoot a three-foot putt that he actually missed it, and—his anger mounting—the follow-up, and the next shot as well! Enraged, he hurled his club fifty feet across the course. Katie was unintimidated. "I'd use an overlapping grip to get those distances,"[27] she teased.* Weekends they sailed the *Araner*, and, when their picture was finished, Sean and Katie went east together to New York and to the Hepburn home in Connecticut, where they spent a month.[28]

Even before *Mary of Scotland*, John had felt dissatisfied in his marriage; now, during his six months with Katie, he probably felt happier with a woman than he ever had. Dan Ford has theorized that they were both "opinionated, pigheaded, and difficult to live with. John's masculine ego would never tolerate Kate's independence, and Kate instinctively knew that John Ford's house had to be a cold and lonely place for a woman. John was better off married to someone who had a stabilizing effect on him, a woman who could tolerate his energies and absences and could make him a home. Deep down, he knew he was better off with Mary."[29] But rather than such inordinate and unlikely pessimism, the real obstacles seem to have been John's children and, when all was said and done, his commitment to Mary, whatever the shortcomings of their marriage. In June 1936, Sean and Katie parted, and she, perhaps to distance herself, embarked on a very long national tour with the play *Jane Eyre*. In a letter the following April, she wrote, "Oh Sean, it will be heavenly to see you again—if I may—and if I may not I can drive by Odin St. in an open Ford and think a thousand things. In my mind and heart your place is everlasting."[30]

Their friendship endured until Ford's death. They avoided the closeness of filming together, although there was talk of her doing a picture with him in Ireland during the fifties and illness prevented her appearing in *7 Women*. It was she who persuaded Spencer Tracy to make *The Last Hurrah* with Ford; there had been some stubborn quarrel between the two men dating back to the early thirties.

Ford's father had died, quite unexpectedly and quickly, in June 1936, three years after his mother. He had been sending them $1,000 per month since the mid-1920s. Years later, he related an episode about his mother that had always interested him, as he said:

---

*Recollecting this incident in 1973, Ford commented to Hepburn, "I was mad at you for a week after that!" But she retorted, "I don't remember you ever being mad at me."

Ford and old woman who may be his mother (who died in 1933).

One of the members of one of our leading families went to Harvard and got a medical degree. He married a girl from Radcliffe. This girl was hooked on planned parenthood. She had a big tea at which she had all the leading doctors and expounded her plan. She said the population of Portland was too great and one of my closest friends—she wanted to know where she could go to, you know, with her theories—suggested that she go to 23 Sheridan Street, which was where we lived.

So she arrived and the ladies were there, Mrs. Mahoney, Mrs. Feeney, Mrs. Myers, etc., they were all there in bombazine in the parlor. They were very polite to this Yankee lady visiting from uptown, and she started talking and asked how many children they had and my mother said she had thirteen and this lady was horrified. "Much too many, Mrs. Feeney!" she said. "All the children can't be normal, they all can't get the proper upbringing!" My mother said, "All the children are normal," and she turned to my cousin and said in Irish, " ——." My cousin says, "Oh, yes, they are all normal except one—the youngest one, Johnny."

The lady says, "Well, you can't expect thirteen normal children. Where is Johnny now?" My mother says, "Oh, he's in a home." "Well, you see, that must be a terrific expense for you to support him in a home." "Oh," she said, "I don't support him." She says, "Well, where does he live? Where is the home?" My mother says, "Hollywood, California." "Hollywood? Why is it so far away?" "Well," she says, "I don't know, he's married, has children." "You say he has a home?" "Oh, yes he has a home—it's a very big, nice home." "Well," the lady says, "what is his work, what does he do for a living?" "Ah," my mother says, "he doesn't work at all. When he was growing up all he did was play football and read books. Johnny doesn't work at all." "He doesn't work?" "No, he just sits in a chair and yells at actors." "Oh! He's a movie director?" "Yes." "Oh."

"Now," my mother says, "tell me about yourself, darlin'. How many children do you have?" "I don't have any." "Well, that's too bad. How long have you been married?" "Fourteen months." "Ah, that's a shame. What's the matter? You better send your husband to see a doctor." She says, "My husband is a doctor." "What's the matter, can't he get his tallywhacker up?"

She arose in horror, and said, "I've never been so insulted in my life!" and she charged out of there. Mrs. Mahoney had nine, Mrs. Myers had eight, and my mother had thirteen—they were all past the age of child bearing.[31]

Meanwhile, Johnny was tolerating the new Hollywood, where it was becoming increasingly difficult for even a John Ford to do things his own way. He granted a rare interview, in order to publicize his dissatisfaction:

We're in a commercial *cul de sac*. We have time schedules, we are ordered to direct a certain story in a certain way because that's what the middle-west wants and after all the middle-west has the money. But the profession on the whole is progressing steadily. . . . Eventually motion pictures will all be in color, because it's a success and because it's a natural medium. And we'll go out to a Maine fishing port or to an Iowa hill and employ ordinary American citizens we find living and working there, and we'll plan a little story, and we'll photograph the scene and the people. That's all pictures should do anyway, and it'll be enough.[32]

It was fine to dream, but the movies Ford was actually making at the time were more studio-bound and artificial looking than ever. The era of the assembly line had come; directorial control was at a low point. Even Fox, Ford's bastion, had been invaded by a Napoleonic tycoon in boots and riding

crop, Darryl F. Zanuck, whose new fangled Twentieth Century Productions had absorbed the venerable but ailing Fox Film Company in August 1935. And the producer system was becoming all-powerful; it was another means whereby studio bosses hoped to control directors who, until then, had enjoyed comparative freedom.

Some directors succumbed to the inevitable; others, like Maurice Tourneur, packed their bags and went home; a few, like Ford, connived to fight back. On *The Informer*, Ford introduced Cliff Reid to his troupe. Reid had collapsed from sunstroke during *The Lost Patrol*, his absence had pleased Ford, and he had asked for him again. "This," he said, gently turning Reid's head to a profile, "is an associate producer. Take a good look at him, because you will not see him again till the picture's finished." (Reid supposedly did show up again, on the last day of shooting, to congratulate Ford on the rushes as the latter sat contemplatively chewing a handkerchief. So Ford spent $25,000 reshooting the scenes Reid liked.[33])

Darryl Zanuck received a similar introduction on *Wee Willie Winkie*, except that this time Ford ordered the studio cop to keep Zanuck off the set. When, later, Zanuck complained Ford was behind schedule,[34] he tore out a bunch of pages from the script: "Now we're all caught up." And he never did shoot those pages. Sam Goldwyn once came on set to suggest, timidly, that Ford add some close-ups; Ford belted him thrice in demonstration of where he would crop close-ups when and if he, Ford, felt like taking them. "Oh, well," said Goldwyn, "at least I put the idea into his head." On another occasion when Goldwyn came on the set "just to watch you work," Ford called an immediate tea break, explaining that it would be very rude for him to go on working while his employer was there. Then, a few days later he sauntered casually into Goldwyn's office and sat down. "Can I help you, John?" asked Goldwyn. "Oh, I don't want anything," said Ford. Goldwyn continued going through his mail, time passed, and finally, knowing Ford was due on set, he asked him what he was doing there. "Oh, nothing, Sam. I just wanted to watch you work."[35]

Because Ford and Dudley Nichols had collaborated on two unusual, arty films at RKO—*The Lost Patrol* and *The Informer*—the theory grew that the RKO Ford was the *real* Ford, whereas the Fox Ford merely drew paychecks. But the follow-up Ford-Nichols RKO films—*The Plough and the Stars* and *Mary of Scotland*—were considered flops, and this was taken as evidence that Ford needed studio guidance. Actually, *Mary* did well commercially, but the quality of both pictures suffered from the most disastrous studio interference Ford ever endured. Contrariwise, his folksy Foxes (the Will Rogers movies among them) were smash hits, but critics never dreamed of taking them seriously. And even though Ford often did not initiate his Fox projects, they were more personal, had greater integrity, and suffered less supervisory meddling than the supposedly "independent" projects at RKO.

A legend grew, too: that Ford, to prevent others reediting his work, would only shoot the precise footage he needed. This was almost true. Many directors shot fifteen or twenty times more footage than ended up in the picture, whereas Ford's ratio was about 2½:1.[36] Yet RKO did reedit *Mary of Scotland,* and could and did take themselves the close-ups Ford avoided. Meanwhile at Fox, Darryl Zanuck outraged Ford by streamlining his movies' pace, but of all the big producers Zanuck was the most sensitive. Moreover, he was a superb editor, and did not interfere until after Ford had assembled his own first cut.

Yet Ford probably won more battles than most directors. "He was a man no one wanted to invoke the wrath of," said his researcher, Katherine Clifton.[37] "They were *very* scared of [him at RKO]," said Hepburn.[38] "John was a terrifying fellow," said Nunnally Johnson.[39] But it never occurred to Zanuck to be afraid of anyone working for him. When Ford failed to implement an order that Warner Baxter drop his phony Southern drawl during *The Prisoner of Shark Island* (actually, Ford was quite frustrated by Baxter), Zanuck stormed onto the set, and Ford immediately threatened to quit. Zanuck screamed: "Are you *threatening me?* Don't you threaten to quit. *I* throw people off sets!" Ford shut up. And a few days later, Nunnally Johnson, who had witnessed the scene, overheard someone ask Ford how he and Zanuck were getting along.

"'Oh,' said Ford, very casually, 'Darryl and I had a little talk, and after that there was no more trouble.'"

"A couple of seconds later Ford turned around and he noticed me sitting there, for the first time. 'That's right, isn't it, Nunnally?' he asked, finally."

"I just nodded," said Johnson.[40]

Another person Ford never could intimidate was John Carradine. The actor was terribly absent-minded and was forever messing things up. Few things made Ford more furious; over and over he would fly into a rage, and go on and on calling Carradine a god-damned stupid s.o.b. and every name he could think of. It did no good. Carradine would watch him with an indulgent smile and when Ford had finished would come over, pat him on the shoulder, and say, "You're o.k., John," and walk away. And Ford would be almost sputtering, because there was no way he could get under Carradine's skin.[41]

3 Second Period (1935–1947): The Age of Idealism

"Who am I? What kind of a person am I to be?" These are questions posed constantly by Ford's people, as they search for, or grasp at, concepts of virtue and purpose in life. Cheyenne Harry, in *Straight Shooting*, found answers in love, and in himself. Later characters find their foundations in family, tradition, duty, occupation, or name.

Judge Priest recognizes virtue by the individual, and sees it manifested by how well a person performs his work: a good man is a good man. But in *The Prisoner of Shark Island*, Dr. Mudd defends himself by his occupation, not by his selfhood. A momentous change has occurred. *Judge Priest* is the last film in which it is enough for a person to do a good job at being himself. Henceforth, in an era of disintegration and chaotic flux, names or appearances are constantly confused with essence, as in *The Whole Town's Talking* and *Steamboat Round the Bend*. Accordingly, traditional values become uncertain and new ethical values must constantly be discovered. The Joads in *The Grapes of Wrath* search blindly for such new values—and Tom thinks finally he has found them in revolution, while his mother, like Huw in *How Green Was My Valley*, holds to the suicidal suppositions of old. For blind adherence to occupational duty, as in *The Hurricane*, breeds ruin. Young

Mr. Lincoln, like Priest, knows truth by knowing the person; and he attempts to redefine encrusted concepts like Law. But to convince the crowd he has to resort to tricks.

The idealism of the Depression decade found new certitude in the valorous struggles of World War II. Ideas seemed brighter and trustier—albeit distant—beacons in the postwar phase, as well. And by 1948, when Ford's third period begins, man has become the servant of myth, at first as a sort of partner, but soon as virtually a puppet.

EXOTICA (1935–1938)

The Informer	5.1.35	RKO Radio
Steamboat Round the Bend	9.6.35	Fox–20th Century–Fox
The Prisoner of Shark Island	2.12.36	20th Century–Fox
Mary of Scotland	7.24.36	RKO Radio
The Plough and the Stars	12.26.36	RKO Radio
Wee Willie Winkie	7.30.37	20th Century–Fox
The Hurricane	12.24.37	Goldwyn-United Artists
Four Men and a Prayer	4.29.38	20th Century–Fox
Submarine Patrol	11.25.38	20th Century–Fox

In mid-1934, as control of the motion picture industry became consolidated in the hands of outside financial interests, censorship, moral and political, was effectively imposed. And in August 1935, as Twentieth Century absorbed Fox Film, a politically more conservative administration took over that firm. Although the Depression had lost little of its vehemence, Hollywood films lost most of the acerbic social criticism. Seven of Ford's recent pictures had assumed antiestablishment views toward contemporary America, but the next twelve retreat into the past, into fantasy, introspection, and allegory, into historical romances set in Scotland, Ireland, India, and Samoa, or during our own Civil War or riverboat eras. This is a period of transition, of renewed, starker, single-mood expressionism, of an operatic, symbolic, and literary style.

Characters are introverted, egocentric, and obsessed with duty, because questions of identity become all-important when society drops out from an individual (Gypo, Duke, Mudd, Mary, DeLaage) and because people not only fail in duty, duty now begins to fail people. Duty and instinct are sometimes identical, sometimes in conflict. Duty is often wrapped up with ideologically governing myths, but these myths (midst the political and economic traumas of the thirties) are increasingly inadequate for human needs; they have become ossified, ripe for revolution, or else violent quarrels arise as to their meanings (totems in *Steamboat*, justice in *Shark Island*, priorities in *Plough*, queenhood in *Mary*, law in *Hurricane*). Whereas the fantasy-reality of social order tended to be stable (if sterile or noxious) in the previous period, fantasy now takes over, isolating individuals beyond hope of reintegration with real values. The hero no longer rises above the herd via alienation, but by primeval instinct stubbornly persisted in, without choice.

There is much stylistic diversity among these movies, but most of them are flawed and uneven, with only a single masterpiece, *Steamboat Round the Bend.*

The Informer (**1935**). Theodore Huff, writing some thirty-five years ago, summed up prevailing critical opinion on *The Informer*: "Nearly every list of 'ten best pictures of all time' includes it. Many consider it the greatest talking picture ever made in America. It is as much a landmark in the history of the sound film as *The Birth of a Nation* is in the silent era."[1] Indeed, *The Informer* had been inundated with awards,* Ford had been acclaimed the high priest of native cinema art, and still today he seems associated more with this than with any other of his films.

But in 1950, Ford told Lindsay Anderson, "I don't think [it's] one of my best. It's full of tricks. No, I think that comes a long way down the list."[2] He reiterated these feelings to students at UCLA in 1964[3] and again to Peter Bogdanovich, adding, "It lacks humor— which is my forte. . . . But I enjoyed making it."[4]

Ford had enjoyed the photography, Joseph August's radiant *Sunrise*-like tonalities; but he had subsequently come to realize that his real art lay in greater variety in mood and style. And today the very qualities that won *The Informer* its place as an official film classic seem even antithetical to Ford's virtues. Its single sustained mood, its heavy shadows and muffled sounds, its pedantic, heavy, slow tempo in acting and cutting, its "painstaking explicitness of a silent film grimly determined to tell its story without the aid of titles—an impression strengthened by Max Steiner's blatant, imitative music"[5]—all these qualities delighted thirties critics, most of whom failed to recall the waves of murky expressionism of the twenties or thirties. For them, *The Informer* stood out as new, different, and artistic, midst Hollywood's assembly-line product.

---

*Oscars: best direction, screenplay (Nichols); actor (McLaglen); score (Steiner); nomination for best picture, best editing. New York Film Critics awards: best picture, best direction. Belgian Crown: Chevalier Order of the Crown of Belgium (Ford); the Belgian Prix du Roi (Ford). L'Académie française: Officier de l'Académie française (Steiner). King of Belgium: bronze medal. International Artistic Motion Picture Exhibition (Venice): cup (Nichols). National Board of Review: best picture. Foreign Press Society of Holland: certificate of honor (Ford, McLaglen). Film Daily Poll: third best. Cinema Jumpo-sha (Japan): among eight best foreign films of the year. Daily Variety Poll rating (by 200 industry figures, 1950): fourth- best film of the first half-century of cinema. (List compiled by James L. Wilkinson), "An Introduction to the Career and Films of John Ford," unpublished M.A. thesis, University of California, Los Angeles, August, 1960.)

Dudley Nichols says he and Ford undertook the picture as "a deliberate and devoted stylistic experiment"[6]—though this explanation is too ingenuous to account for the motives of John Ford, to whom the "experiment" must have seemed pretty derivative, after eight years of conscious imitation of Germanic expressionism. He had met the Irish Marxist writer Liam O'Flaherty in Hollywood* and taken an option on his novel early in 1933, then had had the project rejected as uncommercial by almost every studio in town, until Merian Cooper at RKO decided, October 1934, that it might prove prestigious. Nearly every detail of production was dictated by Ford himself— including the script for which Nichols won an Oscar. Even more than usually, Ford used Nichols as a foil, critic, and sounding board in an exhausting process of countless rewrites during which maximum terseness was obtained. The browbeaten Nichols vowed never to work with Ford again.[7]

Perhaps Ford in 1935 wanted to do something flamingly extreme. Many of his pictures had been fast moving, rambling, variegated in mood and tempo, and quite popular. But it was only when he took on pretentious situation dramas, virtual theater pieces in their literary imagery, that he attracted critical attention for artistry: *Men Without Women, Arrowsmith, The Lost Patrol*. It seems incredible today that anyone could have enjoyed *The Informer* more than Ford's other 1935 films, *The Whole Town's Talking* and *Steamboat Round the Bend*, and, in fact, *The Informer* did earn much less, barely paying its $215,000 cost. (Yet Ford's personal dedication to it was certainly intense; Dan Ford tells us John was so distraught by its negative reception by its first preview audience that he vomited.)

And it was also precisely what tastemakers thought a film ought to be, and which they were evidently incapable of noticing unless bludgeoned. How else can we account for the fact that, seven years and more into the sound era, critics were raving over the use of the blind man's stick's "tap-tap"? Or that they were charmed by that reward poster for Frankie McPhillip,** which manages to blow against the foot of every Irishman in Dublin, and, as if that were not enough, keeps miraculously appearing every time Gypo looks at a

*The two became drinking buddies. Some years later they met in Paris and passed a night in a bar. O'Flaherty, taking no chances, had his own whiskey—Irish—with him in a suitcase, and it was not until 9 A.M. that John got back to his hotel. Alas, he then had to be carried from his bath to a hospital.

**The story: Dublin, one night during the Sinn Fein rebellion, 1922: Gypo Nolan (Victor McLaglen), cashiered from the IRA for failing to carry out an execution and thus left alone and destitute, betrays his friend Frankie McPhillip to the British for £20, for passage money to America for himself and a streetwalker. To shield himself, he accuses another, then nightmarishly carouses away the money. He breaks down before a rebel court, is sentenced to die, but escapes. The streetwalker unwittingly betrays him and, pursued and wounded, he dies in church begging Frankie's mother to forgive him.

We do not know if Ford was familiar with the 1929 English version of *The Informer*, less artily directed by Arthur Robison, and not distributed in the U. S. Ford's version was banned in Peru, because "it showed rebellion against authority."

brick wall. The same critics who raved over Ford's "innovative" use of subjectivity (i.e., the materializing poster; the "tap-tap" representing Gypo's conscience; Frankie's voice in Gypo's mind; the point-of-view camera techniques) failed and would fail to note subtler and more resonant subjectivity in *Pilgrimage, The Black Watch, Salute,* or *How Green Was My Valley.* [8]

Critical enthusiasm for Max Steiner's score is almost as bizarre. Steiner, going against fashion, which had favored on-screen music over background scoring, championed the through-composed movie in which music illustrated every action or object (e.g., Gypo's tinkling coins, or beer gurgling in a man's throat) and expanded a character's slightest emotion. Working from the completed, edited movie, Steiner would measure it and make up elaborate cue sheets detailing each action. From this he wrote his expanded musical commentary, or, as Oscar Levant termed it, his "Mickey Mousing." Perhaps Steiner's unwillingness to trust pictures to express themselves was (and is) justified by audience responses, yet he nullifies music's ability to counterpoint, and underlines *The Informer*'s pedantic heaviness.

Critics approved of Gypo Nolan, because in Victor McLaglen's performance he was a hulking stupid beast of a man, wandering in a friendless, depressed foggy night, and thus representative of the proletarian Everyman whom liberal critics felt Hollywood neglected. In fact, Ford all but eliminated O'Flaherty's protests against capitalist exploitation and British imperialism, reducing them to a generalized situation. And it seems strange that (considering only Ford and leaving aside hundreds of similar examples) the profounder and subtler social probings of the lower classes in pictures like *The Whole Town's Talking, Pilgrimage, Doctor Bull,* and *Flesh* were dismissed as "potboilers," while Gypo's simplistic and endlessly repetitious blusterings were hailed as evidence of a new social outlook.

Lindsay Anderson points out that McLaglen's performance seems "neorealist in its suggestion of actual behaviors," and is thus at odds with the rigid formalism of the production. Of course, this is typical of Ford, whether with Will Rogers, Anne Bancroft, or Francis Ford. And his methods with McLaglen support appearances. He did everything possible to keep the actor confused: mocking him, lambasting him publicly, getting him plastered all night, then surprising him with dawn summonses to work, changing the script at the last moment, having people slip McLaglen Irish whiskey just before asking him to run through new lines. "I just want to get the timing, people have to leave; if you miss a line, just keep going," Ford would say, then shoot McLaglen's fumbling first take without the actor knowing it. [9] The sadism won McLaglen an Oscar, and Ford spent thirty-five years denying his tactics. But such is the public's conception of great acting that no one but Ford seems to have regarded the truth as insulting to McLaglen. And there is, perhaps, a connection between this and the Englishman John Baxter's remark that Ford's "most expressive symbol [of "Irishness"] is the character of Victor McLaglen, a personification of noisy, violent, drunken but loveable Ireland."[10] No one would cite Stepin Fetchit as the most expressive symbol of Negro culture or even Willis Bouchey of Wasp culture. Yet somehow out of all Ford's Irish stock company (Wayne, Bond, O'Hara, Shields, Fitzgerald, Francis Ford, MacDonald, Pennick, Malone . . .), it is the satiric buffoon character one finds identified as symbolic of the Irish. In fact, one wonders at the intelligentsia of the thirties, who could view Gypo as a model of the common man, rather than as an insult to humanity.

No character in *The Informer* is developed beyond the initial definition of his or her simplistic function within the gears and cogs of the mechanistic scenario. Instead, simple little ideas are pompously drawn out. In anguish, we watch an IRA man whimper in fright that he might draw the straw assigning the job of executing Gypo; of course he gets it, and three more chances to exhibit his sweaty whimper when Gypo escapes. This observation aside, neatly contrasted to the professional shooting by another IRA man, nothing whatsoever is told us regarding anything else in his life. This is typical. Commandant Dan Gallagher (Preston Foster) loves Mary and loves his IRA duty. This we learn, and nothing else, some fourteen times. And Mary loves Dan, loved her dead brother, and wants people to stop killing each other. That's Mary. (Ford repeats this winning formula with Foster and Stanwyck in *The Plough and the Stars*.) Ford does nothing to broaden his characters, or to humanize them with little snippets of spontaneity. Types they are born, and types they die.

The Informer takes extreme approaches to the themes and style Ford had been developing. Its society is devoid of heroes; Gypo indeed is the inverse of a Fordian hero. He fails in duty, destroys a family, is utterly determined by environment. Money is merely the proximate cause of his downfall; his true problem (like that of Depression America) is moral, not financial, poverty. Gypo, wholly externalized, lacks selfhood. Once ostracized by the community that defines him, he is prey to every attraction equally, whether vengeance, patriotism, drink, or comradeship. And, with guilt over murdering his friend, Gypo's existence becomes intolerable. He never makes choices. As instinctual as anything else is his dying plea for forgiveness; if this redeems Gypo socially, it scarcely redeems him morally. But social pardon suffices for Gypo. This mechanistic creature symbolizes the inadequateness of his society's sustaining myths—Ford frequently finds spinelessness characteristic of enslaved races, and simultaneously cause and effect of subjugation. But if Gypo is too vacuous to interest us in himself, lack of external reference similarly depletes his interest as mirror of his society: in contrast to the documentary-like detailing of social texture in previous movies, Dublin 1922 is a subjective fantasy, a mood far more than a place, an echo, like the sets of *Caligari*, of Gypo's gloom. Such interiorization marks all Ford movies, particularly those of the next three years, but, thankfully, never so limitingly again; nor are we again asked to participate in the subjectivity of such a troglodytic bore.

Steamboat Round the Bend (1935). In the premises of its plot, *Steamboat* resembles *The Informer*. Both Gypo and Dr. John (Will Rogers)* dwell in ideologically inadequate communities wherein reality and fantasy have merged, moral choices are few, and duty and instinct often conflict. And both Gypo and Dr. John seek solutions for initial failures, the one wandering around Dublin, the other wandering up and down the Mississippi River.

Beyond these premises, the two pictures diverge. That which in *The Informer* is definite becomes transmutable in *Steamboat*; surface denotes essence in one, but in the other, although densely layered, seems merely accidental to reality; one picture is pedantic and gloomy, the other poetic and mercurial.

A gentle morality fable, *Steamboat Round the Bend* reflects the American cinema at its most affable, the age of 1935 in its isolation, and, ever so delicately, the unspoken horrors of rural Southern life. The movie seems inspired by showboat melodrama: the folksy exoticism, the purposefully broad, "showboat" acting (more modulated than in Ford's "city" pictures), the easygoing romanticism, the less ostentatious (though equally inventive) visual technique. Is there anything lovelier or more careless than the way Fleety Belle, her first time at the wheel, yanks the whistle and joyfully calls, "Steamboat round the bend!!"?

Like *Pilgrimage, Dr. Bull*, and *The Whole Town's Talking, Steamboat* ravels itself around change in a static society populated by characters who are sometimes more and sometimes less than they appear to be. The opening screen legend suggests its anywhereness: "Time—The Early 90's, Place—The Mississippi River." Social contradictions are more pronounced than in *Judge Priest*: this is a regimented society where blacks are let out of their segregation cages for Fleety Belle's wedding, and where the train-station door says "Whites"; but it is also a fluid society (like *Straight Shooting*'s or like Vidor's all-black Southern society in *Hallelujah*) in which the principal characters change their occupations and social class every few minutes.

By today's standards, these characters are incredibly open; their simplicity—or rather, their insouciance in venting contradictions— is a major theme. In the very first episode, the New Moses (Berton Churchill, in

---

*Dr. John Pearly sells a cure-all, "Pocahontas Remedy," on his Mississippi steamboat, in the 1890s. Nephew Duke (John McGuire) accidentally kills a man to defend swampgirl Fleety Belle (Anne Shirley—twenties child-star under name Dawn O'Day, later in *Stella Dallas*, etc.), is sentenced to hang, and John starts a wax museum to finance an appeal, which fails. Fleety Belle and Duke marry in jail. She and John hunt the New Moses, who can clear Duke, but encounter a riverboat race, and Capt. Ely (Irvin S. Cobb—*Judge Priest* author, friend and rival of Will Rogers, with whom he ad-libs) taunts John not to renege on an old wager (both boats to winner). As they race, they lasso Moses aboard, burn wax figures and "medicine" for fuel, and win just in time to avert Duke's hanging. (In 1928 Ford was to have made *Captain Lash*, in which a Mississippi riverboat race climaxes when one boat explodes. Victor McLaglen was to star, but title and star were transferred to a wholly different subject ["Black Gang"] and directed by John Blystone.)

bedsheet, beard, and top hat), haranguing Demon Rum, shouts, "A sinner from hell!" and everyone stares at poor drunken Efe (a Francis Ford child-of-nature*), innocently holding his bottle. Efe looks round, shakes his head confessingly, offers his bottle in vain to all, and, as the New Moses utters the pledge, adds, "Me too!" and allows a ribbon to be pinned to his chest. But at the other end of the riverboat, another huckster, Dr. John, is hawking "Pocahontas Remedy," a medicine commercially popular, as it renders its patients unable to work while under treatment. Efe, to ensure his supply of the elixir, goes to work for John, quite happily, until the New Moses reappears to denounce Pocahontas as Demon Rum. Important here is the mania for superficial definitions—Demon Rum, Pocahontas, the New Moses, *Doctor* John, costumes, ribbons, rhetoric—that specify *function* rather than essence, or, rather, that assume function *is* essence. Efe recognizes this truth, which is why he need not recognize the identity of Demon Rum and Pocahontas. There is no paradox.

In this world, names, appearances, myths, symbols, and conventions *are* reality. In Professor Marvel's Wax Show sits "the very whale that swallowed Jonah"! But it is also a world of transmutation. Inside the whale, asleep, lies a Stepin Fetchit character who was baptized David Begat Solomon, changed his name to George Lincoln Washington, but whom Dr. John will call Jonah, of course. The wax figures' names are changed as well, to fit local occasion (Grant becomes Lee, two "old Moseses" becomes the James brothers, etc.). Not only do people mistake wax figures for real people (a mob is silenced when "the James Brothers" threaten), but real people are mistaken for wax figures, by some kids (who think Efe is wax) and even by us (who mistake Matt Abel, standing beside "Little Eva," for "Uncle Tom").

---

*The most developed of Ford's fool-characters, Francis Ford's Boudu-like coonskin wino appears notably in *Judge Priest, Young Mr. Lincoln, My Darling Clementine, Wagon Master, The Sun Shines Bright* and, less symbolically, *The Prisoner of Shark Island, Stagecoach, Fort Apache, 3 Godfathers, She Wore a Yellow Ribbon, The Quiet Man.*

And a farmer, whose sense of reality is as sophisticated as Efe's, accepts a lock of "George Washington"'s hair as an actual relic. Why not?

Simplicity seems gullible. People buy patent medicine, hail the New Moses or the New Elijah, trust that writing it in the Bible makes it so, even trust public institutions known to be corrupt, and declare with the astonishment of first discovery their greater insights: it *is* worth $500 to save Duke's life, decides Dr. John; "I ain't never had nothin' to love in my life, 'cept [Duke]," decides Fleety Belle. And simplicity and openness seem to be epitomized in her—her frank sexuality when Dr. John kisses her, her acute ingenuous passion during the prison-window love scene with Duke, the way her every emotion receives clear play, often physically, or even, as after the trial fiasco, when her blank stare outdoes the eloquence of Dr. John's verbalizing.

But the simple are not simply gullible. Jonah, for example, may seem a mere Uncle Tom stereotype, a fawning menial. In fact, his exaggerations satirize Uncle Tom: wanting to dress up as General Grant, offering a drink of water to the New Moses fished choking from the river, playing "Dixie" for gullible whites—such acts show he is not a witless underling, but (as Peter Rollins notes[11]) one of the country's many hucksters, all of whom (Dr. John, the New Moses, Elijah, Ely, Efe, Professor Marvel, the sheriff) wear several faces.

Such extensive skills at transmutation might seem to indicate a society's durability. But they may also signify moral hypocrisy and ossification. Merely changing names and appearances, while providing a "safety valve" for societal pressures, can prevent actual change, and embalm prejudice and the status quo. Indeed, in *Steamboat*'s world, people often *are* their functions: Jonah, for example, "belongs," as John observes, to the wax show. And Ford, in crosscutting between "General Lee" and farmers petrified waxlike in salute, demonstrates that people may become icons.

Moreover, taking things at face value is dangerous. Dr. John upbraids Duke for slumming with "swamp trash" (Fleety Belle), only to have the girl's family declare *her* irredeemably degraded for consorting with "river

trash" (Duke). Similarly, because Duke has been labeled "guilty," officials who know him to be innocent and pure nonetheless enact with grandiloquent lethargy the government machinery culminating in his execution. Sheriff Rufe Jeffers (Eugene Pallette) is amiable, polite, and roly-poly (like his little daughter, who plays for the wedding, badly but appropriately, "Listen to the Mocking Bird"), but he sports a long buggy whip* and his quip, that it's "too bad" Duke must die, is maddeningly laissez-faire. Similarly matter-of-fact is the tone of the execution official, granting Duke's last request to see the race finish: "So if it's alright with you, Duke, we'll let it go when the *Pride of Paducah* comes around the bend." ("It won't be long," adds Rufe, consolingly.) But Duke accepts fate without murmur or protest; he finds no cause to object that the judge condemns him because of personal animosity toward Duke's lawyer, and he even refuses to escape. Duke is a dupe, a lamb fit for slaughter, trusting, as often in Ford (e.g., *Wagon Master, 7 Women*), his fate to higher authority. Life is what he's got at the moment—which makes it all the more nostalgic.

*Villains have whips in *3 Bad Men, My Darling Clementine, Wagon Master,* and *Liberty Valance. Steamboat*'s officials resemble those in *The Whole Town's Talking.*

But Duke is wrong to be so trusting, for society's welfare depends on individual responsibility. And John's mistake is similar. Against Fleety Belle's outraged protests—"No! He ain't gonna do as you say! We've heard tell of that hangin' judge!"—John counsels Duke to surrender: "Trust me. They won't hang him." But she is right, of course, and John, a practiced huckster, *ought* not to have acted like a witless underling in trusting the corrupt judiciary. But in fact, he even awakens the law from bed, and complains at its lazy, reluctant attitude. "Guess I thought, 'cause I was older, I knew more about right and wrong than you," he apologizes later to Fleety Belle. And in effect, Dr. John is not quite the Fordian hero. He *is* a lonely bachelor, laboring to reunite a family threatened by society, but his wisdom is faulty and his efforts ineffectual. To finance an appeal (still trusting corrupt institutions) he takes on the wax show, revitalizing old myths, so to speak, by their transmutation (as the New Moses does). But John's archetypes, under any guise, are impotent: the appeal fails. And the New Moses (the archetype degenerated into a prohibitionist!) cannot be found.

Only collective iconoclasm will save Duke. For, as in *The Whole Town's Talking*, with its association of a liberated officeworker with the iconoclastic realism of Abelard, the old order has become so tyrannic that mere reform is hopeless. And, fittingly, it is Duke, the innocent lamb, who introduces the violent spark for the revolution, in his "forbidden" transmutation of Fleety Belle from swamp-girl to river-girl. Significantly, she wins John's respect by attacking him with a knife, and he will use this same knife, given him unawares by her, to save her from her swamp family; thus an alliance is formed. But it is Fleety Belle who knew better than to trust the establishment, and it is her goddesslike declaration that Duke shall not die—neither a command nor a prayer—that abruptly transforms defeat into victory and relaxation into raging violence. And many ideals perish as the *Claremore Queen* surges down river. The New Moses, kidnapped by John's lasso, protests, "I've got *souls* to save," but is corrected: he has a *life* to save. John, to keep going without fuel, cheats (making Ely tow him), hacks his boat into kindling wood, and burns the wax show figures. Finally, when only "the power of prayer" can save them, Pocahontas is revealed as Demon Rum, but finds its true function as fuel! As Efe, newly awaken, secretes away a jug, symbols and myths are fed "Into the fiery furnace! Hallelujah!! Glory Be!!!"

Does a new realism result? Yes and no. Duke's trust, after all, proves justified; and Ford's fetchingly brief concluding cameos suggest primeval values abide, even if today they can be achieved only with violence: Dr. John lounges fishing on his new riverboat, and Duke and Fleety Belle have gained Eden. As Duke said (and as all John Ford movies say), "There ain't nothin' nicer than goin' up and down the river."

"*Steamboat Round the Bend* should have been a great picture," grumbled Ford in 1965, "but at that time they had a change of studio and a new manager came in who wanted to show off, so he recut the picture, and took all the comedy out."[12] Such acerbic sarcasm thirty years after the event—the new "manager" was Darryl F. Zanuck, the "change of studio" was Twentieth Century's absorption of Fox—suggests Zanuck's editing was significant. We shall never know. *Steamboat* has less comedy than other Fords, and little of his characteristic wackiness. Zanuck's defenders, Dan and Barbara Ford among them, suggest Zanuck quickened Ford's pacing and eliminated the inconsequential. Yet good Fords are often the sum of their inconsequentialities, and there *is* a peculiar episodic quality to *Steamboat*.

Will Rogers' death, shortly after completing *Steamboat*, ended what possibly was Ford's most fertile creative relationship. Naturally it was not without strains. There is an amusing story that Rogers—after characteristically giving Ford a continuous line of instructions on how to direct and then seeing Ford walk off the set, leaving him in charge—went sheepishly to tell Sheehan that Ford had just disappeared, for no apparent cause. But Rogers, like Carey, brought something more than folksy charisma into a Ford picture, namely an easing of tension and a rechanneling of directorial energy into gentler, more complex, yet less artificial representations of human relationships. The Rogers films are almost the only prewar Ford movies in which one does not sense Ford *making* things happen, but rather *letting* them happen. Not coincidentally, they, like the Carey silents, derive their magic primarily from the nuances with which characters relate in little things rather than from their larger dramas. Only in *Wagon Master* was Ford to recapture this magic, a movie about people first, and about events only inconsequentially.

Quite opposite such guileless art are Ford's next four films, brooding and ambition-heavy, in his *Informer* manner, each deeply flawed, and each dealing with deeply flawed worlds. Values and myths are inadequate for human needs; black expressionism befits conflicts of instinct and duty, in which duty's nature is ambiguous, and in which the combatants' commitment is so bound up with selfhood that, like Gypo, their moral choices seem predetermined, rather than free.

The Plough and the Stars (1936). The least imposing of the four, *The Plough and the Stars*, may well be Joseph August's photographic masterpiece—particularly in its dewy park scene. But like Hitchcock's *Juno and the Paycock*, this Sean O'Casey play, too, translates awkwardly into cinema. His Ireland—of quixotic revolutionaries, of oppressed barboors who loot, of balladeers and weeping women—is reduced to sixty-seven minutes of (often memorable) Easter Rebellion vignettes, unintegrated in their stylistic disparity and highlighted by Moroni Olsen and Arthur Shields. In face of RKO's interference, Ford lost interest. Denied a

The Plough and the Stars (1936). Note Ford crouched by camera at lower left corner of window.

The Plough and the Stars (1936).

cast of *only* Abbey Theatre Players* and forced to star Barbara Stanwyck (who wrought wonders for Capra), he transformed her into an incredibly blah stereotype. She whines repetitiously against her husband's fight for Ireland. But men will go on dying, and women will go on weeping, and neither, as she says, can help it.

The Prisoner of Shark Island (1936). Duty seems indistinguishable from instinct in *The Plough and the Stars,* and equally so in *The Prisoner of Shark Island.*** With the Civil War ending, Lincoln instinctually attempts to rechannel the duty with which the war was fought into a policy of *reconciliation:* upon announcing Lee's surrender, he asks the band to play "Dixie," claiming it for *all* Americans. But other factions instinctually feel that duty demands *revenge:* Lincoln is assassinated.

Dr. Mudd is a Southerner (as Ford's use of "Maryland, My Maryland" reminds us), but he shares Lincoln's positive sense of duty. And just as the accumulated kharma of years of war descends upon Lincoln, so too upon Mudd. A black filmworld evokes a grim epoch of repression, suspicion, cruelty, and hysteria. Beginning with bagged and ironed prisoners confronted, in ramming angulation, by their court, a dramatic nightmare progresses through executions, starkly lit horrors of geometric prisons, sharks, dank holes, and into the ultimate horror of plague.[†] But through it all, Mudd, a weary man, absorbed in duty to family and patients, obstinately defends himself *not* as unacquainted with Booth or Booth's deed, but as duty bound to aid the sick; and in prison, instinctually rejecting rancor, he will aid even his torturers, without hope of reward. In contrast, Secretary Erickson instructs the tribunal that duty demands they condemn Mudd and others accused, regardless of evidence; from duty, guards and the prison doctor instinctually hate Mudd. From duty, the commandant refuses to fire on the flag (to make the ship land medicine); but Mudd does so, because "I gotta look out for things."

This is the typical justification of a Fordian hero, and Mudd, no intellectual, has not reasoned his way to truer insights into society's welfare. He

*Among the Players Ford *did* import were Shields, his brother Barry Fitzgerald (né William Shields), Dennis O'Dea, Eileen Crowe, Una O'Conner, et al. (Backstage glimpses of O'Casey's plays at the Abbey occur in *The Rising of the Moon* and *Young Cassidy.*) Many players, like Shields, had actually been in the Dublin post office when it fell. And, years earlier, use of Irish and English veterans during *Hangman's House* resulted in brick-slinging battles.

**After setting a stranger's leg, Dr. Samuel A. Mudd is arrested, summarily tried, and given life at Dry Tortugas (Florida). Wife Peggy's escape plan fails; Mudd and black friend Buck are thrown into a dank pit; but yellow fever erupts and the commandant begs Mudd's aid. He squashes a black mutiny and fires on a federal ship, forcing its plague-fearing captain to land supplies and doctors. All petition Mudd's pardon. He and Buck return home. (The film follows Mrs. Mudd's biography, but elides the years in prison. Mudd [1833–83] was pardoned by Andrew Johnson on his last day in office [March 21, 1869], but appeals for his exoneration [recently, to President Carter] have not succeeded.)

[†]Cf. *Arrowsmith*'s more harrowing plague. Here, Dr. McIntyre's slow, unwilling body-melt is juxtaposed to an onerous wheel.

merely persists in instinct, arriving at heroic actions simply because his stubbornness leaves no other choice. And, far from canonizing him, Ford omits appeals for our empathy, such as the information that Mudd freed his slaves years ago, and thus turns a scene such as Mudd's peremptory treatment of a carpetbagger into an instance of arrogance and politics. Nor does Ford palliate the refusal of Georgian Nunnally Johnson's script to cater to Northern tastes in racism. Black soldiers, though scarcely guileless, speak in musical, rhythmic patterns, with quasi-balletic gesture; and Ford changes Mudd's maid from a white to a black woman, and has her tremble not as a slave but as a servile woman, as she serves breakfast to Grandpa. Mudd defends, doctors, lives, and suffers with blacks; his friend Buck even enlists in the prison guard to help him escape. Still, Mudd can handle situations Northerners cannot, like quelling a black mutiny:

> — They're gonna take you before the judge, gonna take ya out in the courtyard and build a scaffold, and yur gonna have to build it yurselves too, yur own scaffold. Now when ya get that done yur gonna do some diggin', yur gonna dig yur own graves, an' the law is gonna hang ya. They're gonna put a rope around yur necks, an' they're gonna choke ya, choke ya till yur eyeballs pop out an' yur tongue swells up.

Whereupon a mutineer comments:

> — That ain't no Yankee talkin' just t' hear hisself talk. That's a Southern man, an' he mean it, yessir.

But Mudd ultimately emerges as a shallow, mechanistic character, more like Gypo Nolan than Judge Priest, and the fault lies in Ford's inability to direct Warner Baxter. Baxter's overprojected acting is mere representation; by wholly exteriorizing Mudd's innate arrogance, for example, he renders the character superficial; he substitutes nervousness for relating. In contrast, Harry Carey and Jack Pennick relax and swing their bodies nontheatrically, feeling out to each other, not "acting," but just "letting it happen."

Imagine Carey as Mudd, and note how the movie's emotions are clarified and deepened! In lieu of such humanity, Mudd's function is chiefly thematic, and Ford's overdependence on scenic values cannot compensate for this vapidity at the movie's core.

Also, despite its Ford-like themes and photography, *Shark Island* is a fairly cold, impersonal film. Even a nightmare needs atmospheric variety and more ironic relief (like Francis Ford comically slapping away flies while telling a twenty-yearer, "You'll never make it, Arnold, you're too old. The mosquitos'll get you!"). But Ford was not at ease under Zanuck's domination, had not at all (for the first time?) participated in writing the script, does not manage to interpolate his customary plethora of ritual, and seems rarely able to vivify personalities beyond Johnson's outline. Johnson wrote wonderful dialogue, but his emphasis on action results in fairly stratified characters, giving his work a mechanical, theatrical air. The "simple Fordian characters" of *Shark Island, The Grapes of Wrath,* and *Tobacco Road* are Johnson's, not Ford's, and far less complex and ambivalent. Lacking too is Ford's usual sense of a fabricated biography behind each character; Johnson's people have little past. Also, Ford's direction, in all three Johnson films, is deliberate. He parses Mudd's escape through moody corridors and archways, using barrack routine to heighten illusion and tension "with shrewd care for the pitch and speed of every move, every detail" (Otis Ferguson);[13] but such virtuoso executions seem on repeated viewings less interesting than Ford's visualization of what is not in the screenplay: moments of inconsequence, like Mudd sitting silently at his cell window with his legs curled up beneath him.*

Mary of Scotland (1936). Duty and instinct, synonymous in *Plough* and *Shark Island,* conflict in *Mary of Scotland* and *The Hurricane.* Mary Stuart, both as personage and character, is overwhelmed by the clatter of swords, thumping of armored men, deterministic compositions in monumental sets, ramming angles, and sweeping gestures, and by the cacophony of

---

*Other Ford additions include the freeze-frame of dead Lincoln, the reflection of Peggy's face in the window searching news of Mudd, the visual tour de force of the execution sequence, and the film's ending, when Buck's shadow swoops toward his thirteen kids like some homeward soaring eagle (Johnson had placed Buck's reunion inside, with Mudd's family). In Johnson, after Mudd has been recaptured in front of his wife, we return to Key West, where the child Martha's white nurse is reading to her: "And then the Prince leaned down and kissed Sleeping Beauty on both eyes—and she waked up." Cut to /Peggy coming in the door, then /to a shot of Peggy and her child, and she tells her that daddy and grandpa won't be coming home, daddy someday, but grandpa never. As Ford filmed it, the scene begins with the camera looking out the window toward the sea (= death; hope in afterlife; etc.), then, with the colored maid's voice *off*-camera, it pans slowly 90 degrees and we see Peggy wearily opening the door, while *off*-camera we hear: Maid: "And then the Prince leaned down and kissed the Sleeping Beauty on both eyes—and watcha s'pose?" Martha: "What?" Maid: "Sleeping Beauty waked up." Martha: "Mama!" *Now* Ford cuts to /a general shot of the room and we see Martha and the maid for the first time. One of Johnson's squarer scenes has been turned into something quite lovely.

complex events extended over years and beyond the temporal unity Ford-Nichols attempt to impose. History is a monstrous prop for Mary's collision with the world. She arrives (like so many Ford heroes) alone, in fog and night, and she kneels and prays to rule with "piety and wit"—virtues that will constantly elude her. Her dilemma, the conflict between her personality and office, is prefigured as she crouches helplessly beside a giant globe, and is articulated in Ford's presentation, alternately intimate and distanced—e.g., the familiarity we feel toward her as she greets James seems abruptly a trespass of manners when, in long shot, she mounts the stairs, the guards salute, and majesty is evoked. And Mary herself is girlish, even ingenuous, with only foolish dignity and sorry politics to oppose her ruthless barons and demonic cousin Elizabeth I. As often in Ford, virginity (Elizabeth) is associated with bitchiness, whereas uncontained sexuality (Mary) indicates purity.* And

*Flesh (Lora), Pilgrimage (widows vs. nubile daughters), Stagecoach (Dallas, Lucy), The Fugitive, What Price Glory, The Quiet Man, Mogambo, Donovan's Reef, 7 Women. Both petulant and prim, willful and self-destructive, the Ford heroines Mary most resembles are Shirley Temple, Grace Kelly, and (My Darling) Clementine.

Mary, in terror, will fling away her throne and her God for love of Bothwell ("Aye, and I'd do it again, a thousand times!").

Mary, though she tries, fails in her duty as queen even as she succeeds in her duty to herself. In Fordian terms, this ought to condemn her (albeit 1936 was the year a king of England resigned his throne for love) and, in the absence of any actual societal context, the contextualization of Mary's drama as a disembodied dynastic struggle occurring always in nightmarish castles, night, and fog, almost conceals the embarrassing truth: Mary really has no other cause as sovereign than herself. Having opted for "to thy own self be true," she expects her subjects to fight and die by tens of thousands, not that she might love as she chooses, but that she might rule as well.

Ford does not underline this hypocrisy. (Does he even acknowledge it?) On the contrary, he finds a moral victory in her defeat. She advocates tolerance and the right to marry whom she chooses. Her only alternative to being "a creature of love" is to become a machine like Elizabeth. Thus, in her penultimate scene, her lover dead, her throne gone, her execution hours away, she declares, "I win," meaning her progeny will inherit barren Elizabeth's throne: unlike Elizabeth, she has been a human, not just a queen. (But, alas for thematic sense, Mary's son was born of a marriage of state, not of love, and the victory she cites is political, not the moral one she and Ford accord her.)

Ford is intrigued by ideas, personages, and myths of history as background to Mary's moral odyssey, but almost none of it matches historical truth.* Indeed, *Mary of Scotland*, like Max Ophuls's *The Exile*, is irrelevant to history, retaining only the myths suitable for fairy-tale reflections on kingship and Manichaeanism, for which Charles II and Cromwell, or Mary and Elizabeth, provide the poetic subjects rather than the historical objects. Mary Stuart is a paradigmatic hero of this period: everything is given her—her duty, her glory, her downfall. Her native ingenuousness is under constant assault by a hostile world. Within a milieu determined by pageantry, the one element of freedom granted her is the possibility of rising above despair, through courage of purity.

Ford was unabashedly excited at the ideal casting of Katharine Hepburn as Mary, and he related to Howard Sharpe how he had carefully screened all her pictures, studying "every angle of her strange, sharp face—the chiseled nose, the mouth, the long neck."[14] It was a rare instance of Ford directing a major female star, while for her part Hepburn creates possibly her most multifaceted personage. Less rugged in the thirties and possessing greater range than in her Tracy years, the formality of her intonation and gesture,

---

*Ford's film echoes the Stuart-Catholic party line: villainous Bothwell is ever-pure, and Darnley's death is blamed on Mary's enemies; she herself never has a scheming thought. Also, Mary's long imprisonment is telescoped and she does not age; the real Mary died at forty-five, in 1587. And the meeting with Elizabeth (in Maxwell Anderson's verse drama from which Nichols adapted his scenario) never occurred.

her sense of her body in framed space, perfectly fit Ford's own manner. And she is well supported by an unusually subdued Fredric March (Bothwell), a morosely polychromatic John Carradine (Rizzio), and a bravura Moroni Olsen (Knox).* But the stiff prolixities of Nichols's script bog the movie's sweep, after its first half hour, midst detail and Korda-like dramaturgy. And RKO's reediting—ragged, jarring inserts, mismatched angles, and botched rhythms—produces a travesty of Fordian style.

The Hurricane (1937). In *The Hurricane,*** as in *Shark Island,* misguided duty underlies everything, exacerbated by the order / freedom dichotomy generic to South Sea movies. Governor DeLaage's refusal to allow his heart to influence his inhumane application of French law to an instinctual lifestyle makes him Ford's most irrational law-and-order extremist, and the character is infested with so much myopic arrogance that we may wonder what mitigating traits render him palatable to his wife and doctor, who vainly debate the meaning of DeLaage's ruling myth (order). Kersaint's prediction, that the hurricane will teach DeLaage there are things more important than the French penal code, suggests, along with shards of biblical allegory, that the storm represents God's wrath. Perhaps Depression America read a parable here (like *Steamboat Round the Bend's*): establishment mythology, morally bankrupt, cannot suppress nature. But if this be true, the proletariat is in trouble, for the natives have no function other than as props for DeLaage's confusion, for it is they and their island (and the good priest and his church) who are destroyed and their oppressors who are spared. (Actually, the hurricane seems a manifestation of De-Laage's wrath sweeping, like Walter Pidgeon's destructive id in *Forbidden Planet,* over the world [and priest] that mock his personification of Law.) Afterward, confronted by ruination, DeLaage humbly concedes Terangi freedom.

*Knox's towering robed figure sweeps out of a crowd, bearing a striking resemblance in gesture and costume to Nicolai Cherkassov's Ivan the Terrible (1944), and Eisenstein's admiration for Ford was unbridled. The separate cuts of reluctant lords bowing woodenly to Mary, earlier, could have been copied by Eisenstein even in rhythm.

**Dr. Kersaint (Thomas Mitchell) reminisces about a sandbar, once an island paradise. *Flashback*: DeLaage (Raymond Massey), French governor of Manacura, denies mercy as Terangi's jailbreaks increase a six-month term for hitting back a Frenchman. After eight years, Terangi (Jon Hall) escapes across six hundred miles of ocean to his wife (Dorothy Lamour) and unseen daughter. DeLaage, deaf to pleas by his wife (Mary Astor), pursues—until a hurricane destroys everything.

Oscar to Thomas Moulton (sound recording); nominations to Thomas Mitchell and to Alfred Newman (music).

Before taking a trip, Ford had jotted down some possible names for the studio to look at, among them Charlie, who lived next door to him, was Tahitian and a good swimmer. One morning they were both driving out at the same moment. "Where are you going?" asked Ford. "U.A." "So am I. What are you going to do there?" "Well, I'm going to be in a picture." "What's it called?" "*Hurricane.*" While Ford was away, the studio had taken some tests of Charlie, liked them, and changed his name to Jon Hall. (The story is told by Ford in the John Ford Papers, Lilly Library, Indiana University.)

The Hurricane. Ford directing Dorothy Lamour.

All that, just to teach DeLaage a lesson? No wonder the sandbar set and its painted backdrop look so phoney: such obvious aestheticism recalls Kersaint's eyes' crazed gleam in the film's prologue. Nowhere else are we made conscious of studio re-creation. Yet, a few Samoan background shots aside, everything—village, church, buildings, palm trees—was constructed, for $150,000, on Goldwyn's back lot, even the lagoon (a 600-foot-long tank). Bert Glennon's expressionist photography even struggles to counteract the authentic look by melodramatizing land- and seascapes. And excess typifies this Goldwyn movie: full-blown, injudicious voluptuousness, repelling, compelling—but utterly unerotic. Ford could come no closer to *Tabu*'s spirit than occasional touches and the casting of Murnau's heroine, Reri, in a bit part. The priest (C. Aubrey Smith) declaims like the Bible, usually with organ, as when he says, "This is between me—and Somebody Else," and a heavenly choir bursts through a glorious cloudscape. Massey and Astor are credible, if underdeveloped, as Frenchmen, and Dorothy Lamour is credible, if only physically, as a Polynesian—she is made to mouth colloquially poetic English supposedly representing native mentality. Severity toward such generic wallowing would be thankless, but Jon Hall's bewildered, put-on expressions deal poetic authenticity a fatal blow. (It was Hall's debut, and Ford—trying to sabotage him?—had him beat with real whips and fired upon with real bullets.)

The Hurricane was a box-office smash, due largely to the storm sequence (by Jim Basevi with Stuart Heisler). Huge propellers simulated driving rain "which," wrote Mary Astor, "kept us fighting for every step, with sand and water whipping our faces, sometimes leaving little pinpricks of blood on our cheeks from the stinging sand."[15] Wave machines churned the water. Then, for $250,000, the set was destroyed by a tidal wave created by releasing water from 2,000-gallon tanks mounted on sixty-five-foot towers (controlled by Ford with electric buttons). Detail shots, such as those of the stars tied to the giant tree, were done indoors, with more wind machines, hoses, and a papier-mâché tree suspended in a tank (so that it would turn as though its roots were coming loose).

Ford seems to relish his repeated crosscuts from the horrified face of Mary Astor to the horrifying face of the titanic onrushing wave. But what becomes striking on repeated viewing is less the action of the storm than the serene and lordly pacing of Ford's editing. Never has disaster been so majestic.

Wee Willie Winkie (**1937**). In contrast to the murky, darkly subjective dreamworlds of the RKOs, *Hurricane* and *Shark Island*, Ford's next three movies, all naive little matinee pieces, seem fresh, variegated, and almost documentary-like. And one of them is, next to *Steamboat Round the Bend*, the gem of the period. *Wee Willie Winkie** is so much a portrait of a world, rather than merely a vehicle for the most profit-making star of the thirties, that the viewer would do well to forget about Shirley Temple and think instead of Priscilla Williams.

As she stares wide-eyed from her railroad car, Miss Priscilla Williams is clearly thrilled to be in India. How India might feel about having her there may be surmised from Ford's wry introduction of Priscilla emerging from a smoky gorge. While his intentions might have been less than symbolic, people who *arrive* in Ford movies generally end up fulfilling rather awesome purposes** and, as it happens, Priscilla will in her first few weeks in India

---

*1890s: Widowed American Joyce Williams (June Lang) with daughter Priscilla is obliged to accept hospitality from her father-in-law (C. Aubrey Smith), a British colonel in India. There a young officer (Coppy: Michael Whalen) courts Joyce, and Priscilla befriends a tough sergeant (Victor McLaglen) and the notorious Khoda Khan (Cesar Romero). Thinking her abducted, the regiment is about to storm an impregnable fortress when Priscilla shames the Indians into negotiation. (There is almost no similarity to Kipling's poem.) Release prints were toned sepia for daytime, blue for night. Oscar nomination to Thomas Little (interior decoration).

**Mary Stuart arrives by boat, the Joads by truck, Sean Thornton by train, Wyatt Earp on horse, and Clementine by stagecoach. Colonel Thursday also has a coach, Boats Gilhooley rides a freighter, Amelia Dedham a ketch, Marty Maher has to walk, Ethan Edwards is alone on a horse. Ransom Stoddard arrives once by train, once by stage and buckboard. The Fugitive and Dr. Cartwright have mules. The Nordleys (*Mogambo*) arrive by steamer, Duke (*Air Mail*) by plane. All arrive as loners into alien milieus.

sow flowers where'er she walks, humanize her grandfather, comfort the dying, win a boyfriend, marry off her widowed mother, and prevent a war. In effect, she is a true Fordian hero, celibate, mediating between repression and chaos (Britain and the Petans), and reuniting a family. Indeed, she is Ford's most affirmative hero, for her higher wisdom derives not from tragic experience or innate arrogance, but from an innocence reflecting humanity's innate virtue. Priscilla's innocent eye regards the world as her teddy bear, and therein lies her strength—for who dares disillusion such stubborn innocence? She does not know her mother's fragile naiveté, her grandfather's ruthless martial gravity, MacDuff's brute toughness, nor Khoda Khan's murderousness.

At times her mythology dominates the picture, as when a call grows louder passing from one mouth to another, until the camera jumps suddenly into a gaping close-up of MacDuff's huge orifice—a Homeric simile reflecting Priscilla's imagination. But if Priscilla does not always know how to interpret, she sees with a frankness denied unbiased observers. And Ford provides immense detail for her innocent eye, making *Wee Willie Winkie* as much a study of the British-India military as later films will be of the American.

This teddy-bear-documentary style is apparent in the reveille sequence: an Indian pulls energetically at a bell, the camera tracks along rows of barrack bunks, showing identically arranged kits and rifles chained to soldiers' feet; we follow the men through a raucous washroom scene. Priscilla awakes, sits up in bed and stares, entranced by pipes, drums, parades, cannon. She has a wide view from her window, out past the big tree, of the ferocious native hussars galloping by and the formations of tartaned infantry. (Ford and Shirley Temple repeat the sequence in *Fort Apache* [1948]. Later she visits MacDuff, not knowing he is dying. "Please God, honor the Queen, shoot straight, keep clean," says he, and she sings "Auld lang syne," which a piper takes up, after she leaves; and MacDuff is buried with pomp.

Elsewhere, too, in Ford happiness belongs to the perversely innocent, success to the blindly persistent. And Priscilla, who can mime the imperialist spirit Stepin-Fetchit-like, shares some of the qualities of the blessed Ford fool. But it is frightening that Priscilla is made the regiment's mascot, given a uniform, and trained in ordnance. For ordnance will regulate her spirit and merge her into that pleasant pageantry that is the arrogant, racist, and resented position of the British. We see that position in almost every scene, whether with English ladies shopping, English gentry in a tea shop, English officials supervising native police, English breaking through train-station crowds, or English balls interrupted by attacking Petans. Pax Britannica vs. native rule. Everywhere can be sensed the flag, the cross, and British music. "England's duty, my duty," huffs the colonel. English dominance is occasionally the butt of Ford's Irish amusement—e.g., a huge dour orderly gripping to his imperious chest a teensy-weensy teacup. But the tremendous barriers of rank (and race) seem constantly to terrify even the soldiers themselves.

The scene in which the colonel attempts to justify duty's point of view is set with stunning expressionism in a darkened room, he to the left engulfed in shadow, Priscilla and Joyce in the middle, their white dresses illuminated. The composition lends majesty to his words, but lends them subjectivity, too. He does not quite win his point. For to these Americans not so much India as the British are foreign, and the army even more so. But when Priscilla begs her mother to take her home, mother has to reply, "But this is home" — a line with considerable reverberation within an oeuvre in which the search for home is a constant theme. An old life, husband, and national identity are dead; new beginnings must be made. There is no choice.

One of Ford's finer ingenues, Joyce is hardly twenty-one and when she has to explain to Priscilla about "Indians," "India," and "Columbus," her sweet-serious parroting of history indicates her sheltered gentility. And her series of expressions while serving Coppy's parents tea— fright, bewilderment, anxiety lest she fail to please—are as entrancing as her shaded dance with him later—to a gentle "Comin' thro' the Rye," to camera movements *andante*.

Wee Willie Winkie is among Ford's most seminal prewar films not only because like virtually every postwar picture it studies militarist ethos, but also because it grasps the paradox that one must grow up, one must go on, one must belong, and that this is good, even though thereby one's conscience is arrogated and one is inculpated in collective evil. The future is to be entered into willingly.

Four Men and a Prayer, Submarine Patrol (1938). Neither movie explores any deep theme, yet both display *allegretto* virtuosity, deftly vignetting large casts and variegated modalities. Expressionism is moderated; and, as in *Winkie*, depth-of-field blocking and cutting, graceful camera movements, and animated reaction shots are employed more as in fifties than as in thirties Ford. The scripts, moreover, are trivial skeletons for the director's invention.

Four Men—with its subtle verbal gags, ridiculous costumes, butlers, and chewing gum, with Berton Churchill a hysterically sober tycoon, Loretta Young a Hawksian screwball, and George Sanders a pompous attorney, with Barry Fitzgerald drinking midst Ford's first friendly barroom brawl, every European in India carrying an umbrella, and Alexandrian bellboys wearing "Sphinx Hotel" sweaters—is an affair best appreciated by Ford cultists. Its uncharacteristically lampooning direction makes the story—of four sons globehopping to clear their father's name—almost meaningless.

In contrast, *Submarine Patrol*, which also stars Richard Greene, and studies a military society in miniature, is impressively self-effacing in technique and detail.* A brilliant bar sequence begins as Warren Hymer chains his taxi to a pole (an instance of "invisible humor"—easily missed, thus more delightful if noticed). Midst beery bedlam, "The monkeys have no tails in Zamboanga," and sailors' manic assault on a slot machine, a marine sergeant**, with cocky nonchalance, slips in a single coin, holds out his hat, and exits with his reward, as the sailors futilely resume. Meanwhile Perry absconds with Susan, having locked up morose John Carradine ("Dancing is a sinful pastime!") and discarded the key onto a passing tray. Later, when we find the sergeant dancing with Perry's society sweetheart, we recall a brief flirtation and a wry smile at Perry, and comprehend his cockiness of necessity toward the slot machine. But this subplot is executed with such deft innuendo that it may be all but overlooked.

Similarly subtle is the ingenious performance of the former Keystone comedian Slim Summerville, as Cookie. Cookie lives in a Tati-like world of his own with its private gestures, and the smile he gives the captain at a moment of potential crisis establishes his inviolable independence of even the navy. His gags typify Ford's invisible humor. While the crew pumps away at calisthenics, Cookie brings Quincannon (J. Farrell MacDonald) coffee and donuts, remarking, "That's great stuff! I do it myself every morning before I get out of bed"—a line thrown away and bringing no reaction from Quincannon. For all Cookie's gags occur in a separate universe—as when he steps forward to refuse, and finds himself included among the volunteers who have stepped forward too.

Sterner emotions counterpoint pleasantries: as in *Seas Beneath*, awkward individuality and mechanics dominate a depth-charge attack; fear dominates an *adagio* mine sequence, apoplexy a battle, orgiastic exhaustion its

*1918: Playboy Perry (Greene) and a motley crew shape up in convoy from Brooklyn to Brindisi on a wooden subchaser whose Capt. Drake needs to redeem himself for letting a destroyer run arock. Perry's attempt to wed Susan (Nancy Kelly) is thwarted by her freighter-captain father; Perry wins his respect on a mission, but orders to sail postpone marriage.

Ford once cited *Submarine Patrol* as a favorite, and *The New York Times* (Frank Nugent) gave it a rave review. Richard Greene's debut in *Four Men and a Prayer* won the British-stage import a Fox contract, but after a half-dozen movies he returned to England in 1940 to star there in adventure films and as TV's Robin Hood.

**Setting, song, machine, and character are repeated in *Donovan's Reef*.

aftermath. Schmaltz is juxtaposed to skillfully edited action, sailing past the Statue of Liberty (as in *The Growler Story*), or provides motivation, as when *Anchors Aweigh*, underlining an admiral's (Moroni Olsen's) soft sonorous delivery, conveys the officer-caste tradition behind Drake's determination. And while a lugubrious Italian waiter conducts a gooey "Santa Lucia," Perry and Susan stare straight ahead; he glances at her, then turns away; she does the same; the schmaltz throws their sincerity into relief.

PRE-WAR PRESTIGE (1939–1941)

Stagecoach	3.2.39	Argosy–Wanger–United Artists
Young Mr. Lincoln	6.9.39	Cosmopolitan–20th Century–Fox
Drums Along the Mohawk	11.3.39	20th Century–Fox
The Grapes of Wrath	3.15.40	20th Century–Fox
The Long Voyage Home	10.8.40	Argosy–United Artists
Tobacco Road	2.20.41	20th Century–Fox
How Green Was My Valley	12.?.41	20th Century–Fox

This is Ford's prestige period. These seven movies captured ten Oscars and thirty-four nominations, and in each of these three years the New York Film Critics chose Ford best director. Artistically, the period represents a renaissance after the dark ages of the preceding few years. But it is not without its impersonal tinges. Many of these movies were major studio productions, for which Ford had to contend with assigned scripts and Darryl Zanuck's supervision and editing. And to an extent, Ford played it safe and adapted himself to the tastes of the tastemakers and the instructions of his employers. He had striven for the lofty position he was now assuming—virtually unanimous recognition as Hollywood's foremost director—and he aimed to hold it.

On the other hand, Ford is far more profoundly and complexly engaged in these pictures than in any of the preceding period, which seems in retrospect to have been one of negativity, floundering, and indifference. Much that was contentious then is assured now. The Fordian hero reemerges; duty, no longer ambiguous, is synonymous with destiny; far from having identity problems, characters acquire fortification in class consciousness. Not only in *Stagecoach*, but in all these pictures, an individual represents his specific culture.

Themes of persistence, helplessness, and desperation pervaded preceding films. Themes of *survival* dominate now. This is very much a populist period. And characters are more instinctual, free will less in evidence, than ever before. In *Stagecoach, Young Mr. Lincoln*, and *Drums Along the Mohawk*, societies habitate premythic frontiers, where social structures are still defining themselves, rather than ossified, as earlier in the decade. And Ford's moody expressionism now seems almost a veneer barely containing a vigorous, variegated naturalness right below the surface. Yet matters take a sharp downturn with *The Grapes of Wrath, The Long Voyage Home, Tobacco Road*, and *How Green Was My Valley*. Now people are suffocated, entombed by social structures, and utterly destroyed; yet, even so, those who survive often emerge strengthened.

The period contains films such as *The Long Voyage Home* and *The Grapes of Wrath*, which brought Ford oceans of prestige in 1940, but which now seem fairly minor alongside the period's three great masterpieces: *Stagecoach* is more vigorously intense than any prior Ford movie. *Young Mr. Lincoln* has deepened characterizations and gives a more resonantly complex import to an individual's personality. *How Green Was My Valley* uses cinematic form as "spatial music," and to subvert the narrative's superficial meaning.*

---

*While Ford films and Fox films have a similar "look" (e.g., Henry King's 1939 *Stanley and Livingstone* looks more like fifties Ford than Ford does—except that scenery distracts from characters more than informing them), we ought not blithely to assume that Ford's three-dimensional lighting, fluid compositions, and expressive montage (if not his acting) derive from studio "tradition"—from the corporate talents of an oligarchy of photographers and editors. It is also possible that the Fox look owed much to Ford. Fox's fortunate vulnerability toward seeming a virtual "school" of a great artist had already been demonstrated under Murnau. But Ford was an even more valued and influential studio asset—after twenty-six years there he was still thought worth $600,000 a year. And by the mid-1950s, neither Zanuck nor King retained the Fox "look," but John Ford did. .

Darryl F. Zanuck, looking back on these years, concluded that Ford was "the best director in the history of motion pictures" because "his placement of the camera almost had the effect of making even good dialogue unnecessary or secondary."[16]

Stagecoach (1939). Westerns, churned out in profusion by poverty-row firms for the lowest classes of audiences, had been shunned by big producers throughout the decade. But *Stagecoach* showed westerns could be intelligent, artful, great entertainment—and profitable. Budgeted at $392,000, it grossed over a million its first year, promoted John Wayne into big stardom, and gave Ford's reputation its first real boost since *The Informer*. Today still, *Stagecoach* is one of the freshest of official film classics.

"I found the story by reading it in *Collier's*," said Ford. "It wasn't too well developed, but the characters were good. 'This is a great story,' I thought, and I bought it for a small amount—I think it was $2,500. I tried to sell it to the studios, but nobody was buying. After the studio heads read it, they said to me, 'But this is a Western! People don't make Westerns anymore!'"[17] Ford shopped nearly a year for a producer, trying Joe Kennedy and David

Stagecoach. Ford with the coach and Berton Churchill.

Selznick before finding Walter Wanger, an independent producer releasing through United Artists. After urging Ford to cast Gary Cooper and Marlene Dietrich, Wanger agreed to Wayne and Trevor, relative nobodies, and subsequently had little influence on the production.

Ford's wisecrack to Bogdanovich that the story is really Maupassant's "Boule de suif" is farfetched. In Maupassant, when a coach carrying French refugees is halted during the Franco-Prussian War, the passengers intimidate a woman of reputedly easy virtue into sleeping with the German commandant. But, their release obtained, moral snobbery reasserts itself, and their savior is snubbed. Nor is there any more similarity to Maupassant in Ernest Haycox's *Collier's* story "Stage to Lordsburg" (but there is in *7 Women* and Sternberg's *Shanghai Express*!). Haycox's ending is like the film's, but Malpais Bill (i.e., the Ringo Kid) is not an escaped outlaw and boards the stage in Tonto. Dallas does not deliver a baby (nor do anything outstanding), the banker does not exist (but there is an English hunter), and the whiskey salesman succumbs to the heat rather than to Indians.*

When we think of *Stagecoach* we think of a coach traversing a giant vista of Monument Valley. Monument Valley, on the Navajo lands in northern Arizona, made its movie debut in *Stagecoach* and, always photographed with opulence, became a defining element in Ford's harsh, stony West through nine subsequent appearances. But even this first time, the valley is not simply a valley, but a valley melodramatized; and the coach is not simply a coach, but the historic mythos of "the West." Ford's previous evocations of history's magic moments (*Shark Island, Mary of Scotland . . .*) had usually originated from the diminishing confines of a soundstage; exteriors, curiously, had tended to represent a character's interior culture (the park in *The Plough and the Stars*, the riverbank in *Salute*, the river in *Steamboat*). But with *Stagecoach* a new magnitude of exteriority enters cinema, one touched

---

*Tonto, 1870s. Passengers board a stagecoach: Lucy Mallory (Louise Platt), a pregnant lady joining her officer husband; Dallas (Claire Trevor), a whore being evicted; Doc Boone (Thomas Mitchell), a drunk also ostracized; Peacock (Donald Meek), a meek whiskey salesman; Gatewood (Berton Churchill), a haughty banker. Cavalry ride guard, for Apache are loose. Hatfield (John Carradine), a gambler, goes along to "protect" Mrs. Mallory, and the sheriff (George Bancroft) to hunt the Ringo Kid (John Wayne), who escaped jail to avenge his brother, and who joins the coach outside town.

At Dry Ford Station, relief cavalry fail to rendezvous, but the passengers vote to go on without protection. At Apache Wells, Lucy learns her husband was wounded and Dallas and Boone deliver her baby. Ringo and Dallas fall in love, but smoke signals foil his escape. And, after fording a river, the coach is pursued by Apache across salt flats. Hatfield, about to kill Lucy to protect her, is killed himself, just as cavalry arrive.

In Lordsburg the travellers separate. Gatewood is arrested for robbing his bank. Ringo kills the three Plummer brothers and the sheriff lets him ride off with Dallas into the sunset.

Stagecoach won two Oscars (supporting actor: Thomas Mitchell; score: Richard Hageman et al.) and was nominated for five others (picture, direction, art direction, photography, editing—losing out generally to *Gone with the Wind*). The New York Film Critics chose Ford best director and the National Board of Review cited it as the year's third best. Current prints, however, give a totally false impression of the movie—grey, washed-out, soft, distant, old-fashioned looking, rather than sharp and vibrant.

on previously by *Tabu* and *Nanook*: a consciousness expanding forcibly; an alienated stare at the world's vastness, at an immensity embarrassing our trepidant love (rather like the mixture of passion and alienation with which nature is confronted in Rossellini's Bergman movies). *Stagecoach* in retrospect seems to be seeking heroic sensation and premythic purity, lost qualities needed in 1939, as the world turned toward global war. Scenery, then, is not simply a given, but a participant in drama.

On the other hand, there is a theatricality to *Stagecoach* that may seem to lie at the opposite extreme from this "realism." Story, Monument Valley, the Old West itself, all seem to have been transposed by Ford not into "re-creative realism" but into a dreamworld—to the extent that everything about *Stagecoach* works best when least plausible: the improbable collection of characters, the chase sequence, the 7th Cavalry, the Lordsburg shootout. *Stagecoach* seems to look *back* to Victorian theater's traditions and spectacle (whereas Griffith's movies, to which *Stagecoach* may appear to have stronger-than-usual relation, came *out* of Victorian theater). *Stagecoach*'s characters are as archetypal, generic, and basic as their adventures, and, here more than elsewhere, each character is given entrance and exit. Soon the fantasy takes on a dream's reality; the Old West is gone but *Stagecoach* will never die. It begins and ends with nostalgia—"I Dream of Jeannie"—and sadness is pointedly underlined in the first shot, when couriers emerge from distant vistas and gallop past a rising flag. Subsequent low-angle, deep-focus shots of the offices and streets of Tonto seem to stress that we are there, that this is it; but really the effect is like staring into a Matthew Brady photograph and imagining we are there. This is the *effort* that *Stagecoach* asks and obtains from its audiences, and this is why our belief in it and its impossible characters is as vivid as our belief in the reality of, say, Dickens's world, one now more real than the actual. So *Stagecoach* begins sadly, lamenting a dead world, and taking us back the way *The Lone Ranger* said it would. Lamenting what? Perhaps what Doc Boone says as Ringo and Dallas ride away: "Well, they're saved from the blessings of civilization!"—"I Dream of Jeannie."

Hence, if there is a tendency to think of *Stagecoach* as Ford's first large-sized masterpiece, the reason is less that it is a *better* movie than, say, *Judge Priest* (it is not), than that it is different. It sprawls; previous Fords seem tidy. And it sprawls in many ways: it seems to be three different movies stitched together; it has several climaxes; it has many stories, many cinematic styles, many locations, and many characters, who, for once, resist coherence into a community.

Stagecoach's structure is tripartite and unusually disparate: (1) the town of Tonto, where we meet the nine principals; (2) the journey to Lordsburg; (3) the town of Lordsburg, when the "story" really begins. Each section differs in script-method and cinematic style. The Lordsburg section, the third, is expressionistic melodrama, telling a normal story in parallel sequences (Ringo and Dallas, Luke Plummer in the bar) and then resolving the conflict. The second section, the journey, alternates between scenes en route and the way stations. On the road, Ford repeats the same pattern nearly a dozen times: (1) The coach in long shot rolling along the plain (to "Bury Me Not on the Lone Prairie"); (2) Curly and Buck in two-shot conversing on the driver's seat; (3) The passengers inside, always in isolated crosscuts. Three progressions occur simultaneously: space grows smaller, we pass from verité to comedy to chamber-drama, psychologies become more fragmented. At the way-stations, Ford composes model ensemble sequences. The first section, in Tonto, offers the most freedom for cutting around at will, and is probably scenarist Dudley Nichols's finest triumph:

the introductions are wittily and swiftly done, each vignette possessing a mood of its own and revealing personality and period.

Unfortunately this pace of revelation is not maintained in the second section, in which Ford and Nichols seem less interested in exploring individuals than in interactions. Each character, more than merely a dream-world archetype, represents a culture and class in microcosm (whereas other Fords contrast groups). If they are predictable, it is because they are vivid enough not to require demonstration. The surest route to ruining *Stagecoach* would have been to have cast these roles with vague, everyday-Joe faces, to have suppressed Ford's telltale, clichéd grimaces, gestures, clothing, and motives, and to have spent the movie in defining the characters' types. Ford, unpedantic, starts where another director would have concluded. True, such tight juxtaposing of so many archetypes in archetypal adventures seems an extreme application of Ford's vignette techniques of characterization (whereby a hypertypical cameo immediately defines a character); yet vignetting is blended with extended character development, and the result becomes a sort of archetypal fireworks show of increasing brilliance, as Ford freely plays each situation to an extreme degree of stylization and composes vignette "magic moments."

Interest in the characters stems from their interaction, from subtle details of gesture, intonation, and staging, and from tension between the type and the individual inhabiting it. Let us consider each of them.

Buck, the stage driver (Andy Devine), is a strident, stupid oaf, whose awkward voice makes anything he says sound not worth listening to—although it is, for the fascination of absurdity. But arriving in Lordsburg, he turns to Ringo and says, with a mature empathy that is "off-character," just "Lordsburg, Ringo" and one senses suddenly that Buck's public personality, his oafy side, is not the "real" one. Similarly, Yakima, the Apache woman, changes from a proud siren to a street urchin when she interrupts her song to tell three men (in Spanish), "OK, boys, get goin'!"

Similarly, Doc Boone: this Thomas Mitchell drunk is a variation on Mitchell's drunk doctor in *The Hurricane* and his drunk reporter in Capra's *Mr. Smith Goes to Washington;* and he is a variation on Ford's drunken doctors in *My Darling Clementine* and *The Colter Craven Story* and the drunk reporter in *Liberty Valance.* Yet nuances are brought to the role. When Boone weasels a parting drink from bartender Jack Pennick (Ford's perennial everybody's pal), the staging—he stands in a shaft of light in an empty bar—goes beyond mere cliché, seems *so* archetypal as to be pre-mythic. Rather than trying to be "original" (i.e., different), the character glories in being the "original" (i.e., archetype). But this personage too has distance within it, displayed in the film's last line, when Boone responds to Curly's offer of a drink with, "Just one," and sounds wholly himself for once.

Then there is Ringo, as basic and raw as a hero can be. Yet his magnificent admission, "I lied to you, Curly. I saved three bullets," not only glorifies the archetype (who needs only three bullets to kill three men); it also reflects a deeper side. Of all the passengers, Ringo seems the most community-minded, yet he gave vengeance priority over defense during the Indian chase. In fact, one wonders how Ringo got past the Hays office: for the movie certainly seems to excuse and even to laud Ringo's avenging his brother by calling out and shooting down three men in the streets, and we feel he deserves to ride off into the rising sun and happiness with Dallas. With Harry Carey, Wyatt Earp, or Ethan Edwards, Ford makes it clear that moral reckonings cannot be avoided; but Ringo's moral reckoning is his single-minded duty to vengeance. Untroubled by the complicated personality and social mission of the Fordian hero—he does not mediate, reunite families, or claim higher wisdom—Ringo's archetype (like Terangi's in *The Hurricane*) antedates civilization. Albeit, John Wayne, playing much younger than his thirty-two years, gives the character such laid-back personableness that his "realness," however simplistic, is instantly accepted by audiences.

Hatfield, we are told, has shot men in the back, but we meet him in a gallant hour trying to be again what he once was; his Satanic side nonetheless bursts out occasionally, as when he shouts, "Put out that cigar!" at Boone. Dallas, in contrast, is almost Shirley Temple dressed for a wicked Halloween. She may be an orphan and all but unemployable, yet her disgust at whoring is inconsistent with her persistence in it. Her underplayed bitterness does not flash to the surface as Hatfield's does, and thus at her moment of "transfiguration," when she presents the baby, she compares poorly with *7 Women*'s Dr. Cartwright in a similar moment. Cartwright's whore side is more explicit, her bitterness more matured, but when she gushes over a baby, the transfiguration is not only a greater contrast, it also occurs in a fleeting instant, not as a minor dramatic catharsis. Nonetheless, this catharsis is not as pronounced as in Nichols's script directions:

> The last trace of hardness has vanished from Dallas as she holds the infant in her arms, and there is a glow of wonder in her face. She stands a moment in the doorway, a smile in her eyes. . . . Her experience of the last few hours has deeply affected her, taken all the defiance out of her face, and softened it into beauty.[18]

Ford's realization is less grandiloquent. Dallas has all along been eager to be pleasant; she does not abruptly shift attitudes; she is merely relieved momentarily from self-shame, which soon returns. But Dallas's whole existence is a kind of dream: every moment, not just this one, has its glow or gloom, its warmth or chill; an accepting baby on one hand and a repelling propriety on the other dramatically define the boundaries of Dallas's affective consciousness, and thus exacerbate the vibrant oscillations twixt hope and despair with which Dallas experiences Ringo's presence, when every other moment threatens transfiguration. And it is this melodramatized representation of inner experience that Ford aims for and which reaches its

height in the streaked blackness of the Lordsburg sequence, one of the finest achievements of Ford's career. Dallas is afraid to let Ringo know where she lives and what she is, and Ford's relentless tracking through the red-light district up to a ramp leading down into a nestle of dark shacks emphasizes how her whole life is at stake, and emphasizes the horror of the alternative awaiting her. She is an apt character for Ford's expressionism, for she is affective rather than philosophic; she does not contemplate her tragedy, she shares the naiveté of the youngsters we see in the Lordsburg bar, sheltered by their madam as though by a convent nun. We are not sure whether Ringo is noble or stupid, whether or not he knows Dallas is a whore, but his unflinching simplicity as he walks with her perfectly offsets her confusion. The honky-tonk piano that accompanies their walk contrasts with Richard Hageman's symphonic folk-tune score that elsewhere plays so major a role in making *Stagecoach* repeatedly enjoyable; a sort of apex of stylized populist melodrama is reached with the timpani roars accompanying the footsteps of Ringo and Plummer stalking each other. Dallas's tension climaxes just after the fight; typically Fordian is the way she first hears approaching footsteps and turns gradually around as the camera glides subjectively up to her, until Ringo emerges into the frame, and the storybook-spotted horses pull up with her wedding coach.

Lucy Mallory is typical of many Ford characters whose stereotype, patent at first glance, is ultimately elusive. As Hatfield says, she is "an angel in a jungle, a very wild jungle." A product of her gentle breeding and its unquestioning moralism, Lucy is also intelligent and impressionable. She seems the film's only person who really relates to the land. If her repugnance for Dallas is an indoctrinated intolerance, her repugnance for most of her other passengers comes more naturally. Her subtle pouts and attempts at formal politeness toward Gatewood are uproarious. When she first sees Hatfield she waits impatiently for the first opportunity, then excitedly gasps, "Who is that gentleman?" Her acts of courage are girlish, as when in bed she insists she will go on. Like Clementine Carter, she has come from the East alone, braving a wilderness to join her man. Passion and determination lie at the heart of many of Ford's misplaced gentle ladies, and always with a provocative thrill.

Thus in every character there are elements of contrast, some obvious, some hidden. Ringo, Boone, Dallas, Peacock, and (sometimes) Hatfield are "sympathetic"—no matter what they have done or will do; Lucy, Hatfield (generally), and Gatewood (always) are unsympathetic, their good sides left for discovery. The gentle Peacock, commonly mistaken for a clergyman, wants to "go back to the bosoms," but he is a businessman like Gatewood, with a business (whiskey) that wrought incalculable harm. But for Gatewood there is nary a saving grace. Dissolving from his snarling face to the Law and Order League suggests cause-and-effect, not only between establishment and intolerance, but between the banker's wife and *his* desire to flee town. Yet a forthright banker-villain had resonance in 1939 America.

Contrast and ambivalence create one of *Stagecoach*'s loveliest moments. At the first way station, Ringo has had the (inadvertent) audacity to seat the whore beside the lady. Everyone freezes and stares. Hatfield offers to "find" Mrs. Mallory a "cooler" seat by the window and Gatewood goes glaringly along. We hate them. Then Ford puts "I Dream of Jeannie" on the soundtrack and glides his camera dreamily into a poetic and intimate conversation between Lucy and Hatfield, into the nostalgia of the Old South and lost lives. We love them.

André Bazin initiated a lengthy debate when, after World War II, he lauded as "realistic" the long takes and composition in depth of *Citizen Kane* and *The Best Years of Our Lives* and disparaged in contrast the "classic" Hollywood editing styles of Ford and Capra, which he thought "manipulative."*

---

*Bazin, like other critics, grossly exaggerates *Citizen Kane*'s novelty and its importance as personal style as an end in itself. Said Welles: "John Ford was my teacher. My own style has nothing to do with his, but *Stagecoach* was my movie text-book. I ran it over forty times." (Quoted by Peter Cowie, *The Cinema of Orson Welles* [New York: A. S. Barnes, 1965], p. 27, from article by Dilys Powell in *The Sunday Times* [London, February 3, 1963].) Certainly Welles and Ford have diverse sensibilities, but Welles's visual style seems almost a hyperbolic parody of Ford's; where Ford is subtle, Welles is cramped, exaggerated, and ostentatious. For the record, both directors exploit depth of field, long takes, multiplane composition, avoidance of conventional intercutting, UFA-style expressionism, high-contrast lighting, low-level camera, sharp-focus objects near image surface between us and the main action, cameo cutting,

One might reply that Ford's cutting between and among characters in the coach—this isolating of one or two characters—is more psychologically realistic to one's experience within a carriage, whereas a single distanced long take of everyone would disperse the vividness of individual experience. Perhaps the coach cutting occasionally gets a bit ponderous, so that the laboring montage amplifies the sense of effort in the screenplay, and perhaps the repetitive contrasts are a commercial concession. Yet how enjoyable is this disjunctive editing! And such cutting and staging within ensemble scenes is, through movies such as *Mogambo* and *7 Women*, increasingly a Fordian forte.

Yet, even though *Stagecoach* is a rapidly cut movie (612 shots in ninety-seven minutes = 9½ seconds per shot, or 10½ without the chase), it is a mistake to overlook, as Bazin does, how much *Stagecoach* abounds in long, fluid camera takes and how much more integral to its style than to Welles's or Wyler's is composition in depth. The way-station episode illustrates how Ford synthesizes the two styles—montage and long take—that Bazin took for antitheses.

Dallas the whore has offended propriety by sitting next to Lucy the lady, who, by the morals of the day, must register shock. (To her credit, she hesitates before accepting Hatfield's offer.) Ford combines shots from his own narrating perspective (left column) with subjective shots (right column), which, although from Lucy's perspective, are not at first clearly defined as being from her gaze—even shot 5, of Lucy staring, may surprise some spectators who have missed the matching of her glance (3) with the forward dolly (4). The subjective shots from Lucy are not balanced with matching subjective shots from Dallas (there is no third column)—which emphasizes Dallas's passive victimhood and Lucy's active aggression, and also Dallas's

---

bringing actors into close shots by moving them rather than the camera; broad characterizations, particularly of bit players. Professor Robert Carringer argues Gregg Toland's credit for *Citizen Kane*'s visual style, citing as evidence Toland's similar work on Ford's *The Long Voyage Home* (1940, just before *Kane*). But Carringer's description of *Long Voyage* as "the first film . . . in which there is a consistent use of the deep-focus style" ("Orson Welles and Gregg Toland: Their Collaboration on *Citizen Kane*," *Critical Inquiry*, Summer 1982, pp. 658–70) suggests a profound unfamiliarity with Ford's (and others') visual style, in which we find abundant exploitation of all the skills of deep-focus style from 1929 onward. Carringer also repeats the false but generally accepted argument that it was not until *Kane*'s time that improved lighting, film stock, lenses, and the blimpless Mitchell camera enabled film to escape the "heavily diffused light, soft tonality [and] relatively shallow depth of field" that sound techniques had imposed on thirties Hollywood, and to "return to the sharper, crisper, still-photographic style characteristic of many silent films." But the soft, diffused style began in the late silent years (Charles Rosher, Karl Freund, Ben Reynolds, George Schneiderman, Karl Brown, Ernest Palmer, et al.), not with the first talkies, while, on the other hand, many early-thirties talkies are sharp and crisp (if one sees good prints), particularly Capra, Lubitsch, Vidor, and Ford (*Salute, Arrowsmith, Doctor Bull*)—but only when they wanted to be sharp and crisp. And the blimpless camera was (first?) used by Arthur Miller for *Wee Willie Winkie* in November 1936—four years before *Kane*. There were always ways to get around technical limitations (and a good artist capitalizes upon his limitations), although Bazin, in a fit of metaphysics, assumed things like faster film stock necessarily advanced cinema in that they help to perfect cinema's ability to be an "imprint" of reality—as if Bach's music would be better had he had modern instruments.

Figure 4. *Stagecoach:* **Way-Station Episode**

Objective point of view *(i.e., narrator's, Ford's)*	*Subjective point of view* *(i.e., Lucy's)*

1. **General shot:** room and table: Lucy at head.

2. Ringo offers to seat Dallas (from, approximately, Lucy's perspective).

3. **Closer** (from Dallas's side but not from her perspective): Gatewood (Boone and Hatfield background) and Lucy, who turns and stares toward:

Figure 4. (continued)

Objective point of view (i.e., narrator's, Ford's)	Subjective point of view (i.e., Lucy's)

4=2. **Dolly-in** on Dallas sitting (Lucy's pov).

5. **Medium close-up:** Lucy staring (frontal: i.e., not slanted from Dallas's pov):

6=2. but closer. **Medium close-up:** Dallas, who lowers her eyes under Lucy's gaze.

Figure 4. *Stagecoach:* **Way-Station Episode (continued)**

Objective point of view *(i.e., narrator's, Ford's)*	*Subjective point of view* *(i.e., Lucy's)*

7=3. Four at table. Lucy turns away.

8=2. Dallas and Ringo react. (Same perspective as 2, but no longer under Lucy's gaze: i.e., Lucy is there, off-screen, but refuses to interact.)

9=3. Hatfield offers to find Lucy a cooler place by window.

Figure 4. (continued)

Objective point of view (i.e., narrator's, Ford's)	*Subjective point of view* (i.e., Lucy's)

10=2. Dallas and Ringo react.

11=3. Lucy rises and leaves.

12. **General shot** from head of table, Ringo and Dallas seated left. Lucy, Hatfield, Gatewood seat themselves in rear.

Figure 4. *Stagecoach:* Way-Station Episode (continued)

Objective point of view *(i.e., narrator's, Ford's)*	*Subjective point of view* *(i.e., Lucy's)*

13

13. **Medium two-shot:** Dallas and Ringo (frontal: not former angle).

14a

14b

14. **Dolly in:** Lucy and Hatfield . . .

inferior position. The space-defining crosscutting thus not only underlines Lucy's brutality; geometric space itself graphically represents this brutality —the abrupt close-up (5), the piercing stare dollying-in on Dallas (4).

The shots exemplify what Bazin termed "expressionist montage" and clearly the drama's dialectics could not be so well represented in a single take. As it happens, however, Ford proceeds to reap a long take's advantages, for it seems to take an eternity for Lucy, Hatfield, and Gatewood to leave their seats, relocate, and settle anew; all the while we stare at their subtle interactions and refusals to interact with Dallas, their hypocrisies and confessions. And all this occurs within composition in depth, as they move up screen to the table's far end, leaving the outlaws isolated in the foreground. This distanced perspective (12) comes as a physical relief after the crosscuts. But, as a summary of the previously divided space, it also registers the result of the conflict. And, by its distance, the shot invokes our helpless inability to control the deeds of other people, despite our sense of their wrongness.

There follows, while *our* indignation is strongest, a cut to the sympathetic victims, and their togetherness is brought out in the interactions permitted by the long-take two-shot (such as Bazin likes: we do not know which of them to watch); but in order for their emotions to emerge, Ford had first to isolate them by cutting the others out of the frame. Similarly, he will isolate Hatfield and Lucy together (via a gentle dolly), but, subsequently, the privacy of crosscuts rather than a two-shot better suits their timidity.

Nick Browne, a theoretician, has published an ingenious study of the first portion of this sequence in which, however, he reaches conclusions diametrically opposed to central theses of my own study of Ford's cinema.[19] As Browne reads the shots, we, as spectators, *share* Lucy's gaze and are thus implicated with her; but our emotional identification with poor Dallas prompts us to repudiate Lucy's gaze, along with her moral authority. So strong is this process of identification and implication that, in effect, we experience the film as though we were part of it, and as though it were itself narrated by Lucy. Ford "masks" his activity as narrator, becomes "invisible," and employs Lucy as "a visible persona . . . to constitute and make legible and continuous the depicted space, by referring shots on the screen alternately to the authority of her eye or the place of her body, [so that] the story seem[s] to tell itself [and seems to deny] existence of a narrator different from character."[20] In other words, we experience the fiction directly, without the mediation of Ford's auteur presence. "Ford" does not exist; we are being manipulated; our own moral decisions are preempted.

The impracticality of Browne's propositions, from my view, is that Fordian cinema belongs to quite another syntactical system than those of the cinemas of star-system identification, *Star-Wars*-like sensation, or Hitchcockian subjectivity; rather than unquestioning involvement, Ford exacts empathetic distance, and his narrating presence is, even among auteur directors, exceptionally strong. Browne's tendency to approach Ford as though he were Hitchcock is analogous to approaching Vermeer as though he were Van Gogh. A sequence from Mizoguchi's *Sansho the Bailiff*, similar to the *Stagecoach* sequence, makes the distinction clearer:

Figure 5. *Sansho the Bailiff*

Objective point of view	Subjective point of view
1. The bailiff about to brand an old woman with a hot iron.	
	2. The woman (bailiff's point of view).
3. The bailiff's face as he brands off-camera.	

In neither film are we so implicated with the branders (Lucy; the bailiff) that we need to repudiate them. We see *that* they see and know that social custom decrees that their seeing is far less empathetic toward their victims than is ours! (We see suffering, angelic humans; they see institutions.) Ford makes this particularly clear, showing (shot 4) the victim from Lucy's perspective even before (5) Lucy herself gazes in the direction of that perspective, and having Lucy afterwards (7) turn away and pretend Dallas is not really there—although Lucy's perspective shot remains (8 and 10). (See Figs. 4 and 5 above.)

Importantly, neither Ford nor Mizoguchi shows the brander from the victim's perspective. There is no third column to the far left. The conflict and the terror such a perspective would convey would detract from the greater, philosophic question. Although we scream at one woman's pain and squirm at another's humiliation, these emotions lead our interest to the psychology of the branders (*How can they act that way?!*), not to the trauma of the victim, and for this reason we study the branders from impartial (unconflicting, un-terror-filled) perspectives. Thus neither Lucy nor the bailiff is a narrating persona; they are the *chief themes* of their scenes. Ford's and Mizoguchi's styles are both presentational, not subjective. The objectivity of Ford's shots of Lucy, particularly the frontal close-up (5), evinces his narrative presence. They are not merely "'objective,' or perhaps 'nobody's' shots" (Browne[21]), they are Ford's shots.

Ford's strategic intention, finally, is incompletely stated as "to ally us emotionally with the interests and fortune of the outsiders as against social customs" (Browne[22]), for it is also to solicit our understanding of the *insiders* who, because they cannot escape as easily as Dallas and Ringo, are far more the real victims of social custom. This is why Ford concentrates on Lucy. Lucy can no more socialize with a whore in a lunchroom than she can present her to society. The first impossibility stems from her own unacknowledged intolerance, the second from her newly discovered acknowledgment of the intolerance of her world. Thus the sheriff acts partly as her proxy in letting Ringo and Dallas quit civilization (social custom) after Ringo exhibits his wild-ness (a rival social code) by gunning down the Plummers. But in the 1880s, the only practical form for such tolerance was segregation. *Stagecoach*, then, is more concerned with studying social custom than with revolutionary alienation. And Ford is more concerned with the art of sensibility than with the pseudo art of excitation.

In fact, no other Ford western gives a more cynical verdict on the notion of the West as synthesis of nature and civilization. In *Liberty Valance* (1962), for contrast, Ransom Stoddard spends a lifetime to figure out what everyone in *Stagecoach* already knows: that civilization is corrupting. The idealism, progressivism, and enlightenment shared by virtually everyone in *Liberty Valance's* Shinbone is absolutely absent in malodorous Lordsburg and Tonto — dirty, sleazy, full of mean, intolerant, aggressive people. Doc Boone's drinking and Dallas's prostitution symbolize their intolerable, "hippie" characteristics in a puritanical society. The fact that two do "escape the blessings of civilization" is no more a happy ending than are the conclusions of *The Grapes of Wrath* or *How Green Was My Valley*. Ringo, who ignores society rather than confronting it, who is less outlaw than oblivious, is a dumb god who snatches Dallas off to never-never land. Who of us resembles Ringo? What solution or reason for optimism does he offer *us*, who cannot escape? As always in Ford, happiness belongs only to fools and simpletons, and if we fantasize with Ringo it is only because hope is more primal than realism.

According to John Wayne, preview audiences found the chase sensational. They "yelled and screamed and stood up and cheered. I never saw anything like it."[23] Yet William S. Hart objected that the Indians could have shot one horse to stop the coach. And in other respects—the impossible accuracy of the passengers' six-guns and inaccuracy of the Indians, the trumpeting arrival of the cavalry— the chase, exciting as it still is, may seem a bit of a campy put-on. Such a reaction is not far from Ford's intentions, which, while not desiring suspension of belief, do intend release, release not only from melodramatic suspense, but also from suffocating Victorian repression. The chase climaxes a process (gratifyingly, even sadistically witnessed) during which these diverse types, thrown together and systematically stripped of civilization, pomposity, and inhibition, let loose their true selves. But the trumpet that climaxes the chase marks also civilization's reimposition. For Ringo and Dallas, fortunately, there is yet another frontier to escape to; for us, that is fairyland. The ultimate truth of the Fordian western is its own extinction.

Later Ford westerns repeat ideas from *Stagecoach*,* as *Stagecoach* presumably repeats ideas from Ford's silents. Like the Carey-Ford Universals, it envisions plots and characters in archetypal, mythic terms. Or rather, the

---

*For example: Buck's "legs, eh, limbs" to Lucy shows up in *Donovan's Reef*; both Buck and his coach are essentially the same in *The Man Who Shot Liberty Valance*; the dusty columns of soldiers show up again in *Fort Apache* and *Rio Grande*; the surprise discovery of the Indians via a pan is repeated in those films and in *Wagon Master* (and occurs via a cut in Francis Ford /

terms are *premythic*, in the sense that the characters are not, as in *Steamboat Round the Bend* (or any mature society), echoing myths, but seem to have relatively pure and secure self-identities—particularly when compared with the dependent, disintegrating beings inhabiting the threatening, repressive worlds of earlier thirties Ford films. On the other hand, *Stagecoach* is perhaps still too self-conscious to revive completely the earthy intimacy of those early silents, while its mixture of artfulness and commerciality set it apart from the Argosy westerns, too. Hence it is problematic how personal or typical of Ford *Stagecoach* really is. Coming out of the exotica period, it looks back to the *Men-Without-Women*, *Lost-Patrol*-type situation, and forward to the pretentiousness of *The Long Voyage Home* (all Dudley Nichols scripts), yet with less preciousness than any of the other 1939–41 movies. In some ways it resembles *The Hurricane*, yet with far more variety, speed, and vigor. Probably we shall never know what sort of movie and what sort of reception Ford expected from *Stagecoach*, but if a single quality makes it stand out from his previous work, it might be audacity.

   Young Mr. Lincoln (1939). A deeper, more multileveled work than *Stagecoach*, this film attracted little attention and no awards in 1939, and was not even successful financially. Yet it seems in retrospect one of the finest prewar pictures. It deals, in its prelude, with Lincoln's discovery of Law and his friendship with Ann Rutledge in New Salem, 1832, and in its second section depicts a trial in Springfield, 1837, a success that sets Lincoln on his road to glory.*

   But as in *Liberty Valance* and *7 Women*, the movie's ultimate concern is the dubious dialectic between free will and a deterministic cosmos—

Ince's *Blazing the Trail* (2-reel 101 Bison, 1912); the Plummer brothers anticipate the Clantons of *My Darling Clementine* and the Cleggs of *Wagon Master;* the silent close crosscutting of the badmen recurs in those two films as well as in *Fort Apache;* the newspaper-office joke recurs in *Liberty Valance;* and the shot of Dallas and her lamp in the long narrow corridor is a big moment toward the end of *7 Women.* Ragtime piano recurs in *My Darling Clementine* and *The Sun Shines Bright.* The Dallas-Ringo relationship is probably more typical of prewar Ford (though, cf. Denver-Travis in *Wagon Master*), the Lucy-Hatfield one of postwar Ford. Most prophetic is the startling dolly-up introduction of John Wayne (against mountains), for *Stagecoach* introduced him to stardom. Ford had fought to get Wayne this role, a good-badman role, a Harry Carey role, and Ford, seeing Wayne as a Carey-type, had been urging him to copy Carey.
*The trial depicted occurred in 1857 in Cass [sic] County, Illinois; Lincoln used *The Old Farmer's Almanac* to break down a case against a certain Armstrong. The idea of two defendants derives from a trial covered by scenarist Lamar Trotti as a young reporter in Georgia: the mother of two young men was the sole witness, she refused to tell which one did the murder, and both were hanged.
   The script is essentially Trotti's, but Trotti had worked with Ford on their Will Rogers Americana and much internal evidence confirms Ford's claimed collaboration (e.g., the Francis Ford character who is drunk and spits). Not since 1935 had Ford made a movie he cared deeply about at Fox, and to limit Zanuck's interference, he turned in scarcely a foot more film than he intended to use. Even so, Zanuck deleted shots, humor, and a scene when a young dandy, John Wilkes Booth, leaves a theater playing *Hamlet* and notices "this funny, incongruous man in a tall hat riding a mule" (Bogdanovich, p. 73) wishing he had money to go in.

between Lincoln as autonomous man and Lincoln as agent of history. Here, as in the later films, the case for free will is submerged within hints and glances, and all but overpowered by contexts rendered deterministic by various distancing devices—mood, myth, archetypes, genre, symbol, music, history, and time.

Time weighs heavy, Murnau-fashion, and the mood throughout is gloomy. Although the movie's thrust is passage (from immaturity to manhood, innocence to tainted wisdom, human to mythic stature), history, like God's omniscience, puts everything outside time, into the static determined; life is pilgrimage. And Lincoln seems haunted by this pilgrimage. Haunted, on one hand, by his *past,* by loss of Ann, and by general homelessness, which attract him to the family of Abigail Clay, whose two sons he defends against a murder charge; haunted, on the other hand, by his *future*—for Ford contextualizes the young Lincoln within a conditioning matrix of tenses. Time in various ways contributes a mystic determinism that pervades the film:

1. Cause-and-effect: Lincoln is seized in youth, on the threshold; thereafter all has been decided, with awesome finality, it seems, as Lincoln walks off screen at end.

2. Cause-and-effect bipartite structure: Events in 1837 seem determined by events in 1832. Ann inspires him from her grave.

3. Foreknowledge as cause: We know Lincoln's future, and premonitions of his tragic myth loom in anticipation.

4. Sense of destiny as cause: Lincoln combines ambition with mysticism, belief in free choice with conviction in ordained, appointed destiny; alternately, the character may be seen as a sort of Faust, a plaything of devil-history. Does he pursue his future? Or does his future pursue him?

5. Finally, Rosemary Benet's poem prefaces a future-perfect from the outset:

> If Nancy Hanks
> Came back as a ghost
> Seeking news
> Of what she loved most,
> She'd ask first,
> "Where's my son?
> What's happened to Abe?
> What's he done?
> You wouldn't know
> About my son?
> Did he grow tall?
> Did he have fun?
> Did he learn to read?
> Did he get to town?
> Do you know his name?
> Did he get on?"

Of course *we* know the answers, we tell ourselves, but Ford tricks us, answering every question not in terms of 1865 but of 1837: the son is in Springfield, he became a lawyer, stood for right and mercy, did indeed grow tall, did not have much fun, certainly learned to read, and got to town too; a few of us know his name, and at movie's end he says he'll "walk *on* a bit farther." From our point of view, 1837 is in context of 1865, of what *shall* be; yet the film asks that we grasp 1837's happenings from the mother's point of view, implying that for her 1837 is a truer response to her questions than what happened later, because that future belonged to history, while this present belonged to Abe. It was now that his life defined its course.

In later pictures, John Ford would exploit a future-perfect perspective (vision of the past from a more recent viewpoint) through music in *Wagon Master*, or the flashback structures of *The Long Gray Line* or *Liberty Valance*. Here the poem provides perspective. Only the poem refers explicitly to Lincoln's mother. But it suggests Abe still under his absent mother's gaze, still conscious of that gaze, seeing himself serving a surrogate mother in Abigail Clay. His acceptance of payment from this impoverished mother-figure suggests umbilical severing: taking her money spares her humiliation and confirms their independence. He does not recall her as the woman who gave him the lawbooks in the movie's second scene, in 1832, nor does she remember him; but the circle has come round, and Lincoln enters into manhood, both released from his mother's gaze and launched by it.

[When Ford discussed Lincoln] there was such an extraordinary sense of intimacy in his tone . . . that somehow it was no longer a director speaking of a great President, but a man talking about a friend.[24] [He didn't wish to film Mother Cabrini, objecting,] "I'm a Catholic and I'd treat such a subject with too much respect."[25] [But he cajoled Henry Fonda into being Lincoln:] "You think you'd be playing the goddamn great emancipator, huh? He's a goddamn fucking jake-legged lawyer in Springfield, for Christ's sake!"[26]

The myth of Lincoln also controls the character's freedom. The nineteenth-century theater had bequeathed an onerous tradition to Lincoln depictions, one that films had been thoroughly exploiting, too,* and Ford capitalizes on the tendency of any Lincoln movie to be an apotheosis of its own genre, with conventional mythic elements and shorthand narration. As with his later cavalry epics, Ford's starting point is less actual historic fact than inherited myth, which he reinterprets via history. Ford had Fonda's nose enlarged, played up his long, sinuous body and his big feet: Abe enters a scene a lank woodsman with slung ax and huge boots, and with scenery equally traditional. "Books?" exclaims the rustic youth; then, in typical Ford fashion, re-

---

*Francis Ford impersonated Lincoln frequently in the teens, but never for John. Frank McGlynn, Sr., held the role in *The Prisoner of Shark Island*. Both Fords read Lincolniana omnivorously.

peats, wondrously: "Books!" Or, the tall dark man stands alone silently, while a mob sweeps through streets. Or, from Lincoln's low-level point of view, Ann Rutledge suddenly appears, a mythic apotheosis of loveliness.

Like time, such magic moments, evocative of the mythic Lincoln, threaten, along with the suavity of Fonda, to submerge the real man. It requires the viewer's active participation to detect Lincoln's ignobility, silliness, awkwardness, arrogance, and fear. Comedic frontier roughness exonerates Lincoln for cheating at tug-of-war, or for ruthlessness toward two farmer plaintiffs or toward Jack Cass; and we admire his foxiness rather than his obnoxious guile in the way he dupes everyone during the trial. His silliness, too, is mitigated: as he rides into town, long legs draped over his mule, and tips his hat to the courthouse flag, the humor is a bit neutralized by Ford's characteristically unhurried and reflectively paced treatment, and by the scene's conclusion in a newspaper announcement of the opening of Lincoln's law office—thus bestowing upon the entire sequence an aura of "And so it happened . . . " Nor at Mary Todd's ball does he evince discomfort at finding himself in high society and admitting his humble origins ("No Lincoln I ever knew ever amounted to a hill of beans"). Perhaps he is caught off balance by Mary's offensive and by having to dance, but he does not seem to dance that badly. Ford even spares us the sight of Lincoln courting the venomous Miss Todd: few permutations of character are so extraordinary as their balcony scene when, as Lincoln abruptly tunes her out to stare at the river, bossy Mary docilely retreats to wait in a corner.* Even flirting with Douglas fails to arouse jealousy: Lincoln strums his Jew's harp nonchalantly. It is she who pursues, he whose timidity clothes power.

Yet this "angelic" Abe has a strong ego, can lord it over his fellows, is

---

*The way Mary flirts—leaving room and frame and forcing Abe to follow—anticipates Grace Kelly's similar tactics with Clark Gable in *Mogambo* (1954). Lincoln's ride into town on a mule (or ass?) has been compared by Jean Roy to Christ's entry into Jerusalem, but such an analogy strikes me as less intentional here than in *The Fugitive* or *7 Women*.

secretly, almost obnoxiously confident, and knows how to make the most of an opportunity. Whatever destiny's role, he chooses his road in life, even as he tips the stick on Ann's grave. "I'd feel such a fool," he mumbles then, "settin' myself up as knowin' so much." But scarcely a minute later (screen time) his head eclipses George Washington's portrait while quarreling farmers, behind a rockingchair* foreground, are coerced into peace by a sassily grinning Lincoln in the background. A little later, as he calms a lynch mob, he does not hide his cocky self-assurance, his enjoyment of what he is doing, or his exaltation after the event. In contrast, Judge Priest, in *The Sun Shines Bright* (1953), is nervous, calms a lynch mob with a weary sense of work, and, when all is over, wipes his brow with relief. Lincoln is proud, feels power, calms the mob with guile; the older man needs a gun and a drink.

Yet Lincoln seems dazed—surprised, almost scared—not at the danger he has faced, but by the power and destiny he is uncovering. The dazed expression comes again, more strongly, at Mary Todd's ball, as he stands transfigured on a balcony, suffused by the moonlit river's power, and, more strongly still, when he walks from the courthouse into the bright light and cheers of the masses. Destiny, as we know, is drawing him; but he himself only gradually becomes aware of it. The Lincoln who, at picture's end, strides resolutely up the hill (rather like Christ departing the Garden of Gethsemane) is a far cry from the whimpering, indecisive farmboy who, when he lets the fate of a falling twig decide his future, thinks he is only playing a game!

True, there is already a bit of a haunted look to Lincoln when we first see him lounging on a porch, awkward and unaware, and as he rises, the noisy chatter of a politician suddenly gives way to solemn calm: time will almost always slow down when Lincoln appears (he cannot dance to others' tempo). And Ford's camera watches him, passionately, repressively, yearningly, lovingly, but not innocently, recording every muscle movement all too intently, as young Abe puts down his board, lowers his legs, stands slowly, walks over, puts his hands in his pockets, begins to speak. Gloom, a mystic aura, seems to

*Cf. the rockingchair-as-stability in *The Searchers*.

impose itself, so that this Lincoln seems a dream creature, walking through a dream whose plot he cannot control but whose theme he begins to suspect.

> Fare thee well, my darling lass,
> Fare thee well and gone,
> With golden slippers on.

Ford does not tell us, but Nancy Hanks, like many pioneers, was a forest mystic (and Mary Todd took to spiritualism after Lincoln's death). Not surprisingly, then, Lincoln, in seeking what is in him, would expect to find guidance in Nature herself. Truth exists, within oneself and in the natural world consubstantially; the only "mystery" is the fog that blinds us to it. And Ford *does* tell us about Truth, for as Lincoln wonders, "Law!," gawking at the book, and then repeats, "Law!," the medium shot dissolves, nay, slowly explodes into an immense riverbent landscape, wherein Lincoln lies, against a big tree, reading the book. Thus we know that Law and Nature are one. "Why, gee," he says, "that's all there is to it, right and wrong!"—and thus we know that Law and innate intuitive knowledge are one with Nature, too. Whereupon, Ann Rutledge appears, cut to with a suddenness that marks her apparition as even more miraculous than the explosion of Law into Nature and that suggests she is Truth's angel. She alone, in fact, understands Abe Lincoln, revealing to him his own deepest thoughts:

— "Hello, Mr. Lincoln. Abe."
— "Hello, Ann. Give me a minute to try an' untangle myself."
— "Aren't you afraid you'll put your eyes out, reading like that upside down?"
— "Trouble is, Ann, when I'm standing up my mind's lying down. When I'm lying down my mind's standing up. Of course, allowin' I've got a mind."
— "You've a wonderful mind, Abe, and you know it."
— "River sure is pretty today, ain't it?"
— "You think a lot about things, don't you?"
— "Well, my brain gets to itchin' inside sometimes. I gotta scratch it."
— "Father says you've a real head on your shoulders, and a way with people too. He says it's not all just makin' me laugh. They remember what you say because it's got sense to it."
— "Mr. Rutledge is a mighty fine man, Ann, but if you ask me, I'm more like the old horse the fella's tryin' to sell. Sound of skin and skeleton and free from faults and faculties."
— "I know how smart you are, how ambitious you are too."
— "Ambitious?"
— "You are, deep down underneath. Even if you won't admit it."
— "Gotta have education these days to get anywhere. I never went to school as much as a year in my whole life."
— "O but you've educated yourself. You've read poetry and Shakespeare and . . . and now Law. I just had my heart set on your goin'

over to Jacksonville to college when I go to the seminary there
an' . . ."
— "You're mighty pretty, Ann."
— "Some folks I know don't like red hair."
— "I do."
— "Do ya, Abe?"
— "I love red hair."

The way Ford treats this dialogue—foolish Abe and sweet Ann strolling beside the river in an aura of intense enchantment— virtually overpowers the conflict that, reading the dialogue alone, is so obvious. Lincoln keeps trying to deflect their talk to romance, but Ann keeps turning it back to pushing Abe along, even to the point of using herself as bait. (This, of course, concurs with the puritan ethic. And Mary Todd would later assume a comparable role— pushing Abe on to the presidency.) After their parting, Lincoln's casting a stone into the river indicates a nonchalant surrender to her will (to fate, in effect: the ripples). But this surrender is sealed by winter's ice and Ann's death. Love and sexuality are transformed into duty—duty to the dead, duty to her plans for him, duty to discover "what's in" him. When Lincoln appears at her graveside to consecrate his surrender to her, he already seems a step closer to the legendary Lincoln figure (with his ax and huge boots), and Ford, as he does all his most significant moments between lovers, marks the occasion with a flower put by Abe on Ann's grave.* And the river, so often sacramental in Ford, will constantly recall him to this task. "You sure do love to look at that river," remarks a friend, "Think it's a pretty woman."

Ann points Lincoln's ambition, another woman (his mother) watches over

*Lincoln's consecration to duty foreshadows Wyatt Earp's in *My Darling Clementine*.

him, a third (Mrs. Clay) gives him lawbooks and opportunity, a fourth (Mary Todd) beckons him on. As memories, as ideals, as women, they guide the mystic Abraham, and they confirm his sense of divine appointment. "I may not know much of the law," he chides the prosecutor, "but I know what you're doing is wrong." What *does* he know of the law? "Not enough to hurt me." Indeed, even his knowledge that Jack Cass is lying during the trial is presented as though come from the moon, as it were, via an almanac, which he plucks from a top hat.

A set of melody-motifs (by Alfred Newman) reinforces the aura of divine guidance surrounding Lincoln:

1. "Lincoln's Destiny"
2. "Funny Lincoln"
3. "Mrs. Clay" = rightness (law, lawbooks)
4. "Ann Rutledge" = confirmation (duty, river).

Scene	*Motif*
Campaign speeches	"Destiny" / "Funny"
Mrs. Clay and books	"Clay" / "Destiny"
River: Tree	"Destiny"
Ann	"Funny" / "Rutledge"
Grave	"Rutledge"
Riding into town	"Funny"
Newspaper announcement	"Destiny"
Farmers' case	—no music—
Celebration: Pies	"Funny"
Carrie Sue and Adam	"Clay"
After killing:	
Sheriff and mother	"Clay"
Lincoln appears	"Destiny"
Lynchers and Lincoln	"Destiny"
Bye to Mrs. Clay	"Clay" / "Destiny" / "Clay"
Going to ball	"Funny"
Ball: river balcony	"Rutledge"
Ride out by river	"Rutledge"
Clay farm	"Destiny" / "Clay"

Curiously, no off-camera music at all appears in the film's entire second half (except for "The Battle Hymn of the Republic" at the very end). Even at points where one would expect music, there is silence, as when Lincoln walks out of the courthouse and is cheered. Are we to infer that here, as during the trial and the farmers' case, Lincoln is on his own?*

*The "Destiny" motif is used again by Ford to evoke the tragic Lincoln' in the Civil War episode of *How the West Was Won* (1962) and in *Cheyenne Autumn* (1964) when Schurz looks at Lincoln's portrait; the association of Ransom Stoddard with Lincoln is reinforced in *The Man Who Shot Liberty Valance* by association of the "Rutledge" motif with the cactus rose plant and Hallie and youthful hopes and love, as in the Ann Rutledge scene here. The "Destiny" motif also appears in the Walter Lang–Shirley Temple–Fox *Blue Bird* (1940) when a pubescent Lin-

So possessed does Lincoln seem and so determining does Ford's treatment appear that the editors of *Cahiers du Cinéma,* in a much-paraphrased article in the August 1970 number of their magazine, stated that *Young Mr. Lincoln's* original intention—to be an edifying hagiography of Lincoln as an ideal representative of American (i.e., Republican) ideology—is routed by Ford's "excessive" treatment, which reveals instead the "truly repressive dimensions" of Lincoln and thus of America's ruling ideology. Although supposedly a man of the people and of peace, Lincoln receives Law from God, uses it with violence, and represses most human instincts in himself and others. When not outrightly ridiculous, Lincoln is a mediocrity, a mere agent of truth; rather than a human, he is an unchanging, glacial monster, a sort of Nosferatu.[27]

The tendency of Frenchmen to oversimplify America is an honorable tradition dating back at least to Rousseau and Stendahl; and Abraham Lincoln—sad, haunted, unafraid to look foolish—perhaps is hard to digest as a hero for those accustomed to heroes of the ilk of Louis XIV, Napoleon, or DeGaulle. But *Cahiers'* psycho-Marxist ideology particularly misses the dialectical complexities of the Lincoln myth—and of John Ford. True, tragedy piles on tragedy for Lincoln all his life, turning him into a figure of the night and ultimately killing him. True, it is the force of Lincoln's will, implemented by violence on the most massive scale, that counters the South's desire to secede. And true, Lincoln is ultimately not a man but a monument to will. But these themes, these contradictions, have always been essential attributes of the Lincoln myth.* Lincoln was not a man pulled up by "the banal game of universal suffrage," as *Cahiers* through the mouth of Engels claims, but a man whose ambition and conviction (self-righteous, undoubtedly) drove him on, so that each new tragedy became an impetus rather than a defeat; he accepted the course thrust upon him. There could be no relaxation for Mr. Lincoln: not for him the chance to play Father Abraham, the Great Emancipator, the Great Reconciler—except in legend. The

---

coln (looking Fonda-ish) is encountered in the Land of the Unborn Children; and in a World War II Signal Corps film, *It's Your America* (1944), when Arthur Kennedy muses on the meaning of democracy while studying a Lincoln-head penny as he dog-soldiers through the war; in Fox's *Belle Starr* (Irving Cummings, 1941) and *A Man Called Peter* (Henry Koster, 1955).

*The character of Ford's Lincoln is quite consistent with the Lincoln of the Robert Sherwood–John Cromwell *Abe Lincoln in Illinois* (Raymond Massey, 1939) and the Lincoln of D. W. Griffith's *Abraham Lincoln* (1930). But the latter does offer contrasts. Walter Huston's sprawling, declamatory, loutish Lincoln splits logs while Ann reads him law; Fonda's Lincoln, tidy, self-conscious, lies lazily on his back reading when Ann comes by. Both associate woman-law-nature, but Griffith concentrates on the ax: his Lincoln is the North's hammer, a man of perseverance in a dark psychodrama.

Both also have Mary Todd's ball. Ford's Mary is radiant, her gown freshly white, the ballroom spacious, floors waxed, walls high and clear; the men, all dressed nattily alike, swirl in circle to "Golden Slippers." Griffith's Mary is plain, her lace cream-colored, the room small, cluttered; the men, dressed variously in well-worn clothing, dance a languid waltz. Ford's past is glorious present, Griffith's antique; Ford exalts linearity and motion, Griffith the lovely in the commonplace. His Lincoln is awkward, straggly, vest too small, trousers short; but, unlike Fonda, he goes boldly to Mary and *he* asks *her* to dance.

mythic Lincoln is no monster, but a man ensnared by a potent conspiracy of his own character (formed by his life) and of historical forces (among them the ideological evolution of the "American dream"); both man and myth evolve, emerging out of gloom.

For while it is true that Ford's Lincoln often stands reflectively apart from everyone else—even, as J. A. Place observes, having himself draped like a proscenium arch over many of the trial scenes[28]—it is equally true that he is always being pulled into society. His proximity to tragedy, his duty to his dead, unite him with all who share a sense of loss. But in the world he inhabits there is little sense of "Fordian community"; only Lincoln's illusion of one, only isolation and hardship, and strife. When Lincoln visits the Clay farm and imagines himself a part of their family, he is actually speaking with three women related not by blood but—at the moment—by common tragedy: the threatened execution of the two Clay sons, one married, the other engaged to Carrie Sue. Mrs. Clay, when we first saw her, sparkled like Carrie Sue; a half-dozen years later, she is old, and widowed.* In the letter scene she speaks of those years: all the unremarkable, unquestioningly accepted horrors of pioneer life, the deaths, the unrewarded pain and toil. The letter concludes with a mawkish verse (a nice touch). Then, in a cell the family clings together singing, waiting (we see them in cameos); as Abigail leaves, the sheriff responds indifferently to her curtsy: she is nothing to him, nor does she expect attention from exalted personages. Midst all this, the real miracle is people's buoyancy—Carrie Sue's impetuosity: her unconscious eroticism, country accent, love for Sarah's baby, forwardness (like Mary Todd) in proposing marriage.**

Like Lincoln, the folk dwell in a mystic, forest dreamworld. The "blessings of civilization" have not yet come. People are instinctual, ingenuous; as in *Steamboat Round the Bend*, they are discovering things for the first time—books, law, their country's history as paraded on July 4th. But these "myths," without the hero's mediation, will not yet function properly. Without sufficient civilization, the law is a terrifying machine and the people are an unthinking mob. A Fordian fool (Francis Ford) exemplifies public volatility: a drunk (i.e., like most people, intoxicated by the moment), he will cheer lynchers or weep over a mother; yet Lincoln wants him on the jury.

---

*Alice Brady (1892–1939), Mrs. Clay, debuted on stage in 1911, somewhat against the will of her promoter father (William Brady: boxing and Broadway), then became his star at Brady Motion Pictures in 1914. She made fifty-two pictures (World, Select, Realart) before returning to the stage in 1923, where she was regarded as one of America's finest comediennes. She returned to films in 1933, made twenty-six more, and won an Oscar in *In Old Chicago* (Henry King, 1937). She was dying of cancer while making *Young Mr. Lincoln*, her seventy-eighth and last. Dewitt Bodeen cites her trial scene as "one of the profoundest manifestations of humanity's frightened bafflement before an inexplicable universe ever recorded by the camera." No wonder Lincoln understood her. ("Alice Brady," in *Films in Review*, November 1966, pp. 555–73.)

**The character's function anticipates Sue Lyon's in *7 Women*. Dorris Bowdon (Carrie Sue) receives no screen credit; she evidently replaced Judith Dickens, who is credited. She retired after marrying Nunnally Johnson in 1940 and playing Rosasharn in *The Grapes of Wrath*.

Lincoln appears nourished by the commonfolk; but he knows they are *common*folk. His introversion makes him so self-aware, so conscious of his apartness, of his "priesthood and judgeship," that (like Ransom Stoddard but unlike either Judge Priest) he cannot avoid condescension. He talks down to the lynchers and describes Mrs. Clay as, "Just a simple woman. I've seen [her] three times in my life, yet I know everything there is to know about her." Actually he has seen her four times, and does not know she gave him the lawbooks. For to him she stands for *all* mothers, just as Carrie Sue is like every young girl. (Indeed, the dramatic prominence of Lincoln's subjectivity may tend to blind even us to the individuality of the many "typed" supporting characters—and wrongly so, for it is they who save Lincoln from abstraction. As in *The Fugitive*, they root a hypertheoretical hero.)

Lincoln's sad, haunted, contradictory qualities are (unknown to *Cahiers*) shared by a remarkably large number of Fordian people, particularly from 1935 through 1947, all of whom feel chosen by destiny, secure in transcendental justification, and motivated by a sense of divinely appointed duty: Mary Stuart (*Mary of Scotland*), Dr. Mudd (*The Prisoner of Shark Island*), Casey and Tom Joad (*The Grapes of Wrath*), Wyatt Earp (*My Darling Clementine*), the Dubliners (*The Plough and the Stars*), the British (*Wee Willie Winkie*), the French (*The Hurricane*), the Americans (*Submarine Patrol, The Battle of Midway*). More generally, Lincoln is a paradigm of the Fordian hero of any date: solitary, celibate, almost impotent in grief, yet of the people; independent of logic, he arrogates authority to intervene, even violently, even by cheating, in order to mediate intolerance and to impress his personal convictions upon those whose thinking he faults (again: Judge and Priest); he reunites a family and walks away at the end.

The sense of tragic gloom haunting both film and Lincoln emanates from the shared knowledge (Ford, Lincoln, us) of the unity of life's passage from the necessary past into the necessary future. If Lincoln's belief during the twig episode is superstitious, later events in Springfield make him a more serious believer, until he realizes he no longer has the choice of going back: he must say goodbye to Ann, to Mrs. Clay, to his sidekick, to us and the screen, and "walk on a bit farther, up to that hill maybe": thunder, lightning, "Battle Hymn of the Republic," the Lincoln Memorial statue. But the man has become myth even before he dissolves into marble. That he is not entirely aware of this—nor entirely unaware, either—is evident from the manner in which the famous tall hat is made to dominate the forefront of the frame during the trial, while action occurs upframe from its perspective. We, but not cocky Lincoln, recognize the full irony of his putting this hat on, at his moment of triumph. The hero has been born.

Drums Along the Mohawk **(1939).** Frontier life is depicted similarly in *Drums Along the Mohawk*, which sketches a gloomy series of events undergone by pioneer settlers in New York's Mohawk Valley, 1776–1781. The land is work; Indians attack periodically; farmhouses and crops are burnt; children are born, men march off to fight the British and die. But the land is virgin, the people young, the air suffused with freshness, the gloom something to be brushed aside. Even old widow McKlennan (Edna May Oliver—nominated for an Oscar here), momentarily overtaken by memory of her dead husband as she feeds twigs to a fire, quickly recovers her jaunty spirits. As in the early thirties, Ford shows the social structures that inspire people to endure, and even to die, in order to solidify those same structures. But such traditions—source of all evil elsewhere in Ford—here do not ossify under stress. Traditional male-female roles are constantly exchanged. Each helps the other persevere. Gil provides one home, Lana another. She searches for him after the first battle, and finds him dazed in the night. He, in a 100-second take, searches for her after the second battle—she dons a soldier coat and kills an Indian—and finds her dazed. And unlike *Stagecoach*'s or *Lincoln*'s frontiers, *Mohawk*'s is dense with embryonic institutions and myths. Rituals abound, often grim, occasionally of fairy-tale charm, but, whether the ritual be marriage, a doctor amputating a leg, or a U.S. flag being raised, people sense that what they do for their first time has been done since time immemorial.

But compared to *Young Mr. Lincoln*, *Drums* is artful naiveté, airy and bright in its use of Technicolor (Ford's first film in color and his least expressionistic since talkies began), and seeming a particularly commercial enterprise for Ford—why *did* Claudette Colbert insist on wearing full glamour-puss makeup even while raking hay? Still, it is dotted with magic moments, of which the finest, blending beauty, glory, and sadness, occurs as Lana stands gazing from a hilltop while, small in the distance, a column of troops, her husband among them, marches off to battle, piping "Yankee Doodle."

The battle in question, incidentally, was actually fought by Herkimer at Oriskany, August 16, 1777, against a corps of Burgoyne's army, one of a series of victories culminating at Saratoga October 17, which in turn brought about the French alliance by which the war was won. (Field forces were generally small; Cornwallis at Yorktown had 7,073 men.) The film's siege is fictitious.

Zanuck had been growing progressively more frantic as the date for the troupe's return from Utah drew near and Ford, already over budget and behind schedule, made no preparations for this huge battle—it had been scheduled for three weeks of shooting. He badgered Ford daily with telegrams. Then one day Ford replied: they were caught up, within budget, and the battle had been filmed that morning. What had happened was that Ford, out of a clear blue sky, had turned to Henry Fonda (Gil): "Henry, I have to shoot a battle scene that I don't want. I had a better idea today. You've studied the script and your role, you probably know more about the battle than I do. Sit down and lean against this wall." With the camera aimed at Fonda, Ford fired a series of questions: "So, Henry, how did the battle begin?" And Fonda replied, making up an account. "And Peter? What happened to Peter?" asked Ford; or, "What was it like to have killed that man, after seeing John die?" And Fonda went on improvising, giving a virtual psychoanalysis of the battle. "Cut," called Ford, and told the editors: "Cut out my questions and use it as it is." One long take.[29]

Weather conditions in Utah's Wasatch Mountains caused enormous delays and difficulties. When the light was not changing (making it impossible to match shots), it rained. Frank Baker recalls six days of rain beginning the day he arrived, and Ford's not speaking to him for weeks in retaliation.* To make matters worse, Fox had started production without a completed script. But Ford maintained strict discipline in camp. Beer was allowed only in the commissary and limited to two per man; violators were promptly sent home. Only Mae Marsh and Ruth Clifford were permitted to carry out beer—concealed in their aprons; in return, they knitted Ford socks. Every night Ford sent a bugler thirty feet into the woods to play "Taps"— distantly.

The Grapes of Wrath (1940). Following completion of the shooting of *Drums Along the Mohawk*, Ford's third picture without a break, he embarked, with scarcely a month's pause, upon the *Araner*, on *The Grapes of Wrath* (1940), the film, as Andrew Sarris has written, "that was

---

*Ford typically kept Baker ignorant of his role until Baker found himself leading a column of Continentals into the fort—with no instructions otherwise, so that all the way he tried desperately to divine where to stop and what to do. Such uncertainty was Ford's way of getting that little spark of spontaneity—and of keeping actors on their toes.

single-handedly to transform him from a storyteller of the screen to America's cinematic poet laureate."[30]

A variety of critical tendencies—literary, documentary, and social-conscious—contributed to placing this film on the "one small uncrowded shelf devoted to the cinema's masterworks," as Frank Nugent wrote in *The New York Times* at its release.[31] In 1940 its debt to British and American documentaries was evident, and the same qualities distinguished it from other commercial movies: not merely social concern, but the look of actuality, spare decor, location shooting (some of it), authentic-seeming actors, the understated tone of everything. Perhaps it did sweeten John Steinbeck's bitterness, and maybe its aura of outrage was belated, and some found it an amusing profanity—tinsel Hollywood mimicking the messianic underground. But it was difficult to recall any other movie from a major studio whose tone was anywhere near so "aware." Even today, after the radical-chic social-consciousness of the fifties, sixties, and seventies, few films appear quite so seditious, bitter, and damning.

It remains to be ascertained to what degree social criticism had been repressed in American films after the financial consolidation and stricter censorship codes wrought in the early thirties. True, protests were the norm in allegorical genres like the western and the gangster film, but such rabble-rousing was seldom taken or considered as serious social criticism. *The Grapes of Wrath*—its prestige guaranteed by the highly acclaimed novel from which it derived*—was to some degree unique. Had critics remembered the movies before 1935, they may have recalled the doleful, astringent, iconoclastic, and almost misanthropic terms in which Ford (to speak only of Ford) had depicted contemporary America in *Flesh, Pilgrimage, Doctor Bull,* and *The Whole Town's Talking*, and hence they might have thought *The Grapes of Wrath* less original, though preachier. Ford's wrath had been drenched in exotica since 1935, but he eagerly employed the license given by *Stagecoach* to vilify a banker over gamblers, whiskey-drummers, prostitutes, escaped convicts, street murderers, and marauding Apache.

> This here old man just lived a life,
> an' just died out of it.
> I don't know whether it was good or bad.
> An' it don't matter much.
> Heard a fella say a poem once.
> An' he says, "All that lives is holy."
> But I wouldn't pray just for an old man that's dead.

---

*It won two Oscars (direction; supporting actress: Darwell) and five nominations (best picture; actor: Fonda; script: Johnson; editing: Robert Simpson; sound: a group); New York Film Critics chose it best picture, and awarded Ford best director for it and *The Long Voyage Home*.

Many critics, some of them experts in literature, have compared this film to Steinbeck's novel (see Bibliography). My own tendency is to consider how a script or story serves a director, not how the director serves a script, and rather than duplicate the critical work of others, I have tried to limit my critique to locating Ford's personality in what is, after all, a studio collaboration and one of Ford's lesser movies—considered as art rather than as reputation.

'Cause he's alright.
If I was to pray, I'd pray for folks that's alive,
an' don't know which way to turn.
Granpa here, he ain't got no more trouble like that.
He's got his job all cut out for him.
So, cover him up an' let him get to it.

Casey's Funeral Oration

In *The Grapes of Wrath*, characters are less prototypical than in *Stagecoach*, and the anger they arouse is initially less totemic and, hence, more personally uncomfortable to us. The banker who throws Muley's family off its land seems initially a not-bad sort doing a job he hates. But doubts arise as we study his spiffy car, and as we watch him light a big cigar and drive off deaf to Muley's pathetic protests. Yet Ford mitigates the effect of these gestures by shifting the camera's gaze to the rear, so that the banker lights his cigar with his back to us and in far shot. So as we begin to hate him, we regard him less as a person. This process of alienation does not climax until the banker's second appearance, when he tells the Joads to be off by sunrise, and when we see him distanced and with a sheriff riding beside him. Now it's us against them.

This process of alienation is announced in the opening conversation between Tom Joad (Henry Fonda) and a truckdriver, and is repeated with the banker, the lunchroom people,* and the gas-station attendants, the New Deal camp director, and numberless policemen and contractors. We are led to identify with "Our People" (as Ma Joad puts it) and to regard the rest of the world as alien. Such a process of identification / alienation is essentially revolutionary. In many earlier Ford pictures, when society and its sustaining myths failed, individuals went into identity crises. Paradoxically, in *The Grapes of Wrath*, the opposite occurs: the individual is strengthened not only in self-identity, but in identity as a member of a class. Through this process Tom Joad comes to understand his mission in life, and goes off alone.

In later years Ford went out of his way to downplay this revolutionary side of the picture:

I was only interested in the Joad family as *characters*. I was sympathetic to people like the Joads, and contributed a lot of money to them, but I was not interested in *Grapes* as a social study. I admire John Steinbeck and enjoyed working on it. I bucked to do that picture, and put everything I had into it.[32]

And again:

Before all else, it is the story of a family, the way it reacts, how it is shaken by a serious problem which overwhelms it. It is not a social film on this problem, it's a study of a family.[33]

---

*Rather ironic: two truckdrivers reward with a large tip a waitress who grudgingly gave Pa Joad fifteen-cent bread for ten cents, and five-cent candy for one cent.

Such denials border suspiciously on affirmations. Ford "bucked," his politics are declared, he could hardly have been unaware of the project's uniqueness, and he rests his case on a distinction between a "family study" and a "social study." Furthermore, it had been typical of previous socially conscious documentaries (such as *Hallelujah, Our Daily Bread, Moana, Man of Aran*) to focus on exotic, alien subjects, on the lowest classes, and often on a family, and to employ "documentary" elements only as sorts of dramatic foils. This, of course, only the more hotly inflamed audience empathy.

But Ford is technically correct. *The Grapes of Wrath* is perhaps not a social study, because it concentrates on effects, not causes. The "system" is condemned, but remains unseen; impersonal tractors destroy homes; impersonal signs forbid rides. But oppression assaults the Joads without cessation (other than pointed reminders how much better they have it than others).

In later years Ford more typically concentrates on the causes, often neglecting the effects (e.g., *The Long Gray Line, The Man Who Shot Liberty Valance*), and his central characters are the soldiers or police or others within the power structure, while the oppressed are represented superficially. For example, in the cavalry films, it is the soldiers who are analyzed and the Indians who suffer iconically. But in *The Grapes of Wrath* the reverse is true. The focus is on the "Indians," the Oakies, while the oppressors and virtually everyone else are, if by no means dehumanized, the ones restricted to symbolic gestures. Even the federal camp director is presented as a prototypical New Deal knight.

A number of factors, however, alter the thrust of the film's "politics" of empathy and alienation. Primary is the unavoidable fact that "Our People"— these proud, folksy, hopelessly ignorant Oakies—are so exotic as to be almost unreal, while the classes and attitudes arousing our indignation are in reality our own. Thus audience indignation is inevitably intellectualized.

Secondly, the impact of revolutionary alienation is deflected in plot development. Empathy, as always in Ford, is aroused by situating narrative point of view at the level of the central characters. Usually these characters represent not only themselves but a society to which they belong. Often these societies are "enclosed": by profession—military bases; by geography—islands, towns; by vehicles—stagecoach; or, as in *The Grapes of Wrath*, by caste—the downtrodden. But generally they are less homogeneous than in *Wrath*, even though the society here is only a single family, and individuals achieve richer identities through elaborate patterns of contrast. "Our People," instead, are contrasted only with brutal simplicity, en masse, and as individuals they remain somewhat indistinct and distant (compared with other Ford films). Ford concentrates on one character, Tom Joad, while shoving far into the background most of the others in the family and their particular stories (e.g., Rosasharn). Perhaps it was at one time the intention to anchor the narrative in Tom Joad and his transmutation, through alienation, into revolutionary. A paroled convict, Tom's loyalty is contested between the immediate welfare of his family and the long-term survival of his class, i.e., between his mother and the preacher, Casey (John Carradine). By responding with violence to the martyrdom of the preacher, Tom becomes an outlaw, and must separate from his family, taking up Casey's torch. It is likely, however, that he would have accepted this torch in any case, even if he were not fleeing the law. For, in effect, we are witnessing the birth of a Fordian hero: Tom feels it his duty and destiny to become a mediator between order and the chaos it causes, in order to preserve families; and, like Casey, he accepts celibate aloneness as part of his mission.

It is interesting to reflect that this Christ-like Henry Fonda character carries with him reverberations of young Mr. Lincoln, whom he played for Ford the year before. Once again Fonda must isolate himself from family to a mission both times revolutionary, one to the Law, the other to the Out-law (though both above the Law), and both times he walks off at the end into his destiny. Lincoln's fate is to dissolve into granite mythhood, Tom's to ascend out of family-consciousness into richer (?) selfhood. In *My Darling Clementine* (1946), Fonda-warrior exits down a long road of aridity; in *The Fugitive* (1947), Fonda-priest ascends to martyrdom; in *Fort Apache* (1948), Fonda-Custer gallops to perdition with irony. His part is taken up by James Stewart in *Liberty Valance* and *Cheyenne Autumn*.

In point of fact, the film as Ford shot it did end with Tom Joad's linear separation from his mother, followed by the shot of him going up over the hill.* But, somewhere along the course of production, a counterplot began to mute this revolutionary trumpet: Ma Joad (Jane Darwell) and her feeble attempts to preserve her family midst patriarchal abdication (the preacher retires, Muley stays behind, Grampa dies, Pa goes senile, Rosasharn's husband flees, Tom flees).

Supposedly Ford agreed with producer Darryl F. Zanuck that the picture would benefit from an upbeat ending. A European might have introduced a chorus singing "The International," but Ford sailed off on his ketch, and a few days later Zanuck telephoned to say he had added a concluding sequence, in which Ma Joad delivers her now famous "We keep acomin'. We're the people that live. Can't nobody wipe us out. . . ." Ford liked it and asked Zanuck to direct it.

But even if Ford did like it, and even if, as he claimed, it was his idea to end with Ma, still it is difficult to reconcile Ford's hindsight with his eloquent departure from the set.** What is more, the capacious Jane Darwell

---

*Jean Mitry claims to have seen a print in Switzerland in 1945 that ended like Steinbeck: the Joads are living in a barn, picking cotton for a pitiful wage, and Rosasharn, having borne a dead baby, suckles an orphan. No one else has heard of this version; it is unlikely it ever existed. (*John Ford* [Paris: Editions Universitaires, 1954], p. 101.)

**Ford gives this account in an interview with Walter Wagner. Zanuck's biographer, Mel Gussow, assigns Zanuck credit for writing Ma's lines and using her scene to end the picture, but also quotes Ford as crediting Zanuck for limiting music to Dan Borzage's accordion—surely

had been cast over his preference for the gaunt Beulah Bondi, whereas his preference for the strong Fonda won out over Zanuck's for the flabbier (but more box-office-popular) Don Ameche or Tyrone Power—partly because Zanuck saw the chance to bait Fonda into a seven-year contract. And even though Ma's speech sounds "Fordian," and even though those final shots echo the primal Fordian life-symbol, the parade, Ma's uncharacteristically prolix oration seems a tawdry resolution, in contrast to Ford's refusal to resolve. Nor is such sententiousness generally accorded Fordian characters without equal doses of irony. Of course, in this instance, it virtually destroys the film's trajectory toward inevitable *disintegration* / revolution, in favor of *perseverance* / abidance.

Ford pictures throughout the decade had been tackling social issues, characters determined to act, and instances of oppression, and we have seen how in many instances the natural response to repression and ossified convention (and inadequate myth) was a revolutionary upheaval—a burning of icons in *Steamboat*, a betrayal in *The Informer*, rebellion in *Plough*, revolt and disaster in *The Hurricane*. Persistence is the principal weapon of the oppressed. But persistence in itself is neither necessarily heroic (as Tom says, "It don't take no nerve to do something you can't do anything else *but* do") nor salutary (Hannah Jessop, Terangi, Mudd, Dr. John) *unless* directed toward erection of an alternative ideology (new myths). Ma offers no such alternatives; Tom does.

Grapes "was purposefully photographed black" by Gregg Toland, said Ford—although today most prints are gray—and seldom has a Ford picture been a world so unreal. Not even in *The Fugitive* is there so much abstraction from reality. Everything is submerged within a heavy shadowed mood, a dreamlike world mirroring Muley's insanity, like the desolation following nuclear war in a science-fiction film. Exteriors are carefully photographed to look like soundstages, the characters are lit like statues. People and objects are shorn of autonomy, emotions are *too* externalized (expressionistically). Elsewhere in Ford, subjectivity emanates from characters and it is they who create the spirit-world; here it is imposed a priori. It is unreason-

politely, as Borzage always played on Ford sets. Ford told Bogdanovich that the Fonda scene "was the *logical* end, but we wanted to see what was happening to the mother " (my italics)—which skirts the issue: we are even more curious about what happens to the central character. Tom Stempel, however, on scenarist Nunnally Johnson's authority, states that Johnson's original script ended with Ma's scene (whose words come from various places in the book, and which Steinbeck had enthusiastically approved as an ending, saying he had considered ending the book that way) but that Ford and Zanuck had not decided on the ending and left it out of the actual shooting script. Ford, in his reminiscences, claims Johnson wrote out the lines in front of Zanuck and him. (See: Wagner, *You Must Remember This* [New York: Putnam's, 1975], pp. 55–65; Gussow, *Don't Say Yes Until I Finish Talking* [New York: Pocket Books, 1972], p. 86; Peter Bogdanovich, *John Ford* [Berkeley and Los Angeles: University of California Press, 1978], p. 78; Stempel, *Screenwriter: The Life and Times of Nunnally Johnson* [New York: A. S. Barnes], pp. 78–87; Ford, in the John Ford Papers, Lilly Library, Indiana University.)

able, however, to lament *Grapes*'s expressionism: contemporary audiences perceived the film as gritty actuality; it copies Thomas Hart Benton[34] and photographic styles current in photo-journalism; and expressionism had been prominently exploited in *Potemkin* and such hallowed "documentaries" as *Triumph of the Will*, *Night Mail*, and *Olympiad*. To suggest that a blunt, natural style would be preferable to Ford's eerie lighting is to question the efficacy of art to comment on life.

The problems with *The Grapes of Wrath* resemble those of *The Informer*: the mood is too restricted, too repetitive, too seldom varied. The story itself seems to go on and on, episodically. And prolixity and monomania dominate other aspects of Ford's style. What Orson Welles once said of him—that Ford "does not move either his camera or his actors very much . . . there's little movement in [his films]"[35]—is patently untrue in general of this most dynamic of all filmmakers, but is true in particular of *Grapes*. Takes are long, cutting is slow, actors pose, and Ford will move them rather than the camera when a closer shot is desired. The long conversation between Tom Joad and Casey toward the beginning has a take two minutes forty seconds long, with most movement occurring in the tree-leaves, and is followed by another that is sixty seconds long. There is nothing "wrong" with this scene, one of the better in the film, in fact—it does much to establish the picture's distinctive, morose atmosphere—but, combined with a general fatigue in formal inventiveness, such techniques render *Grapes* a ponderous picture.

The Long Voyage Home **(1940).** Our poet laureate's second prestigious success of 1940* is even blacker and more single-minded than *Grapes*; stylistically, it seems a reversion to 1936.

Although the title could almost sum up Ford's work, the endless quest for a nonexistent home is seldom enunciated elsewhere than here, where most talk and all thought is of "home," and where again and again a death or departure is marked by John Qualen's commenting that someone has "gone home" (a line not to be found among the four Eugene O'Neill plays from which the movie derives). Even the contrast offered by the one seaman not seeking to escape the *Glencairn* is nihilistic; according to Donkeyman (Arthur Shields):

—   The best thing to do with memories is—forget 'em. . . . When a man goes to sea he ought to give up thinking about things on shore. Land don't want him no more. I had me share of things going wrong, and it all came from the land. Now I'm through with the land, and the land's through with me.

Huw Morgan's attitude toward memory, in *How Green Was My Valley*, leads him into an isolation even more absolute than Donkeyman's, but that film's treatment of the memory motif is far subtler and variegated than *Voyage's*, just as its brighter palette and recalcitrant optimism render it ultimately far more pessimistic than *Voyage's* persistent repetition of the same few motifs of cosmic malevolence.

Yet this is a movie Ford was proud of—stills from it decorated his home. Those who delight chiefly in the spoken word relish it. And in 1940 it seemed a distinguished exception to Hollywood's "general worthlessness." Ford consulted with O'Neill and spent six weeks planning the adaptation with Dudley Nichols (a friend and fan of O'Neill, who in 1947 directed the film *Mourning Becomes Electra*); Nichols then locked himself away for twenty 16-hour days, haggled over his first draft with Ford for a week, then worked another month on the final script.[36] O'Neill loved the picture and screened it periodically.

O'Neill's stage words are frequently replaced by movie images. In *The Moon of the Caribbees*, restless men, native girls, a dance, and a fight translate the storyline with scarcely a single O'Neill line. Later, verbal poetry tends to be Nichols's, not O'Neill's. For instance, Donkeyman's "Memory" speech (quoted above) derives from a "land"-less O'Neill sentence ("Not that I ain't had my share o' things goin' wrong; but I puts 'em out o' me mind, like, an' forgets 'em"). Absent also from O'Neill is the grandiloquent cry by Driscoll (Thomas Mitchell), "Is there to be no more light in the world?" whose inspiration seems sprung from the long day's journey into night photographi-

---

*No Oscars, but seven nominations (best picture; screenplay: Nichols; music: Hageman; photography: Toland; editing: Sherman Todd; effects: Ray Binger and R. T. Layton; sound: Robert Parrish). New York Film Critics chose Ford best director for this and *Grapes*.

cally formalized by Gregg Toland's spots and shafts of brilliance midst total black, with the result that, far from the Ford-Toland pictures seeming to illustrate the text, it is rather the text that seems to be verbalizing the pictures—at least until the ineffable concluding sequence, when the sailors return downcast and scraps of refuse paper fly around in the patch of light dockside.

Thus, though fifty O'Neill words get telescoped into five or ten Nichols ones, the effect of Ford's expressionism is expansion, not contraction; each verbal idea becomes a fleshy personality, expressive gesture, or photographic space. Words are concretized even by words, as Donkeyman's "Memory" speech is tied to a "land/sea" theme. Elsewhere, Ole (John Wayne) is given a pet parrot by Ford, and Driscoll learns of Ole's fate by finding the parrot, whereas in O'Neill the news is merely verbal. Even changes seeming to debase O'Neill intentions actually strengthen emotional themes; for example, O'Neill's Smitty (whose letters the sailors steal and read) is just an alcoholic failure, but the film's Smitty (Ian Hunter) is an upper-class hero of the British Empire as well, so that, typically for Ford, he has sought escape not so much from physical weakness as, like Doc Holliday, from shamed social identity.

Characters may occasionally seem like too many Gypo Nolans—dunderheads wandering in the fog, almost too stupid to be pitied—and one might feel that here, as in *Tobacco Road* (Ford's next picture), the fascination with lower-class simpletons typical of this period of Ford's work is demeaning. It is all the more miraculous, then, that the casting of Hollywood "types" like John Wayne, Ward Bond, Thomas Mitchell, Barry Fitzgerald, or John Qualen never lessens credibility nor hints at that dreadful impression of actors "playing down."

Tobacco Road (1941). Scenarist Nunnally Johnson thought *Tobacco Road* "a fiasco," for Ford relied on "old-fashioned bed-slat comedy . . . crude [and] clumsy."[37] Albeit there are magic moments: Arthur Miller's photographic prologue; Bible songs at City Hall and the car dealer's; walking to the poor farm; and Jeeter's final speech. But a condescending veneer of euphoric populism has replaced the uncomplicated gaze with which Ford previously viewed simple folk (e.g., *Steamboat Round the Bend*).

How Green Was My Valley (1941). The film that beat out *Citizen Kane* for Oscars in production, direction, photography, and art direction, is often criticized as a "prestige" commercial picture, a tear-jerking bit of Hollywood gloss that improperly detracts from proletarian issues—as represented by such "realistic" (i.e., politically preachy) films as *Kameradshaft* or *The Stars Look Down*.* "A monstrous slurry of tears and coaldust,"

*Leaving his Welsh mining valley after fifty years, Huw Morgan recalls childhood as youngest in a large, working family. Flashback to c. 1900: Midst increasing economic recession, the valley quarrels over unions and liberal ideas of a new minister. Four brothers quit the valley

David Thomson calls it, and, echoing a common view of John Ford pictures as Pollyanna celebrations of tradition, charges, "Ford dumbly regrets the passing of a make-believe stability that has served as an obstacle to any necessary critical sensibility."[38]

As we shall see, only the most conventional and disingenuous readings of the film could support such conclusions.

Planning of the picture was dominated by 20th Century–Fox production chief Darryl F. Zanuck. Shot at Fox's San Fernando Valley ranch and costing $1,250,000, it was intended to win Academy Awards, which it did, six of them, and to gain wide popularity, which it did, grossing more than any film except *Sergeant York* during its year of release. But the project caused initial misgivings to the politically reactionary Zanuck. According to scenarist Philip Dunne: "Zanuck, Ford, and Nunnally Johnson had come under savage attack by right wingers for making *The Grapes of Wrath*. . . . Zanuck, who persisted in believing that I was much more of a radical fire-eater than I actually was . . . pretend[ed] to wring his hands over the great risk he was taking in turning me loose on a goddamn pro-labor picture."[39]

Zanuck had purchased the rights to Richard Llewellyn's novel, a best seller in 1939, and had at first assigned Liam O'Flaherty, then Ernest Pascal to script it. But in a memo in May 1940, he criticized Pascal's emphasis on the sociological over the human, and proposed taking a "*revolutionary viewpoint* of the screenplay of this story and [telling] it as the book does— through the eyes of Huw, the little boy. We should do the picture with him as an off-stage commentator with many of the scenes running silent and nothing but his voice over them."[40] (In effect, although it was about to become commonplace, voice-over narration by a character was virtually unknown in 1940.**) Pascal was replaced by Dunne, who worked with William Wyler, hired to direct, some three months on the script. In November 1940, Zanuck, having made the key decision for Huw as narrator, made two more critical decisions, writing Wyler that Huw "should never grow up" (Tyrone

---

to find work elsewhere, the eldest brother is killed in the mine, but Huw, who is the first in the valley to receive an education and could become a doctor, chooses to go down the colliery. Sister Angharad's divorce incites her excommunication, the minister (who loves her) quits in disgust, and Huw's father dies in Huw's arms in the mine. But in a second flashback, Huw recalls the good times.

The movie also won Oscars for supporting actor (Crisp), and was nominated in five other categories: supporting actress (Allgood), script, editing, music, sound. The art direction award was two separate Oscars, set direction and interior decoration. New York Film Critics chose Ford best director, and this was almost the only award he showed up personally to collect: he always shunned Oscar ceremonies.

**Kentucky Pride* (1925) excepted, this is the first voice-over narration in Ford. Aside from the documentaries and the special case of *Liberty Valance*, eight later films employ character narrators, but none to *Valley's* extent: *When Willie Comes Marching Home, Rookie of the Year, The Quiet Man, The Long Gray Line, The Wings of Eagles, Gideon's Day, The Colter Craven Story, Sergeant Rutledge*. Noncharacter narrators occur in nine others: *Tobacco Road, The Fugitive, She Wore a Yellow Ribbon, Wagon Master* (the song), *What Price Glory, The Majesty of the Law, Flashing Spikes*, "The Civil War," *Cheyenne Autumn*.

Power was to have played the grown-up Huw) and that "now is the time for us to start talking in terms of drama and audience. I was bored to death by the repetition of the strike business and of starving babies, etc., etc. It all seems old hash to me."[41] By April, with script and casting completed, filming was put off until summer, by which time Ford was to be available.

Aside from its deemphasis of sociology, the script follows the book faithfully, and often word for word, allowing for tightening of time and telescoping of events. Most suppressions are expectable, such as the compromising sexual affairs of the Morgan sons and of Huw himself. Ford's most obvious addition to Dunne's script (which he otherwise followed closely) was the coda, in which idyllic memory triumphs over tragic actuality. Intended to finish the picture on an uplifting rather than depressing note, this "false happy ending" may fool a casual viewer (as it has fooled many a critic eager to accuse Ford of reactionariness and Hollywood of creampuffing social issues) into thinking that the movie is celebrating the very theme its double-leveled story is condemning. It is the movie's emphasis on memory, a motif only gradually enunciated in the book, that is the primary difference between it and the book. Huw's opening monologue

— I am leaving behind me fifty years of memory. Memory . . . Who shall say what is real and what is not? Can I believe my friends all gone when their voices are a glory in my ears? No. And I will stand to say no and no again, for they remain a living truth within my mind. There is no fence nor hedge around time that is gone. You can go back and have what you like of it . . . So I can close my eyes on my valley as it was . . .

is partly original, partly culled from scattered passages in the book, but its sense is quite different in the movie, because of the movie's more intense distinction between fact and fantasy. Huw's gaze looks out his window at the desolate slum his valley is today only to dissolve into his imagination's images of the lush valley of his childhood. The cameo scenes that immediately follow, in which quotidian events are spelled out as the essence of sacramental beauty, tell us what sort of person Huw is and prepare us: what we shall witness is a highly subjective, terribly colored depiction of reality, one in which a child's emotions of remembering take precedence over crass facts. The book's focus upon the change in the valley becomes in the movie the (non)change in Huw. In effect, the conventional stage fiction—that years may pass but Roddy McDowall (playing Huw) does not age—becomes a symbol of the character's and the culture's stasis. It is Huw who unites the myriad disparate persons, episodes, and styles of the movie's storyworld. To his progression from paradise to slag, from sunshine to mine, is juxtaposed his awakening to (and refusal of) consciousness. To experience the movie only as a celebration of Huw's dreamy myopia, denial of reality, and adhesion to tradition is to experience *only* Huw's point of view; it is not to experience *Ford's* point of view *of* Huw's point of view. And it is not even commonsensical. For it is quite clear in the movie that it is Huw's attitude, shared in different ways by his neighbors, that has destroyed the valley and mortified Huw. Huw is an antihero, and Ford, as in *The Man Who Shot Liberty Valance* (1962), calls into question the validity of Huw's point-of-view narrative. These ideas are not in the book.

Such a technique is commonplace in literature, but rare in film. True, almost every movie has shots reflecting a character's point of view or impressions; and dream sequences, too, are frequent. But mind's-eye narration sustained over an entire movie is virtually unknown.* It cannot work in ordinary films because audiences have no narrator to deal with. It is difficult to work in an auteur film—where audience should sense a narrating personality already—because the director must then interpose himself between the audience and the narrating character. What is easy in literature is nearly impossible in film (as the failure of literary-oriented critics to comprehend *How Green Was My Valley* demonstrates), for cinema, particularly auteur cinema, is less like literature than like painting made into music. The operative analogy is thus not with Joseph Conrad—who used narrating characters often—but with Vincent Van Gogh—who never did. Can we imagine a painting by Van Gogh showing the world as experienced by a well-adjusted Dutch businessman? in which both Van Gogh's *and* the businessman's sensibility are apparent? Even a single subjective shot, in cinema, can detract from a director's presence. Thus a Hitchcock always corrects, imposing his own point of view following a shot from a character's point of view. And thus *Citizen Kane* has not five narrators (unless they all see the world in identical echoing, black, deep-focus fashion), but only one, Welles, who is also Kane (and as vacuous as narrator as character).

In *How Green Was My Valley*, Ford's solution—and it is a successful solution for emotionally involved audiences—has been to sustain Huw's "I" both powerfully present and powerfully distanced. To the degree the viewer is conscious of Huw as narrator, he will be conscious of possible attitudes other than Huw's, and there he will find Ford. A large variety of devices, aural and visual, continually affirm Huw's narrating presence and distance the action:

- Most of the movie occurs in flashback.
- Huw's adult off-camera voice narrates (the voice is Irving Pichel's**).
- Scenes are shot from the visual point of view of boy Huw.
- Scenes frame Huw at their compositional focal point (e.g., when the family is presented to Bronwyn [Anna Lee] and Huw sits foreground while

*Only one other comes to mind: Max Ophuls's *Letter from an Unknown Woman* (1948). In *Liberty Valance* subjective distortion is more evident, since the narrator and many of the principals appear in expanded framing sequences.

**G. Dane Wilsonne, who knew Pichel, tells me that Rhys Williams had originally recorded the narration. But Ford, fearing on second thought lest audiences identify the voice with the boxer Dai Bando whom Williams plays in the film, substituted Irving Pichel. As the picture had already been completed, it was necessary for Pichel to match precisely Williams's rhythm and timing. Williams's (superior) version once circulated in Britain.

the others, spreading out before him, move as though in the dream of his persona memory)[frame 1].

• Scenes echo his mood in lighting (e.g., the shadowed corridor, his first day at school [frame 2]; expressionist shadowing emphasizes the interiority of Huw's image of community, his inner fantasy.

• Scenes echo his mood in cutting (e.g., when Huw opens the classroom door, Ford, crosscutting between Huw and the students at their desks, follows the pattern of Huw's timid attempt to take in the situation: in succeeding shots the large mass of students [frame 3] centers gradually on those few closest to him, while, correspondingly, the shots of Huw move closer to Huw; then Ford breaks this pattern and cuts startlingly to a medium close-up of the teacher, hitherto unnoticed, sitting high above and far away: the crosscuts now isolate Huw and teacher from the class, since Huw has now something more terrifying than the children with which to contend).

• Scenes echo his mood in sets (e.g., when Huw visits Angharad [Maureen O'Hara] at the Evans mansion, the gates and door are twice the size they actually would have been [frame 4]).

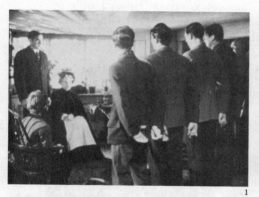

1 2

3 4

Huw's subjectivity, as we have seen, is established in his opening narration, as the adult Huw, gazing at the desolation his valley has become, is pulled back by memory. Harsh reality is swept away for a dream. And no doubt for Huw the same dream repeats itself eternally, has repeated itself these fifty years, and each time its "romance" will be subverted by its plot—the "slag" will come to the valley—until this plot is in turn subverted by renewed memory (the rosy-hued coda).

For Huw wishes to envision life as a succession of miracles; indeed, one such series is among the picture's most inspired stretches: after falling through the ice, Huw, in quick succession, is preached a wondrous sermon by Mr. Gruffydd, is introduced to the wonders of great books (are they the same books adult Huw is wrapping in his mother's scarf at the film's beginning?) while simultaneously Angharad discovers love, encounters the birds of spring, embraces again his mother, sees the whole village singing and his brothers returning home, and is taken by Mr. Gruffydd to a hilltop where, almost miraculously, he walks again [frame 5]. But, alas, Huw's enchanted outlook is the myopia of innocence; the movie is actually a succession of frightening tragedies, failures, oppressions. It is arguably Ford's most cynical and pessimistic film (and we recognize Ford in part by the staggering disparity between events and Huw's innocence). Even Huw's family is a failure, for it cannot tolerate discussion, and communication within it is severely circumscribed by patriarchal absolutism. (One gets the feeling, how-

5

ever, that the Morgan parents are closer and more liberal to Huw than to his much older siblings.)

Huw's view is remarkably distanced (even for Ford): he (and thus we) watch characters, particularly Angharad and Bronwyn, almost voyeuristically, from outside them, without penetrating (as we do matter-of-factly in most movies) into their motives and consciousnesses. This "apartness" in Huw largely accounts for *How Green Was My Valley's* seeming so "staged" an affair. In fact this "staginess'—the carefully noble manner in which the people talk, move, gesture—is one of Huw's chief contributions as "director" of his dream. He regiments his material into a mode of memory.

Consistent with the "stagey outsideness" of the characterizations is that Ford, here more ambitiously than with *Stagecoach*, is attempting (in his capacity as Huw's assistant director, so to speak) to adapt his vignette style of characterization, of comedy style, to the dark modalities of an introverted tragedy. Huw grasps his people in characterizing action: we shall, for example, always think of Bronwyn as Huw does, as she appears in the coda recapitulation of Huw's first encounter—coming round the corner with basket and bonnet, when he falls in love with her—and two or three more such simple vignettes complete her dramatic personality. In fact, we know nothing *about* her, except what seem to be vivid, tactile impressions of knowing *her*. In other words, in the script she is, as a dramatic personage, a nonentity, a simple foil for Huw, but in the picture she is, as a dramatic personage, among the most intimate and sure personalities in movies. Similarly, vignette narration is wondrously successful in the economic concreteness with which Angharad's marriage is sketched. We see her with her husband only as they leave the church, but so vivid later are her emotions in the tea scene with Huw that we in no way miss a scene between them.

But if such successes exemplify some advantages of Huw's distanced, awestruck vignette methods in a large-cast, quickly sequenced, ensemble movie, the obscurity of the Gruffydd personage (Walter Pidgeon) exemplifies its disadvantages in extended study of a *complicated* personality. Gruffydd's actions are rarely comprehensible to Huw (or to us?), yet *his* story, thrust into the background behind the stories of Huw, Huw's family, and the valley, is the film's "backbone." The long cameo exposition concludes in the marriage of Ivor and Bronwyn; here the "plot" begins, for now Mr. Gruffydd makes his entrance before his congregation and now—in a series of point-of-view crosscuts occurring almost without Huw's awareness, "underneath the thread of his narration"—Angharad falls instantly in love with the new minister (as Huw fell instantly in love with Bronwyn). It is by Ford's intervention that some of the lacunae in Gruffydd's tale are filled. For example, midst matters intimate to Huw (Bronwyn is reading to him in his window-bed), Ford's camera retreats discreetly to watch Angharad (out of Huw's sight) and Gruffydd, while keeping Huw and Bronwyn in the frame (6). (Such composition in depth seems infinitely more subtle than the scenes

6

praised by Bazin in *Kane* and *Little Foxes*.*) The presence of multiple narrators in the movie (Huw-adult; Huw-boy; Ford) allows such fascinating play
with point of view in which the fairly blunt ideas of *Stagecoach*'s dinner
scene are developed with delicate, fugal complexity. But other sequences
dispense with Huw altogether: Gruffydd's rejection of Angharad; some labor scenes; the expressionistically caricatured women with teacups gossiping about Angharad's divorce. And Ford's additions allow us to see that Gruffydd's story parallels the valley's, a failure in relationship, a misconception of
the spiritual and the material. We realise Gruffydd is a Fordian hero manqué: celibate, solitary, claiming truth and authority, but a figure of impotence. He sermonizes about virtue and charity midst mountain daffodils,
but in the next scene allows his flock to excommunicate an unwed mother.
His congregation sit in their pews like soldiers in formation, and are shocked
by their minister's attempts at fellowship—singing and drinking and supporting a union. Gruffydd's self-appointed role is to mediate between revolution
and reaction, but he fails, as mediator, goodfellow, and leader, by virtue of an
idealism that, like Huw's, ignores the real world around him. Far from reuniting families, as the Fordian hero is supposed to do, Gruffydd watches
them be destroyed, and contributes to Angharad's own downfall. His inability to accept her love or realistically to acknowledge her, while yet courting
her like some chaste Parsifal, effectively condemns him—and the valley. An

---

*Bazin liked the long takes in *Little Foxes* during which Teresa Wright appears on a staircase behind and above her feuding in-laws. Ford had staged a similarly composed *coup de
théâtre* in *Mary of Scotland*, five years previously, when Mary appears on a staircase behind
and above the feuding Bothwell and Knox—and would repeat it in *The Searchers*, when Scar
appears on a dune behind and above the feuding Ethan and Marty. Such quarreling with Bazin
would be more gratuitous than it seems, did not Bazin specifically cite Wyler's compositional
style as superior to Ford's montage. (See: "The Evolution of the Language of Cinema," in Bazin's *What Is Cinema?*, translated by Hugh Gray [Berkeley and Los Angeles: University of
California Press, 1971], p. 35.)

inexorable chain of cinematic logic links this moment of denial (Gruffydd lights a lamp and notices Angharad in the dark; he flicks out his match as, in contrapuntal motion, Angharad rises to greet him; the rest of the scene is redundant, except as necessary ritual: we know their love is doomed) to Angharad's excommunication, the colliery explosion, the father's death, and the slag heap. As in *The Hurricane*, the cataclysm (storm or mine explosion) seems a sort of wrath of God: the shriveled minds of the valley people incite their just destruction; ironically it is the particularly innocent who are killed (Ivor, Gwilym—as in *The Hurricane*), while the "guilty" are preserved. Angharad will shiver, and Mr. Gruffydd, impotent rather than redemptive, will pose crucified, but it is Huw who will stare out blankly when the colliery lift rises.

The elusiveness of Gruffydd's personality and actions is partly connected to explanations elided by Zanuck. In Llewellyn's novel, unionism plays a more important role, the father is more sympathetic toward it, and less authoritative. The cause of the valley's desolation is analyzed as a combination of economic expediency and the workers' failure to unite behind the progressive socialism promoted by the Morgan sons. Also in the book, when Huw (not, as in the movie, Angharad) protests in chapel the excommunication of the unwed mother, Gruffydd explains that the valley has hitherto been self-governing; it has no police, no courts; the people have lived by the Bible; hopefully in time they will become more educated and kindlier, but until then it is only the sternness of their customs that has enabled them to function as a community without the evils of outside (English) intervention. The movie omits these explanations, instead implying that unionism, along with Gruffydd's new morality, is repugnant because it means change, and change is anathema to sinewy tradition: thus the valley cannot decide to unite in opposition to the diddle-brained mine owner and his dandy scion. Both valley and Huw ossify and decay because they prefer dream to reality.

In fact, the movie omits these explanations not *just* because of Zanuck, but because Huw omits them: the traditionalist attitudes are Huw's. When the dinner ritual is shattered toward the movie's beginning by dispute over the union, Huw protests that *he* has not deserted; and with each successive departure from the valley, Huw reaffirms that *he* shall not desert. (Actually, the father dismisses his sons for their *bad manners* at table, not because he disagrees with their position; but the sons walk out because they feel that being right is more important than manners. This "false" conflict confuses subsequent debate, and leads Huw irrationally to perceive all "new ideas" as threatening to home and tradition.) Conversely, the line "I'm leaving the valley" signals Gruffydd's capitulation. Indeed, Huw's one departure from the valley (going to school) was traumatic, and even at age fifty still there, his decision to leave conflicts with memory. For Huw sees *every* action as ritual, as part of sacramental tradition: coming home from work, washing, dinner, allowance, toffee shop, even just going around a corner becomes ritual—a consecrated, instantly legendary, special magic moment.* Change is mirrored in disrupted ritual: that Bronwyn continues to put out fresh clothes for Ivor a year after Ivor's death evinces her refusal to admit change. And Huw, confronting his heart with reality, tries like Bronwyn to force reality to bend to his heart's needs: tiny details become heart-rending nuances, bigger than life and set in scenes hyperdramatic; a plethora of incidents spin the spectator far out of the duration of normal time (i.e., the movie seems longer than its 118 minutes). It would, for instance, require a page to relate the miniature drama enacted in a few seconds by Angharad as she waits excitedly inside her door for Mr. Gruffydd coming to call; this is a tiny moment, almost a period of punctuation, yet so typical of the picture as a whole.

When the sons leave the table and Huw stays, he pities but admires his father. And the idealism with which Huw views him is inseparable from the aura of defeat he equally surrounds him with. As in the famous "Lord is my shepherd" sequence when father Morgan grieves the breakup of his family, Huw's father is always seen from his son's spiritual and often physical perspective (and Donald Crisp conveys Gwilym Morgan's bilevel presence—as real man and as Huw's fantasy), and this reflects Huw's obligation and (scarcely acknowledged) guilt toward this defeated nobility. Initially Huw is torn between his reactionary father and the progressive Gruffydd; but the choice is not so simple. The father is not so much reactionary as a believer in first principles—that people ought and will perform the duties of their stations and that legislation and institutional strife cannot remedy failure in individual duty. Gruffydd, on the other hand, backs institutions over individuals, fails toward individuals, and sees all institutions—mine, union, church, and family—break down. But Huw *will* not fail; he *will* tend his station. To follow tradition for Huw means not to leave the valley, means to be a miner, as was his father; to leave the valley, to become a doctor or lawyer, this would be to deny his father, to put down his father's life. Or, at least, this is how his *mother* feels. (She and Bronwyn, with baby, stand in a background doorway, in ceilinged depth of field, framed foreground by Huw announcing to his father his decision, which they apparently cause, to affirm tradition; appropriately, the scene is a static tableau.) His father's ardent hope, to the contrary, is that Huw *will* contradict him, will leave the valley, will leave the old ways, will surpass the father, and yet take with him the good in family tradition.

Alas, in this world, the best-laid hopes run aground on the reefs of human instinct. Nothing was ever so necessary as that Huw leave the valley. But Huw misjudges the force of tradition, apprehends only its inward spiral, its negative, closing-out-the-world face, and, intending his life to be an act of consummate purity in devotion to a supreme beauty, he rejects the path of

---

*Lisa, in Ophuls's *Letter from an Unknown Woman*, suffers similarly; and she is also a point-of-view persona narrator, tempting us to believe her "suicide" is merely romantic, rather than also unconsciously sado-masochistic.

growth, chooses that of decay, and thus is ultimately responsible for the end of his tradition's evolution.

In Huw's linkage with his mother in defiance of his father, is there implication that Huw wishes, oedipally, not merely to follow father's footsteps, but to replace father?—as, in fact, he does, just as he replaces Ivor in Bronwyn's house (he moves his bed there). Curiously, the mother-Huw alliance not only shares aversion to change and leaving the valley-womb, but also, like Bronwyn, even to acknowledgment: the mother also denies the father's death, just as she denies the map showing her sons' diaspora ("They are here. In the house!"). And Huw, as he looks, age fifty or more, out his window and glimpses slag and desolation, speaks of leaving this valley at last, wrapping his belongings in his mother's shawl (tradition), but boasting proudly that it doesn't matter, that he can cancel out Now, can close his eyes and remember how it was. And there it is: the whole movie running by in flashback, but the story one of destruction, of dismemberment of the family, of its destruction, and of Huw's guilt — all unacknowledged. Tradition itself has become, unrecognized, the malignant slag, has itself become change; and once again in Ford it is a question of duty and tradition gone astray. Huw's innocence undergoes successive shocks culminating in Angharad's excommunication, Gruffydd's desertion, and his father, in pitted darkness, in earth womb, dying in his arms. Oedipal guilt mingles with utter futility; only suffering has meaning. Huw's blank stare into nothingness, when the

colliery lift reaches light, is (I think) the movie's key shot. The eyes fix inward, not outward, into a desolate soul without a thing to look at, for life has meaning because seeing is a moral act. Evil change has triumphed (as it always shall in Ford), the Morgan family has been slaughtered, as Ivor predicted, the valley turns arid and Huw bereft, which necessitates that he in the mine of his own identity subsist all the more strongly within the fantasy purity Gruffydd (so cruelly?) bequeathed him.

Hence, as the colliery lifts, Huw's heart flees into memory, and is wholly absorbed by it. Reality *becomes* memory, and ignites a rerun of Huw's dream (i.e., the coda in which the valley blooms in youth and Huw walks with the father he has betrayed), and Huw, Gruffydd's appointed successor, *rejects* reality, as do, in various ways, his mentor, mother, sisters, and valley (in contrast to the brothers, who fight and emigrate, and to the father, who bends to events). Huw's act (the coda) is both tragic and courageous. Memory subdues reality, isolates the mind, but at what a cost!

Although scenarist Philip Dunne feels Ford filmed his script virtually without change,* *How Green Was My Valley* is far more John Ford's picture

---

*Nonetheless, as Dunne has acknowledged, Ford's contributions were many. Among them: changing Dunne's two fighters into a comic team, with Barry Fitzgerald as the slapstick part-

than Philip Dunne's script. Ford's cinematization does not merely "realize" Dunne's intentions, it transmutes and even subverts them, and creates an expressionist fantasy of ritual whose subjectivity Ford faults.

The music helps convey Huw's cloying saccharinity, counterpointing here, reinforcing there; yet the music is usually more sentimental than the image, where Ford's rigorous purposefulness, in staging and framing and gesturing eyes, combats the maudlin Huw by clear and simple strength. As usual (although here it is probably Dunne's doing), he makes everything concrete: a dispute between mistress and servant is represented by a tea pitcher. The scenes of valley life opening the film and orienting us have the principal effect of causing sensations of depth, memory, and déjà-vu, of vertical structure during the movie's course, so that as these scenes recur (e.g., the paymaster's window) they take on more intimate significance. But most notably, everything has been choreographed, the better to reflect Huw's notion of life as ritual: everywhere, whether in church or at Bronwyn's presentation, ritual is expressed as flowing geometric motions. The choreography, moreover, constantly opposes motion and stillness, echoing the movie's antinomy of changing reality vs. (Huw's) static idealism. Not only is all motion choreographed within each shot, but (what is rarer) between shots as well, so that shots join into movements of a suite.

An exemplary sequence occurs when the mother (Sara Allgood) comes downstairs after a long recuperation and is reunited with Huw, still restricted to his window-bed: MS: Mother, at bottom of stairs, moves out of frame right, FS (low level): and hobbles across room diagonally down frame toward Huw; /CU: Huw sits up in bed, puts hand to breast. X MCU: Mother opens arms and bends toward Huw: /2MS: they embrace. /GS: The room, with them in far corner.*

Nothing could be more classic than Ford's treatment, the tight opposition of matching close shots exploding into a two-shot, and then the long shot for relief and distance. But the sequence is exceptional in that the cutting seems demanded not so much by dialectic of ideas as by internal motions and gestures within each shot. This is a peculiarity of Ford and of this movie in particular.

Ford's "rule" (though frequently violated) can be seen in the school fight. The two boys move left to a knockdown, /then right / and so on, until Huw, beaten, sinks in a spiraling combination of boy and camera. Here each shot contains a single line of motion; a cut occurs when this single motion is

---

ner; lines like "'Tis a coward I am but I will hold your coat"; the women calling to each other in song; Crisp frowning in disapproval at him when Huw grabs some bread, or putting on his bowler hat and announcing "I'm going to get drunk"—both in imitation of Ford's own father; putting Crisp's feet in a bowl of water when Evans comes to ask for Angharad's hand; having Sara Allgood behave somewhat like Ford's own mother. In addition, Ford participated in most of the picture's casting. (See interviews with Dunne, and with Josephine Feeney, in the John Ford Papers, Lilly Library, Indiana University.)

* / = cut; X = crosscut (matching angle); FS = full shot; MS = medium shot; GS = general shot (bigger); CU = close-up; MCU = medium close-up.

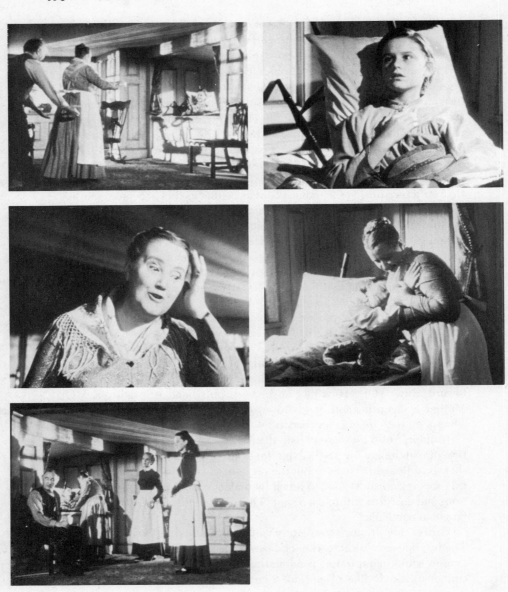

caesuraed. The same rule is employed in the Huw and mother sequence quoted above: one take, one motion.

When a number of characters occupy a single take, their motions may be utilized in contrapuntal vectors. For example, the camera stands inside Mrs. Tossle's toffee shop, looking out onto the street. Huw, outside, moves from window to door; but as he does so two women pass in the background in the opposite direction, so that the two motions (Huw/women) cross in the doorway; the women move on as Huw enters the shop. Such an instant may seem trivial, but the "collision" does not happen by chance. Such devices, frequent and important in Ford's film language, reinforce a principal motion.*

Contrasting employment of stasis is also frequent. Outside their door, suddenly realizing two sons are leaving, the mother shivers and the father is stunned, a portrait of repressed trembling, and the camera prolongs the shot. Similarly treated are the dinner scene, Huw seeing Bronwyn, presentations of the sons to her, Huw's decision to become a miner, the colliery-life group—all tableaux immortalizing tradition.

In the most elaborate scene (not contained in Llewellyn), Ford capitalizes on his one-motion, one-take rule: Ivor (Patrick Knowles) has been killed in a mine explosion and his body is being carried down the road from the colliery, past the cottages on the right, to his wife Bronwyn. On the left, hundreds of miners stream down the hill-road, their passing an obligato of motion through the frame. Above, in the background, the colliery whistle screams and fiery black smoke belches from the hills, sprinkling the valley

*Jean Renoir discusses such devices in his *My Life and My Films* (New York: Atheneum, 1974), p. 156–57.

with cinders. Townswomen swarm distraughtly in black veils. Bronwyn is pushed forward (i.e., down-frame) toward her house by the mass of Ivor's friends carrying his body. She trips on a small stone wall, reacts slowly, then rushes suddenly to Ivor. But it does not matter where she goes, for the parade (and the retreating camera) bearing Ivor dead will not stop till it reaches her door and enters her home. She is led back by Mr. Gruffydd and father Morgan, separates herself, and alone in a halo of space retreats sobbing toward her yard, and then to her door, her path a crazy pattern of zigs and zags. A low picket fence frames screen-bottom. She reaches her door on extreme right, screams "Ivor!" and collapses. Gruffydd and Morgan rush across-frame to her; then Gruffydd rushes back to the left, as the camera pans with him. All this while the stream of miners continues. Reality, motion, change cannot be resisted by idealism, but only by participating in life's flow: next scene, Bronwyn's baby is born.*

Ford never took a second take, recalls Anna Lee (Bronwyn), and the above sequence, like most, was unrehearsed: the men were told merely to keep pushing her back. Instead, Ford fussed over wardrobes. "He would take one of his old handkerchiefs and tie it around your neck, which was a real mark that he liked you, and he'd come up and either adjust something or pick up your apron and tell you to put it in your hand and almost use it as a prop. He'd do all kinds of little things with wardrobe, and he must have had some idea why he was doing it. I never quite got the idea."[42] But it would change her mood. Like Ford's other bizarre tactics—his refusal to explain or rehearse—the wardrobe fetish channeled the actor into attentiveness to milieu, and thus to natural spontaneity.** "I was twelve years old," said Roddy McDowall. "I had already made about twenty films in England, and I wasn't naive. I knew what was going on. What stands out in my mind is that I never remember being directed. It all just happened. Ford played me like a harp. I remember him as very dear and very gentle. . . . He forged a unique sense of family with all of us."[43]

Along with *The Grapes of Wrath* and *Tobacco Road, How Green Was My Valley* may seem to constitute a social-consciousness trilogy. The pictures share a common theme: disintegration of a family, a culture, and part of the earth, due to economic oppression by the larger world outside. In fact, this is not really a Fordian theme and occurs in none other of his films (wherein there are more elements of growth and more multiclass viewpoints) but

*Death/birth juxtapositions occur in *Pilgrimage, Doctor Bull, Fort Apache,* and *7 Women;* cf. *The Long Gray Line.*

**Wyler had hoped to cast Greer Garson as Bronwyn; Ford cast Anna Lee. She feels the role compensated for the brighter career she would probably have had, had she not left her native England. She actually was pregnant during filming of this scene—unknown to Ford—and suffered the loss of a twin in miscarriage. This devastated Ford who, ever after, when casting her, would inquire, using his pet name for her, "Boniface, I want to know one thing: Are you pregnant?" (Anna Lee's real name is Joan Boniface.) (From author's interview with Anna Lee, March 1979.) Maureen O'Hara named her daughter Bronwyn.

doubtless owes its genesis to Zanuck, Dunne, and Nunnally Johnson. None-theless, Ford has been criticized, in each case, for neglecting "documen-tary" for "Hollywood" entertainment, and for emphasizing political *effects*, rather than causes and solutions. One might dismiss these arrant com-plaints, arguing that, even if they were true, people do not themselves al-ways comprehend the forces moving them and that, therefore, it is not nec-essary for us to understand, either, within the movie; in fact, it is more realistic (at least subjectively) if we do not. But, in fact, we do understand. For what *is* specifically Fordian in these pictures (we have seen it before, notably in *Judge Priest*) is the notion that people behave not from logic but from feeling. Facts have no value without character and character is feeling (indeed, a film character is essentially a locus of emotional forms). Social and economic analysis cannot precede merely from concepts and statistics: it requires emotional sensitivity as well; and this is why we have art, despite the efforts of those who would subvert it to political action.

In any case, more sociology would scarcely make *How Green Was My Valley* better, for it is not at all trying to be a movie about labor or even about coal, but rather about psychosis and the dialectics of individuality within family and social change. Moreover, the picture does explicitly pose the question. Why did the green valley turn to slag? And it does provide thorough answers: blind adherence to tradition, resistance to change. What is ironic is that these same complainers cite these movies as instances of *Ford*'s reactionism, as though, in light of his analysis of the valley's decay and Huw's wasted, psychotic life, he were inviting his audience to follow such example, and to "take [their] intelligence down a mine shaft"!

At the time he was making *How Green Was My Valley*, Ford, sensing America's entry into World War II, had already begun training his Field Photo Unit. As the youngest in a big family and as one who had also discov-ered books as a bedridden child, perhaps he identified with Huw, and with Huw's "fifty years of memories." Ford was forty-seven, and he too found it always difficult to let go of the past; but he could not countenance a fantasy isolationism that would lead to slaughter; it was time to quit the valley for-ever. In Ford's next movie, *The Battle of Midway*, the "drama" would lie in the hope to maintain Huw-like purity in face of war reality. But hope is dim in *How Green Was My Valley*; the holocaust looms. By the time of its re-lease, war had come to America.

WAR (1941–1945)

Sex Hygiene	1941	Audio Productions–U.S. Army
The Battle of Midway	Sept. 1942	U.S. Navy–20th Century–Fox
December 7th	1943	U.S. Navy

Numerous training, coverage, and reportage projects (see Filmography).

John Ford in Navy uniform.

Nearly a hundred films are credited John Ford before his war service resulted in his first documentary in 1941. Many of his subsequent documentaries are curious, collective, or anonymous projects, but, especially in the cases of *The Battle of Midway* and *This Is Korea!* (two personal masterpieces), they represent unique aspects of Ford, explore alternate styles of cinema, exploit various dialectical relationships with the audience, and anticipate many of the "modernist" techniques of Rossellini, or even Godard and Straub.

Briefly, Ford's stance is more didactic than in his story films, visual and aural elements are more disjunctively combined, and montage becomes linear and simple, designed, in Vertov's phrase, to describe "fragments of actuality," and from their accumulation to evoke actuality. But greater objectivity is not an aim. Quite the contrary: Ford's documentaries are all propaganda movies (with the qualified exception of *This Is Korea!*), and their attitude is unequivocal compared to the story pictures, wherein military duty gone astray is a constant theme.

Unlike some modernists, Ford did not throw away Hollywood notions of the reality of the cinematic image; but Ford did wish to exploit tensions between apparent actuality and obvious fabrication. Curiously, it is at those points that tension is most taut, at which both oppositions are being most fully exploited, that both cinematic and actual reality are most potently thrown at us.

> I am really a coward. I know I am, so that's why I did foolish things. I was decorated eight or nine times, trying to prove that I was not a coward, but after it was all over I still knew, know, that I was a coward. Courage is something . . . I don't know . . . it's pretty hard to define. All I know is *I'm* not courageous. Oh, we'd go ahead and do a thing but after it was over, your knees would start shaking. I was not gallant or anything else. It just happened that way.[44]

War was another test for Ford. He plunged into it typically, with consuming commitment and total detachment. That was always his tragedy and genius: he was never exhausted by his passions; part of him remained outside, lonely and unsatisfied. Photos of him during the war are often breathtakingly romantic: his eyes hide beneath dark glasses, he wears leather jackets, sports a pipe mythically, his poses are larger than life. But if Ford adored military panoply, he abhorred its stupid slaughter. Perhaps he acted out boyhood fantasies, but he went off to war carrying not a gun but a camera, trading shots of film for shots of bullets.

He had been rejected by the navy during World War I for his poor eyesight, and an appointment as a photographer in the Navy Flying Corps, politically wrangled by his father, did not come through—if it ever did—until after the armistice; but somehow he got a Victory Medal.[45] Through his wife he had many friends in the Pacific fleet; he was given a reserve commission as a lieutenant commander in September 1934. He regularly filed intelligence reports on Japanese activity off the Mexican coast—on land he would stroll from bar to bar, accompanied by Wayne and Bond and followed by a hired mariachi band—and it has been claimed that he was acting as an undercover spy during his two trips to the Philippines. (If so, he fooled George O'Brien.)

Now, to record the history of the coming war, he began in 1939 to plan the most ambitious documentary film project ever undertaken. To this purpose, he recruited and trained his own film corps, consisting of Hollywood technicians each of whom became able to do everything. And they were drilled weekly by ex-marine Jack Pennick. Most were "over age and rich," as Mary Ford said, "people who could never have been drafted, but when Jack said, 'Let's go,' they obeyed him."[46] At first, the navy declined to take them as a reserve unit, but finally Colonel "Wild Bill" Donovan accepted them into the foreign intelligence agency Roosevelt had secretly ordered him to set up. Ford became chief of the Field Photographic Branch of the Office of Strategic Services (OSS, later the CIA); his only superior was Donovan, whose only superior was Roosevelt. "Our job," explained Ford, "was to photograph both for the Records and for our intelligence assessment, the work of guerrillas, saboteurs, Resistance outfits. . . . Besides this, there were special assignments."[47] Ford's unit made a great many films, some of which were only projected once, and in the greatest secret, before a few government leaders.

Sex Hygiene (1941). The first project, apparently undertaken prior to the unit's acceptance, was a curious instructional epic produced by Zanuck for the army and titled *Sex Hygiene*—VD ignorance had caused more harm than all World War I's battle casualties. Ford's first documentary shows tendencies that reappear in the others: the enclosure of the documentary material within an outer narrative or theatrical framework, and repetition. GIs are marched into a theater, where they view a film in which a doctor shows films (films within a film within a film) of pus-oozing penises, raving maniacs, and, as an example of how not to get help, a boy getting a bottle from an evil-looking pharmacist. We learn disease may spread by hand contact while watching Pete buckle his belt beside a statue of Venus before passing his cigarette to another guy. Over the doctor's final warning come fourteen close reaction shots of soldiers, a tiny track inward with each. A musical comedy was being filmed on a stage next to the one Ford was using at Fox, and he caused quite a stir when he sent his syphilitics over in wheelchairs to watch the half-naked dancing girls.

Field Photo was ordered to Washington in September 1941; it consisted of fifteen crews (ultimately, 175 men and 35 officers), a lab, and offices in the South Agriculture Building. Ford's home for two years was "a tiny broom closet of a room" (number 501) in the Carlton Hotel, until he finally found an apartment on the third floor of 1636 Connecticut Avenue. In December he accompanied his crews to Iceland to film a report on the Atlantic fleet and to Panama to report on canal defense. Since documentaries by regular army or navy photo crews would have tended to be whitewashed within service bureaucracy, Ford's OSS unit proved its worth to Roosevelt immediately.

The afternoon of December 7th, Ford, Mary, and Barbara were dining at the Alexandria home of Admiral William Pickens, chief of navigation. "The phone rang," Mary recalled, "and the maid brought the telephone to the admiral, and she called him 'animal,' and she said, 'It's for you, animal.' He said, 'I've told you not to disturb me while I'm at dinner.' 'It's the war department.'

We all bristled up. And he said, 'Yes, yes, yes,' and he hung up. And he said, 'Gentlemen, Pearl Harbor has just been attacked by the Japanese. We are now at war.' Everyone at that table, their lives changed that minute. We all walked out of the dining room. Then Mrs. Pickens said, 'It's no use getting excited. This is the seventh war that's been announced in this dining room.'"[48]

Mary came from "a war-fighting family. Most of my brothers were lost in wars." She was to see almost nothing of Jack or Pat (in the navy) during the next three and a half years. In World War I, she had been a psychiatric nurse, and active in charity between the wars. Now she took over the kitchens at the famous Hollywood Canteen, a free club where celebrities entertained 6,000 servicemen a night; it kept her busy—and stable. *Araner* was leased to the navy for the duration for one dollar. The Fords joked later that they never got the dollar (but the navy did assume large upkeep and repair expenses).

The regular military resented OSS people snooping around. MacArthur never did allow them into his theater, and Ford had tried and failed to countervail FDR's order restricting OSS operations to outside the United States.[49] Ford himself was strongly disapproved of in many circles. He acted as unmilitary as he possibly could, and most of the men in his unit probably did not know how to execute a right-face.[50] He would skip important meetings, was seldom in uniform or even reasonably tidy, ran his branch with his customary disrespect for bureaucratic niceties, generally failed to show proper awe toward chiefs of staff, and outraged navy regulars by dining publicly with enlistees. To win friends, he would invite various officers and chiefs to screenings of his movies, when he would deliver a stock speech: "I've been wanting to see this picture myself. I never saw it after it was all put together." This was in line with his legend—the brash, instinctual Irish hard-nose who could knock off a *How Green Was My Valley* and not bother to look at it. Then after the screenings, Ford would pull out his big white handkerchief, wipe away a tear, and croak, "I'm glad I waited until I could see it with you. I didn't realize it was so moving."[51] His personal filming of the battle of Midway also won him esteem (plus a Purple Heart) for boosting the nation's fortitude as it sent forth its sons to die.

The Battle of Midway (1942). This type of film was virtually lacking formal precedent, one for which Ford had to invent something "new." And it was an occasion when critical reception mattered little but when the reaction of the *masses* to Ford's deeply personal essay on "war, and peace, and all-of-us" mattered terribly. Rarely is an artist given so vast a subject for his canvas, and rarely does his thought receive the interested attention of so vast an audience.

To this aim *The Battle of Midway* is directly manipulative: it seeks a deeper level of consciousness through a fuller exploitation of multimedia art. To be sure, Ford did not abandon staginess altogether, but he did not again stand so far off from his material after *The Battle of Midway* as he did before it. This is the deepening of feeling to which critics referred, after the war. It is the difference, perhaps, between a man who films his ideas and a man who films his experience. His vision expanded, to darken considerably, but also to discover a greater beauty in a cactus rose than was seen in *Stagecoach*. Compared to the moody thirties pictures, *The Battle of Midway* has a broader, more open style—mood contrasts are freewheelingly juxtaposed, hokum mixes with sublimity, man is viewed less transcendentally and more ambiguously.

Whatever else war might be, Ford tells us, it is regardless an ultimate sort of experience of one's life. What is life, or love, or death compared to it?

War at the Battle of Midway (June 4–6, 1942) took place over a three-hundred-mile battle area, the film informs us. It would be impossible to report such an event in cinema, if by "report" we intend a record not simply of events but rather of deeds and thoughts and emotions. War is an experience, but also it is an attitude: whoever experiences war or thinks deeply about it is altered in his thought.

> Ford shot it himself, standing on an exposed water tower and, according to onlookers, yelling at the attacking Zeroes to swing left or right—and cursing them out when they disobeyed directions.[52]

> I was not ready and when the attack arrived I had only an Eyemo, a 16mm camera. I shot film and continued to change the film magazines and to stuff them in my pockets. The image jumps a lot because the grenades were exploding right next to me. Since then, they do that on purpose, shaking the camera when filming war scenes. For me it was authentic because the shells were exploding at my feet.[53]

We frequently see the walls of Ford's shelter.

> I was on this tower to report to the officers who were 50 feet under the ground, to report exactly the position of the Japanese planes and the numbers and so on. I had one boy[54] with me, but I said, "You're too young to get killed," and I hid him away, I thought in a safe place. I just kept reporting. I'd say, "There's a plane up there, one of our planes shot down, man in a parachute, Japs have shot the parachute, the man landed and the PT boat went out . . ." I just reported those things and took the picture. I was getting paid for it. That's what I was in the Navy for.

> I was doing alright till I had a blast of shrapnel that knocked me out. I was wounded pretty badly there, however I managed to come to long enough to finish the job.[55]

Ford's tower was on top of the power house—the first objective in a raid. A wound in his left arm plagued him the rest of his life. And at his funeral in 1973 the flag from his Midway headquarters was draped on his coffin.

It was not a coincidence that Ford was there photographing it himself.

Ford at Midway Island, 1942.

He had asked to be there, to photograph the battle. And the thought is staggering, particularly if one regards Ford as the great poetic chronicler of American history. For this was the biggest naval battle of history, the turning point of the greatest sea war ever fought and, is it too much to say?—the moment when the United States became the dominant global power.

The most significant fact of *The Battle of Midway* is that it is authentic, and Ford at every moment wishes to remind us of this. The film goes as far as possible toward being an exception to Godard's dictum of the similarity of documentary and fictional cinema (i.e., that, once images reach the screen, there is no essential difference between a "real" Nanook building an igloo ["documentary"] and a staged Hitchcockian murderer lurking in the shadows ["fiction"]). There is all the difference in the world between the historical films of Ford and Rossellini and this actuality; and all the difference in the world, too, between filming the actuality of Forty-Second Street and filming the actuality of the Battle of Midway. The twin facts of its historic importance and of the ultimate nature of war draw us more deeply into its documentary than would otherwise happen. There is a unique sort of "reality" here; there is a closer proximity to life than exists in Ford's fiction films. The confrontation is starker, more vivid, more deeply encountered.

And it is personal. Since Ford was there, he reports the deeds, the thoughts, the emotions of this ultimate experience, reports them as he felt and experienced and performed them. It is even a sort of autobiography, for war is an extension of one's cognition, down toward hell, up toward heaven, and broadly across a horizon no longer two-dimensional.

Ford is filming philosophy along with experience. One thinks constantly of what it is to kill, to be killed, to be in deadly peril, to be a mechanic fueling death. Is it heroism? How scared are they? Do not misinterpret Ford's sentimentality: it is a sign of his breadth, not of his simpleness. These are our people, our friends, or they could be. The voices of the narrators throw us into the terrifying mundane reality of it, of war unthinkable. They speak directly to us—"You!" Like it or not, we are forced to respond.

There is a dialectic to this film that is posed to us constantly, one that turns itself into an argument for the justness of this war by one who hates war with profound feeling. Yet Ford argues not so much with logic as with senti-ment. There are streams of emotion that run the gamut of nearly every emo-tion. The succession of emotional forms—from peace to war to victory, from heroism to fear to courage, from individuality to paranoia to commu-nity, from innocence to sin to redemption, from dawn to night to dawn— constitute a reflective philosophy written into cinema and as such untrans-latable into words. The film's title symbolizes a struggle of conscience.

The Battle of Midway is a symphony in its succession of tones of light, of tones of emotion, of tones of movement. The wonderful score is inextricably woven together with the images involved at a given moment, the cutting, the words spoken by the narrators. The two battle sequences are not long, but for me real time slows, and each shot seems to last a hellish eternity. There are no dead bodies, and no blood; no more than Sophocles does Ford need to resort to such devices.* Here, as in battle scenes in all his other pictures, he relies on an intense, often surreal, "impressionism." *The Battle of Midway* is a picture that demands deep concentration and total involve-ment to yield its riches. It is not a movie for a small screen, or for soft speakers. The music and battle sounds stand in relation to the pictures somewhat as a rich musical accompaniment stands to a vocal line; the two are equally important and reciprocally supportive. If a formal precedent be sought, it can be found in the battle compositions so popular in nineteenth-century music. Only Beethoven's *Battle of Vittorio* (*Wellington's Victory*) is widely known today, but there were many such pieces, often for piano solo, and their tripartite structure (presentation, battle, aftermath—each of fairly equal length) is the same as that of Ford's picture. In cinema, there was

---

*Compared with most U.S. war-propaganda film, *The Battle of Midway* emphasizes death, danger, and vulnerability. *Fighting Lady* (de Rochemont–Steichen, 1945), for example, bor-rows much from *Midway* but is calculated to make parents think their sons are in capable hands against an inept enemy—with little sense of danger.

Eisenstein's *Alexander Nevsky* (1938), which, unlike Ford's film, places the Jubilation *after* the Lamentation, leading one to observe that all battle pieces may, by that choice, be divided into those who leave one celebrating or lamenting war. In any case, Ford's musical movie exemplifies the operatic Ford, an aspect of his style occurring at the high point of most of his movies, particularly—on a through-composed basis—in *The Black Watch, Mary of Scotland, Wagon Master,* and *The Sun Shines Bright.*

Nothing happens by chance in this film. And Ford's calculation in getting it released exactly as he wanted, and to the widest possible audience, belies the image of a man who would "just go out and shoot it" and then take off on a yacht trip leaving everything in the hands of the studio. After stopping in Hollywood to have the film processed, he flew straight to D.C. "His left arm was still bandaged, he needed a shave, and he looked as though he hadn't slept for a week," recalls editor Robert Parrish.[56] There was need for secrecy and haste. Word had gotten out of Ford's exploit and there was danger the film would be seized for interservice news pools. To prevent this, Ford dispatched Parrish and the film to Los Angeles—without orders— telling him to hide out at his mother's.

Ford assembled a rough cut, gave Parrish further instructions (one wonders how much initiative was Parrish's), brought in Phil Scott to dub sound effects and Al Newman to provide a score (Ford supplying the tunes). Dudley Nichols stayed up all night writing a florid commentary, which Ford had James Kevin McGuinness (a Metro production head) rewrite more folksily. Henry Fonda, Jane Darwell, Donald Crisp, and Irving Pichel came upon instant summons; Ford, reading from notes, told them what to say, and they said it into a microphone, imitating him—a twenty-minute session. During the editing, Parrish omitted McGuinness's lines, spoken by Darwell, about getting the boys to the hospital, which he found maudlin, and a furious debate ensued. "It's for the mothers of America," Ford explained. "It's to let them know that we're in a war and that we've been getting the shit kicked out of us for five months, and now we're starting to hit back. Do you think we can make a movie that the mothers of America will be interested in?"[57]

Because of interservice rivalry, it was important to give army, navy, and marines equal footage. When Parrish told Ford they were five feet short on the marines, Ford pulled from his pocket a five-foot close-up in 35mm color of the president's son, marine major James Roosevelt. That night, they took the print to the White House, FDR's support being necessary to get it released. He chatted all through the movie, then suddenly froze into silence when his son appeared. At the end Eleanor was crying, and the president proclaimed: "I want every mother in America to see this picture!"

Most of them did.* Ford, to prove a point, ordered Parrish to attend the

---

*Not without further difficulties: Eastman-Kodak, according to Wilkinson, at first claimed 16mm Kodachrome could not be successfully blown up to 35mm. Ford suspected the company feared cheaper production methods; after a month dragged by, veiled threats of government seizure helped loose the film from the lab. Then Technicolor made five hundred prints.

Radio City Music Hall premiere. "*The Battle of Midway* was the first film of its kind," said Parrish. "It was a stunning, amazing thing to see. Women screamed, people cried, and the ushers had to take them out. And it was all over the material that we had fought about. . . . The people, they just went crazy." And the film went on to win an Academy Award.[58]

Never was Ford to make a film more cinematically and formally perfect than *The Battle of Midway*. The concision of its seventeen minutes never demands concession to amplitude.

Titles. A legend emphasizes: report, actual, authentic. A map situates Midway Island midway in the Pacific.

I. Exposition. (1) *Midway Island.* Bright blue Kodachrome sky and lively music induct one into the movie. Crisp's voice addresses *us:* "Our outpost. Your front yard." (2) *The Marines.* But cutting abruptly closer to a marching marine column, just as a male chorus enters the instrumental hymn ("*First* to fight . . . "), Ford produces an operatic effect: the future heroes present themselves. This is a necessary device in an epic; but we know some of them will actually die, soon. (3) *The Birds.* Crisp: "These are the natives of Midway. Tojo has sworn to liberate them." But our flag dissolving into blue sky and birds (whose voices abruptly follow the "Hymn"'s cadence) suggests they are *American* birds, free as the sky. (4) *Sunset Before Battle.* "The birds seem nervous." A sailor plays "Red River Valley" (dubbed by Dan Borzage) as others gaze into a sunset whose red flames suggest the Japanese battle flag: muffled explosions.

(5) *The Air Force.* As B-17s are prepared, Jane Darwell exclaims: "That fellow's walk looks familiar. My neighbor's boy used to amble along just like that. Say, is that one of them Flying Fortresses?" Henry Fonda: "Yes, ma'am. It sure is!" Darwell: "Why it's that young lieutenant! He's from my home town, Springfield, Ohio. He's not gonna fly that great big bomber?!" Fonda: "Yes, ma'am! That's his job! He's the skipper!"

Darwell's and Fonda's voices play a different role than Crisp's and Pichel's. The latter are informed commentators; the former seem to speak from the audience, speaking *to* the film. They engage us in actuality, in a dialectic with it, and help us admit these soldiers as representative of our friends and neighbors. (Also, Darwell and Fonda were readily identifiable as folks from *The Grapes of Wrath*, while Crisp carried patriarchal authority from *How Green Was My Valley*.)

But Darwell's role is more complex: she questions the film and it replies to her. When she says, "Will's dad is an engineer. Thirty-eight years on the old Ironton Railroad," the film obediently dissolves, with homey music, to Dad oiling a locomotive, then turning in a closer shot to look into the camera. (Gregg Toland shot the "Ohio" scenes.) Darwell, not so much narrating as

Figure 6. *The Battle of Midway*

Timing	Divisions	Music /(Sound)
0:30	**Titles**	"My Country 'Tis of Thee"
4:56	I. **Exposition**	
1:00	1. Midway Island	"Anchors Aweigh"; "Yankee Doodle"
0:22	2. The Marines	"Marine Hymn"
0:35	3. The Birds	(Bird sounds); bird motif
0:35	4. Sunset Before Battle	"Red River Valley"; (bombs)
2:22	5. The Air Force	
0:50	a. Council	"Columbia, Gem of the Ocean"; "Off We Go"
0:40	b. Crew and flash home	Homey folk tune
0:52	c. B-17s take off	(Engine sounds)
5:35	II. **The Battle**	
3:35	1. U.S. Defense	
1:25	a. Japs attack, bomb	(Gunfire, plane drones, bombs falling)
0:35	b. Flag-raising	"Star Spangled Banner" (explosions)
1:35	c. Jap planes shot down	(Battle sounds)
2:00	2. U.S. Counteroffensive	(Battle sounds) "Anchors Aweigh"
4:50	III. **Aftermath**	
1:00	1. Flyers return	"Anchors Aweigh"
0:35	2. Birds still free	"Marine Hymn"—slow
0:20	3. Search for survivors	"Anchors Aweigh"
0:55	4. Survivors return; hospital destroyed.	"Anchors Aweigh"; "Onward Christian Soldiers"
2:00	5. Funeral on land; on sea; recapitulation.	"My Country 'Tis of Thee"
0:50	**Coda**	"Off We Go"; "Anchors Aweigh"; "Marine Hymn"; "Over There"

16:51

talking privately to someone else, continues: "And his mother. Huh, well, she's just like the rest of us mothers in Springfield, or any other American town." Mother sits knitting, red flowers beside her, a service star on the wall; then we see a girl talking on the phone, a red ribbon in her hair: "And his sister Patricia! Eh! She's about as pretty as they come!" Fonda: "I'll say so!"

As the B-17s take off, Darwell calls, "Good luck! God bless you, son!" Again Ford wants to engage us, but even if we do not support Darwell's sentiment, we must relate to its ramifications. Eight consecutive pans of B-17s taking off set a tone of mechanical strength thrusting forth. The constant birds increase their association with America: like the airmen, they amble and fly.

　　　II. The Battle. (1) *The U.S. Defense* (3:35). 1/Sky, five Jap planes. Crisp, hurried: "Suddenly, from behind the clouds: The Japs Attack!" (Din of battle noises.) 2/Soldier with field glasses looks from foxhole. 3/Sky. 4/AA gun-barrel fires from foxhole. 5/Japanese plane flies through shrapnel. 6/AA gun again. 7/Plane through shrapnel. 8/Two boy soldiers at AA gun in foxhole.

　　　9/Two USMC planes take off, pan right. Unidentifiable male voices call, "There go the Marines!" 10/Pan right with two more USMC planes. 11/ Again, several more. 12/=2: soldier with field glasses looking up. 13/Planes directly overhead. 14/Two boys in foxhole, from above. 15/Their AA gun firing. 16/From Ford's hut: plane flies along beach, suddenly there's an immense EXPLOSION; film slips sprockets, rights, camera shakes. 17/In long-focal lens and perhaps slow motion: debris floats through air (cf. Antonioni's *Zabriskie Point*). 18/Plane swoops overhead in CU. 19/AA gun firing. 20/Sea and sky full of shrapnel. 21/Two boys. 22/Their gun again. 23/Planes above; EXPLOSION loosens film; explosion on beach and its smoke. 24/Overlooking base, fires and beach. 25/Similar. 26/Island ground: fire and wreckage. 27/Hangar, burning, pan right into smoke. 28/ Plane above: EXPLOSION, loosening film; looking out from hut, debris falling. (Instrumental strains of "The Star Spangled Banner" begin just after this explosion.)

　　　29/Men running rapidly through fiery debris. 30/*A flag detail is attaching U.S. flag, while others race by seeking shelter. Behind them a marine with field glasses kneels on one knee looking up at sky. Choir enters with,* "And the rockets' red glare . . ." *The flag is raised, slowly, the camera panning up in steady steps: a lengthy shot midst rapidly cut ones. As the flag is raised Irving Pichel's voice says,* "Yes, this really happened." 31/White sky

The Battle of Midway (1942).

with bursting shrapnel—". . . bombs bursting in air . . ." 32/Fiery smoke-cloud—". . . gave . . ." 33/The flag, frame filled with black smoke—". . . proof through the night . . ." 34/Long shot, slightly tilted up, the brilliantly sunlit *flag*, its pole; the *blue* sky filling upper left diagonal, the *black smoke* churning through right diagonal. A few *birds* fly through smoke—". . . that our flag was still . . ." 35/Quick shot of plane flying through fiery smoke—". . . there!"

36/Beach, abrupt EXPLOSION. (End of music.) 37/Fiery smoke-clouds. 38/Black smoke. 39/Billowing fire and black smoke. 40/Two boys in foxhole shooting. 41/Shrapnel-filled sky. (Plane drone, distinct.) 42/AA gun-barrel firing. (Drone continues.) 43/Droning plane in air is hit and explodes. 44/Jeep careens through fiery debris. 45/Tremendous EXPLOSION on ground rocks film; camera jerks around to left, then pans right to medic attending man. 46/Plane flying in air. Camera pans around base; sound of bomb falling, then EXPLOSION. Film jumps and when it steadies, camera looks out from hut toward base. 47/Again, from the hut.

48/The base, with huge black smoke-cloud, pan up along it. One bird flies through. (During this shot begins distinct drone of plane, which will occupy the soundtrack through shot 55.) 49/Long shot: hangar, billowing cloud of fire pours from it, and out of the fire pours the huge black smoke-cloud. (Drone continues.) 50/Closer shot of fire-cloud. (Drone . . .) 51/Two boys in foxhole firing AA gun. (Drone . . .) 52/Air filled with shrapnel. A metallic CLANK. Camera rocks. The clank stops the droning sound: now the plane is heard to cough a few times and then starts falling earthward. This sound continues in ever-rising crescendo for almost fifteen seconds. 53/During this crescendo, the camera looks over burning installations, smoke rising, then pans slowly leftward. 54/The two boys—crescendo nearly deafening. 55/Looking up to sky from sandbag ridge in foxhole: plane careens diagonally across sky, crescendo increasing; it hits earth, rocking camera, which jerks. 56/Plane wing: fire burns in circular Japanese emblem. (Fire sound.)

It goes without saying that, while the footage is actual, the soundtrack was added later.

(2) *U.S. Counteroffensive.* In terms of the film, the flag-raising inspires courage, the plane-downings signal the turn of battle, which now switches to the sea. Planes swirl dizzily above, but Ford keeps cutting to the carrier men fueling ammunition, their guns flaring the film red; he is fascinated by men and their might, by mechanical discipline in crisis, by the job of war, by the impersonal, unseen enemy. On our men's faces we glimpse intense excitement, happiness beyond intoxication. Strains of "Anchors Aweigh" succeed an immense explosion. We dissolve to Ford's hut window: the shot says "I was there. I am safe." (Lt. Kenneth M. Pier shot most air/sea footage.)

III. Aftermath. (1) *Flyers Return.* As pilots gaze joyously at the camera, Pichel says: "Men and women of America, here come your neighbors' sons. . . . You ought to meet them." But his phrase "home from a day's work" is disturbing. War may be a job, but killing and winning are not so intoxicating for us as for those living it. The faces alienate while attracting. Ford is fascinated: they are heroes, but theirs are deeds difficult to comprehend. (4) *Survivors Return.* As Crisp speaks of pilots "eight days . . . nine days . . . ten days without food or water," the film flares red between his words, as an exposure-shocked survivor emerges, expressing painful endurance. Others arrive, Pichel's stern naming becomes epithetical, mythic. The melody "Onward Christian Soldiers" enters, cutting and panning take on lofty, jubilant rhythms. "Logan Ramsey." Pans with a stretcher, cut to another . . . ; the hymn swells. "Frank Sessler." As two enter an ambulance and it pulls off, the hymn begins a glorious canon; Darwell: "Get those boys to the hospital! Please do! Quickly. Get them to clean cots and cool sheets. Get them doctors and medicine and nurses' soft hands. Get them to the hospital! Hurry. Please." A choir enters the hymn on "clean": "*Onward Christian soldiers, marching as to war! With the cross of Jesus marching on before!*" Meanwhile we pan a destroyed building; as the choir sings, "*war,*" the pan switches direction, ending on the red cross that was to have safeguarded the bombed hospital. Poignantly, the movie has tried to respond to Darwell with images. The hymn is a prayer; it says: "*Be* Christian." It is a hope. Ford seeks reassurance, justification, for war. Darwell's plea is part of this dialectic; these soldiers are "ours": how would *our* mother react were we in the ambulance?

With tolling bell, the red cross fades into (5) *The Funeral.* Deep-hued light of late afternoon, the camera tilted up toward faces shadowed by dusk and history. PT-boats churn through sea deeply blue, as a choir sings the second chorus of "My Country 'Tis of Thee"—"*Author of liberty*"—directly over a coffin draped in gleaming red flag. Even the white-topped waves rise and fall with the hymn, as we pan up to billowy clouds ("*Freedom's holy light*"), then down to the island ("*Protect*"), dissolve into a pan in opposite direction, following three planes to center on a shot recapitulating

four themes: a soldier kneeling with field glasses (*watchfulness*), birds flying (*freedom*), both oblivious to the huge black smoke-cloud (*danger*); the planes (*strength*) ("*and Guide Thy might*"). Cut to a scene overlooking the base ("*Great God our King*"), then to the flag, its colors strongly etched against black smoke, but this time the camera is not tilted upward: the difference between courage and faith, hope and security ("*Amen*").

A coda, added at FDR's request, swishes paint across three successive signs tabulating the Japanese vessels destroyed.

Meanwhile, after accompanying Doolittle toward Tokyo and participating in raids on Marcus Island and Wotje, Ford in August 1942 flew to London, and checked comfortably into Claridge's. (His flight had laid over in Ireland, where John had joked, "There are only two neutral countries in all of Europe: the peace-loving Irish and those cowardly Swedes."[59]) His job in England was to prepare Field Photo crews for the invasion of North Africa—at Oran, Algiers, and Casablanca, November 8—and for this purpose his men were sent to commando schools in Scotland. Ford himself reached Algiers November 14 and a few days later encountered Darryl Zanuck at Bone. Zanuck, now a colonel in the Signal Corps, was going through the war in such luxury and with such intense self-promotion that he was later singled out as an example of a "Hollywood Colonel" and forced into inactive service—one reason Ford took care to document his own contributions. At Bone Zanuck snapped a satiric photo—from behind—of Ford astride a donkey, then had it published in all the newspapers, to Ford's disgust. They had a sole cigar between them when a bomb nearly blew them to kingdom come; "Did it hurt the cigar?" Ford asked.[60] After Zanuck departed, Ford followed the American advance to Tebourba, where Field Photo filmed a gargantuan tank battle. On the way, near Souk El Arba, while photographing a dogfight directly over his head, Ford captured a downed German fighter, turned him over to Free French forces, then repossessed him when the French began torture. By late January Ford was back in Washington. He was responsible now for nearly six hundred people. Jack Pennick moved in with him, which made life a bit less lonely.

Around this time, Ford saw *The Ox-Bow Incident* and sent a note to director William Wellman congratulating him. And he added: "The only thing in the picture that didn't strike me as being real, Billie, was my brother Frank refusing a drink and making such a fuss about getting hung. After all, most of his ancestors have been hung and I just can't see Frank refusing a drink."[61] That June, Frank, aged sixty-one, dyed his hair and enlisted in the army, noting he had been too old for World War I. All went well during basic training at Fort Ord, until Frank tried to cash a Social Security check—and got discharged.[62]

Son Pat had gotten married in Maine and received a commission in the navy; but his eyesight was wretched and to his disgust he found himself stationed in Los Angeles as a public information officer. Only toward the end of the war was Ford able to pull enough strings to get Pat headed toward intelligence work. Mary was up to her neck in the Hollywood canteen and also was worrying over Ward Bond and John Wayne. Neither was in the service; they were both over the draft age, Bond was epileptic, while "Duke" (the nickname came from a dog he had had as a boy), with four children, had waited until too late to apply for a commission and was unwilling to enlist as a private. Ford got Wayne onto a USO tour in MacArthur's theater in the South Pacific—where the OSS was banned—and then had Wayne write up a report for the OSS.[63] But much of the time Duke and Ward were hanging around Ford's house engaged in antics. Duke set Ward's bedclothes on fire to wake him up once, and another time, after Ward bet him he could not knock him off a newspaper and then closed a door between them, Duke punched Ward by driving his fist right through the door.[64] There were more serious problems, too. "Can't you write and try and beat something into Duke's head," wrote Mary to Jack. "I've practically been sitting on Josie [Wayne's wife] to prevent a divorce but now guess she will have to get up for decency's sake and try and save a little for the kids before it's too late. He has gone completely berserk over that Esperanza Bauer and cares for no one. Thinks he is the hottest set in pictures and says he is madly in love and nothing else matters. It's a damn shame that with a war going on he has to think about his lousy stinking tail. I only think of those gorgeous kids. It's really tragic. Bond is drunk three-fourths of the time and as Pat says, 'When the cat's away how the mice will play.' Guess without you they're bound for destruction. . . . [One of Duke's leading ladies] was talking about him the other day and said (this is funny), 'I tried to help him. I knew he couldn't act without being coached. He said Ford took him home at eight and helped him with his next day's scenes. I tried that too but it didn't work.'"[65]

Meanwhile in Washington, Ford was under considerable opprobrium. Soon after Pearl Harbor, Donovan had ordered Field Photo to film a secret report on the attack—what happened and who was to blame. The perilous situation of OSS units poking into that sensitive affair had been further exacerbated at Pearl by the somewhat undiplomatic manner of Gregg Toland, famed cinematographer of *Little Foxes, Grapes of Wrath, Citizen Kane,* etc., whom Ford had assigned to direct. (Ford went out to Pearl in May 1942 and is listed as co-director.) The finished film, *December 7th,* a bitter exposé of how administrative oversight had left Hawaii vulnerable, was judged outrageous and politically disruptive. It was confiscated, never released, and Roosevelt issued a directive subjecting all future Field Photo material to censorship, lest it injure national morale. Disgusted, Toland had gone to Rio to film a report on Brazil (Ford visited him there during a month-long trip in May 1943). And Donovan, to avoid having Ford officially reprimanded, got him out of the way by putting him on an unescorted munitions freighter that left New York October 4 and reached Calcutta November 25. While Ford's men were puzzled why they had not flown, Ford himself was glad for the rest and, as usual, loved a fifty-five-day sea voyage.[66]

December 7th (**1943**). The eighty-five minute, unreleased version of *December 7th* survives in the National Archives. On December 6, 1941, a character called "U.S."—a traditionally garbed Uncle Sam (Walter Huston)—is musing about "Hawaii, Territory of Heaven," but white-suited Mr. C (for Conscience: Harry Davenport) suggests U.S. is complacent. U.S. narrates the cultivation of Hawaii, comparing it to the winning of the West. Sugar cane, pineapples, big business. From grass huts to modern Honolulu, its university libraries, schools, arts academy, streets, homes, trees, churches, hotels, beaches, ports (typically repetitive: e.g., not *one* exemplary church, but eight different churches), businesses. "The Big Five" companies: "Castle & Cook, Alexander & Baldwin," etc., "the nerve center . . . of the territory. Grandsons, aunts, held together by blood ties and interlocking directorates. Scratch one and the other bleeds."

But, says C, the laborers are mostly Japanese, 37 percent of the population, at work in fields, restaurants, flowermarts, their streets, slums, Japanese telephone book, magazines, banks, their own "Big Five." Thirty-two(!) Japanese shop signs, with superimpressions of street life. Japanese boy scouts salute the flag. But the Japanese language is taught, too, "along with their morality and their culture" and their Shinto churches. Declares a monk:

— In Shintoism we worship the first Japanese emperor, whose
  creation started the world of mankind. . . . [Emperor Hirohito] is
  the mortal image of our immortal deity. . . . Shintoism preaches
  honor of the ancestor, thereby keeping alive the fires of
  nationalism and preserving a racial and social bond with the
  unbroken and divinely descended Imperial dynasty. To be a Shinto
  is to be a Japanese. This is not, nor can it be, a matter of choice. It
  is a duty.

Seventeen thousand Hawaiian children are registered for Japanese citizenship; the consulate carries on extensive espionage. We see various eavesdropping Japanese: a gardener outside a men's room, girls in a barbershop, a chauffeur, a girl on a date. A Nazi tells the consul how overheard club talk helped him sink a destroyer (a frequent "plot" in propaganda films).

But U.S. remains optimistic. Nine lovely girls represent minority groups; children perform ethnic customs; six girls say "Aloha." But U.S. dreams of the war in Europe. And, Sunday morning, the squadrons appear, "swooping down like flights of tiny locusts," as Japanese envoys confer in Washington. Ten minutes of battle footage.* Fifty of two hundred planes are downed,

---

*All this footage (accepted as actual for years) was staged by Toland and Ray Kellogg, mostly at Fox, using rearscreen. Similarly, actors and studio sets were employed for much of the background material. According to William T. Murphy ("John Ford and the Wartime Doc-

but 2,343 Americans die. The camera frames a grave. "Who are you boys? Come on, speak up some of you!"

A voice identifies itself as Robert L. Kelly, USMC. We see his picture on the wall at home. He comes from Ohio, he tells us, and introduces his parents. The *same* voice continues through six more dead soldiers, each representing different services, different regions, different racial origins. Iowa parents pose American-Gothic-like before their silo; a black mother hangs laundry. "But, how does it happen that all of you sound and talk alike?" "Because we *are* all alike. We are *all* Americans." Notably Fordian is the funeral held on a shore midst white sand and flags (terribly beautiful photography). A tenor sings "My Country 'Tis of Thee"; an elderly officer and wife stand in attendance, she struck with such fragile sorrow that, though it looks actual, one suspects Ford posed her in his patented way; tracking shot looking up at palm trees.

From a map of Japan a radio tower arises, a Godzilla-like monster sprouting waves: our narrator corrects Tojo's victory claims. Before-and-after shots chronicle salvage operations. "Who is that saucy little girl . . . ? [A small ship sailing past.] By George, it looks like . . . Yes! It is! The mine-layer *Oglala* . . . !" *Now* Hawaii prepares for attack. Barbed wire, tunnels, drills, children in gas masks. Some Japanese buy war bonds; others are forced out of business, others arrested. But not a single act of sabotage. All traces of Japanese language are removed, all those signs changed, temples closed.

In Arlington Cemetery a Pearl victim talks to a Marine casualty, who points out where everyone's buried. "I saw the General the other day," he says, meaning Washington. The World War I vet is cynical but the sailor says, "I'm putting my bets on the Roosevelts, the Churchills, the Stalins, the Chiang Kai-sheks!" Twenty-four UN flags pass in review.

In 1943, Ford eliminated *December 7th*'s finger-pointing, changing it from an investigation to a paean of the navy's ability to bounce back. This thirty-four-minute version omits U.S., Mr. C, and the analysis. And it won Ford his fourth Oscar in a row.

After some time in New Delhi, Ford, always accompanied by Jack Pennick, flew to Rangoon where Field Photo was making a propaganda film in support of Mountbatten (*Victory in Burma*, directed by Irving Asner). In Rangoon he met Donovan and together they flew to Assam. Donovan insisted on parachuting into Nazira, and Ford of course was obliged to parachute too, with some fright. The next day he saw planes landing at the airstrip and realized Donovan and he could have as well. Colonel Carl Eifler

---

umentary," *Film and History*, February, 1976, pp. 1–8) there was no actual U.S. film of the attack, only Japanese, C. Daughtery, however, shot two hundred feet in 16mm and Lt. Comd. Edward Young shot one hundred feet of 8mm Kodachrome, and this footage was lent to Field Photo as reference, according to documents in the John Ford Papers (Lilly Library, Indiana University).

was in command of OSS operations in the Far East, and Donovan wanted to prove to Congress that the OSS's daredevil guerrilla activities behind Japanese lines deserved support. Here in the jungle a priest, James Stuart, was training Kachin tribesmen as guerrillas, and Ford, deciding to incorporate the Kachins into the Mountbatten film, left Guy Bolte, Bob Rhea, and Butch Meehan with Father Stuart; a few months later, Meehan was killed in action. Ford and Donovan went on over the Himalayas to Chungking and Kunming in order to establish OSS operations in China. Field Photo began an extensive program of aerial mapping, and Ford spent a month there training his men.[67] He also visited Tibet. After one camera crew was killed parachuting, Ford had to send in a second. In mid-January, he and Pennick flew back to New Delhi, and then, in a nine-day series of hops (Karachi, Masira, Aden, Khartoum, El Fasher, Maiduguri, Kano, Accra, Ascension Island, Natal [Brazil], Belem, Georgetown, Trinidad, Boringuin, Miami), they reached Washington on January 23, 1944.

In March, Ford took two weeks' leave at home—his only leave thus far, except for two days after Midway—and then in April was off for London, for D Day. Ford was in charge of U. S. Navy, U. S. Coast Guard, British, Dutch, Polish, and French camera installations—all seaborne photography for the United Nations.

When Ford had left Mark Armistead in charge of Field Photo in London, his only orders (for two years) were, "Do a good job for the OSS and the navy." Armistead's group made a few documentaries, but their chief labor was in the invention of reconnaissance methods, such as photographing through submarine periscopes. Armistead's biggest task was to develop aerial mapping techniques, for the Allies possessed no detailed maps of the Normandy beaches. (Later, after D-Day, with five planes known [but not to Ford] as "John Ford's air force," Armistead mapped most of Western Europe and had started on Russian-held portions, when Allied governments, realizing at last what valuable military information the U.S. was gaining, put a stop to it. Ford had to save him from a court martial, but Eisenhower told Donovan that Armistead's work alone justified the whole OSS.)[68]

The day before the invasion, Ford sent cameramen Brick Marquard and Junius Stout (Archie Stout's son; he was killed some months later) onto Omaha Beach with the Rangers, to prepare camera positions; others were sent in on the first wave. Armistead had mounted springwound cameras on five hundred landing craft. Ford rode a destroyer in the first attack. (There is a story, perhaps apocryphal, that he was commanding an observation vessel and, receiving a signal to turn starboard, he turned to port instead. A message came: "You turned the wrong way, you idiot." Ford read it and handed it to an aide. "Take this down to decoding," he ordered, "and have it translated immediately."[69]) Later on D-Day, Ford joined Armistead in a PT boat commanded by Johnny Bulkeley (the hero of *They Were Expendable*), where he spent the next five days. Bulkeley piloted Ford into some excursions with the French underground—experiences Ford recreated comically in *When Willie Comes Marching Home*—and Ford, keeping a promise, brought back some wine for director George Stevens, whom he had placed in command of British photography. Then he returned to London and got uncontrollably drunk.

Ford participated with Bulkeley in a PT boat operation in support of Yugoslav partisans, on the side of Tito's anti-Communist rival, Mikhailovitch. Ford groused that the business was "too full of lousy Oxford dons and aristocracy, princes and dukes and God knows what kind of White Russians."[70] Then he was detached by order of the secretary of the navy to make a propaganda movie about Bulkeley and the PT boats, *They Were Expendable*. When Ford got back to the real war, in July 1945, it was almost over. He went to Budapest to assist in the repatriation of Jewish refugees, filmed French forces entering St. Nazaire and Bordeaux, and sent a detail from Field Photo to cover the Nuremberg trials (see Filmography). On August 11 he was promoted to captain and on September 29 was detached from service.

As a condition of making *They Were Expendable*, Ford had asked MGM's Louis B. Mayer for the highest price ever paid a director, all of which he would contribute to the "Field Photo Farm." Sam Briskin, a Columbia Pictures executive, owned a twenty-acre estate in the San Fernando valley with a five-bedroom house, swimming pool, stables, and tennis court. Ford wanted to turn it into a clubhouse for his unit. He told Mayer that Mayer had been making money and movies while others had been fighting Nazis; now was the time to pay his bill. "Just pay me two hundred fifty thousand dollars. That will be my contribution. Then you throw in another two hundred fifty thousand to show that you are grateful to the lads for suppressing Nazism, and I'll direct *They Were Expendable* and get John Wayne to star in it. We'll get Cliff Reid as associate producer. . . . He's the best goddam associate producer in the business. Did a hell of a job on *The Informer*."[71]

Ford's motives were mixed. The war had made him no less egotistical than he had been before it, but, in almost everyone's opinion, it had made him a much *kinder* person. He wanted to perpetuate his leadership, and his unit's *esprit de corps*, into civilian life, but he also wanted to provide for his men. Any of them could live at the Farm free of charge, and this was initially a boon to those whose marriages and lives had been disrupted by the war. The Farm also served as a recuperation center for paraplegic veterans condemned to nearby Birmingham Hospital. Mary Ford organized regular entertainments for them. Christmas Eve and St. Patrick's Day were big, family occasions, with stars like Wayne, Fonda, or Andy Devine as Santa Claus. A small barn was converted into a chapel, a replica of Washington's at Mount Vernon, with stained glass windows from the church set of *How Green Was My Valley*. Here the central service of Ford's life was enacted each Memorial Day. Everyone from the unit (and most of the Ford stock company) was expected to be there. Bagpipers would march, a black choir sang "The Battle Hymn of the Republic," and the honor role of the dead was read. Ford knew every member of his unit, their wives and families, and supported many of the paraplegics, in addition to subsidizing the Farm by about $10,000 a year. Ford, said Mark Armistead, "was the only one of the Hollywood directors that fought who did not forget his men."[72]

Thirteen of them died in action; more than half were decorated.

POSTWAR: TRANSITIONAL PHASE (1945–1947)

They Were Expendable	12.20.45	Metro-Goldwyn-Mayer
My Darling Clementine	11.?.46	20th Century–Fox
The Fugitive	11.3.47	Argosy Pictures–RKO Radio

While all of the second period, 1939–41 in particular, is marked by themes of survival and persistence, Ford's three postwar films meditate on ruination, rather than on the victory culminating World War II and the preceding decade of social strife. *They Were Expendable* stares at destruction and regards survival as an onerous duty; *My Darling Clementine* allegorizes the war and loss of innocence; *The Fugitive* ruminates on destruction caused by attempts to impose justice (postwar foreign policy) and sees hope only in God. Thus, these movies are blacker than ever. Consciousness seems expanded, bolder, less facile, with a greater sense of evil and a searching quality. Also, expressionistic style seems fiercer, montage more articulating, and the operatic side of Ford in the ascendant. But these are sad films, there is a sense of waiting; this is a transitional period.

A dialogue with destiny begins. In contrast to the transcendental assurance with which duty was previously regarded, its source now seems more imminent. The hero may be mistaken about his duty, feel incapable of it, or wonder what it is. Free will returns, slightly.

In March 1946, Ford, seeking independence as numerous filmmakers were doing, incorporated his own production company, Argosy Pictures. In addition to eight brilliant Ford movies, the company also made *Mighty Joe Young*, with Ernest Schoedsack as director. The principal investors, besides Ford (chairman) and Merian Coldwell Cooper (president), were all OSS veterans: William Donovan, Ole Doering (a member of Donovan's Wall Street law firm), David Bruce (married to a Mellon and variously ambassador to England, France, Germany, and China), and William Vanderbilt.* So eager was Ford for this independence that he turned down a Fox offer guarantee-

---

*Argosy Pictures Corporation was capitalized at $500,000. Ten thousand shares were issued. Upon dissolution in 1956, Ford and his wife held 2,475 shares, Cooper and his wife 1,130, with another 1,095 in trust for relatives, Bruce and his (?) wife 1,992, Doering 2,000, Donovan's lawfirm 250. Sixteen other shareholders held small blocks of stock.

ing $600,000 per year. (His first attempt at independence—a cooperative group called Renowned Artists formed in June 1937 with Tay Garnett and Ronald Colman—had failed to get off the ground.) Argosy had actually produced *The Long Voyage Home* in 1940 and, very unofficially, *Stagecoach*, both through Walter Wanger. Its initial distribution agreement with RKO specified backing for *The Quiet Man* if its first picture were successful, but *The Fugitive* failed, and then Howard Hughes took over RKO. A new agreement with Republic was similarly formulated, but this time Ford made a western first. To hold down costs, and to bail out from *The Fugitive* disaster, Ford was especially sparing with film, perhaps exposing no more than one and a half times the finished length of *Fort Apache* and completing it and *She Wore a Yellow Ribbon* for about a million dollars *under* budget. Long disputes with Republic over *The Quiet Man*'s earnings—it appeared Republic was underreporting them—eventually resulted in a large settlement in Argosy's favor ($546,360.25 as I read the papers, twice that according to Dan Ford[73]), but the company ceased production in 1953 after Republic butchered *The Sun Shines Bright*. The new era of the superproduction made companies like Argosy less viable, even aside from the problems that were encountered with Republic. It had, however, realized a 600 percent capital gain for its major-risk investors, 30 percent for its minor-risk investors. Ford, in addition, had been paid approximately $1.5 million in salary, Cooper about $500,000. Cooper again worked with Ford on *The Searchers*, this time with C. V. Whitney money. Cooper's immense importance as Ford's producer, in handling myriad administrative details, became painfully evident in later years when Ford had to perform these tasks himself.*

---

*Cooper (1894–1973) was born in Jacksonville to a Scotch-Irish plantation family; his lawyer father became chairman of the Federal Reserve Board in Florida. After Lawrenceville and Annapolis (whence he resigned in his last year because of excessive exuberance), Cooper was a merchant seaman, a midwest reporter, a national guardsman fighting Pancho Villa, and an army flyer in France, where the Germans shot him down in 1918. He got shot down again, fighting Bolsheviks with Poland's Kosciusko Squadron, but escaped Russian prison after ten months, making it to Latvia with two others in twenty-six days. He worked for *The New York Times* and did a quasi-autobiography, *Things Men Die For* (Putnam, 1927) under the pseudonym "C." He then enlisted with cameraman Ernest Schoedsack in Edward Salisbury's round-the-world exploration; their movies of Ethiopia were burnt up in Italy, they wrote a book, *The Sea Gypsy* (1924), then with Marguerite Harrison filmed the 350-mile migration of Iran's Bakhtiaria tribe. This became the famous documentary *Grass* (1925), whose success inspired Paramount to finance Cooper and Schoedsack in *Chang*, in Thailand, and *Four Feathers* (1929). Well advised, Cooper had invested in aviation stock and soon found himself on the boards of Pan Am and several other airways. In September 1931 he became production assistant at RKO, taking over Selznick's job as production chief in February 1933. Along with the Whitney brothers, he invested heavily in the new Technicolor process, teamed Fred Astaire and Ginger Rogers, brought John Ford from Fox to make *The Lost Patrol*, and, with Schoedsack, made *King Kong*, in which transparencies were first used. In May 1933 he married Dorothy Jordan (Lucy Lee's mother in *The Sun Shines Bright*, Martha in *The Searchers*), resigned as production head, but continued to produce specials, such as *The Last Days of Pompeii*. In 1936 he became vice-president of Selznick-International but, failing to interest Selznick in a Technicolor *Stagecoach*, quit to form Argosy, bringing along some Whitney money. During the war, he was Chennault's chief of staff in China, assisted Whitehead's airborne invasion of New Guinea,

They Were Expendable **(1945).** The story is drawn from a short best-seller by W. L. White, an account of America's disastrous defeat in the Philippines from the viewpoint of a torpedo squadron and its commander, Lieutenant John D. Bulkeley (= Brickley here), edited from interviews with the second in command, Lieutenant Robert Balling Kelly (= Rusty Ryan).* Ford:

> What I had in mind was doing it exactly as it had happened. It was strange to do this picture about Johnny Bulkeley—I knew him so well. He was the fellow in Guantanamo who, when Castro cut the lines off, quickly installed the water system. During the [world] war, my district was around Bayeux, practically on the Coast, and it was pretty well populated with the SS and Gestapo. So instead of dropping an agent in, we took a PT boat, which Johnny always skippered himself—he refused to let me go in unless he skippered the ship. We used to go back and forth— we could always slip in there, if the signals were right—because the Resistance had told us the Germans never thought of guarding this one creek. We'd go in there on one engine, drop an agent off or pick up information, and disappear.[74]

Among the film's most ardent champions was the English critic (now director) Lindsay Anderson, who discussed it with Ford in 1950:

> Ford's attitude toward [*They Were Expendable*] so dumbfounded me that a whole tract of conversation was wiped from my memory. As a matter of fact, we were both dumbfounded. He was looking at me in extreme surprise. "You really think that's a good picture?" He was amazed. "I just can't believe that film's any good." I was amazed. "But—didn't you want to make it?" Ford snorted. "I was ordered to do it. I wouldn't have done it at all if they hadn't agreed to make over my salary to the men in my unit." He added: "I have never *actually* seen a goddamn foot of that film." I told him that horrified me. "I'll use the same word," he said, "I was horrified to have to make it. . . ." "Didn't you feel at least that you were getting something into it, even though you hadn't wanted to take it on?" He scorned the idea. "Not a goddamned thing," he said, "I didn't put a goddamned thing into that picture." He had been pulled out of the front line to make it, had just lost thirteen men from his unit, and had to go back to

---

then became deputy chief of staff for all air force units under MacArthur. He produced the first Cinerama spectaculars with Lowell Thomas, but left, with the Whitneys, when Warner Brothers took over. In 1952 he was awarded a special Academy Award "for his many innovations and contributions to the art of the motion picture." (See Rudy Behlmer, "Merian C. Cooper," *Films in Review*, January 1966, pp. 17–35.)

*A lawsuit followed the film's release: Commander Kelly was awarded $3,000 for John Wayne's "libelous" portrayal of him, while Lt. Beulah Greenwalt won $290,000 for Donna Reed's portrayal of her.

Robert Montgomery (Brickley), a navy officer, had actually commanded a PT-boat squadron in the Solomon Islands. He also directed the last few days of the movie (some back-projection plates) when Ford broke his left leg falling twenty feet from a scaffold and spent two weeks in traction.

Hollywood to direct a lot of actors who wouldn't even cut their hair to look like sailors. I said I found this particularly extraordinary because the film contains so much that needn't have been there if it had been made just as a chore. "What, for instance?" I made example of the old boat-builder (played by Russell Simpson), who appears only in a few shots, yet emerges as a fully, and affectionately conceived person. Ford relented slightly: "Yes, I liked that. . . ." He shifted his ground: "The trouble was, they cut the only bits I liked. . . . Is that scene in the shell-hole still there, between the priest and the boy who says he's an atheist?" "What priest?" I asked. "Played by Wallace Ford." "There's no priest in the film at all." This surprised him. I said I found it extraordinary that one could cut a whole (presumably integral) character from a story without leaving any trace. "M-G-M could," said Ford. I said: "But *Expendable* runs two and a quarter hours as it is. . . ." Ford said: "I shot that picture to run an hour and forty minutes—it should have been cut down to that." I said that this could not be done without ruining the film." "I think I know more about making pictures than you do," said Ford.

He asked me what the music was like; he had had fierce arguments over it. "But surely—it's full of just the tunes you always like to use in your pictures." But Ford had found it too thickly orchestrated, too symphonic. "I wanted almost no music in it at all—just in a very few places, like 'Red River Valley' over Russell Simpson's last scene. We played and recorded that as we shot it. Otherwise I didn't want any music; the picture was shot as a documentary, you know. No reflectors were used at any time, and we kept the interiors dark and realistic." He asked if that last shot was still in, with the aeroplane flying out, and the Spanish tower silhouetted against the sky; and what music was over it. He seemed satisfied when I told him it was "The Battle Hymn of the Republic."

But chiefly Ford was amazed at the thought that anyone could find *They Were Expendable* an even tolerable picture. "John Wayne had it run for him just recently—before he went back to the States. And afterwards he said to me: 'You know, that's still a great picture.' I thought he was just trying to say something nice about it; but perhaps he really meant it."[75]

Three years later, Anderson persisted in another article:

But made with reluctance or not, it is evident from the result that the subject and theme stirred [Ford]. . . . The film he made . . . had from the beginning to end the vividness and force of profound personal experience. Although (presumably) a recruiting picture in intention, it transcended its origins completely: fundamentally, the values and human responses of the film were those of *The Grapes of Wrath*—love and comradeship, devotion to a faith, the spirit of endurance that can make victory out of defeat. In its sustained intensity of expression, it was perhaps even superior as a poetic achievement.[76]

A month after their chat, Ford sent Anderson a telegram: HAVE SEEN EXPENDABLE. YOU WERE RIGHT. FORD. But thirteen years later, at UCLA, he again claimed he disliked it.[77] His ambivalence is understandable. He had been pressured into doing it, by Frank Wead and Jim McGuinness for over two years, then by Secretary of the Navy Forrestal. Meanwhile, he had met and come to admire Bulkeley and had tried to distill into the picture his own war reflections and experience. "Jack was awfully intense on that picture," recalls John Wayne, "and working with more concentration than I had ever seen. I think he was really out to achieve something."[78] Then MGM hacked away.

It is easier to imagine what MGM hoped to achieve: support for reconquest of the Philippines, with MacArthur beginning that task. But the war ended sooner than expected and what had been urgent present became historic past, a memory of sacrifice. The film now ends in 1941, with a lighthouse invoking the hopes of those left behind, and a preface by MacArthur recalls us to times gone. It is difficult not to believe that this was what Ford intended all along, for nothing in this plaintive, meditative movie seems calculated to arouse war fervor. And although almost every writer on Ford states that *They Were Expendable* was a critical and popular failure due to its release some months after the war had ended, when no one was in the mood for war pictures—Dan Ford writes it lost money and was soon withdrawn, Andrew Sarris claims it marked Ford's estrangement from the cultural establishment—in actuality *They Were Expendable* ranked among the year's top moneymakers. Like *The Grapes of Wrath*, it is a tale of disintegration and employs a protracted documentary-like approach, mingled with touches of expressionism. But, judging by the box office, Americans were overwhelmingly more stirred by Ford's lamentation for the war than by his lamentation for the Depression.

They Were Expendable resembles other Spig Wead scripts—*Air Mail, The Wings of Eagles*—an all-male world, almost self-sufficient, to which women contribute awkwardly. Men stand watching as comrades sail off to battle, then feign nonchalance at medals and tales of derring-do. For it's a job to be done— in this case, a sacrifice "bunt" to be laid down—and it's the team that counts. Which makes it all the more affecting that the team disintegrates through no will of its own: bases are deserted, men reassigned, boats junked, till only a few men remain, on foot yet. Along with materiel, life's normal rituals, too, are disrupted: dances, romances, phone calls, funerals. Only the professional, sporty traditions of duty and team remain. "Take care of him," says Brickley to a soldier, in parting, because—the final ignominy—the commanders, the coaches, are ordered to desert their own team.

All this Ford dedramatizes as much as possible. Rather than a charging plot, *They Were Expendable* is a series of quotidian episodes moving unemphatically but inexorably toward nullity. For these are the little men who see only the war in front of them, and rarely see even that. No Japanese are seen; the struggle is interiorized. Only the evacuation of MacArthur—not even the battles—takes on dimensions of an "event," and this for the man's symbolic value, rather than for the trip itself, which Ford elides. And so much is the emphasis on the group, not on the individual, that characterizations are extraordinarily recessive for Ford. Even in Robert Montgomery's Brickley it requires our aggressive attention to discern tics of personality, to discern an unprepossessing hero and a study in the art of command, as that command slowly evaporates.

Yet the picture's worth depends precisely upon our insights into those privileged instants when the individual does emerge in the group-member (and through his individuality reconsecrates the sanctity of the whole). Performances are gentle, laid back (but with some jaunty one-liners). As in *Wagon Master*, Ford enjoys extended two-shots of people chatting, but most dialogue here gets exchanged during "moments between," as though passing in a corridor or while awaiting a bus. Thus character seems all the more fugitive and precious a quality.

The victories Ford perceived in this defeat—proof of the PT boat and proof of moral fiber—are, however, exceeded by mortification that it happened as it did. Much of his outrage was deleted,* as with the censoring of *December 7th,* but much of it remains still: words of puzzlement that we were so unprepared, that the Japanese attacked so easily, that the navy ran away and the air force was gone, that so many men were expended to no purpose, in obedience to orders from an invisible and seemingly uncaring command on high.

Perhaps the reason Ford felt *They Were Expendable* a failure is that it is too protracted. No more than Lindsay Anderson can I suggest where Ford would prune thirty-five minutes, but even the dedramatized, episodic quality of the film would gain from concentration. As it stands, *They Were Expendable* lacks two qualities typical of Ford's best work: it is too seldom rich in invention (notably excepting its last fifteen minutes) and, partly because of MGM's ubiquitous jaunty march tune, there seems to be little sense of progression in its modal textures. Documentary style for Ford, after all, always meant not the unvarying flatness of Grierson but the structured variety of the "cinephonic" suites of Murnau or Jennings. Some moments of intense expressionism—the mysteriously lit face of the admiral issuing orders as retreating troops pour by in the background, or the fire-bordered road near the end—suggest Ford may have intended a film wierder, more psychotic, more like *Arrowsmith*, than what we have. At present, the battle scenes are so unintegrated into the atmosphere we experience that some critics have questioned whether Ford even wished them in the movie at all. He surely did, but as in all his other war pictures, as interludes of exhausting, preternatural catharsis, not, as now, as mere kiddie-matinee-like action.

*Sinclair (pp. 118–22) writes that the script had called for "voices" to ask questions about American unpreparedness, that Ford shot a bitter farewell address by Brickley to his men, and that "Ford's private message about valiant self-sacrifice for inscrutable commands" is perverted by the studio's having added "The Battle Hymn of the Republic" at the end.

My Darling Clementine **(1946).** With *They Were Expendable*
and *The Fugitive*, *My Darling Clementine* forms a dark trilogy of sadness,
hope, endurance, and yearning, of Manichaean drama pitting light against
darkness. While all three react to the experiences of World War II, *My
Darling Clementine* approaches allegory. Wyatt Earp (the U.S.) gives up
marshalling in Dodge City (World War I), but takes up arms again to combat
the Clantons (World War II) to make the world safe. Victory is horrible, and
Wyatt must return to the wilderness, to his father (confession; reconstruction), leaving innocence, hope, and civilization (Clementine) behind, "lost
and gone forever," a distant memory (the long road) in Tombstone (the world
of 1946).

So familiar is the mythic iconography of the hero within generic conventions of the western, that one may take Ford's mythicizing of Wyatt Earp a
bit too much for granted, even though *My Darling Clementine*'s black, expressionist, music-drama style, closely resembling *The Fugitive*, is remarkably self-conscious and exaggerated, even for Ford. Earp (like most Henry
Fonda roles for Ford) is a hero pure who knows his mind, talks seldom, lopes
calmly, gazes steadily, gets the job done; his very name inspires gapes of awe.
Initially, in the wilderness, he is framed with upward-gazing angles, sky-
backed poses, and Monument Valley monuments. Indoors, counterpointed by
mournful honky folk tunes, he inhabits a blackness streaked by clouds of cigarette smoke and spotted by gaseous lamps, and is sighted along distant lines of

perspective. Wyatt combines the godhood of Lincoln, the passion of Tom Joad, the directness of the Ringo Kid. Like many another Fordian hero, he comes out of the wilderness, rights wrongs, and goes on his way.

But Ford's topic is less the hero as archetype than the archetype's moody sensibility within a world of contradictions. Outwardly, Wyatt is perennially in passage—from black wilderness to white civilization—and in this he resembles Tombstone, which Ford typically seizes upon at a moment of transition in the making of America. "Wide-awake, wide-open town, Tombstone! You can get anything you want there," says Pa Clanton. But the nightly atmosphere of sinful roisterousness, in which nomads throw each other out of town and Jane Darwell's madam represents distinguished stability, is quickly giving way by day to a community of schools, churches, and Clementine Carters.

Inwardly, as Wyatt passes from one world to the next, his sensibility (like the community's) comes more and more into scarcely acknowledged conflict with itself, conflict between the Wyatt dutiful to the "high moral codes" of the wilderness actually existing and the Wyatt yearning for the values of civilization. Just sitting is a sensual, soulful pleasure, as for Judge Priest on his porch, Ole Mose in his rocker, Lincoln anywhere. But Wyatt's loafing, like his shave, poker, and (three!) meals, is repeatedly interrupted by violence and by duty (always paired). Duty disrupts his journey home to stop in Tombstone, and duty calls him back into the wilderness when that job is done. Wyatt embodies the Fordian hero's traditional urge to squat with his traditional obligation to wander. He likes to think of himself as an "*Ex-marshall*," but he becomes one again to find his brother's murderer. The weary gloom with which he accepts this duty, the self-consciousness with which he casts himself as an angel of vengeance and order, are not unfamiliar qualities for the hero, but the contradictions they imply are dwelt upon with unaccustomed emphasis (no doubt reflecting Ford's reaction to the war). Wyatt consecrates himself at James's graveside to the loftiest goals of civilized utopia ("When we leave this country, kids like you will be able to grow up and live free"), but he equally consecrates his personal vengeance, his honor of family, as lawful authority. Nobility in Ford seems often a virtue blooming in hypocritical soil: Huw's loyalty, Lincoln's bossy assumption of truth, the Fugitive's of martyrdom. We do not object to Wyatt killing the Clantons, nor even to his assumption of right to do so; what is worrisome is his alliance of implacable vengeance with legal and moral justification. Although he is in the community, even defines it, and helps establish civilization, he is actually a wilderness figure just passing through; he cloaks his wilderness moral code with the laws of civilization, and leaves a bloodbath behind him. He stays in Tombstone only four days, with motives initially opportunistic and only belatedly communal: i.e., he quiets the drunken Indian to get a shave, takes the marshall's job for family honor. True, he finds himself drawn to communal involvement: reversing earlier priorities, he ignores Brother Morg's plea to finish dinner, because he has "got" to get Doc to bed, and, characteristically, he allows himself to be seduced into attending the camp meeting, while his brothers exclude themselves from the community to pursue their private visit to James's grave. But when it comes to Wyatt's chief purpose, to get the Clantons, he seeks to exclude the community (the mayor and the deacon)—"*strictly* a family affair."

If Wyatt is aware of his contradictions, he is not perplexed by them. His simplicity encloses his philosophy. "*What kind of* town is this?" he exclaims. "*What sort of* town is this where a man can't even get a peaceful shave?" "*What kind of* town is this that sells liquor to Indians?"* Such lines are jokes, because Wyatt utters them with the sincere amazement with which Louis XIV once remarked, "I almost had to wait!" But Wyatt's lines also typify the questioning, Tom-Joad-like mixture of emotion and morality with which he confronts life. "Have you taken it into your head to deliver us from all evil?" someone asks; and Wyatt replies, "Not a bad idea. That's what I'm being paid for." Hamlet's soliloquy is not out of place midst this muddle of duty, vengeance, right, and doubt. Just what sort of world *do* we live in? And how do we define our answers? Does new awareness entail political consequences? Must we take up arms? As for Hamlet, the cost for Wyatt of "quietus" is bloody: a second brother's life is sacrificed to family honor. But we get the feeling Old Man Earp would agree with Old Man Clanton, that family duty precedes everything. This is the West, and moral codes rise monumentally out of the wilderness. Wyatt is enslaved to them. But can a land where people "live free" be built on such codes? Can civilization be founded on wilderness law?

This heart-of-darkness inquiry particularly permeates Ford's postwar films, notably, of course, *Liberty Valance*. Its irony is underscored in *My*

---

*"What kind of . . ." phrases occur often in Ford, often as dramatic-rhetorical devices—e.g., "What kind of man am I that . . . ?"

Darling Clementine with graphic expressionism. In frame 1 (p. 227), the need to arrest his friend Doc Holliday and the onus of avenging his murdered brother weigh heavily on Wyatt: the bar ramming massively against his guts symbolizes his duty, conscience, and heavy recognition of his own moral world determining what he shall do; he seems all the more heroic for being so humanly puny. So strong is the dynamic force of the bar-line across the screen, that when the Clantons lumber in from off-frame, their motion across the screen seems uncomfortably contrapuntal—the two compositional ideas seem more dissonant than complementary. And in fact, with the Clantons lined up along the bar (upper left) like feathers on an arrow, the bar no longer symbolizes Wyatt's superego, but an external hostility independent of his awareness. From being a crushed human enduring self-inflicted martyrdom, Wyatt becomes a portrait of comic myopia. Obsessed idealistically, he is oblivious to actual, threatening evil.

The same point is made earlier, when Ford sets an encounter between Wyatt and the Clantons, just after Wyatt takes the marshall job, in an eerie series of confrontational close-ups:* the Clantons' knowledge (they seem to be waiting for him) and Wyatt's intent obliviousness enclose them and him in worlds absolutely disparate, albeit momentarily tangential. People, in this movie, do not live in an objective reality, but in subjective ones enclosed by the limits of their knowledge, moral philosophy, and, above all, their sensibility. Subjectivity may be communal—e.g., the Clantons, the Earps, Tombstone, individual relationships. But by and large solipsism and loneliness suffuse this precommunal, precivilized world ("Ten thousand cattle gone astray," sings Chihuahua); people live separate lives and relate to divergent experiences. Ford "creates" these disparate emotional worlds cinematically, through composition, cutting, music, and acting styles, and by modalities mirroring subjectivity as they shift from *film noir* nightmare to poetic realism. The movie is virtually a series of skits, or turns, illustrating mostly abortive attempts at community: the Clantons vs. Earp; the Clantons and the Shakespearian actor; the deliberate grouping in one theater box of a bizarre collection of stereotypes; the actor's wacky embrace of the town drunk ("Great souls by instinct to each other turn, demand allegiance and in friendship burn. Good night, sweet prince"); the silhouetted argument between Holliday and Clementine; the crosscuts between Holliday operating and Chihuahua being operated on; the interrupted dinners; Clementine's pretending not to notice Wyatt when she gets off the stage; his farewell kiss to her; and, perhaps most spectacularly, this remarkable series of vignettes:

*180-degree crosscut CUs recur in *Wagon Master* between the goodies and the even more evil Cleggs who, like the Clantons, are given as degenerate, are motherless families with four perverted sons, whose father dies last trying to sneak a shot. Cf. *Two Rode Together, Liberty Valance* —more degenerate motherless families.

1. Pa Clanton leaves his empty, crypt-shadowed room. (His son Billy lies dead abed; Pa has just murdered Virgil Earp in revenge.)

2. Chihuahua: long-held close-up; melancholy after being operated on without sedation.

3. Doc Holliday, happily victorious after managing to perform the operation, is toasted by Wyatt. (The jovial town madam, who never has any trouble relating, points up the awkwardness of everyone else.)

4. But Clementine, at the saloon door, is snubbed trying to congratulate him.

5. Wyatt and bartender Mac (framed foreground, the Clementine-Holliday doorway scene occurring way downscreen between them) discuss romance.

In each case, the frame is the character's world, its atmosphere an extension of his personality; his or her viewpoint becomes the "only truth." Hence we pass from Clanton's black dementia, to Chihuahua's mortal despair, to Holliday's elation, to Clementine's depression, and now to Wyatt's jubilation— for Clem's failure with Holliday leaves her available for Wyatt. "Mac, have you ever been in love?" he asks, happily. "No," replies the bartender, con-

cluding this series of solipsistic vignettes, "I've been a bartender all my life."

Diversity of sensibility, one setting another in relief, is consistent with Ford's penchant for juxtaposing scenes of contrasting moods. Pa Clanton brutally whipping his sons sets into relief the magical scene next morning, when Wyatt balances his feet on the porch post, then awkwardly rises and takes off his hat as Clementine Carter (Cathy Downs) steps out of the stagecoach. From his reluctance to speak and from his lithe body's measured movements lofting her trunk, you know he has rarely felt so self-conscious—though his back is turned. Two Indians glide by on ponies, so quietly is the scene drenched in the air of vivid awareness. The gruff joke of Brother Morg (Ward Bond) ordering a gargantuan breakfast counterpoints this mood, but then everyone stares: a lady, civilization, has come to Tombstone. Being from Boston, she will start a school, and it is she, or perhaps what she represents, that entices Wyatt into their enchanted Sunday walk toward the tolling bell of the church-to-be and singing choir ("Shall we gather at the river," aptly). Their walk is prefigured earlier, as Wyatt escorts her down a hotel corridor toward Doc's room: its churchy shadows, like the walk to church, predict an alliance between Clementine and Wyatt, which will, however, probably never be, and predict the hallowed fulfillment of her lengthy quest for John Holliday, which will, however, be futile. The way she fondles John's things, in a room describing his personality, recalls the fondling of loved ones' objects in *Straight Shooting* and *The Grapes of Wrath*, except that there is a hint of repressed sexuality in Clementine's immersion of self into John's room. It is she who is evoked by the film's title, because it is darling Clementine who personifies the hopes and dreams of both men, one decaying, the other rising: their yearning for what is lost irretrievably—whether as Wyatt gallops down an endless road, destined to wander forever toward some mountainous fate as Clementine waits forever within the town fence

("I'll be loving you forever, O my darling Clementine!"), or whether as Holliday spurns her attempts to reach out to him:

— "You *are* pleased that I came . . . ? My coming has made you unhappy."
— "It was ill advised."
— "Was it ill advised the way you left Boston?"
— "How'd you know I was here?"
— "I didn't. Finding you hasn't been easy. Cow town to cow town. One mining town to another.* I would think that if nothing more, you'd be at least flattered to have a girl chase you!"
— "Look, Clem, you've got to get out of here . . . "
— "But I won't!"
— "This is no place for your kind of person."
— "What kind of a person am I, John?"
— "Please go back home, Clem, back where you belong. Forget that you ever . . . [coughing fit]. The man you once knew is no more, there's not a vestige of him left. Nothing!"
— "You can't send me away like this. Now I know why you don't care whether you live or die, why you're trying to get yourself killed. You're wrong, so wrong. You have a world of friends back home who love you as I love you."

"What kind of a person am I?" If John Holliday does not understand Clementine, she understands him even less. Now, destroying himself, dying from consumption and alcoholism, his lost ideals undimmed in memory, his stuffed bookcases and diplomas belying the stereotype he has become, he is the opposite of the Boston physician she recalls. "In fact," observes Wyatt, "a man could almost follow [Doc's] trail from graveyard to graveyard."

*The eliptical dialogue is typical of Ford.

Clementine has been pursuing a fantasy and, rebuffed, decides to go home.

"If you ask me, you're giving up too easy," says Wyatt. "If you ask me," she retorts, "you don't know much about a woman's pride." Her gentle control of her voice and refinement of gesture always contradict the passion of her words. Ford has made her manner opposite to her character. Clementine is from *Boston* (we know what that means, in Ford): she is willful, pushy, has crossed a continent all alone in search of her man, will found a school. It is she who asks Wyatt to church, and she who hints he ask her to dance.*

The situations of Wyatt, Holliday, and (the absent) Clementine are focused in the "To be or not to be" sequence. The pretentiousness of inserting Shakespeare into a western mirrors the advent of culture in the wilderness, and is both undercut and underscored by staging the soliloquy on a saloon table with a drunken actor (Alan Mowbray) and an uncomprehending savage audience (the Clanton boys). For once, Shakespeare is directed for maximum expressivity and intelligibility, as Ford has Mowbray speak slowly and with long pauses (indicated by □), and uses music, from an on-screen pianist, to accompany exactly, balance the verse into musical quatrains, and expand the actor's voice-pitch into melody of sorts.

> To be, or not to be: □ that is the question: □
> Whether 'tis nobler in the mind to suffer
> The slings and arrows of outrageous fortune, □
> Or to take arms against a sea of troubles, □
> And by opposing □ end them?

Wyatt, of course, opposes troubles (ought he to?), and Clementine and the Clantons also decide to take action. But Holliday prefers

> To die: □ to sleep; □
> No more; □ and, by a sleep to say we end
> The heart-ache □ and the thousand natural shocks
> That flesh is heir to, □ 'tis a consummation □
> Devoutly to be wish'd. □

Is not Wyatt in a kind of "sleep"? Holliday in a nightmare? Clementine in a kind of dream?

---

*Commentators are wont to contrast Clementine and Chihuahua as Ford's opposite female stereotypes. Clementine does resemble Grace Kelly (*Mogambo*) and many early ingenues, while good-whore Chihuahua resembles freely friendly Charmaine (*What Price Glory*). But to reduce Ford's women to two stereotypes is as superficial a criticism as it would be to reduce Ford's men to goodies and baddies. As always, the stereotype only begins to define a character. It is curious, though, how both women, with ambivalent mixtures of fickleness and survival-instinct, switch their gazes quickly from their hearts' desire to new lovers (Chihuahua to Billy Clanton, Clementine to Earp). In contrast to Hawks's western women —who are treated essentially as erotic fantasies and whose eroticism is always updated to the era of the film's release (e.g., the women in *Rio Lobo* are 1970-like Californians)—Ford's Clementine has her feet firmly planted on the earth. She pursues Holliday not simply from desire but to help him; rejected, she is independent enough to stake out her own future in Tombstone.

> To die, to sleep; □
> To sleep: □ perchance to dream: □ ay, there's the rub; □
> For in that sleep of death □ what dreams may come
> When we have shuffled off this mortal coil, □

These are thoughts that haunt Holliday specifically. Thus he silences the mocking Clantons—at whom the actor spits:

> Must give us pause: □ There's the respect □
> That makes calamity of so long life; □
> For who would bear the whips and scorns of time, □ . . .
> . . . the law's delay, □
> The insolence of office, □ and the spurns
> That patient merit of the unworthy take[s], □
> When he himself □ might his quietus make □
> With a bare bodkin? □ Who would fardels bear, □
> To grunt and sweat [under] a weary life, □
> . . . life . . . , life . . . *Please help me!*

And Holliday takes it up:

> But that the dread of something after death,

Although he has forgotten how to be a doctor, he remembers his Shakespeare and, as Wyatt watches with wondering concern, Holliday gives soul-searching resonance, with clouds of tobacco smoke swirling around him, to the next three words:

> The undiscover'd country □ from whose bourn □
> No traveller returns, □ puzzles the will, □
> And makes us rather bear those ills we have, □
> Than fly to others that we know not of? □
> Thus conscience does make cowards of us all . . .

Whereupon he breaks into a coughing fit.

Thus, *My Darling Clementine* concerns a search for a dream of justice, oblivion, or love, and breathes the langorous airs of loss. As if looking for answers, the camera stares at the sky after the battle and down the long road at the finish, at the moment that picture's title—and theme—become clear.

For a sad movie, *My Darling Clementine* is invigorated by much humor, invention, and sudden shifts of mood. Although Ford is at his best at moments of digression, Dan and Barbara Ford claim that Darryl Zanuck markedly improved the movie by reediting Ford's original cut frame by frame, deleting some humor and "sentimentality" (thirty minutes in all), and thus strengthened the storyline and pace. At this point the picture was previewed to an audience of two thousand that was immensely appreciative up until the final minute. Then, however, they laughed at Ford's original ending, wherein Wyatt shakes hands with Clementine rather than kissing her. Accordingly, but to Ford's chagrin, a kiss was inserted.

The real Wyatt Earp used to visit friends working at Universal during Ford's apprentice years, and Ford claimed to have recreated the Battle of the OK Corral according to Earp's account. Today, however, historians consider the movie's once respected sourcebook, Stuart N. Lake's *Wyatt Earp, Frontier Marshall*, to be a tissue of untruths designed by an Earp relative to create a legend around an unsavory character. Actually, Earp, Holliday, and the Clantons were leagued in a holdup racket; disagreements led to the OK Corral incident, which was a massacre, not a battle; afterward, Wyatt and Holliday quit town and the Clantons' bodies were left hanging in the butcher's shop. It was brother Virgil, not Wyatt, who was the sheriff in Tombstone; his wife's account is in Frank Waters's revisionist history, *The Earp Brothers of Tombstone* (New York, 1960). Ford's truer, and utterly different, portrait of Wyatt in *Cheyenne Autumn* (1964) probably reflects his reading since *My Darling Clementine*.

The Fugitive (1946). For his first independent production, Ford chose Graham Greene's *The Labyrinthine Ways* (or *The Power and the Glory*) which he had been planning to make before the war at Fox, but with C. V. Whitney financing it and with Thomas Mitchell as the priest. Most of what made Greene's novel famous—a fornicating, alcoholic priest drifting into ambivalent martyrdom—could not be filmed because of the Production Code,*and in a letter to Zanuck in 1946 Ford confessed, "It is really not a sound commercial gamble but my heart and my faith compel me to do it."[79] So, Henry Fonda was cast as the priest, and, with Dudley Nichols, Ford wrote a sort of Passion Play allegory as a screenplay. But once in Mexico, Ford jettisoned most of the script and, giving leave to his fancy, made a highly abstract art film. *The Fugitive* lost considerable money, caused a rift between Nichols and Ford, and has posed problems even for Ford's most devoted followers. Only the director himself consistently defended it. "I just enjoy looking at it."[80] "To me, it was perfect."[81]

And in terms of composition, lighting, and editing, *The Fugitive* may be among the most enjoyable pictures. For example, the opposing internal angles of frames 1 and 2 interlock with an interesting dynamism and, in bringing the peasant forward while placing the interrogating police lieutenant behind the peasants, the compositions reverse each man's actual power and

---

*The film: Pursued by a tormented police lieutenant (Pedro Armendariz), a priest (Henry Fonda) holds furtive baptisms, is nearly betrayed, almost escapes but returns for a dying man, is arrested trying to buy Mass wine, watches a hostage die in his place, is aided by the lieutenant's ex-mistress (Dolores Del Rio), and an outlaw (Ward Bond). Free at last, he is tricked into returning for the dying outlaw, and executed.

Two curious ironies of our prejudices toward film vs. literature: what was prohibited on the screen was widely assigned reading in Catholic schools; and rights to the picture have now reverted (as provided), not to Ford, but to its literary forebear, Greene, who, however, wrote me: "I have never been able to bring myself to see the film as it was a total travesty of my book, perhaps due to Ford's Irish type of Catholicism. The illegitimate child was given to the police officer instead of to the priest!" (March 7, 1979.) There is little reason to approach Ford's picture as though it intended to be a staging of Greene's novel rather than as a work in itself.

1　2

illuminate their psychologies: the threatened lieutenant, the secure peasant. And some of the more brilliant technical feats in film may be found in
The Fugitive, such as the police attack on the peasant market, or the moment when a gramophone horn is swung away and a dancer, in one close *brio*
pan, gets chased into a saloon, into a soldier's arms, and is lifted up onto a
bar, where her legs begin to dance.

But Lindsay Anderson, among many, attacks "the over-luscious images [as]
frequently vulgar in their sentimental appeal; a lame child in a church doorway, holding a lighted candle."[82] Could not Ford have been less obvious with
such holycard images, however typical they may be of naive Catholicism? Yet
Ford's artfulness is intimate rather than synthetic; he celebrates openly cultural aspects that repel Anglo-Saxon sternness. Just as the movie's marvelous
score, which might initially seem overly expressionistic, is an emanation from
the characters rather than a "Hollywood" touch, so too the pathos of the images emerges from their content rather than from Ford's direction. His camerawork during crowd scenes resembles the realism of Rossellini or Buñuel
during the next few years, rather than the contrivance of a Goldwyn; and
music in Rossellini and Buñuel is certainly no less emotional.

An attack from opposite grounds comes from Jean Mitry: "A theoretical
drama in theoretical reality . . . depersonalized . . . cold." Perhaps Ford is
excessively iconic (even the credits underline such intentions: "*a* fugitive, *an*
Indian woman, *a* lieutenant of police . . .") but his abstraction of his characters from their milieu is deliberate. They are persons depersonalized in a cold
world. A terribly fractured world, in the cutting, a terribly shadowed world, a
terribly formalized world. Yet it is their world, the most subjective of any Ford
movie—and, I suppose, in that sense, theoretical. The priest's dilemma, we
might say, lies in trying to reconcile substance and appearance, or in trying to
control his monstrous imagination, which so often runs away with him—as in
the (much imitated) temporal ellipses as he debates whether to board the
boat or go with the boy, or as he flees the city. In an ultimate prolongation of
Ford's vignette techniques, the priest's subjectivity swamps objective reality:
he cannot palliate the excruciating torture (unbearable equally to us!) of the

3

hotel-room scene. Or, try as he will, to the priest, Diego (J. Carroll Naish)
appears snakelike, Judas-like, repulsive; Maria Dolores seems a sort of Mary
Magdalen seeking out iconic poses as refuge; and the inner agony which El
Gringo's bluff refuses to acknowledge is patent to the priest in the way the
outlaw keeps his chin thrust in throughout. Beauty midst this agony—little
children singing with big happy faces, a refugee doctor (John Qualen) utter-
ing placidities—only serves to remind the priest (and us) of the *constraint* of
the film's world, of its theoreticalness, its subjectivity—and thus naturalness
seems prodigiously unnatural. Where is truth? The question sounds pompous. But the priest's dilemma revolves far less around the ultimate ramifications of God's presence in the world than around the priest's inability to separate the subjective colorings of his perceptions from "actual" reality. Do the
peasants he is baptizing really smile up at him so humbly—or is that partly
the way he conceives the event? (In 1960 I heard an American priest sermon-
ize of a visit to Mexico in terms every bit as "over-luscious" as Ford's—and I
wondered then at the accuracy of his impressions.) How isolated this priest is!
Five years in such a country, traveling from village to village, the only priest in
the land, adored on one side and hunted on the other, the adoration more
isolating than the pursuit. The discomfort that Mitry and Anderson and
Fonda have remarked in Fonda's performance is—why should it be necessary
to point this out?—precisely what Ford wanted. It is just this discomfort that
renders the character palpable. Frame 4 is held for over a minute and requires

4

Fonda, against accepted portrait technique, to hold his hand outstretched, thus distorting his torso proportions (more in the movie than here). Spatially, we know he is sick, indrawn, involuted, feels awkward, tiny, helpless. His head is too big; he is even "outside" his body (the hand). His hand represents an annoyance, something bigger than himself. His speech is self-flagellating:

> It wasn't courage, Doctor, it was only pride. . . . I began to lose grace. . . . I began to think I was a *brave* man, who knows? a martyr. I suddenly realized I was the only priest left in the country. . . .

The Doctor pooh-poohs: "Oh, don't be so hard on yourself, Father. A man is entitled to a little pride." The priest's agitation mounts:

> Not in my profession. I was building a fine lie, wearing it like a proud cloak. . . . [But] when the first real test came I couldn't measure up. I let men die for me. . . .

Indeed, the priest flees throughout the movie, first in one direction, then in another. His cowardice stems from the quality that Ford's pictures (*The Quiet Man, 7 Women*) identify as the clergy's essential problem: pride, moral arrogance, separation from the world. In short, a hypocrisy—but a hypocrisy perhaps necessary to the profession—and it is with this *abstract* flaw that Ford has replaced the *concrete* flaws (alcoholism, simony, fornication) of Greene's novel. The priest's flight is from his own impurity, and from that there is no "sanctuary" in the doctor's hospital; there is sanctuary only in martyrdom. He flees safety to do what saints are supposed to do, knowingly. He is not discouraged when he learns El Gringo did not write the note asking him to come and does not want the sacraments. Is he mad? Like Ingrid Bergman in Rossellini's *Europe '51*, he is obsessed in isolation, is posed with solipsistic dilemmas, is marching to the step of a different drummer. As in the Bresson-Bernanos *Diary of a Country Priest*, flight leads to a sort of gnosticism ("All is grace"): a thunderclap and a rainstorm give courage and recall him not only to God by the experience of power, but also to the cosmos by the experience of having an eternal, if tiny, spot within Being. "I want to live my death," he says.

Don Rafael, the lieutenant, is the priest's Doppelgänger. He too engages the peasants in rituals (but sermonizes them, whereas the priest is tongue-tied), is depicted riding (but a horse rather than a donkey), is obsessed with cowardice and his abstraction from everyone else's reality, and like the priest is constantly associated with geometric backgrounds, divine shafts of light, and doorways (leading through labyrinthine ways to God). More marked in his hypocrisy, he believes in the revolution, believes he is "making a better world," but leaves trails of blood in his wake; his release is violence. He is frustrated by officials who profit from blackmarket liquor, and by his own people: "I'm an Indian like you are," he harangues, riding back and forth, "Stand up straight! I want to give you—Everything!" Yet he is unable to acknowledge his child by Maria Dolores. Frame 5 shows her defying him by genuflecting; her action relates to the foreground font, in which the child has been baptized, to the lieutenant's chagrin; the zig-zagging angles through four layers of depth, and the contrapuntal angles of light and wall, create multitudinous relationships between the characters and their situations. The lieutenant's men become beasts when he is not present, and in battle bloody madness possesses him as well, as sometimes seems to happen to Third-world revolutionaries today. But, given that Ford tells us little of anticlericalism's good reasons in Mexico, the lieutenant does not come off badly. The priest tells him, "I'm the sort of man you lock up every day, and give money to."

The outlaw, El Gringo (Ward Bond), may have started out in Nichols's treatment as a sort of Good Thief. In the movie, he shows no sign of faith or repentance, but represents the ostensibly accidental but actually providential figure that brings priest and lieutenant together and to God (cf. the Cleggs in *Wagon Master*). As in St. Augustine's theory of history, God's ways are mysteries. Almost all *The Fugitive*'s characters are outcasts, yet they are ruled by formalized codes. Warmth and integrity exist in their Sternbergian world, but any real communication between them can occur only in stolen instants, in subtleties of expression and glances within codes. Yet Sternberg does not erect such formidable barriers of obviousness, abstraction, and Latin Catholicism. What are we to think of the scene when the priest, after riding up to the hillside on his mule, returns to his ruined church and stands

5

gazing at a high round window streaking light into the darkness? Later, Don Rafael confronts this same window and laughs hysterically. The priest in prison will find comfort through a similar window. God is the light of the world, and shadow, which seems at first His antithesis, is perhaps really another, labyrinthine, way. The grace that flows into rooms flows also into souls who confront it, and it illuminates these souls dramatically. Were the priest, or Don Rafael, not the sort of persons who react the way they do, the symbolic light would be merely pompous. But Ford is trying to capture the level of their existence: a Latin priest who thinks he is a saint, a Latin revolutionary who thinks he is destroying God. The priest can no more escape the light than he can escape the myriad arches that, as signs of formalized culture (i.e., of his belief in a rational, God-inhabited cosmos), follow him everywhere—the arched aqueduct on the plain (frames 6, 7), the arched sidewalks in the city (8), the arched tree-shadows at the river (9), even the arched walls in prison (10*). The horrible question, of course, is whether these are signs *from* God or only signs *for* God. No matter; for the priest the world's architecture is a sermon: myriad angles jutting inward hound him

*This frame forms part of a remarkable montage: /Full shot (as here): the priest sees: /LS: hostage and cops crossing courtyard. /Medium CU: the priest gawks: /Full shot (frame shown), drops buckets and runs /into a long shot chasing the cops. The varying of space (between CU, FS, and LS) and the dropping buckets create a crescendo of motion, while the stasis of the principal figure is relieved when the priest drops the buckets, then runs.

6 7

8 9

10 11

12

toward his duty, angles spreading outward conduct him heavenward—as in frame 11, when he ascends to execution. Nor is the lieutenant spared similarly continual assaults by the physical world, which violently attacks him at the moment the priest is killed (12)—at which point he crosses himself, testifying to superstition, to belief, to proof of God, to who knows? For the priest, the dilemma between appearance and substance is solved only in surrender, when truth becomes legible.

Simple definitions, simple people with simple paradoxes, yet paradigmatic of every culture's inherited dilemmas; these are simplicities that become almost unmanageably complex because of the intensity and profundity of people's belief in them, simplicities that drive people mad, and whose intense profundity must be felt also by us: a difficult task, since it all seems so alien and so simple.

Don Rafael bursts into the cantina, screams at the dancer, "What kind of woman are you?!" (like Wyatt Earp asking what sort of town this is). Then he sees who it is. Maria Dolores drops her fan, he bends to pick it up. "I don't know, Don Rafael. What sort of woman am I?" An instant of gallantry, when each stands helpless in love and defiance, and when, as throughout the film, everything is washed with the melancholic dreams of a past world. *The Fugitive* is already *The Man Who Shot Liberty Valance*. With great passion it looks back, as did *How Green Was My Valley*, to a more innocent world (specifically to the world before World War II—for *The Fugitive* is an allegory for Reconstruction). The fugitives are outcast by time and history, and they are searching, half in the old world, half in the new, for ways of coping.

It is such resonances as these, along with the way characters' souls emerge together with their public poses, that give pungency to *The Fugitive*'s flat, stark dialogue. The conversation between the priest and Maria Dolores is composed of an ingeniously inventive series of reverse-angles and two-shots:

— "Will there be churches again, Father?"
— "We must hope so."
— "In the village they have no hope. They say . . . the Church is dead."

And the priest climbs to the rooftop and rings a bell.

From *Tabu* to *The Passenger*, films like *The Fugitive* have sought out privileged and private landscapes and have dressed themselves in the most formalized expression in order to evoke the most unformalized realities of life.

Although *The Fugitive* presents unique difficulties, its stylistic invention is typically Fordian, only concentrated. If in its allegoric, operatic ways, it resembles *The Battle of Midway*, in its unanswered questions it is closer to *7 Women*; or, it can be seen as a journey to God such as *3 Godfathers* and *Wagon Master*, or even *Mogambo*—a mixture of the quotidian and the mysterious. But basically *The Fugitive* is a western: land, Indians, army, robber barons, outlaws. Otherwise it resembles *My Darling Clementine* (*film noir*; do-gooders moved by divinely appointed duty), *Stagecoach* (the Gringo's theme is "Bury Me Not on the Lone Prairie"), *Fort Apache* (arrogance), and *When Willie Comes Marching Home* (mindless patriotism).

Funerals

When Will Rogers had died in an air crash in 1935, Ford had gone to pieces; and for the next couple of decades he wore a hat with a funny hole in it Rogers had given him. When Tom Mix died in a car crash in 1940, Ford had rushed to the wake, placed a Stetson on Mix's head and interceded with the War Department for burial in the flag. (Technically, Mix had been AWOL since the Spanish-American War.) Ford always came on strong at death—whatever life's disputes.

Harry Carey's last years had seen memorable roles in *The Last Outlaw*, *Mr. Smith Goes to Washington*, *Duel in the Sun*, and *Red River*. But he had worked with Ford only once since 1921, in *The Prisoner of Shark Island*. They had drifted apart partly due to rival tale-carrying by two old bachelors, Joe Harris and J. Farrell MacDonald. When the Careys and Fords would get together, about twice a year, Dobe used to wonder why his mild-mannered father would get so excited. "Now, Jack, that's a lot of crap!" Harry would exclaim, slamming down his fist, "For Chrissake! *I* wrote that story, the story was *my* idea!" "No, it was *my* story," Ford would rebut. And on they would go. Dobe took Harry to see *Stagecoach* in 1939, and all through it Harry hardly ever stopped talking: "We did *that*! We did *that*!"[83]

But Ford was at Harry's bedside, September 24, 1947, the day he died. Afterward, Ollie Carey went and stood on the porch. "And I remember Jack came out and he took hold of me and put his head on my breast and cried, and the whole front of my sweater was sopping wet. For at least fifteen or twenty minutes he cried, just solid sobbing, solid sobbing, and the more he cried, the stronger I'd get. It was very good for me, it was wonderful. Oh, God, he shook and cried. I thought, it's chilly here and here I am sopping wet all the way down."[84]

Harry's death gave Ford a chance to fulfill his dreams of having a wedding or funeral at the Farm, and an Irish wake, too. Four uniformed sailors stood guard all night outside the Field Photo chapel, with Carey's horse, Sonny, tied to the hitching post. Ford, Wayne, Bond, and Spencer Tracy were pall-bearers. Dan Borzage played "Red River Valley," and John Wayne read Tennyson's "Crossing the Bar." *3 Godfathers* was in production at the time, a remake of Ford's favorite of his movies with Carey, *Marked Men* (1919), and Ford prefaced it with a dedication. A lone rider appears, half-silhouetted in the dusk, and removes his hat: "To the memory of Harry Carey—Bright Star of the early Western Sky," reads the legend, while "Good Bye Ole Paint" (". . . I'm a-leavin' Cheyenne"—a reference to Carey's Cheyenne Harry character) is quoted musically. And Ford used *3 Godfathers* to promote Dobe's stardom as Harry Carey, Jr. (Henry George "Dobe" Carey yielded reluctantly to billing as Harry Carey, Jr., on pressure from Ford and Wayne; he had appeared briefly in three earlier films—notably *Red River,* but without meeting his father on screen. The rider on the horse, however, is Cliff Lyons, and Wayne rather than Dobe assumes Harry Carey's former role.) "I think he felt duty-bound by his higher power to launch me on a film career," said Dobe. Was this in compensation? "Yes. And I think that's why he caused me so much hell. When we got back to town he was marvelous, but in Death Valley he was really tough. I used to think, 'Gee, if you were mad at my dad, don't take it out on me.' "[85]

Ford's next funeral of atonement came with Francis Ford, who died, painfully, of cancer, September 6, 1953. Shortly before, Dan Ford, then a boy, recalls stopping beside one of Hollywood's giant studios. "John and Francis exchanged a look. Then Francis turned to me and said. 'I used to own that studio.' For a moment he smiled and the old twinkle was there in his eyes. Then it faded away. 'You know,' he said, 'I've really had a very wonderful life.'"[86] But jobs had been scarce for the aging actor. His wife had written John a year earlier, "I am terribly worried about Frank. He hasn't worked for over one year . . . He walks the floors constantly."[87] Some years before John had lent Frank money to open a saloon, but business went poorly, Frank got discouraged, and so one night he locked the doors and drank all the booze. John was scarcely uncaring, but his pathological attitude toward Frank, which so infuriated Harry Carey and other old-timers, continued to the end. Once John was sitting back acting nonchalant as a procession of people admired a camera setup he had arranged. Then Billy Ford, Frank's son, took a look. "Whadya think?" asked John. "Well, it's great but it looks just like something my father once . . . " John threw him off the set right then and there.[88]

The funeral was a grand affair. Frank Baker had never attended funerals, not even his wife's, but he went to this one. Afterward, he did not speak to John, but sat across the street in a car. Ford, while chatting with various groups of people for five or ten minutes, kept staring silently over toward Baker. Some weeks later they met. "Were you at Frank's funeral?" Ford asked, immediately. "You know very well I was there. You saw me." "We gave him a good send-off, didn't we?"

Baker made no reply. Yet for the next few years, every time Ford saw him, he would ask, "We gave Frank a good send-off, didn't we?" He knew Baker as among those most critical of his treatment of Frank and hoped for approval of the funeral. He never got it.

John Ford probably felt guilt toward any friend who died. His ability in life to bestow affection was impaired by his self-protectiveness. He hid. Toward women he could be utterly tender, but men he loved combatively— and how much more so Frank, who was probably the person in his life he held most in awe.

4 Third Period (1948–1961): The Age of Myth

"From *Fort Apache* on," writes Andrew Sarris, "Ford's films seemed to have abandoned the Tradition of Quality for a Cult of Personality."[1] As the critical mainstream veered increasingly toward astringent social relevance, the ex–poet laureate looked increasingly irrelevant, holed up in Monument Valley churning out matinee westerns. In fact, the bitterness of social comment in Ford's movies was more acerbic than before. The thirties revolutionary had not embraced the establishment. But what Ford had to say, America did not wish to hear. To his credit, he no longer sought prestige by couching his thought within trendy styles. His pictures instead became intensely private, formulated within well-worn commercial genres, fraught with myth, irony, and double-leveled narratives. Still today, many a casual critic, underestimating Ford, misses not only the subtlety, but misconstrues denunciations as celebrations.

BRILLIANCE (1948–1956)

Fort Apache	3.9.48	Argosy Pictures–RKO Radio
3 Godfathers	12.1.48	Argosy Pictures–MGM

She Wore a Yellow Ribbon	10.22.49	Argosy Pictures–RKO Radio
When Willie Comes Marching Home	2.50	20th Century–Fox
Wagon Master	4.19.50	Argosy Pictures–RKO Radio
Rio Grande	11.15.50	Argosy Pictures–Republic
This Is Korea!	8.10.51	U.S. Navy–Republic
The Quiet Man	9.14.52	Argosy Pictures–Republic
What Price Glory	8.52	20th Century–Fox
The Sun Shines Bright	5.2.53	Argosy Pictures–Republic
Mogambo	10.9.53	Metro-Goldwyn-Mayer
The Long Gray Line	2.9.55	Rota Productions– Columbia
Rookie of the Year (TV short)	12.?.55	*Screen Directors Playhouse*
The Bamboo Cross (TV short)	12.6.55	*Fireside Theatre*
The Searchers	5.26.56	C. V. Whitney Pictures –Warner Bros.

This period is distinguished by the vitality of its invention, at every level of cinema, but with particular intensity in montage, motion, and music. Ford at his most energetic intellectually is also Ford at his most optimistic. The defeatism of the preceding period has been largely rejected—or, at least, recontextualized. Although virtually all the pictures take place in the past (or in Africa or Korea) it is evident that Ford felt some hope in America. This is the period of *3 Godfathers, Wagon Master,* and *The Sun Shines Bright.* But it is also the period of *Mogambo*—is man different than the ape?—and it is evident Ford finds more to criticize than to praise in American society: *Fort Apache, When Willie Comes Marching Home, The Long Gray Line.*

In this period the community theme in Ford is in ascendance, a period of social analysis, akin to the early thirties pictures. Military or military-like societies are chosen because they provide clear sets of the customs, ideologies, and structures relevant to America. Although ten prior pictures dealt with such groups, only *Wee Willie Winkie* and *Salute* had attempted quasi-documentary approaches to such communities. But of the thirty-three films made after 1948, eighteen are directly concerned with studying the problems of military communities, while nine others treat, in much the same terms, quasi-military communities (wagon trains, missionaries, political parties, police), while two others have military life as a background (*The Searchers, Donovan's Reef*). In all thirty-three films the specific question is, What makes people tick? Why do they do what they do? or, twenty-nine times, What makes people fight?

There is less determinism and more free will than elsewhere in Ford in this period. Duty, previously regarded by the hero as divinely appointed, henceforth resides in the group and is socially assigned.

Previously people lived in idealistic commitment; individuals might die but the Idea would endure (e.g., Ma Joad). This theme continues, but the static concept is replaced by a dynamic antinomy and given concrete representation: *subsistence* and *change*—and an uncertain change—become the matrices through which all other themes must operate. And henceforth the films of John Ford essentially constitute a cinema of passage, whose central symbolic antinomies are the parade and the house.

Expressionism virtually disappears in its purer forms, and though Ford exploits operatic cinema more than ever, most of his mannerist tendencies are subsumed into brighter palettes and cleaner compositions.

But the films grow progressively darker. A few old men sustain the viability of society, only faith can find an ontological distinction between man and ape, the parade is a substitute for the insufficiency of reason. The films dwell on the coercive tendencies of society, of instruments becoming malevolent institutions. The period concludes with *The Searchers*, a farewell to youth and the entry into Ford's work of acute ambivalence, of a dialectic equivalent to pessimism and uncertainty about Good and Evil. Yet even so, these eight years constitute a period of glory, of stability and sureness, more blessed with masterpieces than any other period.

Five Westerns

"I made four or five westerns . . . , potboilers, but they served a purpose," said Ford.[2] "I had to do something to put my company back on its feet after what we lost [with *The Fugitive*. *Fort Apache*] was a very concocted story. But very good box-office."[3] "[It] is a variation inspired by Custer's last battle. We changed the tribe and the topography."[4]

Ford's prewar reputation had been based on "quality" adaptations of literature conceived to tastemakers' appeal. Now, needing to appeal to new, wider audiences, his style became more forceful, his palette more colorful; his better instincts were refreshingly liberated. *Fort Apache*'s style owes more to *The Battle of Midway* than to *The Grapes of Wrath*, or even to *Wee Willie Winkie*—although it was the notion of making a movie about the intimate life of an isolated cavalry post that had led Ford to purchase James Warner Bellah's Kiplingesque story, "Massacre." Army-post pictures had been common enough in Hollywood. But when the troops ride in and out of their garrison in Curtiz's 1936 *Charge of the Light Brigade*, music and countryside are dramatically banal in contrast to the dynamic significance of Ford's folk tunes and Monument Valley. What Ford brought new to the genre—and what now enters more intensely into his work—is a conscious vivification of his material as mythic actuality. The land, its indigenous inhabitants, quotidian ritual, and documentary detail assume awesome symbolic roles. The complex social forces that formerly determined Fordian people are henceforth concentrated into myth. Myth rules man.

Fort Apache (1948). Here began a long association with Frank S. Nugent, who had been hired as an in-house critic by Darryl Zanuck back in 1940 (in order, some gossiped, to stop Nugent's pans of Zanuck films in

The New York Times), but who, like another newspaperman, Dudley Nichols, had not written a script until hired by Ford.

> [Ford] gave me a list of about fifty books to read—memoirs, novels, anything about the period. Later he sent me down into the old Apache country to nose around. . . . He made me do something that had never occurred to me before—but something I've practised ever since: write out complete biographies of every character in the picture. Where born, educated, politics, drinking habits (if any), quirks. You take your character from his childhood and write all the salient events in his life leading up to the moment the picture finds him—or her. The advantages are tremendous, because having thought a character out this way, his actions, his speech are thereafter compulsory; you know how he'll react to any given situation. . . . Bellah's short story, *Massacre*, touched the character and provided the ending. But the first 80 percent had to be worked back from the ending—and the key to it was in the character development.[5]

Indeed, *Fort Apache* is dense with character interrelationships and prior biography, ethnicity, religion, manners, and mores. Innumerable happenings—riding lessons, dances, drills, drinking bouts, romances, visits, punishments, home-makings, serenades, dinners—have been "concocted" to detail documentary, along with a multitude of richly individuated personalities—five sergeants, two corporals, four officers, four women (plus Francis Ford doing his famous spit). There is a Grand March* (to "St. Patrick's Day") and some magical dancing (to, as so often, "Golden Slippers"). And there is Shirley Temple, absolutely right and beautifully subtle as Philadelphia Thursday, an ingenuous, rascally sixteen, fresh from school in Europe, devoted to her father and unafraid to express frank thrills for a dashing young lieutenant ("Wonderful!").** Indian-killers though they be, the soldiers engage our warmest sympathies. As we watch Sergeant O'Rourke (Ward Bond) deliberately finishing his Bible-reading before raising his head to greet his son returned home, every detail of the home—its textiles, plates, religious statue, fireplace, and lighters—articulates the man's identity and aids our affection. We know the moment fulfills a lifelong dream: an immigrant's son has become an officer.[†]

Despite this achievement, Colonel Thursday justifiably discourages courting of his daughter by O'Rourke's officer-son, because the latter, as an enlisted man's son, will never advance. And all life at Fort Apache is domi-

---

*Similar to but not so fine as in *The Sun Shines Bright;* Ford's first Grand March occurred in *The Prince of Avenue A* (1920).

**John Agar (Lt. O'Rourke) had actually married Shirley Temple shortly before the film. Alas, the fascination of *her* eroticism was not of the stuff that created adult stars in 1948. But Ford recreates an episode from their 1937 *Wee Willie Winkie*, when she wakes up her first morning, goes to her window, and sees the flag being raised, the cannon shot, horse, wagons, dust. She was paid the same salary as Wayne and Fonda—$100,000. McLaglen got $35,000; Bond $25,000; O'Brien $15,000; Kibbes $12,000; Withers $7,500; Lee $7,000; Rich and Agar $5,000.

[†]A similar scene occurs in Francis Ford's *The Burning Brand* (1912).

nated by the military's caste system. Alcohol, for instance, is always be-
stowed from a higher rank to a lower (Thursday buys drinks for the men at
the way station; officers spike the noncoms' ball punch; Thursday orders
Meachum's whiskey "destroyed"; Thursday offers Collingwood a drink;
York gives Sergeant Beaufort a drink at the canyon). A higher-ranking soldier is always in authority, in military thinking, and reality must conform to
theory. Thus, when a recruit is thrown from his horse and chases after it, his

sergeants shout, "Hey! Where are you going with that horse! Come back here with that horse!" Here, as generally, Ford's slapstick is making a point. In fact, another gag virtually explains the whole film: Sergeant Mulcahy (Victor McLaglen), cautioned to behave at the ball, pledges: "We'll be the morals of decorum!" For, in actuality, decorum dictates the only morality they have.

For the people of Fort Apache serve a system, in which group, duty, and order are more important than individual, morality, or life itself. They are warrior-priests. But they will be destroyed by the system, by duty gone astray; willingly, they will charge into a canyon of slaughter, led by a man particularly dedicated to ritual glory. Even though Colonel Owen Thursday (Henry Fonda) has been told the Apache wait in ambush, the soldiers obey his orders, knowing him wrong, and they die.

The Indians are outside the system; they are the Other, the enemy (by definition rather than cause); they are like the land, something to be controlled. And dust is their constant ally: dust thrown by Cochise as sign he will engage the cavalry (conveying sorrow at having to fight, in contrast to Thursday's elation, and telling us also that the soldiers are already dead); dust clouds warning York the Apache are near; dust clouds squaws create to fool Thursday; dust engulfing the trapped regiment; dust into which the Apache disappear after planting the destroyed regiment's banner in front of York and which then rolls over York's men. Cochise tells Thursday the Apache had surrendered, but then came the Indian agent:

— He is worse than war. He not only killed the men, but the women, and the children, and the old ones. We looked to the Great White Father for protection: he gave us slow death. . . . Send him [the agent] away and we will speak of peace.

Thursday has previously indicated his disgust for the agent, but, insulted by Cochise's threat of war, he calls him a "recalcitrant swine . . . without honor"—though it was Thursday who was just now about to attack treacher-

ously under a flag of truce. A martinet, stiff-backed, hungry for glory, shamed to fight "breech-clad savages," affected with his cigars, Thursday's arrogance is motivated by the blind prejudice of his racism—which Ford instances in Thursday's attitude toward the Irish (forgetting O'Rourke's name twice and calling him O'Brien or Murphy); need it be said, Thursday comes from Boston, like most screwballs in Ford.

Ford sees the cause of army barbarity in disgruntled officers trying to make a name for themselves so they can return east. But glory is an acceptable goal in the system, as Mrs. Collingwood (Anna Lee) proves by refusing to call her husband back from the fatal campaign when a long-awaited promotion to West Point comes through, even though she has a premonition of his death ("All I can see is the flags"). And glory is the response the system makes to Thursday's mass suicide.

In the picture's last scene, the camera dollies back from the B Troop banner, an oil portrait of Thursday, and his saber. Captain York (John Wayne), whose oath to Cochise Thursday betrayed, whose advice of the ambush Thursday scorned, talks with two reporters:

Rep. 1: [Looking reverently at the portrait:] He must have been a great man. And a great soldier.

York: [In an official but convincing tone:] No man died more gallantly. Nor won more honor for his regiment.

Rep. 1: Of course you are familiar with the famous painting of Thursday's Charge.

York: Yes, I saw it the last time I was in Washington.

Rep. 2: That was a magnificent work. There were these massed columns of Apache in their warpaint and feather bonnets, and here was Thursday leading his men in that heroic charge.

York: Correct in every detail. [In fact, the description *is* exact.]

Rep. 2: He's become almost a legend already. He's the hero of every schoolboy in America. But what of the men who died with him. What of Collingworth . . .

York: Colling*wood.*

Rep. 2: Oh, of course. Collingwood.

Rep. 1: That's the ironic part of it. We always remember the Thursdays, but the other men are forgotten.

York: You're wrong there. They aren't forgotten, because they haven't died. They're living, right out there. [York has moved to the window; ghosts of the cavalrymen appear superimposed on the pane—"Battle Hymn of the Republic."] Collingwood and the rest. And they'll keep on living, as long as the regiment lives. The pay is thirteen dollars a month, their diet beans and

hay—they'll eat horsemeat before this campaign is over—
fight over cards or rotgut whisky, but share the last drop in
their canteens. The faces may change, and the names, but
they're there, they're the regiment, the regular army, now and
fifty years from now. They're better men than they used to be.
Thursday did that. He made it a command to be proud of.

Thus the archdemon becomes a hero, and the individuals are proud, un-
disturbed by the murder committed upon them; in fact, O'Rourke, whose
father Thursday sacrificed, has named his son after Thursday. How can this
be? The answer is that their lives *are* the system; life is not questioned; no
additional act of the will is required to honor Thursday.

And the epilogue of *She Wore a Yellow Ribbon* consists of a similar epi-
taph, narrated over a color brigade in Monument Valley:

— So here they are, the dog-faced soldiers, the regulars, the fifty-
cents-a-day professionals, riding the outposts of a nation. From
Fort Reno to Fort Apache, from Sheridan to Stark, they were all
the same: men in dirty-shirt blue and only a cold page in the history books to mark their passing. But wherever they rode, and
whatever they fought for, that place became the United States.

We may not like these conclusions, but Ford's intentions are to give accurate
depictions of the system, not to give us "happy endings." What sounds like
a paean to American imperialism happens to be simple truth. These *are* our
heroes, our forefathers who have given us what we have today; in a way, they
are ourselves. A Kubrick applies placeboes to our consciences, showing us
that evil, warped men cause evil; but Ford makes us uncomfortable, showing us that fine, noble people cause evil—and reminding us that, however
much we decry what they did, we are not about to undo their work. Thus,
Ford shows us facts, but also an "inside" perspective on those facts.

> *Bogdanovich:* The end of *Fort Apache* anticipates the newspaper
> editor's line in *Liberty Valance*, "When the legend
> becomes a fact, print the legend." Do you agree
> with that?
>
> *Ford:* Yes—because I think it's good for the country.[6]

Really? How come, then, that in both movies Ford "prints" the facts, while
exploding (and explaining) the legends?* His portrait of the cavalry is a
scathing indictment of arrogance, idiocy, racism, and caste-ridden inef-
ficiency. It is puzzling that so flagrant an irony as *Fort Apache*'s is commonly
mistaken for chauvinism by so many of Ford's critics.

---

*Peter Watkin's *Culloden* had a similar conclusion: despite the ruination Bonnie Prince
Charlie's arrogance visits upon them, the Highlanders continue to venerate him as a rallying
symbol of national identity.

And the movie is also one of the few in which Indians emerge both honorable and victorious. That they remain alien testifies to Ford's honesty.* He certainly does them no injustice. But here and in *She Wore a Yellow Ribbon* he sights them across the gap of culture and history, and lavishes upon them some of the finest epic photography of his career. John Ford:

My sympathy was always with the Indians. Do you consider the invasion of the Black and Tan into Ireland a blot on English history? It's the same thing, all countries do the same thing. There's British doing it, Hitler doing it, there's Stalin. Genocide seems to be a commonplace in our lives. But it was not a systematic destruction of the Indians. All I know is the cavalry got the hell kicked out of them, and the Indians practically destroyed themselves. It was the loss of the buffalo that wiped them out.[7]

Fort Apache is the first (and maybe the best) of the so-called trilogy of 7th Cavalry films—all based on James Warner Bellah stories. Stretches of it meander and there is some careless mismatching of shots due to haste, but much of it is first-rate Ford, with powerful photography (frequently on infrared stock). More impressive even than the credit sequence's sweeps across Monument Valley are the vast, epic compositions of Thursday leading his columns, backed by thunderous skies, with Archie Stout's camera scarcely a foot off the ground.

Fort Apache's action, at the time of Custer's 1876 Battle of the Little Big Horn, chronicles a fresher, more meaningful cavalry era than the later, mopping-up operations of *Yellow Ribbon* or *Rio Grande*. It is, relatively speaking, a picture of actuality, whereas *She Wore a Yellow Ribbon*, the second of the "trilogy," celebrates the generic ritual established by the first.

Here, in *She Wore a Yellow Ribbon* (1949), the nostalgic dreamworld, the old man's reverie of *Rio Grande*, the third of the series, is confronted in the bright sunshine of Technicolor. We can thus trace, in the span of three years and three pictures, a retreat into mythic re-creation. Gone already are the documentary reenactments of nineteenth-century life. The palpable feel of grit and guts is transposed into the purely iconic, icons stunningly recreating the colors and movement of Remington (other icons, other myths),** visually actual and executed with bold romantic panache, but already given within the context of a leading character grown old, to whom the present (1876) is a pale remnant of the Old West, and whose living memories find their most natural companionship beside the grave of his wife and children—like Will Rogers's Judge Priest.†

---

*An accurate Indian movie, in which everything is viewed through an Indian consciousness, would, language aside, pose insurmountable problems for our comprehension—not to mention commercial disaster. Nicholas Ray made a (heavily compromised) attempt to do this, with Eskimos, in *The Savage Innocents* (1959). Ford attempted honest pictures from *our* viewpoint.

**Ford and Carey's *Hell Bent* (1918) opened with an author contemplating a Remington canvas ("The Misdeal") that comes to life to start the story.

†Just after Custer's massacre, Fort Stark is threatened, and Capt. Brittles, due to retire,

The window of Captain Nathan Brittles's quarters at Fort Stark looks "out" onto the close-set wooden posts of the stockade—two feet away. On a printed calendar (curiously lacking a month name), each day is crossed out as retirement approaches, but really Brittles's life is marking time until death reunites him with a happier reality, with that family whose portraits he falls asleep with on his lap. Meanwhile the man is indistinguishable from the jargon and protocol of military duty. His motto is, "Never apologize. It's a sign of weakness," and, just like George Washington, he stays mounted and in clear view during battle. The mentality of a professional soldier has become his second nature. And because of this, we understand the depths of his mortification at the manifold failures of his last patrol, even though such a mentality is, like that of many Fordian heroes, not the sort many of us would be comfortable with in everyday life. Brittles, however, comes

---

leads his last patrol. But, escorting two ladies, he cannot intervene when he sights Arapaho, arrives late for one rendezvous to find men dead, late for another to find the stage burnt and more dead, and cannot stop a white trading rifles to Indians. Leaving a rear guard, he returns dejected. Since he retires at midnight, he is denied permission to lead the relief. His men give him a silver watch and he sees them ride off. But he takes command on personal authority and, when a parley fails, stealthily drives away the Indian horses, thus ending the war-threat. At 12:02 he retires, officially. And he starts west alone, but Tyree is sent after him, with news of appointment as chief of scouts. A dance is held in his honor, but he prefers to visit alone the small cemetery where his wife and children are buried.

through as a more palpable, "brittle" human being than did Wyatt Earp or Colonel Thursday, and, unlike them, his interventions save lives and bring peace, rather than wreaking havoc and death. Ford:

> Some years ago Douglas MacArthur asked me to stop by to see him in Tokyo. "We're showing one of your films tonight, *She Wore a Yellow Ribbon.*" He added that he had it shown at least once a month and that he still wasn't tired of it.[8]

"I'll be back, men, I'll be back," calls Captain Brittles as he leaves his troop to guard a ford, and, later, "Old soldiers," he says, "how they hate to grow old!"

At the time of the action, the redmen, spurred on by the destruction of Custer and the miraculous reappearance of the buffalo, are enjoying the illusion that history can be reversed, and, for moments during his last patrol, Brittles intersects this Indian summer, and the days of his youth are reborn under the bright sun. Coincidentally at such moments the picture, dropping its mask of theatricality, rises to a high level of present-anterior actuality: in the distance an entire tribe of Arapaho moves nomadically across the plains; later a herd of buffalo grazes with much the same naturalness. Sergeant Tyree gallops across the prairie pursued by Indians, and jumps a ravine to escape, one man alone in the wilderness. At Sudrow's Wells, Private John Smith dies and is buried with a general's honors: he was Rome Clay, CSA. Like Tyree ("I ain't gittin paid fer thinkin"), many of the cavalry's common soldiers are former Confederate officers who, like Brittles, seem to regard the army as a kind of monastic retreat from a bitter world. Even Pony That Walks* finds himself ignored by his younger tribesmen, and, when Nathan says, "Old men should stop wars," the chief replies, "Too late," and suggests they go away together to hunt buffalo and get drunk. And when the troop sights the herd, a soldier exclaims, "Sure hanker for a piece of buffalo meat!" "Me too!" adds a second soldier, "'Hain't never had none." But before this reference to the passing wilderness rings too sententiously, a third soldier interjects, "Beans is safer!" Couples may float deathlessly into a sweet slow waltz midst the dark, glowing colors of the final reception, but a new age is at hand. No wonder Brittles retreats to his graveyard.

John Wayne carries the drama single-handed, virtually, with more dialogue than ever before or since. His roles in *Stagecoach, The Long Voyage Home,* and *Fort Apache* had been small, taciturn, and distinctive, but his performance in Hawks's *Red River* had convinced Ford he could act, and in *3 Godfathers* Wayne recited the longest monologue in any Ford movie. In *Yellow Ribbon,* he has the added novelty of playing in makeup a man a

---

*Played by Chief John Big Tree (1875–?), 100 percent Seneca, who in 1912 posed for the Indian-head nickel and from 1915 appeared in innumerable pictures, including *Drums Along the Mohawk.*

generation older than himself. At times, like the movie alternating between storybook theatricality and realism, he gets a bit hammy, but that is the character.

Ford westerns tend to be epitomes of the genre, rather than variations upon it. Brittles exemplifies this tendency, as does the photography—the expressionistic black-and-red skies with bright low-drifting night-clouds; or the day-for-night stampede, sepia, black-and-white, traced with blue*— and as do the gags. Speed makes Victor McLaglen's hammy barroom brawl one of Ford's best friendly fights (what else would army types do for recreation?). For Quincannon, who retires himself in two weeks, this is the final "battle" and his blows seem inspired by Dumas's description of Porthos's Herculean death. But this tendency toward epitome seems to handicap *She Wore a Yellow Ribbon*'s attempts toward being a Fordian comedy. The rugged, crass, even vulgar professionals of Ford's cavalry movies are all-of-a-piece types; they lack the ability of *Submarine Patrol*'s citizen sailors or of *When Willie Comes Marching Home*'s pixilated Punxatawnians to explode readily into chimeric manifestations of individuality.

Magic moments aside, however, the fact remains that *She Wore a Yellow Ribbon*, and *Rio Grande* even more, were made to make money from kiddie-matinee audiences. They were shot hurriedly, and their scripts are concocted banalities played at the broadest levels. Never was Ford more careless with his players. Joanne Dru, fascinating in *Wagon Master*, has the least personality of any Ford female, and John Agar and Harry Carey, Jr., are correspondingly simple. Takes are long, with little of the inventive montage or composition of Ford's more personal movies.

Rio Grande (1950), Ford's seventh western in eight pictures, was undertaken because Republic would not back *The Quiet Man* without a successful first project. But if Ford began with indifference, warming up O'Hara, Wayne, and McLaglen for the Irish movie, he seems to have grown enchanted eventually. And, after all, the Argosy westerns' magic is inseparable from their rawness and careless production—one notes even more mismatching of infrared than in *Fort Apache*.

Rio Grande is so obvious technically, yet so successful, that many may find here an initiation to Ford. It is a storybook movie, accessible and privileged, cozy and strong, almost a chapter of reveille in an old man's fireside reverie, a mixture of epic and corn. It is a textbook in the rendering and exploiting of empathy.**

Victor Young's melodies yearn over vast strong valleys; the wide swift river inculcates rhapsodic beatitudes. A color brigade bursts dustily

---

*Winton C. Hoch's Technicolor won an Oscar—despite his formal, written protest against shooting the famous thunderstorm sequence, which Hoch was certain would not come out.

**Texas, 1878: Midst rescuing children captured by Apache, Lt. Col. Kirby Yorke is reunited with his family after fifteen years, when wife Kathleen comes pursuing their son Jeff who has enlisted.

through a gate, and the camera pushes forward to stare commandingly at an approaching horseman. Such dynamics evoke Remington or Delacroix, but mostly Matthew Brady: actuality mingling with theater (i.e., those Civil War soldiers could not have been as mysterious as Brady portrays them). Cut closer: he is dirty, unshaved, weary, but a small gesture he makes—straightening, trying to look proud—affords us immediate entry into the human being within the professional. Partly because of the moustache, it takes effort to remember this is John Wayne.

Knee-level camera angles both distance and personalize; but empathy is secured chiefly by extensive use (most atypical for Ford) of point-of-view camera. Kathleen (Maureen O'Hara) stands in close shot while soldiers ride off behind her; /she pops into an empty frame after her son rides out of it; /the reverse-angle shows a desert vista with a speck of a rider, before we cut back to /Kathleen gazing.

Jeff (Claude Jarman, Jr.*) combines sensitivity, cuteness, and lanky toughness, almost erotically, and Ford promotes identity with him. He sits singing in a tent with three buddies, but only his face faces the camera and only he is spotlit and not shadowed: our experience is his. When, of all people, his mother walks in—she was supposed to be back in Virginia—his embarrassment almost overpowers the humor, because we are still meant to identify with him (he is spotlit, his mother is in the crosscut). His wake-up is entirely in reaction shots:** Jeff wakes, looks, /Heinze smiles, /Jeff reacts, /Tyree and Boone smile, /doctor offers spoon, /Yorke looks in window, /Doc gives spoon, Jeffs says "ough," /Yorke smiles—all over a bugle blowing reveille. Later: Yorke leads sorties down the Apache street: /Indian takes aim /Yorke /Indian shoots /Yorke falls off horse /close shot: and onto ground, writhing QUICK DISSOLVES high-angle long shot: horsemen form circle around wounded leader. /High-angle CU: Yorke. X low-angle CU: Jeff. X Yorke: "Pull it out, Jeff." X Jeff hesitates. /Low-angle two-shot: Tyree and Boone: "Get it done, Reb." "Yo," adds Boone. /Jeff yanks; X Yorke cringes. X Jeff wipes nose. /Long shot: Yorke is helped to horse, bugle sounds recall. This is textbook crosscutting; the matching high-/low-angles mirror growing intimacy between father and son; the cut-aways to friends supply moral support; "Yo" and Jeff-wiping-nose are devices milked throughout the movie.

Ford crosscuts between Kathleen and Yorke when they first see each other, and even puts "I'll Take You Home Again, Kathleen" on the soundtrack, but the moment is more perfunctory than Earp seeing Clementine or Marty Maher meeting Mary O'Donnell. Kathleen is so vague, her life a void except for quadruple repetition of the he-burnt-her-plantation story;[†] she seems summed up by her gazes into off-space. She is affecting when most wifely, when she finally joins the plain-faced young wives and overalled boys waiting on the road for their men, and when she spins her parasol while the band plays "Dixie." There's nothing vague about Jeff, though, and his scenes with Yorke have the chemistry lacking between husband and wife. Low-angles add seriousness to their first conversation, and crosscuts ascending to close-ups add intensity. *Rio Grande* is a succession of intimacies with pungent dialogue: "What kind of man is he, mother?" "He's a lonely man."

---

*Jarman (1934–) starred in *The Yearling* (1946), *Intruder in the Dust, The Great Locomotive Chase*; recently directed the San Francisco Film Festival.

** / = cut. X = crosscut, or reverse-angle.

[†]"Silent as death she was, with her babes in her arms," says McLaglen. Ford's wife's Carolina ancestors had their house burnt by Sheridan.

"They say he's a great soldier." "What makes soldiers great is hateful to me." Sacrifice of self to duty is explicit in the uniform.

Sheridan (J. Carroll Naish) is depicted almost as mythically as MacArthur in *They Were Expendable*. His spiffy horse belies his personal dirt, and, after being serenaded ("We may have more great men but we'll never have better . . . Glory-O!"), queries, "I wonder what History will say about Shenandoah?" "I can tell you what my wife said about it," quips Yorke, but the magical moment of history and humanity has had its effect, and when the scene concludes with Sheridan pouring himself coffee, we are programmed to wonder at the Great Man's simplicity.

Tyree (Ben Johnson) echoes myths more archetypal. Silent and capable, he gallops free and sovereign across the horizons of Monument Valley, summing up, like the cactus rose later, Ford's West. At one special moment, as Tyree's charger careens into an unsuspecting Apache happily pursuing a soldier, the epic mythologies of Ford join those of Buster Keaton.

Archetypal, too, is the status, largely symbolic, of women, who exist for the warriors' repose. Yorke wanders along a riverbank: Wayne, as instructed, keeps his face blank, thinks nothing; the moonlit water and haggard twilight tell us he is thinking of Kathleen. Later he stands in the dust watching his wife's wagon depart; presently we discover the music is coming not from the soundtrack, but from a sentimental tribute by the men of the fort. In such a world, poor Kathleen will find no peace until she accepts her prescribed role within the army. But then, no existential choices exist for men, either. All is duty.

Rio Grande is Ford at his best and worst. Its images rest in the mind—a little girl yanking a church bell, Jeff holding his swooned mother, wives tramping beside stretchers—and at worst it has at least the virtues of intimacy. Ford must have felt some pride: the mounted bugler on the horizon under the words "Directed by John Ford" is scarcely modest.

3 Godfathers (**1948**), and *Wagon Master* (1950) both stand in marked contrast to "the cavalry trilogy," being freely structured around historical and biblical myths, rather than demonstrative of institutional dynamics. Particularly dear to Ford was *3 Godfathers*'s story, of three bad men who, after robbing a bank and escaping into the desert, rescue a newborn baby and, guided by the Bible, take it to New Jerusalem, two of them dying on the way. The good badman, as we know, was a frequent Ford character, as was also a trio of badmen, whom he would usually liken to the three magi. Besides *Marked Men* (1919), his first filming of Peter B. Kyne's story and his favorite of his films with Harry Carey, *The Secret Man* (1917) and *Action* (1921) have similar stories, and there is a 1915 Francis Ford two-reeler, *Three Bad Men and a Girl*, in which Jack and Francis play two of the badmen. Three good badmen show up in *3 Bad Men* (1926) and there are similar triplets in *The Iron Horse* (1924) and the cavalry trilogy sergeants, not to mention the three magi in *Donovan's Reef* (1963).

As in *Donovan's Reef,* everything in *3 Godfathers* looks forward to Christmas, as to a moment of universal renewal. The badmen are ingenuous and respectful, and far too inept for the wilderness (one gets shot, they drink all their water, lose their horses, have to consult books for advice, and fumble into suicide). And civilization has provided a train by which the posse outflanks them. Yet it was clear at the outset, when B. Sweet (Ward Bond) emerged from behind his flowers and picket fence, that badmen have become anachronistic less by triumph of history than by triumph of virtue. This is the Mormons' promised land. The town "Tarantula" has changed its name to "Welcome" ("Welcome to Welcome") and, as in Mrs. Sweet's coffee, "egg shells . . . settle the grounds." As in *Liberty Valance,* the desert had bloomed—and in glorious Technicolor. But *3 Godfathers* tends to be a minor movie, its long stretches of desert monotony redeemed by magic moments, of which by far the best is the finale, when sparkling cutting and framing rhyme spunky, swingy girls singing "Bringing in the Sheaves."

That *Wagon Master* (1950), one of Ford's major masterpieces, grossed about a third of any of the cavalry pictures surely came as no surprise. It was a personal project, with no stars, little story, deflated drama, almost nothing to attract box office or trendy critics. The story, resembling the Carey-Fords of the teens more than a fifties western, was written by Ford himself, the only such instance after 1930, and he was ruthless with the script. Said Frank Nugent: "We did not work at all closely. . . . His script cutting—especially of dialogue—was rather harsh."[9] Of all his pictures, said Ford, "*Wagon Master* came closest to what I had hoped to achieve."[10] It is "the purest and simplest western I have made."[11]

The magic that places *Wagon Master* among Ford's most enduringly rewarding movies tends, alas, to elude many viewers, particularly upon first viewing and particularly because purity and simplicity define that magic, for such qualities are far from those usually associated in the public mind with Great Motion Pictures. But *Wagon Master* is more poetry than drama, weaving together the West's purest myths with the simplest, most natural characters.

The opening (credit) sequences pose the themes:

1. The *Cleggs:* over their own "Wanted" poster rob Crystal City express office and kill clerk in spite.

2. The *Mormons:* wagons ford sparkling river. (Evil vs. good; association of Mormons with river image.)

3. The *Cleggs:* ride on twilit horizon.

4. The *Mormons:* camera pans thrice as Mormon wagons pass. (Evil vs. good again; accent on family [women and children in wagons] of Mormons, as opposed to femaleless Cleggs.)

5. Sister Ledeyard (Jane Darwell): blows her *bullhorn:* dissolve:

6. Longshot: *Horsetraders* Travis Blue (Ben Johnson) and Sandy Owens (Harry Carey, Jr.) driving with horses *toward* Crystal City.

7. The *Cleggs:* riding *away* from Crystal City.

8. Crystal City: horsetraders sell horse to marshall and meet Mormons: Elder Wiggs (Ward Bond), Elder Adam Perkins (Russell Simpson), his daughter Prudence (Kathleen O'Malley).

Note the mediating role of the *bullhorn* between the *Mormons* and the *horsetraders*, framed by the *Cleggs* on either side. This prefigures a later sequence: the Mormons, as Wiggs puts it, are heading for "the San Juan— to a valley that . . . that's been reserved for us by the Lord, been reserved for His people, so we can plough it and seed it and make it fruitful in His eyes." They need a guide, however, and Wiggs suggests that Travis and Sandy are the answer to this prayer. But the boys decline, and the Mormons set off alone, yet Wiggs, scratching his head, gives it another try (note the blend of corn [scratching] and apotheosis [words]): "Kinda wishing those young horse traders had given the Lord a hand! Sister Ledeyard! Supposin' you blow that horn again!" She does, and, as though answering her prayer, we dissolve to Travis and Sandy riding up to a fence, on which they sit to watch the wagons pass; suddenly, in *song,* they decide to take the job.

Note how the reprise of the prefigured image of the bullhorn as linkage between Mormons and horsetraders (and Cleggs) suggests not only that the Mormon-horsetrader alliance is divinely preordained, but also apotheosizes into poetic themes the various social groups. These groups correspond to the basic mythic elements of the West, and throughout the movie will be interwoven in similarly forthright fashions:

A. The Cleggs, outlaws

B. The Mormons, the ordained

C. Travis and Sandy, horsetraders (cowboys), drifters, and agents of the Lord

D. Marshall and posse, the establishment, who persecute A, B, and E

E. The showfolk

F. The Indians

Wagon Master meditates on the *difference* of these thematic groups. A and B are presented almost as two polarities of sonata form, with C as a bridge or catalyst. In the second movement, B, C, and E climax in the communal harmony of the dance scene. Thirdly, the Cleggs intrude and oppose everyone, and then the posse intrudes, also opposing everyone. In the fourth movement, B, C, and E combine to climb the last mountain, then in a swift sudden gunfight C annihilates A. A coda reprises in free combinations of B, D, and E—a sort of *stretto*.

The showfolk (a patent-medicine salesman, two loose women, and Francis Ford as a drummer) are, like other groups, outcasts, expelled from Crystal City. Ford's West, just like America itself, was colonized by urban refuse— outlaws, religious pilgrims, whores, swindlers, and free-spirited youngsters; not surprisingly, the wilderness knows its own: the Indians are friendly.

Two "obbligatos" add dimension to the allegorical mythos of the social groups. One, of course, is the land. Details of geography and time are vague, the better to be mythic, but the journey appears to take about a week and cover a hundred miles. * And the westward parade is persistent. Over and over again the off-screen chorus repeats, "rollin', rollin', rollin' . . . Goin' West, goin' West, goin' West . . ." In one key, minute-long sequence, the pilgrims trudge wearily through the dust toward the end of a forty-mile waterless trek, and here as elsewhere Ford strikingly sharpens the elements of mineral (desert—Monument Valley) and vegetable (brush) to contrast animal and man. The Mormons with children, horses, and dogs (ever-present on the soundtrack) are a herd in migration, a people pushed on by social and elemental forces, and by their will to find paradise. "We're just a small group of families," says Wiggs. And they *walked* West, step by step. Small in number, humble with faith rather than heroic, nothing could better explain the invincibility and inevitability of the conquest of the West than these images of walking people. Their columns form a parade, glorious, tawdry, and religious, but primarily their phenomenon seems lustily biological. The wilderness, in contrast to the civilization of Crystal City, seems to cradle man and to welcome him as a means to its fulfillment.

Music adds additional dimension: legend. "A hundred years have come and gone since 1849," sing the Sons of the Pioneers, and their unmistakably 1949 sound disturbingly distances the movie's pictorial action. That Ford's oxymoron is intentional is evident from the juxtaposition of the chorus's references to "the mighty wagon train" whose "thunder echoes in the sky" and the actual group of eleven or twelve wagons and sixty people. The blatant

---

*The San Juan River is some hundred miles northwest of Crystal (= Crystal City?), New Mexico. After fording a river, the Mormons encounter the showfolk (stranded without water, but evidently too far from Crystal to walk back). The next water is now forty miles, or two or three days as the wagon master says. After reaching the river, they entertain the Cleggs for about three days before entering their valley. The action is anterior to *3 Godfathers'*, in which the Mormons and Ward Bond are settled and growing flowers.

artificiality of this Stan Jones music apotheosizes the you-are-there authenticity of the images, underlines the stuff of legend (cf. *Fort Apache* and *Liberty Valance*), and serves a narrative function. Alas, it also seems to alienate
many audiences completely, who, in trying to ignore the music, miss both
the historic dialectic and *Wagon Master*'s essence as a *music* drama (or horse
opera?). Music supports its tendency to epiphanize everything into primal
symbology: the colt mounting the riverbank, the Cleggs' arrival, a gallop
over the prairie, a lovingly prolonged shot of Travis taking his horse for a
bath, even a bed or a rockinghorse. (Still, it seems a shame that at the dance,
the participants' folksy instruments are faded out for a studio band and the
Sons of the Pioneers.)

It almost seems as though Ford tried to promote Ward Bond, Ben Johnson, Harry Carey, Jr., and Joanne Dru; he listed their parts next to their
names in the opening credits—the only time he was ever to do so. And each
of them gets plenty of evocative cameo shots, with the three men frequently
lined up in front of the camera to trade remarks and gesticulate. But normal
Hollywood star-creation employs quite different techniques: high-energy
performances rather than laid-back ones, and subjective rather than distancing camera techniques. For example, in an Errol Flynn film, in contrast
to Ford, we see everything from Flynn's point of view; we are encouraged
toward empathetic "identification" with *him*. But in *Wagon Master* folks just
"be." And we watch. For as always in Ford, symbols, apotheoses, and poetry

are counterbalanced by the relaxed "realism" of individuals, although no-where else to this degree of simplicity, purity, and naturalness. Here above all is where *Wagon Master*'s magic resides. Watching Ward Bond whittle becomes wonderful, and the moment on the fence when Travis and Sandy sing to each other becomes one of the miracles in Ford. As in *Steamboat Round the Bend* and *How Green Was My Valley*, it is *Wagon Master*'s thesis that each little happening is grace.

Singing, for example, in John Ford pictures, besides its importance in ordinary community rituals such as marriages and funerals, is often sym-bolic of the most intimate act of social commitment a person can be capable of. Sons serenade their parents in *How Green Was My Valley* to mark resto-ration of family togetherness, peasants come serenade their priest in *The Fugitive* and their queen in *Mary of Scotland*; singing signifies Sean Thorn-ton's acceptance into the community in *The Quiet Man*, becomes the sign of fellowship in *Up the River*, and even in *Straight Shooting* (1917), the act of listening to a recording together becomes quasi-mystical. (Contrarily, at-tacks on phonographs reflect broken unions in *Air Mail*, *The Wings of Ea-gles*, and *Donovan's Reef*.) Yet more intimate by far are the few occasions in which characters actually sing to each other: Helen Chandler's teaching William Janney "Anchors Aweigh" in *Salute* sums up deep traditions of ro-mance and social duty intermingled; Will Rogers's joining the blacks in "Old Kentucky Home" in *Judge Priest* momentarily transcends all barriers of rac-ism; Colleen Townsend and Dan Dailey express fellowship that redeems their utter conventionality in their song and dance in *When Willie Comes Marching Home*.

In *Wagon Master*, Travis and Sandy's resort to song to express a decision to guide the Mormons has at least three significations. By its formality, it suggests a commitment to the Mormons and an acquiescence in "the Lord's will"; by its connection to music's role throughout the film, it suggests mythic adventurousness; but more importantly, it suggests their friendship. This male-male partnership, lacking combativeness, macho manners, or

sexual overtones, is a rare thing in American movies. Showing such a relaxed and natural friendship is what Ford had in mind by "pure and simple."

Meanwhile, the two romances proceed with tender economy. The mystery of a Fordian character is not the mystery of what he will do next; it is the mystery of his life such as it is at a given moment. It is not so much what happens to him that matters, as what he is; not so much what he does, as what he is in doing it. Thus Ford's peculiar power to evoke the atmosphere of a frontier era, with characters and culture father to our own, yet alien to us. Sandy ("carrot-topped") begins gazing at Prudence ("red-headed") at their first meeting, in Crystal City, and she quietly avoids and seeks his eyes; the relationship throughout is developed subtly to the side of whatever other action is occurring, so their courtship is the sort of event one might not wholly notice on first viewing the picture.

The Travis-Denver (Joanne Dru) romance, though given more prominence, is also articulated in undertones. Ford had taken the Ringo-Dallas love affair from *Stagecoach* (1939) and sublimated it. Travis is a steadier, quieter, and more intelligent sort than Ringo*; Denver seems attracted partially by her inability to fluster him.** Without overtly displaying it, they enjoy each other—which is what makes watching them interesting. Sexual innuendoes are especially covert: for example, the way Travis mounts his horse to bathe in the river, after telling Denver he will "join her." When Travis, like Ringo before him, offers marriage and a lonely life on a cattle ranch to a prostitute, Denver for an instant gazes joyously, then rushes wildly away, as the camera tracks with her in a tear-wrenching motion (eight seconds); she trips and falls, but the camera never stops its relentless motion—one of Ford's most extraordinary scenes. Then, instead of explicating her reasons as he did with Dallas, Ford dissolves to a twenty-five-second study of Denver slouched in the back of her wagon, puffing once on a cigarette then throwing it away (like Ava Gardner, *Mogambo*, or Anne Bancroft, *7 Women*, both of whom she resembles in style).

The Cleggs, though fleeing like the Mormons and showfolk, are not in search of peace; their goal resembles the biblical snake's. Long, secure shots give way to eight frightened and frightening rhythmic close-ups and eerie, hymnal music, to mark their intrusion into the Mormon dance. The close-ups recall Ford's similar parsing of a confrontation in *My Darling Clementine* between Wyatt Earp and the Clanton family. Both Clanton and Clegg

*Ben Johnson (Travis) (1919?– , Oklahoma) is more properly in the line of Ford's relaxed naturals stemming from Harry Carey and Will Rogers than is Wayne. Curiously, he used to be impossibly nervous, but "once Ford relaxed him, he stayed relaxed," recalls Dobe Carey while demonstrating how Ford aped relaxation by standing in a grotesque droop. Johnson entered films as a stuntrider, catching Ford's eye when, doubling Wayne in *Fort Apache*, his quick thinking saved some lives. Alas, his type of hero was as out-of-date in his day as Harry Carey would have been, and he did not get the recognition he deserved until his grossly inferior role in Bogdanovich's *Last Picture Show* (1971).

**Joanne Dru (1923–), a friend of Ford's daughter, starred in Hawks's *Red River* (1947). In contrast to her cocky slinkiness there, she was rather nondescript in *She Wore a Yellow Ribbon*, but achieved her most real-to-life presence in *Wagon Master*.

families are womanless, number four sons (Fred Libby and Mickey Simpson appear in both), and are ruled by despotic patriarchs hostile to all the world, who whimper their dead sons' names at the end, then try to draw and are themselves shot dead. Of the two fathers, Shiloh [sic] Clegg is the more deranged, and his family has an insular criminality closer to that in such seventies films as *Bloody Mama* or *Dirty Harry* than to 1951's *White Heat*. But Shiloh is well rounded with sardonic wit: "The Lord will bless you for [taking us in], brother," he tells Wiggs; "He marks the sparrow's fall." Shiloh, of course, was to be one of history's bloodiest battles.

As the wagons climb the final mountain at the end, instead of the expected apotheosis, Ford runs through another series of close-ups of the Cleggs, preceded by one of Wiggs, thus anticipating for us the Clegg decision to kill Wiggs and destroy the seed grain. "Grain is more valuable to us than gold itself," Wiggs had said (reviving an antithesis Ford exploited in *3 Bad Men* in 1926), inadvertently giving Clegg means to avenge the whipping administered Reese Clegg. To the Clegg sense of things, it mattered not that Reese had outraged an Indian girl in an Indian camp, that Wiggs's quick punishment prevented general massacre, nor that the beating was not so severe that Reese rode his horse less well next day, nor that the Mormons have saved the Cleggs from the posse and given them freedom. The whipper is shot dead, for family honor, as the express-office clerk was shot dead for *disrespect;* rudeness is sacrilegious. When Shiloh assumes control, his haughtiness has the majesty of an ancient autocrat. There is no need for Charles Kemper to play the part satirically or in an overblown Rod Steiger fashion, for Shiloh is self-righteous beyond display, able to slap Wiggs with his hat in the same calm, sane, unpretentious manner one would govern a horse. (In contrast, when Wiggs realizes he has unjustly yelled at his horse for tripping in quicksand and throwing him, he says, "Sorry, horse.")

The Cleggs represent the absolute evil of myth. They ooze dementia, foreboding fatality for whomever they meet. We have not yet discovered their purpose (nor that of the "snakes" in *The Fugitive*). Perhaps they have none, are only a "mistake." Yet they rekindle the age-old theological mystery of evil and divine omniscience. For their encounter with the Mormons seems preordained—in the film's first shots. "Providential," Cleggs terms this encounter, and his blasphemy proves true: innocence obliterates him. Yet the Mormons are lambs, not willing to protect themselves. Without Travis they would have maintained their pacifism, Wiggs would have died, the grain would have been lost and the colony destroyed. Yet—and this compromise of ideology for practicality fascinates Ford—the Mormons will accept protection from a shepherd, thus (a trifle hypocritically?) maintaining their innocence.* "No toil nor labor fear," sing the people; "The Lord will provide," affirms Wiggs.

---

*The same notion appears in *7 Women* (1965), but then the myth is less pure (or perhaps more pure), for the sheep are saved, but their innocence, where intact, is turned into psychosis.

Travis is an odd sort of Fordian hero to mediate between order and chaos, for, reluctant to draw on a man ("only on snakes!") and seeing violence as violence whatever its rationale, he intervenes more from instinct than from higher knowledge. He is, reluctantly, the instrument of the Lord, the gun is appropriately supplied by a small child (an angel), Travis uses it only to prevent a second murder, and even then Sandy forces his hand by throwing the gun at him. The violence—scarcely the film's only "action"—is so swift and sudden that it is over almost before we realize it has begun. And Travis throws away his gun, disgusted at having the snake-killing job thrust upon him.

In contrast to the depressed quality of his prewar work, Ford's optimism reaches a beatific apex in *Wagon Master*. Here, surely, is paradise gained. The debt to constant struggle is acknowledged, and man becomes in some sense the creator, the molder of destiny, while equally the shriven pilgrim gathered at new rivers. The deserts seem constantly in bloom, and the valley entered with innocence and purity intact is the Lord's own and needs only man for its completion. It is not Eden; it is better than Eden, for the "snakes" have been killed by Travis, the Lord's agent, "the answer to a prayer."

As Travis throws away his gun, Ford fades into a clutching moonlit shot of a lush virgin valley and glimmering river (one of the finer moments in constantly fascinating photography by Bert Glennon and Archie Stout). A Mormon hymn (off-camera) accompanies:

Come, come ye saints, no toil nor labor fear,
But with joy wend your way.

Though hard to you this journey may appear,
Grace shall be as your day.
'Tis better far for us to strive
Our useless cares from us to drive;
Do this and joy your hearts will swell—
All is well! All is well!

Dissolve: a vast high-shot of the wagons and of the people walking in a mass away from them. Dissolve: an intentionally theatrical, black-drop night shot: they mount onto a small platform of stones and gaze forward joyfully at / unbridled horses drinking tranquilly from the valley river. / Mormon men and women drink the vision rapturously; / among the children, Elder Wiggs stands in foreground and, along with the final lines of the hymn, he (Ward Bond) takes off his hat and says twice with boyish gusto, "I'll be dog-gone!"—what filmmaker today would venture such accurate simplicity? Quick fade into the recapitulation shots of the finale, with rollicking chorus.

More, perhaps, than any other film, *Wagon Master* is less interested in where it is going (plot), than in where it is (the moment). Still, obviously, it is a movie about *passage*—a "parade" West. Only briefly is "home," the antinomy of passage, suggested. And immediately upon its suggestion, it is abruptly refused by the film, which obstinately cuts back into flashbacks, back to passage rather than fulfillment, back to the past, to distance. And the movie fades out during a pan as a young colt steps up onto firm ground after fording a river—an image of eager progeny that sums up *Wagon Master* in the forward motion of life.

Three War Films

Three war films pass, like the westerns, from social study to mythic evocation. The three employ widely disparate styles of, respectively, comedy, surreal farce, and documentary. But in each case Ford's purpose is identical: a critical portrayal of the virtually unacknowledged ideologies that—in, respectively, hometown America, the frontline army, or national consciousness—establish war's possibility. (The theme is taken up again in *The Long Gray Line*.)

When Willie Comes Marching Home (1950). Ford called *Willie* "one of the funniest films ever made," and in later years would often lament, "I feel I'm essentially a comedy director, but they won't give me a comedy to do."[12] (Of Ford's postwar films, only *The Quiet Man, Donovan's Reef*, an episode of *The Rising of the Moon*, and a TV show, *Flashing Spikes*, could also be classified as comedies.) *Willie* resembles Ford's silent and prewar comedies—economical production, a huge cast of nearly fifty speaking parts, wacky gags, abundant detail, and invention. It would almost be comprehensible as a silent picture. Signs often substitute for spoken words: four newspapers with headlines, successive officers introduced by name plaques (lieutenant, captain, major, colonel), besides seventeen actual signs. More series dot the movie: drinks (wine, rum, whiskey, cognac, bourbon, sherry, compared to milk and ice cream at home), vehicles (trains, planes, fighters, parachutes, boats, motorcycles, bicycles, jeeps, taxis, hay wagon). The hero progresses through all enlisted ranks, while progressively encountering all officer ranks. And there are series of maps (2), radios (3), chasing dogs (2), a "Who's that?" gag (2), parades (2), and parties (3).

Yet *Willie* is chiefly a document on hometown American war fever.* Its obvious serious point is that war pictures never celebrate the guys who do not get into battle. "I'd rather fly dawn patrol in an F-6," declares an ace pilot, "than fool around with a bunch of rookies—that's rough stuff!" But everyone in town ignores poor Kluggs. Near-fatal training accidents are ignored, people ridicule him, small dogs attack him.

Willie's less obvious serious point is yet another Fordian essay in social dynamics, on his "Why They Fight" theme. But satire is more obvious. Punxatawney is a platitude, as are its citizens, institutions, buildings, rites, lifestyle, and attitudes (like Sternberg's masterful short, *The Town*, and Preston Sturges's *Hail the Conquering Hero* and *Miracle of Morgan's Creek*). Our hero loves the girl next door and runs across their yards like True Heart Susie. Their two houses are identical, differing only slightly in tasteful but unadmirable lower-middle-class decor. The two mothers (Evelyn Varden and Mae Marsh) are hilarious models of pixilated lubby-dub. Kluggs's father's every gesture affirms his stereotype—like grabbing a cigar out of his mouth when the radio broadcasts news of Pearl Harbor, or carrying the bass drum in the American Legion Band. Rituals, too, are repeatedly lampooned—church collections, parties, and tearful train-station good-byes. And when Ford builds up to one of his typical finale-revues, the obvious irony is that Kluggs is leaving: both times Willie came marching home he was greeted with suspicion. And Ford's TV-style pans and dollies mimic the platitudinous material, as do his patterns of master shot followed by crosscuts. The latter, typical of Hollywood cheapies but not of Ford, is capitalized on for the opportunities for variation afforded by its formal clarity. Performances, too, broad and satiric but subtle and economic in gesture, mimic the platitude. In marked contrast to other Fords, characters do not

---

*Punxatawney, West Virginia, 1941: Bill Kluggs (Dan Dailey), first to enlist, gets a hero's send-off and a welcome-home party after training, only to spend a miserable war as a gunnery instructor at home watching others leave. Finally, opportunity comes, but his B-17 has to be abandoned. Kluggs, asleep, bails out later, is captured by French partisans photographing a V-2, gotten drunk, quizzed in London, quizzed in Washington, exhausted by forced drinks, and finally hops a freight to escape a psychiatric ward, only to be clubbed by his father who mistakes him for a spy when he climbs in his kitchen window—four days after leaving. But MPs will escort him to Washington for a presidential decoration, and Kluggs leaves a hero.

Sy Gomberg was nominated for an Oscar for original story. Lt. Gomberg had actually left an air base Friday noon on a B-17, been strafed by a Japanese plane that he then shot down, and found himself home and haggard Monday.

surpass stereotypical expectations, except in exaggeration, and society is homogeneous rather than stratified. Even national differences are incidental: the war mentality is the same whether French, English, German, or American.

The French village is an equivalent of Punxatawney. It has the requisite picturesque square, the inn, and cross-section of indigenous types, all exactly as they ought to be—even the Germans. The partisan Yvonne (Corinne Calvet) is young, beautiful, sexy, pert, and mysterious; she wears lipstick, low-necked blouse, and gunbelt; she puts Kluggs's bracelet down her bosom and stores her notebook there too. Ford pokes fun over the French word *impossible* (meaning: I-don't-want-to) and Dan Dailey's double-takes over a question about the "Yonkees" imitates Ford's own tomfoolery with British interviewers. But Kluggs himself cannot speak standard English: quizzed who Dick Tracy is, he replies, "A flatfoot, a cop, a *gendarme*." What is comic in Punxatawney, however, here has the depressed earnestness of a neorealist war drama, with the intimate proximity of war. All the same, hidden amidst the melancholia occur the same gags, the same pompous seriousness so absurd in the context of Punxatawney. The Frenchman looks silly when he kneels with his gun to cover friends fleeing into a crypt. A German officer kicks down a farmhouse door, then carefully hides behind as his men barge in shooting. The gray-suited *madame le professeur* blinks her eye comically when cautioned. But nothing is funny, least of all the farewell to Yvonne, her hair wafting in the wind, the flat grassy hills and low-lying clouds. Even photographic style has changed: subdued Renoiresque light, white skies, restricted depth of field, giving poetry to bare tree branches. And music, rare elsewhere, has melodramatic functions in France.

From the dark silhouettes of the French coast, we progress to seacoast dusk, then to London and the Thames, somewhat brighter but with blimps hanging in the sky and sirens sounding, while over Washington, the Pentagon and Potomac, the sun shines bright and strong. Clothing, too, progresses toward lighter colors. Those back home can only make believe, and so paranoia steadily increases. The elder Kluggs (William Demarest) assumes the Germans would go to the trouble of spying on his kitchen. And the gruff MPs who show up clubbing and pounding their way into his home resemble the Nazis seen earlier. That scary suggestion culminates Ford's satire. MPs act like MPs, soldiers like soldiers, good patriotic civilians like good patriotic civilians. Such was the structure of society during World War II and everything follows from that. Sang Kluggs, "I say hello to the people I know in a vague sort of way. Baffled and blue I go stumbling through the day." And the band plays, "We're poor little lambs who have gone astray, baa, baa, baa."

Ford presents the platitude that today we name "Middle America," how those who live within this platitude are uncritically conditioned by it, how

innocent they are, and how dangerous. Despite humor, the portrait is distinctly melancholic and would be overtly cynical, were the characters less affectionately drawn. As it is, we may remember best how Kluggs mimics Fred Astaire's pointing hand and top hat, doing a period song and dance, how he and Marge (Colleen Townsend) swing with delighted rapport, graceful and marionettelike, how Ford treats this—the sole classic-musical sequence in all his films—with élan and fun, panning and cutting with rhythmic symmetry from his proscenium-framing camera.

What Price Glory (1952). The original idea had been to remake Raoul Walsh's celebrated silent as a musical, but Fox executives from Darryl Zanuck down were surprised when they saw what Ford had wrought. "If you want music, *you* put it in," said Ford, as he walked out.

There *are* musical numbers, mostly at the beginning, though fewer of them than were shot. But, neither fish nor fowl, the movie was received coldly and dismissed as a weird miscalculation by the maker of *The Quiet Man* (which had debuted the day before in New York). Among a surfeit of war movies, this one seemed neither sufficiently pro- nor antiwar to a public fatigued by Korean "police actions." For, like *This Is Korea!*, the support-the-boys documentary Ford had made the year before, *What Price Glory* is a eulogy for the dog soldier, and not a defense of the politics of war.

Of the 1926 version, Walsh has written that his message was

> that war is not only futile but a dirty, bungled mess. There was no glory
> for the men on the rifle pits and the trenches. They had to launch or repel
> an attack against the enemy because their generals and congress said it
> was their duty.[13]

Ford, whose war experience was intimate, intensifies this message. But instead of belittling the soldiers for their helplessness, he stands back in awe
at their persistence. Whether, as Flagg wonders, there is a kind of religion
to the profession of arms that a soldier can't shake loose from, or whether it
is merely that the drums, the bugles, and the marching columns offer a more
rational order than the farcical hysteria of life behind the lines, Ford finds a
kind of nobility in these men. Their "glory," their "truth" that "goes marching on"—cited in the opening tableaux—is more universal than the heroism of military duty.

Flagg's type of soldier is not a normal human. He and Quirt bitch incessantly, go nearly insane with paranoia at the front, but they have no other
life. "I almost got married . . . 25 times . . . but I was saving myself. From
what? From what?" For war. War, Flagg wails, "was alright when you had
30 or 40 men in the hills who knew their jobs, but now there are so many
little boys, little boys who have no business being here at all." Yet war's

infection is contagious. The wounded boy who shrieks, "What price glory now, Captain Flagg?" hobbles out the door with his gun a few minutes later.

Actually, what he walks into is a theatrical mist lit bright red, with a hymn on the soundtrack, a more intense version of the artificiality of the gold wheat field and its bright white clouds against pink skies, or the blue-tinted night scenes. And this artificiality continues into the hysteria of the acting. In the midst of this surreal hell, there is a moment of happiness when Flagg and Quirt capture a German colonel. Now they can go home. The comedy Ford introduces here (Keaton's salute joke) aims to mirror their mood. But like much of the picture's comedy—and like the love song (substituting for Walsh's chewing-gum scene) that Marisa Pavan sings to Robert Wagner—it may strike us as a bit excessive and misplaced. (When Ford fails, at least he does not fail timidly.) In *What Price Glory* both comedy and melodrama are contrasting species of the same hysteria, and serve to equate Ford's odd style with his theme: that war is an extension of reality into farce, and also into lunacy, and yet seems, deceptively, more purposeful and rational than the ambiguous games of peacetime. This is portrayed in the poker game, when Flagg's hysteria bursts even *his* ample bounds. These soldiers grasp, without option, for the only *raison d'être* their lives possess: marching on. "We don't know where we're going—nobody knows."

The parade as a substitute for reason is, like duty earlier, an important metaphor in most of Ford's postwar pictures (the journey of the Mormons in *Wagon Master*, the dragging home of Maureen O'Hara in *The Quiet Man*, the parades in *The Long Gray Line*, the search in *The Searchers*). Life is a constant passage without a map, and with only immediate purposes; the seduction of the moment gives life its vitality. Since the opposition between the precariousness of freedom and self-responsibility and the surety of order and prescribed duty is strongest in the military, it is hardly surprising that Ford almost always chooses disciplined social organisms for his subjects. But the sense of duty that sustains his individuals also commonly leads them astray into aberrations or death. Racism becomes a function of society, like war. If the army exists for war, Ford's pictures also show us that war exists for the army.

Although all Ford's movies of the early fifties are eccentric, *What Price Glory* is the weirdest of the lot. Perhaps it is too much of a good—or horrific—thing. The concentration on the frightening process by which individuals coalesce into a fighting organism deprives the picture of deep peaks and valleys of contour. Despite the contrasts between love and war (prefiguring in their extremity the films of Ford's transitional period), the modal variation is insufficient to relieve a certain erosion in interest. And unlike most Fords, the last act is the weakest of the three.

Both Flagg and Quirt are hollow heroes for Ford. Since neither of them has any life beyond the histrionic, Ford is forced to develop Lewisohn, a weak minor character, in compensation. But it does not work. Curiously, Ford never spends time mourning the dead; he focuses intensely on the living, and the scene between Flagg and Nicole, about Lewisohn's death, is strangely flat.

What Price Glory is the *volte face* of *When Willie Comes Marching Home*, and it works best when closest to comedy. Act I has a gag nearly every ten seconds, some broad, most subtle sleight of hand. James Cagney and Dan Dailey slouch throughout the picture and deliver their intensity from the neck up. This reinforces the spring-wound tautness of Ford's farce, and of course adds to the impression that *What Price Glory* relaxes too seldom.

Ford had wanted John Wayne in the part of Flagg (Wayne had played the role in Ford's 1949 stage production of the play—see Filmography) and his mood was not improved when Henry and Phoebe Ephron, the scenarists, took one of his off-handed barbs to heart and walked off the set in a huff, mistakenly convinced he was anti-Jewish. Unable to work with any of his usual scriptwrights, Ford largely ignored the Ephron text.

This Is Korea! **(1951).** No genre of film arouses such controversy as poetic documentary. Distortion of fact, fabrication, omission and commission, prejudicing viewpoint, blatant chauvinism, all supposedly anathema to documentary, are in fact the modus operandi of *Potemkin*, *Listen to Britain*, *Triumph of the Will* (and, perhaps less consciously, TV news). Distance (aesthetic and geopolitical) may, for some viewers, excuse Eisenstein, Jennings, or Riefenstahl (and myopia disguises the news). But with America's own John Ford, so much do his films seem personal statements and so prevalent is the tendency to confuse Ford's intentions with his characters' (as in misreadings of *Fort Apache*), that distance contracts to confrontation, when his mythicizing treatment of history (through aestheticized images and idiomatic dialogue) deals not with storybook past but with newsreel now, as in *This Is Korea!*

That picture's failure in the fifties to earn its cost (financed by Republic, not the republic) was surely due less to politics than to awkward length and thoroughly depressing mood. But it suffers irrelevantly when those determined to see it as propaganda point out (correctly) its scarce success explaining an unpopular war or engaging homefront solidarity with the boys over there. For closer inspection reveals, superficial evidence to the contrary, that anything so practical as propaganda was merely Ford's excuse, not his purpose, for a project initiated wholly by himself: to document a moment, an attitude, that even today seems shrouded in poetry.

Thus he is not concerned with detailing strategy, movements, dates, or statistics; merely the soldiers' worm's-eye view. Nor for Ford the journalist's heady assumption to report truth, or both sides, of a war; more relevant to capture the spirit of his own side (distinct, at least). For Ford the consequential mythology of the Korean War lay not in judicious debate over its wisdom, but in our dominant ideology, as represented in the attitudes of those defending the Pax Americana.

It was "Christmas in the year of grace, 1950," and marines were giving bubble gum to kids and dying for them thinking of home; they were retreating in desolate cold and tending myriad war machines and killing people, and all this was for God, mother, and orphaned children, for Christmas and the flag and things that make life worthwhile. Still, they wondered why they were there; something seemed wrong. It was a job to be done, duty, and there were the kids, but, god, it was awful. There are glimpses of heroes: MacArthur in silhouette, Chesty Puller growling ("Put some more fire down on those people! Thank ya!"); but mostly there is marching, drudgery, and, above all, machines: again and again Ford cuts away to name weapons. The enemy in person is almost never encountered; but others keep returning dead or maimed. * We go on, leaving cemeteries behind, one hill after another, endlessly, until space and time merge into dreary sameness and it no longer matters whether we are "advancing" north or south or whether it is now or then.

This is the attitude Ford shows, and the movie is more distanced, less folksy, and not at all optimistic, compared with *The Battle of Midway*, and the soldiers never come disarmingly alive as they did there. That was Ford's war, not this. But this was Korea, this was the cold war. Ford arrived January 1, 1951, two months after a million Chinese hurtled across the border pushing UN forces into desperate retreat midst snow and ice; a month or so later our counterattack began. Characteristically, Ford had found the moment of defeat. No past film of his, not *The Informer* and not *The Long Voyage Home*, has such long-sustained sensuousness: somber, sober, empty. But bleakness is not conveyed through sacrificing aesthetic brilliance; instead of desaturating color, he found a yellow-green-blue option to create mood. Pale greenish fields fade into yellowish hills blending into bluish skies; wintry landscapes, otherwise pretty, are framed behind gnarled trees. Only when orphans jump for bubble gum do bright reds and other gay colors appear. But there is a cut-away to a deep-hued hospital ship, and deep tones paint a scene in Tokyo as command officers reenact historic moments with stiff superconsciousness (recalling the independence proclamation in *The Plough and the Stars*). Meanwhile, retreat and weather worsen, and white skies haze everything; marines, unlike the 7th Cavalry, are not etched against the sky but blended in *sfumato* to the earth. Carrier planes take off into stark skies, with motor and water sounds replacing music. Through the night the *Missouri*'s cannon** flash and thunder (as in *The Wings of Eagles*).

*Ford once lamented not being able to show the Chinese attacking at night; but the enemy's absence has Sophoclean eloquence. (The Chinese are never mentioned in the film.)

**The scene of the battleship firing all its sixteen-footers simultaneously—referred to by several biographers—is not in the movie.

Quickening montage and crackling fire-wind climax long seasons in hell as marines plunge into maelstroms of flame and acrid smoke ("For this is Korea, chums. This is Korea. And we go in"). The camera watches from doorways, anticipating Ethan's descent into hell in *The Searchers;* no wonder Ford's next movie, *The Quiet Man*, is so Edenesque.

Outside any context but this, the effect of a small boy's wry grin as Korean nuns accept him into an orphanage might be bathetic ("You'll be alright now!" tenderly). Elsewhere we see an endless road of refugees ("Now look at this, and look at it, and look at it!"). Korean faces stare frequently at the camera (at us), blankly or inquisitively, whilst GI faces tend to ignore us. It is the familiar Fordian theme of privacy invaded—usually by the hero, now by us.

The movie concludes quietly, in perhaps the most refulgently haunting montage of Ford's career. There is no glorification here; but in this infinite purgatory, what magnificence! what weary, Iliadic persistence and sacrifice to undergo, so that somewhere way around the world in some semi-stone-age nation, little kids can have bubble gum. Such an effort is inseparable from the preppy cold-war jargon of the narration, which makes us wince, yes, but which Ford was so right to use. For this is a definitive memento of the uncertain hope that America could make things all right in the world.

The Quiet Man (1952). Like so many other Ford heroes, Sean Thornton enters this movie by arriving on a vehicle (a train), a touch personal to Ford that confirms the intimacy suggested by the credit sequence's warm tones, dark waters, and cello motifs. Sean arrives in Innisfree from Pittsburgh and has his buggy stop on a little stone bridge near a small cottage, and he hears in his mind his dead mother's voice:

— Don't you remember it, Seannie, and how it was?
  The road led up past the chapel and it wind and it wound.
  And there is the field where Dan Tobin's bullock chased you.
  It was a lovely little house, Seanin,
  and the roses,
  well, your father used to tease me about them,
  but he was that fond of them too.

Quips the coachman, "Ah, that's nothin' but a wee humble cottage." But comes the reply, "I'm Sean Thornton and I was born in that little cottage. I'm home and home I'm going to stay." *The Quiet Man* will be the reverse of *How Green Was My Valley*.

Ford liked to say he was born *Sean;** his parents came from this part of Ireland and he had made trips there as a boy. "I shot it on my native heath," he said; "the actors were old family friends."[14] Indeed, they were more than

---

*He had Irish cousins named Thornton, and dubbed Jack McGowan's runty character "Feeney."

that: *The Quiet Man* so abounds in family ties that its communal "feel" arises naturally. Besides Ford's brother Francis and son-in-law Ken Curtis in the cast, daughter Barbara and son Patrick participated in the production. Barry Fitzgerald and Arthur Shields were brothers in real life (and old friends of many of the picture's Abbey Theatre players), Bond and Wayne had gone to school together, and four of Wayne's children (Ford's godchildren) sit at the race with Maureen O'Hara, whose brother is Charles Fitzsimmons. Other old acquaintances included Merian C. Cooper, Archie Stout, Mae Marsh, Harry Tenbrook, and Victor McLaglen, whose son Andrew was assistant director.

Ford had wanted to make *The Quiet Man* for many years and had almost done so back in 1937 in association with a co-op called Renowned Artists Company. And then had come the financial problems of Argosy Pictures. "Remember," Ford told Lindsay Anderson, "that with all these pictures [the Argosy westerns] I wasn't just working to pay off on *The Fugitive*, but to make enough for *The Quiet Man* as well. Of course, it'll probably lose the lot; but that's the way it always goes."[15]

But when Ford got to Ireland in 1951 things did not go well. Lindsay Anderson, who interviewed him just after location shooting in Cong, reports Ford's remarks:

> Injuries inherited from the war gave him, intermittently, a good deal of pain; they had put him out of action for a few days on *The Quiet Man* [when Wayne and Patrick Ford shot the race sequence], and generally made studio shooting—in the glare and oppressive atmosphere of a sound stage—a penance. "I was out in Korea before coming to Ireland—I made a documentary there called *This Is Korea*—and oddly enough I never had a twinge. But out at Cong it really got me down."[16]

No doubt the weather was the cause; it "was photographed in the rain—or Irish mist, as they call it in Ireland. That helped the picture a lot."[17] But, Ford continued,

> "The unit seemed to go soft too; they started standing about looking at the scenery. I had to start watching for points of continuity—people looking out of windows, that sort of thing, which no one else noticed. Then, of course, our technicians work a lot faster than yours. It was really too big a job for one man to tackle on his own."[18]

"I'm just going back to making Westerns," Ford concluded, and even mused about quitting films entirely: "I want to be a tugboat captain."[19]

Perhaps no Ford picture has been so popular as *The Quiet Man*.* But when François Truffaut wrote of his dislike for Ford's "slap-on-the-rump"

*The Quiet Man was Ford's top-grossing picture to date. It won Oscars for direction and photography, and was nominated in six other categories: best picture, supporting actor

style of comedy, he summed up both a prevalent critical antagonism and a popular enthusiasm. Yet both attitudes miss the forest for the trees. According to Ford,

> The customs shown in *The Quiet Man* are true and prevail in Connemara, which is the poorest county in Ireland and the only one Cromwell never conquered.[20]

Indeed, the picture's commercialism and intoxicating Technicolor tend to obscure its documentary and Brechtian aspects. Ford moves rapidly through an analysis of Innisfree society. We go from train station to countryside to town to church to pub, meeting trainmen, coachmen, priests, aristocrats, squires, the IRA, drinkers, field hands, Anglican clergy. But again, the many characters provide such atmospheric vignettes (and their theatrics and comedy are so engaging and funny) that the community's sociologic complexity—despite the picture's obsession with public custom—is not readily apparent. Yet Connemara is a Third-world culture, fundamentally Gaelic-Irish, but with the Roman Church and England superimposed upon the palimpsest.*

Well may Widow Tillane maintain that "Innisfree is very far from being heaven." She will never be believed. Thick though it be with stultifying formalities, to Sean (and to us, after World War II), this land of simplicity and community, where horses and bicycles are the means of transport and life is close to the soil, seems Shangri-La, without Shangri-La's asexual intellectualism. Yet Ford's story should be evident enough: a peaceful American returns to his native village, but can only find peace there after bullying his wife and brawling with her brother; until then he will feel himself an outsider, confused in his manhood, a gentleman surrounded by peasants and clergy.

The Reverend Peter Lonergan is among the more interesting characters. "What I detest more than anything are the Irish priests," Ford told Tavernier, adding, "The parish priest [of Innisfree] has more money than the Lord Mayor of Dublin."[21] And in opposition to the amiable tones of Father Lonergan's narrating voice, Ford in pictures, without doing anything overt enough to offend the Legion of Decency, depicts Lonergan in his first meeting with Thornton as repressed, twisted, and sanctimonious. I cannot reproduce the grotesque shadow his hat casts over his face, nor the lurid sound of his voice:

(McLaglen), screenplay (Nugent), art direction (Frank Hotaling), set decoration (John McCarthy, Jr., and Charles Thompson), sound recording. The Screen Directors Guild gave its crown to Ford, and the Screen Writers Guild its to Nugent, the National Board of Review and Look Magazine chose it best film, and it was one of three runners-up at Venice.

*Ford said: "This is a very sexy story, you know. I like good lusty sex but I object to dirty innuendoes. . . . I was born in Cape Elizabeth, Maine, but I went to school in Ireland for a while and was brought up to speak both English and Gaelic. Every Irishman is an actor. The Irish and the colored people are the most natural actors in the world."

Lonergan: Ah yes. I knew your people, Sean. Your grandfather. He died in Australia. In a penal colony. And your father. He was a good man too. Bad accident that. And your mother.

Sean: She's dead. America when I was twelve.

Lonergan: [Piously:] I'll remember her in the mass tomorrow, Sean. [Sternly:] You'll be there. Seven o'clock.

Sean: [With Yankee ingenuousness:] Sure I will.

And come next morning Sean is there in church. And Ford's floor-level shot down the nave is the strongest image in the film, and indicates the curious power of an institution that has integrated itself with local custom: Mary Kate will use Gaelic to confess her marital difficulties, and Lonergan, with an appetite for violence beyond his calling, hypocritically performs penance by upbraiding his effeminate curate. (A similarly practical morality consists in forbidding sale of intoxicating liquors at horse races—but just during the race itself.)

Ford called *The Quiet Man* "a love story, a mature love story"[22] and "a very sexy story."[23] And as one might expect, he exploits a love story's traditional archetypal situations—skipping through fields, embracing in a cemetery during a storm—with artful novelty, but not with such novelty as to make us forget them as symbolic reminders of the repression within which the romance is enacted. The first glances occur within painterly formality (green foliage and sheep, then the scarlet-skirted redhead), ecclesiastical formality (the holy-water font), or atavistic longing (Thornton's balletic sex-

ual clash with Mary Kate's blue blouse and red skirt at night in his cottage).
When Sean comes to call he is greeted with formulaic phrases and Mary
Kate (as often) is framed by a window.* Formal courtship is initiated with
the whole village gazing in witness; the wedding itself is given Victorian
distance as they pose for their portrait (Lonergan narrates, "So they were
married—in the same little chapel I gave them their Baptism") and flash
powder explodes. But the dispute over the dowry disrupts the love
"process"—as indeed Sean's Yankee ways so often disrupt Gaelic custom.

In one of the few scenes in which he and Mary Kate talk reasonably, Sean
is working in the yard. "Roses?!" she gasps, "Are you plantin' roses?! Fine
farmer you are—not a turnip or a cabbage or a potato on the place. . . ." "Or
children," says Sean. She changes the subject to getting a horse for the
ploughing; Sean suggests a tractor. "A tractor!" she responds, "Nasty, smelly
things, an' besides, they're an awful price. With a horse you get other advantages. . . ." "For the roses," says Sean, handing her a buttercup.

The scene, though one of the least overt in a declamatory movie, is one of
Ford's finest. The flower symbol is particularly dear to his work and conveys
major ideas in more than twenty pictures: Hannah Jessop is given flowers to
carry to France in *Pilgrimage;* families hold pieces of heather in *The Black
Watch* as they bid farewell to sons off to war; Lana throws her bouquet in
Drums Along the Mohawk; Lincoln puts a flower on Ann Rutledge's grave;
Dr. Mudd returns home to flowers in *The Prisoner of Shark Island;* Joanne
Dru brings John Wayne a plant for his wife's grave in *She Wore a Yellow
Ribbon;* cadets bring flowers for old Marty Maher in *The Long Gray Line;*
Minne's flowers get Spig Wead to move his toe in *The Wings of Eagles;* a
single flower is carried in the slum church in *Gideon's Day;* the Irish mistake
the British couple for newlyweds because of their flowers in *A Minute's
Wait;* Frank Skeffington puts a fresh flower daily beneath his wife's portrait;

*The scene recalls Mr. Gruffydd outside Angharad's window in *How Green Was My Valley.*

Tom Doniphon gives Hallie a cactus rose in *The Man Who Shot Liberty Valance,* and half a century later she gives one to him; in *Donovan's Reef,* in one of many floral metaphors, Dr. Dedham's outcast children lay flowers on his lawn Christmas morning; in *7 Women,* Woody Strode picks flowers for Dr. Cartwright.

Sean's mother's voice spoke of the roses she used to grow in this very same yard. But Sean not only wishes to renew a tradition; in the form of the buttercup he expresses his wish to give roses to Mary Kate, roses that now express all he wishes to be and all he hopes for. Indeed, this sequence began inside the house, with a lengthy, formalized shot of their empty dining room, a large bowl of red roses (the same red as Mary Kate's skirt) prominent on the center-set table. Now she fastens Sean's buttercup to her lapel.

Earlier, red roses were thrown away by Sean when Danaher rejected his courtship. Later at the wedding, Mary Kate's bouquet is a prominent motif; then, when he brutally carries her to the bedroom and she momentarily submits to him, she embraces him with this bouquet; then, thrown upon the bed alone, she cries with it.

It is significant that Ford externalizes their conflict. The statuesque crowds that gather for each step of the battle remind us that in this society no relationship is private. And when Thornton and Danaher at last confront each other by the field oven, the village women standing veiled and separate from their men remind us that the stick both Mary Kate (by the fireside) and an older woman (coming from the train) offer Sean is no mere prop of Fordian-concocted comedy. The parade back from the station (with the "kick-on-the-rump") is not only a form of the Fordian parade, as in *What Price Glory* a substitute for reason, it is also a graphic illustration that marriage is a community function. Mary Kate wants her things about her because it is the *inside* of the house that is the woman's power base. Sean fails to grasp this, because he fails to grasp that, *external* appearances to the contrary, in Ireland the man merely reigns: it is the woman, controlling bed and board, who rules ("They'll be no dinner tonight," saith Mary Kate). Thus for today's audiences, *The Quiet Man,* like many Fords, poses the worrisome proposition that primitive sexism might not be without advantages; for liberation is often another form of compulsory conformity, one all too often deracinating the individual. In Innisfree, Sean *must* conform; and when he does, Ford hits high gear for his wonderful finale-revue of cameo portraits. There is irony, to be sure, but more profound than bitter. For is it ever possible to watch those smiling, cheering faces, shot out at you with the brazenness of Eisenstein peasants, and the moment when Mary Kate throws away Sean Thornton's stick and they join hands and run at last into their cottage and the bagpipes come in to climax, is it really possible to resist Ford's poetry?

Ford is still an expressionist, and in *The Quiet Man* emotions are not merely represented, but articulated. One notes the lovers' balletic clashes, or (an almost more typical instance) the way Mary Kate interrupts a lengthy, sedate conversation with the marriage broker (Barry Fitzgerald) to jump to her feet and race to the forescreen (the camera cuts rapidly backward to expand the frame), both camera and actress giving kinetic and spatial articulation of her reaction to Sean's words (that she come "with the clothes on her back—or without them"). Equally expressionistic is Ford's use of color in his artful, closed-formed, painterly compositions. One might argue that in *The Rising of the Moon* (1956), Ford's second made-in-Ireland film, the subtle black-and-white photos have a more "realist" air and better serve to document Ireland's countryside; but we should beware falling sophomorically into the illusion that "realist" is innately superior to (or more truthful than) "expressionist." Three-strip dye-transfer Technicolor was (like Rimsky-Korsakov's orchestration) generally used not for naturalism but for glorious artifice. The deep scarlet of the roses is one such example, the greenness of the fields another—Ford was actually accused of having painted the fields. But similar logic is a mite less successfully applicable to the scores of the two pictures. *The Rising of the Moon*'s discreet use of tenor and recorder weighs less heavily upon its (admittedly less fortified) images than does Victor Young's richly symphonic one upon *The Quiet Man*'s; a few snatches of accordion and spinet are all we get of on-screen music, alas.

In the original story, by Maurice Walsh, Sean Thornton is a featherweight whose size belies his ferocity, and no one can imagine his skill. In Ford's version no one doubts John Wayne's strength, they only think him a quaint American, perhaps a coward. Obviously Ford's "quiet" man is different from Walsh's, and it is difficult to say whether the decision to alter the character's size was for the best, although there is something to be said for Ford's eliminating a facile gimmick in favor of a subtler structure of *moral* tensions. Wayne, in any case, tended to be vulnerable rather than domineering in Ford pictures—perhaps reflecting their original relationship as a polite college boy working for a famous, patriarchal director. Wayne's Sean Thornton is closer to the shy, sensitive brother in *Salute* (1929) than to the cocky, bossy older brother who lectures him to grab what he wants and fight to keep it. This, of course, is what Sean Thornton is reluctant to do. Thus, while on one hand, it is he who upholds the tenets of liberalism against his wife's traditional sexism, on the other hand, Wayne's low-energy, suppressed, dead-rhythmed performance, especially juxtaposed with Maureen O'Hara's passion and the flamboyance of all the Irish, marks Sean Thornton as a dead man emotionally. "That was a goddam hard script," said Wayne. "For nine weeks I was just playing a straight man to those wonderful characters, and that's really hard."[24] Indeed, in his emotional repression, Sean resembles the Fonda heroes in Ford (Lincoln, Tom Joad, Wyatt Earp, the Fugitive) and is in fact a typical Ford hero trying to moderate intolerance. But this time the hero's inability to join the community derives not from his priesthood or even from the moral principles Sean espouses, but from his inabilities to accept reality (the reality of himself as one who killed and one who likes to fight, the reality of Innisfree and of Red Danaher and their traditions); the true hero does not shrink from violence, whose salutary place in life he concedes. Sean Thornton, like so many Ford characters (and particularly after World War II), has learned to forget the horrid, violent past, and to return home (thus the deep significance of the scene behind the film's title credits); but he is one of the few who actually make it home and find rebirth there, albeit ironically, as a macho male.

Francis Ford plays the next-to-last of his twenty-nine appearances in brother John's pictures: Dan Tobin, an old man with long white beard who jumps from his deathbed to see the fight. Francis's parts had progressively less dialogue as the years rolled by—he was a marvellous mime—and his last spoken word here comes toward the middle, during the wedding sequence when, echoing Danaher, he says, "Without further eloquence." It would make a better story to say he never spoke again on screen, but in fact in his large role in *The Sun Shines Bright* he does say a single word, "refreshments!" The cameo of brother Francis, incidentally, is *The Quiet Man*'s penultimate: he's jumping for joy.

The Sun Shines Bright (1953). John Ford:

> Maybe there's one that I love to look at again and again. That's *The Sun Shines Bright*. That's really my favorite. At Republic, old man [studio head Herbert] Yates didn't know what to do with it. The picture had comedy, drama, pathos, but he didn't understand it. His kind of picture had to have plenty of sex or violence. This one had neither, it was just a good picture. But Yates fooled around with it after I left the studio and almost ruined it.[25]

The Sun Shines Bright is one of two or three John Ford pictures one would like to call his finest. Yet it never had a New York first run, was dismissed by the *Times* as so many sentimental clichés, and was quickly cut from ninety to sixty-five minutes. Its failure contributed to the demise of Ford's Argosy Pictures, and even today its depictions of blacks may, wrongfully, incite indignation. Any treatment of this obscure film must try to evoke its artistic magnitude and to clarify its attitudes toward race.

It might well have been titled *Intolerance*, not alone for its theme, but for its formal complexity as well. Unlike Griffith's film, however, its structuring antinomies are simultaneously thematic and formal. And its complex subtleties are hidden beneath an air of effortless ingenuousness. For, despite four intricate story lines and twenty or so distinct characters, the movie's narrative, composed in tidy sequences with a Mozartian concision and nakedness of technique, unfolds most of the time midst dancing and parading through suites of beautiful and intriguing compositions. Rarely has a movie been so inventive—and playful—with montage.* Yet each separate shot seems a

---

*Minus titles, the film runs 88 minutes 33 seconds and has 640 shots (8.3" average). But, leaving out a 60-second shot and the slowly cut funeral (7'15", 16 shots), there are 623 shots in 80

Figure 7. *The Sun Shines Bright*

A small western Kentucky town c. 1905

ACT I. The First "Day"—Morning
1. Levy. Ashby Corwin comes home, and romances Lucy Lee Lake.
2. Courtroom. Judge Priest prevents his opponent Maydew from persecuting banjoist U. S. Grant Woodford (whose rendition of "Dixie" causes patriotic bedlam) and town madam Mallie Cramp.

ACT II. The First "Day"—Night
1. a. As he has for eighteen years—ever since Dr. Lake brought home his granddaughter Lucy Lee, whom he does not recognize—General Fairfield refuses to attend the CSA veterans meeting.
   b. Priest tells the eleven vets he will take home their portrait of the general and his wife, lest Lucy Lee see it and realize who she is (for she looks exactly like her grandmother).
   c. And Priest returns to the USA vets their "captured" flag.
2. Outside. Drunk, Ashby sees Lucy Lee, then whips Buck for gossiping about her, but Priest explains General Fairfield's son was killed in a riverboat fight over her mother.
3. The mother arrives in town, collapses on her way to Mallie's and is taken to Dr. Lake's, where, glimpsing Lucy Lee, she fulfills her dying wish.
4. Lucy Lee runs to Priest's home, spies the portrait, and realizes who she is. Then the sheriff arrives: Mendy Ramser has been raped and the bloodhounds treed U. S.

ACT III. The Second "Day"—Morning.
Jeff fetches Priest, who confronts a lynch mob outside U. S.'s cell.

ACT IV. The Second "Day"—Night
1. Mallie comes to see Priest, who promises "the Lord will provide" the dead woman a proper funeral.
2. Ashby takes Lucy Lee to the festival dance, but discreet stares chase her out, just as
3. The sheriff arrives: Mendy has identified Buck, who her father shoots, Buck flees in Lucy Lee's carriage, is shot by Brother Finney, while Ashby rescues Lucy Lee.

ACT V. The Third "Day"
1. Maydew's election-day oration is interrupted by
2. A white hearse, a carriage of whores, and Priest. Eventually, a hundred townsmen join him.
3. At the blacks' church, General Fairfield joins Lucy Lee, and Priest recites the parable of the woman taken in adultery.
4. Maydew is confident, but the lynch mob tie the vote for Priest, and he votes for himself.
5. That night: the whites parade past Priest's door, then the blacks come serenade him.

---

minutes, for a 7.7" average. Republic's prerelease excisions—including a scene in which Priest chats to portraits of the dead—are presumably lost for all time (?).

complete little movie in itself—like Lumière's one-shot films. And each shot *tells*: we are not merely *shown* a storyland, but are led, *by means of* Ford's narrative and cinematic textures, into an analysis of the class structures of Fairfield, Kentucky, 1905, its people, their manners and civilization, and, finally, into their collective consciousness.

The small world of Fairfield is fraught with divisions: the Southern faction, holding firmly to the Old South's traditions and the CSA's glories; the Northern faction, sometimes miming progress in carpetbagger terms and maintaining GAR traditions; the Negro population, not far enlightened out of slavery's traditions and rigidly segregated; the ignorant, tough farmers from the Tornado District; the prostitutes, the military-school cadets, the temperance women. There are the aristocrats, the businessmen, the politicians, the townsfolk, the farmers and the subproletariat, the blacks. Within each of these groups, ingenuous adherence to tradition sets the stage for intolerant persecution not only between factions but even within families. Various aspects of intolerance are illustrated in the four story lines (in two of which it is the appearance of the steamboat—Fairfield's link with the outer world—that precipitates crisis): (1) Priest's reelection campaign against Republican Maydew—who employs labels to stigmatize people and discredit tolerant attitudes; (2) Ashby Corwin's return to Fairfield and romance with Lucy Lee—the bitter profligate humanized by the outcast orphan; (3) U. S. Woodford's near lynching for rape—the true culprit incites racist hatred but is thwarted by Priest and exposed; (4) The mystery of Lucy Lee's parentage, revealed when her mother, a whore, returns to Fairfield to die—moral intolerance dividing families and persecuting an innocent child. *

Fairfield's whites are depicted as militarist and rambunctious—by means of uniforms and deportment, but chiefly by music: when they dance they also march; in the funeral procession they march; even standing in place they march. Only thrice do they produce their own music: march

---

*The picture claims to derive from three of Irvin S. Cobb's many Judge Priest stories. In Cobb's "The Sun Shines Bright," Dr. Lake tells how young lawyer Priest faced down with a gun some whites wanting to "coon" young Pleasant Woolfolk. Later, Priest is about to lose his first election, when Pleasant brings all his people to vote. The only element used in the movie is that after the election the blacks began to sing "Old Kentucky Home" and 1,500 whites joined in around Priest in the street.

"The Mob from Massac" is the movie's Tornado gang, but the Jim they try to lynch is unrelated and unknown to anyone. Priest faces down the mob as in the movie, but with fewer words. The true culprit, another black, dies confessing and the eighty-four Massac men vote for Priest—who does not need his own vote.

In "The Lord Provides," Mallie Cramp visits a half dozen churches by streetcar before coming to Priest. The dead woman has no connection to anyone. The funeral procession resembles the movie's except that Lake and the equivalent of Amora have been carefully alerted. The Lord provides the other mourners. In Priest's short sermon, he decides *not* to tell the adultery parable and instead quotes the verse, "Suffer little children. . . ." Ashby Corwin, "a nobody, financial or otherwise," says a prayer. No election is at stake. Neither Lucy Lee nor the general is referred to in these stories, nor Buck or U. S. Woodford.

tunes, at the GAR meeting ("Marching Through Georgia"), Maydew's brassy parade ("Hail, Hail . . ."), Priest's brassy victory parade ("Dixie"). And their funeral procession has only mechanical sounds—until it reaches the blacks.

For it is given to the blacks to supply music for the whites. Jeff plays harmonica on Priest's porch (steps!) and at the CSA meeting; U.S. plays "Dixie" in court; the blacks sing black hymns at the funeral, play for the steamboat's arrival, play for the whitefolk's dance, and sing "Old Kentucky Home" at the end.

The abiding peacefulness of the blacks contrasts to white militancy, politics, lynch mobs, class strife, haughty mien, and endless parading. None of the four black principals is discontent. Uncle Zach has a coach business. Uncle Pleas carried his master's body back from Chickamauga and now looks after drunken Ashby. His nephew hangs around the levee strumming banjo. And then there is Jeff Poindexter, played by an aged Stepin Fetchit with the squeaky voice, bent head, and bumbling gestures of the comic darkie. But unlike earlier Fetchit characters, this one is not *quite* the traditional Fordian fool who, in *The Black Watch, Salute,* or *The Searchers,* satirically reflects establishment values. Even in Fairfield, Jeff, like Priest, seems a type who has survived beyond his era, only to find his fashion obsolete. None of the other blacks share his "comic" traits. Yet Jeff is not funny in what he says or does, and he continually earns our respect. Nor do the whites find him silly, although by habit they condescend toward all blacks. Even Judge Priest addresses the noble, gray-haired Uncle Pleas as "boy." And the mark of oppression exists in every black action, in the un-underlined contrast between their part of town and the whites' part, in the attitude (or nonattitude) of whites toward them, in their own acquiescence to their state. In the peaceful coexistence of a segregated society the mechanics of racism are most apparent. But they are less apparent when an audience, due to its own racism, sees Stepin Fetchit's character as merely a comic darkie and misses the man.

As always, it is the Fordian hero who mediates community tensions, searching for a middle way between chaos and repression—a way of tolerance. He is celibate, lonely, willing to resort to violence; he reunites a family, then walks away at the end. And Judge Priest, possessed by long experience of higher wisdom, always acts judiciously, if paternalistically. Unlike impractical reformers, like Governor DeLaage, Mr. Gruffydd, or Mary Stuart, whose immoderate idealism leads to failure, Priest knows when to accept reality. We see him often recoil smilingly from a shock: e.g., Pleas's war recollections, Lucy Lee's discovery of the portrait, the vote tally showing him behind by sixty-two and particularly after Brother Finney shoots Buck when the camera tracks rapidly up to a close-up of stunned Priest (a rare technique for Ford), who then decides, melancholically: "Good shootin'! Saves the expense of a trial."

Fairfield needs Priest's paternalism. It is no lovely, peaceful haven, but a town torn by class feuds, racism, violence, lust, and hypocritical social standards. Political opposition, the GAR, is led less by the noble banker, Colonel Jody Habersham, than by the Nixon-like prosecutor, Horace K. Maydew. Forever orating, or shouting for "Order!", Maydew proclaims:

> It is a great and glorious day for Kentucky, when no longer, no longer, can an empty sleeve or a gimpy knee serve as a blanket to smother the progress of the twentieth century . . . [Cheers]

To gain political capital, Maydew persecutes people—Mallie Cramp, Brother Finney, U.S.—as though they personified vice, moonshine, and indolence. His haughty Northern racial intolerance contrasts with Priest's tolerant racism. But Priest labors quietly, tolerating some disorder, and respecting individuals. Now, when he walks into the town hall to vote for himself and win the election, he walks toward a picture of George Washington. But there are strong intimations that the Republicans, younger and more numerous, will win next time. Thus it seems the last victory for the Confederacy, the Last Hurrah for an old order (and for America?), the twilight before the Maydews take over. The picture ends at night.

Sound and Sight. Sound's role is prominent. More than half the movie has music, all but five minutes from on-screen sources (far more than most musicals). Effects include things as minor and foxy as crickets outside Priest's house or something like the footsteps we suddenly *hear* over reaction shots of Priest and friends *before* we *see* Mallie Cramp at the gate. Ford repeats this scheme often: ten reaction shots of terrified blacks and a grinding turbulent score with added barks, guns, and female screams, before we see the lynch mob; hearse sounds and Maydew's reaction before the procession; in the "Dixie" number, Bagby in his smithy reacts to the bugle before we see Priest blowing it—and Ford builds to the climax of this joke by having Lake, Bagby, and Felsburg burst consecutively into the courtroom and stare, before reverse-cutting to the scene of mayhem. In 1935 in *The Informer* we knew what was going on when we heard tapping, because we had previously been introduced to the blind man and his cane; but in 1953 we do not know to what the sounds refer. Reaction shots before the fact are used elsewhere in postwar Ford (and in *How Green Was My Valley*); he generally gives temporal precedence to emotional form over facts, to effects over causes, for his cinema is largely one of reactions. This allows audience thought to flow from reflection rather than articulation. For example, by the time we finally *see* the lynch mob and come to know the cause of commotion, some of the rawer emotion has been drained, and the "thought" of the scene clarifies: i.e., the horror of violence.

Sound is used impressionistically while Ashby walks Lucy Lee to school (see Figure 7:I.1), and this emphasis on the subtle and close-at-hand sounds of a rural lane enhances by contrast the sudden cut from the close tracking to the open-space long shot of the schoolhouse, and the effect is further underlined by the flock of small black children who run gaily diagonally downframe toward Lucy Lee like a fan unfolding. Elsewhere, during the funeral procession, we hear almost nothing for six long minutes but hearse wheels, hooves, and the remarkable, steadily augmenting volume of human feet as the procession grows. Elsewhere, some marvelous rag piano accompanies the mother's walk to the whorehouse (as in *Stagecoach*). Her arrival in town is presaged by an off-camera steamboat whistle during the preceding scene between Ashby and Priest, just after the latter says, "You can't suppress truth" (II.2), and thus the whistle seems a sort of divine intervention.

Providence seems also represented through the tune "Genevieve," which (like the strum tune in *Donovan's Reef* and the jungle sounds in *Mogambo*) seems also to conspire that truth come to light. "Genevieve" occurs six times:

1. Soundtrack, Lucy Lee in buggy outside Ashby's (II.2).
2. Soundtrack, her mother cries for her (II.3).
3. Jeff's harmonica, Dr. Lake tells Priest "somebody" has come back to town (i.e., the mother) (II.4).
4. Soundtrack, Priest goes to look at portrait of Lucy Lee's grandmother (II.4).
5. Soundtrack, same sequence, just after Lucy Lee recognizes grandmother.
6. Banjo band, when she dances with Ashby (IV.2).

"Genevieve," then, seems associated with mothering, or, perhaps more precisely, with the prodigious consequence of a child wrongfully separated from its parents—one of Ford's major themes, for nothing more acutely manifests intolerance. It is fitting that when in the last instance Lucy Lee rushes out of the ballroom, "Genevieve" seems to be chasing her. Her attendance at the dance (so wrongfully counseled by Priest and his cronies) is an attempt to overcome shame, to brave public gossip, in short, to refuse to recognize that the whore who has just died was her mother. Dancing the day her mother dies! Lucy Lee forfeits her innocence, applauds heinous hypocrisy, and will have much to expiate; fortunately for her, her guilt will have the consolation of communal contrition.

Angles. Judge Priest may be the "star" of the picture, but he never quite dominates his scenes. An exemplary sequence occurs in his courtroom dialogue with Uncle Pleas:

Priest: Uncle Pleas Woodford . . . ! Are *you* the boy that brought Bainbridge Corwin's body back from Chickamauga?
Pleas: Yessir, judge. You remember. I brought him all the way back in these two arms. [*Wistfully:*] Don't you remember?
Priest: [*Grave nostalgia, nodding:*] Yes. I do.

Pleas: [*Extreme melancholy:*] O what a time that was.
Priest: [*Suddenly cheerful:*] Yeah! Ha ha!

As Ford crosscuts between them, one is left free to view each character both within and without the other's prejudicial view. We are not permitted to "identify" with Priest; his subjectivity does not dominate the scene: Ford remains narrator.

But at certain brutal confrontations, Ford employs a character's point of view. The recognition scene (II.4) warrants extended analysis:

Lucy Lee rushes into Priest's hallway. The camera stares down-hall; a doorway left leads into the room with the portrait of General Fairfield and his wife. (If Lucy Lee, who resembles her grandmother, sees it, she will know who she is.) Priest comes out this door, into the shot of the hall. A lamp inside the room and off-camera lights the *left* side of the frame (Priest) but puts most of the *right* (Lucy Lee) in shadow:

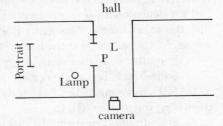

Lucy Lee: Uncle Billy! Uncle Billy . . .! I had to see you, Judge. I must know what's going on. Who am I? I know Dr. Lake loved me like a daughter, but tell me, Judge, who am I?
Priest: Why, you're his adopted daughter, honey.
Lucy Lee: That's not enough anymore, Uncle Billy.
Priest: You're mine, too. You belong to every one of us, every man jack that ever rode for Gen . . .

The camera position cuts to one *inside* the room, in fact, from the point of view of the portrait! It now looks out into the hall doorway, and Lucy Lee has changed position in the frame. Now she is on the *left* and he is on the *right*! Priest, startled, stops talking when he sees her see the portrait. The cut across the axis* exemplifies the drama of the event, and simultaneously Lucy Lee moves her face forward out of the shadow and into the light. Ford crosscuts to the portrait briefly from her perspective, then comes back to the previous shot. She now goes into the room, up to the portrait, and Victor Young's music illustrates her "awakening":

1. /MS, side: Lucy Lee approaches portrait on left.
2. /MCU: Priest steps forward in concern; his face enters light and moves into CU.

---

*For sake of smoothness, characters ordinarily maintain identical relative position during shifts of camera position between shots. If their positions are exchanged (e.g., Lucy to Priest's right in one shot, to his left in the next), the transition is rough and confuses space—and is termed "cutting across the axis." Another example: showing a motion (a car moving) first from its left, then from its right, so that on screens it appears to reverse direction.

3. /CU, 180°: Lucy Lee, staring.
4. XCU, matching, 180°: her grandmother's identical face in portrait.
5. X(= 3)CU: Lucy Lee.
6. /(= 2)CU: Priest wipes perspiring brow.
7. /(= 1)MS, side: Lucy Lee moves a step closer to portrait, and lifts drape, thus revealing General Fairfield.
8. /(= 6)CU: Priest, smiles now (an instance of his coming to terms with reality).
9. /(= 7)MS, side: Lucy Lee leaves portrait, and
10. /(= 2)MCU: kisses Priest: "Thank you, Uncle Billy. Now I know who I am."

The music follows the melodrama step by step, building up to a Straussian *Verklärung* during the 180-degree crosscut close-ups, then a cello moves gently into "Genevieve," consolingly. This is Ford's unabashed operatic manner. The crosscuts, however, are severe, both in closeness and angle, and are previously used by Ford only during the menacing confrontations in *My Darling Clementine* and *Wagon Master*. Here Lucy Lee confronts truth, herself: significantly, and this is the point of the 180-degrees, *she* not only looks at the portrait, the portrait looks at her. The portrait, like that of Manulani in *Donovan's Reef*, thus plays a providential role, along with "Genevieve" and the mother's return. The portrait's sudden appearance is particularly unexplained, but this only emphasizes its *deus ex machina,* or providential, intervention.

The clarity of this sequence—each shot *tells*, and is perfectly composed and lit, so that each shot is a miniature drama in itself—the clarity is deceptive. Ford so subordinates plot explanation to the individual moment, and the nature of Lucy Lee's mystery unfolds in such slow stages, a line here, another there, and with such lack of emphasis, that many have found the plot line baffling on first viewing. This is rather typical of Ford, who hated plot exposition; *The Sun Shines Bright* demands highly active attention. But Ford seems to be mocking himself at the CSA meeting, when, as the veterans deliberate mysteriously about what to do with the portrait, Ford cut to a little moment between Brother Finney and Mink in the back. Mink looks quizzically at Finney, who shrugs a pantomime equivalent of, "I haven't the faintest idea, either, of what they're talking about."

Depth of Field. Ford regularly divides his compositions into three distinct planes of depth. Action commonly occurs in mid-field. Both lighting and placement of objects and people contribute to the impression of depth. Ford's compositional style becomes a play upon internal angles. The screen, the camera's focal plane, may be regarded as the stable side of a box, whose rear wall, almost never parallel to the screen-wall, forms an oblique angle to the screen, thus accentuating depth of field and interior angles. Characters are placed within this box in lines or in a bent line forming an angle of its own; such angles, in relation to the screen-plane, form triangles and pyramids. Ford's pictures make us look *in*—into these angles and pyramids—but because they do so, they also make us continuously jump out, to view the screen as a whole.

At the CSA meeting (II.1), frame-top and frame-bottom are darkened; the gray-bright middle draws us into the depth of field. As Priest enters the room, the camera, distantly gazing over rows of empty wooden chairs, pans 40 degrees with him across the hall, then reverse-pans left, then right again, as flags are fetched. The deep-focus panning accentuates the empty chairs. At this long take's end, the camera stares down a striking alley (formed by wall, chairs, and men in gray, and punctuated by objects, such as a cannon, in the darkened foreground); then, at the moment of salute, Ford cuts deep into this alley, into a tenser alley of men and flags. Silver-gray textures reflect the poetry's image: "Dashed with honorable scars, lo in glory's lap they lie. Though they fell, they fell like stars, streaming splendor through the sky." Space informs emotion.

Nowhere is Ford's montaged choreography of motion in deep space better achieved than at the Grand Lemonade and Strawberry Festival, the finest of his dance sequences and an exemplary definition of Fordian cinema. Tonal values again play counterpoint to kinetic and musical ones: the Negro banjo band alternate black suit, white suit; the twenty cadets wear gray coats and white trousers, their partners light-shaded long dresses. Spectators line all four walls; march and dance take place *within* this square

of townspeople, within the community. Additional "boxiness" (the camera, with floor and ceiling, views five box-sides and itself forms the sixth) amplifies kinesis within each shot composition and across seams of montage. A dazzling suite of shots during the Grand March ends with a frontal shot overlooking five rows, eight abreast, stiff at attention. With a banjo tattoo, Ford cuts snappily closer, accentuating militarist qualities and reinforcing the music change (to "Golden Slippers"). * With the downbeat, the dancers clack their heels and in a rapid flowing wave from rear rank to front, jump into the dance with leaping gusto—O how the girls love it!

Similarly: when Ashby and Lucy Lee make their entrance in a beautifully conceived pan and track from the rear of the auditorium up to Amora Ratchitt (who tells her, as she has told every girl tonight, "Why Lucy Lee! You're the prettiest girl at the party!" and Mae Marsh adds a long shrieking, "Yeeessss!"), Ford doesn't wait for laughter. The banjo band has just started "Genevieve," sprightly. Lucy Lee, in the midst of her curtsy, rises in the same movement and joins with Ashby to swirl into the melee. Space and motion inform emotion.

The Gift to be Simple. A Ford character may be a simpleton, or a person who never amounted to much, or someone we don't like; but he claims our attention by sensitivity and activity. Emotions are implanted into his every gesture and posture. When Lucy Lee and her father come out of their house (I.1.ii), it is one instance among hundreds of a stylized portrait Ford wishes to eternalize. It is not simply the occurrence that may attract us, it is Ford's narrative presence, as though he were telling us, "Lucy Lee and Dr. Lake walked out into the street . . ." and we were feeling in his voice the meanings and memories of the event. As with dramatic situations, so with the characters themselves: elemental generic structures provide palpable qualities that are then vivified by invention. Each "point" is made separately, but in retrospect the number of points is vast. Several personages illustrate this.

Ford's brother Francis appears in the role of Brother Finney (the name is close enough to their family name, Feeney). It was his twenty-ninth appearance for John, his last on film (he died September 6, 1953), and the final development of his latter-day screen persona, a tattered coonskin remnant of former glory. He could spit across a room and make the spittoon ring. He was usually drunk, he was always good-natured and as cooperative as a leaf in a breeze, and more and more he came to be a character of silent pantomime (as befits a silent screen star). Jeff, at the CSA meeting, recognizes Finney's sidekick Mink and asks Priest if he remembers the little boy at Shiloh: Finney nods his head and shakes, and beats his hands as though holding drumsticks while imitating a drum roll, "*Bssss-bzzzz.*" Otherwise

---

*Ford uses similar techniques to punctuate voice entry into "The Marine Hymn" over the color brigade in *The Battle of Midway.*

he speaks only a single word, the last of his career: "Refreshments!" He personified a variety of raw instinct, the Fordian idyllic human being, irresponsible and innocent in a nature supremely simple. It is he who shoots Buck Ramsey in the back, and the exchange of shots afterward between a horrified Priest and a gleefully proud Finney says much about the differing natures of the two. Apparently only "Brother Feeney" can kill and retain his innocence, and Priest's decision to accept it for the best adds to the suggestion that Finney acts for God and Brother John. Indeed, Finney and Mink are the only whites who, like the blacks, resist Fairfield's white society. Finney even brings a jug to the temperance ladies' dance, and later we see him drinking happily beneath a campaign sign, "Maydew will drive out the Moonshiners"!

Two others contain Finney's simplicity but contrast markedly. Ashby Corwin's (John Russell*) woodenness is the soul of his character and reflects his discomfort when obliged to step out of the narrow confines of his cliché nature. He (*Ash*-be) has the aristocratic gesture-and-do of the dead Confederacy without its depth of personality; glory is denied him because his proper epoch died before his birth. General Fairfield, on the other hand, is a magnificent relic, a recluse who writes his memoirs in full-length smoking jacket in a study crowded with mementos half a century old. When "Trumpeter" Priest

---

*Russell (1921–) played Tytyl in *The Blue Bird* (1940), *Rio Bravo* (1959), etc.

comes to call, he enters like a soldier, marches to the desk, and becomes a boy. It is the most stylized sequence of an extremely stylized movie, and James Kirkwood's* posture and voicing yield not an inch to legend, myth, or humanity. When last we see him he stands watching Priest's "Dixie" parade like a tin soldier, straight and proud, his drawn sabre held arm's length at his side. In a single shot Ford evokes the flower, grace, and lustrous glory of vanished aristocracy. And the parade is passing by.

Procession. The funeral procession is a tour de force of angles. Itself a line, it traverses Ford's box in nearly every possible direction. Twice Ford cuts across the axis and the procession, without disequilibrium, changes direction across the screen: first, at shot 22, when GAR Habersham takes his place beside Priest— the *first* person to join the tiny procession of Priest, the white hearse, and the prostitutes. By the second cut across axis, shot 48, the procession has become a vector (a line in motion, a force) to which a good part of the town has fastened, like an arrow gathering feathers. Now, as Lucy Lee, acknowledging her mother and sin, joins the procession, its direction again changes across the screen.

Equally, the procession is a culmination of Ford's vignette methods. The whole of *The Sun Shines Bright* resembles a riverboat melodrama, in which each scene is a skit, every shot a turn, and every character a cameo. And the procession is a procession of cameos—Priest, the prostitutes, Bagby, Felsburg, Habersham, Amora Ratchett, Mae Marsh, the jeering women with parasols, ** a farmer, Lake, Redcliffe, Finney, Mink, and dozens more—a congregating of cameos into a community. En masses they announce their guilt.

This climax is formalized in a panorama. As the procession snakes downframe into a large open space between white and black quarters of Fairfield, Ashby runs in from the right; the camera begins panning leftward with him, then shot at 60 cuts to a matching pan as he joins Lucy Lee. For twenty-five seconds the slow pan moves leftward, only 90 degrees, but seeming greater, for its arc is tangent to the procession's curve. And gradually the tight shot of the carriage opens into a long vista, down whose right side the procession files toward the colored church and a small Negro choir.

---

*Kirkwood (1883–1963), a flamboyant, hard-drinking, legendary show-business figure, went from stage to pictures as actor and later director under Griffith. He appears in the latter's *A Corner in Wheat* (1909). Before marrying actress Gertrude Robinson, he briefly romanced Mary Pickford and later directed her in nine pictures at Majestic (1911) and Paramount (1914–15); he directed a number of Mary Miles Minter vehicles at Metro (1916) but did not direct again in film after 1919. He was wiped out in 1929 and after the mid-thirties he found it impossible to get work. "He lived out a precarious alcoholic existence until his death at eighty," writes Jack Spears (*Hollywood: The Golden Era* [New York: Castle, 1971], p. 167), and quotes actor John Griggs: "'I recall Jim Kirkwood not so much for his illustriousness as for the fact that never in a lifetime have I seen an actor so gallant in adversity.'" His son authored *A Chorus Line* and many other plays.

**Ford was fond of parasols' visual effect: women on the boat deck at the beginning; a yellow one in *Mogambo*, red in *Donovan's Reef*.

The white sound of marching feet joins the black sound of song. The choir sways earthily to "Swing Lo," but the procession marches even in place. This contrast is reiterated: "Detail, halt!" cries Priest; "The first three ranks will fall out, act as pallbearers." But Uncle Pleas comes forward to sing "Deep River." His action is a typically Fordian device: it combines music and movement, underlines sentiment, and changes—by his stepping forward from his place in the line— the simple diagonal line of the choir into an angle, thus realizing a static composition's dynamic potential.

As the camera shifts position, it seems that casket and mourners funnel away from us and upward into the chapel. This, and the fact that inside the chapel is stony and cavelike, is appropriate for the goal of a symbolic journey. The blacks stand outside, not by custom of segregation, but because this is a ceremony of *white* penance. Priest's sermon will transform public confession through absolution into redemption. Whatever his motive for choosing it, the black chapel is the perfect site for humble confession of intolerance. The whites enter into this black womb, so to speak, and thus acknowledge that the basis, heart, and conscience of their community is black.

"'Whosoever receives a child into his arms receiveth me,'" quotes Priest from Saint Mark, referring to Lucy Lee's mother; then, after General Fairfield enters like a repentant child, he continues the parable of the woman taken in adultery.

— You remember, Jesus raised himself up, and he looked those
accusers in the eye. And this is what he said: "He that is without sin
among you let him first cast a stone at her." . . . And by and by . . .
every last one of them common scoundrels were gone! And only the
woman herself stood there! And he said to her . . .

Here we cut from Priest (and coffin) to /the front row of the chapel, where sits the strange combination of General Fairfield, Lucy Lee, and Mallie Cramp, with Ashby standing protectively (but displaced) behind Lucy Lee. It is with these four framed, and the casket significantly unseen, that Priest, looking them in the eye, says:

— . . . "Woman, where are those, thine accusers? . . .

Cut back to /Priest:

— . . . "Hath no man condemned thee?" And she said, "No man,
Lord." And he said unto her, "Then neither do *I* condemn thee!"!!!

Shouting ecstatically, Priest slams shut the Bible in triumph.

Thus would he anneal his community and bring it into the innocence and light of God. Yet innocence is at the root of the community's endemic intolerance: duty gone astray (as always in Ford). It is simplicity that is pernicious, whether in the indignant righteousness of General Fairfield, Ashby, or Maydew, or in the pagan Finney, who, flowing with chance and fate, carries a gun, is drunk, kills without pang, yet remains pure. Well might Ashby pray God to "pity . . . simplicity," for this funeral is a ceremony not of puri-fication but of guilt. All share place with the whores; no man lives immune to this contagion, blameless for his innocence of (i.e., unconscious responsi-bility for) almost infinite guilt—not even Judge Priest, who most of all in this community confronts moral choices consciously, is capable of real sin, and embodies Ford's notion that principled good intentions lurk behind most human tragedy. Such knowledge breeds caution: Priest always carries an umbrella. Warily, defending U.S. with a gun, he, unlike cocky Young Mr. Lincoln, does not feign cuteness or reason with a lynch mob, nor glory in forcing them back: he wipes his brow and begs for a drink. He has the prac-tical sense to acknowledge, in acquiescing in Buck's murder, violence he cannot control, and takes concrete steps to atone for his silence's share in the wrong done Lucy Lee's mother. And, judge, soldier, and priest, he is also, as friend Felsburg says, "a cunning, unscrupulous politician," and wisely ships off the prostitutes right after the funeral. * Yet even Priest is innocent (un-aware) of his own racism.

Parade and House. Priest wins reelection by one vote (his own). The band plays "Dixie," Brother Finney grabs the stick to beat the drum himself,** properly, and music and picture dissolve into the victory parade past Priest's house that night.

It is a movie of parades: funeral parades and victory parades. The Tor-nado boys parade to a lynching and, later, to vote. Maydew's band parades twice (so that "Hail, Hail, the Gang's All Here" frames the funeral se-quence!). There is a Grand March at the dance. Lucy Lee and Ashby have several little parades all to themselves, while her mother's solitary trail is marked by Uncle Zach as she limps toward Mallie Cramp's. Now, finally, the whites parade past Priest in groups: the CSA, the GAR, the band, the Tor-nado boys ("He saved US from ourselves"), the cadets, two-score women with fans. Cinematically a parade is an angle, a vector, an image that is simultaneously the dramatic core, formal figure, and primary symbol of Ford's film. The people parade, the compositions play with vectors, and life is dynamic subsisting, form its manifestation, providence its rule.

This is an Augustinian viewpoint. Ford's people are pilgrims, and in *The Sun Shines Bright* (curious name for a movie that could be titled *Intoler-ance!*) he relates to his material while suggesting a more perfect City of God. Although Priest's victory parade resolves complex plots and relation-ships into a single gesture of communal unity, it also gives formal expression to a yet existent disunity. For the blacks who come at the end sing a different tune—"The sun shines bright on my Old Kentucky Home," not "Dixie."

* In *The Soul Herder* (1917—Ford liked to think it his first picture), Cheyenne Harry cleans up *his* town by giving whores money to go away and "start a new life." Harry too was a fighting clergyman, like Capt. Rev. Clayton in *The Searchers* and many another of Ford's characters.
** "The first [movie] part handed to me was that of a fresh drummer"—in 1907!—wrote Francis Ford in 1914 (in *Universal Weekly*, December 20, 1913, p. 4).

And they do not march; they stroll, softly—in the opposite direction. Nor does the sun shine bright; it is night. And while crosscuts twixt Priest and whites are nearly level, when he looks at /the blacks, the camera gazes up at him gazing down.

But this is a 1952 picture about 1905, and, unless we favor Maydew, we realize that the world's problems are not to be solved in a few days, and that, meanwhile, such men as Judge Priest, albeit racist, are to be treasured. Hence as Priest retreats through one door of his home, then another, carrying his lamp deeper into successive rooms and then disappearing at last, Jeff, the black man, sits outside on the porch steps, serenading and guarding this white "motherless child," just as blacks have guarded and serenaded whites throughout Fairfield's history, and as Judge Priest has guarded them.

As silhouettes of Lucy Lee and Ashby pass off the frame (she having prevented his intruding), the camera, having panned slowly to the left as though taking a deep, slow breath, releases itself quickly rightward and into an expansive embrace —the most benedictory camera movement in Ford's oeuvre. Except for Jeff's fingers on the harmonica, all motion has ceased. The parade has passed. The town glistens in white and black like some jewel, the bushes seem suddenly green, the bricks red, and the white frame house of Judge Priest glows abidingly.

> My most beautiful pictures are not westerns; they're little stories without big stars about communities of very simple people.[26]

Judge Priest vs. *The Sun Shines Bright*:
How Does Ford Change?

Rather than occurring randomly throughout his career, Ford's best pictures (those most inventive and emotionally balanced) tend to date from four narrow points:

1933	*Pilgrimage, Judge Priest* ('34)
1939	*Stagecoach, Young Mr. Lincoln, How Green Was My Valley* ('41)
1952	*Wagon Master* ('50), *The Quiet Man, The Sun Shines Bright, Mogambo*
1962–65	*The Man Who Shot Liberty Valance, How the West Was Won:* "The Civil War," *Donovan's Reef, 7 Women*

There are, naturally, fine pictures in between these points (especially *The Black Watch, Steamboat Round the Bend, The Battle of Midway, My Darling Clementine, The Fugitive, The Searchers, The Majesty of the Law, Gideon's Day,* et al.), but each of the four points epitomizes the spirit of one of the four periods of Ford's career.

Comparisons between the four points are tempting, but fraught with danger. Received wisdom has it that Ford's work "evolved" into deeper expression, deeper self-consciousness, deeper style, deeper criticism of his material. Indeed, it seems a virtual truism among genre critics that sometime around 1960 happy Hollywood became neurotic New Wave and that John Ford repented of his Pollyanna simplicities. Closer inspection, however, reveals 1952 as a rare burst of optimism midst the general depression of Ford's output. Nineteen thirty-three offers scant evidence of simplicity, Pollyanna spirit, or dearth of self-reflexivity, and no western, not *Liberty Valance* and certainly not the parodies of Peckinpah or Altman, proffer estimates of the West *more* critical or cynical than does *Stagecoach*. Perhaps there are other ways, equally facile perhaps, of characterizing the four periods:

1933	dark; humane characters (organic)
1939	black; ideal characters
1952	light; iconic characters
1962+	fiery; humane characters (metallic)

From 1948 on, Ford's compositions are generally more classical, less mannerist, while the pictures of the final period are striking demonstrations of the range and variety classical styles may assume. Compared with *Judge Priest* and *Stagecoach, The Sun Shines Bright* and *Liberty Valance* have more straight lines, more flat surfaces, more rectangles, flatter lighting, and compositions less filled, whether by props or by modeling light. Thirties Ford is more Murnauian. Everything is more curved, pliable, rotund,

fleshy. Not only is there more scenic clutter, the clutter itself is more clut-
tered: contrast the randomly scattered candy-pull lanterns in 1934 (*Judge
Priest*) with the neatly patterned strawberry-festival lanterns in 1952 (*The
Sun Shines Bright*) with the geometric fishnet Lelani peers through in 1964
(*Donovan's Reef*). Light in the 1930s is a thing of great interest; rather as in
Caravaggio, it has mannerist depth and seems three-dimensional. Blurred
chiaroscuro plays upon walls or forms pools through which characters move,
or encloses them in haloes; space is less distance than an illuminated mist.
The vast quantities of stylization in thirties Ford evince intense self-
consciousness: style itself is clearly a distancing device, requiring us to
come to terms with an interpretation rather than with simple reality.

In one aspect, at least, "improvement" can be sensed. The cutting of
1933, though insightful, conceptual, and playful with contrasting moods and
worlds, is nonetheless off-hand, abrupt, and even crude in comparison to
the cultivated, musiclike cutting of 1939 and after, so that here one may
make analogies to the "evolution" of Mozart or Beethoven and suggest that
"improvement" is a matter of each "note" coming to seem more expressive
in more ways.

But in another aspect, as his characters become less anatomical and more
iconic, Ford perhaps loses something. There is a fleshy sprawl to the people
of 1933 and a patience in their voices and gestures that in later years seems
sacrificed to greater purposefulness: even Jeff Poindexter (Stepin Fetchit)
seems leaner and more "edited" in 1952 than in 1934. It is true, perhaps,
that later Fords have vaster visions, place buglers on horizons and fire in the
night, and sense the flow of historical destiny in ways that 1934 does not yet
even dream of, but sometimes their characters seem distanced to Cimabue
proportions and reliant, Godard-like, on specific signifying gestures, alongside the more naked, mercurial, and sensual presence of 1933's characters.
As the later Ford sometimes seems unwilling or unable to build his art as
much on Henry Fonda and John Wayne as he formerly did on Harry Carey
and Will Rogers, so too he grows progressively more contemplative toward
landscapes, so that a Rossellini-like dialectic with "raw" reality almost
seems to compel Ford, as it does Bresson, to treat his actors iconically.

If Ford becomes less mannered, less intrigued by his actors, more puzzled by land, it is partly because he becomes more distanced, and not only
in style but personally as well: simply put, he grows older. The dreams of
youth are more valuable but less immediate. Decreased physical participation with his characters is the price Ford sometimes (but not always!) pays
for more understanding —and for a heightened sense of *in*comprehension,
too. It is perhaps true to suggest that awareness of complexity and contradiction and dialectical struggle is more clearly and completely written into
the scripts of late Ford, whereas it is more sensuously contained in the actors of earlier Ford. *The Sun Shines Bright* is easier to talk about than *Judge
Priest*. But there are prewar and postwar pictures that belie this facile dis-

tinction: *Stagecoach, Young Mr. Lincoln, How Green Was My Valley, Wagon Master, Liberty Valance, 7 Women.*

Mogambo (1953). Shortly after the release of *Mogambo*, Jean Mitry questioned Ford about his penchant for introducing a group of people into a difficult situation, and Ford replied:

> For me, it's a way of confronting individuals, of bringing them face to face. This situation, the tragic moment, permits them to define themselves, to become conscious of what they are, to rise above their indifference, their inertia, their conventionality, the "mediocrity" they'd be without that situation. To find the exceptional in the ordinary, heroism in everyday life, to exalt man "in depth," this is the dramatic device I like. And also, to find humor in tragedy, because tragedy is never totally tragic. Sometimes it's absurd. I'd love to do a tragedy which would turn ridiculous, very seriously . . . What interests me are the consequences of a tragic moment upon diverse individuals, to see how they behave, respectively, in confrontation with a crucial fact, or in an exceptional adventure.[27]

We shall see that this applies to *Mogambo*.

Deep in Africa, c. 1953:

Day 1: Vic (Clark Gable) traps animals for zoos. He has an affair with Kelly, a stranded playgirl (Ava Gardner).

Day 2: Vic summarily kicks her out a week later when safari clients arrive: anthropologist Donald Nordley (Donald Sinden) and his wife Linda (Grace Kelly), who's fatally attracted to Vic. Kelly returns when the boat busts.

Day 3: Linda spars with Kelly, takes a walk, is rescued by Vic, flirts with him; complicated repartee at dinner.

Day 4: Safari in jeep: more repartee. Flirting in camp.

Day 5: Mission station: Vic undergoes "Ceremony of Courage" (natives throw spears); Kelly confesses to priest.

Day 6: Linda rebuffs Kelly's friendship; on river; Samburu tribe hostile at Kenya Station; Kelly confides in Brownie; Linda kisses Vic at waterfall; bitter tent scene with Don.

Day 7: Mountains of the Moon. Gorillas: Linda, frightened, grabs Vic; later they plot to tell Don.

Day 8: But instead Vic saves Don from gorilla attack. Later he gets drunk with Kelly, Linda sees and shoots him in arm, and Kelly tells Don Vic was making passes.

Day 9: The Nordleys leave. Vic and Kelly will marry.

Mogambo is a comedy of manners, blarney, and sophistication, set in the jungle. It is an essay on ethics, uncertain that "ethics" is not merely a synonym for "cultural instinct." It observes four orders—land, animals, primitive tribes, cultured whites—wondering whether the same law (a Hobbesian law of the jungle) governs each, or whether man possesses power to impose a higher law of his own.

Donald Nordley is an anthropologist. "He studies man, man's development . . . he examines heads." He wants to study the giant gorillas because he has a "theory of derivative evolution." He says, "I can't wait to see them in their natural habitat: the truest exemplary link between modern man and his primitive derivation." "Yes," opposes a priest, "I think you and I could have a lusty debate on the origin of man."

In the key sequence the question is only partly resolved: Waiting for the gorillas, Vic, instead of telling Don he is taking Linda away from him, saves his life. At the first sound of gorillas, Ford cuts back to a proscenium shot of the jungle clearing, announcing a "stage." And after Vic shoots a gorilla, dead silence reigns for the first time; he walks up and stands behind the fallen beast, the camera tracking in to a three-quarter shot of him, then / crosscutting to a high-angle shot, from Vic's perspective, of the dead gorilla's face. Then /back to the shot of Vic. He brushes off Don, "Do you think I planned this?! The last thing I wanted to do was to knock him over [i.e., metaphorically: Don]. Let's stop the chatter." And Brownie says, "Sorry, Vic, the little one got away [i.e., the baby ape; metaphorically: Linda]."

In Ford's syntax, the track-in on Vic is a momentous figure of style reserved for key moments of confrontation, a moment when interior and exterior realism join. (Such a track occurs, for example, in *The Sun Shines Bright* when Judge Priest sees Buck Ramsey shot dead—Figure 7: IV.3.) Vic has been constantly associated with beasts, pictorially and verbally; the ambivalence inherent in crosscutting* allows him to be read either as equivalent or opposite to a beast. But in shooting the gorilla has he denied the beast in himself? Has he acted sensibly, persuaded by Don's words of Linda's unsuitability? Did he act nobly, or only by a cultural conditioning that made him instinctively save a life that by jungle law he ought to have let the gorilla take?** Kelly says, twice, "You went noble." Vic says, "I went yellow." Did he fail in courage, or did he act like a man? (And what is man?)

Mogambo is somewhat vague. The land and animals, which play so constant a role in the movie, act, of course, without moral qualm or responsibility. Nor are the tribes *seen* as much better; rather they are primitive, corporate, alien, and with (to the whites) arational ethical systems; they offer no ethical contrast to the land and animals—with the single exception that they will not follow Vic into "that strange territory . . . the Mountains of the Moon" until he passes the "Ceremony of Courage." That is, the gorilla country represents truth (anthropologically, for Don; ethically for the film; confrontation with reality, for the characters); "Africa" is the test.

---

*When a shot of one person is paired with, for example, a gorilla, we will sense either comparison or contrast (or both). Similarly, crosscuts between people can indicate either comparison or contradiction.

**Vic's dramatic itinerary closely resembles Tom Doniphon's in *Liberty Valance*.

But the question of the possible uniqueness of man is confused in that each of them is a "split" personality. Vic is not a hunter, he is a trapper who loves animals; he is passive rather than active; he loves the wilderness but encages it for zoos and circuses; he cannot confront Don; he cannot confront reality. And he is split between two women. His two assistants, kindly Brownie and bestial Boltchak, reflect also his split.

But the film, Africa, will bring each of the four principals into a forced confrontation with reality, and in each case passion (*mogambo*) rather than rational decision will prompt the confrontation and acceptance. Each character's "moral itinerary" is prefigured in a short sequence before repeating itself at greater length (the characters have their own cyclicism). In Vic's case, the film's prelude serves as an allegory: the prey is trapped but escapes because the net is too weak. His prefiguration sequence is also Linda's.

Linda is twenty-seven, looks younger (and in fact is: Grace Kelly was twenty-four), has been married seven years to a boy she has known since they were five. She is sheltered, wealthy, pampered, ingenuous; in manner she is either too correct, bitchy, or disarmingly girlish. Of all the characters, she is psychologically the most complex. It is Linda, ostensibly the most civilized, whose repressed savagery, once released by Africa, wills Vic's involvement with her; by coming to Africa she falls into a situation, actually a trap, which at first (and then again) seems idyllic but which also will bring her (twice) into the savage's jaws.

Linda and Vic share a prefiguring sequence that is parsed in classic montage. She walks into the jungle and at first is enchanted, an innocent in paradise, crosscut with monkeys and birds (frames 1–3) and happily leaving the frame (3A). Then Vic rushes after her (4), and the idyll is interrupted; Linda, turning, is crosscut with fighting animals and becomes frightened (5–15). In panic she falls into a pit-trap (18)(one of *Vic's* traps). A black panther on a tree limb snarls downward, as Linda, looking upward in crosscut, cringes and shrieks (19–20). But this pair of shots is crosscut with Vic, in a low-angle shot (matching that of the panther, thus suggesting their mutual interest in Linda); he takes aim and kills the panther (24–25). Then he comes to the pit and pulls /Linda out. Ford breaks this action into *two* shots (26–27), typically, because the experience of being pulled out of a pit is different from that of standing beside Vic (27A, the continuation of shot 27).

Rescued, Linda seems to want to be taken. She stands emotionally naked (27A), then strolls off swinging her sweater and obliging Vic to follow (28). Then (29), simultaneously thrusting out her bosom while retreating her body, glimpsing up with her blushing, downcast eyes, she plays at seduction, coy, teasing, girlish. "Donald's one husband who's believed everything I've told him since I was five years old." She taunts Vic with remarks like, "That could be the remark of a cynical man . . . of a lonely man." Again walking off (30), she almost skips, and forces Vic to follow her. She poses (31) weakly and birdlike against a fallen trunk, and her feelings seem reflected in

1   2   3

3a   4   5

6   7   8

9   10   11

12   13   14

15   16   17

18   18A   19

20   21   22

23   24   25

26   27   27A

Ford's composition, wherein Vic appears twice her size, and in the subsequent crosscuts (32–33), sexually menacing—with a low-angle for him and a high-angle for her. A fierce storm begins, she falls, so that Vic lifts her, whereupon she throws her arms around his neck—intercut with images of wind, river, rain-swept trees. At her door he closes in on her, trembling and wet (35). Vic has become the hunter again, and he pulls her scarf off, leaving her (35A) naked emotionally, her head birdishly tilted; she quickly retreats inside after an all-revealing glance. (The same figure of birdlike neck and scarf recurs in *The Horse Soldiers*; Ford found necks attractive.)

As in this sequence, *Mogambo* often creates dialogue between its "stage-play" artifice and its jungle "documentary." But the two are distinct, even though at times comparable or equivalent. The big ensemble scenes occur in rooms or tents, around tables, beds, or piano; and this melodrama is marked off from Africa by studio lighting (or, in closer exterior shots, by lamps and reflectors). The women come with full wardrobes and change for virtually every scene. The script is Ford's talkiest; lines snap with sardonic wit, weaving intricate networks of double entendre. But purposefully and metaphorically, much of the dialogue is *chatter*, the whiteman's sound, just as land, animals, and tribes possess their sounds. In terms of the film, stageplay vs. Africa is the question of external and internal realism. Africa not only brings out the unconscious of the characters; its juxtaposition also gives the stageplay whatever aesthetic-ethical meaning and realism it possesses, by placing its artifice within a context of actuality. Africa, on the other hand, may possess actuality, but it gains meaning only in juxtaposition (through the montage analysis) with the stageplay. *Mogambo* is full of magic, deeply intimate, and emotional exchanges between its characters. Time and again they gaze into the off-space, into Africa, seeking meaning, and then turn back to the surer comforts of human society. Such moments in *Mogambo* are fleeting instants, scarcely accentuated, when time seems suspended. Quickly and impassionately these moments are absorbed into the chitter-chatter of the stageplay and into the vastness of Africa. No one in *Mogambo* sings "Shall We Gather at the River," but rivers punctuate repeatedly with the varied metaphors their presence bestows.

What seems contemptible, sinful, in Linda is her lack of courage, her deceit. After her second love scene with Vic, by the waterfall, she returns to Don in the tent and repulses his advances. The camera looks through the tent from the rear, past Linda and Don and their cots, left and right; beyond the tent-flap doorway, the campfire sends smouldering white smoke into the night sky. Crickets, instead of the waterfall, are the background sound. As Donald talks to Linda he shines a flashlight into her face (twice), blinding her and making her cry. Across the rear of the tent is mosquito netting; the camera looks through this netting to Linda, whilst it sees Don through an open flap of the netting. The netting serves as a theatrical scrim: the backlight from the fire throws the shadow of Linda's head onto the scrim above her actual head, thus giving her two heads. He asks her calmly, "Lin, darling, are you still my girl?" "Don't be childish!" she retorts, moving hurriedly toward the door. "That's good enough for me," he says, stretching out on his cot.

Comparable to Donald's flashlight is the flash of his Leica. Twice, before and after this scene, he surprises Linda with his flash, each time freezing her in deception; the second occasion she stands in wide ensemble scene, holds her pose with an indescribable expression of naked truth for three or four lengthy seconds. (At picture's end, marriage reaffirmed, he snaps her picture without a flash.)

How much does Don suspect? This is an intrigue the movie poses. He is a scientist who does not leap to conclusions, and a proper British gentleman who presumes others are honorable until contrary evidence becomes overwhelming. Donald too has a "split." He observes reality, records it via film, tape, and notebook, but another side of him prefers the myth. (He and Linda are alike: each feels sophisticated and thinks the other innocent and innocuous.) *Mogambo* permits three interpretations of him: he is naively trusting; he is suspicious but afraid to discover the truth; he is all-knowing. In the third interpretation (which I lean to), Donald is seen as coldly setting up a "test" for Linda when he sends her back to camp with Vic after the first encounter with the gorillas; and he is seen as deliberately manipulating Vic's emotions during their talk before the second encounter with the gorillas. This interpretation suggests the moral deficiencies of the scientific method when applied to human relations. In the subsequent scene with Boltchak (when he gets mad at Boltchak for saying what he already suspects or knows), the natives in the background are dissecting the dead gorilla, and the scene is staged with images of decadence. In any case Donald's conduct is frighteningly efficient. He puts just the right amount of pressure on Linda. He preserves the trust-bonds of their wedlock through his deceitful trust (thus the significance of taking her picture without the flash). He clearly makes the right (i.e., human as opposed to jungle) choice when he "accepts" her innocence and the Vic-Kelly lie (cf. *Fort Apache, Liberty Valance*: preference for myth over fact when the former is more utilitarian). And he effectively disarms Vic. His motives, however, are rooted in passion.

A second question is whether Donald's "survival" abilities bring him closer to the beast or to man. He suggests that certain compromises must, and ought, to be made in life. Hypocrisy is sometimes laudable (as in Renoir). Everyone unites in the lie that will preserve Linda and her marriage, and yet she is the least responsible and the most culpable. She throws onto Vic her own obligation of confessing to her husband. When she feels she has been tricked, she reaches instinctively for a gun and fires at Vic. Is her reversion to jungle law duplicated by her civilized husband? "If she hadn't [shot you] I'd have done it myself!" But Linda is restored to Donald's comforting arms, to "home and Devonshire" and "raising that family." She will never learn the "truth" about Vic, but she has learnt the dangers of "Africa" and thus a "truth" about herself. *Mogambo* itself happily mocks the clichés of its fantasy drama. When Linda catches Kelly in his arms, she pulls back the tent flap (= stage curtain) and Vic says:

> Listen Mrs. N, you're not gonna tell me that you've been taking all
> this [love affair] seriously, are you?! You know how it is on safari—
> it's in all the books— the woman *always* falls for the White
> Hunter, and we guys make the most of it. Can you blame us?
> When you come along with that look in your eye there's no one
> who . . . [at this point Linda shoots him.]

The gorillas are described as unpredictable and dangerous. In their fascination they prompt us to question ourselves (man/beast) and to wonder what is real. In *Mogambo* the apes were photographed by a second unit equipped with 16mm equipment using the same methods Donald does.

(There are a couple of 16mm shots of natives beating bush in costumes different from those beating bush in 35mm.) What is curious, however, is that these 16mm shots (recognizable by their paler color) are *almost* (the operative word in discussing *Mogambo*) always crosscut with Donald's Bolex 16mm movie camera, so that the cinematic result *suggests* we are seeing the film he is taking. I say "suggest" because obviously we are not: Donald's film is still in the camera and Ford does not provide the usual masking that would indicate it. *Mogambo* is essentially a story of a bunch of people who make a long arduous trek (pilgrimage, parade) into strange territory in search of gorillas (truth, home). Linda finds fear and excitement—she cringes but keeps looking. Vic, crosscut with a (35mm) dead gorilla, finds himself. Don finds only a paler (i.e., 16mm) image. Cinema, like life, turns in upon itself. Artifice and document, man and ape, theater and life, myth and reality, white and black, are equated, divided, subtracted, and multiplied.

Kelly alone does not go to see the apes. She has come to Africa by mistake in the first place. Besides, she was unwillingly stuck at Vic's a week, she was again prevented from leaving by the Kenya Station tribal revolt, and even in the last scene as she climbs into the canoe, Brownie asks her, "Are you sure you're ready to go?"

Kelly is a bit like Father Josef (even including his sanctimonious side); she is Catholic, learns to avoid dangerous animals (devils?), and is close to knowing the beast within herself. As Brownie says, she has "scars" (cf. the Indian named Scar in *The Searchers*). She is the legitimately tragic figure in *Mogambo,* Linda is the playgirl.

Kelly is initially presented as a brainless toy; Vic says:

> That's playgirl stuff, Brownie. I've seen 'em in London, Paris, Rome. They start life in a New York nightclub and end up covering the world like a paint advertisement. Not an honest feeling from her kneecap to her neck.

She jokes about her "split": hearing Brownie describe an anthropologist as someone who examines heads, she quickly parries, "He could have examined both of mine!"

In Kelly's "prefiguration," she takes a shower, approaches dangerous animals that look cute, refuses to discuss her scars, goes after Vic, falls for him, and is jilted. Then, after her confession, she gathers water from the river, tells about her scars, ignores the gorillas, and finally, at first refuses to fall for Vic a second time, then pushed by passion gives in, plunges into the river, and wades to him.

What motivates her confession and change? One presumes she confesses fornication and was moved by the shock of her encounter with Vic, her battles with Linda, the initial encounter with a primitive tribe threatening to kill her, the availability of a priest, the need to confide. But there is another element, one subtly presented, that brings her moral adventures into parallel with Vic's: they both would like to see their rivals dead.

Kelly allows Linda to take her walk without warning her about the dangers of the jungle. Since Kelly has been there a week, she must be aware of these dangers. And as Linda leaves, Ford inserts a shot of Kelly's watching; not only does the camera look at Kelly from behind a bamboo curtain (staging used frequently throughout *Mogambo* to indicate hidden motives), but also the camera tracks up to Kelly (we have already discussed this figure of style in reference to Vic). When, however, Vic brings Linda back, Kelly, standing with rain pouring down in back of her, realizes her scheme has backfired. ("Scheme" is much too strong a word: after all, she herself tells Vic about Linda's walk.) Ford follows this shot with a strange tracking shot of Kelly walking in the rain in a black raincoat and black rainhat—strange colors for Kelly but ones which in the psychochromatic terms of *Mogambo* suggest a state of sin. The subsequent juxtaposition of the confession scenes and her attempted apology to Linda suggests action motivated by advice given by Father Josef.

Kelly is the one courageous member of the quartet. Her second confession, to Brownie, indicates her "great strength of character" after her husband's death; in the jeep scene we see her fighting back tears. She says constantly what no one else will say, cutting through the polite innuendos with which Vic and Linda masquerade their hypocrisy. She has one of her finest moments after the famous dinner scene. Standing beside the piano in her white gown, with Don and Brownie gathered 'round, she uses her white handkerchief as a prop while singing "Comin' thro' the Rye." The song's words accurately taunt Vic and Linda, who flee into the shadows, and the words also capture Kelly's dilemma, placing it in context of Vic's polygamy:

When a body meets a body comin' thro' the rye,
If a body kiss a body, need a body cry?
Every lassie has a laddie; none they say have I.
But all the boys they smile at me, comin' thro' the rye.

Kelly represents Western culture at its best. She has the savoir faire to lie at the proper time. Least prepared for Africa (as Etula says, she "can't even cook an egg"), her toughness and openness make her the least incompatible with it (she joins in the native chant and dance). She best suggests the sort of harmony into which the various ethical dilemmas merge at the end. A rainbow is in the sky and as at the end of *The Sun Shines Bright* order reigns as best it might in a beautiful, wild, and changing world.

It is difficult to ignore Ford's use of color in the female costuming. Vic refers to Kelly as a "paint advertisement." Offset against white, black, and tan (jungle colors) are patches of red, pink, and yellow. There is virtually no blue in *Mogambo*, except the sky. These colors operate psychochromatically, though again not with total consistency: they reinforce what is already there, rather than themselves producing something. Red may be equated with attack, yellow with cowardice, green with harmony. That is, Linda and

Kelly wear red or yellow depending on how they are faring toward Vic. Kelly assumes a green blouse after her conversion, white for her scar talk with Brownie, and green when she accepts Vic at the end. Colors are used to great effect in the crosscut dinner scenes. One might cite the declaration of blood implied by Kelly in her white gown pouring a glass of red wine. (True-blue Brownie wears a blue kerchief.)

Although *Mogambo* possesses not a note of an off-camera musical score, it is through-composed: on-camera native chants, Kelly's song, the sounds of the jungle and the land. This "score" is of considerable importance.

Ford was not considered a woman's director. With the exception of *Mogambo*, he worked with major female stars on only five occasions in the sound era: *Arrowsmith* (Helen Hayes), 1931; *Drums Along the Mohawk* (Claudette Colbert), 1939; *Mary of Scotland* (Katharine Hepburn), 1936; *Tobacco Road* (Gene Tierney), 1941; and *7 Women* (Anne Bancroft), 1965. Hardly an imposing collection of "sex goddesses." In *Mogambo* Ava Gardner is cast quite differently from her customary siren and vamp roles: more tenderness, health, and layers of depth. Her character closely resembles Bancroft's in *7 Women*, and they both perform during dinner scenes. Grace Kelly had stellar roles after *Mogambo*—*Dial M for Murder, Rear Window, The Country Girl*—but had not yet earned star billing at the time of *Mogambo*, the picture that *made* her a star: both she and Ava Gardner received Academy Award nominations for it; Grace also got a Metro contract. Ford had insisted on Grace Kelly over the Metro hierarchy's opposition; *they* thought her "ordinary, drab and uninteresting" in her minor role in *High Noon* and a Fox screen test. "As far as this test," argued Ford, "Darryl [Zanuck] miscast her. But this dame has breeding, quality, class. I want to make a test of her— in color—I'll bet she'll knock us on our ass."[28] Hitchcock came upon Kelly after *Mogambo* and used her mechanically, subordinating her personality to fairly iconic conceptions; under Ford she is looser, with more humor, relaxation, and complexity, more physically projecting and improvisatory, and she appears to greater erotic effect than with any of her other directors. Her feigned English accent—although quite good— adds another dimension to the artifice of Linda. It is a pity Ford did not direct "sex goddesses" more often.

Mogambo was also a major picture for Clark Gable. His career on the wane, Metro had not planned to renew his contract, but *Mogambo* put "the King" on top again.

The role of the packboat skipper, Captain John, played by Laurence Naismith, was probably intended for Francis Ford, who had died a few months before.

The production safari, one of the largest safaris of modern times, left Nairobi November 1, 1952, and in eight days traveled a thousand miles to the Kagera River in Tanganyika, near the Ugandan border, a hundred miles from the west shore of Lake Victoria. Footage was also shot in Kenya, Uganda, and French Equatorial Africa. Interiors were filmed in London.

Not atypically for Ford, he molded the screen personages partly upon characteristics in the actors themselves, in this case managing to find more sensitivity and sweetness in Kelly, Gardner, and Gable than they displayed elsewhere. Many of the episodes in the movie reflect actual events of the production. A leopard did walk into Ava's tent one night, and she cooked for everyone once, too. The absurd luxury of Vic's safari (tons of vanity luggage, two or three chairs in each tent, etc.) was mirrored in Metro's, except that some of the stars stayed in hotels in Kenya and flew back and forth each day to location (then bragged how they "roughed" it). Various rumors (never substantiated) had it that Kelly and Gable were having an affair; other rumors (even vaguer) had it that she was allowing *two* men to seek her favors—consequently fostering considerable tension on a production already potentially troubled by Frank Sinatra hanging around trying to patch up his marriage with Ava.

Mogambo holds the record for first-year grosses of all Ford's pictures. Artistically it is a worthy companion to *The Sun Shines Bright* and *The Long Gray Line*. It is a remake of an earlier Metro, *Red Dust* (Victor Fleming, 1932), in which Gable plays his same role; Jean Harlow, Gardner's; Mary Astor, Kelly's. The two movies have little in common.

The Long Gray Line (1955).

> We're always afraid of what we do not know. I'm curious why people love military marches. Why do people follow them automatically, marching quite naturally in step? Simply because each time we hear a march we know, we know what's coming next, and this gives us an absolute confidence in the next minute, while in obscurity we're all afraid. We need to have confidence in the second, the minute, the hour which is coming. And with a march we know that second, that minute.   JACQUES TOURNEUR

The questionable sense, or worth, of life, a frequent Ford theme, receives increasingly pessimistic treatment in his later years. *The Long Gray Line* suggests a philosophy that, while seeking to transcend the bewildering contradictions of life's ordeal, is yet rooted in the immediate existential moment. Tidily summed up in Old Martin's parting blessing, "Subsist, subsist," this notion of *balance* is central to Ford's oeuvre. All creation is in passage, man is a pilgrim ever in motion; at times we may feel a moment that is "out of time," but really we are caught up in powerful and mysterious currents, can never stop, rest, and take our bearings, arational chaos can erupt at any instant, but the wise man subsists.

Marty Maher is a bit of a simpleton; his life is basically an experience of sentiment. He is thus an apt character to illustrate desire for order midst life's dazzling confusion. A parade catches him up, he follows its step, and in this engagement of self into the pace set for him by the parade—an engagement requiring repeated renewals of persistence—he finds subsistence. But has he chosen the right parade? At the parade's heart, how can he know?

        Subsistence. Affection, too, dazzles, but provides its own satisfaction. Unpalatable truths lie frequently within bonhomie, particularly in Ford. Old Martin is a typical "wolf in sheep's clothing": Donald Crisp makes him so engaging, one happily agrees to disregard how obnoxious, rude, intolerant, egocentric, chauvinistic, and domineering he is. "When I was a lad," he tells Kitty seconds after meeting her, "a girl that cluttered up her head with education was sure to turn out flat-chested and with a squint" (whereupon she removes her glasses). Milburn Stone's John J. Pershing is so mythic that we overlook how terribly *nasty* a sonovabitch *he* is. Marty and Mary have an abiding love; nonetheless, she is something of a nag. And so on. Things are not obvious in *The Long Gray Line;* they merely seem so.

    Now, John Ford failed Annapolis's entrance exam but ended up an admiral anyway. He appreciated a cadet's decision to enter West Point and as a "professional soldier" himself subscribed to duty; yet such moral subordination did not conflict with his clarity and honesty as a moviemaker. Hence, *The Long Gray Line* pleases, on one level, militarist viewers, while yet, on another level, it is objectively a critical, damning portrait of the "heart" of the military. In this picture the wisdom of hindsight can see not only explanation for the Vietnam War, but also—in showing what "made" (Marty's phrase) Eisenhower—the picture enlightens us about certain qualities of fifties America.

Figure 8. *The Long Gray Line*

<table>
<tr><td rowspan="5">Part I</td><td>A
B</td><td>Parades (Titles), P1ª
Marty and Eisenhower.</td><td>1954</td></tr>
<tr><td>C</td><td>(1) Arrives at Point, P2. (2) Breakfast hazing, plates. (3) No pay; plates.</td><td>1896</td></tr>
<tr><td>D</td><td>(1) Enlists. (2) Paints ball. (3) Dance sentry P3. (4) Punishment P4; fights Rudy; guardhouse. (5) Boxes Koehler, cadets; Mary. (6) Asks Koehler for (7) kitchen work. (8) P5, picnic. (9) proposes.</td><td>1900?</td></tr>
<tr><td>E</td><td>(1) Mary welcomes home; flag 1. (2) Father and Dinny, prayer. (3) Swimming; Red. (4) Dinner for Red and Kitty; Old Martin and superintendent. (5) Notre Dame game, P6; locker room, and Church. (6) Dinny's new car; Mary pregnant. (7) Hospital birth. (8) Walk home with Old Martin; party; death. (9) Bar and cadets. (10) Punishment 2, P7. Mary in hospital, P8.</td><td>1913

1914
1915</td></tr>
</table>

<table>
<tr><td>INTERLUDE</td><td>(1) Parade Review, P9
(2) Graduation 1915
(3) Parade Review, P10</td><td>1915</td></tr>
</table>

<table>
<tr><td rowspan="4">Part II</td><td>E</td><td>(1) Red and Kitty married, P11. (2) Station—off to war, P12. (3) Marty refused combat; Old Martin tries to enlist. (4) Posting of casualties. (5) Black ribbons; Kitty and Mary. (6) Armistice; Red dead; quits army. (7) Farewell to Old Martin. (8) Visits Kitty and baby; decides to reenlist.</td><td>1917

1918</td></tr>
<tr><td>D</td><td>(1) Red, Jr., sworn in. (2) Marty and ball; hazing. (3) Red, Jr., off to "hop." (4) Pearl Harbor announcement. (5) Marty and Mary at son's grave; Red, Jr. (6) Red confesses honor violation to Marty; Mary and flag 2. (7) Night argument between Marty and Mary over Red; Red and Kitty: Red off to war as sergeant. (8) Marty tells off governor about tradition. (9) Mary's death, P13.</td><td>1938

1941</td></tr>
<tr><td>C</td><td>(1) Marty in church; crèche. (2) Walks home in snow. (3) Alone; cadets; Kitty and Red, Jr. (now captain) give him party.</td><td>1944</td></tr>
<tr><td>B
A</td><td>Marty and Eisenhower.
Parade Review, P14</td><td>1954
(Actually: May 23, 1946)</td></tr>
</table>

ª*P* = Parade

"What a fine ruin it would make!" exclaims Marty, and his original observation remains as true as the attacks by "the youngest governor in the United States" on tradition vs. reality. Life may go on outside, but at the Point everything stays the same (almost): the cadets (with a couple of exceptions) are wooden, uninteresting, and impersonally similar (or so they would seem to Irish Marty); a man here has a good chance to end up a monument (like Major Koehler). West Point's justification is that it *works*.

Marty Maher is an immigrant; like his wife, he arrives in America wearing his ticket (for entrance, for life's journey). "Things are cruel hard in Ireland . . . but not for a man that owns a pub in a hard-drinking community." But West Point, the only America either of them knows, "is a fine proud place." A place of absolute order: "A prison, an insane asylum!" Marty calls it. "What!" he says of his father, "Himself? Him that's always lived free—bring him here among the regulations . . . ?!" In truth, Marty longs to return to Ireland; he does not like the army. What keeps him?

1. He joins to avoid losing his earnings by paying for the dishes he breaks as a waiter (Fig. 8: I. D. 1).

2. Koehler tricks him into reenlisting by his desire to win Mary O'Donnell (I. D. 8, 9).

3. He reenlists when Mary is pregnant; then, the baby dead, he is trapped midst reminders of dead hopes (I. E. 10).

4. During World War I Marty is needed at the Point (II. E. 3).

5. Pershing calls West Point the "heart" of the army (I. D. 1.); but at war's end Marty sees it as a death factory and quits. But like a good Irishman he sees in another what he cannot in himself. Kitty's baby is a link to the future (as Ford demonstrates by dissolving from Old Martin ["Subsist!"] waiting to

die to the little naked baby), and the child's duty ("to follow in his father's glorious footsteps") also provides Marty with a sense to his own life, past and future. So he reenlists.

6. Finally (I.B.), Marty tells Eisenhower, "It took me thirty or forty years just to get the hang of it [army life], you know." Now, says Marty, sitting posed with a vase of *flowers* left rear and a large *urn* right rear, "Everything that I treasure in my heart, *living* or *dead*, is at West Point. I wouldn't know where else to go."

The Point's holding power is clarified in the hospital sequence that concludes part I (and complements the Christmas party concluding part II). There is a crescendo of motion: cadets march in to bring Marty home from the bar; his shadowing father walks behind in the dark; next morning cadets walk punishment duty for having gone off-limits for Marty—a sort of formal symbol of a funeral procession; Marty comes with flowers, whose symbolism is dual (and which the nurse bars from Mary's room). Then, after momentary stillness in the hospital room, comes the gargantuan parade outside.

Multiple dramas unfold, in that stillness, between husband and wife: sorrow for dead Martin Maher III; Marty's fury that he will never have a child (cf. Old Martin's "I'm on my way to becoming an ancestor!" and the continuity expressed in the joke that the babe will be named not after Marty Jr. but after the older man); Mary's sense of empathy, but also of guilt at her barrenness; the mutual need for comfort, which they seem unable to give. In the silence, a faint drum beat, slow and ominous, then, eventually, some fifes, and finally the marching tune loud and clear (the same tune cadets sang going to breakfast the day Marty arrived, and even then it suggested permanent motion). Down below, from afar down the long straight campus road, come four-abreast columns of cadets. The loudness of the drum beats is exaggerated. And the portentousness of the confrontation is marked by Ford with (1) no less than three exchanged crosscuts, plus (2) a dolly-in on Marty (which we know as a Fordian figure marking coming-to-terms with reality), and with (3) virtually the only "impossible" camera angle in postwar Ford (i.e., the window is on an upper story), an unnaturalness accentuating the rational act portrayed. Says Mary, in the crosscut from outside the window, "It's a cruel thing, but try to find it in your heart, Martin, to accept the will of God . . . or would [these cadets] only be putting you in mind of the son we had for such a little while . . . so that you'll wish you could go away from here and never have to look at them again?" Marty's face, in fact, is shadowed, but Mary's is lighted, for of course the parade means not only doom but also that life marches on; her heart flies to it for succor. But this grim, implacable parade, though Marty does not know it, is really what seals his fate and defeats his desire to leave the army and to live "free";* it indicates the inexorable power of the tradition of military discipline—and tells us why men will kill and die.

*Sgt. Rutledge, another racial underling, also rejects "freedom" for the army.

More than an institution, West Point is a giant family, and the friends who half a dozen times come to console mark the links of love that bind. When Kitty, expressionistically shadowed with Red's Medal of Honor, bitterly complains of her widowhood, "Professional soldiers are trained to die, is that it?" Marty replies, "They're trained to do a job, Kitty. Some die young and some don't, but they all give their lives for their country, they're ready when they're needed. They set the example—and their wives, Kitty!" "Alright," she says, with flat desperation, "I'll set the example too." The baby cries: dissolve to his enlistment as a plebe. Did this Red, Jr., whom at movie's end Kitty will proudly present on crutches as a "professional soldier," ever have a choice? "The *Corps*!!" proclaims the title music—a hymn, solemn and implacable.

Marty shares many of the characteristics of the Fordian hero: celibate, even impotent, able to "balance," able to keep atop the maelstrom; but he lacks the authority and critical consciousness of the true Fordian soldier-priest. Having made the initial move, by casually walking into West Point, he spends the rest of his life watching as others walk (or parade) into it. He is oft separate in the movie, often spatially, because he is an observer, a feeler, but not quite an outsider. He is an Irishman among Yankees. He is West Point's oldest living tradition, but he can never graduate. The real Point, the cadets, pass in review through half a century, always changing; Marty grows old, people die, and he will soon; the institution is permanent. West Point, one might say, becomes a woman, a womb. To leave the Point is like leaving the womb: some die, some are injured, some become great men. But Marty cannot leave. He prepares others to leave and die, but remains on the sidelines. Even midst celebration of his son's birth, Marty sits typically to the

side, contemplating a dress sabre given him by the cadets to mark the occasion. Little does he imagine the sword symbolism (death; phallus), for the doctor has not yet come announcing death, and Marty has probably forgotten how, years earlier, he was ordered to report to "the Master of the Sword" (i.e., Major Koehler).

The cannon at West Point are harmless. Marty tells Pershing the balls don't fit (and is told to mind his duty). The cannon suggest aggression, but they cannot fire. The biological image of Marty sitting abreast the barrel and dropping a ball between his legs suggests the barrenness of his issue, intimates the coming scandal of Red, Jr., reminds us of futility: of the questionable worth of our life when we turn ashen gray, of the cruelness of renewing seasons and of brass cannon, which, dumb as they are, have a permanence denied to us. One would not read too much into these cannon, but they appear in two other important scenes: dominating, from above, the parents, suddenly grown old, as they watch Red's oath-taking; leaned on by Marty and Red, side by side, as Red confesses. Implacable, almost sinister cannon.

In a film full of dinners and luscious inviting food, it is strange that Marty never eats: he never tastes that cake with the light green icing (Fig. 8: I.D.7); Mary's picnic basket goes to Rudy Heinz (I.D.8); when Old Martin and Dinny arrive, Marty's dinner is forgotten and they all go to the living room and pray; he takes not a mouthful during the dinner for Red and Kitty. In the flashback's last sequence (II.C.3), he burns an egg (!) that he tries to cook; Kitty asks him when he last ate and orders the cadets to work: they place Marty in an armchair, holding a fork and an elaborate pipe he has just been given, they put a pillow behind him and Mary's old shawl on his lap, they place a tray and eggs in front of him, and around his neck, as a bib, they tie a red-checkered napkin exactly like the one Mary had in Rudy's picnic basket, they give him Red, Jr., a hero, set up a Christmas tree, decorate it, and sing him a serenade.

Still Marty does not eat. What he does do, throughout the movie, is smoke his pipe. He does not fully join with life, but he subsists, smolderingly, an image of West Point tradition. The barrenness of Marty's life seems particularly strong in this last act, in that house so amazingly changed with Mary's departure, in colors turned brown and blue-gray, a brown barrenness even a Christmas tree cannot redeem. Yet how important *things* have become, things like the cannon, the house, the uniform. As Mary died, Marty placed her glass on a shelf and dropped her shawl on the floor. How important they seemed, being there as Marty clung to Mary's dead body, dead traditions pointing like the Point itself to death. Far brighter is the gold statue of Mary Queen of Heaven holding the infant Jesus, with the Christmas crèche below it, to which Ford dissolves across the years after Mary's death scene: an image of spiritual rebirth corresponding to the renewal of the seasons on earth, another tradition, a "response" or "answer" to the question posed by Mary's death.

Cyclicity. Figure 8 illustrates *The Long Gray Line*'s structure, which may be conceived of in various ways:

1. It is circular: the structure mounts, then regresses toward its beginning. The keystone of the structural arch is the 1915 graduation ceremony, flanked by two parade reviews. Parades begin (I.A) and end (II.A) the film; the scene in Eisenhower's office is both the second (I.B) and penultimate (II.B) sequence. These (A and B) "frame" the flashback; but within the flashback itself, the archlike structure is continued.

2. It is additive: a flashback (*b*) not only occurs within bracketing present-time sequences, *aba*'; a flashback is also an equation, $a = b$, because such a structure suggests causal (and other) relations between past and present. In fact, Marty tells his story to prove he ought to be allowed to stay at West Point: here has revolved his life's struggle, the "thirty or forty"-year process of changing a "free" Irish immigrant into a unit of that alien society of "regulations . . . sobriety . . . duty."*

3. The second section repeats the first. The first son died, the celebration party was interrupted; the second son enlists, has Marty pin on his officer's bars (as Overton, in 1917, requested his first salute), and the second party concludes successfully, with the same song sung at the first:

> Come fill your glasses, fellows,
> And stand up in a row,
> We're singing sentimentally,
> We're going for to go.
>
> In the Army there's sobriety,
> Promotion's very slow . . .

As events occur and recur, repetition appears predestined.

For example: Red, Jr., is not only the son of two close friends (one dead) and a substitute for Marty's own dead son, he is also intended to fulfill hopes that, like Ward Bond's in *Fort Apache*, are really Marty's own desire to relive his life as a cadet rather than just a coach. We dissolve from Marty's reenlistment decision to Red, Jr., and his class taking the enlistment oath, which corresponds to: the 1915 graduation, Marty's 1896 enlistment, the fulfillment denied Marty's baby. The next scene finds Marty astride a cannon dropping a ball as in 1900, and Red, Jr., is hazed with identical recitations of 1896 by sons and grandsons of cadets Marty knew back then. And as Marty places flowers on his son's grave, Red, Jr., confesses he has broken his oath (by marrying before graduation) but plans to conceal his violation (the marriage was quickly annulled). But those cannon and the Hudson's granite cliffs and, of course, Marty himself are implacably hostile to Red's dishonor; Marty watches the flag lowered to half mast (as he watched decades earlier) and in Rembrandtesque darkness tells Mary he wants to quit: failure.

***The Man Who Shot Liberty Valance*'s similar (*aba* ; $a = b$) structure also explains the present by the past, and shows the present to be a result, or product, of the past.

Thus events occur and recur over fifty years. But as Marty ages, their pace quickens. Autumns pass into winters, springs turn barren. More and more, each scene contrasts starkly with its neighbor, happiness thrust against tragedy.

Parade. Such dialectical clashes are the structuring motifs of postwar Ford. Change and subsistence; parade and house; chaos and order; theater and reality. In *The Long Gray Line* parades frame the story; a parade celebrates Marty's courtship of Mary; another mourns his son's death and another provides courage to go on living; the parade suggests madness, as troop-trains depart for World War I and crowds surge in wild confusion behind Marty; the parade bridges the gaps of years; and, manifested by only its distant sounds, the parade signals the coming of death to Mary O'Donnell. (Parades are indicated on Figure 8, the plot diagram, by *P.*) Antinomally, the image of the house has been almost as frequent, along with a dying father's parting blessing to "subsist," advice that Marty, searching frantically for something to say as Red, Jr., hurries off to World War II, suddenly and intuitively finds to repeat to this *his* "son"*—while Mary gazes bereftly.

The four-and-a-half-minute parade review for Marty (with Irish tunes) with which the picture concludes bursts almost like a miracle the dialectical tensions of *The Long Gray Line.* As in the finale of Renoir's *French Cancan,* we enter rare realms of evocative spectacle, poetry, and symbolism. At any rate, this is clearly another world: we are struck by the sudden proliferation of automobiles and buses onto these hallowed grounds, and by the new bleachers overflowing with tourists. The grass is green, the military is benign, innocuous, overflowing with good fellowship. The squads of cadets now seem like toy soldiers; the music provides the glory, the pictures are of cute, sprightly, but faceless, mechanical toy soldiers. And Marty's dead appear: Mary, Old Martin, Koehler, Red, Sr., Overton! The only disturbing,

---

*Red, Jr., scarcely notices these words, and Marty himself utters them almost without thought. The disorder of the scene contrasts markedly with the original, careful ritual when Marty walked to his father, saying, "I ask for your blessing, daddo," and there came the formal, but magically prophetic response, "You'll always have that, my boy. Subsist, subsist."

*un*theatrical element in the spectacle is Marty himself, forever dropping out of attention, shaking hands, reaching out for his ghosts, crying. He alone seem "real." When Kitty answers her son's "It's been a great day for Marty" with "It's been a great *life* for Marty," her delivery is deliberately shorn of dramatic nuance; the essential question of the film (Does life make sense?) is answered affirmatively in negation of its patent tragedy, and for the simple reason that experience itself is precious. The contradictions of life at a death factory, of course, are not resolved; they are lifted instead into a higher order. The parade substitutes itself for reason, an arational, atemporal framing of Marty's flashback narrative of his life. He knows now, reaching for his ghosts, that the past *is* present ($b = a$), tradition is now, human experience is essentially permanent within memory, whose reality, in this "Viking's Funeral," transcends that of death—as in *How Green Was My Valley*. The sequence dazzles, then, not by apprehension of a preternatural miracle, but of a natural one: consciousness of the import of one's own existence as a permanent particle of time. The final shot is not of the parade but of Marty breathing heavily beside two generals. Like us, he has become a spectator of his life.

The Long Gray Line has fared badly with critics, and although it certainly is not a movie without faults,* it *is* one of Ford's most ambitious works, and complaints of its supposed chauvinism, sentimentality, and manipulative facility misconstrue the movie's nature, which is allegorical (rather than realist) and subjective (rather than objective).

The appearance of Marty's dead during the parade finale ought not to surprise us. We should recall the montage earlier, during another parade, as

---

*A couple of marginal scenes threaten to blight one's appreciation of the whole: absurdities like someone soaping the kitchen ramp—when Marty slides and falls—while waiters serve breakfast, or that half a dozen cadets disappear during swimming class. We could dispense with the swimming scenes and with Old Martin trying to enlist (albeit modeled on Ford's sexagenerian brother Francis). It is a shame Ford's determination to remain within Marty's point of view deprives us of a wonderful dance sequence just because Marty is outside on sentry duty: true, he is always outside, but he could have peeked. At least we do see the lovely young girls throw their boys bouquets, framed fittingly in an archway.

Marty, from behind a tree, watched Mary O'Donnell and her picnic basket (Fig. 8: I.D.8): two-shot: Marty and Mary at bench / LS: parade / two-shot again / MS: three cadets, in parade, salute / two-shot again. Ford's remarkable interjection of utter nonrealism here, the saluting cadets midst a love tryst, allegorizes the tryst much as Renoir allegorizes a tryst in *The River* by using *Invitation to the Dance* as background music. The whole of *The Long Gray Line* unfurls within this allegorical dialectic between life (the parade) and Marty's subjectivity.

But characters here do not so much develop as watch themselves exist through time and other people. With Marty as central persona, we learn that life is not so much ours to live, as for others to live for us. No doubt Marty's narration reflects his Irishness, lowerclassness, and "redneck" immigrant mentality; no doubt he distorts some portraits (e.g., his animated wife, in Maureen O'Hara's marvelously full-bodied stylization, contrasting with Tyrone Power's woodenness—Marty's passivity). No doubt Ford romanticizes events, and chooses to relate the precious moments, and those only, the moments of utmost feeling. But far from passing facilely through many intoxicated incidents, Ford typically fills out each episode with density of decor (e.g., the love and detail of the Maher living room) and disciplined performances that often vivify (Ford's typically) taciturn scripting: e.g., Mary steps down a step, turns her neck in that Irish birdlike way of hers: "Is it sorry you are already, Martin Maher?" "It's sorry I'll never be, Mary O'Donnell" (I.D.9).

Ford's virtues are often his most attacked features: his up-front showmanship, degrees of unabashed stylization of actors and emotions never attained even in Metro musicals, bold clarity in gesture, frightening precision in effects. Each shot has beginning, middle, and end. Even the simplest reaction shot receives inventive treatment (e.g., Rudy Heinz, watching Koehler box with Marty, leaps on an exercise bar). Marty, first entering West Point, is struck by the cadets marching in the quadrangle (I.D.1); in the parade finale, Koehler and two cadets strut into a low-angle proscenium shot and tip their hats like Pall Mall boys. Such effects evince confidence in emotions. Perhaps Koehler's swimming instructions ("There are four things to remember: confidence, timing, relaxation, and breathing") apply also to cinematic technique. (But when Marty falls into the pool, his friends save him from drowning.)

Ford's subtle structuring of moods and emotions appears in sequence II.E.5: During World War I, Marty puts a black ribbon next to Overton's yearbook picture; as he mentions Rudy Heinz was also a casualty, the camera shows Mary reacting to the news. The doorbell rings, she stands still a moment, then walks straight back to open the door. Ford cuts on the door movement to Marty's reaction, hearing Kitty's voice. When we cut to a general scene of the living room and see Kitty, Marty is already coming into the room. Now, a lesser director would have shown us Kitty's entry; by sticking in the reaction shot, Ford preserves Marty as the central character: had he shown Kitty bubbling into this sullen scene he would have turned our attention to her. Now Kitty and Mary sit gossiping, and Marty, to his chagrin, must set table for tea, and, outraged at a tea ceremony while his boys are dying and he's stuck at the Point, he stalks off in fury. By having the two women chatter at a frenetic pace, Ford: 1) contrasts stylized, satiric comedy to the sullen mood; 2) preserves a juxtaposition to set off Marty's weightier mood while preserving his primacy; 3) provides a telling moment in a throwaway reaction: Kitty gleefully reports news of "Cherub Overton" in Paris— "Imagine! In Paris!!" But Mary O'Donnell lets fall not a hint that Overton is dead.

The Long Gray Line was Ford's first picture in Cinemascope, a format he disliked at the time. He felt compelled to use extremely long takes and to shoot entire scenes in single shots with characters framed full length. Five hundred and fifty-seven shots in 213 minutes results in about 15 seconds per shot, deceptively low because of some quick sequences; versus a deceptively high average of 8.4 seconds per shot for *The Sun Shines Bright*. There are less than forty camera movements, most tiny, and early Cinemascope's shallow focus constrains Ford's usual depth of field (but clever staging partly compensates). Pictorial style otherwise resembles *The Sun Shines Bright*, but however creative Ford's long shots (and most are indeed wonderful), Ford without cutting is Ford sorely lacking.*

Though ostensibly based on Marty's autobiography, *Bringing Up the Brass: My 55 Years at West Point* (1951), and proclaiming itself "The *True* Story of an Enlisted Man Who Was There for 50 . . . Years," virtually all of the movie is pure invention. Marty Maher enlisted in 1896 and retired in 1946, when the parade review was held in his honor and when, by order of the commander-in-chief (Truman), he was allowed to stay at West Point. He was still alive at the time the picture was released, but I have not found accounts of his reactions. In actual fact, the Mahers had no children, but adopted a niece; the Red Sundstrom characters are not in the book, nor are most of the other incidents. Instead the chronicle is a fairly unreadable collection of locker-room stories and talk of old Ireland—with a foreword by Eisenhower.

The Searchers (1956). Texas, 1868, a solitary cabin: Ethan Edwards returns from the Civil War and Mexico still a Reb; affection for brother Aaron's wife makes him an outsider. Indians massacre Aaron's family, but Ethan vows to find little niece Debbie, who may be captive, and is joined by Martin Pawley, an orphan Aaron adopted whom Laurie Jorgensen hopes to marry. For seven years the living suffer while the (probably) dead are

---

Cheyenne Autumn (1964) is also in long takes, appropriately; but *7 Women*, Ford's third anamorphic feature, shows complete adaptation to scope format and is among his most rapidly edited pictures.

Figure 9. ***The Searchers***

The division below is somewhat arbitrary. But within each "act" there is considerable unity of time. By merging together the three middle acts, a tripartite structure is revealed: exposition, development, resolution.

1. Exposition	**ACT I**			
	1.	Edwardses'	Ethan arrives / living room / dinner / fireplace and gold / bedtime	Day 1: evening
	2.	Edwardses'	Breakfast and rangers / departure	Day 2: morning
	3.	Desert	Indian grave: posse splits	Day 2: afternoon
	4.	Edwardses'	Indians heard; Debbie at tomb	Day 2: evening
	5.	Edwardses'	Ethan and co. / Edwardses' ruins	Day 3: morning
	6.	Edwardses'	Funeral	Day 4
	7.	Desert	Swamp / chase and battle / posse splits off	Day c. 5
	8.	Desert	At cliffs	Day c. 6?
	9.	Desert	Brad's death	Night 6?
	10.	Desert	Snow	Much later
2. Development	**ACT II**			
	1.	Jorgensens'	Arrival / home scenes / Texacans	2 years later
	2.	Jorgensens'	Home scenes, leave	Day "2"
	3.	Futterman's	Bar	Later
	4.	Desert	Rock ambush	Evening
	ACT III			
	1.a.	Jorgensens'	Letter arrives . . .	2 years later
	FB-1	Desert	(Trade with Indians / Look)	(Day 1 . . .)
	1.b.	Jorgensens'	. . . Letter continued . . .	---
	FB-2	Desert	(Bed, Look / morning)	(. . . night 1 . . .)
	1.c.	Jorgensens'	. . . Letter continued . . .	---
	FB-3	Desert	(Killing buffalo / slaughtered Indians / 7th Cavalry / lunatic captives)	(. . . much later)
	1.d.	Jorgensens'	. . . Letter concluded	---
	2.	Desert	Wilderness sunset ride	Every day
	ACT IV			
	1.	Cantina		3 years later
	2.	Scar's camp		(7 years from start)
	3.	Debbie, Scar's attack		
	4.	Cliffs and wounds		
3. Resolution	**ACT V**			
	1.	Jorgensens'	Dance and wedding / Ethan and Marty arrive / fight / Mose and lieutenant	Some months later: Night 1
	2.	Desert	Night camp debate / rope / night march / Scar killed / attack: Ethan and Debbie / slapstick	Morning 2 Morning 2
	3.	Return home		

searched. Then Debbie is found, married to her mother's assassin, Comanche chief Scar, and only Marty's intervention and Scar's attack prevent
Ethan killing her. Their return, after five years unseen, stops Laurie marrying another. They join rangers to destroy Scar's band and Ethan is about to
kill Debbie when, lifting her as he did seven years ago, he hugs her instead
and takes her "home."*

In order to distance Ethan (John Wayne), and to define him within his
culture, Ford and scenarist Frank Nugent have placed a "letter scene" in the
middle of *The Searchers*.

III.1.a. Jorgensens': The only letter Laurie (Vera Miles) gets from Marty
(Jeffrey Hunter) in five years is delivered by Charlie McCorry (Ken Curtis).
In a comic sequence, she is forced to read it aloud in front of Charlie (an
oaf courting her) and her parents. Marty writes how he acquired an Indian
wife . . .

Flashback 1: (Laurie reads, voice-off.) Ethan and Marty trade with Indians, then find a chubby girl following them, a wife Marty has unwittingly
purchased. "Come on, Mrs. Pawley!" jokes Ethan. They call her "Look."

1.b. Jorgensens': Charlie is overjoyed ("Hawh! Hawh! So he got himself
an Indian wife!"); Laurie throws the letter into the fire. Her father retrieves
it, scolds her, pitilessly orders she read on. "'She wasn't nearly as old as
you'!" she reads, fuming . . .

Flashback 2: That night, Look tries to lie with Marty, who kicks her
down a hill. At mention of Scar she shows terror. Next morning (Marty
narrates) they follow her trail marks.

1.c. Jorgensens': Laurie, eyes filled with tears.

Two points deserve note thus far. First is the intricate structure of narrative points of view. *We* are watching *the movie* (Ford) wherein *Laurie* reads
Marty's words about *Ethan's attitude* toward *Look*. Secondly, each character
offers a contrasting sensibility. We are at once aware of the disparity between
Laurie's comprehension of Marty's letter and what actually happened.
Within her home, we see her distress contrasted by Charlie's oafish opportunism, her father's obliviousness, her mother's wish that Laurie forget Marty. In
the flashback, we may feel inclined to participate in Ethan's humor at Marty's
plight. If so, we do so because we perceive Look through the filters of others'
sensibilities (all of them racist: Ethan, Marty, Laurie). Our lack of regard for
Look's feelings parallels the general lack of regard for Laurie's feelings. Empathy is rare in the world of *The Searchers*, as in our own. Ford hopes, by
means of the intricate contrasts of this letter scene, to make us aware of how
each person's attitudes color reality. To do so, he must "distance" us from the

---

The Searchers was shot in 1955 in fifty days, all over the West from Gunnison, Colorado
for snow, to Edmonton, Alberta, for buffalo. Its producer and backer, C. V. Whitney, had, with
John Hay Whitney, been a Selznick backer and was frequently involved in projects with Merian
C. Cooper.

sympathy we automatically feel for the John Wayne character and must turn our participation in Ethan's callous racism against us:

Flashback 3: (Marty, voice-off:) They lose Look's trail in snow. Later, Ethan slaughters buffalo, to deprive the Indians. Then they come upon an Indian camp raided by cavalry, with corpses everywhere: men, women, children, and Look. (See Fig. 9)

Ethan kills buffalo to kill Indians; soldiers kill Look. Do we now feel sorry for laughing at her? But this sequence's chief effect is to distance Ethan. As we dissolve from Laurie into a long shot of Ethan about to slaughter buffalo, Marty's voice tells us we are about to see something that he still has not been able to figure out: the way Ethan goes wild killing the buffalo. This episode, then, and in fact this entire third act, is a sort of "medical report" on Ethan. Elsewhere, Ethan tends to be the dramatic focal point of *The Searchers* and an empathy-identity figure for the audience; but in this act we see him through others' eyes, others comment on him, his deeds are complexly contextualized, his sanity is dissected, he becomes a phenomenon to be studied, and is least able to guard from view the tenderness and terror inside him. As a result, not only is our compassion for him enriched, but his actions are objectified against the tapestry of his culture.

Flashback 3 (continued): Later, they sight the renowned 7th Cavalry, with flags, beautiful horses, and a bright Irish jig. At the fort entrance three peaceful Indians, each in different-colored blanket, enter the frame as silent onlookers. The music dies into tough-faced soldiers whipping captives, herding them like cattle into the stockade.

Ford *shows* the 7th Cavalry in its mythic glory, because its myth is an essential portion of its historical actuality. And he shows the Searchers responding to that glory, because that is how they felt about the cavalry. But Ford does not thereby glorify the cavalry. On the contrary, he "frames" the evocation of their glory between scenes of massacred Indians and whipped captives. Without its glory, properly contextualized, the 7th Cavalry cannot be understood. Thus Ford treats it as he treats Ethan. And Ford shows reasons for their brutality:

Flashback 3 (continued): In the fort Ethan and Marty inspect whites rescued from Comanche. All are half-crazy; perhaps one is Debbie. In a sustained close-up, Ethan's eyes react to the broken humans he sees and the lunatic howls he hears.

Everyone inhabits a private world: Laurie, her father, her mother, Charlie; the 7th Cavalry, the captive Indians, the peaceful Indians, the indifferent sergeant (Jack Pennick) who shows Ethan the rescued whites. The privacy of the lunatics may differ in dimension from this universal solipsism, but does it differ in kind? Where is truth midst such myriad solitudes? In all probability Debbie is a lunatic, too: why does Ethan persist in his search? Perhaps because he recognizes something of himself in others' lunacy: his stare outward at the terrified lunatics is really the stare inward we noted in

Huw at the end of *How Green Was My Valley*. And Ethan had a similar moment earlier (resting his horse and gazing anxiously across the desert toward his brother's house [Fig. 9: I.3]) when his sensitivity broke through his armor. His vision of a comfy home is impaired by his vision of "wilderness" (in his threatened family, in the lunatics, in Debbie, in himself), but his kindnesses—his concern for Martha and Mrs. Jorgensen, his stopping Marty and Brad from seeing their dead—explain Ethan's unbridled hate as a form of terror, a terror he can only control by exteriorizing it into the search for Debbie.

III.1.d. Jorgensens': Marty's letter offers not a word of love; Laurie is disconsolate. Her father takes the letter, folds it into his pocket, and exits nonchalantly smoking his pipe. Laurie stares bereftly out the window (a stare mirroring Ethan's), but Charlie, strumming guitar, saunters coyly to her side, singing, "Gone again, skip to my Lou, my darling."

2. Laurie's thoughts are visualized by a long dissolve into a sunset vista of Ethan and Marty riding the wilderness. (See Fig. 9)

The worst fears come true: cruel waiting, endless searching, lack of empathy, hostility, deaths of whites and reds, brutality, torture, all ending perhaps in lunacy. Ford shows the cause and effect of these phenomena in each personage. Through comic techniques the viewer is indicted as a participant in the mechanics of racism. The glory of the 7th Cavalry is a paradox—like any man's justification. Empathy is almost nonexistent: whites have no feeling for reds, nor has Marty much concern for Laurie, Laurie for Marty's cause, Jorgensen for his daughter, or Charlie for anything but his opportunism. Ford shows each autonomous point of view and contrasts them, thus throwing them into relief. The juxtaposition of wilderness horrors against home's comfy fireside makes us both question the quest and comprehend its necessity. Laurie's authentic tragedy is not diminished by a comic presentation necessary to contrast it with the starker horrors of the hostile world outside. All this is Ethan's context.

There is need to insist upon this context, and to present it as a sort of conglomerate of tunnel-vision points of view. For in 1868 Texas homesteads are dispersed, people gather (seldom) for weddings and Indian hunts, survival discourages empathy. In place of a dramatic world constructed upon ever-present multitudes of interlocking relationships, it is mostly an arid wilderness that Ethan wanders, with social bonds more theoretic than concrete. Few westerns inhabit grimmer worlds. *The Searchers* is an atypical Ford movie in its concentration on a solitary hero rather than a social group and in its emphasis on the bright open spaces of the desert rather than the angulated chiaroscuro of rooms. It could be classed among Ford's allegorical pieces—*The Fugitive, Wagon Master, 3 Godfathers*—but even more than they it is a morality play, in which all hostilities of wilderness and man flow from a consummate sin.

Intolerance was always a major Ford theme, and racism became a dominant motif (generally misunderstood by critics and thus increasingly strident)
in *The Sun Shines Bright, The Searchers, The Last Hurrah, Sergeant Rutledge, Two Rode Together* (1952–61). In *The Searchers*, racism first destroys
Debbie's family, then nearly destroys her; not until Ethan overcomes his racism will he regain Debbie. Meanwhile, the community leader, Captain-
Reverend Samuel Clayton (Ward Bond), totes both Bible and gun* (the tools
of American expansion according to Ford), and few greater pleasures exist
than killing Indians. Even fleeing women and tiny children, we see, are exterminated joyously. "O Lord, for what we are about to receive we thank you!"
prays Mose Harper (Hank Worden) just before a slaughter. Of course Ole
Mose is a "fool," and accepted as such, but like his alter ego Ethan his actions
represent the actual morality, if not the decorum, of the whites.

For attitudes in *The Searchers* are externalized and theatricalized. The
movie itself, with each bright Technicolor frame organized into painterly,
definitive portraiture, expressionistically composed and lighted, and with
the yearning tune "Laurina," is not realistic but symbol of reality; everything
is saturated in myth, everything is a commentary upon myth.** "I used
a Charles Russell motif," said Ford,[29] as if to remind us that his own myths
are based on the myths devised by others. Perhaps *The Searchers'* "Texas
1868" looks nothing like the *real* Texas; but it does look the way "Texas"
ought to look. And who has made a more mythic entrance into a movie than
Ethan's slow ride out of the distance? Ethan, in a repressed but incessant
ascent toward fury, dominates *The Searchers* through strength and stature
(in his back and walk), through fragility (in his voice and eyes), and through
humanness (supporting performances are more stylized comically, expressionistically, even statuesquely); but most of all Ethan dominates as the focal point of mythic tensions. All these qualities of style combine in some of
Ford's finest moments, fully choreographed to affecting music, such as the
way the Edwards family walk to their porch positions to see Ethan arrive, or
Ethan's background farewell to his sister-in-law Martha while gruff Sam
Clayton stands foreground sipping coffee with feigned unmindfulness; in
both instances, characters frozen on the porch or at the table stop time,

---

*One of many Fordian soldier-priests.
**Technicolor is itself a medium better suited to mythicization than to realism. In addi-
tion, Ford organizes his 1:1.65 VistaVision compositions far more expansively than the nar-
rower ones of *The Sun Shines Bright* or *Mogambo*. Frame space favors the horizontal: tops and
bottoms tend to be darker, the center swath brighter; characters are posed horizontally, horizon lines and scenery and props also emphasize the horizontal. All this frame-space-to-be-
traversed fits the notion of a search. But the effect is mitigated in 16mm (and of course on
television), where side-space present in 35mm is cropped and aspect-ratio consequently reduced to 1:1.33. VistaVision was originally a "high fidelity" process by which a larger image
was obtained on the film by printing frames sideways rather than vertically, resulting in a much
sharper image.

emphasizing the import of Ethan's arrival or departure. And well they might. Insofar as myths are conflicts safely sublimated for the reasonableness of daily life, nothing is less comfortable than a myth incarnate.

During Ethan's first evening home with Aaron's family, the rockingchair, its back to us and its face to the fire, dominates the scene with Ford's usual subtle obviousness (cf. young Lincoln's hat). Ethan jumps out of it, never to return to it, in fury over Aaron's remark that Ethan, before the war, seemed anxious to leave the farm. Ethan, curiously, takes this in exactly the opposite sense, and replies that he is perfectly willing to pay for his stay now. Then next morning, Mose arrives, grabs the rocker, departs saying to Martha, "Grateful to [sic] the hospitality of your rockingchair," and then grabs the chair again, during the scene outside the smouldering ruins of dead Martha's home [Fig. 9, I.5], whilst Ethan goes stalking off. To have his own rockingchair becomes the nomadic Mose's dream. And repeatedly throughout the movie, the rockingchair-by-the-fire is contrasted (by camera, script, and character) to Ethan's never-ending motion across arid open space. Even the peaceful, trading Comanche possess a rockingchair, in contrast to Scar's nomadic band. As always in Ford, happiness is for fools and society is for the simple, not for the idealists, the romantics, the hyperconscious, like the widowed Judge Priests or the haunted Lincoln.

"What makes a man leave house and home and wander off alone?" asks the title music, announcing once again the familiar Fordian antinomy of passage / subsistence, parade / home—and, as in *What Price Glory* and *The Long Gray Line*, the parade (the searching) seems a sort of *substitute* for reason as well as a *search* for reason. For Ethan, who like Tom Joad keeps trying to return home, paradoxically leaves home to search for home, deserts humanity to discover what humanity is, gives up meaningful existence to seek out meaning. As in *Mogambo*, a long trek is a search for "man," and the hero has a "split" within himself as a social and interior being; Ethan's confrontation with Scar thus parallels Vic's (Clark Gable's) confrontation with the dead gorilla, in that the hero really confronts the ambivalence in himself (civilized or savage?). This paradox too is proclaimed in *The Searchers'* title song: "A man will search his heart and soul, go searchin' way out there." Only metaphorically can Ethan's soul be "way out there." His inner search—for home, for resolution of fury, for peace—manifests itself in the outward search for Debbie.*

The wilderness Ethan wanders is metaphorical as well, not, as in Hawks's *El Dorado* or as in the familiar "wilderness / civilization" antinomy some

*These lyrics *were* specifically chosen by Ford.

 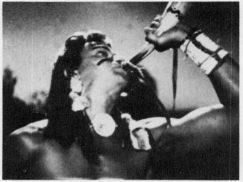

critics ascribe to Ford, a territory in which anything is permitted and to which civilization has yet to come. In Ford, wherever man is, he brings with him his culture, laws, and codes. The Comanche are not linked to absolute wilderness but to their own, rival culture—as our first, hypericonic glimpse of an Indian emphasizes; indeed, with feathers, horn, and warpaint, Scar sports all the totemic paraphernalia we expect in a Fordian vignette. Reiterated crosscuts between Scar and little Debbie contrast cultural icons while presaging their future importance in each others' lives; he picks her up from a cemetery and takes her into another world—but not exactly into a "wilderness." The Indians of *The Searchers* are constantly paralleled with the whites—riding abreast of them, in battle, or parleying. As with Look, our tendency to look upon Indians as totem poles is reversed against us when we finally meet Scar intimately (Fig. 9, IV. 2), discover that he is human and that his racial hatred is equated with Ethan's. (Scar's raid on the Edwards was in revenge for sons killed by whitemen; now he lives surrounded by the trophies of his hate: his scalps, the medallion, and Debbie.) The struggle between reds and whites is thus an all-or-nothing war between two civilizations, with the land as both prize and battlefield. For now, the Indians and their tepees blend into the landscape like integral parts of its rocks, towers, and pinnacles. The whiteman is the invader, the stranger in this land: witness the peculiarity of the Edwards house, perched in nowhere. But the whites will conquer this land and transform it, so that no longer will they seem strange here, transforming the land as now the Comanche transform white captives. "Whoo whoo whoo," sings the crazed woman to her doll, as Ethan gazes numbed by the frightful fragility of the human mind: how utterly we are like weeds. It is fear, a psychological wasteland, that is the wilderness Ethan wanders. He emerges from and returns into this wilderness not because he, like Shane or like Vidor's Man Without a Star, is a wild thing, but because he embodies quintessentially human longings for which society offers no fulfillment. His longings all symbolize an *excess* of civilized values rather than wilderness ones. Society deserts Ethan as much as Ethan deserts society. Others give up; he persists. "That'll be the day!"—his favorite retort—virtually defines him: Ethan is someone who does not change, does not give up, does not miss a shot, does not get parties thrown for him, cannot be seriously threatened by the likes of Marty or Brad. He appears to be a loner, yet his absence from home is motivated by desire to preserve a family that his love for Martha might threaten, just as, subsequently, desire to preserve that family's remnants keeps him apart for the course of the film. He appears, like the dead Indian whose eyes he shoots out, doomed "to wander forever between the winds." His love of family, his need to restore it by rescuing Debbie, his racism and intolerance, all assume a purity and persistence that set him uncomfortably apart. If character is fate, feelings are character: his persistence through seven years of obsessive love/hate causes a crisis, a "split," in Ethan. Unable to reconcile his love of family with his outrage that this white child has given herself to her mother's red despoiler, he is impelled to destroy her.

Ethan's conflict mirrors ideally the racism of society. Brad Jorgensen gave up his own life, unable to deal with the thought that his beloved died less than pure. And Ethan's desire to see Debbie dead is endorsed by almost everyone, particularly by Laurie, who tells Marty that Debbie's mother (Martha) would *want* Ethan to put a bullet through the girl's brain. The captain-reverend endorses this attitude *but* also endorses Marty's effort to preserve Debbie's life; he is a captain-reverend, after all (and similarly, earlier [Fig. 9, I.7], he shoots attacking Indians and, as opposed to Ethan, spares retreating ones). Mose Harper also combines both attitudes, but in a more exuberantly theatrical manner (just as he mirrors Ethan's rocking-chair-vs.-wandering duality). The captain-reverend and Ole Mose can tolerate the essential paradoxes of racial violence, however, and so can society as a whole —the Edwards family fondly watches their boy's central placement of Ethan's sword over the hearth. But in Ethan, who is extraordinary in being a student of his hate—an expert on the Comanche and even speaking their language—the desire to kill that which is most essential to him produces acute conflict, obliging him finally, as he hurls Debbie above his head to kill her, to confront a racism that society accepts unthinkingly.

Ford aptly described *The Searchers* as "a kind of psychological epic,"[30] and it is worth noting that the Comanche—who have the mythic qualities of being constantly discussed, feared, and pursued, of marking their passage as violently as possible with ravaged and stricken victims, but of being themselves virtually never *seen*—appear almost magically when they *are* seen. A dead Comanche is found beneath a stone; Scar is suddenly *there* in the cemetery; the Comanche who battle the rangers are suddenly *there* on the horizon; an Indian is suddenly *there* to shoot Ethan, saving Debbie.

The Comanche, then, appear as shocks of terror, as an element Ethan cannot control. And they become associated with even deeper terrors within him. And with another chain of images:

When, in *The Searchers'* first shot, Martha opens her door from blackness to the bright world outside, the equation of home with blackness suggests (as is subsequently confirmed) that within the doorway dwells our innerness, heart and womb, our vulnerability, even our unconscious. On this occasion Martha is opening herself to Ethan—the imagery accounts for the sequence's extraordinary emotional power—but the necessity to protect, to seal off our interiority from the world outside, from other people, produces psychic isolation, the consummate sin from which stems all the lack of empathy we noted in the letter scene, and all the intolerance, racism, opportunism, obsessive hate, and insanity of *The Searchers'* world.

Martha and her home seem the prime desires of Ethan's interiority. But they are also the prime frustrations: Ethan is left outside alone at night as Aaron takes Martha indoors to bed. The languorous timidity with which Ethan rode up to the house is contrasted with the robustness with which Marty charges up and bolts through the door, and with the way the children suddenly burst open a door to tease Lucy and Brad kissing, and, later, with the way Laurie teasingly and uninhibitedly bursts into Marty's bath.

Doorways, then, are linked to sex, and usually with a degree of shock, for sex is another feeling Ethan cannot control.

The doorway image in all its connotations recurs, now associated with the Comanche, as the worst conceivable nightmare, as a screeching searing of consciousness: Ethan, midst swirling smoke, stands framed by Martha's burnt doorway, within which lies her body, dead and dead after unthinkable torture. All Ethan's terrors unite; from this moment, unable to face them, he goes insane. The seven-year search he now undertakes is thus a search for peace of mind; but in the meantime Ethan's mind is anything but peaceful. Two goals torment him. He pursues Scar to avenge the murderous rape of the woman he himself could not possess. And he pursues Debbie not only because she is Martha's child but also as a sublimation of his inability to have Martha, of his impotence in *anything* that matters to him.

The searches for years are for unseen ideals—ideal evil and ideal good. Then Ethan finds Scar and enters his tepee. His eyes follow the camera's pan along the rod of Scar's collection of white women's scalps, and Debbie is suddenly there, holding it, appearing magically, with a shock, out of nowhere, like a Comanche. That she has become a Comanche she herself confirms after she appears a second time, again like a miracle, on the horizon of a sand dune. Beautiful, nubile, but unharmed, she has evidently given herself freely to Scar. No wonder Ethan wants to kill her.*

---

*At the base of the sand dunes, just before Ethan tries to kill her (but is himself shot by Scar [IV.3]), Debbie, at first speaking in Comanche, tells Marty she had hoped for years they would come, then gave up, is now Indian, they should go away. Does Debbie, then, *want* to go home?

And so, later, he hurls her above his head. But the setting is a doorway—a cave entrance—and the sand is swirling in duplication of the smoke that engulfed Ethan outside dead Martha's ruins. Does he recall lifting Debbie the night before that massacre (I:1)? Regardless, he finally *touches* Debbie, grasps the *person* rather than ideas, and all his hate, fury, and insanity is transmuted into love.*

The moment and the image are justly among the most celebrated in American cinema. Ethan, in an iconic gesture that is strikingly original yet rooted in tradition and myth, personifies a new moral awareness of self and humanity. In rising above the universal racism and solipsism, he acts as surrogate for his society—and for us, too.

Fordian heroes tend to act as surrogates. They have seen themselves as agents of the Lord (Travis and Sandy), the law (Lincoln), justice (Rogers), medicine (Mudd), high ideals (Huw Morgan). They must purify the world: right a wrong, restore honor, purge disease, avenge crime, purify law, uphold ideals. But Fordian heroes are lonely; isolation and self-exclusion are the prices they pay. Tom Joad cannot rest while society's outcasts tread the road; Mr. Gruffydd must leave the valley. All are obsessed by duty, all be-

---

Can she be a white woman? Are not the whites about to destroy her second family much as the reds destroyed her first family? Given what we see of other captured whites (here and in *Two Rode Together*), Debbie's physical and mental health can be accounted for only by a miracle—or by extraordinary gentleness on Scar's part. We do not know the answers to these questions, nor can we say to what degree she has found peace with the man who perhaps displays her mother's scalp (as he displays the scalp of Marty's mother). But Debbie has come not to chat but to warn of Scar's attack. Does a fourteen-year-old have clear ideas of what she wants, after seven years of rigorous conditioning to be an Indian, when she suddenly finds infant fantasies close to fulfillment? She does begin to hope again, for later (V.2) she embraces Marty joyfully when he tells her he is taking her home. (In Paul Schrader's 1979 *Hardcore*, *The Searchers* is remade as a modern Methodist [George C. Scott] trying to rescue his daughter from slavery to a porno producer; she too instinctively refuses at first to return home.)

*Lifting up Debbie = pulling down the branch in Mizoguchi's *Sansho the Bailiff* (1954). In both cases a gesture repeated years later restores a hero to sanity, family, and first principles.

come "priests," take vows equivalent to chastity, give up everything for their task. And over the years Ford's concept of his hero evolves toward ever more pronounced obsession and introversion. The heroes played by Fonda illustrate this evolution—Lincoln, Tom Joad, Wyatt Earp, the Fugitive priest—and the process continues through the Wayne heroes, climaxing in the suicides of Tom Doniphon (*Liberty Valance*) and Dr. Cartwright (Anne Bancroft, *7 Women*). The hero's ability to moderate intolerance becomes progressively more questionable, and the cost to him more ruinous.

Among these heroes Ethan is distinctive not so much by his neuroses (he may even seem fairly normal alongside DeLaage, Terangi, Rankin, Arrowsmith, Mary Stuart, John Knox, Muley, Gruffydd and Huw, Lincoln, the Cleggs, and the Clantons) as by the resonant complexities of his contradictions. It is true that he so thoroughly perverts the hero's traditional tasks—to moderate intolerance and reunite families—that Marty has to stay by his side to hold him in check. Although in many respects Ethan's alter ego ("He-Who-Follows," Scar names him), and with even his own set of doorway images, Marty, part Indian himself, does not share the common horror at racial pollution, and is the only person to recognize the absurdity of granting ideology dominion over human life—only begrudgingly do the rangers permit him to slip in ahead of their raid to try to save Debbie. But Marty is not a Fordian hero. He has no affect on Ethan; his attempts to save Debbie fail (Scar saves her the first time, Ethan abducts her the second); Ethan, not Marty, saves the family; and Marty's devotion to duty does not cost him Laurie. We ought not, then, discount Ethan for his neuroses. His hate is cogent, his loyalty to a dead woman noble. No one finds him absurd. A man with very human qualities, he is forced to deal with his surroundings in a superhuman way. The arguments that he should care for the living, that Debbie is dead or "the leavings of a Comanche buck" (Laurie) are refuted and Ethan vindicated when Debbie is found. Even Ethan's hate appears ultimately as the other face of his compassion. Thus when he rides up to the Jorgensens holding Debbie, her arms childishly around his neck, we must, I think, feel awe and admiration for him. He did what no one else would bother to do. His loneliness and sin humanize his heroic stature and heroize his humanity.

The Searchers, initially so grimly antiromantic, comes, with the improbable recovery of a healthy Debbie and the nullification of Ethan's hate, to reassert hope with expressionistic vehemence. The miracle recalls *Wagon Master*'s apotheosis. Even the wandering old Moses has gained the promised land—the rockingchair. But, unlike in *Pilgrimage*, the resolution of inner conflict culminating a journey does not mark reconciliation with society. Ethan, the new Moses, modern man, stands outside, grasps his left elbow with his right hand, and turns and walks away, as Mrs. Jorgensen's door closes to end the picture in the same darkness out of which Martha Edwards opened her door to begin it. Why did Ethan not enter?

Many explanations are plausible, from ones traditional to the western (distant horizons beckon; new duties call; the task is done; the hero belongs to the wilderness), to ones particular to *The Searchers* (Ethan is doomed to wander; happiness is for the simple; his new moral awareness excludes him from the older order). And there is the special explanation (as noted earlier, pages 22–23) that the arm gesture Ethan makes was the signal gesture of Harry Carey, who often walked away at the end of pictures, and who greatly influenced Ford and Wayne—and, in fact, the house Wayne walks away from here is Carey's widow's (Olive Carey, playing Mrs. Jorgensen). Wayne's homage acknowledges debts and links Ethan to past Fordian heroes.

But, on the other hand, why—beyond the requirements of a happy ending—should Ethan *not* be left alone? Is he to live with fourteen-year-old Debbie? Surely she is better off with the Jorgensens. Is he to live with the Jorgensens? They are relative strangers. No, as in our own world, people live separately, not in utopian communes: Ethan walks away for the most commonplace of reasons. That his walking away *seems* extraordinarily meaningful, that his arm gesture seems an admission of impotence, is perhaps because, in a moment, the hero disappears and only a lonely, aging man is left.

Ford and Politics

Once at Goulding's Lodge in Monument Valley, Ford hired a gorgeous woman to wait on Ward Bond's table, act enamored of him, and give him devoted service. One evening she told Ward her husband would be back next day; this would be her last night alone; he should bring a six-pack and a watermelon. So that night, with six-pack and watermelon, Ward set out for her bungalow. Little did he suspect that Ford, Wayne, and four others were waiting with blank-loaded pistols. When he opened the door, they started firing. Ward dropped the six-pack and raced away for his life, still carrying the watermelon.[31]

Ford and Wayne were constantly thinking up tricks to play on Bond. Because Bond *strove* to be pretentious and was always griping about his role, his room, or whatever, he was Ford's pet patsy, with Wayne as the audience. No insult could dent Bond's thick hide. And, consciously or not, he was a superlative actor, perhaps the most underappreciated in films. He was also among the Ford family's most intimate friends, godfather to Jack's children and grandchildren. He even got married on the *Araner*.

But Ward Bond was president of the Motion Picture Alliance for the Preservation of American Ideals, an organization determined to root out Communists and "fellow travelers" and to aid the House Un-American Activities Committee in its witch hunts. This caused problems for liberal thinkers. "I didn't know if I should like Ward," said Dobe Carey. "I didn't like that outfit. But I did like Ward. Ford said Ward would do anything that made him feel important, even at the expense of stomping on people, 'cause he was just too thickheaded to really analyze it and see what a phoney thing it was. It was terrifying. But I don't think Ward knew what he was doing. As Ford used to say, 'Let's face it. Ward Bond is a shit, but he's our favorite shit.'"[32] Indeed, Bond was infamous for putting his foot in his mouth. Once while Ford was shooting a scene for *The Searchers*, the power suddenly went off. People scrambled hither and yon to find out what had gone wrong. It turned out Bond had innocently unplugged the camera so he could take a shave.[33] Ward, said Ford, "was a great, big, ugly, wonderful guy. But he was . . . the greatest snob I have ever known."[34]

John Wayne, an equally close friend, was reputedly an authentic Jew-baiter and Red-baiter in the early fifties. Ford, who seems to have regarded him as something of an intellectual lummox only fools could take seriously, used to rib him endlessly.[35]

Ford, as a child of immigrants and a member of a (then) persecuted racial and religious minority, tended to ally himself with blacks or Indians or anyone victimized by discrimination. He came from a time when loyalty to family, friends, country, and principles counted more than life itself. Thus he did not turn his back on cronies who descended into bigotry. But he did not support them in it either.

While Ford was principled, he was basically apolitical and would rarely voice an opinion. But if someone's integrity or job were at stake, he was the first to speak up. The speech he made in 1933 to the Screen Directors Guild (an organization he had helped organize) was such a case:

> In the past few weeks, despite the most profitable year that the motion picture industry has ever known, there have been more studio people fired than at any other time. Hundreds have been let go at all the studios. Directors and assistants, writers and stock players, craftsmen and office

workers of every classification. Now, after this eminently successful financial year, just why is this going on? Why are so many people being let out? The usual answer is, of course, business depression. Stock market is going down. Business is bad. I don't believe it. Your Board of Directors doesn't believe it. President of the United States doesn't believe it. The Attorney-General's Office in Washington doesn't believe it. Their investigator, Mr. Jackson, doesn't believe it. In fact, he boldly states that the banking industry is going on a sit-down strike. Why? To bring about a financial crisis. So that wages and wage-earners can be pushed back to where they were in 1910. . . . How does it affect this Guild? Look, Gentlemen, I don't think that we are stupid enough to deny that the picture racket is controlled from Wall Street. All right, last year, again I repeat, the most profitable year of all, this Guild was unrecognized. Big finance won the first round. Now they are going to try to win the second round. They are going to keep us unrecognized in bad times. . . .[36]

At the same time, intolerant of endless committees and infighting, he avoided the 1930s wars between the studios and the incipient trade guilds. Behind the scenes he helped; and Mary Ford aided the unemployed through the Assistance League.

The blacklisting of the McCarthy era disgusted him.* "Send the commie bastard to me, I'll hire him," he'd say.[37] He had the Military Order of the Purple Heart condemn the 1947 HUAC hearings as "defamatory and slanderous . . . witchhunts."[38] When in 1951 the Department of Defense charged Frank Capra (of all people!) with Communist involvement, Ford retorted, "I never heard him [object] to the Congressional Investigation of Hollywood Communists. I don't believe he did. Frankly, I objected to it loudly and vociferously. I'll now go on record as saying I think it was a publicity stunt and taxpayers would have saved a lot of money in railfares if the investigation had stayed in Washington."[39] In 1950, he refused to back Cecil B. DeMille's loyalty oath for the Guild; DeMille proposed that names of those declining to sign be sent to the studios. Then, to confound opposition, DeMille rumored that Guild president Joseph Mankiewicz was "pinko" (then a serious charge) and attempted a quick coup by sending recall ballots—only to his allies! But the liberals forced a general meeting, at which Ford's intervention, concluding four hours of debate, was decisive. He identified himself for the stenographer, "My name's John Ford. I am a director of Westerns," and declared himself "ashamed" at "what looks to me like a blacklist. I don't think we should . . . put ourselves in a position of putting out derogatory information about a director, whether he is a Communist, beats his mother-in-law, or beats dogs. . . . I don't agree with C. B. DeMille. I admire him. I don't like

---

*Ford discovered Anna Lee had been blacklisted for a year, due to confusion with another woman of similar name. For subsequent jobs, producers obliged her to sign a disclaimer that she was not "Ann Lee." (Author's interview with Anna Lee, March 1979.)

him, but I admire him." The assembly passed Ford's motion for DeMille's resignation and endorsement of Mankiewicz.[40]

Cultural identity, to Ford's generation, was something to be profited from, preserved, and celebrated. But in popular jargon after the mid-fifties, it was confused with racism, and "integration" seemed often to imply cultural uniformity. Strangely, what began as an effort to assure individual rights threatened to turn into ideological fascism. The depiction in movies, even in historical setting, of communities whose attitudes the new ideology deemed racist, jingoist, or antifeminist was declared "offensive." Since Ford's pictures deal obsessively with themes of race, ideology, and class, it was easy for well-meaning observers to mistake the man himself for a racist and a reactionary. Such damnation was infuriatingly ironic, for no other film artist had sought so persistently to uncloak society's noxious patterns and to sift out existential freedom. For Ford it was always a question of inquiring into the tensions and adhesions between an individual, his origins, and his present situation. Whether Irish, Negro, Indian, British, Wasp, or whore, the individual was always played against his stereotype. Ford's detractors saw only that stereotype. It is a pitiable reflection on American criticism that Ford, virtually the *only* filmmaker to concern himself with racism before it became commercially fashionable to do so, is virtually the only filmmaker whom critics attack as racist.

One reason he filmed so often in Monument Valley was that his Navajo friends needed the money his projects brought them. He paid them union wages at a time when Indians were not commanding even fifty cents a day. He studied their language, played their sports, was adopted into their tribe, and named Natani Nez—"Tall Soldier." A blizzard covered the Valley in the fifties, and Ford got army planes to drop food in. "To the Navajos," said Harry Goulding, who operated a lodge there, "Mr. Ford is holy, sorta."[41] Indians, in Ford's movies, are both noble and savage, just like the whites. "They say I took pleasure in killing Indians in the movies," said Ford, late in life. "But while today film people shed tears over the fate of the Indians, write humanitarian pamphlets and make declarations of intention without ever, *ever* putting their hands in their pockets, more humbly I gave them work. . . . More than having received Oscars, what counts for me is having been made a blood brother of various Indian nations. Perhaps it's my Irish atavism, my sense of reality, of the beauty of clans, in contrast to the modern world, the masses, the collective irresponsibility. Who better than an Irishman could understand the Indians, while still being stirred by the tales of the U. S. Cavalry? We were on both sides of the epic."[42]

The complexity of Ford's treatments of blacks and the military—core themes best considered in context of the pictures themselves—was obscured by his public career as a naval officer. An Air Medal gained making *This Is*

Korea! had earned him retirement promotion to rear admiral in 1951, and he would periodically train navy film crews at sea or make a documentary, not so much in support of a war, as of the men fighting it. For him the muddled ambiguities of Vietnam were overshadowed by his immersion in those of the past. Ironically, his defense of the notion, in all its simplicity, that this was a struggle for freedom against tyranny embarrassed official hypocrisy, for the government withdrew his movie enunciating this simplicity.

In 1937 Ford had contributed $1000 for an ambulance for the Loyalists in Spain, and had written his nephew Bob Ford, "Politically, I am a definite socialist democrat—always left. Communism to my mind is not the remedy this sick world is seeking. I have watched the Russian experiment with great interest. Like the French commune I am afraid it might lead to another Buonaparte [sic]. Mussolini was in early manhood an anarchist, Hitler almost."[43] His name appeared on the masthead of liberal antifascist organizations such as the Motion Picture Democratic Committee. If he later seemed to drift to the right, it was because its ideological purity occasionally seemed preferable to the general carpetbaggery. More than ever, he was basically uninvolved with politics. He was unusually candid during a visit to Paris in 1967, as Bertrand Tavernier reported: "I'm a liberal Democrat. Mostly, I'm a rebel." His favorite presidents? "Lincoln, Roosevelt and John Kennedy. I adored Kennedy . . . but Johnson is a detestable person, a murderer." Bob Kennedy he thought "an ambitious opportunist." "In the last elections, I didn't vote. Goldwater had no serious program and I hated Johnson." He opposed organizations like the American Legion mixing in politics. "I hate people who try to dictate your conduct." Asked about the McCarthy purges, Ford replied, "I was the first to protest." Tavernier continues:

> Several times he spoke vehemently about communists, like a middle American. Nonetheless, when we introduced Samuel Lachize, from *l'Humanité*, as a communist critic, Ford didn't blink. "Let him come in . . . I'd love to talk with a communist . . . I'm a liberal."
> And then, to our great astonishment, the conversation unrolled beautifully. The two were instantly sympathetic and Ford didn't play games with Lachize's questions. He responded at length, a very rare thing, and only became angry when Lachize told him some people thought (wrongly, added Lachize) there were racist aspects in his work:
> "The people who say that are mad, insane. I'm a Northerner. I detest segregation and I've employed hundreds of blacks at the same wages as whites. I got the production companies to pay a tribe of Indians, who were starving, at the same rate as the highest paid Hollywood extras and I saved them. Racist, me? My best friends are blacks: Woody Strode and my servant who's lived with me for thirty years. I've even made a picture which exalted the blacks. . . . No, I'm not a racist. I consider the blacks as completely American."
> He came back to the subject a number of times, and we had immense difficulty trying to calm him down. He even mentioned how Jews were

treated in the USSR, the only time he made a critical reference to his questioner's ideology. The tone remained very cordial, but the reference had struck him. All at once, he called me in a stentorian voice and asked me to bring him his rosary. [Ford was receiving in bed, with his dirty night shirt, cigar butts and chocolate bars.] When he had it in his hand, he gave it to Lachize, saying, "Take it, it's a gift. Join our group."

Lachize was stupefied. Ford took back the rosary. "I'll pray to Our Lady for you."[44]

DECOMPOSITION (1956–1961)

In 1952 *The Quiet Man* had been released to universal acclaim, and Ford had won his final Oscar. All six of his Oscars were displayed in his office or home, although publicly he feigned disinterest and had always skirted attending award ceremonies.* But Ford had ceased since the war, as Andrew Sarris has observed, to exercise fashionable leadership. One did not look to Ford for films like *Key Largo*, *On the Waterfront*, *The Country Girl*, *Rebel Without a Cause*, *Man with a Golden Arm*, or *Psycho*. His ideas no longer resounded within the new ideology, but seemed instead to be backward-looking. True, Ford movies continued to be popular, almost all popular movies seemed far more backward-looking than Ford's, and Hollywood as a whole was even less concerned than Ford with the latest fancies of New York critics, who themselves scarcely reflected the mainstream. But Ford was a special case. The rites of his cult obscured the newness and evolution of his work. Fashionable progressives did not want careful analyses of functioning racism and mythmaking; they wanted to see suffering minorities screaming for justice and myths rejected. Conservatives, meanwhile, were blind to Ford's ridicule and revisionism, and saw only celebrations of tradition; their interpretations reinforced progressive rejection of Ford. For example, *Fort Apache:* here is a picture glorifying the Indians and debunking myths of the 7th Cavalry; yet it is incessantly cited as a typical example of exactly the opposite and of everything wrong with John Ford. Such failure to communicate seems due neither to directorial or audience incompetence but to the role ballyhoo plays in shaping not only how we see movies but our ideologies and national politics as well. Ford's image was linked to the establishment and his pictures were too strongly within the classic mainstream for his wisdom's subtle complexities to be perceived.

The Ford aura of these years was linked to the image of John Wayne kicking Maureen O'Hara, to Victor McLaglen's drunken bluster, and to the director's endless cigarsmoke-laden games of "pitch" with piles of silver dol-

---

*But he had accepted an honorary doctorate from the University of Maine, Orono, in 1947, and an honorary master's from Bowdoin College the same year. Williams College offered him an honorary master's provided he show up to accept it; he went to Brazil instead—May 1943. Maine schools only, apparently, although he may have received LL. D. from Brandeis.

lars and such macho stalwarts as Wayne and Ward Bond. (Humphrey Bogart joined the gang occasionally. Once, having been slipped the Queen of Spades during a game of Hearts, he flew into a towering rage, swore never again to set foot in the house, and stormed out. He returned, sheepishly, after fifteen minutes: it was his own house.) Ford's hard-nosed, man's-man image and his wild eccentricities hid the real person. It was more fun to contemplate his slow, theatricalized antics chewing handkerchiefs and lighting his pipe, the long silences prefacing explosions of sarcasm. But as Anna Lee, to whom he gave candy on Valentine's Day, has said, people neglect what a kind and wonderful man he was—if he liked you; if he did not, he could be very unkind. Lindsay Anderson wrote these impressions in 1951:

> It is natural that anecdotists should concentrate on his wild Irish temper, his fondness for horseplay, the violence of his conflicts with producers and high-stepping actresses; and there is no reason to suppose these stories exaggerated. (Ford has only to protest "I'm a quiet, gentle person" for one to be quite sure they are not.) But besides the stampedes, the war parties, the knockabout fights, there are those quiet moments in his films, equally characteristic, of tenderness and insight; and these too his presence reflects. This was the Ford I found in Dublin—a man of fascinating contradictions; of authority in no way diminished by a complete rejection of apparatus; of instinctive personal warmth as likely to evidence itself in violence as in gentleness; confident of his powers, yet unpretentious about their achievement. A patriarchal figure, sitting among friends; it was easy to understand the devotion he inspires in those who work for him.[45]

We must, then, accept Ford anecdotes within context of his immense charisma. No one could have gotten away for decades with being so abusive and such a prima donna in the petty-petty ego-glorious worlds of Hollywood and the navy had he not possessed a fascination that more than compensated. Kindness and humor were his chief traits. Even midst aggravation, the madder he got, the wittier he became.

People so often approached him expecting the worst and emerged charmed. Robert Parrish's journalist aunt had been meeting popes, statesmen, plutocrats, and celebrities for thirty years; after chatting in Gaelic with Ford, she remarked he was among the most delightful people she had ever met—but it was a pity he had not continued his studies for the priesthood (!).[46]

Allan Dwan, after some four hundred films beginning in 1911, had adopted a rather casual approach to direction by 1949. Then one day Ford, who had worked for Dwan as a prop boy back at Universal, came into his office. Dwan, sixty-four, was about to start *The Sands of Iwo Jima,* and Ford, Dwan relates, said, "'Will you throw yourself into this one? Will you really *do* this one? For me, will you do it?' Like a coach talking to a guy who was going to play halfback for him. He pepped me up so much I said, 'All right, for your sake I'll make a good picture.'" Ford then talked John Wayne into starring in it, and *The Sands of Iwo Jima* is today the picture that Allan Dwan is best remembered for, out of all those four hundred.[47]

Yet even in 1954, surrounded by friends, wealth, medals, and unparalleled prestige, Ford's self-esteem was prey to the same anxieties that had made him ill during previews of *The Informer*. Filming of *Mister Roberts* had begun in a party spirit as the Ford regulars, and *Araner*, too, gathered in Hawaii for Ward Bond's marriage to his friend of many years, Mary Lou May. Henry Fonda, who had been out of films since *Fort Apache* in 1948, was there as well. He was to play the title role in *Mister Roberts*, as he had in the play's Broadway production. Unknown to Fonda, Warners had thought William Holden or Marlon Brando would be better box office and had consented to Fonda only when Ford threatened not to make the movie unless they did so. But Fonda had spent seven years playing *Mister Roberts* and now quickly became disgruntled with Ford's approach: "I didn't like the kind of roughhouse humor that Pappy was bringing to it. . . . Pappy shot it all wrong. He didn't know the timing. He didn't know where the laughs were and how long to wait for them to die down. He had them all talking at once, throwing one line in on top of another. When I said something he just handed me the script and said, 'Here, you wanna direct?'"[48] The producer, Leland Haywood, sided with the actor, and during a meeting of the three of

Mr. Roberts (1955). Cast and crew relaxing.

them, Ford socked Fonda in the jaw, knocking him across the room. He apologized an hour later, but the rift never healed.

Of course, what is best for the stage is seldom best for a film, and an actor who thought he knew more than the director was scarcely a novelty. One would expect that "hard-nosed" Ford would have surmounted discord this time as he had so often in the past. But instead Ford started drinking and, as the weeks passed, he became more and more morose; he took to retreating to the *Araner,* and finally hid there, refusing to eat or see anyone. Production was shut down for five days. Ford sobered up and got back to work, but shortly afterward his gallbladder ruptured and he was hospitalized for an operation. Mervyn LeRoy was brought in to replace him. *

The "betrayal" of a friend is not enough to account for Ford's behavior; fear of failure is a likelier explanation. His ability with comedy, which *he* thought his strong point, had always been questioned. He was taking a large risk in transmogrifying a fashionable Broadway play into the quite different thing that is a Fordian comedy. He lost confidence in himself. His need to achieve was undiminished.

There were many reversals in the fifties. Besides Francis Ford's death, the fights with Republic, and the dissolution of Argosy, home and health came under attack. After thirty-four years in their unfashionable Odin Street home (to which they had occasionally added extra rooms), the Fords were summarily given sixty days to vacate: the City of Los Angeles wanted the hill for a Hollywood Bowl parking lot. Protest was useless; so was a two-week binge on the *Araner.* They moved in May 1953 to a Mexican-style Bel Air house, 125 Copo de Oro Road, formerly owned by the William Wylers, and by the Frank Lloyds before that. Very Hollywood, it did not seem like home.

Both *Araner* and Ford were deteriorating physically. The $100,000 he spent repairing the boat's dry rot was only the beginning of a constant financial drain. Ford's attack of "shingles" in 1949 was probably just a means of getting out of doing *Pinky,* a film he disliked. But there was nothing phony about the gallbladder attack that forced him off *Mister Roberts* in 1954; his stomach blew up like a balloon. He suffered also from periodic pain in his

---

*Ford shot most of the exteriors, but there are few of these, and many of them are integrated with studio work, so that there are virtually no significant sequences of Fordian cinema, with the editing Ford intended. His segments are recognizable by their faster tempo, spiffier style, greater physicality, and more inventive employment of space. The LeRoy segments—long, sparsely edited, talky, and static—lack visual interest and resemble a filmed play, as Fonda wished. Ford can be distinguished during the nurses' visit; in the altercation (in crosscuts) between Fonda and James Cagney over shirtless sailors; and in individual shots of the Liberty Port sequence. Ford evidently intended a speedier, many-charactered portrait of a crew, and more ambivalence about duty and obedience. His Roberts, in contrast to the fairly simple one of LeRoy and Fonda, would have enriched contradictions: his druggy pomposity and thirst for glory that make him prefer to be the crew's hero rather than an effective intermediary. Ford had wished to eliminate the scotch-making and the laundry scenes—which Joshua Logan directed after LeRoy left. Some of the slapstick comedy Ford inserted—such as the drunk sailor riding a motorcycle off a pier—was cut out by Fonda and Haywood and then restored by Warners.

left arm (where he had been wounded at Midway) and, more seriously, from his eyes.

His eyesight had always been terrible. He had begun sporting his famous black eyepatch in the early thirties, partly for its rakishness, partly to protect his light-sensitive left eye; but he wore it only now and then and would lift it up in order to read. Dark glasses and the eyepatch also kept others from seeing the tenderness that all who knew him well found in his eyes. And naturally he profited from no one being quite sure how much he could see. Sometimes he would not see something six feet in front of him; but if he were filming and an actor readjusted his hat a hundred yards away, he would stop the shot. In Africa, however, blurred vision and amoebic dysentery had led him to shorten *Mogambo*'s location shooting schedule; planned exteriors were moved into tents and filmed later in London. Mary then accompanied John on a holiday drive down to Naples, from where, on April 2, 1953, they sailed home on the *Andrea Doria*; but Ford's vision had grown worse, and he spent the voyage in his darkened cabin. On June 30 he entered the hospital for a critical operation; he was afflicted with conical myopia and with external cataracts on both eyes. The operation gave him the experience of total blindness for a number of weeks and only slightly improved his sight.

The effect on Ford of these multiple afflictions is apparent in the pictures of the next five years.

Decomposition: The Films

	Filmed / released	
The Rising of the Moon	Spring '56 / May '57	Four Province Prodns. – Warner Bros.
The Wings of Eagles	Aug. '56 / Feb. '57	Metro-Goldwyn-Mayer
The Growler Story (documentary)	Nov. '56 /	U.S. Navy
Gideon's Day	Spring '57 / Mar. '58 (G.B.)	Columbia British Prodns.
The Last Hurrah	/ Nov. '58	Columbia
Korea: Battleground for Liberty (documentary)	Fall '58 /	U.S. Dept. of Defense
The Horse Soldiers	Fall '58 / June '59	Mirisch–United Artists
Sergeant Rutledge	May '59 / May '60	Ford Prodns.–Warner Bros.
The Colter Craven Story (TV)	/ May '60	Wagon Train series
Two Rode Together	Nov. '60 / July '61	Ford–Sheptner Prodns.–Columbia

The films comprising this period are distinguished by disequilibrium, stark modal contrasts, cynical pessimism, and experimentation. These are pictures with myriad magic moments, but (except for *Gideon's Day*) without overall coherence. Often one feels Ford is uninspired and merely doing his job.

It is an era of confusion in the movie industry, of the disappearance of the studios, of independent superproductions. Without much difficulty we can discern the itinerary of Ford's private life, his struggles with the decay of age, his search to reconcile his religion and the world's evil, his faltering faith in America.

In contrast to other divisions in Ford's oeuvre, the boundaries of this transitional period are somewhat vague. *The Long Gray Line* and *The Searchers* contain incipient traits of "decomposition." And similarly, at the other end, *The Man Who Shot Liberty Valance* is flawed by traces of misanthropy.

All of these movies, from *The Searchers* on, concern themselves with persistent heroes in increasingly malevolent worlds. There is, as a result, a growing polarization between the sweet and the horrible, which Ford, attempting to expand the dimensions of his realism, tries to embrace with altered expressionistic techniques—and fails, fails because his style is inordinately strained. The solution, aesthetically and philosophically, will be found in the final period, in a transcendent approach capable of containing otherwise incommensurate contradictions.

The Wings of Eagles (1957).

The title was lousy [recalled Ford]—I screamed at that. I just wanted to call it "The Spig Wead Story." . . . I didn't want to do the picture because Spig was a great pal of mine. But I didn't want anyone *else* to make it. I knew him first when he was deck officer, black shoe, with the old *Mississippi*—before he went flying. . . . We did quite a few pictures together. He died in my arms. I tried to tell the story as truthfully as possible, and everything in the picture was true. The fight in the club— throwing the cake . . . , the plane landing in the swimming pool—right in the middle of the Admiral's tea—[all] that really happened.[49]

The Long Gray Line dealt with West Point and an immigrant outsider's subsumption into its culture. *The Wings of Eagles*, Ford's only other extended biography, deals with the navy (like *Salute*) and with Spig Wead's efforts to fit into life—navy, marriage, writing.

Ford concentrates on Wead's inner itinerary. His public life, in contrast, is narrated so obliquely*—via newspapers (three), film clips (three), off-screen narrators (two, three times), meetings, a marquee, a chartroom, and battle (like *When Willie Comes Marching Home*)—that one may well finish the movie wondering who Wead was to have a movie made about him. ** But then

---

*For example: attention is called to insignia whenever promotions occur, but ranks are never identified. This is probably an inside joke, since fewer people recognize navy than army insignia. Similarly, names are carelessly given. Clark Gable is never identified in the *Hell Divers* clip. Admiral John Dale Price, an actual Wead friend who (played by Ken Curtis) narrates the movie and is credited as "technical advisor," is referred to in the movie only as "Johnny Dale."

**Besides naval aviation and devising World War II's "jeep" carriers (to replace disabled planes), Frank Wead, Jr., after recovering from total paralysis, received credit for some thirty-

The Wings of Eagles (1957). Ford talks to Ward Bond (imitating Ford) and John Wayne.

it is typical of "transitional" films that they provoke questions and leave one with incoherence. This picture, and Spig, gravitate around four motifs whose correspondence is, annoyingly, suggested but ultimately unclear (to me, at least): illusion/reality and friendship/separation. The key would appear to be that Spig is destructive to himself and to others; this is the reality, which he attempts to avoid through situations of irreality and isolation.

Military life, and Ford's least attractive portrait of it, is part of irreality—poke-in-the-ribs rivalry among rah-rah locker-room jocks unimaginable outside their own weird world. Wead, like his peers, fights, as though playing football, for money and power for his service, and Ford, whatever the merits of Wead's crusade for air-power, displays the mechanics of self-perpetuating military institutions run by brotherhoods of jingoistic myopics. Even the classic defense is given to the particularly unsympathetic Willis Bouchey, a perennial Ford heavy here playing a senator:

two Hollywood screenplays, from *Flying Fleet* (G. Hill, 1929) to *Blaze of Noon* (Farrow, 1947). For Ford: *Air Mail, They Were Expendable.* Also: *Ceiling Zero* (Hawks), *Test Pilot* (Fleming), *The Citadel* (Vidor), and many service pictures. Wead died in 1947.

— We've got a country yelling pacifism at us, disarmament, the world is going to live together like one big happy family, there'll be no more wars, the Army and the Navy are going out of business. Now, you fight maybe one war every generation, but we have to fight those voters every blame two years.

There is, in addition, a strange self-consciousness about military things. One finds oneself wondering what it would be like, every time one entered a room, to have somebody run ahead, shout "'Tention!" and have everyone stand stiff. Perhaps because Ford participated in many of these events (he ducked the cake), perhaps because this bland, broad, tough lifestyle was one side (of many contradictory sides) of Ford, his choice of dramatic tone is often uncertain and distanced. The free-for-all fight, for example, prompts less laughter than puzzlement—especially after two rival noncoms call a truce and drink beer instead. Why these strange pleasures? Does their energetic and artificial existence breed an unfulfillment that finds release in a good fight? Ford's friendly fights are blatant sadism. Those in *The Long Voyage Home* and *Mister Roberts* gain eroticism from repression, but elsewhere (*She Wore a Yellow Ribbon, What Price Glory, The Quiet Man, Donovan's Reef*) heterosexual needs seem secondary to male comradery. The first lines of Johnny Dale's voice-off narration—"Spig knew he wanted to fly and I knew I wanted whatever Spig wanted"—set the tone for this

portrait of a friend: Spig is always viewed from slightly uncomprehending third-person distance, but he is viewed always with devotion.

Partially because Spig prefers the world of men, partially because Minne is the only Ford service wife unwilling to accept her subservient role, Spig is never able to integrate career and marriage. This dimension of impotence becomes more palpable with paralysis and his final ride down the cable. In one sense Spig's dilemma is the familiar Ford theme of outside forces determining an individual (as Ford said of Wead, "Life disappointed him"), but here it is also a quasi-sexual theme, and military life, if not labeled deviant, is at least viewed as destructive. Wead is compared to Frank Merriwell, a foolish hero who leaves confusion in his wake (as is Mr. Peter in 7 *Women*). Wead proceeds from slapstick* through melodrama to tragedy, but his era is portrayed as sad and subdued (consistent with Ford's contemporary movies) and so is he: "Half man, half worm, half wit," he describes himself. "Damn the martinis, full speed ahead . . . star-spangled Spig," his wife calls him. For an obstinate persistence replaces *The Long Gray Line*'s theme of subsistence. Spig persists, but fate (?) has a will of its own.

Reality, illusion, and friendship. Unfortunate in not having a more compatible mate, Spig suffers as deeply as Minne but never gives up hope—nor surrenders his independence. Ford does not simplify (or clarify); at least three motives might explain why, paralyzed, Wead sends her away: the heroic gesture of sacrifice, the despair and neuroses induced by sudden helplessness, the unbearable pain of being an object of pity.

Spig endures hell (reality). Ford's matured expressionism, the sun and rain, the shadows, the bright white streak across the mattress, the burning-yellow coloration, Wead's horizontal pose, all convey a state of soul. He is forced to accept help, because Carson, unlike Minne, is not the sort to be sent away. "I'm gonna help you through this little trouble," declares this paragon of friendship. The principles of military training are adaptable to every situation: for days, and even with music, Spig chants, "I'm gonna move that toe!" From this lugubriousness springs an oddly heroic distance, bringing into relief a polyphony of strong emotional motifs, emphasized in Ford's unusual Mizoguchian tracking shot back from the window, over Spig, and across the room, a gesture of classic distancing wedded to Murnau expressionism—awed withdrawal.

To this point, newspapers and newsreels have hinted at the film's play between irreality (e.g., seeing Daddy on a moviescreen—a movie within a movie) and brute evidence (being paralyzed). Now the simile accelerates. Always the myopic, always living the immediate moment, Spig looks into the mirror that Carson places under him and, at first—it's a gag—sees not his toes, but the names written on the mirror's surface; Carson obliges him

*The airplane stunts repeat gags in the Ford-Wead *Air Mail* (1931).

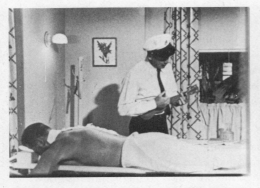
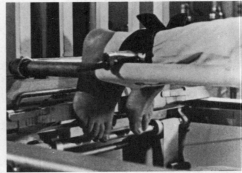
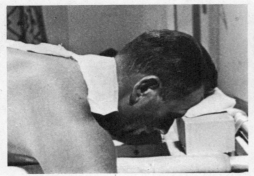

to look deeper into the reflection. And Wead, persisting in his chant, eventually turns deeper into himself: the second time we see the mirror he is looking at his own face in it. But this is not all. Wead must learn he *needs* others. The third time we see the mirror he sees in it the roses that Minne (he knows) has sent anonymously: now he moves his toe. Once again flowers play an important role in Ford. Earlier, when Spig comes home to a messy living room, he throws a bouquet into the wastebasket. Minne, wandering home tipsy, discovers it there and realizes Spig is back. The bouquet continues to counterpoint their reconciliation as Minne throws it beside Spig, washing dishes in the kitchen, and he typically puts it in a vase and plops it down in front of her.

Spig inspires devotion, but he is afraid to admit his need for friends and is never seen giving back as much as he receives. Typically, we never hear him tell Minne he loves or wants her. Typically, he replies, "That was yesterday, what do we do now?" when Carson complains Spig has not written in years. Typically, he forgets all about Johnny Dale when Dale provides the key word, "jeep," to solve a tactical dilemma.

This last incident is bathed in irreality: a darkened chartroom in which Wead, sleeping there in search of solution, flashes his flashlight on and off around the room; whenever the door is opened, alarms ring and glaring lights pop on. But there does not appear to be an exact correspondence in the movie between Wead's treatment of friends and the motif of reality / irreality. Yet reality is generally hostile. The Victrola (representing reality) that spits records at Minne* when Pearl Harbor thwarts her reunion with Spig is the same sort of symbolic idea as recurs, benignly, with the slot machine in *Donovan's Reef*. War has provided another intrusion of reality, and, like paralysis, comes clothed in its own artifice.

Midst the potent expressionism of the authentic battle scenes (Kwajalein, January 1944), the 1956 scenes of Wead (Wayne) during the battle contrast obviously; thus it is not surprising that Spig emerges unscathed, but that Carson is wounded protecting Wead.

Spig gets Carson wounded, but Carson rejects from Wead (again coming too late) assistance similar to that which Carson gave Wead earlier. Again the motivation is complex: pride, anger, a hint that Wead should retire. Spig has a heart attack, and now comes the climax: a rapid montage of seventeen shots of sea battle at night, cannons thunder, balls of fire streak gold-red through the pitch-black sky. Reality replies to Spig with persistent repetition of its own, with a dreadful might that achieves the most implacable figure of hostile determinism in Ford, and which, while dwarfing even the indomitable Spig** and proclaiming the folly of any individual's independence, simultaneously reverses itself and becomes the formalized expression, again, of Spig's state of soul.

He decides to retire; death is approaching and he has caused enough damage. "Let 'em think I'm licked." But clearing out his desk, photographs (i.e., illusions) of Minne start him dreaming of happier times. The black-and-white photo dissolves, with the fantasy sparkle of thirties Hollywood, into hazy color flashbacks of life with Minne. As in *How Green Was My*

---

*Perhaps in vengeance for a record broken in *Air Mail*.

**Spig's strength is apparent when he holds a telephone—the old, heavy metal type—aloft and steady with one hand, keeping the arm above its cradle, while dialing with the other hand.

Valley, some we have not seen before (but we did see Spig taking one he is now fantasizing over), and all memories are glorified. Yet the memories and parade concluding Spig's life lack the affirmation of those concluding Marty Maher's in *The Long Gray Line.* In place of that optimism, it now seems (as it will again in *The Last Hurrah*) that at the end all you have, and the best any man can hope for, is friends. Lined up on deck to see Spig off, these admirals and generals set a seal of moral redemption to Wead's life; but they also attest to its failure. The old buddies have grown into their uniforms to the point that they look almost alike, all of the same mold, while Spig, at last reduced to tears of friendship and public avowal of incapacity, melts into an outsider: a human being first, a soldier not at all.

★

Another thing Spig persisted in was writing: through thirty-nine(?) rejections. Writing, says Carson, "is just a bunch of lies wrapped up in paper," so Spig ought to be able to do it well (i.e., irreality again). The Hollywood director he goes to work for is called John Dodge in the film; in real life it was George Hill; in actuality it is Ward Bond imitating John Ford. Ford claims this was Bond's idea, but Ford was more than cooperative. We see the Old Man's Oscars, his hat, pipe, whiskey-holding cane, prize Mexican saddle, pictures, and who knows what else. Bond imitates Ford's boots, his white handkerchief that he played with, and walk, and numerous small tics. The way Bond-Dodge-Ford gives Wead instructions—just write about "people, Navy people"—recalls Frank Nugent's account of his first *Fort Apache* story conference with Ford. Earlier, when Wead asks John Dale, "How does he know I can write?" Dale (i.e., Ken Curtis, Ford's son-in-law) replies, "Well, he knows *he* can't!"—a line whose truth is confirmed by Nunnally Johnson's account of Ford's frustration at not being able to write. Dodge's secretary of twenty-two years has her counterpart in Ford's. And on the office wall are pictures of Harry Carey and Tom Mix. The little skit with the matchbook during *Hell Divers* has the look of another Ford imitation, used in *Rookie of the Year*.

At one point, trying to warn Wead away from the theater, Dodge cites his own experience, throwing a copy of *The Odyssey* onto the table:

> *Dodge:* I even played in this thing once.
> *Wead:* *Ulysses?* You played in *Ulysses?*
> *Dodge:* Yep, Bowling Green, Kentucky. I played Robert E. Lee.

Does this joke have any meaning? Apparently not. Does Wead's life have any meaning? Apparently not. *Meanings*, perhaps, to those who knew him and to himself. But for us . . . ? We are struck more by its incoherence, its defeats and failures. It remains a mystery marked by persistence, endurance, and more than a hint of futility. Wead may remind us of Sisyphus, but we do not think of him as happy.

Such a vision of life may be realistic. But is such irresolution consistent with the needs of art, in which we expect aesthetic completion? Can the film have meaning, when its subject does not? The question nags at Ford's film in this period. He had always sought to *equate* form and meaning. But now meaning begins to disintegrate, and so form decomposes, too. Peter Bogdanovich found a message in these movies: "glory in defeat." Of course, in Wead's case, glory may have been in his life, but certainly was not in his defeat. Nonetheless, the theme, scarcely hinted at in previous pictures, lurks throughout these years. Initially, when defeated heroes survive, as in the opening story of *The Rising of the Moon*, glory appears redemptive. But by *The Last Hurrah* and *The Horse Soldiers*, when defeated heroes die, glory resounds emptily as mere rationalization of waste.

> *The Rising of the Moon* (1957). The relative optimism of *The Rising of the Moon* and *Gideon's Day*, scarred though it may be, derives also from their being made in the British Isles, where Ford, taking no salary, was able to escape professional and personal problems in America and to make movies his own way. *

---

*Producer of both (and actual, though uncredited, producer of *The Quiet Man*) was the Lord Killanin (Michael Morris), hereditary peer, Shell Oil director, one of the world's leading aspirin distributors, and, recently, head of the World Olympic Committee. His barony adjoined Ford's father's birthplace, and there were blood ties between the families. With Ford, Killanin formed Four Province Productions, including Roger Greene, Brian Desmond Hurst, and Michael Scott, and struggled tirelessly to promote filmmaking in Eire. There were ambitious plans (see the list of unrealized projects at the end of the Filmography), but none of them materialized. *The Rising of the Moon*'s negative cost $256,016.53, and with distribution costs it netted a loss of around $250,000. World grosses scarcely exceeded $100,000. Before deciding on "A Minute's Wait," Ford had thought of doing "Ghost Story," with Katharine Hepburn. *The Rising of the Moon* was controversial in Ireland: it was banned by the city of Belfast and caused protests among IRA sympathizers in the South.

Uncommercial, ethnic in character, with an almost overwhelming sense of place, and employing Abbey Theatre Players, *The Rising of the Moon* was originally called "Three Leaves of a Shamrock." The shamrock was once the symbol of Irish resistance, and the movie's three stories have revolution as their—covert—theme. In "The Majesty of the Law," Inspector Dillon follows narrow lanes into the country, along a stream where sunlight and tree-shadows ripple gently.

Come back, Paddy Reilly!
. . . The Garden of Eden has vanished, they say,
But I know the lie of it still . . .

sings a background tenor, with recorder. We glimpse an old man walking stiffly, and a moonshiner, indicating a ruined tower, quips, "From there to a wee thatched cottage." "'Tisn't the cottage that makes the king," replies Dillon, and Mickey J. echoes, as if savoring poetic wisdom.

The old man, in rhymed motion, throws himself backward into the air while slamming his hat to the ground; just then, the inspector bursts into and across the frame. All this equals "Welcome." The extravagant warmth and sincerity of Dan O'Flaherty (authentically overplayed by Noel Purcell) suit the granite will his arthritic movements reflect. A certain Feeney called him a liar, accordingly Dan bashed his skull; Feeney sued, Dan will not pay the £5 fine. So Dillon has been sent to arrest him. This is revealed midst vehement fireside prolixities on every subject under the sun: mostly tradi-

tions lost, songs, secrets, cures. * Much of the movie's charm lies in the lilt of its dialogue. But, as Mickey J. demonstrated, running round the tower enclosing his still while the inspector waited for him to complete his circle instead of chasing him, the inevitable cannot be evaded.

Friday evening Dan sets out for prison, kissing his stone as neighbors stand silent witness. Suddenly Feeney appears, hobbling in bathrobe and bandages, begging to pay the fine himself. O'Flaherty's cane implacably bars the frame:

> I will punish you, you weak snivering man. I will lie on bare boards for you. I will suffer for you, so that neither you nor your children nor their children after them will be able to raise their heads for the shame of it! Who walks with me to the top of the hill?

Farmwomen bow; poor as he may be, he is their king.

"The Majesty of the Law" bids hail-and-farewell to heroism for lost principles. The reactionary old man today is revolutionary, as the moonshiner represents sedition, and the inspector a reluctant instrument of alien codes superimposed on native order. **

---

*The notion of youth's loss of traditional knowledge recurs in *The Long Gray Line* when cadets forget Maj. Keough, and in *The Searchers* when young Pat Wayne cannot locate places not mentioned on maps, and in *Liberty Valance* when newspapermen have never heard of Tom Doniphon.

**Dialogue was added to Frank O'Connor's story, wherein "Dan Bride" was a simple farmer, without the royal ancestors Ford adds; the rebuke to Feeney is announced to the in-

The other two stories seem less significant. Yet "A Minute's Wait," a delightful train-station vignette comedy, demonstrates deft virtuosity with some twenty characters. And the residual oppression of modern Eire depicted in the first two stories becomes overt in the stark contrasts and vertiginous angles of "1921." A patriot escapes prison disguised as a nun, then Ireland disguised as a balladeer. * A policeman, distracted by his wife, allows the escape, and comes in the process to a consciousness of self and oppression—the first step toward revolution.

Gideon's Day (1958). "The freest, most direct, least fabricated film ever to sprout from one of Her Majesty's studios," was the verdict of the prestigious *Cahiers du Cinéma*.[50] But when the picture got released in America, its title had been changed (to *Gideon of Scotland Yard*) and it was relegated to the "art house" circuits of the day (then specializing in Margaret Rutherford and coffee), and rather than go to the expense of Technicolor prints, Columbia distributed it in black-and-white.

Yet *Gideon*, following a Scotland Yard inspector through a single day, with thirty episodes and fifty speaking parts tidily compressed into ninety

---

spector, not in confrontation, and the fight resulted from an argument: there was no question of being accused of lying!

*Francis Ford's 1916 *The Cry of Erin* concerns an Irish peasant escaping execution by changing clothes with a priest, then sailing from Cork.

minutes, is among Ford's most personal and ambitious movies, although costing only $543,600. One senses how delighted he was with his cast of English actors, especially Jack Hawkins (Gideon), whom Ford, extravagant with praise, called "the finest dramatic actor with whom I have worked."[51]

This particular Gideon's day gets a high score: a rapist, two mobsters, a female con artist, a murderer, a corrupt policeman, three bank robbers. But Gideon gets the wrong fish—an old haddock instead of the fresh salmon his wife requested. And his personal life is ill-fated: he loses his morning bath to his daughter, gets hit with a ball coming downstairs, gets a traffic ticket, forgets his concert ticket (and the fish), can't find a parking space, rips his coat, has a drink thrown in his face, is interrupted at breakfast, at morning tea, lunch at home, porkpie in pub, sandwich in office, and midnight dinner at home. Customarily frantic—he literally spends the whole movie going in and out of doors—often driven to fury by crime, he nonetheless has that strange English ability to relax totally when his job calls for him to interview someone. Yet as the opening shots tell us—beautiful Technicolor of sunny happy London, followed by a beshadowed Gideon burning the night oil in his bare drab office—Gideon is a hero because he deals all day with things everyone else can afford to ignore, and because when he gets home he has no stories to tell. Not that he is untainted: he is overly alarmed when Kate tells him "some young man" took Sally home from her concert; his job deprives his family of his presence, and its problems make him difficult. As Sally says, "Just because something's gone wrong—we all have to suffer!"

Kate is like one of Ford's cavalry wives at some remote outpost and, thanks to Anna Lee's beautifully poised and assuredly modest performance, she does her job with hardly an unangelic whimper. The world's "wrongness," however, afflicts women with much suffering. "Promise me one thing. Never marry a policeman," says Kate. But love and compassion for Gideon shine in her eyes, and Sally, answering "Yes mother," gazes dreamily after Constable Farnaby-Green, thus proving Gideon's daughter's love for her very human father. The charm of these home scenes (the happy light-greens, yellows, and red-checked tablecloths of Kate's kitchen, balanced by her blue dress) makes them the picture's nicest parts. Indeed, George Gideon is one of those rarest of Fordian people—a man with a wife, family, and real home at film's end. But, as in *The Searchers*, this cheer exists to contrast the hostility beyond.

Ford's sole tragicomedy, *Gideon's Day* is about London, the British, and 1957, about the claustrophobia, craziness, and complacent despair of modern life ("London Bridge is falling down . . ." mocks the theme tune—and it is surely not unintentional when we glimpse a headline about the H-bomb). Yet if *Gideon's Day*, of all the 1956–61 films, comes closest to solving the aesthetic problem of molding such wildly disparate material into modal forms with overall coherence, this is because its tone is generally light and its characters deep and clear.

The humor is often Ford's traditional, understated wackiness: the squeak of Farnaby-Green's shoes and his slightly Chaplinesque walk; the chief's obsession with his moose head; the way the vicar's daughter enters the church carrying one large flower; Sergeant Gully snapping to attention when Gideon enters, and the latter's bemused reproof that the war has been over for years. One relishes the way Farnaby-Green, giving Gideon his ticket, remarks to his daughter with polite snottiness, "The law, Miss Gideon, allows no distinction between high-ranking police officers and other members of the public," and the way Gideon repeats the same words to Farnaby-Green in the last scene. Eighteen-year-old Sally Gideon is delightfully puckish, particularly mimicking Farnaby-Green to his face.*

The characters, as an interview with producer Killanin clarifies, owe more to Ford than to their conventional scripting**:

> *Killanin:* You more often than not suggest types quite different to that indicated in the script.
>
> *Ford:* But don't you see, I am interested in *people*. That is why [in] a picture like *Gideon's Day* and, indeed, *The Rising of the*

---

*In the last scene, the way Gideon pushes back his hat and throws away his match, when it turns out Farnaby-Green has forgotten his license, is an imitation of Ford by Hawkins.

**By T. E. B. Clarke, whose credits include Ealing comedies, *Hue and Cry, Passport to Pimlico, The Lavender Hill Mob*.

Moon where we had some 50 speaking characters, all the parts "sing." I certainly don't like type casting. I like casting for individuals, for I photograph people.

Killanin: Both the eventual pictures have gone a long way from the shooting script.

Ford: Because as the basic story develops one must develop each character in the actor, besides the mood and the tempo, so that the drama is correctly mixed with humor.[52]

Ford's point is paraphrased by Louis Marcorelles, in *Cahiers:*

> For anyone who takes the trouble to open his eyes, to follow the progression of each shot and each detail in the shot, nothing happens in Ford except that which is rigorously desired, willed not by some higher decree of the scenario, but because each personage possesses his own internal logic, and is inscribed according to very precise limits onto space and time.[53]

Each portrait receives detailed care, in Ford's vignette method. For example, a decorous middle-aged secretary Duke interviews among three reports we see of an investigation into Joanna Delafield's past—surely a minor character if ever there were one!—grabs our interest: she tells nothing of

Gideon's Day. In the Gideons' kitchen: Jack Hawkins, Ford, Anna Lee, Anna Massey, and visitor John Wayne (without toupee).

Joanna we have not observed ourselves, but she chooses to complain of the same faults of character apparent in herself.

The quiet matter-of-factness of Ford's staging captures events as they are to their participants, thereby intensifying the horror of our passive witnessing. And comedy's *allegretto* tempo has an advantage over tragedy's *adagio*, in the effects to be gained through agogic emphases to serve as contemplative points of relaxation or tension. To cite a few instances: The second or two the camera rests on Mason's dead body; Mrs. Kirby's closed door after Gideon's terrible visit; Sayer climbing the stairs (deprived of all suspense because we know he will kill Dolly); the moments stolen to watch Sergeant Gully crease Gideon's hat; the half-startled glance Mrs. Kirby gives Gully when he brings her tea and announces, "Milk and sugar" (a bit like the fleeting instants of sweetness in *7 Women;* in fact, Mrs. Kirby resembles Agatha Andrews). Similarly, when Gideon hears the rape-murderer of a fourteen-year-old is on his way to London, his remark is trite, "Well, let's hope he gets here." But Ford has him walking slowly across the room as he says it, has him pause to fiddle with his pipe as he says it, and then has him walk out of the frame (then cutting back to him immediately!), and has Hawkins recite the line with a manly matter-of-factness that barely masks inner fury, so that what resonates is psychological insight into a character whose sense of purpose is even more potent and terrifying than *The Searchers'* Ethan Edwards's. And as with Edwards, a forward dolly to Gideon's eyes shows crusty professionalism has not inured him from caring deeply.

As Gideon's day darkens with nightfall, Ford becomes giddy, the craziness facile, color combinations jangly, discordant. And just violence in green contrasts with unjust violence in red. A slum church bathed in green light (exotic expressionism) with painted backdrop, neon lights of downtown London, jangly red, gold, white, and black of the Delafield apartment: color and artifice climax when the affectatious Fitzhubert complacently fires three bullets into Mason, a sympathetic vault guard, whose red blood Ford links with Fitzhubert's red carnation. This is one of few studied death scenes in Ford: he wants to impress evil's actuality, to make us hate it as Gideon does nearly slamming his fist into Fitzhubert, but above all to convey banality. Both the clichéd mad painter and Fitzhubert *bore* Gideon: he has seen such triteness-posing-as-genius hundreds of times. (Accordingly, Ford throws away his only action scene in one long dark take.) "You're due for a promotion—in ten or twenty years," Gideon cracks to one of his men, quoting from some John Ford western he must have seen.

Because one aspect of *Gideon's Day* is that it is a "crime prevention" film, Ford is able to elaborate his belief in justice "when it is virile." For justice, the police must be respected, as honest as effective. Unlike most police in pictures, Ford's bobbies never stumble. Nor are they ever particularly intelligent or heroic. Instead it is all routine performed with the placidity of a short-order cook.

The Last Hurrah (1958). Gideon & Co. are nonetheless fighting a rear-guard action. The relative absolutes that previously secured society are crumbling, to be replaced by brief moments of love midst general carnage. Still, in London *Gideon's Day* manages to find *some* hope within a psychotic world's ordered chaos, whereas in the chaotic order of Boston, *The Last Hurrah* finds only cynicism, misanthropy, and despair. (It becomes clear, at least, why Ford had avoided subjects dealing with contemporary America or with cities since *The Whole Town's Talking* in 1935.)

The personages surrounding Mayor Frank Skeffington—the potent cast surrounding Spencer Tracy—are mere satellites of an aging Irish king, whose unscrupulous ambition has for decades promoted the welfare, security, and future of his people. His ethnic patriarchal system has survived past its time, however, and Skeffington's defeat for reelection marks the emergence of a new—but unsecured—order. Skeffington is a Fordian hero in the Judge Priest mold; but this time the Maydews take over.

As in "The Majesty of the Law," tradition and ethnicity are heavily emphasized in the Ford-Nugent screenplay, but not in the literary source. "You wouldn't have me break with tradition, would you?" asks Skeffington. "Remember the day we took office. Frank Skeffington is available to every man and woman in this state." But only the last sentence is in Edwin O'Connor's novel, not the evocation of tradition. And far more than O'Connor, Ford sees this Dan-O'Flaherty-like majesty leading a bitter, dirty, racial strug-

gle. All opposition, as far as Ford's Skeffington is concerned, is motivated by "the fact that the city is no longer yours [the Wasps']—it's ours." Skeffington is often contemptible (and Ford tastelessly misanthropic), as when black-mailing a slum-clearance loan by making the chief banker's mentally deficient son fire commissioner. But a Fordian hero always employs violence, and more often Skeffington is lovable, as when meeting his nephew's wife:

— Do you know? Your mother was the most beautiful woman I ever saw. Except for one. Your grandmother Ellen. And, you know? You look exactly like her.

Tradition for Skeffington is a living force, spearheaded by himself. He takes his nephew on a pilgrimage to his childhood tenement (another scene not in O'Connor):

— I was born here, Adam. Your father-in-law, the eminent Sir Roger, was born down there—oh, that of course is before it became a Chinese laundry. See that window: Martin Burke. ["You mean the Cardinal?!" interjects Adam, as the soundtrack quotes a tune associated with Donald Crisp in *The Long Gray Line*.] Yes. This is it. We were all born down here together, then drifted our different ways. [He strikes a match to peer at initials carved in a heart on a post:] Still there. I guess I was about six years old when I met your Aunt Kate. I've loved her ever since.

But tradition has not ennobled the younger generation. Cocky, foolish and superficial as Ford's young men are wont to be (in the postwar pictures), they never fare worse than in *The Last Hurrah*. Adam (Jeffrey Hunter), slightly urbane, slightly arrogant, slightly vapid, is the best of the lot; beyond loyalty (to his uncle) and contempt (for politics and numerous people) he almost never commits himself to a point of view. The pampered obliviousness of Skeffington's wishy-washy playboy son and the enemy banker's idiot son illustrate the dangers of patriarchy. It weighs too squarely on the shoulders of old men and enfeebles everyone else. Skeffington's victories have been obtained at too great a moral cost: there is ironic justice that his generation's corruption gives birth to the class-traitor who defeats him — the marshmallowy Kevin McCluskey (whose TV appearance seems a Fordian lampoon of Nixon's Checkers speech).

In *Drums Along the Mohawk*, a pastor warns a girl against an unfit suitor, praying, "He's a Massachusetts man, O Lord, and Thou knowest no good can come from Massachusetts!" *The Last Hurrah*'s host of misanthropic characters would not alter the pastor's mind: McCluskey's wife, Amos Force, Roger Sugrue, undertaker Johnny Degnan, among others. "I certainly do know Boston* and those people," said Ford. "Half of them are half-witted and half of them are bright, but there's always a couple of kooks among them."[54] Indeed, most of the kooks in Ford — Colonel Thursday, Doc Holliday, Amelia Dedham — come from Boston. And Ford's bitterness extends even into the unsympathetic satire of the Irish wake.

Skeffington, glorious in defeat, announces his candidacy for governor as he concedes the mayoralty. Yet he walks home alone, as McCluskey's victory parade passes behind him on a direction of its own: passage and continuity. He feels his heart give at home and (another interpolation) looks beseechingly toward his wife's portrait before collapsing down the stairs.

An ethnically authentic ritual has been established around this portrait of the dead Kate Skeffington. A lonely and isolated man, despite his active life, Skeffington places a fresh flower in front of it each morning. Now the parade of his supporters troops slowly into the house bringing him flowers. Adam, after Skeffington's death, puts a new flower beneath the portrait. But the action does not promise survival of tradition. Instead, the parade returns finally to Skeffington in the last shot when, from outside the door, we watch his old sidekicks and their shadows parade mournfully up the staircase to view their dead leader. As in *The Wings of Eagles*, life's ultimate achievement is having friends at the end.

---

*Though the picture says only "A New England City," one senses Boston, and O'Connor's novel was supposedly based on the career of Congressman, Mayor, Governor James Curley, who sued Columbia and settled for $25,000 in damages, then $15,000 when the first check went mysteriously astray. But Ford's picture never accuses Skeffington of personal corruption — beyond his blackmailing through a loan. (For Curley, see Francis Russell, "The Last of the Bosses," in *American Heritage*, June 1959.)

The Last Hurrah, in its major moments, develops Fordian symbology into a dark despair of dissolved traditions and social orders. Life and ideology seem futile—except for flowers.

But the picture as a whole is weak. "Something went out of it in the cutting," said Anna Lee, adding that Ford was disappointed with the picture and had not been permitted by Columbia to supervise its editing.[55] Perhaps it is not the editing's fault that the Adam character is a useless bystander, not even a narrator. But it is the editing's fault that *The Last Hurrah* is lethargic and long (121 minutes), with the lengthiest sequences and shots of Ford's career. No wonder his interest seems often merely casual, and cynicism rather than inspiration spikes banality. It should be a beautiful moment when Skeffington, inviting nephew Adam to watch the last old-style campaign, leans against the window and says, "The last hu-rrah." But it is tepid. The long monologue is essentially expository. Ford always avoided exposition and kept things stationary when words were important. Here, however, Skeffington wanders awkwardly from spot to spot, within a continual long shot, and energy and character are dissipated. Ford-Tracy's Skeffington is more symbolic than O'Connor's, but he is far more shallow. Tracy conveys worlds of emotion through restrained visceral force, but, with Columbia's editing, he seems an actor without a director.

The Horse Soldiers (1959). Similar problems—and greater ones—haunt *The Horse Soldiers*. "No! I don't want to make great sprawling

pictures. I want to make films in a kitchen. . . . The old enthusiasm has gone, maybe. But don't quote that—oh, hell, you can quote it."[56] Ford's usual postfilm depression was justified. *The Horse Soldiers* sprawled all over the South, its 250-page six-corporation contract had taken dozens of lawyers half a year to iron out,* Ford was deteriorating physically, had never felt enthusiasm for the script or hit it off with his producer-scenarist Martin Rackin, and stuntman Fred Kennedy had broken his neck during shooting.

Yet, as Louis Marcorelles concluded, after a highly unfavorable review in *Cahiers du Cinéma*, magic moments mitigate *The Horse Soldiers'* failure:

> Ford in cinema has attained summits difficult to equal, not so much by totally perfect works as by instants of unbearable beauty, where man calmly turns back into himself, harmonizes himself with the world, and goes off to continue the struggle. . . . Judged by the standard of elegant defeatism in nearly all contemporary cinema, *The Horse Soldiers* is still passionate. Both as filmmaker and man, Ford always releases that same Herculean force, tempered with tenderness. But the contours are increasingly blurry. Ford is very close to imitating himself. But, for the unhappy souls, it should be made clear that, at its best moments, *The*

---

*Wayne and Holden each got $750,000, Ford $375,000 plus 10 percent of the producers share after it reached twice negative cost. The six corporations belonged to Wayne, Holden, Ford, Mahin-Rackin, Mirisch, and United Artists. Moviemaking was becoming a craft for dealers, not moviemakers. Similar problems drove Frank Capra into retirement.

Horse Soldiers struck us as quite superior to both *Stagecoach* and *How Green Was My Valley.*[57]

The picture's faults begin with its story, a free adaptation of Harold Sinclair's account of Colonel Benjamin Grierson's 600-mile, sixteen-day raid from La Grange, Tennessee, to Baton Rouge during the Vicksburg campaign, April 1863. A story of incidents, the film never passes beyond the incidental. Lacking a fixed locale, it lacks depth in character and culture. Unlike other "travelogues," such as *Stagecoach* or *Mogambo*, the principal characters are vapid, they lack biography, their subdramas are tawdry. Cameo vignettes are shallow, for Ford, and there is little evocation of the past. Thematic ambiguities are incoherent, symbols often are without referent, interrelations are obscure.

Particularly noisome is the heavy reiteration of doctor-hatred by Colonel Marlowe (John Wayne) and his consequent running feud with Dr. Kendall (William Holden). Marlow's explanation—how he held down his young wife while doctors cut her open for a nonexistent tumor and killed her—is undercut by juxtaposition to the slaughter of Confederates and Kendall's efforts to save the wounded. The subplot becomes macabre: Kendall treats a soldier's leg with tree moss, Marlowe scoffs, soldier removes moss, gets gangrene, dies after amputation.* Marlowe mocks Kendall, and Ford ridicules their fight by intercutting it with boy cadets parading to battle. It is difficult to care about this talky subplot, but it and some tangential concoctions between Marlowe and Hannah Hunter (Constance Towers**) constitute the movie's internal drama.

The Horse Soldiers could be transposed to Monument Valley, with the Southerners becoming Indians combating manifest destiny, except that mythic stylization of the blue-coats is tempered and key types made repugnant. Major Gray (Walter Reed) is a less empathetic version of the glory-hungry lieutenant, Colonel Secord (Willis Bouchey) an obnoxious Colonel Thursday, Sergeant Kirby (Judson Pratt) a disgusting version of Victor McLaglen's amiable sadist, Marlowe a repressed Nathan Brittles without Brittles's compelling humanism. Ken Curtis, Hank Worden, Jack Pennick, O. Z. Whitehead, and Hoot Gibson[†] bestow moments of personality, but briefly.

---

*Similar images of physical helplessness recur frequently in late Ford. Cf. *The Wings of Eagles, The Last Hurrah, 7 Women.*

**The real Hannah was in her sixties. Towers in her twenties brings beauty and amusement to the role, but Ford repeats many Maureen O'Hara gags.

[†] Ford and Gibson were ex-roommates and Ford directed his first feature, *Action*, in 1921. The great B-western star was fondly remembered in Tennessee. The day Wayne and Holden arrived, the *Natchez Times* banner-headlined: "Filming Stars. Hoot Gibson, Others Arrive"; and next day, still snubbing the superstars, a four-column picture was headlined, "White Haired Hoot Star Attraction." Hoot got $5,000 for his tiny part. (*The New York Times Magazine*, September 20, 1959, p. 62.)

In contrast, the South is bathed in myth. The long rebel column passing on the distant far riverbank (singing "For Southern Rights Hurrah") recalls the migrating Arapaho in *She Wore a Yellow Ribbon* (and Wayne hides his men both times). Southern cameos are strong and empathetic: magnificent one-armed Jonathan Miles (Carleton Young) carrying the Stars and Bars alone at the end of the Battle of Newton Station; the headmaster (Basil Ruysdael: another reverend-colonel) carrying a Bible to battle; the proud sheriff (Russell Simpson) nearly hung by dastardly deserters.

When we think of the industrial North, its politicians and carpetbaggers, its dirty cities and sober citizenry, it is easy to forget that the Confederate constitution sought not only a slave-based economy but also hegemony over the vast majority of whites by a landed plutocracy. Yet the racial theme is minimized* and the populist one neglected entirely. Though the blacks look threadbare and famished, the Southerners are virtually never depicted as slavers or racists; they fight for "Southern rights, hurrah!" As for the Union forces, Hannah mocks their pious talk of "preserving the Union," calls them "plundering pirates," while they themselves only say they're doing a job.

*After the battle, Union troops pass a Negro congregation outside its church. "Jubilo," an emancipation song (used also in *Sergeant Rutledge*) is on the soundtrack, but the blacks only remove their hats, expressionless. Then two CSA snipers accidentally kill Hannah's black maid (Althea Gibson). Why? Cut to next scene: no explanation. This is an instance of the referentless symbolism referred to earlier.

One might, therefore, conclude with J. A. Place that "Ford's sympathies are with the South throughout,"[58] but this, like Place's claim that Ford is saying that war is senseless, simplifies too much.

The episodic narrative has two unifying elements: both appear in the last shot—a cabin and a passing column of horsemen. In most scenes, horsemen move, foreground or background, usually Northern, but here they are Southern. Their carriage suggests triumphal heroes, whereas they are actually vanquished minor players. In any case, they pass by and are gone, and their oddly inconclusive image is confirmed as the familiar Fordian parade, transitory life. What remains on the screen is the cabin.

"A house divided against itself cannot stand." The cabin represents subsistence, the effort to save the Union. It looks just like the cabin a few scenes back that is blown up by Confederate cannon, while the boy cadets attack the Yankees. Now, the cadets are able to attack because Marlowe has paused in his flight to destroy some salt deposits ("as valuable as ammunition"). Midst the conference deciding this, Deacon (Hank Worden) stands in the background, the exact image of ole Abe Lincoln. For it is the divine Lincoln who is directing this war, and Ford subtly invokes him to justify more destruction. Deacon, in fact, saves the Yanks. After Newton Station, they are three-hundred miles within Southern territory with a large CSA force on their tail. Their fate seems sealed. But Deacon used to live hereabouts and smuggle runaway slaves through the underground railway, the swamp: "The Garden of Eden had its sufferin' too. Follow me, Brother Colonel, through the swamps, all the way to the River Amite. 'Lead kindly Lord!'" Thus, as in *Wagon Master*, the voyagers are saved by an angel of the Lord. (And an underground railway is provided for the railway engineer who destroys railways.)

True, the Yanks are the invaders; housewives throw dust at them. Some Yanks enjoy their orgies of murder, whereas the South is always depicted in desperate struggle (e.g., the many Southern hands vainly trying to ignite a cannon during the final battle). Marlowe himself, tough as nails but refusing to carry a gun, is horrified at bloodshed, and, as a railroad engineer, shamed to be destroying railroads. But Grant has told him that failure to destroy the Confederate supply station to Vicksburg "might cost us 100,000 men, might cost us the war."

A word more about those gallant boys, whose heart-catching action is the movie's highpoint:* Their uniforms and presentation recall *The Long Gray Line*, but now they not only look like toy soldiers, they effectively are toy soldiers. Why are they sent against Marlowe's men? In order to sacrifice themselves by delaying Marlowe, so that the grown-up rebels can catch him. Which side, then, engages in senseless killing? Or at Newton Station?

---

*Such incidents did happen, except that the boys usually got killed, whereas here Marlowe prevents sadist Kirby killing the minister, orders retreat, and gives the cadets a gallant charge. The incident of the drummer boy sneaking out of his mother's window occurred as early as 1913 in Ince's famous *Drummer of the 8th* (1-reel Broncho, May 28, 1913).

Aren't those heroic rebels engaging in one of the stupidest suicidal exploits in cinematic war?

The South's glorious gestures are repeated by the Yankees, but with subdued treatment. We see the Rebels massacred charging Union guns, we see their flagbearers killed again and again but the flag is always raised again. And we see their children march off to war. But it's the Union soldiers we see die in close-up (the boy in the hospital; the man with gangrene). The Southern struggle is invoked verbally, but it's the Union men we watch enduring a six-hundred-mile campaign. They too charge into the mouth of a cannon, their flag is lifted again and again too, and they have an equivalent

to the one-armed Southern colonel in Major Grey, who toasts quoting *Richard III*, replies "Thank you for the opportunity" when ordered to charge, cries "Blow, trumpet, blow" when fallen wounded, and will now, like other Northern casualties, be sent to dreaded Andersonville prison.

Ford's Civil War references generally "side" with the Yankees: no portraits of Lee, but many icons of Lincoln; Grant, Sherman, and Sheridan are the great men who fascinated him.

In the final sequence, Marlowe has neither time nor words to tell Hannah he loves her. But he pulls off her bandanna, revealing her neck (like Sean Thornton in *The Quiet Man* with Maureen O'Hara, or Clark Gable in *Mogambo* with Grace Kelly). She watches him gallop across as the bridge explodes behind him. "Laurina" (the *Searchers* theme) peals forth in sound and picture as she puts her hand to her eyes, looking after him. "Laurina" appeared earlier, at another river, just before encountering Hannah, intimating Marlowe's quest to heal wounds left by his wife's death.

The Confederates cannot catch the Yankees now, but they will try. Their general salutes Kendall gallantly: "Can our regimental surgeon be of any assistance to you, Doctor?" and then races off. These twin treaties of war-transcending humanity are combined, midst the theme music, with the twin images of moving horsemen and stationary cabin, until we are left with only the cabin. An ending as mysterious and beautiful as Ford ever achieved.

Sergeant Rutledge **(1960).** In contrast to *The Horse Soldiers*, *Sergeant Rutledge* never opens up to the natural world. It is shut up in tortured subjectivity, which nature merely mirrors, and Bert Glennon's photography makes it Ford's most expressionistic color film (and possibly his most brilliant—characters set against black, light-streamed fog, trains roaring through the night). Even out-of-doors, emotions are intense, angry, pent-up; even in Monument Valley emphasis is not on the sky but on grim red clay; even lovers are furious. The movie is molded of space between people, space enclosing them, constricting space, constraining light, a world of terror and loneliness. It is not a movie of dialogue between man and environment (like *Wagon Master*): Mary runs to the tracks, looking out into space as people did in *The Searchers;* but this time there is nothing there.

Sergeant Rutledge sets an episode of a black cavalryman's life within a trial, ostensibly a trial for rape and murder, actually a farce for white passion to release itself upon a Negro whippingboy. High-angle shots, numerous close-ups, foreground figures glaring wrathfully downscreen toward background figures, all add portentous tones quickly undercut by their own exaggeration, as well as by the court's idiotic dickerings, by prosecutor Shattuck's racist demagogy and caricatured mannerisms, and by Cordelia Fosgate (Billie Burke) befuddling his name—Shattuck, haddock—and calling him Captain Fish.

Sergeant Rutledge takes up the theme, broached by *The Sun Shines Bright, The Long Gray Line,* and *The Searchers,* among others, of a militarist society's hostility toward anything not held in sway by its moral tyranny. Few pictures depict "order" so distastefully or the military so repugnantly. The violence in themselves that the whites disguise as order and do not acknowledge, they project into the land they strive to dominate—the inimicably inhospitable landscape of arid stone, red like the Indians who strike back like the furies of white subconsciousness—and they project into the blacks they do dominate—the blacks who the whites in their repressed sexuality think want to rape them. When the real rapist, a white man, confesses, his personality collapses completely, he pounds the chair on his knees—"I had to, I had to"—and chaos erupts. Is civilization, then, merely a cloak for savagery? or does it encourage savagery? Denial of reality produces violence, and propriety cloaks the prurient. Ford's exaggeration and humor exemplify these hypocrisies: the rhetoric disguising racism, the clock the colonel snitched during the burning of Atlanta, Cordelia's ladies fanning as they contemplate rape, the judge's whiskey that everyone calls "water." As in *Steamboat Round the Bend,* discombobulation between names and things signifies social rot. Thus when Mary Beecher (or another) testifies facing Shattuck across the frame, with the five judges along the rear, and the court is given a proscenium frame with lights dimmed theatrically, leaving the witness spotlit and her voice echoing, it seems the court rather than Rutledge that is on trial.

As in *The Sun Shines Bright* the blackman is the surrogate for white self-flagellation and conscience. Ironically, while the Indians and their land wish to keep the whites out, the blacks wish to join white society more fully. "Someday," we'll be free, says Rutledge (Woody Strode). "Someday" your little girl will be awfully proud of you, he tells a dying black. "Someday" this will be a *good* land, Cantrell (Jeffrey Hunter) tells Mary. But not yet, not now.

Freedom, indeed, is hauntingly evoked midst strains of "Jubilo" (a song of the black emancipation), but Rutledge rejects it (a chance to escape) and returns to constriction. Why? "Because the 9th Cavalry was my home, my real freedom, and my self-respect, and the way I was deserting it, I wasn't nothin' but a swamprunnin' nigger. [Sobbing loudly, always in close-up, he leaps to his feet, the camera arching up toward him.] And I ain't that! Do you hear me?! I'm a man!"*

Rutledge's decision resembles Captain York's at the end of *Fort Apache.* There is no "someday" outside of society. And even though public hypocrisy has thoroughly corrupted established order, truth will still be found in the emotions of the pure of heart. Rutledge, like Lincoln and Judge Priest,

---

*As with McLaglen in *The Informer,* Ford tricked Strode into getting drunk the night before, then called him at 6 A.M. for his big trial scene.

knows facts cannot be argued against prejudice. And like Sternberg's Shanghai Lily (*Shanghai Express*) the only response he makes to a friend's accusations is his own character. Of what value, ask Ford films repeatedly, are mere facts compared to character? The little gold cross at the crux of *Sergeant Rutledge*'s murder mystery symbolizes burden, salvation, and the inner truth that someday will bring someday.

"Taller than a redwood tree," sing his comrades of Rutledge, a sort of underground Fordian hero. "I've never gotten over *Sergeant Rutledge*," said Woody Strode (Rutledge) years later. "It had dignity. John Ford put classic words in my mouth. . . . You never seen a Negro come off a mountain like John Wayne before. I had the greatest Glory Hallelujah ride across the Pecos River that any blackman ever had on the screen. And I did it myself. I carried the whole black race across that river."[59]

But *Sergeant Rutledge* was not a commercial success. It was half-heartedly marketed as a suspense picture, with no one allowed to enter during its last five minutes—a tactic that must have highlighted the movie's most annoying flaws. Theoretically, suspense is served by the eerie lighting, stark angles, and dozen flashbacks, which dribble "facts" piecemeal and backwards. (Not until the sixth flashback do we learn Rutledge's crime, not until the twelfth do we learn his side of the story, and all the while false suspicions are shoddily implied by interruptions at crucial points.) But suspense is not Ford's forte, and, anyway, *Sergeant Rutledge* is too much a discombobulation of genres— suspense film, western, racial melodrama, theoretical expressionism. We know almost immediately that Rutledge is 100 percent good, our interest in the murder mystery quickly evaporates, and the last-minute histrionic confession by an all-but-new character seems contrived. Granted, all this is Ford's intention: to reveal the farce and exalt character. But it destroys the suspense film, so that, in practice even more than in concept, *Sergeant Rutledge* shares the problems of other Fords of the period—weird, uneven, strident, dispersed in effects, ultimately incoherent. And, unhappily, the script's structural premises are unfulfilled: the twelve flashbacks do not reflect their six narrators' personal knowledge (i.e., events occur outside their sight and contrary to their description), while the only instance of real tension between narrator and event occurs with Cordelia's reminiscence of her attitude toward Lucy. Given that subjectivity is at the heart both of prejudice and nobility, it is curious Ford did not exploit the possibilities inherent in multiple subjective narration. Finally, Ford never seems at his best when, as with *The Informer*, he forces a single mood of constriction to dominate a film without large doses of off-setting humor. The few instants of hope, far from trying to balance grimness, possess a crazed disequilibrium—the scenes heroizing Rutledge at campfire, the awkward, unrehearsed spontaneity of the love scenes. This lack of balance is a consistent problem throughout this period, a problem solved in the years ahead.

Two Rode Together (1961). According to Ford, he undertook
Two Rode Together as a favor to Columbia's Harry Cohn, hated it, and "just
tried to make James Stewart's character as humorous as possible."[60] According
to Dan Ford, Ford did it for the money ($225,000 plus 25 percent net
profits) and lost enthusiasm while working on the script with Frank Nugent.
Whatever, once again, despite magnificent passages, themes (including that
of "moral ambiguity") do not cohere. It is not clear even to whom the title's
"Two" refers.* The bitterness, revisionism, disjunctiveness and experimentation of this transitional period climax in this film.

It is a grim, claustrophobic movie, set mostly at night against solid black,
occasionally in overcast daytime. The Comanche are ignoble rabble (compared to *The Searchers'* Comanche), willing to sell a white boy who has
become a warrior in their own tribe, subjecting their women to dreadful
slavery. Midst blackness and fire, Stone Calf orgiastically invokes his war
gods, while Quanah Parker sneers, "He still thinks buffalo shields can turn
away bullets!"

The redman's myth-ridden paranoia is matched by the whiteman's obsessive fantasies. Families dwell in guilty pasts, outside present reality, their
lives and relationships suspended, their search for missing members kidnapped by Comanche also a search for personal redemption. Grief-crazed
Anna McCandless is martyring her husband. Marty Purcell (Shirley Jones)
blames herself for her brother's capture, though she was a little girl at the
time; she is a tomboy, doesn't go to dances, confesses, "I used to pray to be
changed into a boy. At times I still do"—to compensate her father. The
motherless Clegg boys have grown into uncouth effeminate roughnecks.**

It is strange the army does not convince these people of their futility, of
what happens to youngsters reared as Indians. In *The Searchers* Debbie
came back safe and sane, but in the more realistic *Two Rode Together* Hannah Clegg refuses to go back; Freda Knudsen is too daft to return; Running
Wolf is savage and hates whites (due to difficulties growing up Indian) and
has to be locked up; Elena (Linda Cristal), having accepted slavery proudly
as Stone Calf's woman, allows herself to be taken back as though changing
masters, but is greeted as a degraded freak. The last dance scene in Ford
masks poisonous inhumanity: Elena prefers to return to the Comanche,
McCabe (James Stewart) denounces the assembly. Simultaneously, Running Wolf, having quite naturally killed the psychotic Anna, is "tried" and
hanged. Instinct replies to instinct. The whites release pent-up rage against
not only Comanche but also their own fantasies. But on his way to be
hanged, in one of Ford's finest sequences, the boy hears Marty's music box

*The Gary–McCabe dominant storyline is intimate but a nonrelation: they do not in-
fluence each other, cooperate only once, and McCabe, manically asserting independence,
once threatens to kill Gary. At the end, McCabe rides off with Elena, together, while the
"ride" with Gary remains a fleeting incident.
**Like *My Darling Clementine*'s Clantons and *Wagon Master*'s Cleggs.

(already established as a fantasy object from the past), rushes to it shouting "Mine," and is dragged away just as Marty realizes he is her brother. (Ford's counterpointing of stasis and propulsion to convey Marty's terrible multifaceted realization creates the picture's catharsis.)

If *Mogambo* shows men as different from beasts, *Two Rode Together* shows them as weeds. Reality is subjective, morality too, and they and personal identity depend upon the conditioning milieu. Instinct and necessity determine everything. No other Ford picture is played so constantly at a level of gut response. Elena, reluctant to leave the Indian camp when there, accepts McCabe as her savior once out of it; but when McCabe kills Stone Calf she hurls herself onto his body wailing a Comanche dirge and streaming sandy soil through her upraised hands—until McCabe shouts her back to consciousness. Similarly, Running Wolf reveals himself slave to conditioned reflex when he jumps for the music box and speaks his first English word, but in him split nature is total and inimical. Hannah Clegg (Mae Marsh) alone in the movie seems to have a transcendent awareness of her situation—"I am dead," she says.

As Running Wolf is hanged, Ford cuts back to Marty and Jim Gary (Richard Widmark) separated across the space of the frame. She rises to her feet, sculpturally, and comes to embrace him. This and the following shot to which Ford will dissolve—an altar boy ringing a bell—resolve the catharsis. And since the movie began with boy-and-bell, the Fordian notion that life is an ongoing journey (people ride together in *Two Rode Together* but they do not parade) is expressed in consolation.

The love scenes between McCabe and Elena (particularly the lovely one when he plays with her hair and encourages her to go to the dance) and even more so, the Gary and Marty scenes, are played on a high level of spontaneous ingenuousness typical of Ford's experimental representationalism, in order to contrast the general grimness and rabid constriction.* They come off like cute innocent teenagers. Naturally this comedic style seems more artificial than the grim, sculptural *verismo*. Long single takes are used, too, such as the three-minute fifty-one-second riverbank chat between McCabe and Gary, improvised by the actors when they thought they were rehearsing. All this marks Ford's return to his roots; he said in 1964:

> Since actors used to play natural roles simply, people always assumed they were lousy actors. But, in those silent westerns, look how much more natural and "modern" their acting is, compared to the romantic stars of the time. Critics, however, seem to think acting is better when it's self-conscious.[61]

McCabe—who lounges on a porch, feet balanced on a railing, and sees gamblers tremble at learning his name—seems a cynical parody of *My Dar-*

---

*Less defensible, to my tastes, are the comedy of Widmark's fight with the Cleggs and Andy Devine's stomach buffoonery.

ling *Clementine*'s Wyatt Earp, for McCabe is a mercantile marshall who gets 10 percent of everything. And it would appear that James Stewart (McCabe)* has taken over the intellectual-hero roles Henry Fonda used to play. But McCabe is really a corruption of the traditional Fordian hero, and of *The Searcher*'s Ethan Edwards in particular. He rides off in the end, but uncelibate and rejecting—rather than barred from—society. Also, unlike the Fordian hero, McCabe refuses to play God: he *does* reunite families, even brings people "back from the dead," but does so for the sake of money rather than principle. And it is because McCabe, with unacknowledged hypocrisy, disclaims godlike arrogance that he dislikes Wringle (Willis Bouchey). Wringle is willing to pay $1,000 for "*any*" boy, in order to appease his wife and get himself out of the wilderness and back to business. And yet, is this not an instance of Ford tricking us, his audience, by using our facile willingness to define characters at face value?

The *obnoxious* Wringle is apparently contrasted with, but actually mirrored by, the *nobly sympathetic* McCandless, who is willing to dupe *his* wife out of pity for her. But we ought not to judge methods by motives alone. And, in fact, McCandless's action of adopting a boy (sixteen years old?) he knows is not his own amounts to racist enslavement (so, explicitly, Ford depicts it— the boy must be encaged), whilst *only* Wringle has the moral sense to do the right thing: "Send the boy back where he belongs," he shouts, obnoxiously, "Let the past bury the past." Again, good intentions are the true evil.

By means of these hypocrisies, and through Elena, McCabe discovers his own mercantile morality is not so bad after all. The major, a figure of supposed righteousness, breaks the bargain he made when he hired McCabe to ransom the captives: he refuses to honor McCabe's deal with Wringle, refuses to repay McCabe for the goods traded the Indians, and when McCabe protests, has him thrown into jail! When Gary protests, the major utters, profoundly, what (save for our auteurist insight into the Fordian hero) may be the most incomprehensible non sequitur in Ford: "I thought McCabe might be able to teach you what I was never able to—that only God can play God!"** Has Ford rejected the Fordian hero—which Gary wanted to become? Or has this transitional period, like the 1935–38 one, been merely one of reassessment and of heroes manqué?

---

*"Wayne, Cooper, and Gable are what you call natural actors," said Ford. "They are the same off the screen as they are playing a part. Stewart isn't like that. He isn't a thing like he is on the screen. Stewart did a whale of a job manufacturing a character the public went for. He studied acting." (Quoted by George Capozzi, Jr., *The John Wayne Story* [New Rochelle, N.Y.: Arlington, 1972.])

**Gary is called "Natani Nez" by Quanah Parker—Ford's own Navajo name, meaning "Tall Soldier."

5 Final Period (1962–1965): The Age of Mortality

John and Mary Ford made several trips to Europe, to Spain, Paris, and Rome, but most of the free time was passed aboard the *Araner*, now moored in Honolulu. While moving through a harbor, John found it almost impossible not to indulge his love for military pomp. With *Araner* flying his admiral's burgee, he would make a point to sail past any navy ship lying at anchor, whereupon the navy ships would have to pipe their crews to attention and dip their flags. And John would round up his guests (those not smart enough to hide in the galley), stand them in line at attention, and proceed to inspect them, straightening a tie here, readjusting a hat there.

As always, he was a night person. Although he generally held court in bed, he also had a sacred chair, a leather one, surrounded by countless piles of books. When not alone, he was addicted to bridge and poker. Come morning, to wake him Mary would play blaring music, and not infrequently she would have to get Jack Pennick to lift him out of bed; the first half-hour on set was a bit groggy. He wore his navy baseball cap nowadays, and had given up pipes for cigars—Irish Castle brand. His walk was still strong and jaunty—the walk John Wayne made his own, it is said.

As a father he had been rather distant. Father and son were never close, although they tried to be when Pat worked as producer, writer, or assistant on

Ford's pictures. "Pat is leaving Friday," Barbara wrote her father on the occasion of *The Quiet Man.* "He's certainly thrilled. You were awfully sweet to ask for him. He's a different person already."[1] Ford's indulgence, coupled with stern admonitions to prove oneself and stand on one's own feet, was an onerous heritage. Pat tried to copy his father's personality, but in his case it alienated people. Drink and gambling, according to Frank Baker, compounded Pat's problems; John would give Pat money on Monday, on Tuesday he would borrow from someone else, and for long periods he would disappear.[2] The collapse of his first marriage drained Pat financially—there were two sons—so that he had to abandon his dream, with his new wife and daughter, of buying land in Kauai (where *Donovan's Reef* had been filmed; Pat's high school had also been in Hawaii), and his father felt unable to lend him $15,000 toward a house in California.[3] John had written Pat into many of his production contracts, and Pat had often helped make up for the loss of Merian Cooper; but a bitter fight between Pat and producer Bernard Smith during *Cheyenne Autumn* virtually severed relations between father and son.

Barbara got closer to her father and made a career as an editor under Zanuck (and on some Ford pictures). With her, Jack would discuss his movies at length while he was making them. He liked to immerse himself in period music during preparation, and Barbara would find the records for him. Barbara's first marriage, an elopement at Catalina to actor Robert Wagner, was annulled after five weeks, on the grounds that Wagner had "no intention of consummating the marriage."[4] On June 1, 1952, she phoned from Las Vegas to announce her marriage to Ken Curtis, an actor-singer in many Ford pictures. Barbara had no children, and divorced Curtis in 1964.

John's own marriage, despite the tempest of the Hepburn period and periodic ups and downs, had long ago settled into mutual tolerance. He was permitted his extramarital affairs, of which there were not a few, including one as late as his sixty-fifth year with a young and exceptionally elegant Korean lady. But this side of Ford's life was conducted with extreme circumspection—Mary wanted no knowledge of it—and apparently with consistent grace and dignity.

Says Dobe Carey: "If you were in Big Trouble, Ford'd be the first guy you'd go to—rape, murder, assault. But if you just wanted to gossip or talk about girls, you wouldn't tell it to him. He set it up that way, then was almost sorry he did. No, he wasn't a fitter-inner, sort of an outsider. If there was one part of him that was unhappy it was that he wasn't one of the boys. All the kidding around would stop the moment he'd show up, and he wanted to be in on that. I think he was always that way." Merriment halts when clergy enter parties in *How Green Was My Valley* and *The Quiet Man.* But sometimes Ford's heroes were what he himself wanted to be. He liked to brag, liked to tell outrageous stories about girls making passes that everyone knew were untrue. He would get "voice-drunk" and give everyone a pain in the neck. He liked to say he was Bull Feeney as a kid because he was a tough, two-fisted, hard-drinking Irish sonovabitch, and so he used people like O'Brien, Wayne, and McLaglen in his films and as poker companions. But, as Dobe Carey says, "there was that incredible tenderness, poetry, and pathos underneath all that muscle. Dad would get sarcastic, 'Gee, he loves to take guys' shirts off with the muscle!'"[5] There were rumors of this sort—a stunt-boy once quit after Ford slapped him on the rump[6]—but they were simply inevitable consequences of Ford's secretive ways. "He wouldn't let you see those eyes: so soft and tender." As he hid his feminine sensitivity, so too he hid his erudition and intellectual subtlety, for nothing could be more damning in Hollywood. He once confessed being able to speak German to Hedda Hopper, then added, "You know, I don't want this to get out—I pose as an illiterate."[7] To be an artist, he had to hide artistic intention. At other times, of course, he hid because it was fun, manipulative, or just easier. "I take exception to your remark, 'he doesn't give a hang,' etc., etc.," wrote Bea Benjamin, Ford's business manager, to Henry Yeager, his captain of the *Araner.* "Mr. Ford keeps in touch with all of his financial business but likes to create an impression of indifference to deliberately confuse or befuddle the listener or to pass the buck."[8]

Some who knew Ford thought him a basically happy person, indeed a blessèd one. Others saw darker sides as well. "He was never relaxed, never mellow, never allowed you to relax either," said Frank Baker. "He was always unhappy. He never had a day's happiness. Will he find peace? Lonely spirit! What was he looking for?"[9]

Religion he approached with minglings of piety, casualness, and Celtic superstition. He felt debts to the dead. He carried a sort of necklace on which were his navy dogtag, a St. Christopher medal, a rabbit's foot, a Star of David, an elk's tooth, a small black ring of rhinoceros hair, and others; if he were talking to a Catholic or Jew or whatever, he would shamelessly pull out the appropriate charm. Scripts had to be worked over on the *Araner,* in his "lucky spot." He distrusted clergy and his movies focus on their hypocrisy, but he depended on them, too. The parish priest—a Jesuit—was frequently called into family affairs. And when on location, Ford would arrange for services and sometimes serve the Mass himself. But he was not above putting a five-dollar bill in the collection and telling the priest afterward he had not been able to find change for the twenty he had contributed. Once in Honolulu Jack stopped to call on Cardinal Spellman; Mary, who had never met him, waited in the car, because she was wearing jeans. "This little man walked over to the car," she recalls, "and he said, 'Are you Mary? Why don't you come in.' 'I can't go in there. Look how I look.' 'If it's the Cardinal you're afraid of, don't give it a thought, because I'm the Cardinal.' And he had some strawberry shortcake he'd saved for me. That would convert anyone!"[10] It did convert Mary.

Some Universal executives, all dressed like undertakers, came onto Ford's set. "I'm an associate producer," said one. "Gosh!" said Ford, "Are you really? God! For years I've been wanting to meet an associate producer! Tell me all about what it is you do!" Ford was reminded not to give extras dialogue, for by union rules a full week's actor's wage would have to be paid. Well, *Flashing Spikes* had a baseball game in it, and Ford found a couple of words for every player and nearly every spectator.

Once, as usual, Frank Baker found himself about to play a scene he knew nothing about. "Ford would never tell you anything!" "Okay," called Ford from atop a boom, "Ready?" Baker gasped: "But what do I say?" "You say, 'Father Sister Father.' Okay? Okay. Ready!" Only halfway through the scene, as he watched things happen, did Baker unfathom the cryptic line. Ford snarled afterward: "So! You figured it out, did you?!"

This was on *The Bamboo Cross,* but was typical of Ford's methods. Sometimes, though, he would casually walk through a scene himself, but without announcing he was doing it. Old-timers knew to watch, and knew if they did not copy exactly, he would not say what was wrong, but would just make them try again. When Ford went through a scene in *Liberty Valance*, he ended with his hand *drooped* over a railing. Edmond O'Brien noticed, but deliberately placed his *on* the railing. Forty-two times. Ford would not give in and tell him.

Photographer William Clothier said:

> Ford used to wear the same clothes day after day. Christ, he wore the same hat for 20 years. He also had things he'd say all the time, commonplace things like, "I guess I'll have to pull a rabbit out of my hat," whenever a scene wasn't going well. One day we were doing a tough scene in *Cheyenne Autumn* and the Old Man must have taken 30 minutes moving Carroll Baker and Richard Widmark around, trying to get the scene to work. Nothing. So he turned to me and said, "This isn't going to work, is it?" I said, "No." So then he said, "Well, I guess I'll have to pull a rabbit out of my hat." So he took his hat off and pulled a [toy] rabbit out of it! He must have had it hidden there all morning."[11]

"Nuttier than a fruitcake and a genius," Widmark called him.[12] But he was growing old. He had always kept everything in his head making a film; unlike other directors, he had never depended on his assistants or script girl. But as he aged, he became forgetful and it would have been contrary to habit to turn to others for help, even had there been people to turn to. And Hollywood had changed. In an era of independent production, he was obliged to make "great, sprawling films" to get backing. Months spent setting up deals would exhaust him and myriad tedious details previously handled by line producers fell now upon him. Then the financiers would intervene and spoil his best efforts. It was not simply due to old age that he would get bored and throw away pages of script.

But "directing's like dope addiction," he moaned to Hedda Hopper in 1962, "something you can't leave. The only thing is now that the present cycle has rolled around, I have no choice but to make westerns. Talk about moral bankruptcy! In the past 18 months I've had three good stories okayed at the studios—warm, human stories. It's not the studio that turned them down, but the Madison Avenue and Wall Street people who do the financing. They sent them back saying there wasn't enough sex and violence!" He offered to ghostwrite a sports column for Hedda.[13]

In the late years of old age and accumulated tradition, filming with Ford became an even more intense celebration of community. Partying had been inherent in his methods, even in the teens. Players made it a point to be on set every day, for they never knew when Ford might invent some marvelous business for them unforeseen in the script. *Donovan's Reef*, in Hawaii, climaxed this tendency, with old friends and children gathered together. Yet every night Ford would have Frank Baker accompany him on a drive up to a cliff, where he would pass several hours in utter silence, staring out to sea.*

TRANSCENDENCE

The Man Who Shot Liberty Valance	April '62	Ford Prodns.–Paramount
Flashing Spikes (TV)	October '62	Alcoa Premiere TV series
"The Civil War" (in *How the West Was Won*)	November '62	Cinerama-MGM
Donovan's Reef	July '63	Ford Prodns.–Paramount
Cheyenne Autumn	October '64	Ford-Smith Prodns.– Warner Bros.
7 Women	November '65	Ford-Smith Prodns.–MGM

If, as Ford's films have shown, so much of human response is determined by societal environment, is there any hope of finding a firm basis to support claims that life is worthwhile, struggle for virtue justified, and free will not an illusion? For many Ford characters, service to ideas offers hope, whether in duty to regiment or job, or in the commingling of loyalty to a loved one and vision of a better world expressed by a cactus rose upon a coffin. Man is often propelled upon his "unceasing search for something he will never find"[14] by such goals, substitutes for lost home and childhood. But if all vestiges of home and, indeed, of civilization disappear (all those things that it is usually the Fordian hero's duty to preserve and purify), then what? Implicit in all Ford, these problems are increasingly explicit in this and the preceding period, and in *7 Women* most particularly.

---

*Baker in 1962 had been suddenly summoned to *How the West Was Won*'s location battle scene, where Ford told him to climb a tree and go to sleep. When he awoke, everyone had gone home. Next day he received $1,000 for two weeks' work. It was a typical Ford stunt for a friend in need. Often though, Baker would deliberately goad Ford out of his "guru" implacability, Ford was forever firing him in the middle of scenes, whereupon Baker would refuse to return without a personal apology. And Ford, stuck with half a scene, would have no choice.

In contrast to the transitional years, Ford now reconciles classical, balanced style with thematic ambiguity. He finds a moral vision able to contemplate anguish and uncertainty without destroying itself. It sees the individual within an intricate nexus of determinants, but sees him both intimately and transcendently, both empathetically and dispassionately. A person's inner self is often at odds with his actions and social manifestations; similarly, the chaotic, determining manifestations of the world beyond the individual (society, the cosmos) are often at odds with the ordering principles whose existence one posits. Thus the "transcendent" is both beyond and within, both God and the inner ego. And Ford's vision may be interpreted either as Catholic or materialist or both.

Just as this final creative effort is one of conscious revision and summation thematically, so too it strives for summation formally. Of such formal summation no description, in the instance of Fordian cinema, seems more apposite than "kinetic sublimity." *The Man Who Shot Liberty Valance, Donovan's Reef,* and *7 Women* represent John Ford at his apex.

The Man Who Shot Liberty Valance (1962). The picture opens with a small steam train churning its way across a plain, blowing its whistle: coming.* The movie will close with the same train on a larger plain, again blowing its whistle: going. It is the train that is the film's principal protagonist, the train that changed the West. We might also think of the train as relating to the Fordian symbol of the parade in the more general sense, a formalized progression, a *passage.* Life keeps going; the motion is constant and to a certain extent unfocusable: good and evil, happiness and sorrow, gain and loss, all blend into one another.

This is the first of three masterpieces of Ford's last period, in which earlier ambiguities—intensified yet viewed from a heightened perspective—are subsumed into a higher level of consciousness, one in which struggle seems only another phenomenon—perhaps. *Liberty Valance* and *Donovan's Reef* (twin in many respects) do seem an old man's pictures; but less vigorous inventiveness is compensated, as in many great artists' last works, by deftness and vision.**

The Fordian hero is now more than ever restricted by his inability to act freely. There seems something above man, call it fate, motion, society, or history, but there is a dynamism in human society that moves society without its ken or will. Ford's Augustinian notion of man as pilgrim has been retained, strong as ever for the individual, but with an ironic touch, for the pilgrim has become a spectator of his own life, an actor in a play whose ending he cannot anticipate.

*Most 16mm prints have an aspect ratio of 1:1.33, which crops off the sides from images intended to be 1.65, with the result that the entire movie loses much of its subtle distancing.

**Frank Baker stated to author that the scenarios of both pictures were substantially improvised by Ford from day to day during production—*Liberty Valance* more so.

Familiar themes have grown in ambiguity. Evil is still associated with chaos, and good with order. But without chaos there is no freedom. And order may inhibit freedom, ossify hope, and destroy the wild and heroic beauty of man. Duty has become entirely immanent and personal. Memory is no less vital than present experience, as in earlier Fords, but now it tells far too many lies, and each lie, like each action, reverberates endlessly through history. The hero has gone into exile and been forgotten; the Maydews have inherited the earth.

Ford has a reputation for spacious landscapes, somewhat undeserved since his art has been to use vistas effectively rather than frequently; but *Liberty Valance* lacks exteriors almost entirely. Its manner is theatrical— long scenes of talk—and it focuses on the town, as opposed to the range; statehood as opposed to territory, civilization as opposed to wilderness; words (law and education) as opposed to the gun. The application of all of this to the USA, 1962, or today, is implicit, and a major intention of the film: the past as prelude.

If there is little in the way of landscape, there is not much more in the way of "action." Yet much happens with intensity in speechless scenes, on the level of gazes between characters, on such levels as the slow unwinding dances enacted by Vera Miles and Woody Strode when they recognize each other in the coffin room. This, it seems to me, is properly the world of a great movie, one in which the bodies of the actors, their eyes, and the spaces between them become the chief forms of expression.

As the train moves across the plain at the beginning, the soundtrack music is martial, almost like gladiator music (it resembles *7 Women*'s score). From this low-angled long shot Ford cuts to old Link Appleyard (Andy Devine) waiting at the depot, then crosscuts to the depot itself, the tracks stretching diagonally up screen, and the train pulls in, nearly filling the screen. Link moves into range, and we cut briefly to him, age and expectancy written on his face.

Hallie Stoddard (Vera Miles) and Senator Ransom Stoddard (James Stewart) descend slowly from the train, pause to take in their bearings, and then Hallie, carrying a hatbox, walks slowly down a descending diagonal up to the camera, where Link is standing. Just as she reaches him we cut to a medium close-up as they embrace.

The beauty here is subtle. We are given an opposition between Link in close shots and two people in distant ones. We are given a town quiet and still, except for the train's sounds, its smoke, the low incessant tolling of its bell and, occasionally, almost inaudible muffled timpani thumps on the soundtrack. Everything speaks of age, not the characters' makeup so much as the calculation with which they move, the intensity and selectivity with which they give their attention, their presence, to something or someone. The Fordian absence of extraneous movement has been pushed to an extreme of simplicity. One thing happens at a time and the result is clarity.

This abstract richness in motion and cutting becomes as soulful as Mozart's music for Sarastro. When Ford shows Hallie descending, almost falling, down the screen, and then cuts around to the medium shot of his two characters together in one filled space, the effect is at once a resolution and explosion of everything the preceding compositions had been working to achieve.

In *The Man Who Shot Liberty Valance* one concentrates on the eyes of the characters, thence their souls, and thence their world. It is a world so methodical, so simple in its cinematic manifestation that as our characters walk slowly along the street, their every step a calculation, their participation in where they are so total, the town so quiet (save for the tolling bell*) that everything reveals a shattering intensity of repression somewhere between awareness of life and awareness of death. It seems, here, that a sudden movement, a jerk in the camera's slow ponderous motion, might burst self-control into chaotic convulsions.

There is something terribly unsettling about this scene. Just as the actors appear to be looking inward while at the same time trying to take in the external world, so we are faced with an image whose motion reveals each new detail, unmasks each new "framing." The intensity is quiet but no less borders upon the shattering; it is a combination of a viewpoint that attempts to *grip* objects while at the same time leaving them behind: passage.

As always Ford detests exposition. Not for nearly two hours will we learn precisely why these people have come to Shinbone. Now, though, a newspaper editor (Carleton Young) questions Stoddard. We learn Stoddard is a fa-

---

*The bell was tolling too, but differently, during a similar walk through town in *My Darling Clementine*.

mous senator, once from this town, here now for the funeral of Tom Doniphon, an old friend no one has heard of. This fails to satisfy the editor, so Stoddard reluctantly goes off to talk, while Hallie goes to a buckboard with Link Appleyard.

The same deep silence reigns as they sit together on the buckboard, Link's eyes toward the floor, Hallie's on the hatbox on her lap. As they begin stilted conversation the camera moves us closer into their dispositions:

> *Hallie:* Th' place has sure changed. Churches, highschool, shops.
> *Link:* Well, the railroad done that. Desert's still the same.
> *Hallie:* The cactus rose is in blossom.
> *Link:* Maybe, maybe you'd like to take a ride out desert way an maybe look around.
> *Hallie:* Maybe.

During this strange, terse dialogue, they do not move or look at one another. As Link starts off, we cut to gaze down the street: the overhead electric wires, the buildings, the town they were discussing.

Somewhere outside of town, gazing at burnt ruins Hallie and Link sit silently, her hat's black veil softly waving in the breeze. Crosscut to some cactus plants, then back to them:

> *Hallie:* You knew where I wanted to go, didn't you?
> *Link:* Well, you said you wanted to see the cactus blossoms. There's his house down there, what's left of it, blossoms all around it.
> *Hallie:* He never did finish that room he started to build on, did he?
> *Link:* No. Oh well, you know all about that.
> *Hallie:* There's a lovely one there.

Link labors down from the buckboard, moving as always with weary exertion; Hallie puts her hand round the hatbox.

On the soundtrack appears a nostalgic melody, the same nameless tune Ford used in 1939 in *Young Mr. Lincoln*, associated with Ann Rutledge, as Lincoln talks to her grave. Its connotation is the same now, although it is a woman rather than a man that lives. But just as we do not know these cactus plants have any importance, so too we do not know that the melody has: it is Ford's general principle that he makes you *feel* first and understand afterward.

At the paper, Stoddard sees the buckboard return. The reporters follow him and his wife down narrow streets, past wood houses, down an alley and into a stable, through it and into a backroom doorway. Crosscut: a coffin; then back to them. An aged Negro (Pompey: Woody Strode) sits alone looking up at them. Pan in as he rises—the same "gladiator music" as at the film's start—and Hallie starts toward him. Through this series of crosscuts repressed stony faces melt laboriously into recognitions of old friendship. Stoddard opens the coffin, asks the undertaker angrily what has happened

to the corpse's boots, and orders they be put back on, his gunbelt and spurs, too. Then he sits; but there is no room on the bench with Link, Hallie, and Pompey, and he sits alone, perpendicular, not parallel, to the coffin.

The editor intrudes, demanding an explanation. Stoddard looks at his wife. She nods and so, with evident feeling of painful necessity, he gets up and goes out with the editor. Hallie, with great care, takes the hatbox from Link and starts to open it. Cut to the outer room, to Stoddard and the newspapermen.

As before with the hatbox, we do not yet know even that it is important. We do not think about it. We are more interested in Stoddard and the reporters. They gather round a stove. Behind them is an old stagecoach. Stoddard wipes dust off its name, "Overland Stage Lines," and discovers it is the same vehicle that carried him West years before. (It also looks like the vehicle used in *Stagecoach* in 1939.) He tells how as a young lawyer he came west, following the *words* of Horace Greeley, "Go West, young man, go West! And seek fame, fortune, adventure!" Dissolve into a flashback: the stagecoach hurtles through the night, into a clearing.

This flashback continues for all but the last few minutes, giving *Liberty Valance* a form similar to *The Long Gray Line*'s, almost entirely flashback. And as in that picture, *Liberty Valance* is essentially a montage of its two sections, the one resulting from the other. But there is an eeriness to the style of this flashback (and not until much later shall we understand why). It is composed of long, loping sequences, and of takes uncommonly long for Ford, shot for the most part in general shots. People move somewhat as in a dream. The artificiality is subtle, as is the contrast with the acting style in the "modern" sequences. The playing is freer, almost haphazard. While Stoddard is presumably in his early twenties in the flashback and Hallie perhaps still a teenager, only a token effort has been made to make them look young (Miles was thirty-three, Stewart fifty-three) and this is purposeful. There is precious little decor in the sets. Nearly all the scenes occur in town, indoors and often at night. William Clothier's black-and-white photography is mostly medium gray tones, unlike Ford's usual richness (as in the "modern" sequences—although Clothier's style is always less opulent than Glennon's, August's, Stout's, or Schneiderman's).

The stagecoach is halted by robbers headed by Liberty Valance (Lee Marvin). Valance rips apart Stoddard's lawbook (chaos /order). Their brutality is emphasized, rather than mitigated, in Ford's direction (which generally avoids dwelling on violence), and as Valance begins to whip Stoddard* orgiastically, the camera quickly dollies to a close-up of Valance's face making horrible gestures. It would be easy to dismiss this as simply a device to hide the fact that Lee Marvin is not actually whipping James Stewart but, just as in Mizoguchi's *Sansho Dayu* when the bailiff brands an old woman and the camera moves in to gaze steadily at the bailiff's face, Ford is intent on the psychological truth of violence. In addition, he departs from his usual practice, and shows the event from *Stoddard*'s viewpoint; we shall see why.

Next night, in town. "Genevieve, Sweet Genevieve" comes from a bar nearby; a rider (John Wayne) comes from the darkness down the street, leading a buckboard with Stoddard lying in it, some horses behind. As he rides slowly across the screen, the camera, on the porch, pans along porch-posts and around a corner. This is one of Ford's moments that gain so much from seeming like awestruck religious contemplations. Here it specifically anticipates Dr. Cartwright's entrance into the mission in *7 Women*, the point being that in both instances emphasis is put upon a normal unselfconscious action that in retrospect has great meaning for those involved, although Ford's art is here again creating an *aura* of significance without our yet knowing the significance. In the present scene there is first of all the nostalgic re-creation

*Stoddard is leaning against a wagon wheel, a Ford symbol of suffering.

of passed time, the Old West, into which the sentimental music invites us. Second, the moment will have far-reaching consequences for the John Wayne character. Third, Valance will later be driven *out* of town lying dead on a similar cart. Fourth, there is the contrast between Wayne's entrance and the two entrances (now and years later on the train) by Stoddard. In any case, entrances always have great import for Ford.

Wayne stops beneath a window and calls Hallie, who looks out and calls his name, Tom Doniphon. Now we learn who the man in the coffin is (will be) and the iconographic significance is great, for Wayne has assumed in the public eye (and to some extent in Ford's) a position as the archetypal hero of the West and as representative of certain aspects of the American character. Now he lies dead in a coffin without his boots and nobody knows his name. We shall learn he was a Fordian hero.

"Wayne actually played the lead," said Ford; "Jimmy Stewart had most of the scenes, but Wayne was the central character, the motivation for the whole thing."[15] (One can also understand the film profitably by placing Hallie at its center.)

Doniphon takes Stoddard into the kitchen of a restaurant owned by Hallie's parents, Peter and Nora Ericson (John Qualen, Jeanette Nolan), Scandinavian immigrants with accents.* Of the six sequences composing the hundred-minute flashback, the first two center around the kitchen, the others a schoolroom, a bar used as assembly room, a convention hall, all gather-

---

*In *The Searchers* Miles was also Qualen's daughter and then, too, they were Scandinavian.

ing places of a settled society, of which the kitchen is perhaps the symbolic heart. In contrast to these town scenes, those few of the "outside" suggest, like the stagecoach holdup, a wilderness of insecurity. The townspeople gather in their town, an artificial world, for protection from a menacing and chaotic outer space, from which they isolate themselves.

Ford had dealt frequently with closed worlds: *The Lost Patrol, Stagecoach, The Long Voyage Home,* most notably, but equally it is implied in pictures like *Doctor Bull, The Hurricane, Drums Along the Mohawk, The Informer, My Darling Clementine, The Sun Shines Bright, The Long Gray Line, Donovan's Reef,* and *7 Women.* More than simply a treatment of confined characters it is a treatment of confined space, of a virtually closed society both sufficient and insufficient unto itself. In a sense, the world beyond does not exist. We deal with the interaction between this closed space and society, between individuals and society and how they mutually determine one another, and how the social island is determined by forces from without. But these forces are seldom seen. They are spoken of and their effects are manifest. The railroad is yet to come to Shinbone, and we do not see the cattlemen and their ranges (any more than we saw battlefields in *The Long Gray Line*).

Lying in the kitchen, his wounds being swathed by (first Hallie, then) Doniphon, Stoddard reveals he is a lawyer, with even a shingle: "Ransom Stoddard: Attorney at Law." Doniphon mocks him: Liberty Valance respects only the gun. "I don't want a gun," moans Stoddard sententiously; "I don't want to kill him. I want to put him in jail." "Out here a man solves his own problems," humphs Doniphon. "You know what you're saying to me?!" cries Stoddard. "You're as bad as he is! What kind of a community have I

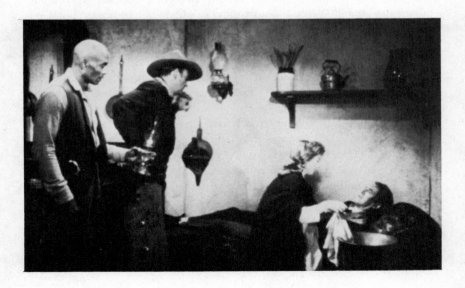

come to here?" he wonders, echoing Wyatt Earp in *My Darling Clementine*, and echoing himself asking Valance, at the holdup, "What kind of man are you?" "Now what kind of man are you, Dude?" Valance replied.

Here an essential conflict is enunciated: the battle between orders imposed by words (law) and by force (guns). Already the name "Liberty Valance" is a word-play: the "valence" of liberty depends on force (which is why order and liberty are not identical). In line with this, and moreover typically, Ford has gone to the trouble of providing a representation of Stoddard by his own device—his shingle, *words*—both his trade and his weapon represented by *actual written* words. Words play a significant part in this allegory of the establishment of law and order. Recall that it was Horace Greeley's *words* that sent Stoddard west. (Two years hence, in *Cheyenne Autumn,* words will be seen as the whiteman's chief and treacherous weapon in genocide of the Indian.)

The Man Who Shot Liberty Valance abounds with words in the form of signs: the funeral parlor has its sign, the newspaper, the stagecoach, Doniphon's ranch, the restaurant ("Peter's Place—Home Cooking"), all have their signs. And each person has his prop, as Valance has his whip, and his product. As always in postwar Ford, each abstract idea has a physical correlative. No character in Ford ever acts in simple space; it is always in direct relation to another person or object. Everything receives physical representation.

Doniphon seems engaged to Hallie, and is building an extra room onto his ranch. But their relationship strikes us as less than entirely comfortable. Doniphon seems to regard her from a distance with equal proportions of presumption and fear. When Stoddard is given whiskey as medicine, Doniphon takes the bottle and jokes about not letting Stoddard drink alone; Hallie impersonally pulls it away and goes about her business, but Doniphon smiles coyly, happy to get attention.

Link Appleyard, the town marshall, comes into the kitchen. Although in the "modern" sequence the character is entirely serious, in the flashback he is the drama's buffoon, whose bits of slapstick are slipped into the general austerity to engage the audience. But at times this slapstick seems tasteless, as with O. Z. Whitehead as a man-child always licking lollipops. Alas, "good jokes" get encored, for example when Link's hat, which he has neglected to remove, is snatched off by Doniphon onto the floor. Joke number one. Then as he reaches down for it Hallie walks by and kicks it across the room. Joke number two. And the marshall is forever eating on the cuff, and each time Nora checks another X on the blackboard already crowded with twentysome X's following the name "Marshall"; and this joke is encored later with a much bigger X. This ilk of comedy does, however, provide contrast.

Of course the implication is that the Law is a buffoon in Shinbone. (Equally: the Law is a "Link" to bring "Appleyards" to Shinbone; but for now Law has many X's against it.) And hence Ransom Stoddard will ransom the Law, while "Stoddard" suggests his stubbornness. In fact, when Link enters Doniphon quips, "Here comes Mr. Law and Order himself!"

Stoddard wants Link to arrest Valance, but the marshall babbles, ". . . Put Liberty Valance in jail . . .?!"

"Somebody better listen to somebody about Liberty Valance!" shouts Nora.

"I'm only the town marshall," whines Link, "and what Liberty [sic] does out on the road ain't no business of mine."

Doniphon takes his leave, but before he does there is a rare moment between him and Hallie. Shot close up, he tells her she's pretty when she's mad; crosscutting to her we see from her reaction that she does love him.

The next sequence, again at night, begins on the street, and things are hopping inside the bar. To a honky-tonk "Golden Slippers" a drunk is bounced out of the saloon and rushes in again. Through his office window we find Dutton Peabody (Edmond O'Brien), editor of "The Shinbone Star." He frightens the marshall on the way to the restaurant, where he lectures Hallie on silverware placement, only to be mocked as superstitious. (The scene relates to the limitations and artifice of the order coming to the West.)

In the kitchen Stoddard is washing dishes. Behind him we can see Hallie through the doorway taking orders. He wants to show her in his lawbook (now *taped* together after Valance's manhandling) that the marshall does have jurisdiction. Her mother pushes them together, and they sit with a lamp between them (a common Fordian suggestion of hope). Hallie with hot embarrassment has admitted she cannot read.

The scene is one of those extraordinarily ingenuous ones that occur occasionally between Ford's men and women (e.g., in *Steamboat Round the*

Bend or *Two Rode Together*). Hallie is simple and modest; reading to her means the Bible. What occurs between them is personal more than physical and in such moments Ford encourages broad playing (though, as we shall see, there is additional reason for their wide-eyed manner). "Do you think I *could*? Do you think I *could* learn to read . . .?" "Why *sure* you can, Hallie!" Ranse's face lights up in a patented James Stewart glow; and the Ann Rutledge melody appears.

And here begins (if it has not begun sooner) a second conflict; Hallie becomes torn between Stoddard and Doniphon, and not simply between them as individuals but between what they seem to represent. While Doniphon might conquer by competence, charm, and simple dominance, Stoddard does so ingenuously by his idealism (and by his *words*): she admires his learning and feels accordingly inferior to him, just as she reacts toward Doniphon's granite strength. Yet at the same time she can mother Stoddard whereas Doniphon poses a sexual threat. The picture's two themes will develop in parallel; as legal order changes, so too will the order between the sexes.

The scene is broken up when Link yells for a second steak and when Doniphon enters with his devoted lackey Pompey. He has brought Hallie a cactus rose plant, which Pompey (in this action symbolizing the blackman's role in American history?) takes out back, plants, and waters. She calls Ranse to admire it.

"Hallie, did you ever see a real rose?" he asks, again unintentionally shaming her.

"No," she replies at last, and then gaining confidence, "but maybe some-day, if they ever dam the river we'll have lots of water, and all kinds of flow-ers!" This motif of making the wilderness bloom recurs at various moments in *Liberty Valance*. And recall the climactic sequence in *Wagon Master* when the Mormons enter their promised land in religious glory, or in *The Grapes of Wrath* when the Okies gaze at California to "Red River Valley," or Mrs. Jorgensen's impassioned speech in *The Searchers*. For Ford the land is a great neutrality waiting for man to come and establish there his order, to give it form. And words play a role in this.

Tom Doniphon has taken a seat with Peabody. The editor is anxious to publicize his engagement to Hallie, but Doniphon holds him back—proba-bly he noticed the vase of flowers on the kitchen shelf where Stoddard keeps his shingle. Liberty Valance and his two dirty henchmen come into the res-taurant, typically bringing violence and chaos; they throw out some diners and arrogate their places.

Ford cuts unabashedly to a reaction shot of Hallie: she turns around and looks scared, and as she does so the camera describes a quick dolly around her and up to a medium close-up of her surprise and alarm. Ford could scarcely have been more obvious in the tricks of his trade, and there are hundreds of similar reaction shots in his pictures. But it fulfills its main purpose here, which is to depict *fear* and to influence the viewer to experi-ence the body of the sequence within an aura of fear. Just a bit later, in the same scene, there is another reaction shot, in which Link suddenly jumps up and scrambles out the door when he learns Valance is present. Here the slapstick contrast produces a laugh (and whether the laugh is with or at the joke makes no difference).

Stoddard backs in with Doniphon's dinner on a tray, and spots Valance's leather whip, the one with which Valance beat him. Ford frames it close-up on the white table. Valance sticks out his foot, tripping Stoddard, who sprawls lengthwise on the floor on top of the food. Valance stands over him, hand on gun, malevolently commanding, "Pick it up, Dude!" Stoddard stares back from the floor, his face masked with fury.

We'll never know what might have happened, for Doniphon, seated at the far end of Stoddard's body, rises: "That was *my* steak, Valance. *You* pick it up!" Valance starts for his gun, but Doniphon indicates Pompey covering him from the kitchen door. Cut to Pompey who cocks his rifle with a menac-ing motion of chin and mouth—typical of Ford, this simple, precise, and deliberate narration.

Stoddard and Valance think Doniphon intervenes from friendship for Stoddard or desire to impress Hallie, but Doniphon seems eager to find any excuse to kill Valance. He says he intervened because of "my steak, pil-grim," but Stoddard probably misses the (probably) unintentional pun: Doniphon has a "stake" in this town, Hallie, and Stoddard doesn't yet.

(Oddly enough, the point is made that *everyone* at the restaurant eats steak, big ones too, but on Ranse's plate, as he tells Hallie about reading, there is no steak: just two slices of bread and some beans.) In any case, as Tom and Liberty stand in tense silence—Ford crosscutting between them—Doniphon with his polished black suit, his white hat and vest, his tie, and his gently mocking smile, is the shining knight, indomitably strong, inviting Valance to die, but always within the etiquette of chivalry. He will not take Valance on principle, only when actually threatened.

But Stoddard, alas, prevents the skirmish. *He* picks up the steak, announcing he does so in the name of common sense and reason (lawyer, order, words); but later, when Doniphon quips, "Thanks for saving my life, pilgrim!" Stoddard's real motives come clear: "That isn't why I did it: *Nobody fights my battles!*"

Valance sneers, knocks over some chairs and people, sweeps a few tables and, thrashing his lackeys, leaves. Outside they throw a bottle through the window, fire some random shots (all duck but Stoddard), and ride violently out of town.

Liberty Valance is rather unique in Ford: a singular example of an absolutely one-dimensional character: pure unadulterated violence and chaos without hint of redeeming feature. But it is not shameful, dramatically, that all his gestures and words are clichés, that he himself is a cliché. This is the point: Liberty Valance types do exist, are clichés, and do respect only force. But evil though he be, within the film's symbolic drama he manifests his violence within society and as such his actions are sacerdotal. For he, as much if not more than anyone else, will be an architect of the future order.

Stoddard has retreated disheartened to the kitchen; Hallie runs to comfort. Doniphon enters, sees he is interrupting, and announces he will be away a few days. Just after he exits Hallie runs to the door, feeling a bit lost, perhaps sensing that their relationship is changing and she is losing something irretrievably. In a beautiful contemplative scene we see her standing outside the back door, lit white midst surrounding blackness, watching, staring out into the distance alone. It is a reprise of a typical Fordian moment. How often before have we seen him evoke this magical nostalgia of someone watching another departing—and always the emphasis is on the person gazing. This haunting blank stare is itself practically a John Ford signature. It is the only exception to the rule that his personages always relate to an object or person; thus the shock when they confront nothingness. His characters stare when someone leaves, when someone dies, when a reality is becoming suddenly memory. But it is usually the stare of a lost soul who can find nothing to look at. Life has meaning because seeing is a moral action.

But Hallie's future is presaged via the dissolve into the next sequence, daytime weeks later: Hallie's image, framed in her doorway saying goodbye to Tom, is momentarily superimposed within *another* doorway: Stoddard's law office.

Her image vanishes as Stoddard pulls a carriage up outside the Shinbone Star. His shingle now hangs beside the door. He is nattily dressed and his self-esteem noticeably higher, and when he praises Peabody's statehood editorial, the editor laps up every word. Hallie tells him class is waiting; she rings the bell for the students.

Stoddard takes the newspaper into a connecting room, where a class of various ages awaits. He rings the bell, calls to order, says hello to a ranch hand (who stutters that he is there because they cut cards and he lost), and stops someone smoking ("None of us smokes here!"). He nods at Hallie and she leads the children through the alphabet song. (There are classes of children in some earlier Fords [e.g., *How Green Was My Valley, Air Mail, Rio Grande*] but the class as an important *theme*—the young being educated— only becomes obsessive in his last movies: here, *Cheyenne Autumn, 7 Women*, and, humorously, *Donovan's Reef*. In each case, education is seen as indoctrination and as a method of imposing repressive order.)

Stoddard sits in front of a blackboard (an Overland Stage Company timetable board) on which are written the words, "Education is the basis of law and order." There is a flag and a picture of George Washington. He reads Peabody's editorial, commenting how statehood will mean safety and schools and development. He asks Pompey, standing beside a picture of Lincoln, to recite the preamble to the Constitution. Pompey starts, "We hold these truths . . ." but stumbles, forgetting "all men are created equal."

— "I knew that, Mr. Ranse, but I just plumb forgot it."
— "That's alright, Pompey. A *lot* of people [*sneer*] forget that part of it."

So here we have more of the words theme, words as a means of indoctrination, as a *force* of order, education as the peculiar American method of fulfilling the dream of an age of idealism.

Words are also Stoddard's means to power, his authority within the society of the town and the weapon he hopes to use against Valance. Note how he rules the classroom by force of ego, how in praising the editor he wins respect for himself and is considered qualified to judge and in some manner superior. There is something slightly pompous in his posture as a teacher, the self-righteousness with which he corrects the smoker, passes over a little girl who always knows the right answer, his condescension toward Pompey. All men may indeed be created equal, but it is rather late for Pompey: he never loses his master/slave attitude; education prejudices everything and gives power into the hands of those who possess it.

The class is broken up when Doniphon comes by to order Pompey back to chores; he brings news of atrocities committed by Valance, whom the anti-statehood cattlemen have hired to terrorize the townsfolk. Peabody hurries to print the news. "Print that and Valance'll kill you," says Doniphon. He advises Hallie to avoid the school for her safety, which infuriates her; he tells her again she's pretty when mad, then exits. And she sees Stoddard *erasing* the words on the blackboard; he repeats in disgust Doniphon's parting words: "When force threatens, talk's no good anymore."

Stoddard leaves Hallie alone in the classroom. She fondles the bell on his desk, sadly, and then walks around the rows of benches fingering the books lovingly. The Ann Rutledge melody again appears, recalling the linkage between hope and learning (in *Young Mr. Lincoln*, too) and manifesting her love for Ransom. (There were, to this effect, some telling scenes of her earlier, as she gazed up at him during class.)

Then from the window she sees Stoddard riding out of town and learns in horror he has been practicing shooting in case of another encounter with Valance. She runs to the porch, the camera subjectively pans right with her as she looks out and off (into outer space, it seems) and calls desperately, "Tom, Tom Doniphon . . . !!!" As she calls, the camera juts up a fraction.

The shots, almost the words, it seems, are suspended through a long dissolve into the next scene, of Stoddard's buckboard speeding along in the country being overtaken by Doniphon on horseback. It is a typical Ford ellipsis, the dissolve suggesting cause and effect, or, "And so it came to pass that Tom Doniphon went galloping after Ransom. . . ." You never see her asking Tom, just the result.

They go to Doniphon's ranch, where Stoddard denies he is after Hallie and fails to hit a tin can. Confronted with Doniphon's authority and out of his own element (the town) he seems as incompetent as Pompey in class. Every time he steps out of shelter he gets into trouble. Now Doniphon, demonstrating as warning how well a gun can be handled, shoots three paint cans, splattering Stoddard. Pompey laughs: Doniphon's honor is his. But Stoddard charges diagonally across the distance up to Doniphon and swings a colossal rounded punch, following through. The follow-through gives a slight pause to the shot before the cut to Doniphon falling back: a well-timed cutting effect. As Stoddard, furious still, climbs onto his buckboard, good-natured Doniphon pitches him his gun; usually he calls him "Pilgrim," now it's "Gunslinger."

The townspeople gather in the saloon to choose two representatives for the Capital City statehood convention. Outside, two officials check off those who enter. Pompey leans against a porch-pole, rifle across his lap, hat on his knee, eyes half closed.

Pompey recalls Stepin Fetchit's character in *The Sun Shines Bright*. During production, when Ford asked Stewart what he thought of Woody Strode's costume, Stewart replied it seemed a bit like Uncle Remus. "And what's wrong with Uncle Remus? I put that costume together—that's just what I *intended!*" Ford called some people over, continuing, "One of the players seems to have some objection! One of the players here doesn't seem to *like* Uncle Remus! As a matter of fact, I'm not at all sure he even likes Negroes!"[16]

Peter Ericson and his wife arrive and he proudly exhibits his citizenship papers. Such naiveté was considered dated in 1962, but here, as in a comparable instance in *Donovan's Reef,* Ford employs Ericson's ingenuous pride as part of the film's nostalgia, part not only of the lost idealism of the age but also of the knowledge that there is some reason for lessened pride in American citizenship today.

A wino in coonskin, Kentuck (Shug Fisher), comes along and the judges make him leave his jug outside. The character is a homage to the dead Francis Ford's coonskin type. But Francis, unlike Kentuck, never had to leave his jug outside; he even had it in the jurybox in *Young Mr. Lincoln.* How times have changed!

Inside it is Tom Doniphon who grabs the mallet, pushes people to seats, enforces the bar's closing ("This is a democracy, isn't it?"—again the ambiguity of liberty and law) and pushes Stoddard into chairing the meeting. "We want statehood," proclaims Ranse, "because statehood means the protection of our farms and our fences, and it means schools for our children and it means progress for the future."

The nominations follow. Stoddard puts up Tom's name. Ford cuts to a general shot placing Stoddard in posture as chairman, the theatrical distancing (Stoddard seems upon a stage) suggesting historical nostalgia and underlining the import of Doniphon's refusal: "'Cause I got other plans, personal plans." This is Doniphon's curious nature; he provides the muscle to get things done and yet stubbornly declines responsibility. While this suggests democracy's tragedy, that those who are strong and good are often reluctant to assume duty, it is Doniphon's adhesion to his concept of personal freedom that makes him act as he does. His world and Stoddard's are mutually exclusive and belong to different ages. Stoddard is from the East, Doniphon probably from Texas. The triumph of one will entail the eclipse of the other, just as only one of them will get Hallie. Doniphon's glory, and that of his order, is that he will continually bring about destruction of himself and his order by remaining true to his notions of chivalry: for he must defend those who are against force, those who are loved by those he loves.

So he seconds nomination of Stoddard ("Not only because he knows the law, but because he throws a good punch") and of course Stoddard accepts. Dutton Peabody also accepts, after a drunken oration about how the press (like the knight?) should stand apart from politics.

Meanwhile Valance and henchmen enter, strewing chaos, and he tries to force his own election as delegate. (Pompey again appears to contain Valance; when he clicks his gun the marshall jumps.) Note the symbolic evocation of Valance spotlit (like Jack Palance in Godard's *Contempt*) against the wall brandishing his whip high over the heads of the voting assembly. He loses, Doniphon laughs, and Valance challenges Stoddard either to get out of town by nightfall or else to meet him on the street with a gun. Then he stalks out, throwing a chair.

The meeting adjourned, everyone rushes madly to the bar. The band plays "Ring, Ring the Banjo." Again Ford punctuates with humor. Stoddard hears

Doniphon's advice (to leave), then walks out, through the swinging doors. This shot is held some time and is carefully composed. Doniphon in the foreground gazes after Stoddard down the screen's diagonal, toward the swinging door (through which we can see Valance ride by). The scene is held long because it will be paralleled later when Doniphon stands outside swinging doors watching Stoddard walk back into the convention for the nomination (and Hallie). For us the second scene underlines the import of the first, not simply as intimation of fate, but as a decisive moment in Doniphon's tragedy.

That night Peabody is in his office, drunk as usual. (It is curious that this word man is always intoxicated. We are intended to infer that words are untrustworthy: Peabody is as intoxicated by words as by liquor and it may justly be asked who is the master, Peabody or liquor, Peabody or words. And we shall see that words do eventually dominate those who use them. As order dominates liberty.)

Peabody notices he has misspelled a headline ("Liberty Valance Defeeted")—surely an omen of coming disaster, this breakdown of words! (Significantly the paper has no date or place name: had Rossellini made this picture he might have titled it *America Year Zero*.) Discovering his jug is dry (that too!), he quips, "What's this? No courage left? Well, courage can be purchased at yonder tavern!" Music (*My Darling Clementine*'s sombrero song) comes from a Mexican bar next door and as Peabody extinguishes his lamp to the accompaniment of this yearning music, he says—and the words are suspended meaningfully—"Go West, old man, and grow *young* with the country!" Peabody is rather old for that pilgrimage.

Meanwhile in the kitchen Pompey and Peter urge Ranse to leave, and he quarrels with Hallie about meeting Valance, in the midst of which he corrects her grammar (surely his character!) and she retorts in fury, "'Isn't,' 'ain't'—what difference does it make?" So again, words are questioned.

Peabody wobbles back to his office, quoting *Henry V*'s Crispin's Day speech, and, illuminating his lamp, he finds Liberty Valance in the shadows with the offending headline. "What have we here," Peabody jokes, "Liberty Valance and his Myrmidons? Liberty Valance taking liberties with the liberty of the press?" Rather than fearful, Peabody derives joy from his pun, as though he were a martyr and the puns a cherished crucifix. Valance beats hell out of him and tears up the printshop, spilling typeblocks all over the floor (the enemy of words). His henchman, giggling fiendishly, vividly experiences something resembling a sadistic orgasm; once again Ford concentrates on the one who *does* violence. Peabody is left with his paper planted on his face; the lamp is thrown through the window (the symbol of hope crashing through the *word* "STAR") and Stoddard's shingle is half shot down: the sign is split, the words "Attorney at Law" drop, the name "Ransom Stoddard" remains hanging.

Hallie sends Pompey for Doniphon. Stoddard, finding Peabody, sends Link to tell Valance (winning at poker in the bar—but with a "dead man's hand") he is waiting outside with a gun. "You all heard it," says Liberty, "A clear-cut case of self-defense!" He quaffs whiskey and crashes his glass on the bar; the scene cuts from *clash* to the *click* of Stoddard's gun, as he cocks it in medium shot. (This familiar technique, often used obviously, is here nearly "invisible," since our attention is concentrated on the characters.)

Stoddard, who earlier said he did not want a gun but just wanted to put Valance in jail, is confronted by his half-destroyed shingle. The shingle is first shown close up at an epic angle, and is then crosscut with Stoddard looking at it. Shall he be true to his concepts of law or shall he take the law into his own hands? Note that Ford *shows* this. Stoddard tears down his sign, his name, throws it to the ground, and walks off, leaving us looking briefly at the broken sign.

The camera tracks in front of him, as he roves around and encounters two farmers, one of whom stutters, comically. This bit of humor is subtly conveyed midst mounting intensity; the further breakdown in words is not underlined and the pun that the valence of liberty is coming right now is scarcely perceptible.

(Though I have been at pains to indicate symbolic progressions, Ford never permits his symbology to intrude, and an analysis such as this one risks obscuring that a movie is meaningful chiefly because of the humanness of the gestures and speeches of the actors. That an audience may be oblivious to deeper ambiguities or to this picture's real subject, that some would even dismiss it as a "yeoman-like western" [Judith Crist] is a tribute to Ford's skill as an entertainer. An audience will feel these many subtleties even if failing to understand them consciously. It is, I think, only the cavalier fashion in which Americans view westerns and segregate art and entertainment that hinders deeper appreciation, except when, in cases like *High Noon*, the pretense is inescapable.)

So at last Stoddard and Valance confront each other. Valance, drunk, plays with Stoddard, calls him "Professor," "Dude," and shoots a wine jug hanging on the wall, splattering Ranse as Doniphon did earlier. Finally, in long shot, they fire at the same time. Valance drops and sprawls into a spot-

light on the street (the livery stable light). Ford cuts back and, in a beautifully evocative use of contrapuntal motion, has Stoddard, holding his
wounded arm, stumble off toward the left as people rush in (in the opposite
direction) in the background, and horses rush by, all converging round Valance's body spotlit at rear: "It's Liberty! Liberty's dead!"—a scene of historical transition, fraught with motion (i.e., passage, the parade).

The camera crosscuts to Stoddard walking up the step to the restaurant
and Hallie. Back where Valance lies dead: Ford goes immediately to comedy. Doc Willoughby shouts, "Whiskey! Quick!" A bottle is handed him, he
takes a snort, kicks over Valance, exclaims, "Dead," and walks off.

In the kitchen Hallie once again kneels before Ranse binding his
wounds. Again the Ann Rutledge melody recurs. "I feel so guilty," Hallie
sobs. "I didn't want you to run away, I wanted you to stay." At the sound of
the door opening they both look up, worried. Doniphon enters on the side,
the gladiator music melancholic now; he apologizes to Hallie that he came
too late to help, then, seeing he is an intruder, he leaves.

Outside the camera pans 45 degrees to the right in extreme long shot,
following Doniphon and Pompey. Meanwhile a cart carrying Valance's body,
his legs dangling from the rear, is driven in from the right, moving opposite
Doniphon's direction. When it reaches screen-center the camera, having
finished its pan to the right, moves back leftward with the cart, following it
off and down the street. Gay music comes from the saloon, some Mexicans
pass singing and strumming guitars, and someone throws Valance's hat onto
the wagon. Again Ford matches music and contrapuntal motion evocatively.
And note, of course, that Valance and Doniphon exit simultaneously.

But first Tom stomps into the bar, in a terrible state of mind. "Come on
home, Mars' Tom," begs Pompey, but Doniphon gulps whiskey. One of Valance's men shouts for a lynch mob to hang Stoddard, and Doniphon throws
him out of the saloon, the camera swaying to echo his fury. The second bad
man faces up to him, inches apart. Cut to a close-up of the bad man's face,
then an abrupt swift drop down to his gunbelt as he grabs his gun from its
holster, then a rapid cut to a medium shot, as Doniphon *kicks* the gun out of
his hand. He hands the vermin over to Link (who now, ridiculously, brags of
his prowess) and, shouting at the band to continue and throwing them coins
and pushing Link out of his way and into a window (which breaks), he dis-
gustedly stalks out.

Reaching his ranch, he stumbles into the room for Hallie, splatters whiskey around, throws a lantern into it, and crumples into a corner as flames
erupt everywhere. Pompey drags him into a buckboard (like Valance).

Cut to a "WELCOME" banner on the woodframe convention hall in
Capital City.* Bands play, parades pass. (Cutting from day to night, to here

---

*Ford has been quoted to the effect that *Liberty Valance*, like *Fort Apache*, is based on "an
historic fact" (*Positif* 82, March 1967, p. 17). Just which historic fact is unrevealed. A letter in
the *Village Voice* (quoted by Sarris, *The John Ford Movie Mystery* [Bloomington: Indiana Uni-

from Doniphon's burning house, amounts to a moral-historical statement: destruction of the old order gives birth to the new.) Ranse and Peabody (bandaged) walk to the door, Stoddard loitering to gaze like a kid at the parade, until an official extends a hand in enthusiasm: "Well, now, I sure do want to shake the hand of the man who shot Liberty Valance!" which instantly destroys Ranse's poise. He is clearly feeling qualms of conscience.

The convention scenes seem to drag on forever, perhaps because Ford dislikes politicians; certainly these satiric festivities are the picture's weakest minutes. After the cattlemen's tempest Peabody nominates Stoddard as a champion of law and order. When the rival orator (John Carradine) replies that Stoddard's sole qualification is that he killed a man, a tumult breaks out and Stoddard ducks away.

Meanwhile Tom Doniphon has slunk into the hall, dirty, unshaven, disheveled. As Stoddard goes out the door Tom throws away his cigarette, John Wayne fashion, and follows him into a coatroom.

— "Pilgrim, where're you going?"
— "I'm going home, Tom. I'm going back East where I belong."
— "What is it now, Pilgrim? Your conscience?
— "Isn't it enough to kill a man, without trying to build a life on it?"

But Doniphon tells him he didn't kill Valance, and as Stoddard gawks, he lights a cigarette and, blowing smoke into the camera, says, "Think back . . ." and the smoke accompanies a dissolve into a flashback: Stoddard and Valance on the street, but this time from an alley perpendicular to the street where they stand. Pompey throws Doniphon his rifle and he fires as they do, dropping Valance. The geometric setup concentrates two vectors of order on Valance as the valence between them. Neither Stoddard nor Doniphon can any longer tolerate Liberty; but Valance's vector is aimed only at Stoddard, for he could exist with Doniphon. The flashback not only corrects Stoddard's notion of who killed Valance; it corrects a geometry that was incorrect in terms of the allegory. Of course both Ranse and Tom compromise their principles: Stoddard by resorting to gun-force and taking the law into his own hands (Valance was technically correct calling his part self-defense), Doniphon by violating chivalry. "Cold-blooded murder. But I can live with it. Hallie's happy. She wanted you alive . . . Hallie's your girl now. Go on back in there and take that nomination. You taught her to read and write, now give her something to read and write about."

It is at this point that themes and symbols reach their penultimate collision. The players have all along acted not from choice but from dictates of their philosophies. Ultimately they are controlled by these philosophies. As representatives of two different orders of society they could be said to repre-

---

versity Press, 1976, p. 179]) from James D. Vizzini states that the "picket wire" referred to in the film is a cowboy bastardization of the Purgatoire River in southeast Colorado.

sent a Fordian philosophy of history. But it is not so simple. Fate, or the unperceived forces of society, plays the game it will, but plays it with human agents, persons who to some extent (what?) exercise free will. It is this free will that will alter the nature of fate somewhat, even if it cannot change its course.

Had fate had its way (if one may use such a phrase), Stoddard might eventually have prosecuted Valance or Doniphon killed him fairly. Instead Stoddard tries to kill Valance because of abhorrence of Valance's deeds (i.e., devotion to order even above the law) and, the major reason, because Valance has challenged Stoddard at his most sensitive point, his vanity. So here we might say that the "valence" lies in the imperfection of mankind. It is Stoddard's pride that causes him to break the law to establish order, his tragic flaw that will corrupt liberty so that the triumph of order will also be a loss of idealism. Thus Stoddard is the man who shot Liberty Valance.

Doniphon's case is a more legitimate double bind. He could have allowed Stoddard to die and thus obtained Hallie. But his knight-and-lady attitude forces him to follow her wishes and to protect Ranse without showing Ranse up (as he did earlier in the restaurant). To do so entails dishonoring himself. No matter what he does he loses Hallie. See how strangely fate closes in on him, how the forces of history converge upon him and erase him. Heroically he chooses the "love-death" alternative. With him one order of liberty dies and another is born, one less free in the absolute sense. For liberty entails disorder. Thus the ironic truth to the shout, "Liberty's dead!" Valance, as long as he lived, represented a potential for either order to succeed. His perpetuation in the world represented an alternative between liberty and order. Thus Doniphon is the man who destroyed (shot) the valence.

One might equally say freedom destroys itself through its abuse. Valance brought about his own destruction, as did Doniphon. Order is a necessity, not just from the viewpoint of those humans who wish it but from the nature of this philosophy of history: all elements move toward cohesion. Thus free will was, perhaps, irrelevant.

Must a government that seeks order through law (words) employ guns? In fact, just before the critical shooting, words, threatened by force, had been failing all over the place. And this occurred not by fate but by human agency, by free will. If order entails a loss of liberty it is because of the imperfection, the sin, of man. Liberals may be more coercive than those who simply use guns. Education is the basis of law and order, and also a tool of totalitarianism.

Words are a higher form of social order than force, for they can only exist where force is not present: they require civilization. The triumph of words appears inevitable, fate will take care of that. But the opportunity still exists for man to corrupt their meaning.

Stoddard's triumph, however, is ironic. He will go on to a glorious political career on the strength of words, the publicity that his vanity has won him, that he is "the man who shot Liberty Valance," words that in the sense intended, are in fact *not true*. But no matter. Stoddard has made himself the tool of words; and in place of his apron gets a spiffy suit.

Doniphon, through the "letter" of the law, has absolved Stoddard of conscience pangs just enough for his ambition to trample his scruples. Here Stoddard exercises free will: he lies. He scoots back into the convention hall and goes on to fame and power on the strength of a lie; goes on too to get Hallie, thus robbing Tom.

She, it appears, is true to her hero-worshipping and inferior-feeling nature, and chooses the "braver warrior" and the higher star. She can in addition relate ideally to Stoddard, while to Doniphon her relationship would have been more primitive. She is always mothering Ranse, tending his wounds; she is sexually awed by Doniphon, and dependent on his strength. She may not have had a choice, however, for Doniphon, his pride lost, has given her up. And so again the nature of society changes and something is lost. The woman chooses security over passion, law over nobility.

Had Stoddard not chosen to go after Valance, had he not broken his own codes, he would not have forced Doniphon to intervene, he could not have forced Doniphon to compromise himself, and he would not have gotten Hallie by default.

And so, when Stoddard returns in old age to Shinbone, he must in some sense come as the murderer of Tom Doniphon, but he does not yet appear to realize this. Hallie, on the other hand, does recognize responsibility for the destruction of a man who loved her. We do not know when Ranse told her Doniphon shot Valance (for she seems to know). But she did not rush to

Doniphon in his moment of need as she did to Stoddard, and it is implied she has not seen him since. Ironically, it was Doniphon who had the more basic need for her; it is hardly imaginable that Stoddard's ambition would have been affected had he not gotten Hallie.

Thus when they arrive in Shinbone at the beginning of the picture, it is Hallie who wears the Fordian stare, looking inward, silent and grave. Stoddard in contrast is his garrulous political self, goes off to talk politics with the reporters, and seems disturbed by his life (that is, seems anxious to prove he did *not* kill a man, even though, by establishing his innocence of possible murder, he establishes his guilt of fraud), rather than conscious of the relationship between Hallie and Tom.

"Shinbone" is so called because it is where liberty stumbled (and even suggests a biblical "rib bone," Adam's sin for Eve). And it stumbled through Ransom's egomania—his "stoddard," his persistence ("a persistent cuss" is what Tom calls him). His stubbornness ransoms order (himself) in exchange for liberty (Tom). Similarly, he has ransomed Tom's love for Hallie. But in contrast to whatever one may read into Stoddard's name, Tom Doniphon is just plain Tom Doniphon. Yet, true to his myth, the Fordian hero, attempting to mediate between order and chaos, has intervened for higher good; and now, having united the lovers and sealed his own celibacy, he goes off alone.

When Stoddard goes back into the convention hall the saloon-type doors continue to swing open and shut for a long time afterward as Doniphon, throwing off a cigarette again, watches Stoddard and then exits, plainly, without fanfare. But standing there he is ironically juxtaposed with big campaign posters, "Vote territory and the open range." It is obvious some preternatural Fordian hand keeps these doors swinging long after they ought to have stopped, but it does not matter: the device underlines the actual significance of the scene: like a stop-motion film, the continual interruption of our seeing what is happening inside the room beyond the doors (just people jumping up and down and making noise) with Doniphon's quiet departure outside increases our feeling that time is passing, that something is happening. And this, after all, is the point.

At long last the scene dissolves back into the "present." Senator Stoddard finishes his story, sitting guiltily outside the room where Doniphon lies bootless and gunless and spurless in his coffin, sitting beside the stagecoach that started it all.

It is immediately obvious that things are, literally, much brighter in the present: we're back into the brighter and more contrasty style of photography and decor, back into a style of acting in which the players seem more vital and stylized. Or rather, into a style of behavior more "educated": the characters in the flashback seemed more physical, their movements more rounded, their consciousnesses more vegetable. Now people act as though they are not limited to the town, they project their personalities more forcibly, they think more intellectually, they move more angularly, more self-consciously.

It is noteworthy too that in all the flashback little occurs that Stoddard himself has not witnessed. Some of the few exceptions are events he could well have imagined: Hallie alone in the schoolroom; Valance in the bar and what Doniphon did after the shooting. Only one shot, that of Hallie outside the kitchen watching Doniphon ride away, strikes one as being beyond Stoddard's narration. It is not, in any case, necessary that Ford have followed slavishly the point of view of Stoddard as narrator; it is sufficient that his point of view be constantly suggested, that the "surface" reflect his limits while the "underneath" express (Ford's) deeper reality.

And, in fact, the flashback is pretty consistently distorted by Stoddard's subjective memory. Hallie, interestingly, is never seen alone with Tom. To the contrary, we have noted a definite ellipsis of such a moment before the shooting lesson. Doniphon's appearances are always handled matter-of-factly. In the key scene in which Doniphon presents a cactus rose plant to Hallie (the importance of which will be clear momentarily) no dramatic or rhetorical emphasis whatsoever is placed upon Doniphon's role: it is just something that happened in between things more important to Stoddard. In fact one has to look hard and deeply at the scenes in which Hallie and Tom are both present to detect a rapport between them. On the other hand, the moments in the flashback that are most alive and intense and on which the greatest amounts of poetry and music are expended are those involving Ranse and Hallie.

Each of the characters of the various personages is colored toward Stoddard's bias: Valance is irredeemably despicable, utterly outside the protection of the law, totally evil incarnate—Stoddard seems less troubled that he killed a man than that he broke the letter of the law; Peabody is lovable but a lesser and foolish rival in the game of words; Pompey despite his heroic side has a slave mentality; Link is a buffoon; everyone looks up to Ranse. Tom Doniphon is relatively incomprehensible, almost a blank mask (superficially), and in his scenes with Hallie wooden, cavalier, seemingly uncaring, even awkward; he is overbearing toward Pompey and ambivalent toward

Stoddard. Hallie is always radiant, soft, and kind, always looking up at Ranse (recall the high-angle shots down at her in the classroom), always looking up to him to form her, but not particularly erotic. The camera generally takes a position proximate to Stoddard's point of view. Recall, for example, the concentration of the face of Valance whipping him.

In the modern sequences, however, we immediately see that Hallie is more independent and more Stoddard's equal. Link is not a buffoon. Pompey is meeker and more subservient, older; and Stoddard is more condescending toward him: when he leaves Pompey in the coffin room, he will squeeze money into his hand, and when Pompey tries to decline it, Stoddard will mumble, "Porkchop money, Pompey"—patting his hand professionally. And, in fact, the sun does shine occasionally in Shinbone.

Ransom Stoddard himself now seems even more pompous and even more a caricature of a politician than he was during the flashback, where, as painstakingly shown, these qualities in him were always hinted at: his was a passage from "Pilgrim" (as Tom saw him) to "Dude" (Valance's truer estimate!). To his credit Stoddard recognizes his failing, if not its full dimension. But his tragic realization and comeuppance are approaching.

Meanwhile, the editor concludes Stoddard's history: "Three terms as governor, two terms in the Senate, Ambassador to the Court of St. James, back again to the Senate, and a man who with a snap of his fingers could be the next vice-president of the United States!"

— "Well, you're not going to use the story, Mr. Scott?"
— "No sir! This is the West, sir. When the legend becomes fact, print the legend."

So it is too late. Stoddard cannot change his lie now. The consequences of his action cannot be undone, nor the falsity of his fame. Words and time have conquered. And thus, more basically, the newspaperman is correct (though we are free to disagree): the real truth is that which has become fact and the legend has indeed become fact. The historical truth is merely a footnote, and, need it be said, this is the problem. Every student of history (and Ford was one) must continually marvel at the disparity between historical fact and tradition. People prefer fantasy and, often, they need it.

A similar point was made by Ford in *Fort Apache* (q.v.), yet in both pictures, though he says he agrees with the notion of printing the legend, he himself "prints" both the facts and the legend. He would maintain that the ideals that form society are more important than the functionaries of society.

Ranse now turns and goes toward the door to the room with the coffin. As he opens the door the camera shoots from the point of view of Hallie, sitting still on the bench against the wall, opposite the door. The camera gazes at a low level across the length of the casket (whose side is in the bottom foreground of the shot: thus definitely Hallie's seated point of view) and up at a gentle angle to show Stoddard at the door. Prominently sitting on the closed casket is a cactus rose plant (like the one Doniphon gave to Hallie years before: it is this that she carried back in a hatbox from the charred, wilderness-overrun ruins of Doniphon's ranch). It dominates the scene, but subtly (like all Ford's symbols) because it is naturally Stoddard who draws our attention and because the prior references to the plant have all been *sotto voce*.* Stoddard notices the rose plant but acts as though he does not see it. The crosscut now shows the room with Hallie sitting on the bench, the camera gazing down at her from Stoddard's point of view, with him in the foreground. She rises and walks toward the camera and out of the room with Stoddard, the camera following her around so that it now looks over the casket toward the door. She exits first, followed by Stoddard, but he looks back again, frowning, at the cactus rose, then closes the door. But the camera stays, moves up closer to the cactus rose and holds that frame. (One recalls this as the stylistic reply to a matching dolly-up to Stoddard when he entered the coffin room at the beginning of the movie.)

This peculiar gesture has several facets. The camera dollies in not simply to draw our attention to the plant, but rather as a (typically deliberative) narrative device. By means of this emphasis Ford tells us something about the plant. Naturally we sense its importance, but without fully divining its meaning. Secondly, the sustained image suggests that, as is the case, both Hallie's and Stoddard's thoughts remain on this rose plant after they leave the room.

The close-up of the cactus rose dissolves into the final sequence, a medium shot of Hallie and Ranse seated alone in a railroad car, the countryside passing by in the window to the right, Hallie beside it, Stoddard on the left. Their eyes and expressions are clearly displayed. Now Stoddard too wears the Fordian stare, along with his wife, but with *The Man Who Shot Liberty Valance* the stare has changed from a stare outward to a stare inward.**

---

*If proof be needed of subtleness: when the picture was nationally telecast some years ago on NBC only one cut was made: the scene in which Doniphon gives Hallie the cactus rose plant! This of course makes nonsense of its role.

**A similar transition from outward to inward stare occurs in *The Wings of Eagles* (1957) with Spig Wead and his mirror. Cf. Huw in *How Green Was My Valley*.

Something appears changed in his manner, he is more sober and austere. They are both deep in meditation, a great silence reigns, broken only by the clatter of the train wheels. When they speak, their words are soft, heavy, and careful, the rhythms flat, the expression repressed.

— "Hallie, Hallie, would you be too sorry if once I get the new irrigation bill through, would you be too sorry if we just up and left Washington? 'Cause I, I sort of have a hankering to come back here to live, maybe open up a law office."

(Note the terseness of the following dialogue:)

— "Ranse, if you knew how often I dreamed of it. [*Pause*] My roots are here. [*Short pause*] I guess my heart is here. [*Long pause: her eyes, but not her head, turn slightly toward the window*] Yes let's come back. Look at it. [*Short pause*] It was once a wilderness, now it's a garden. Aren't you proud?"

There is a long pause. Stoddard does not reply and Hallie does not change her gaze. He just sits there without moving a muscle and you know that he is not feeling proud now. Finally he replies,

— "Hallie, who put the cactus roses on Tom's coffin?"
— "I did."

The camera holds the shot a few moments, holding her voice suspended over the scene.

The camera cuts back to a higher fuller shot, as the conductor comes by, interrupting and getting an ashtray for Stoddard. He tells the senator that "these tracks lead straight to Washington" (once again Stoddard is going contrary to his intentions) and that he has wired ahead to clear the road, so that they may go as quickly as possible.

Stoddard, a big cigar in one hand and a match in the other, bows his head pompously, back in his politician character now, and says, "Thank you, Jason, thank you, and I'm going to write a letter to the officials of this railroad and thank them for their kindness and for going to all this trouble."

"You think nothing of it! Nothing's too good for the man who shot Liberty Valance!" replies the conductor as Stoddard strikes his match and brings it toward the cigar in his mouth while the conductor is walking off. The camera dollies in closer to Stoddard.

Hallie has reacted just a bit to this remark, but she returns to her poise immediately and sits motionless. But Stoddard stops his match in midflight to his cigar, holds the cigar just out of his mouth, his mouth slightly open, frozen for a moment by the conductor's words, then weakly blows out the match and lowers the cigar. There is no escape. The camera holds the scene for a long time.

It is clear, then, that while the long caesura of the flashback was necessary for Stoddard, the talker, to exercise his duty toward Doniphon, it was not necessary for Hallie. For her the cactus rose represents Tom Doniphon and represents as well hope for the future, hope perhaps that held a dream finer than the one fulfilled. Of course it is age looking back upon the dreams of its youth, but one might suggest too that perhaps Ranse has not lived up to her expectations.

And for Stoddard the cactus rose seems to have awakened him to an aspect of Hallie—her love for Doniphon—that he had not before recognized (judging by his narrative), and perhaps, too, to an aspect of himself.

For them both it is an acknowledgment that something beautiful and natural to those rugged days of youth, that something and someone have died, that a better dream existed. We see death written all over the modern sequences, though nowhere more deeply than on the faces of Ransom and Hallie at this moment. We see not only their age (contrasted to the "garden" that has bloomed), but we see that the world is passing them by—but not only going by outside their window, and not only in the transformation of the wilderness (their world) into a garden. Their true death is that, despite the garden, they have ultimately failed, each of them, in deep personal ways. It was a failure they shared, and like some Adam and Eve they have sacrificed their innocence and idealism for something less than their idealism.

The close-up of the cactus rose was sustained in order that it might balance, might hang suspended, over the conversation between Hallie and Ranse on the train—thus the dissolve between the shots. The result of the combination of the two shots suggests that, beyond being a tribute to an old

love, the plant sums up thematic threads: the duality of order and liberty, the better dream, the loss of innocence, youth, perfection, beauty, the loss of a wilderness for a garden, of the physical for the verbal, the loss of what Tom would have given Hallie and which Stoddard has not. And then it is Tom who deserves the symbol of fruition.

The shot of Stoddard and Hallie cuts to the last composition of the film. It is a sort of crosscut, an answer, to the shot on the train, and comes just after the train whistle begins to blow. At a low angle, but on a rise, the camera gazes over stalks of wheat and takes in an immense plain. The train is heading upscreen, the tracks wending across the screen, near the bottom, from left to right and then vertically up the right side. The train, the railroad that has changed the West, is billowing smoke and blowing its whistle. On the soundtrack is the Ann Rutledge theme.

It is the final triumph of fate: things go on: passage. Whatever may happen to Ranse or Hallie or Tom, whatever happens in life or history, the parade goes on. Our sadness remains with us.

Donovan's Reef (1963). The South Pacific island Haleakaloha is, like many Fordian societies, cut off from the world but equally a nexus (and uniquely a resolution) of everything the outside world offers. It is a polyglot society, with strata, an apparent paradise, like Innisfree, but overflowing with flaws ("busted things"), a portrait of imperialism, racism, and hypocrisy. But *Donovan's Reef* never ceases being a comedy; its characters are unfashionably middle-aged and banal, and Haleakaloha's dark side is whimsically reduced to symbol.

Its theology is pantheistic: everything is god. The universe is alive. Animation and moral force belong not only to people, their institutions and communities, but also to weather, to land and sea, to flowers and music, to machines, to pictures, to colors. Every prop has its personality, its influence—particularly the portrait of the island's dead princess, Manulani. As in *Liberty Valance,* there seems a certain ordering principle at work in the world—especially in Manulani's Haleakaloha—which ultimately exerts control over our lives. Slight events partake of epiphany; accord is inevitable; meanwhile, *Donovan's Reef* unravels like necessary ritual. Mythicizing lighting transforms all—emphasizing depth, extending shadows, endowing persons (and occasionally a prop) with consecrating illumination while darkening surroundings, so that actions assume sacerdotal significance. *Donovan's Reef* is close to a cinematic experience of pure form (particularly its last third), moving stubbornly twixt chaos and (repressive) order toward harmony, inexhaustibly gifted with visual beauty (dynamic form). Idealistic and artificial, *Donovan's Reef* is a love affair with a best of all possible worlds. When a flaw is created in "paradise," by the introduction of racism into the family core, these gods become reproving: broken music, slot ma-

chines, leaky roofs, thunder and lightning, pratfalls. But the gods are benign, and everyone is equipped with an umbrella—quite a contrast to the
way things turned out in *The Hurricane*. The gods are righteous, but tolerant, and their order transcends the optimism of *Wagon Master*, the pessimistic optimism of *The Sun Shines Bright*. The bestial in man, so worrisome in
Mogambo, is now a variant no more condemnable than a lightning storm as a
variant of weather. Even Liberty Valance (i.e., Lee Marvin) ends up happily
married, settled, and playing with a toy train, whose intrusion he formerly
opposed. The off-duty law, the anarchy and violence that in *The Man Who
Shot Liberty Valance* were intolerable are in *Donovan's Reef* not only tolerable, but condoned and rewarded. Implacable, historical fatalism has
changed to cozy, animistic predestination.

    Donovan's Reef is of the suitelike, operatic Ford. But what was once ex-
pressionism has evolved into a purer sort of classicism (the shot, for example, of the native blowing into a seashell—a homage to Murnau's *Tabu*). The
structure is generally tripartite, not only in sequencing, and in the fluid
fashion many sequences divide themselves into three scenes, but within
each scene, montage and gesture describe a rhythm that, balancing two
alternatives, moves toward a third state of accord (i.e., a "pax"—a peace).

    Much as *The Sun Shines Bright* began with a riverboat and *Liberty Val-
ance* with a train, *Donovan's Reef* begins with a merchant ship at sea—a
closed society's link with the world. Gilhooley (Lee Marvin), shanghaied,

Figure 10. *Donovan's Reef*

ACT I.   1.i.   At sea: Gilhooley jumps ship.
           ii.   Island riverbank: Dr. Dedham's goodbye to kids and Donovan in canoe; DeLage dictates transfer request; DeLage greets kids and Donovan, sees Gilhooley coming; Donovan leaves.
          iii. Gilhooley greeted on shore; converses; DeLage.
        2.i.   Donovan leaves kids at their home.
           ii.   Gilhooley enters saloon; Donovan coming.
          iii. Gilhooley and Donovan (fight); Dedham.
        3.i.   Boston: conference.
           ii.   Donovan et al. confer in saloon about Amelia coming.
          iii. They interrupt piano lesson; tell Lelani of deception play; she runs to her bed.
    (Interlude) Moving parade.

ACT II.   1.i.   Amelia greeted; she and boat captain; Donovan helps her into canoe; on shore she meets Gilhooley.
           ii.   She has her picture taken outside saloon.
          iii. At her father's house, she sees Manulani's portrait.
          iv. Rain that night; priest in chapel.
           v.   Amelia awakened by storm and open doors, finds Luki and Donovan.
        2.i.   Next morning: DeLage lends Amelia his car and Eu.
           ii.   Saloon: Cluzeot and Gilhooley and jukebox; Amelia asks Donovan for boat, makes pax; jukebox; she visits terrace; and meets kids and Cluzeot.
          iii. General store: she meets Lafleur and buys swimsuit.
          iv. Water skiing with Donovan; pax.
        3.i.   Later: cutting Christmas tree in mountains; Manulani.
           ii.   On return, Donovan leaves kids at saloon; Manulani.
          iii. That night: Eu sees Donovan and Amelia canoeing;
          iv. and, during Lafleur song at saloon, plots with DeLage.
           v.   After love scene with Amelia, Donovan throws Lafleur out of his bed.
        4.i.   Later: Donovan and Gilhooley signal Dedham from lighthouse about Amelia.
           ii.   Dedham lands and meets Amelia.
          iii. At home, she displays Christmas tree and its lights.
          iv. Long talk over tea is interrupted by hospital call.
         5.   Christmas Eve service.

ACT III. 1.i.   Sunrise and Cluzeot; Amelia sees servants honoring Manulani; bicycles to hospital; questions Cluzeot at cemetery: Manulani.
           ii.   Luncheon with DeLage.
          iii. Christmas saloon fight; Cluzeot and jukebox miracle.
          iv. Pageant honoring Queen Lelani: Amelia discovers all.
           v.   She brings presents to saloon, fights with Donovan.
        2.i.   Later: Cluzeot fixing chapel roof.
           ii.   Amelia escorted to pier for departure.
          iii. But she returns to fight and pax with Donovan.
    (Coda) Moving parade.

clubs the bo's'n to escape, and the latter's slapstick reaction announces the movie's acting style: comic, theatrical, (chaotic?), broadly forward, in contrast to *Liberty Valance*'s measured tragedy. The first hints of symbolism are subtle: it is December 7 and Gilhooley wonders what people at Pearl will say; *later,* we learn Gilhooley and Donovan (John Wayne) were both born this day and have been celebrating the event for twenty-two years with annual birthday brawls. (No one tells us, but twenty-two years before 1963 is December 7, 1941: the Pearl Harbor attack.) Gilhooley is a figure of instinctual anarchy—like Liberty Valance, or resembling a development of the Francis Ford character. An eternal cigar-in-mouth marks his oral personality; when not kissing or drinking from bottles, "Boats" Gilhooley enjoys playing soldier with "Guns" Donovan. The two fought the war on Haleakaloha. Donovan now owns a bar there ("Donovan's Reef") and Dedham, a third buddy, is a doctor with three young children.

But as with December 7th, the narration is extremely oblique. Everything in the picture's first sequences anticipates the Donovan-Gilhooley meeting, but the telltale lines of dialogue are not marked off. Individual events overshadow suspense, and it requires a bit of work to figure out what has happened and why. Typically, for example, it is left for us to reflect that Gilhooley has come halfway round the world to keep his birthday ritual.

In any case, as the lines and angles of character placement in the prefight portion of the saloon scene (see Fig. 10: I.2.iii) illustrate, *Donovan's Reef* is basically a movie of motion and beauty. Its seminal articulation comes as the native girls swarm shoreward to welcome Gilhooley (I.1.iii): 90-degree pan right to left; at midpoint we gaze out to sea, down the pier, centering on two Polynesian totem posts. As the pan began girls ran right-to-left down toward the pier; when the pan reaches the far side, a second stream of girls runs left-to-right down toward the pier, to join the others. They start to sing as the camera reverses its motions, panning back toward the right to center on the posts.

This tripartite structure (left/right—back to center) is imitated in the montage frequently in the picture's course (shot/countershot—two-shot), wherein it is stated also thematically (fight/fight—pax; male/female—couple; chaos/order—harmony). *And* it is imitated as well in sequencing: In I.1: Gilhooley/the island and people—their combination. In I.2: Donovan/Gilhooley—their combination, with Dedham added from part one. In I.3: Boston/island reaction—*subtraction!* The remainder of the picture labors toward resolution of the formal deficiency of this opening triptych (I: 1, 2, 3), suspending until film's end this dissonance (the subtraction of the Dedham children). The movement is toward accord.

In I.3, we cut to Boston. The board meeting of the Dedham Shipping Company is one of Ford's finest comic sequences: mythically lit, highly stylized and pungent, and his penultimate satire of the New England dotard.

Four paintings* summarize four aspects of the Dedhams: /portrait of a nineteenth-century businessman; /of a sea captain; /of a nineteenth-century minister; /tilt down from a portrait of a pirate, past a wooden ship model, to Amelia Dedham, very proper in blue suit, glasses, and hat.** The decision is made that she will visit her father, whom she has never met, in hope of discovering moral turpitude sufficient to disqualify his inheritance of a controlling interest of Dedham stock.

Meanwhile in Haleakaloha the decision is made, in Dedham's absence, to pretend his half-caste children are Guns's, from fear of a Bostonian rather than from suspicion of her mission. To this end, the children's piano lesson is interrupted (a bad sign in itself) and Lelani summoned to the living room. Dissolve: The camera frames Lelani at a high angle, then tracks back across the room as Donovan concludes, "So you and the kids must move in with me and pretend you're mine." "But Uncle Guns, I don't understand. First you tell me I have a sister coming from America, and then you say we're to leave home . . . Wouldn't it be proper for me and my brother and sister to welcome her here, in the absence of my father?" The scene exhibits Ford's "postexpressionism": the slow track-out from Lelani, the high angle (un-

---

*These pictures, as well as the Manulani portrait, as well as all other portraits in Ford (e.g., the one in *The Sun Shines Bright*), seem painted by the same hand. Whose?

** / = cut.

usual for Ford), the obtrusively theatrical lighting, all accentuate her position in the center of an arena, surrounded; stark shadows are outlined on the
floor; a few touches of primary color are offset, in the brilliant color coordination of costumes, by white and black: one of Ford's loveliest color scenes.
Cluzeot protests, "Monstrous," but is ignored (like *The Hurricane*'s priest)
and Lelani understands: "It's because I'm not white!" (As in *Stagecoach*'s
dinner scene, when Ford turns our hatred of characters to empathy,
Donovan's pain as he tries to comfort Lelani turns our alienation at his
"cruelty" to empathy: the eternal Ford portrait of a person suffering
through his own misplaced value systems.) In a sad parade, with a strum
tune (a recurrent musical motif), the children move out of the Dedham
house, each character carrying an attribute: Cluzeot (music books), Luki
(baseball stuff), Sally (dolls), Lelani (ceremonial gown: cf. III.1.iv),
Donovan (their luggage), four servants (the piano), Gilhooley (cigar and piano stool). With this "sin" of subtraction, in which racism and family separation, two favorite Ford themes, are combined, *Donovan's Reef*'s first "Act"
concludes.

Amelia's arrival (on Ford's ketch, *Araner,* captained by Frank Baker) du-
plicates the singing-girls business previously staged for Gilhooley. But this
time, more solemn angles and Mizoguchian pans (which seem mystic revelations of reality) underline this ritual—an indication it contains meanings of

a permanence transcending its human agents. This solemnity is extended in the formalized fashion in which, on the shore, the children, Cluzeot, and two nuns *walk* (always this motion into and out of frames!) *into* a shot screened by a net, or André de Lage* unfolds a bright red umbrella, or Lelani, in a perfect instance of Ford's "postexpressionism," wipes away a tear, framed behind the fishing net. In contrast, Amelia, now and throughout, wears red, white, and blue. Her first hint of the mystic comes when finally she finds herself alone in her father's house; a Polynesian hymn accompanies a camera track as she enters the mythically lit living room and stares at the portrait of a native woman (Manulani): crosscuts between Amelia and portrait work as does similar montage in *The Sun Shines Bright* when Lucy Lee sees her grandmother's picture: Amelia starts wondering. In point of fact, Amelia meets nearly everyone in crosscuts, exchanges that stand out both as rare moments of relating and as rare quasi-point-of-view shots. But the Manulani portrait is key: there is no "mother" on the island, only this *idea* (and ideal), which will always be related to native music and forces of nature. Now Manulani's disapproval is suggested in a dissolve to Cluzeot praying in church beneath an umbrella, in protection from the same storm that wakes up Amelia. And prayers and storm lead to the bringing together of Luki and Amelia, and thus to resolution of conflict.

A strum tune and crosscuts accompany a gently satiric cigarette tryst between stuffed-shirt Amelia and redneck Donovan; romance, of course, becomes possible the instant she learns he is a man of means. Rising, they switch sides in the frame, and, in the shot/countershot/two-shot pattern, make "pax," extending their hands across the distance. The delicate agogics in play and montage both here and in the following patio scene (accompanied by the *Don Giovanni* minuet—from Lelani's off-screen piano) make these some of the most entrancing scenes in late Ford. On the minuet's final

*This French governor's name is sufficiently close to DeLaage, the French governor in Ford's other South Sea movie, *The Hurricane*. Among his titles, the Marquis de Lage lists Baron de Fienne, a reference to Ford's birth name.

note, they enter the children's room (all white and black) and Amelia meets Lelani, then Sally, in crosscuts: "Well," she exclaims with effusion, "You're a little *doll!* What's your name?" "Sarah, but they call me Sally." "*Sarah!* Well, my name's Amelia, Sarah. Nobody ever called me Sally!" "No?" This is typical Frank Nugent dialogue. Like the line "Raincheck?" in the saloon and like many other lines it invites figuring out meanings not immediately clear. Nugent has characters express themselves in codes of their own class. Amelia, coldly raised, believes in proper names (she calls Guns "Michael") but her baby talk is typical of her condescension toward everyone.

Instances of her attitude came just before the patio scene, as she ignored Gilhooley and questioned the Chinese pumping the slot machine despite the three signs—one of them in Chinese: "'*Dérange*,' 'Out of Order,' and so forth. Explanation?"

> *Donovan:* Slot machine. Was shipped in here six years ago, busted. It is still busted.
> *Amelia:* Well . . . why . . .?
> *Donovan:* I do not attempt to explore the depths of the Oriental mind, Miss Dedham. [*Turning toward Mr. Eu standing stiffly beside them*] Perhaps your Ivy League chaperon here could explain to my clients again that it's busted.
> *Amelia:* That's reasonable. Mr. Eu!
> *Eu:* I will try to explain it to them, in their *barbarian* tongue!

Evident here is Donovan's caustic racism, Amelia's formidable impersonableness toward Eu, and Eu's own, colonialized (satire of) racism. For like the children whom Cluzeot calls "Monsters" when they twist to "Frère Jacques" the moment his back is turned, there is a monster side to everything on the island: chaos veneered with order. Lelani and Sally wear sailor suits, which could also be Catholic-school uniforms; these "half-castes" are being raised as proper Europeans, which marks, as in *Cheyenne Autumn,* a stage in white imperialism. The whites live in palaces and control: government, religion, commerce, medicine, gambling, liquor. The priest is a private priest, apparently instructing only the children of aristocrats (the children are, in fact, native royalty). Notable by its absence from Ford's little community here is a school for the natives. Instead, the Polynesians operate like a sort of chorus, in the background; church and medicine excepted (for imperialism has its good sides), they are ignored by the upper-class whites,* and judging by the few references (Cluzeot to starvation, Fig. 10: I.1.iii; Dedham to sickness, II.4.iv) their condition is precarious. Note that the shopkeepers and saloon-folk, the petit bourgeois, are Chinese rather than Polynesian. They have, however, a mystic service within Ford's pantheist allegory, for although there is little

---

*But note the native who suddenly races by with a towel when Amelia swims to shore, confirming the suspicions aroused by the singing-greeting girls that the island caters to the tourist trade.

(alas!) of the sounds of ocean and wind (which one got in *Mogambo*), there is much symbolically present music (as in *the Sun Shines Bright*), the "voice-off" presence of the Polynesians who, like the land and the flowers, survey everything and conduct it to accord. Cluzeot's function in this scheme is not quite clear to me. He has a passion for music (a moral good) and is encouraged to regard the slot machine as a lamentably broken jukebox; but he is also the puritanic suppressor of violence, chastizing the kids for cheering at the Donovan-Gilhooley battle, and he believes beauty must be taught through discipline. He is, then, the Ransom Stoddard of the movie, and he *always* carries an umbrella: one never knows . . .

Mysticism returns (after a boring too-absurd water-ski sequence, climaxed by a pax) when, as Guns chops a Christmas tree atop gargantuan vistas of mountains, valleys, waterfalls, Lelani *sings* a Polynesian prayer, "thanking the goddess of the canyon for our tree," as she explains to Amelia. "*Goddess?!*" chortles Amelia, "You believe in gods and goddesses?!" "Well, I believe in the one god as we all do. But I respect the beliefs and customs of my people." This with snotty sententiousness, as Lelani struts away from Amelia, who stares puzzled. What may sound like bad acting by little Jacqueline Malouf is actually appropriate: whether or not we have figured it out yet, the serious, lofty Lelani is Haleakaloha's reigning queen.

Mystic and melancholic, the strum tune accompanies Amelia's marveling at the valleys' power, echoing the pantheism of Rossellini's *Stromboli*, and summoning her toward a war memorial, which, as it threatens to reveal the Manulani secret, Donovan hastens to block from view. His voice grows vicious, his face hard, and Ford has them posed against the sky, as he talks of the war here. The Japanese are gone now, but Americans, French, and Chinese remain, and so, somewhere below, do the Polynesians midst the silent vistas toward which Lelani chants. Somehow the Americans are repeatedly associated with war and destruction—the anachronistic World War II jeep doubly so, since it tears ugly ruts in the sod. Donovan and Gilhooley fight for pleasure, and celebrate a war day as their birthday. Amelia was marked as a pirate imperialist, and associated with the degenerate French governor in constant red, white, and blue.

But perhaps because Dedham is "one of their own," the natives do not perform their ritual for his return—the picture's third arrival and of them all the most lovingly composed. The camera pans down from the beach's rise, following nurses and natives, slowly to the surf, the strum tune melancholic on the soundtrack. Each of the thirteen shots uses motion, within the frame; this is Ford's "kinetic sublimity." Amelia *enters* (theatrically), from the rear, a medium-high-angle shot. At the surf, a patient is carried from a longboat, laid on a stretcher; others start up the beach and exit the frame, for the camera pans only with Dedham, small in the shot, who walks behind the others. The effect is languorous and the beach is all but deserted by the time the pan moves far enough to include Amelia at far right. Crosscuts, next, of

her moving gradually toward him, but from head-on, not from the side, and of Dedham staring at her, before they embrace, between the pax posts (the totem poles on the beach). The choir comments approval, with one word twice: "Haleakaloha."

Ford cuts marvelously to a bright, lively interior. The Christmas tree has been decorated and gifts lie wrapped beneath it. "Look," cries Amelia, flashing on and off the tree lights, "generator's working!" And darkish soundtrack music alters to a slow, premonitory "Jingle Bells," presaging the film's formal resolution and the end of "monstrous" segregation. The list of broken things, among other deficiencies, is awesomely long: besides the generator, a busted photo, busted record, busted bottles, busted slot machine with upside-down sign, leaky chapel roof, starvation, poverty, war, fights, monstrous children, distorted looking glass, backfiring jeep, rain, the United States of America, off-duty law, Donovan's racial fear, Eu's racism, nets, de Lage wishing transfer to Miami Beach or Hollywood, broken mirrors and sixty-three years' bad luck, misspelled words, legion/legend, the bump on the road, Amelia's six pratfalls, elitism, Maydays, Limeys, mispronounced Irish names, wrong words (dove, legs), rose and thorn, the "reef," and a broken piano. But now, finally, something is working. The flashing lights and the "Jingle Bells" look forward to flashing lights and bells and whistles to come, all of which will celebrate the arrival of . . . Christmas!

This and the following sequence are among Ford's finest. The latter consists of three "scenes," the first of which is an interesting étude on the formulaic treatment of a conversation in crosscuts. Dedham is struggling to explain to Amelia that the "little half-castes" are his and why he never told her dead mother's family he married Manulani. The exchange of shot/countershot, pivoting (upon some flowers) across a table, occurs twelve times, but then, as Dedham speaks of war-time dangers, the flat countershot of him is replaced by a deeper, low-angle one, whose depth and rhythm (it is repeated twice fairly rapidly) suggest torpedoing and darkness. But the shot is deeper also because Dedham is *approaching* the "truth," of course, *is* Manulani, whose portrait is, for the first time, present in the depth of this low-angle shot of Dedham. Manulani's portrait forms both (1) the end point of a perspectival, truth-searching line running from Amelia's back, through the flowers, through Dedham, and thence to the portrait, and also (2) the reverse line: Manulani, in back of Dedham, reaching out toward Amelia through Dedham and the flowers. Manulani and the flowers are, recall, both sorts of gods: they represent passions and transcendent forces. The flowers operate somewhat as light does in *The Fugitive* or as the lamp does in *Liberty Valance*. Amelia is altered by contact with Haleakaloha, by its beauty (the flowers), and thus becomes receptive to Donovan, to her father, and eventually to Manulani and her half-caste siblings. Thus the flowers properly act as the axis upon which the crosscuts turn.

The rhythms of the montage are quadruple: the actual time of each shot, the placements of the low-angle shots, and the psychological times: the quantity of words and gesture, and their (agogic) quality. Alternation of patches of color propose rhythms too, of course, for here as often elsewhere in *Donovan's Reef* color is a kinetic gesture.

Dedham's attempt to confess is interrupted when the kids lay flower wreaths on the lawn; Amelia watches through a slatted screen (as her siblings watched her through a net). Intending to fetch them, she leaves the frame; pan right with Dedham, who swallows some rum and, with Manulani's portrait behind him, says, "Amelia," in the picture's most intimate moment; "Yes?" she responds from off-camera; "Well," he continues, " 'The time has come, the Walrus said, to speak of many things' "; " 'Of sailing ships and sealing wax,' " she adds, reentering the frame; and Dedham concludes melancholically, " 'And cabbages and kings.'* I'd been here about . . ." but is again interrupted: the hospital bell; and he leaves the frame, the camera resting on Amelia, then panning with her, alone, as she goes to the door. From the window until now, a single take has marked passage from Amelia at the drama's center, to Dedham, and then, through her just-aroused curiosity, back again to Amelia. The shot's "discourse" is contained in this entering and exiting; it is not a crosscut conversation, nor a two-shot, but rather an attempt at accord. The sensitive agogics of Jack Warden's delivery and gesture take on an almost decorative import; it suffices that they trade lines of poetry, for the words themselves have no use except poetically. One is tempted to call the shot Ford's finest "magic moment."

The Christmas service recalls *The Fugitive's* baptism (community in song, expressionism) and *The Sun Shines Bright's* funeral, but in *Donovan's Reef* all the community's groups are present (cf. the funeral's excluded blacks): Americans, French, Chinese, Polynesians, businessmen, religious, government, medical, military, children, rich and poor, aristocrat and commoner.** As for Lafleur's song sequence earlier, hurricane lamps suggest a theater. The children dressed as angels parade to "Silent Night" in Polynesian, and André reads, "And from the East came three wise men, three kings,† bearing gifts." Each country is represented by its attribute. "The King of Polynesia"— Sergeant Munk (Mike Mazurki)—comes barechested and wreath-crowned with a basket of fruits, to /kneel before the crèche. "The Emperor of China"—Mr. Eu—comes in oriental robes with tea service and rice, to / kneel. And "The King of the United States of America"—Gilhooley—in white sheet and gold paper crown with the antique phonograph, to /kneel. Gilhooley's entrance is underlined by its position (last), a new and heroic

---

*Perhaps the sailing ships are the navy, the sealing wax the marriage to Manulani, the cabbage the kids, the kings Dedham and Manulani. Ford quotes Lewis Carroll also in *Doctor Bull*.

**Dedham, however, is called to hospital just before the pageant; i.e., the Dedham family is yet to come together.

†Once again Ford invokes his favorite myth of the three (*3 Bad Men, 3 Godfathers*, etc.).

angle, flaming torches behind him, stark shadows, and the stately loving manner in which de Lage draws out the U.S.'s full name; all this, combined with Gilhooley, his cigar, and the benign, musical symbol of the phonograph, suggest a deliberate nostalgia for the *idea* of America. Gilhooley is spotlit upon the sanctuary stage, evoking the symbolic dimension across time and space of America's role and man's genuflection before God. Similarly expressionistic shadows fall across the congregation, and they have occurred earlier in the movie whenever Amelia or the house-servants approached the Manulani portrait, and when Lelani is told she must hide from Amelia.

But the cozy warm community's offerings are not accepted. "All is calm," Lafleur sings, followed by thunder, lightning, and rain; "All is bright," and the chapel goes dark and the umbrellas come out. A heavy stream of water cascades onto Gilhooley's head, toppling America's crown. "Steady on, men! Steady! Sing out!" commands Pat Wayne, and all obey.

It is uncertain how much Amelia knows by Christmas dawn. Maids Yoshi and Koshi place wreaths before Manulani's portrait and, theatrically shadowed, bow ritualistically three times, but flee when Amelia spots them. She places flowers there herself and exchanges quizzical crosscut stares with the painting. A series of paintinglike images, unusually beautiful even for this movie, narrate Amelia's bicycle search for information; at the cemetery she demands "the truth" from Cluzeot, while the camera, independently, tracks into a close-up of the cross on Manulani's grave. Earlier, it panned from Cluzeot, to Amelia watching him, and then back again to Cluzeot; this double-motion is exceedingly rare for Ford (who generally limits pronounced movements to one per shot), and suggests a linkage comparable to the attempted accord in the "Cabbages and Kings" scene. Everything leads to Manulani; she is the *contrechamp* of the pan, the chief god, the cactus rose. Everyone tries to keep Amelia away from her, but at every turn she finds her.

Meanwhile at the Reef a miracle occurs. After a song ("Waltzing Mathilda," which music Ford translates into motion),* and a grand Christmas brawl, Cluzeot refuses a coin, given out foretellingly by the clobbered slot machine during the fight, insisting that it belongs to the "juke box." "Music! Comme ça, musique!" he says, throwing the lever; Donovan and Gilhooley, on the floor, watch in awe as a mighty fountain of coins gushes forth. "Whoop, whoop, whoop!" sings the slot machine, jingle-jangling and flashing red and white. Expressionistic shadows mark what is, in many ways, the climactic moment of the film. The machine is a sort of god; the persistence of the Chinese (and Gilhooley), despite the signs, indicates hope and stubbornness (traditional Fordian virtues). Oddly, Donovan has neither put the machine out of reach nor emptied its treasures; instead, he respects the laws of chance. The machine discharges because it is Christmas. All man's most destructive and sadistic temptations may today be joyfully indulged as

---

*Sung by Dick Foran, a singing cowboy star of the forties.

tolerable exercise of "liberty"; even the Lee Marvin character (whom Cluzeot calls a "devil" and whose haircut is indeed satanic) is tolerable; even the piano's destruction can be condoned today. The black-caped priest, leading the police, a puritanic enforcer of harmony, musical and otherwise, appears a benign agent of order (in contradistinction to Sergeant Munk who, like Link Appleyard, is always off-duty). As in many other Fords, it is the innocent who reaps the fruits of others' labors. Cluzeot asks nothing from the machine but music; he says the money *belongs* to it, and renders unto god.

And all of this happens because it is Haleakaloha's national day; Lelani sits enthroned; a choreograph of motion, music, color, and flowers pay her homage.* *Donovan's Reef*'s natives exercise a redemptive power; Amelia finds her family; all is brought to accord (indeed, formally: Amelia curtsies to Lelani in syncopation with a curtsying double line of natives). And, as in a commedia dell'arte, there comes the curtain-call procession: The *Araner* is in harbor, Captain Martin is loading Amelia's luggage. The camera gazes from the surf up at the pier and its two posts, as though a spectator up at a stage, and most of the players—Amelia, the kids, Dedham, Cluzeot, nuns, nurses, natives—walk slowly forward to stand in line; the strum tune, happy, accompanies. But, challenged by her father, Amelia goes back to say goodbye to Guns (whom she clobbered with her umbrella in the last scene).

---

*A subtle but important instant: Dedham and Amelia, instead of mounting the dais to pay homage, stand conversing; but the Polynesian master of ceremonies raps his staff commandingly. Would so authoritative an interruption, of a white by a native, be conceivable any other day?

As she starts back, Dedham calls her, and, "pax-ly," their arms stretch across the screen as she surrenders her umbrella.

Passing Donovan, she falls off the jeep and onto her ass once again. Midst fights and paxes they agree to wed. Her reference, "If what you said is true," refers to his "I made a human being out of you"—by treating her like a woman. In fact, this is true. She is lordly and condescending with everyone, maintaining a genteel decorum also with her father. But with Guns she has no control: her voice, particularly, betrays her, becoming with Donovan squeaky and mousey, enraged, or low and vampish. Their hit-and-kiss skit* endorses neither Donovan's chauvinism nor Amelia's, any more than the barfight,comedy endorsed macho sadism. Donovan's and Amelia's lifestyles were established at the beginning, and their affair has progressed with stated satire. The irony, akin to *Liberty Valance*'s, is that the Bostonian has succumbed to the call of the wild. Does Donovan, as he spanks her, say, "I wear the *pants* in this family" or "I wear the *pax* . . ."? Surely the latter. And "pax" is truer. Those who decry such sexist behavior in this film might ponder that the essence of comedy rules that this "happy ending" need only be acceptable to the characters involved, not to us. Why does this ultimate succession of fights and paxes accelerate in this long, balletic tracking shot, only to conclude at a weed-infested, dry fountain?

*The skit was used, a bit differently, in *A Minute's Wait*.

The conclusion, as happy as could be wished, is ironic. Money solves everything. Amelia (= USA) will become the new mother-figure, the new Manulani—as the crosscuts between her and the portrait suggest. A long parade, as earlier, wends down the path to the Dedham house, returning the kids' possessions. Once again Ford concludes with his primal antinomies: parade /house. The camera's pan does not come to a halt; it still moves slowly across the screen as the picture fades and the movie ends: a long "Alōhaaa."

No sooner had Ford arrived in Hawaii to begin production of *Donovan's Reef* than he learned that Paramount had pulled out of their financing arrangement with him. Rather than abandon the picture, he became his own producer. But, strange to say, here even more than with *Liberty Valance* there was no real script and Ford more or less improvised from day to day. Perhaps his nightly trips up to the cliff for twelve weeks with Frank Baker, when he would brood silently, were meditations for the next day's work.

To some, *Donovan's Reef* showed signs of dotage. Ford once got set up to shoot a scene only to be reminded, when he called for action, that the dialogue had not been written yet. Back stateside, crews readied studio retakes, only to have Ford walk in, yell, "Finished. Pau!" and walk out. On the islands, so many old friends and children were present, that the affairs took on airs of a last reunion rather than of a film production. Indeed, *Donovan's Reef* is a picture whose claims to greatness seem recognizable only to the initiate, and by no means even to many of them. The comedy seems often terribly broad, the children overly indulged in, and, as may happen while watching a movie, the presence of two or three weak and relatively inane sequences tends to elongate and devalue the entire movie. Lastly, there are those who find the scene of Wayne spanking Elizabeth Allen to be inexcusably offensive.

Yet flawed as it is, and perhaps *too* deceptively shallow, *Donovan's Reef* ranks with Ford's sublimest work for at least 89 of its 109 minutes. It combines and advances upon thematic and articulative figures from *The Hurricane* (nature as mysterious transcendent), *The Fugitive* (theocratic labyrinth, expressionism), *Wagon Master* (moral grace, use of music), *The Sun Shines Bright* (social analysis, racism), and *Mogambo* (man and nature). *Donovan's Reef* is the reverse of *The Man Who Shot Liberty Valance*: tragedy /comedy; black-and-white /color; man comes west to establish order and kills liberty /woman comes east to steal and discovers liberty; continent /island; repression /anarchy; pessimism /optimism; long shots and scenes /fast paced; verbal /pictorial; looking /acting; death /birth. . . .

Perhaps, as Jean-Marie Straub and Danièle Huillet once observed, the operative comparison is with Jean Renoir's *The Golden Coach*.[17] Both have somewhat similar pictorial styles, ethereal musical movements and gestures, and a commedia-dell'arte-like stylization of stereotypes and situations. Both are symbolic in anthropology and politics; both are materialist, Brechtian-like critiques of reality and society.

       Cheyenne Autumn (1964). As Ford sank into old age his public persona became more quarrelsome and obliviously irresponsible. Yet it is hard to see how he could otherwise have gotten away with making such determinedly philosophic and abstract films as those of his last five years. It would be stretching the point to suggest that the old man's spells of drunken depression were merely theater cleverly plotted to get his way in the end, but it is true that such spells were scarcely new and that his Hollywood career had been theater from early on. Ford liked sports and poker, but his basic idea of a good time was to retire to his boat and read undisturbed. In the 1960s, Ford's act, his pose as a hard-nosed antiintellectual who magically turned out good pictures, grew progressively more outrageous, while his pictures became less than ever similar to his public character. With *Cheyenne Autumn*, Ford's act backfired.*

       Critical essays rarely deal with the film itself. They deal instead with obstacles Ford encountered. Supposedly, his producers vetoed his plans to treat the Cheyenne as a kind of alien Greek chorus unable to communicate to whites, and insisted on casting the middle-aged Quaker schoolteacher with nubile Carroll Baker and the principal Indians with Caucasians. Supposedly, Ford did not work happily with Ricardo Montalban or Sal Mineo, was forced to retain Karl Malden footage he did not want and to jettison Sal Mineo footage he did want, and had a "bad score" foisted upon him. Supposedly, location shooting was arduous on the sixty-nine-year old Ford, who started shooting before the script was solved and who lost interest before he had finished.[18]

       Some of these stories may be true. It is certainly true that Spencer Tracy, as Schurz, fell ill and was replaced with Edward G. Robinson, and that, it being impossible to go back onto location with hundreds of extras to restage the

---

    *1878. The Cheyenne nation, reduced by disease and starvation from 1,000 to 286, all its appeals ignored, escapes its Oklahoma reservation and begins an 1,800-mile trek home to Dakota. A young Quaker teacher, Deborah Wright, goes along. Capt. Thomas Archer's troop reluctantly pursues, but when Maj. Braden attacks with artillery the major is killed and their horses lost. Dull Knife, appointed war chief by his dying father, swears celibacy for the duration and watches Red Shirt, son of his elder brother Little Wolf, woo his young wife. Back East, the press hyperbolizes facts and Interior Secretary Schurz is under fire. Archer catches up to the Cheyenne, but Lt. Scott's impetuous charge loses a battle. The starving Cheyenne beg food en route—and are murdered for sport by trailhands—and they find the buffalo herds slaughtered.

    Interlude. Archer's troop enters winter camp but renew pursuit when the Cheyenne trail is discovered. But the Cheyenne, dying in the snow from hunger, split in two. Most of the women and children surrender but, brutalized by Capt. Wessels and the War Department's demand they immediately march back to the reservation, they escape again, many dying in the attempt, and rendezvous at Victory Cave. There, only the presence of Schurz, summoned by Archer, prevents their massacre by an army battalion. Afterward, Dull Knife kills Red Shirt in a duel and rides into exile; Wright and Archer send a little girl home to her tribe.

430 · JOHN FORD

treaty scene, Robinson's body was collaged awkwardly onto existent footage. But problems plague most productions, and few movies adhere to their first script concepts. To cite such problems as excuses—as Hitchcock does in complaining to Truffaut of miscastings spoiling his original concepts[19]—is to ignore art's need to capitalize on limitation (Hitchcock should have altered his concepts). Some of what *Cheyenne Autumn* bystanders took for problems may not have been problems at all—Ford never explained—and others, like nubile Carroll Baker, now seem inspired choices.

The pseudocriticism lavished on *Cheyenne Autumn*'s production "problems" of course had a purpose. The film lost money, even critics were bored, and rather than accept the fact that, having gone expecting another *She Wore a Yellow Ribbon*, they had got another *Fugitive* instead, they clung to the meta-film they had wanted. The $4.2 million movie had been ballyhooed as the master's farewell to Monument Valley, only *this* time from the Indian side, and even Andrew Sarris assumed it was "a failure simply because Ford cannot get inside the Indians he is trying to ennoble."[20] Perhaps suspecting Ford had not been trying to "get inside," Sarris later retrenched, noted that no filmmaker has ever seen the West through the eyes of an Indian, and that Ford "had always scrupulously respected the dignity and honour of the Other in the remorselessly racist dialectic of the [Western] genre."[21]

Ford himself had contributed to the confusion, telling Bogdanovich, "I've killed more Indians than Custer, Beecher and Chivington put together,"[22] and even his apologists have blithely assumed Ford needed to expiate injustices done Indians in his earlier pictures. True, those who like *Soldier Blue* (Ralph Nelson, 1970), in which every white atrocity is parsed, will never be content with John Ford. But *Soldier Blue*'s Indians are stupid, misguided, and semisavage, while its whites are troglodytes from whom we can comfortably dissociate ourselves. *Fort Apache*'s Indians, in contrast, were clever and victorious, and the soldiers—unavoidably empathetic and like ourselves—were unwitting instruments of their ideological conditioning. Finally, Ford kept insisting that *Cheyenne Autumn* told "a true story, authentic, the reality as it was,"[23] whereas in fact the movie bears only slight resemblance to the historical facts in Mari Sandoz's well-researched book of the same name. *Her* story is far grimmer, the characters quite different, most events quite otherwise; even in the last scene Ford has changed matters: Dull Knife actually killed "Thin Elk" (not "Red Shirt") in a trading post, not a tribal ceremony; Lone Wolf was drunk, not a noble warrior, and the girl in question was his daughter, not his wife. Afterwards, he went up into the hills, the Elk family destroyed his lodge, and he was no longer chief. And Carl Schurz was basically uninvolved in the Cheyenne affair, and did not come West to parley with them.

Let us, then, put aside worries about the movie John Ford did not make and deal instead with the one he did. What is the *Cheyenne Autumn* we have?

The actual *Cheyenne Autumn,* not surprisingly, corresponds to what our study of Ford would lead us to suspect from him at this date. Its action is not so much genocide as the sway of absurdity, with the Cheyenne as its victims. Almost nothing occurs *with* reason. The Cheyenne parade homeward seeking reason, the cavalry pursue without reason, the parade more than ever substitutes instinct for reason. A major shoots cannon at children, a lieutenant charges for glory, the eastern press goes berserk, the telegram spouts instructions for genocide, sportsmen slaughter buffalo, the army worships orders— all act instinctually. When finally Schurz asks, "Just one question, General. Do you enjoy killing Indians, women, children?" he misses the point. It is comforting to imagine that genocide is the product of evil, sadistic people and so to shift the blame for a holocaust away from ourselves. Alas, Ford indicts every white person: the brutely mechanical army is merely the visible agent of policies engendered by government, press, and average citizen. But they are not sadists. Even Wessels, the archcaricature, is humane and compassionate, a student of Indian culture, while the trailhands who shoot Indians for fun are no more sadistic than rabbit hunters. No reason explains genocide—except that the Cheyenne want to live and that everyone is myopic.

Those who know Ford will not be surprised by the Dodge City episode strangely inserted into the middle of the picture. Comic absurdity offsets absurd tragedy frequently in Ford's work, the novelty in *Cheyenne Autumn* being that the snappy, immediate farce is concentrated together rather than interspersed throughout, the better to throw into relief *Cheyenne Autumn's* ponderous distanced dirge. The episode repeats gags from *My Darling Clementine* as Wyatt Earp tries to have a quiet game of poker. But there is an air of moral decadence, Wyatt's character is a bored selfish cynic rather than a stimulated idealist, and familiar pictorial motives, like the long shot along the bar, are exaggerated into parody. The Ionesco-like dialogue and pantomime—a marvelously intense, volatile vaudeville of pouts between James Stewart, Arthur Kennedy, and John Carradine, triply offset by skits by Elizabeth Allen's whore, the gassy trailhands, and the panic-struck mayor—requires no further justification.* But its point is surely our solipsism, our inability to think or even to see beyond the clichés of our specific cultural determination. The theme goes back beyond *Tabu.* Intolerance is not cruel, it is a limitation of sensibility whereby we protect, define, and assert ourselves. Horribly, genocide of the Indian was not a policy or even a conscious act but the natural voraciousness of a youthful culture's expansiveness, just as the Cheyenne pil-

---

*There are those who judge this episode one of Ford's greater miracles and regard Warner Brothers' extermination of its second half as a loss greater than the complete *Greed.* In the missing portion Earp and Holliday lead Dodge City's citizens out to battle the Cheyenne but, sighting a lonely Indian scout, they rush back home and hide in their cellars. (Ford corrects some facts: in *My Darling Clementine* Earp is young in 1882, having left Dodge City for Tombstone, where he meets Holliday. Now Earp is older, it is 1878, and he and Holliday play poker in Dodge City.)

grimage is the primal urge of a dying nation. A tiny herd collides with a gigantic one; is anyone responsible?

This is the familiar Fordian scheme, the same ravaged world we knew in *Pilgrimage*, but with contradictions vaster, action less immediate, and beauty deepened. But, as in other late Fords, the Hero is problematic—the tasks are greater, their significance overwhelming, the hero's means almost nonexistent.

Is Deborah Wright the hero? She alone possesses higher knowledge of right and wrong (and puts out flowers, but no one comes), and she rejects convention and family to go off alone with the Cheyenne to strive to preserve their children. But she is not terribly successful. Miss Wright is right to teach the Cheyenne to write; without history reason has even less hope. And she teaches spelling while drawing pictures: a buffalo, later a train, thus conceptualizing why Indian life is doomed. (The train brought sportsmen who exterminated the herds on which Indian civilization depended.) Yet also, Miss Wright assures white domination by teaching its language. Education as indoctrination is an obsessive theme in late Ford (Ransom Stoddard, Father Cluzeot, and Mr. Pether labor in classrooms to impose *their* values), and words are never to be trusted. Dull Knife claims he learned words "when white men still spoke truth" (when was that?), but treaties lie, newspapers lie, telegrams are absurd, and all Wessels's book knowledge fails to raise his consciousness. "Confidentially—I want to know the truth," whispers Schurz, but the truth is words, words that, as in *Liberty Valance*, control men and are distorted by men. Words, the conduit of civilization, are the amoral instrument by which intolerance imposes itself. (It is worth noting that Ford's concern with the relativities of point of view and the validity of language anticipates by almost a decade the "modernist" attitudes of Jean-Luc Godard.)

Is Archer (Richard Widmark) the hero? He seems particularly impotent, cast reluctantly as the Cheyenne's most immediate enemy, forgetting the names of his men, shirking moral responsibility, trying to shift it onto the doctor; and when Archer does at last accept higher knowledge, he must run to Schurz to do anything. Back in 1948, *Fort Apache*'s Captain York expressed outrage less verbosely than does Sergeant Wichowsky (Mike Mazurki) in his vaudevillian tent dialogue with Archer (likening the army to Cossacks), but York rode into battle under protests and threats of arrest, whereas Wichowsky, after his binge, reenlists because he cannot resist "Boots and Saddles."

Then is Schurz the hero? Yes, but despite his looking for guidance to Lincoln (midst Lincoln's melody from *Young Mr. Lincoln*), Schurz is a magnificent *deus ex machina*, appearing from nowhere to mediate between a few dozen Cheyenne and an artillery-equipped army battalion bent on their destruction. The cigars he hands out when the Cheyenne admit they have no tobacco for their peace pipes seem ironic proof of white victory. If the land that needs a hero is unhappy, what may be said of the land that needs a *deus ex machina?* Fordian heroes, while never plentiful, formerly sprang up organically.

The world without heroes lacks glory as well. No bands play or voices sing as E Troop parades across Monument Valley. Ben Johnson's "Yoh" and horsemanship have lost their youthful zest. And none of the soldiers nor any of the whites outside Dodge City (save Schurz, the god) possess the cameo individuality we associate with Ford. Toned down, recessive, their actions seem progressively more dehumanized enactments of ritual patterns.

Yet the "truth," the Cheyenne story, is still more distanced. Their gilded statue during the titles, the opening legend, and a history-book narrator frame them in their mythic past. Viewed almost always from immense physical distance, in meditative stares, with a presentational style such as Noel Burch would ascribe to prewar Japanese cinema,[24] the individual Cheyenne are purely iconic, recalling *The Fugitive*'s most abstract moments. Their story, particularly the love story, appears virtually in subtext. Again, the heroes are clay footed. Red Shirt, whose shirt is almost the only bright color in the main film, has the ridiculous glory of a truly lost cause—he recalls Ashby Corwin in *The Sun Shines Bright*—but he also epitomizes the moral decay of the reservation years, arrogating rights to fire first shots and to steal his chief's wife. Dull Knife struggles too for heroism. But his leadership as his people trek homeward has witnessed repeated disasters and when, upholding right, he kills Red Shirt, his violence exiles him from his community. More than any hero, Dull Knife must ride away at the end, barred from the promised land.

Like *This Is Korea!* or *The Fugitive, Cheyenne Autumn* works not so much in terms of theme or character as by the presence of its physical beauty. (Needless to say, it must be seen in full Cinemascope; anything else completely alters Ford's magisterial distance and pace.) When, as it did in *Rio Grande,* the troop rides into winter quarters and the women stand sun-streaked watching in the dust and autumn foliage, Victorian tenderness beats in the frame; but there is a similar awe at beauty in even Ford's most implacable scenes, as when he stares Antonioni-like at the pastel tints of desert bush and sky while the slimy trailhands shoot Cheyenne for sport. We are not so far from the expressionism of *Pilgrimage* when Ford blackens the sky over the bone-laden plain of dead buffalo, or, mournfully, as the hospital's bluish grays chill into the muted reddish grays of prison and then into the ocherous grays of "Victory Cave." Ford never evades his obligation to aestheticize human tragedy. When Little Wolf raises his knife in threat of suicide and pale light refracts softly off the statuesque faces of the Cheyenne chorus surrounding him, it is not merely the picture that is iconic; the moment is as well. Similarly, from outside their prison we see Cheyenne faces peering out through frost-framed windows; the scene is almost totally dark, save for a lamp, which then too is extinguished.

This is the nadir. But blackness in late Ford also means torches blazing in the night—in *Two Rode Together, 7 Women, Vietnam! Vietnam!*, and here, along with cannon in the night in *The Wings of Eagles* and "The Civil War," and candles in the night in *Donovan's Reef.* These images—out of Blake?— tell us that however elusive truth or useless reason, however dependent we ultimately are in miracles that do not come, the obligation to strive remains. The young—Deborah and Red Shirt—do not question this. And as the Cheyenne wend their way toward extinction, they gradually doff their Western clothes and don Indian ones, achieving victory of sorts in their finale, which Ford sets on a meadow against a Renaissance-like perspective of background wilderness, and in which rejuvenation, violent purification, and funeral are combined.

The Dodge City sequence aside, *Cheyenne Autumn* maintains a style of stern formality: figures engulfed by landscape alternate with iconic figures posed against landscape. As in *The Fugitive*, soft breaths of humanity occasionally break through this grimness—generally as confessions of helplessness: the old Quaker sitting uncomprehendingly in the sunstream, Schurz gazing woefully at Lincoln's portrait, O'Carberry wishing he were a better doctor, Little Wolf staring at his brother who has just killed his son, the little girl running home.

"The Civil War" (1962). Cinerama was a three-camera process (now generally seen in anamorphic editions that crop its frame's top and bottom) which, as it suffered from elongated depth perspective, befitted travelogue epics and roller-coaster rides. Merian Cooper was one of its backers, however, and Ford contributed a twenty-five-minute episode, "The Civil War," to Cinerama's 162-minute *How the West Was Won* (1962):

> The Civil War erupts, Zeb's pa was off at the first shot to join the Union army, and now the eager youngster leaves his Ohio farm, Ma, brother, dog. / Shiloh, night: heaps of dead, mass graves, hospital gore. A friend in the dark warns Zeb not to drink from the pink stream and suggests they "jus' leave this war to the folks that want it." Outside the church-hospital, mid cherry blossoms, Sherman urges Grant not to give up, and Zeb knifes his (Rebel) friend before the latter can kill Grant. Bombs and battle scenes. Zeb comes home by riverboat, finds Ma buried beside Pa. He leaves brother on the farm, and heads west.

It is as epitomizing and anthological as anything in Ford: how a youth came off a farm, discovered the world; how this experience killed the past and thrust the will toward expansion. Vast tides of history are concentrated at their point of transition into the immediate emotions of a single individual. Everything is said; and with such formidable elegance and concision that the neighboring episodes of "The Civil War" (behemoths by Henry Hathaway and George Marshall) seem like so much bad disco momentarily ceasing for the *St. Matthew Passion*'s final funereal chorus.

A somewhat similar approach to history was taken in *Liberty Valance*, and would have been taken in a picture Ford desperately wanted to make, but never could, *April Morning*—about the battle of Lexington and the American Revolution.

> I'd devote most of my work to describing the daily life of the future Americans of that time, the life of those farmers just starting to get attached to this new world, taking root here, the existence of those farmers who then begin to revolt against the English soldiers. This aspect of the birth of the United States, rustic, rural, interests me much more than the battle, which is only its crystallization. It's this approach to history that stirs me. I like to make my pictures about the little people, who begin to feel the thirst for self-respect growing within themselves, who become aware of their belonging to a community.[25]

U.S. Grant makes a brief appearance in "The Civil War." Ford thought Grant's life "one of the great American stories—but you can't do it. You can't show him as a drunkard, getting kicked out of the Army."[26] But Ford, in a poignantly elegant and, at nine minutes, even *more* concise episode in *The Colter Craven Story,* had shown Sam Grant coming home in disgrace to Wilmette and being denounced by his father in front of his wife, then suddenly taking charge of some raw volunteers who march off to war piping "Johnny Comes Marching Home," while Sam goes off to a clerical job "sharpening lead pencils." Later, his friends from Wilmette meet him at

The Rookie of the Year. Wayne protects son Pat Wayne. James Gleason watches.

Shiloh in deep despair, and realize what became of Sam Grant. The episode, made for Ward Bond's long-running TV series, *Wagon Train* (a spin-off of *Wagon Master*), was Bond's twenty-second appearance in a Ford picture—and his last in any film. He died November 5, 1960. John Wayne plays Sherman in both these sketches of Shiloh, and he also turns up umpiring a baseball game—with outrageously hammy calls—in *Flashing Spikes*, a hilarious TV episode starring James Stewart. Wayne had played a reporter in an earlier, also inventive, Ford TV baseball film, *Rookie of the Year*.

    7 Women (1965). "Ford represents pure classicism of expression in which an economy of means yields a profusion of effects," wrote Andrew Sarris,[27] and nowhere is this truer than in *7 Women*, in this culmination of Ford's vignette methods, where every gesture, every word, every object resonates into the indefinably symbolic. Each of its characters contains worlds, each of their actions permits multiple interpretations, each of them relates to each of the others on so many diverse levels as to invite virtually endless dissection. And, given the quality of Ford's work during the ten years preceding *7 Women*—the noticeable slowing down, the weariness, the pessimism, and even the misanthropy—*7 Women* is astonishing for its vitality. It may be the most quickly cut of all Ford's movies; it is certainly the most inventive, as rich in detail and revelation as any picture ever made. It constitutes not only a summation of all Ford's prior career; it is also, as so often before, a new beginning, as far above and beyond *The Man Who Shot Liberty Valance* as that picture was in relation to *Two Rode Together*. Each moment confronts us with unequaled virtuosity and unsurpassed depths of humanism.

    But, before continuing in this vein, it should be noted that my view is, alas, in the minority. More typical was *The Morning Telegraph*'s comment in 1966: "A maudlin, mawkish, gooey, dripping hunk of simpering slush"; or Arthur Knight's enlightened chuckle in the *Saturday Review:* "I suspect that his admirers among the *auteur* critics will be hard put to it to explain away this work of The Master."[28]

    Its commercial* and critical failure, and Ford's plaintive remark in *Cahiers du Cinéma*, "I think it's one of my best, but the public didn't like it. It wasn't that they wanted,"[29] moved me to write him how much I liked it. And he responded with the letter reproduced here.

    7 Women scored critical successes in England and France, as an art film, but in the U.S. Metro abandoned it long before release. Its New York debut came after four or five months showcasing around the country as a cheap thriller, and then at a Forty-Second Street theater on the bottom half of a double bill with Burt Kennedy's *The Money Trap*. Its subject, typical for the thirties, alienated 1965's pseudosophisticates and camp followers in com-

---

*7 Women's negative cost $2,308,190. Ford was paid $262,258. With distribution costs it had lost $2,300,000 by 1970. Grosses *worldwide* came to only $937,432 by then.

JOHN FORD

My dear Thomas Gallagher =

Thank you for your very kind
letter. Perhaps its only us
Irish that can appreiate good
cinema fare (I was born Sean
Aloysius O'feeney).

Hollywood now is run by
Wall St. + Madison Ave who
demand "Sex + Violence". This
is against my conscience + religion.
again my heartfelt thanks

John Ford.

P.S. Just now I received a most
imposing diploma from the London
film festival notifying me that
"Seven Woman" has been chosen as
the out standing American film !!!
Is This ironic? Or is it just Life?

J. F.

mand of trends in taste. Audience psychology is a fragile affair; a few detached cynics can easily condition everyone, so that people laugh instead of cry. Yet an all-black audience in Philadelphia's colored ghetto was perfectly in tune with 7 *Women,* even applauding at the end, and I have never known it not to make a profound impression upon anyone to whom I have introduced it.

Superficially, adverse reactions are comprehensible. 7 *Women* is pitched continually on the brink of bathos; its dialogue is a string of terse clichés, its emotions embarrassingly naked. Though distinctly a film of interior realism and dark tragedy, it is on the surface an essay in pure fantasy with a constant obbligato of humor and satire. What at first glance might excusably be mistaken for an overly broad, obvious, and emphatic work is in reality an affair of infinitely subtle distancing.

7 *Women* derives from Norah Lofts's short story, "Chinese Finale" (1936). Miss Argent narrates; all the women are English, and the Pi Lung mission is forewarned that Dr. Cartwright is a woman. She wears a skirt, not pants; her hair is short, but she has no interest in fashion; her motives for wanting a faraway job are not specified. Miss Andrews (without the Agatha) is a typical unremarkable mission chief, without Margaret Leighton's extraordinary characteristics; thus Cartwright's abrasive manners are not balanced by excesses in Andrews and must stand on their own merits. There are no refugees; an influenza epidemic lasts three weeks; Andrews retains her authority throughout. But Cartwright spends two days drinking alone in her room, drives Andrews to tears, and decides to leave.

That night she and Argent see the town afire. She goes to town with Arthur Pether, is wounded in the arm, and returns with news of his death; but Florrie's never told. Next morning the women awake to find themselves prisoners

Figure 11. *7 Women*

Numbers following each entry indicate duration in minutes (e.g., 7:32 or just in seconds (e.g., 95″). Numbers in parentheses indicate number of shots.

ACT I	30:00(246)	Shot average = 7.3 seconds.
	1:35(7)	Titles: Mongol cavalry.
Day One	7:32(65)	
1. Morning	2:45(25)	Courtyard 87″ (19). Dining room and letter 78″ (6).
2. Afternoon	4:47(40)	Classroom 48″ (12). Andrews and Emma 100″ (13). Porch and tree 139″ (15).
Day "Two"[a]	21:53(174)	
1. Evening	2:00(17)	Children sing; Cartwright arrives; meets Florrie.
2. Dinner	4:15(48)	
3. Clinic	3:37(31)	Cartwright, Florrie, Pether.
4. Office	3:14(21)	Andrews cautions Emma against Cartwright.
5. Courtyard	3:51(29)	Kum-cha refugees arrive.

Figure 11. (continued)

6. Diningroom	1:37(13)	Andrews and British.
7. Office	2:25(15)	Cartwright lectures Andrews on Florrie.
ACT II	17:30(107)	Shot average = 9.5 seconds
Day Three	11:22(75)	
1. Morning & c	4:11(29)	Clinic: cholera! courtyard 166″ (18). Vaccinations and clothes firing 85″ (11).
2. Night	6:51(46)	Binns relieves Cartwright 60″ (5). Pether digs grave 34″ (2). Pether leaves Florrie's tray 72″ (11). Andrews and Cartwright: Emma sick 88″ (8). Andrews and Cartwright under tree 157″ (20).
Day "Four"[a]	6:08(32)	
1. Road	0:08(1)	Plague sign removed.
2. Dinner	3:50(25)	Cartwright drunk!
3. Night	2:30(6)	Cartwright and Pether see village burning.
ACT III	38:30(232)	Shot average = 9.95 seconds.
Day Five [b]	12:30(77)	
1. Courtyard	2:07(14)	Army retreats. Pether and Kim to village.
2. Courtyard	5:07(36)	Packing 67″ (7); bandits arrive 230″ (29).
3. Night	5:13(27)	Massacre 162″ (7); bandits arrive 230″ (29).
3. Night	5:13(27)	Massacre 162″ (18). "Ransom" demand and Florrie's labor 151″ (9).
Day Six [b]	15:01(124)	
1. Morning	4:05(32)	Hut: Cartwright calls 64″ (7); dining room bargain for medical bag 85″ (15); meditates 46″ (6); returns to hut 50″ (4).
2. Afternoon	5:25(29)	Tunga hears of birth 24″ (3); goes to hut 138″ (13). Cartwright to Tunga 77″ (6). Woman in hut 86″ (7).
3. Night	7:27(63)	Hut: Cartwright and food 167″ (15). Woman in dining room 111″ (12). Wrestling 169″ (36).
Day Seven	9:02(42)	
1. Morning	2:53(15)	Women, Cartwright and Emma.
2. Evening	0:46(7)	Riding in gate. Women.
3. Night	5:22(30)	Cartwright in corridor; releases women 137″ (5). She watches them leave in cart 71″ (18). She in corridor 20″ (1). Gives poison 94″ (6).
	0:30	End titles.
Total:	86:00(485)	Shot average = 10.63 seconds.

[a]Time is elided for dramatic unity.

[b]Nonanamorphic television editions of 7 *Women* run 100 minutes. Editor Leon Selditz says Ford did not intend to use this additional footage. And some of these scenes, added to make the film optimum television length, are redundant or even not by Ford (such as the Mongol attack on the town surreally suggested by birds, sun-streaked branches, wasp sounds, horse hooves, and shadows). Nonetheless, the Ford-Selditz edition may have been shortened by MGM for theatrical release. For example, while it is clear that Ford shot the riding sequence, it is problematic whether he intended to retain it: it is lovely but redundant, and it destroys the formal unity of never leaving the mission. (Cartwright, Tunga Khan, Lean Warrior, and two Mongols ride out gate. /Extreme LS: Lean plucks flower. /Tunga reacts. /MS: Lean gives Cartwright flowers. /LS: Tunga grabs flowers, swats Lean. /Lean reacts. /LS: They gallop off.)

of Tonga, but there are no executions. They're taken away in a wagon, and the second night, in some town, in a fetid room and without any water, Florrie gives birth. After repeated attempts, Cartwright obtains an interview with Tonga, rides with him, and the women are moved to clean rooms. Andrews, become somewhat vague with Tonga's arrival, objects sternly (but not vociferously) to Cartwright's conduct, and after three days goes crazy and mumbles incoherent verses. Miss Clark, otherwise unmentioned, joins Andrews in turning her face to the wall when Cartwright enters.

Cartwright wakes up the four women to tell them they are going. She has gotten Tonga drunk, and has found a man, who was to have his head chopped off the next day, to drive them away in a wagon; by the time Tonga awakes, they will have escaped. Cartwright's wound has infected her and she expects to be dead within a day. Argent concludes:

— She nodded to the driver, who picked up his whip. I saw through the tears that were pouring down my face the lonely figure at the gate, the Chinese coat—evidently Tonga's present—gleaming in the lantern-light. I thought of the poison being carried with every beat of her pulses. . . . I knew that I should never speak to Miss Andrews again.

Tyger! Tyger! burning bright
In the forests of the night,
What immortal hand or eye
Could frame thy fearful symmetry?

Religion and the search for God is a major theme in only one other Ford, *The Fugitive*, and there too were the problems of evil, of God's silence, and the labyrinthine ways. In both instances the subjects are missionaries, religious who regard themselves as privileged, while being tormented over their conscious inadequacies.

Agatha Andrews (Margaret Leighton) is a bit like Colonel Thursday in *Fort Apache;* she takes things too seriously. She refers to herself often as "the head" of the mission, and indeed it is her head, forever twitching nervously on her spindly neck, that attracts our attention when we first see her, from the back, driving into her mission. Superficially, on the broadest level, Andrews is offered as a dislikeable character.

As in Ford's military pictures, Andrews's colleagues are a motley crew. But, she says, "They have all enlisted in a war. They are soldiers in the army of the Lord." Miss Binns (Flora Robson), the head of another mission, is equally severe when she reminds Mrs. Russell, "When you joined the mission at Kum-cha, you shut the door on your life with Colonel Russell. Leave it shut!"

Juxtaposed to Andrews's army of professionals and amateurs is, as in *The Horse Soldiers*, a doctor, and the clash between ideologies is immediate and fiery. Expected to be a man, Cartwright (Anne Bancroft) turns out to be a woman and unreligious; worse, she appears riding a mule, in britches, carrying a riding stick, with short hair and coarse words. Within two days, with cholera raging, Andrews finds herself deposed and obliged to place her hopes in science rather than in God. Cartwright's common sense appears in refreshing contrast to the kookie pietism of the religious,* and she is offered as a sympathetic character.

As the picture proceeds, still reading it on its broadest level, the contrast between Andrews and Cartwright is intensified. Andrews becomes psychotic and isolated within her own repression, while one by one the other missionaries turn against her. Meanwhile, Cartwright becomes increasingly heroic and beloved.

But neither matters nor morality are so simple. The question of empathy and likeableness is only relevant because the characters, their deeds and dispositions, are placed constantly in question. Starting with the simply definable, Ford quickly passes into the ineffable, to the beyond-good-and-evil within each character. And so perhaps because there is so much that is repellent in Agatha Andrews, she emerges as the most empathetic of all, at least for me. Margaret Leighton does lovable things when she gives tangerines to the children, or sits under her tree. (The tree scene recalls *Stagecoach*'s lunch-table scene: in both pictures Ford alternately arouses our antipathy and sympathy for a given character.)

Ford, as we have seen elsewhere, has a fondness for turning the tables on his audience, and Emma Clark is a fascinating instance. A girl of about eighteen, pretty, healthy, enthusiastic and outgoing, she always stands out from her shriveled, embattled colleagues. She seems the most nearly "normal," "the only one who still has a chance in life." Emma's supreme innocence is due to her sheltered life; both her father and two brothers were ministers. She is mentally young for her age; she has evidently been subjected to a rigorous upbringing, has been trained to be agreeable, has been trained to mime approved sentiments.

Now, Sue Lyon rose to stardom playing Lolita, and there is something still of Lolita in her Emma Clark. The traces of lesbianism, which we may read in Andrews's crushed and complex affections for Emma (daughter-figure, disciple, herself young again) and which make Emma nervous, can also be found in Emma's cautious transference of her affections to Cartwright (as superwoman, glamor, the real world, and manliness). Emma, however, loves babies best.

There seems a certain shallowness in Emma, one suggesting insincerity and detachment from reality. She bursts out of the hut when the children are shot, but it seems odd that, a few seconds later, she looks up from her noisy sobbing and says, "Dr. Cartwright! Now I know what evil really is!"

---

*The sign on the mission says that World Headquarters are in "Boston, Mass., U.S.A." which should tip us off about what to expect to find inside.

What has been criticized as horribly bad acting from Sue Lyon (who could hardly be expected to shine alongside Dunnock, Leighton, Bancroft, Robson, Lee, and Field) is perhaps the reality of the character herself (Ford capitalizing on Sue Lyon). Looking back as she rides off in the oxcart, Emma announces, loudly: "Dr. Cartwright! I'll never forget her as long as I live!" It is difficult to believe that Emma's love, either for the children or for Cartwright, is terribly deep.

Does Emma really have no idea at all of what is happening? How ingenuously she watches Cartwright go off to Tunga Khan, and how excitedly she asks, "What's going on? Where's she going? Isn't she coming back?"! But, by the time Binns has finished her delicate explanation ("Dr. Cartwright has taken an oath to preserve human life"), Emma has turned her attentions back to the baby and seems to have forgotten her question. "Whatever doctor's doing," she lectures Andrews, "is for our good, and you should be thankful!" *"Whatever"?!* Are we to conclude that of all these missionaries Emma has the *least* contact with reality? When Cartwright comes to liberate them, Emma spurts out again: "What are you . . . why are you staying here? Why aren't you coming with us?" (Emma always speaks ten times faster than anyone else; each character has her particular tempo.) "Beat it," answers Cartwright; and even when Emma is riding in the cart, she does not seem to have thought out what has happened. Emma's character wears like a prayer shawl, and her concentration on babies to the avoidance of any other reality has a sort of instinctual quality to it, a survival instinct that contrasts markedly with Andrews's physical psychosis.

Some justification for Andrews acting like "a small-time dictator" is the lamblike nature of her flock. "Though He slay me," quoth Charles Pether, "yet will I trust Him!" (Which is just what happens to Pether.) "Yes, Jesus loves me, We are weak but He is strong," sing the children. "Give us what Thou wilt, when Thou wilt, as much as Thou willest; Thou alone knowest what is good for us," prays Andrews at grace. The missionaries, sitting in the room, wait to be slaughtered, sing hymns, and dream of Christmas, Thanksgiving Day, and home. Their danger is actual. But, at the same time, they have hope in Cartwright, and the situation is quite similar to the Mormons in *Wagon Master* who, unwilling to soil their own hands, leave the immoral task of killing to the "Lord's angel," Travis. Andrews, uncharitable to a fault, at least has the virtue of consistency, in refusing to touch the "contaminated" food and in refusing to condone prostitution.

Often in Ford it is the empathetic fool who delivers the gut punch. Emma runs up to Cartwright and says, uncharacteristically purposefully, "Dr. Cartwright, you got us out of the hut. Maybe you could get the baby away from here altogether?" Cartwright stares at Emma, then looks away, surprised and perhaps even angry, then (deciding Emma has no inkling of what she is suggesting?) she pats Emma on the arm, calls her a "good kid," and leaves to carry out the suggestion. What comes next is obscure to me. Emma leans against the door and breathes deeply, almost as if to say, "Well, that's done!" and then walks slowly across the room and back to the baby. Ford is making a point with this scene, but what? Is Emma less naive than she puts on? Do the glances that the other women make at her indicate their willingness to accept, and hope for, Cartwright's sacrifice?

In any case, we make allowances for Emma, just as we do for Tunga Khan, and also because Emma is young, has never had a choice; but the same is true of everyone. Florrie and Charles Pether (Betty Field, Eddie Albert), both graying in their forties, are still mental teenagers. Their normal lives were suspended, waiting for Pether's invalid mother to die; now they are married, now Charles may fulfill his dream of being a missionary (every bit as much a "Frank Merriwell" gesture as his foray into the village: Charles is lovably awkward in everything), and now Florrie can have a baby. She is both frightening and compassionate when she exclaims: "All my chums at school had babies! Betsy Chapman had twins! Now it's my turn!" As we saw as early as 1933, in *Pilgrimage*, Ford realizes that people never grow up inside. And *7 Women* is a film made by a man struggling against the decay of his own body, struggling against the despair fomented in him by the world, and yet also possessed of a faith, inexplicable even to himself, and therefore of a value that he doubts but cannot avoid affirming, which allows him to acknowledge death confronting him and the evil in the world.

When Agatha Andrews recites that grace—"Give us what Thou wilt . . ." —she does not suspect that a cholera epidemic and Tunga Khan are about to be given, nor does she realize that the positive gift, Dr. Cartwright, has already arrived. Dr. Cartwright will furnish the cart in which the seven women will leave their mission (and only of Miss Binns could it be said that she acted as a Christian). It is for this reason, and because we know what it signifies, having seen the film, that the arrival shot of Dr. Cartwright riding her mule into the mission courtyard is one of the loveliest images in Ford. The children are singing "Yes, Jesus loves me," and here is the proof, as it were, arriving in an unexpected form (female) and at an unexpected time, though no one knows this yet, and though Cartwright does not know that she has found her mission (though she does know it, but not in the more real and symbolic sense—her destiny). But fate blows the leaves this way and that, and the threads of life are as variegated as the row of multicolored bobbins set so beautifully on the dining room windowsill, and which serve as a background to Cartwright's meditation before submitting to Tunga Khan, and after she has bid the seven women goodbye. Cartwright is the eighth woman, first because she seems like a man, secondly because as soon as she trades her riding britches for a gold robe, as soon as her female sex betrays her to Tunga Khan (as it made it impossible to get a decent job as a doctor, and as a tragic love affair had set her on the run), Miss Ling is thrown

Dr. Cartwright (Anne Bancroft) announces she will give herself to Tunga Khan (Mike Mazurki).

back among the women to raise their number to seven again.* Now she has become "The Scarlet Woman, the Whore of Babylon"; now also she carries the lamp in the darkness. The corollary to her arrival shot is that of her standing golden, with her lamp, at the gate, watching the women leave her alone, while the camera tracks hopelessly away from her; and then she turns

*The baby is another instance of substitution: for the baby dead from cholera, the old man dead from cholera, the children shot by the Mongols, and his father, Charles Pether.

to go through the gate, and into a mission that is now, ironically, exclusively her own.

When Cartwright takes the vial of poison, Argent protests, "Don't, please don't, it's a sin, it's a sin against God, it's a sin." "Then pray for me," replies Cartwright. But if she cares little for this concept of sin, she cares mightily for her oath to preserve life, for the profession to which she has sacrificed her life as completely as Agatha has sacrificed hers. The two hero-ines are frequently parallel. Not for nothing does Agatha mean "good." *Blessed are the clean of heart, for they shall see God.* But this is torture, Agatha's eyes almost always have tears in them. She must fill her life, and God is not enough. Nor is medicine. And neither lady has a vocation to celibacy. Both are imperious, both do everything "too much," both drive frail bodies by sheer will, slouching wearily (Cartwright with dangling ciga-rettes), neither has free choices. Agatha, by being consistent to the letter of the law, violates the spirit of Christianity; even so, her barren psychosis attains an Old Testament grandeur. Cartwright, by being consistent to her oath, finds herself confronted with two choices: either to stay on as Tunga Khan's mistress, until he tires of her, or else to kill them both, as she does; Cartwright's murder and suicide are violations of her oath, acts of ultimate despair, defeat, and negation, but there is a pagan glory to her, and a Chris-tian one too. Her moral abnegation of self to save her "family" mark her as

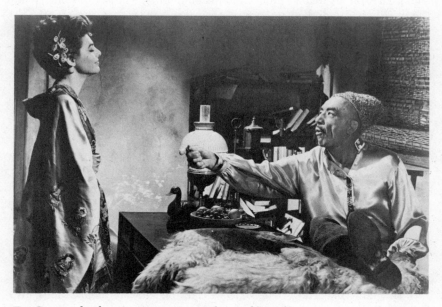

Dr. Cartwright about to poison Tunga Khan and herself.

the Fordian hero in the tradition of Carey, Rogers, Fonda, and Wayne. But the hero's traditional celibacy now has an ironic twist, and the decision to intervene entails, even more forcibly than for Tom Doniphon, exclusion from life itself. Yet this was her "case," so she stayed. So simple. And her manner at death . . . do we not all see our death this way—as a thing we violently detest yet wish we could assent to? She assents, and her suicide seems heroic, an ultimate act of defiance and submission.

Andrews ought to have been proud. "I founded this mission, and I made it a part of the life of the entire province." Education appears to be the prime task; as usual in Ford, the white man conquers with the alphabet. It is easy to judge the missionaries racist, for they seem so displaced in this "last place on earth," "this Chinese hole-in-the-wall"; they are all homeless searchers. As Miss Argent puts it, "We're not like those poor creatures in the village." One may see a questioning of the role of American imperialism here, though there is no denying the sacrifice, poverty, and humane intentions of these missionaries. And the truth is, as in *Cheyenne Autumn* and as in much of the world today, Western civilization's triumph (and often its welcome) is infinitely greater than any attempt at assessing the balance of gain or loss or good or evil.

Yet these missionaries fail, as the French failed in *The Hurricane* (the bandits are like a hurricane), and the implications of many traditional Fordian devices have turned funereal in *7 Women*. The children, as they flee the plague, sing "Shall We Gather at the River" as though it were a desperate *"Dies Irae"* rather than a celebration of community. The favorite image of the parade has dwindled to a procession of refugees, to a doctor and her coolies, to an oxcart of expelled missionaries—and yet, also, has exploded to a hoard of savages roaring across the screen in slashing diagonals. The antinomal image of stable subsistence is almost absent; only a restless serenity is found beneath the large tree in the yard. Life has become more consuming than ever; Marty Maher's pipe is replaced by Cartwright's innumerable cigarettes. But then comes the baby.

All is paradox, like the problems of evil and God, and Ford has no private revelation to communicate. Regardless of right or wrong, historical necessity, as in *Liberty Valance*, is not to be denied. As Tunga Khan gawks quizzically at the rockingchair on the mission porch, the white head of the nomad's horse juts into the frame, reminding us that, as in *The Searchers*, wilderness and civilization confront each other across an abyss. The Mongols are not insensitive to beauty: of the scenes missing from the theatrical edition of *7 Women* the least expendable is the moment, all in long shot, when Lean Warrior jumps from his horse to pluck a bunch of flowers for Cartwright. Yet the Mongols are savages, they kill little children and laugh. The women will all die in a ditch, predicts Florrie Pether, "like animals," and they nearly do, and Charles was "shot down like a dog," and Andrews calls the baby an "animal" and calls Cartwright the "mother of hogs." As in *Mogambo*, the humanity of man is placed in question. For it seems that neither the whites nor the Asians have much more than a shred of free will within the determining forces of culture, history, biology, libido, and profession.

Nothing is revealed, all is mystery. What remains is the image of gold midst black, of a flaming torch passing by, of bright threads, of flashes of vibrant, all-feeling persons who shine in the intimately awesome beauty of human interior life, and who then pass on. This is the immanent transcendent into which Ford has merged his terrible, Blakean ambiguities. Gone is the misanthropy of *Liberty Valance;* the only palpable truth is individual consciousness.

Much of *7 Women*'s artistic interest is difficult to discuss on paper. One small example: we cannot reproduce here the manner in which Mildred Dunnock delivers a line such as "Everybody has turkey [*pause*] on Thanksgiving Day," and it is surprising how difficult, if not impossible, it is to imitate her, even if one tapes that line and listens to it a dozen times. Virtuosity is often greatest in the simplest of things, and complexity is properly the clear combination of a multitude of simple articulations.

The complexity of *7 Women*, a movie that, like its individual characters and their actions, utterly evades description, is due largely to the integrity of character presentation. As in playing a melody, or delivering a verse, the highest art in direction occurs when, through total stylization (clarification),

the subject emerges with a separate life peculiarly its own. Ford and Renoir are similar, in that they both start with simple particles of elements, and then produce ingenious combinations; but generally they are also dissimilar, in that Renoir's particles often have an indefinable nondimensionality to them, while Ford's often have a certain definiteness and squareness. But 7 *Women* is a film in which Ford comes closest to Renoir's manner. Or to Murnau's cinema of presence: for character in 7 *Women* is no longer a conception, but a manifestation, a phenomenon, in which distance no longer disunites actor and role. Thus the fascination of the dining room scenes, in which we can watch the chameleonlike comportment of ten individuals whom we know fairly well, yet who are surprising us constantly. Ford's art is to have each nuance of articulation reveal something novel and interesting (and yet consistent); a character's initial typing becomes the basis for the diversity his personality later manifests.

To the paradox of style/realism correspond other paradoxes: God/evil, opinion/fact, the mission/the world, faith/science, free will/determinism, woman/man, Christian-medical mores/Mongol savagery, and, most especially, interior life/social life. Irish Catholicism has within it a deep streak of Manichaeanism, which Ford manages to pose here at every second, while yet subsuming the polarities of "soul" and "matter" within a mysterious, labyrinthine unity into which they dissolve. To this effect, the feminist angle on 7 *Women* is interesting, because it points out that the life of an individual is a constant struggle against definitions imposed not only by immediate society, but also by history and even by one's own body. Age shall wither, regardless of the youth of the mind.

When Agatha Andrews enters Emma's room, Ford rests his camera for a long time upon Agatha looking, before cutting to what she is looking at (Emma washing). The pause is meditative, rather than suspenseful; it establishes Agatha, rather than Emma, as the scene's emotional center. For Emma will arouse our empathy far more easily than Andrews, and the pause on Agatha intends to correct an imbalance before it occurs. She enters slowly and uncertainly, because Emma is in her bra. The pause at the door engenders conflicts of desire and guilt; she wants to touch Emma's hair, but pulls back her hand.

Crosscutting often indicates conflict. When Andrews and Cartwright argue in the office, angles, subtly oblique at the outset, grow parallel as their mutual fury reaches its height. But, more frequently, the cutting's alternation of isolation and combination suggests the struggle, so continuous in each of these people, to liberate the self from its impediments. Formally, the struggle resembles a concerto grosso—alternations of *soli* (cameo vignettes) and *tutti* (intricate ensembles)—while the vertical (i.e., simultaneous) juxtapositions of disparate emotions attains a quasi-fugal complexity. Tempo slows and shots become longer in the movie's course, simply because the women are forced together by Tunga Khan. In this context, a camera movement may be more precise than a cut, as in expressing Agatha's dual dilemma of mental isolation and inability to escape from forced community.

Since, most of the time, these people are awkward, since they usually communicate something different than what they would like to, the brief moments of nakedness are all the more telling. Such moments may make us wince, as Cartwright winces, when Florrie tells the story of her life in one cliché ("What's a woman without a child?") or when Pether juts his chin out into the frame and declares, "For the first time in my life I'm not scared." Or the moments may be voyeuristic, catching a character unawares, like the placid figure Miss Argent makes eating her rice and trying to hide from the battle of wills raging around her. Or they may be tiny things that later become important, like Mrs. Russell staring at Pether, but avoiding his helping hand, when she climbs out of the oxcart on her arrival at the mission. Or they may come with sudden unexpectancy, as experiences revealed as devoutly wished, like the combination of silver (Argent) and gold when Miss Argent, remembering to love, returns to embrace Cartwright, and Cartwright kisses passionately in return, grateful for a little friendship, the need for which she, in her bereft loneliness, has kept concealed.

Cutting often establishes connections that we would otherwise not make: the surprising image of water being poured over Tunga Khan is followed by the sound of the baby's cry; both image and sound stand out as life symbols. Or, Cartwright surrenders herself to Tunga Khan, then we see the baby being oiled: biological cause and effect. In the first act of the picture, Cartwright says, "It'll be a miracle if that baby lives." Then, in the third act, that baby is born, and Cartwright is on her way out the door to fulfill her deal with Tunga Khan, but finds her way barred by Miss Binns. But, in her role as ingenuous agent, Emma carries the baby between the Cartwright-Binns confrontation, and says, "Isn't it a miracle! He's alive and he's breathing!" And Binns lets Cartwright go, for it is both a miracle and not a miracle.

Seldom has Ford been so exciting in his organization of ensemble movement within a scene; the careful choreography of past films is often replaced by brief, spontaneous contrapuntal gestures: Emma leading the children to the fields, while Cartwright races around in the background; Binns jutting her head into the left-bottom foreground of a scene to offer assistance during the plague, causing Cartwright in the center to pivot away from Andrews at upper-right, thus marking Andrews's fall from authority; the commotion in the hut, when Florrie begins her labor pains, and Ford pans with Argent away from cringing Andrews, over the group on the floor, then follows the excited Emma searching for a stick for Florrie to bite; Cartwright stalking into Tunga Khan's room, simultaneously surrending her body and asserting her authority "simply by striding toward the camera and forcing three people to react to her movement within the same frame. This movement triggers a series of abrupt actions with explosive force. When Ford finally does cut back and forth between [Cartwright and Tunga Khan], the

Eisensteinian collision is supplemented by a more supple sensibility capable of transmitting a touch of tenderness between two deadly antagonists" (Sarris);[30] or, the conclusion of the wrestling match when, in four quick shots: /Tunga Khan reaches down to the ground, seizes Lean Warrior's head, lifts it up to the camera and twists it and throws him down dead; / abruptly Ford cuts to a flute and drum playing cheery folk music; /a wide shot of the fight-circle, Tunga Khan striding toward Cartwright searchingly, as Lean Warrior's body, lifted high, is carried out Viking-fashion; /Cartwright on the porch, throwing away her cigarette and strolling off.

Seldom have Ford's images been so beautiful. The colors pass from orange-brown, to the Vermeer-like blues, purples, and slanting white light of the women locked in the dining room, to the gold and black of Cartwright in the corridor. And the vitally inventive, quickly cut exploitation of anamorphic wide screen's possibilities contrasts glaringly with the comparatively stilted long takes of *The Long Gray Line*.

Seldom has Ford's music been so apt. Elmer Bernstein's score makes *7 Women* into a virtual tone poem. The Mongol theme (recalling *Liberty Valance*'s "gladiator" theme), the intimations of derangement, the excited signals of warning as Cartwright examines the sick refugees, the ominous cantus firmus beneath "Shall We Gather at the River," and, most of all, those lovely fragile passages of quasi-serenity bring to fulfillment this spiritual odyssey of John Ford. For visually, too, *7 Women* is music: organization of time and space to purify, isolate, and interrelate gesture. As lines of motion parade across the frame and characters traverse from one blocking toward another, agogic pauses mark their solitary pilgrimages through life as quests—no sooner attained than denied—for understanding, fulfillment, and closeness to another soul.

7 Women was Ford's final picture. "I think he was ready for it," says Anna Lee (Miss Russell), "because he was absolutely charming to everybody. We'd break for tea as we always did at 4:30 and have the table brought out and the teapot and the cakes. He was particularly gracious on this one, never raised his voice." (The only explosion came when Flora Robson protested her dressing-room door lacked "Dame" before her name; and she would argue with Ford. "I saw her being absolutely shredded, because she did not realize you could not argue with or question Mr. Ford. It was always like that when someone was new.")

The picture was shot in continuity, in order to get good performances; for the same reason, Ford exposed three and a half to four times as much negative as he eventually used. *7 Women*'s scenarists were in France and would telephone portions of the script daily during shooting. Producer Bernard Smith, recalls Anna Lee, "would come over to the long table [where

Ford introducing *The Rookie of the Year* (1955).

the cast gathered] with new pages hot off the wire. Ford would lift his patch and look at them, study them for a few moments, and then deliberately, right in front of Bernie Smith, he would tear them up, throw them on the floor, and say, 'Now, what are we going to say?' From then on he would give us ideas and we'd start improvising the dialogue, and that's why I don't think probably more than a dozen pages in the original script were ever used.* He would say, 'Well, I think you should say this,' and we'd make notes. He'd give us a line and Anne [Bancroft] would say, 'Well, I think I'll say it this way. . . . ' "31

Shot on a sound stage, sparing Ford the fatigue of location, *7 Women* came out just as he wanted. But, even though directing was like "dope addiction," he was not to have another chance at it. The gossips said he was senile, *7 Women* could be cited to prove their point, and production insurance was hard to obtain for sickly old directors. For whatever reason, Ford's

---

*Actually, comparison between the film and preliminary scripts shows Ford followed the screenplay quite exactly. The points of departure are in the precise ways things are staged (e.g., the script calls for Cartwright to stand up in shock when Tunga Khan breaks Lean Warrior's neck, whereas Ford merely has her indicate bored disgust) and in that every third line is rewritten to make it less literary, slangier, and more clipped. The line "So long, you bastard" is not in the script.

Patricia Neal began the picture as Cartwright but was paralyzed by a stroke after a couple of days' shooting.

Ford being interviewed by Philip Jenkinson.

next picture, *The Miracle of Merriford*, was scrapped by Metro in October 1965, scarcely a week before shooting was to have begun. A few years afterwards, his marginal involvement in two minor documentaries, on Vietnam and on Marine General Chesty Puller, were taken as evidence of his isolation. Many feature projects came tantalizingly close to fulfillment, only to have backing dissolve at the last moment. John Wayne was reluctant to involve himself in a film with Ford. As late as May 1973, Ford was quoted as having always dreamed of filming Conan Doyle's *White Company*, which he claimed to have read each year since he was eight.[32] In his hands, it would have resembled his Civil War episode: the bright hopes of youth go off to war only to find disillusionment and unsought-for wisdom.

Personally, he was as messy as ever. Clothes and piles of books would be strewn everywhere. He consumed chocolate bars and tobacco like a glutton. He liked watching movies, but if he did so critically, he never let on.* Natu-

---

*A "ten-favorite" list Ford compiled for *Cinema* in 1964 is whimsical: (1) *The Birth of a Nation;* (2) *The Honor System* (Walsh, 1916—a thief is let out of prison on his word, and returns); (3) *3 Godfathers* (Ford); (4) *Ninotchka* (Lubitsch); (5) *The High and the Mighty* (Wellman), (6) *Tol'able David* (King, 1921); (7) *The Song of Bernadette* (King); (8) *Lady for a Day* (Capra); (9) *Going My Way* (McCarey); (10) *The Alamo* (Wayne). (Always extravagant with public praise, Ford once said: "*The Alamo* is the greatest picture I've ever seen. It will last forever,

rally he enjoyed pictures friends had made, and complained he never could be objective about his own work. Asked his favorite, his choice would vary: *The Sun Shines Bright, Wagon Master, Young Mr. Lincoln, The Fugitive*. He told Tavernier he liked "Leo McCarey—I love *Make Way for Tomorrow*—Frank Capra, and then people like Raoul Walsh, who's a bit like me, but more seductive and pleasing to women, Tay Garnett, Henry King. I also like Sammy Fuller a lot, a fine fellow with great integrity. I don't like John Huston, who's a faker."[33]

In 1966 he made a tour of duty in the navy, sailing from the Mediterranean to the Philippines and then to Vietnam. One grandson, Timothy, was in the merchant marine; the other, Dan, had received a battlefield promotion in Vietnam. In 1968 the *Araner* was sold. It was in ill repair, too old, and costing a fortune to maintain. Ford considered himself lucky to get $25,000 and some Hawaiian resort shares for her. In 1970, he and Mary celebrated their fiftieth anniversary by being married again, in the Field Photo chapel, and she pronounced her advice to young couples: "Believe nothing you hear, and only half of what you see."[34]

The Farm itself had been sold in 1965. Its purpose had become less compelling as the veterans grew into lives of their own. Funerals, such as Ward Bond's in 1960, had become its chief events. Although half the land had been sold in 1961, the financial burden on Ford became immense, and there were tax problems, as well. The $300,000 it fetched, together with the chapel, intact, were given to the Motion Picture Country Home, a lavish industry-endowed retirement community in Woodland Hills. The sweeping portrait of Ford that once dominated the Farm's tavern room now hangs in the lodge.

Ford's acknowledged debtors, among directors, included Elia Kazan, Sergei Eisenstein, Samuel Fuller, Jean-Marie Straub, Peter Bogdanovich, Budd Boetticher, Mark Donskoi, John Milius, Lindsay Anderson, Orson Welles, Bertrand Tavernier, Ingmar Bergman, Frank Capra, Douglas Sirk, and Howard Hawks. In Japan, Akira Kurosawa wore dark glasses while directing, not to protect his eyes, but in order to look like John Ford. In Paris in 1967, and at Venice in 1971, Ford was fêted royally.

But in America he no longer counted for anything. His last years were lonely, and he suffered from forced retirement. And he was aging rapidly. A broken hip put him into a wheelchair in 1970 and compelled him to move from the Bel Air house to a single-level one Katharine Hepburn located in Palm Desert, near Eisenhower Hospital, where he was receiving radiation treatment for cancer.

---

run forever, for all peoples, all families, everywhere." Anything for a buddy.) On another occasion he cited Laurel and Hardy's *The Battle of the Century* (McCarey, 1927) as his favorite. And he was so taken by Renoir's *Grand Illusions* (1938) that he wanted to remake it in English, with English prisoners.

There was not much time left. In October 1972 the Screen Directors Guild staged a salute to him — Ford chose *How Green Was My Valley* for the occasion. Katharine Hepburn came for a week's visit. And finally, on March 31, 1973, the American Film Institute honored him with its first Life Achievement Award. It was his last hurrah, and was telecast nationwide. President Richard Nixon appeared to wheel Ford around, present him with the Medal of Freedom, and promote him to full admiral. Ford talked, cried really, about the prisoners of war returning home from Vietnam and, for this, prayed "God bless Richard Nixon!" The remark disconcerted those who had forgotten the stinging satires of Nixon in *The Last Hurrah* and *The Sun Shines Bright*; but Nixon was president, and needed blessing.

John Ford died in his sleep, attended by priests, August 31, 1973, at 6:05 P.M., in the house on Old Prospect Trail in the desert. Cancer was the cause. He was alert until the end, using painkillers only during the last two weeks. He was survived by Mary, who had Parkinson's disease, their children, and a sister, Josephine.

His will, signed March 31, 1973, left an estate of $500,000, excluding real estate, to be divided, after his wife's death, half in trust to daughter Barbara and half to son Patrick's two children. Patrick himself was excluded, without explanation, but $10,000 was bequeathed to Pat's daughter by his second marriage. (A few years later, Mary Ford brought suit for $4,100,000 against the executors, charging they had sold the Rolls Royce and the Copa de Oro house for less than true value and had made the will in a tax-costly fashion; the suit is still pending.)

Ford, out of pure cussedness, would fight the IRS even when his lawyers said not to. But money, as his business manager, Bea Benjamin, said, was something "he never cared about."[35] The *Araner* was his sole extravagance — he spent $75,000 prettying her up for *Donovan's Reef*, in return for a $5,000 leasing fee — and aside from her, his lifestyle was modest indeed by Hollywood standards. Not only did he turn a deaf ear to most tax and investment advice — such as real estate — but he never exploited his name for gain. Compared with Hitchcock, for example, who did pursue wealth, Ford earned barely 5 *percent* as much money during the fifties and sixties. What Ford pursued was the freedom to make his kind of movies. He not only turned down an offer from Zanuck guaranteeing him $600,000 per year, he went ahead and made, independently, *The Fugitive*, *3 Godfathers*, *Wagon Master*, and *The Sun Shines Bright* — projects which, from their conception, he knew would be lucky even to earn back their cost. Subsequently, when he was commanding $250,000-plus per picture, he chose instead to do *The Rising of the Moon* and *Gideon's Day* for no salary at all, and then *Young Cassidy* for only $50,000. His personal charities were considerable, even apart from the $300,000 donated to found the Field Photo Farm and the annual subsidies he gave to maintain it. His war service, too, cost him heavily: from averaging around $175,000 before the war, his yearly earnings dropped to $27,000, $14,000, and $23,000 in 1942, '43, and '44. He griped constantly, of course, about the sums Mary spent—and they appear to have been fairly lavish—but he never restrained her, at least not for long.

The funeral was held September 5, at Hollywood's Church of the Blessed Sacrament. Richard Koszarski reports that, before the service, the church was empty except for the coffin and a single mourner, Woody Strode—a scene out of *Liberty Valance*.[36] On the coffin lay the flag from Ford's headquarters during the battle of Midway. He was buried in Holy Cross Cemetery, Culver City.

His last public appearance had been for the Memorial Day services at the Motion Picture Country Home. Frank Baker:

> "When he said goodbye to me, it was a very touching thing. He had enormous respect for my wife, Helen Broneau, whose picture is here, and who'd worked with him around 1916. I didn't approach him up there at the chapel. I was sitting here [in my room at the Home], and I heard a car draw up out there, and a knock came on the door, and there was a warrant officer who was taking him around. And he said, "Admiral Ford is in the car outside, and he would like to see you." I said, "Sure, bring him in." So he came in in his wheelchair, and he was sitting where you are. And I didn't have any liquor in the place—I don't drink myself. And he was dying; he didn't have many days to live. He said, "Have you got a drink, Frank?" And I suddenly realized I didn't have one. Now some months before a girl from Australia, a girl named Joan Long, had been out here, and was going to do a picture on my family. And she'd brought me a bottle of Scotch, so I suddenly thought of that—and she was a great admirer of John Ford's work. So I took it out, and to excuse my mess-up, I told him the story of this girl's film, and that he had been her favorite director or some damn thing. And Ford went back into the past. He was dragging up figures that I'd forgotten, speaking with a terribly deep sentimental feeling about them. And bringing up Frank again, and Frank in an entirely different light. And I was hoping he'd just get out and not say goodbye. And he kept staring at this picture, and he was looking at her. I'd poured him the drink, and he had it in his hand. And he wanted to say, "So long, I won't be seeing you again," and he didn't know what to say. He always brought my wife into everything. My wife, he'd get her advice. Certain stories he wouldn't do till she had read them. Suddenly he said, "Well," and he's staring right at her. And he wants to include me, but he can't bring himself to. And he suddenly raises that glass, and he's staring right at this picture, "To . . ." and he's going to say Helen, my wife, and he knew that would shock me I guess, for he says, "To Joan Long." And we downed the drink. And then he looked around for someplace to throw the glass, you know, so it wouldn't be used again. I told him I'd take care of it. He said, "Well, I guess all good things must end. Quartermaster!" and he went out, never shook hands with me or any-

thing. He went out and got in the car, and I stood down there. He's just staring right ahead, and the car starts to move, and he didn't turn towards me, but he raised his hand in salute as he went by. And he did a funny thing, as he started going out, the petty officer left us for a moment to go and open the door and he turned around and he started to put his hand out. And he said a very strange thing which I today value very much, knowing Ford. He said, "Well, I guess this is it. I'd like you to know that you're one of the very few people I ever respected. You never crawled on your belly to me."[37]

Mary Ford, 1977:

To me, he was the greatest man that ever lived in every way. I just thought he was great because he had a wonderful sense of humor; he made me laugh. I'd seen a lot of misery, a lot of unhappiness. I don't know, there was something about him. It certainly wasn't his looks. I just fell in love with him . . . Oh such a life. It was like a dream . . . I wouldn't change a day in my life. Each one has been so perfect. Up in my room, I have a large picture of Jack, and people say to me, "Why do you sit and look at that?" Because every minute of it was a laugh, something worth having.[38]

6 Conclusion

*People are incorrect to compare a director
to an author. If he's a creator, he's more
like an architect. And an architect
conceives his plans according to precise
circumstances.* JOHN FORD

The notion of a Hollywood director as auteur, author, architect, or central creative force of a movie is complex. For a Hollywood director rarely wrote his own story or screenplay, chose his actors, designed his
sets, or edited his shots. Even in telling actors where to stand, the director
had often to bow to the wishes of a producer or star. Yet only when a director
does succeed in imposing his will over the various contributions to a picture
is he considered an auteur.

Broadly speaking, we can discern three types of such auteurs: the collab-
orator, who keeps a low profile (e.g., Cukor); the author, who dominates
completely (Welles, Sternberg); the architect, who reigns (Ford, Renoir).

Ford had the advantage of entering his profession in the teens, when
directorial authority was greatest. Four years' apprenticeship to brother
Francis had already earned him a reservoir of friends within the industry
and a thorough technical acumen. His liberty, during five years and thirty-
nine pictures at Universal, was secured by the facts that his stars (Harry
Carey, Hoot Gibson) were coincidentally close friends and the studio's biggest moneymakers and that front-office interference with low-budget westerns was minimal. He continued to avoid day-to-day supervision by trans-
ferring to a "director's studio," Fox, and by establishing himself as their

"fair-haired boy." In the thirties, when filmmaking became less personal, Ford lost considerable independence, but his box-office record and personal authority still allowed him uncommon control. Even in 1936, at the height of the assembly-line studio system, Howard Sharpe could write in *Photoplay* that Ford "works directly with each department during [preparation]. His hand draws the design for a set fireplace.* His own suggestions are the inspiration for certain gowns and coiffures and uniforms—and most important of all, much of the dialogue (especially in his Irish portraits) comes from the Ford typewriter."[1]

In all but five or so of his films, Ford worked intimately with his scenarist from the movie's inception. He tended to work with the same people through many decades—writers, cameramen, technicians, actors, editors—and they knew what he wanted. Far from squashing these individual talents, Ford had eccentric ways of putting them on their own and goading them to surpass themselves. Yet at the same time Ford fashioned these collective efforts into a movie-world as detailed a product of his imagination as the Paris of Balzac or the London of Dickens.

How did he manage to do this?

Ford's Working Methods

Actors.　Ford sets had a special air to them. For most people it was a reunion, for newcomers it was often trial under fire. "You had to be able to do everything," said Frank Baker. "He didn't care for the rules of the Screen Actors Guild. He'd have you playing a major part, and suddenly say, 'You're doing nothing, I want somebody to sit on that seat there, and when the coach goes by, get up and walk across.' And you'd better do it too, otherwise he'd ride you. He picked on people. He always picked somebody at the beginning of a picture, and he'd let them have it. You couldn't do anything right. You could *not* do anything right! I've seen big Victor McLaglen stand there and cry like a child, and I've seen Duke Wayne do exactly the same thing. Blubber like a child, and Ford just sitting there, humiliating the hell out of his star player. He was doing it for a purpose all the while. He's getting the best discipline out of that company than any company that ever went before a camera. He just had to open his mouth, and 'Yes sir, yes sir.'"[2]

Yet his sets were not tense. An atmosphere of seriousness, of reverence, even, would often prevail, enhanced by Danny Borzage's accordion music, and punctuated by the ritual traditions of afternoon tea and the director's humorous eccentricities—the scapegoat, the chewed handkerchiefs, the long pauses leading up to sarcasms. However disconcerting to the uninitiate, these were among life's stranger joys to the cultists. And Ford's sadisms were the exception. More often he was the soul of kindness. His troupe

---

*This was *Mary of Scotland*'s fireplace, which reappeared in Xanadu in *Citizen Kane*.

became affectionate families and years later many would still speak of the time they were making a Ford picture as one of the most enjoyable experiences of their lives.

"After photographing several John Ford pictures, I didn't notice any pattern or method. . . . He could not be compared even to himself from one day to the next," said Arthur C. Miller.[3] "This man directs less than any man in the business. As a matter of fact, he doesn't direct—he doesn't want any actor to give an imitation of him playing the part. He wants the actor to create the part—that's why he hired him, because he saw him in the part. You'd sit at a big coffee table in the morning—everybody was there, whether you worked that day or not. You'd drink coffee until you couldn't swig it down any more."[4] They would discuss anything, from football to aviation, and occasionally Ford would interject something concerning the picture. "He'd start telling *you* about some scenes, and suddenly a guy over *there* would realize that he was talking about the character *he* was playing—but he'd be talking to you. Now the actor would start using his imagination—I caught wise to this after a year or so—and you could see it, he wasn't listening to the conversation any more, he'd be thinking. This was the way Ford got performances out of people."[5] According to Miller, "There were never any long rehearsals, especially in the dialogue, nor did I ever see him act a piece of business for an actor, or tell when to look at someone, or read a line. There were no marks on the floor for the actors to position themselves [—they might look down for the marks]; he simply gave them a general idea of where to be. I heard Ford tell a writer that if he gave detailed instructions, all he would get would be a well-rehearsed line of chatter. I am sure that this is the reason he never had drilled rehearsals and was displeased when he had to make a second take of a scene, which he seldom did."[6]

Miller photographed *How Green Was My Valley,* among others, and it seems a miracle that Ford obtained the control he did with these methods— every scene and gesture so meaningfully choreographed. But others confirm Miller. "[Ford] doesn't like to talk about it," says Henry Fonda, "there's practically no communication."[7] "He never talked the part you were playing," said Pat O'Brien; "he'd tell you what he wanted . . . , 'I hope you can get it,' he'd say, with that patch over his eye and chewing that handkerchief. When you failed, he'd say, 'that wasn't what I wanted. Try to get what I wanted.' When it was finally good, he'd go over and hug you. 'Why the hell didn't you get it in the first place?'"[8] "'Laconic' is a good word for John Ford and his technique of direction," wrote Mary Astor; "no big deal about communication with John. Terse, pithy, to the point. Very Irish, a dark personality, a sensitivity which he did everything to conceal, but once he said to me . . . , 'Make it *scan,* Mary.' And I said to myself, 'Aha! I know you now!'"[9] "I know I never worked with another movie director who knew as much about acting as he did or cared so much about performance," wrote Raymond Massey; "to me he rarely made a direct comment or suggestion. It was mostly brief innuendo, laced with Irish wit and always constructive, frequently confidential."[10]

Ford centered attention on himself, as actors hoped (sometimes desperately) for a hint of guidance. "You become so tuned to him," said Maureen O'Hara, "one word of his becomes a volume. You become aware that he understands the story and knows how to get it out of you. It's a frame of mind he creates. He puts you at ease and sets you free to think, and you can move easily."[11] "He wouldn't tell you what to do," said Anna Lee, "but you'd find yourself doing things that obviously had come from somewhere. It was some kind of thought transference that he did. And I think that's why he liked people who worked with him to be totally absorbed in him as a director, in other words, not to have too many ideas yourself. You were the vessel in which he injected what he wanted, and then it sort of flowed out of you." Occasionally Ford would walk through a scene, without telling you he was doing it. Nonetheless, you were expected to imitate his tiniest gesture. "People who worked with Ford a lot, like Duke Wayne or James Stewart, have so adapted themselves to his mannerisms," says Anna Lee, "that now, if I see Jimmy Stewart on a talk show, I'm looking at Jack Ford. I mean the way he moves his mouth. And I found this with my sons, when they were little; they'd copy the way Jack Ford would mutter."[12]

Ford's direction was sometimes mechanical, as when during *Rio Grande* he instructed John Wayne to keep his face blank and allow the scenery to provide the thought, or as during *The Battle of Midway* when Ford took notes from his pocket and told his four "voices": "When I point to you, say what I tell you to say," and in twenty minutes they were done.[13] But he could go to the opposite extreme and have Henry Fonda improvise a long, long monologue during *Drums Along the Mohawk* while shooting questions to him from off-camera. And Ford, at other times, might employ the intimate associations that are part of "Method" acting. Ruth Clifford was playing a Comanche captive in *The Searchers* who goes berserk when she sees a doll, and Ford confided to her almost off-handedly, "You know, I'd almost whisper it. She's . . . just . . . lost her . . . No English." Ford sensed Ruth was thinking of her own lost child; he put a piece of wood in her arms, and told her to let go her emotion midway through the scene. It played searingly. "I'm proud of you," he whispered afterward. But such praise was rare.[14]

Ford "rehearsed, rehearsed and rehearsed till you could practically do it blindfolded," says Dobe Carey.[15] "I never remember being directed. It all just happened," says Roddy McDowall.[16] Anne Bancroft:

We realized why he is considered to be one of the greatest directors in Hollywood. He arrives each morning knowing exactly what he intends to film and with every scene visually worked out in his mind. He is never in a hurry, yet doesn't waste a minute. His rehearsals are so thorough that more often than not he will film the most difficult scene in one 'take,' rarely more than two. . . . If there were any differences of opinion as to how a scene should be played, the actor invariably ended up agreeing with Mr. Ford. He is infinitely patient in explaining his reasons for what he wants. At the same time, he is in command and can be firm when necessary.[17]

Often he would rewrite lines, Dobe Carey recalls. He would say, "Come on, kids, let's get chairs and gather round here. Has anybody got a script?" They would run through the dialogue, and this would give him ideas. Then they would start again, and he would point to you and say a line. "And if you didn't catch on, if you didn't know how he'd work, it would infuriate him. The minute he would point to you and say, '*I ain't taking that from you,*' you were supposed to say it right back at him." Then, they would block the scene for the cameraman, relax while the set was lit, and rehearse five or six more times. Ford would never use typical director-talk like, "Jump on your cues! Pick it up! Pick it up! Let's have a lot of energy, kids!" He had *body language*, says Carey. "He'd get very grotesque looking (people would snicker, which would infuriate him); he'd act things out for you in an extremely exaggerated version of what he wanted."[18]

Thus Ford's methods varied radically. But one does note, grossly simplifying, three main "modes" of play: tragic, or epic (in which every superfluous movement was repressed); comedic, or natural (more spontaneous); and slapstick (broad, exaggerated, often used for perverse actions). While the individual actor was usually given liberty to discover himself, "in sequences with a large number of people he [paid] attention to every movement and gesture, almost as though he was directing a ballet," said Flora Robson.[19] Indeed, Ford's direction is most discernible in the choreographed fashion five or more people will move about a room.

Actors were never permitted to view rushes, and though the scenarist might have traced a complete biography for his character, the actor might not even know which part he was playing till just before shooting. Ford delighted in throwing disconcerted actors in otherwise carefully prepared scenes.

In 1936, he used a silent camera 40 percent of the time. "I can talk while a scene is shooting," explained Ford, "and give suggestions about expression or movement; as a result I don't have to make so many takes. I've discovered that if you rehearse a scene too much it looks artificial and—well, *rehearsed.*"[20]

Ford was obsessed with adjusting actors' clothing, particularly hats. He would stamp on hats, crumple them, then put them back on the actor—and grab his hand if he started to readjust it. "The lines of the costume react on the lines of the face just as in music a note has its overtones," writes art historian Frederick T. Weber; "this is why artists are always glad to use scarfs, furs or anything they can themselves arrange on their subjects."[21] No actor dared suggest it, if he wanted a particular hat. But, according to Wayne, if you gave your hat to wardrobe and let it get mixed up with all the other hats, nine times out of ten Ford would pick that one for you.

According to Katherine Hepburn, it was Ford's sensitivity that made him a great director of actors. He could always sense what people were feeling — even across a room (and if he sensed hostility he would get up, go over, and find out why). With this sensitivity—which amounted to an ability to read minds, almost—Ford could prompt an actor to do what Ford wanted him to do, but in the actor's own way. Similar ability, to some degree, has been possessed by many great directors—especially by those who do not treat their actors as marionettes.

Photography. "I think first as a cameraman," said Ford.[22] "He knew more about photography than any other man who ever worked in the movies," declared cinematographer William Clothier.[23]

It may come as a surprise, then, to understand that Ford, like many other good directors, almost never looked through the camera. Gabriel Figueroa, who shot *The Fugitive*, explains how this worked. He met with Ford and they discussed the film's general ambience and looked over the sets. The first sequence was to be shot the following day. Ford gave him some instructions, and said, "Gaby, find the best set-up for a long shot."

Next day the basic lighting was ready when Ford arrived.

I asked him if he would like to check the set-up through the camera. He looked at me, and after a puff on his pipe, simply answered:

"I am just the director, you are the photographer. But tell me: which lens are we using?"

"28mm." I said.

"Okay. So you are cutting here and there," and he began to indicate the imaginary limits of the space covered by the camera lens. It took Ford years of experience to be able to do this, and it made my staff and me aware of the kind of person we were going to work with.[24]

Ford's favorite cameramen—Joseph August, Arthur Miller, Gregg Toland, George Schneiderman, Bert Glennon, Archie Stout—each had recognizable styles of their own, yet their work for Ford *also* looks Fordian. A Ford movie, it cannot be overstressed, is first of all an aesthetic pleasure visually; it demanded beautiful images. Often it is the painterly style of Ford's pictures that first distinguishes him to audiences. At times this painterly manner has fallen into fashionable disrepute, and people have claimed preference for, say, the newsreel-like straightforwardness of De Sica or the extremely desaturated color of the early seventies. Yet Ford believed that "pictures, not words, should tell the story,"[25] and the conscious aestheticism of his compositions is not separable from his narration.

He preferred black-and-white. "You can get a guy off the street and he can shoot a picture in color. But it takes a real artist to do a black-and-white picture."[26] And he liked a rich array of gray tones, from a velvet black to an ermine white. He liked to brag about his lighting, which tended toward a rich chiaroscuro, with pools of light and dark. No other director so consistently exploited the sides, corners, and depth of the frame. Action was staged, usually, triplanarly, with the principal subject in midground.

Ford's reputation for getting "all outdoors" onto film was a matter of effectiveness rather than quantity. Indeed, his interiors are far more creative, simply because he had more angles, shadows, and objects to play with.

He had a reputation for being cheap with film. The typical practice in Hollywood in the thirties was to film a "master shot" of a scene, five or ten times, then move in and cover all the parts of the scene in profuse variety of medium shots and close-ups. All of this footage would then be delivered to an editor who would play around with it until he came up with a way of putting it together that met the approval of various committees of producers. To get this ultimate two minutes of screen time, the director may have exposed two hours or more of negative.

Not Ford. "I don't give 'em a lot of film to play with. In fact, Eastman used to complain that I exposed so little film. I *do* cut in the camera. Otherwise, if you give them a lot of film 'the committee' takes over. They start juggling scenes around and taking out this and putting in that. They can't do it with my pictures. I cut in the camera and that's it. There's not a lot of film left on the floor when I'm finished."[27]

Not only did Ford expose just a little film (say, two and a half times his final footage), but he only shot the precise pictures he knew he would use, and he tended to stage scenes in (short) "sequence shots," moving actors in to close shots, rather than adding inserts later. In Hollywood of the twenties and thirties, Ford's methods were revolutionary and deeply influenced masters as diverse as Vidor and Capra.

Robert Parrish explains what it was like to edit a Ford film:

I was once given a sequence of *Drums Along the Mohawk* to edit. It was the first time I had done that kind of work and I really worked hard at it. I sweat blood and water. Suddenly Ford came into the cutting room and asked me how it was going. I told him it wasn't going well. He stared at me and said simply, "If, with the stuff I've given you, you can't manage, go learn some other job." Since I was gawking at him, surprised, he added, "All you have to do is cut at the frames where I say [on the film], "Start!" and at the frames where I say, "Cut!" and to splice one shot onto the next. That's all." And he left. It was true. Ford didn't need an editor.[28]

Ford, said Lefty Hough, his assistant over many decades, "was such a different character than any of these other fellows—the Capras, the Wellmans. Much smarter director. Very brilliant man. Only director I ever remember walking on a set and never see this guy open up a script. . . . He knew exactly what he was going to do. . . . He had every cut in his head [even] on *The Iron Horse* [back in 1924]—he didn't have it [written] on a dialogue [page of the script]." Ford could not understand why his assistants would not remember shots when he would recite what they were going to do.[29]

Ford did his own editing in the teens, parts of the thirties, and frequently after World War II. At Fox, Darryl F. Zanuck occasionally reedited his films, at times to Ford's grudging approval. ("My father was the second greatest editor who ever lived," said Barbara Ford, who worked many years as a Fox editor; "Zanuck was the greatest."[30])

What is amazing about Ford is not simply that he did not have to compose his pictures in the cutting room (as many directors did—and do), but that he never went to the opposite extreme and storyboarded. Storyboarding—a fairly standard technique today—is best exemplified by Hitchcock's films: the entire movie is first drawn, like a comic strip, with the composition of each shot (or camera movement) precisely indicated. Subsequently, the technicians on the set need only duplicate the drawn illustrations; and, later, the film is cut according to the storyboard. "No wonder Hitchcock's films look like that!" was Barbara Ford's comment. Ford pictures look nothing like Hitchcock's because they never have Hitchcock's mechanicalness. Ford composed the picture entirely in his head, without even a written outline of the shots he would use.

Scriptwrights. "I think John Ford almost dies because he can.t write. It just runs him nuts, that he has thoughts and ideas and has never trained himself to put them down on paper."[31] Thus Nunnally Johnson, who did not collaborate with Ford on their three pictures together. Frank Nugent, who did collaborate, remarked on Ford's "astonishing flair for dialogue." Ford—who admittedly could not sit down and fill a sheet of paper—used a writer as a sounding board, and as someone to perform the drudgery of producing successive drafts of material to be worked on. Anywhere but Hollywood he would automatically have received script credit.

Writing conferences were lengthy, often extending through weeks on Ford's boat. Ford behaved like "a real tyrant, needling and picking away at you," said James Warner Bellah.[32] "Sometimes," noted Nugent, "he is groping, like a musician who has a theme but doesn't quite know how to develop it. I've had the feeling often—in story conferences—that he's like a kid whistling a bar of music, and faltering; then if I come up with the next notes and they're what he wanted, he beams and says that's right, that's what he was trying to get over. . . . Usually a script is written scene by scene, gone over, discussed, rewritten maybe, then okayed—and you don't go back over it again—which, again, is good for a writer."[33] "I'm not sure, but I suspect that when he starts thinking about a story, he calmly devotes himself to personal research, gets hold of the music of the period and, generally, comes to his office well provided with a mixture of facts and fancy, so that he can tussle, if the occasion arises, with the scenarist, costume designer or anyone else who comes within range of his Celtic eye."[34]

Ford hated expository scenes, and would cut dialogue so brutally that talk in his movies usually resembles some elliptical pidgin English. "He loves to tear pages out of scripts," said James Stewart, "cut scenes down to phrases and phrases to words."[35] The finished film, notes Nugent, is "always

Ford's, never the scriptwriter's." After shooting *Wagon Master,* Ford told him, "I liked your script. In fact, I actually shot a few pages of it."[36]

The remark was not a joke. To understand the script's role in Ford's methods, we must reexamine Johnson's notion that it frustrated Ford that he could not write. In America, with our literary biases, we tend to conceive of movies as fundamentally illustrations of stories and words; in fact, our copyright laws allow ownership of the pictures to the person who wrote the original plot (even after the plot is mangled)! For Johnson, for most critics of the old school as for most academicians, the script elements *are* the film. Ford's cinema, on the other hand, is almost unique in rarely giving the impression of having been born via translation from prose. His movies seem rather to have been conceived directly in visual terms (and not so much antiliterary, as aliterary, in origin). Ford never outlined what he was going to do on paper, and he treated his finished script almost as a preliminary outline. Once on set, huge quantities of pages would be discarded, much dialogue would be improvised, all the staging and cutting (rarely indicated in the script) would be "invented." Thus the question of whether or not Ford was capable of writing his scripts alone should be weighed against the more important question of whether it would have been desirable. In fact, Ford believed a director profits more than he loses by not having had to restrict his creative vision first of all to a page of words, and by being able to bring a degree of critical detachment into his utilization of a scenario not entirely his own. For example, Ford thought Sam Fuller's work suffered because Fuller wrote his own scripts.[37]

In point of fact, Ford "grew up" within a collaborative process. Francis Ford collaborated with Grace Cunard, and Ford wrote his films at Universal in collaboration with Harry Carey. This was his preferred method, which he was able to practice in all but four or five instances (Johnson's *The Prisoner of Shark Island, The Grapes of Wrath, Tobacco Road,* and Philip Dunne's *How Green Was My Valley*).

Some of the Dudley Nichols scripts of the prewar years were followed rather slavishly, but these were products of intense collaboration. Ford himself appears to have written most of *The Informer,* and Nichols's influence generally seems to have been more theoretical than conceptual. Paul Jensen, for example, notes Nichols was impressed by a line from O'Neill's *Strange Interlude,* "The present is a strange interlude in which we call upon the past and future to bear witness that we are still living."[38] But Ford liked O'Neill, too, and the line's notion is evident in the pre-Nichols *Black Watch, Hangman's House, Salute,* even *The Iron Horse,* and especially in the non-Nichols *Young Mr. Lincoln,* wherein Lincoln is pulled by his future and pushed by his past. And Joseph McBride has observed that in Ford, "Moments occur in the eye of eternity to be re-enacted in the mind forever."[39]

The Ford-Nichols movies were characterized by literary pretense, theatrical values, and heavy Germanic stylization. Nichols provided Ford, in some instances, with script-architecture, character interaction, and more complex dramatic structures than possessed by Ford's simple, storybook pictures of the twenties. In contrast, the postwar collaboration with Frank Nugent was less schematic in verbal revelation of character, but Nugent's ability to capture a character in a single nugget of unliterary dialogue better suited Ford's vignette techniques.

"Two of the most beautiful things in the world," Ford was fond of reminding his scenarists, "are a horse running and a couple waltzing."[40] His late movies are richly but sparsely scripted, almost epigrammatic in their economy, and their "action" is subtle but direct. "With Ford," said Flora Robson, one of the 7 Women, "the actor is continually conscious of the fact that he is making a motion picture and that it must move, move, move. His scenes are never static or dominated by the dialogue."[41] "When movies are best," said Ford, "the action's long and the talk's short. When a film tells its story and reveals its characters to us in a suite of simple, beautiful and animated shots, that's a movie."[42]

Characterization. A typical Ford drama centers on a group rather than on one or two characters, and is enclosed within a greater drama, that of a society, as represented by a dozen or more well-defined characters. For this reason, Ford's characters are designed for easy recognition, for memorableness. As Jean Mitry put it, they are "almost always strongly typed, indeed, stereotyped. [But then Ford] gives them life and realism by stuffing them with a thousand details, a thousand original or singular nuances, nuances which burst the seams of the ready-made clothing the characters wore at first, when it was necessary to define them and situate them dramatically."[43]

"What makes someone a type," wrote Stanley Cavell, "is not his similarity with other members of that type but his striking separateness from other people."[44] The alternative to using such types is to present characters who are amorphous and undifferentiated and then allow them, during the film's course, gradually to reveal their individuality, so that, at film's end, they emerge as stereotypes. This sort of characterization has been modish in recent years; in a sense, it ends where Ford begins. Sometimes, by initially presenting a character as belonging to an *archetype* (a symbolic personage evocative of universal myths), Ford can not only construct dramas of primordial resonance, but can play that character against his generic type.

Ford *was* highly dependent most of his career upon cameo, or vignette approaches to characterization. The term *vignette* is used here not in the sense of a *masked* photograph but in the emphasis put in such photographs on posing the subject in ways strikingly characteristic. Thus, a single medium shot may instantly convey volumes of information about its character—somewhat akin to a Norman Rockwell portrait. Hence Ford's description of himself as fundamentally a comedian is profoundly true, for his native capabilities were early and consistently displayed in *comedy* skills: in vignetting, accent, deftness, in quicksilver shifts of moods. He had to struggle to master techniques of the tragedian, groping to find a suitable manner, whereas his comic technique required comparatively slight development from *The Shamrock Handicap* in 1925 through *Donovan's Reef* in 1964. Not surprisingly, his finer tragedies, e.g., *7 Women*, are constructed like his comedies, not like such (for him) misdirected approaches as *The Informer*, whose single-minded efforts are antithetical to those of the comedic Ford. Indeed, ability to create an extended study of a complex character (one embodying contradictions, or conscious of existential ones) long eluded Ford. Correspondingly, his cameo technique not only aided him in developing his unique sort of "all-star" ensemble drama, but in fact made this type of movie the *only* fertile direction for his talents. He thus capitalized upon his major limitation, while continuing to experiment in search of extended characterization.

The validity of cameo characterization, so richly a part not only of Ford but of Walsh, Capra, Renoir, Ophuls, and Vidor as well, is often missed midst the craze for mistaken notions of "truth" in art inherited from the nineteenth century. Even George Bernard Shaw saw the critical trend inherited from Wagner and Ibsen as "all along . . . a pious dialectical fraud, because it applies the test of realism and revelation to the arts of illusion and transfiguration."[45] And Jacques Barzun observes that "the truth of a character does not depend on any particular substance or mode of presentation, but on his fitting the purpose and environment provided by his creator. If you take an interest, *any* interest, in Lysistrata or Gulliver, they are real to that extent and for that purpose. Panurge is real in Rabelais and would be false in Meredith, and the converse is true about a Meredithian figure. As for 'real life,' it is impossible to say whether it furnishes Meredithian or Rabelaisian or Shavian characters in the raw. Fictional life is so much harder to live than actual life that most people would wither away in the rich atmosphere of Hamlet or Mr. Pickwick."[46]

"He made me write out complete biographies of every character," said Frank Nugent,[47] for story considerations were secondary to those of character, and it was necessary to give a sense of "life lived" to these cameolike apparitions. "You've got to tell your story through the people who portray it," insisted Ford. "As the basic story develops one must develop each character in the actor, besides the mood and the tempo, so that the drama is correctly mixed with humor."[48] "You can have a weak, utterly bad script— and a good cast will turn it into a good picture. . . . With the exception of the stars who [were in the thirties] signed for parts by the studio in advance, I insist on choosing names for myself. And I spend more time on that task than on any other."[49]

Thus much of Ford's work was done before actual rehearsals began, which explains how his laconic, indeed uncommunicative methods nonetheless achieved results. Often he constructed a screen character by building on foibles or eccentricities already there in the actor.* Thus, for example, Harry Carey became more Harry Carey than he actually was, i.e., more charismatic and relaxed, while in Harry Carey, Jr., the notable characteristic was stumbling over things or walking into walls.[50] Thus Ford was usually less concerned that an actor speak the exact words written for him than that he be comfortable saying them; dialogue, too, tended to be "cameo-typical."

The same care was expended casting minor parts, and it was in this way that the "Ford Stock Company" originated, for he had a penchant for casting ex-celebrities such as Mae Marsh, Russell Simpson, or Francis Ford in small roles. Though columnists played up this stock company as early as 1931, community filmmaking had been a general practice in the teens, when a director had "his company," consisting of stars, bit players, cameramen, and grip. But by 1936 Ford had to explain the practice: "Ex-stars will, after all, give a better performance even in the smallest part than any casual extra would; and it's my contention that the bits in any picture are just as important as the starring role, since they round out the story—complete the atmosphere—make the whole plausible. . . . The other, and just as important reason, is that when I was starting out in this town those people were kind to me. I want to repay a little of that if it's in my power."[51]

Ford's subordinate parts tend to be quite broadly played—"in the English theater style," as Anna Lee describes it[52]—and this is a quality disconcerting to those who mistake "realism" for the apparent absence of stylization. Equally puzzling to modern audiences can be his fondness for mixing actors of theatrical sophistication with untrained ones (e.g., Sue Lyon in 7 Women).

Framing and Cutting. Ford had a reputation, fueled by personages such as Orson Welles, François Truffaut, André Bazin, and Andrew Sarris, for long takes, slight camera movement, and "invisible" editing.** In fact, Ford's typical shot lasts about ten seconds, often less, which is brief indeed by any but Potemkin standards, and probably one out of four Ford shots involves camera movement. True, Ford avoids like poison the showiness of a Lelouch or a Welles, but such quantitative comparisons have little mean-

---

*Concentration on Ford as director may obscure his role in creating stars or launching careers. To name a few: Harry Carey, Harry Carey, Jr., Hoot Gibson, John Wayne, Ward Bond, Spencer Tracy, George O'Brien, Grace Kelly, Jon Hall, Dorothy Lamour, Richard Greene, Barry Fitzgerald, Arthur Shields, Vera Miles, John Carradine, Ben Johnson.

**Ford early on attracted attention for avoiding close-ups and maintaining long shots where others would cut to a close-up, and for moving actors in relation to the camera, sometimes into close-up, rather than cutting to them. He was also reputed one of the first to use long takes in ensemble scenes. Long takes were normal during the early sound era (1928–31), when Ford avoided using them statically, but by 1939 montage style was the rule, 1931 seemed a thousand years ago, and anyone departing from current fashion was regarded as a pioneer.

ing in judging aesthetic articulations; Mozart's music contains fewer dissonant chords than Stravinsky's, but Mozart's dissonance is more stinging.
Ford's cuts, rather like Mozart's progressions, match smoothly enough that
people determined not to perceive cutting will seldom be bothered by them.
But to watch a Ford movie without *feeling*—physically, emotionally, intellectually— his cutting is like listening to music while being oblivious to rhythm
and harmony, or like looking at Renaissance painting while being oblivious to
composition. Cutting and framing are Ford's most basic aesthetic articulations; until perception of them becomes a vital part of one's movie watching,
the cinema of John Ford will remain essentially unexperienced.

Before discussing Ford's montage, however, we must single out three
"heresies" that have worked their way into montage theory. The first of
these is the axiom that the individual shot has no value in itself, that all of its
meaning and emotive force derive from its linkage with other shots. While
the axiom *is* sufficiently true to justify such an overstatement (for people
seldom recognize montage's power), still, at the same time, it *is* an overstatement. The dialectic between shots that conditions each of them can,
obviously, only be as rich as the richness of each shot. To concentrate solely
on the *relation* between shots in discussing montage is to put the cart before
the horse. Secondly, montage has fallen into ill repute through its ability to
govern our ideology and manipulate our emotions. Such suspicion of montage is valid enough and, in essence, goes back to Plato's distrust of art. But
the remedy lies neither in expulsion of art from the republic nor in expulsion
of cuts from films; it lies in the moral responsibility of the artist and the
intelligence of the perceiver. Despite Bazin, "invisible" editing only exists
in the decision of one who will not see. Thirdly, the need for literary-
minded critics and semioticians to reduce films to "narratives" has resulted
in approaches to movies that are excessively conceptual, whereas the more
vital aesthetic functions have been overlooked: montage's ability to isolate
moods and emotions. We all know the trick of cutting to express emotional
change—from calm to surprise; more important is the cut that accords each
emotion its due—from surprise to calm, for example. The example is simplistic, but by this route cinema may effect an *aesthetic* dialectic between
shots. Why is this important? Because despite much effort, human beings
do not confront the world or each other in terms of logic or even in clear
conceptual terms. If we think back in our lives to an event that was personally vital to us, our visual memory of what happened and our aural memory
of what was said are likely to be considerably more vague than our aesthetic
memory of what was felt. And for this reason those who truly want to understand life do not limit themselves to the social sciences or the semioticians
but consult art as well.

Returning to Ford, we have seen how the major influence in his evolving
utilization of the semiautonomous shot as a modal element of montage was the

work of F. W. Murnau. Although Ford did not adopt Murnau's florid camera (for reasons we shall examine presently), he did adopt Murnau's intense exploitation of characterizing body posture, poeticization of spatial relationships within the frame, and moody, chiaroscuro lighting—all techniques whereby compositional form is aestheticized. And Ford further intensified Murnau's tension and movements—dynamics that in Murnau favor the *curve*—by placing them within a geometry of *straight* lines: most signally within the triplanar space generated by Ford's depth of field, planar lighting, and arrangement of props (with actors generally in middle ground).

Ford's cutting, next, extends and develops the emotional/compositional ideas begun in the individual frame. Let us take a terribly simplistic example to demonstrate how this works. The pattern of three shots—John × Mary/John and Mary—is among the most formulaic in cinematic syntax, and Ford uses it often.* What distinguishes his use of it is first of all the degree to which he relates motion, gesture, and graphics so that the reverse-angles rhyme; when the paired crosscuts conclude in a two-shot, the opposition of their contrasting angles is neutralized. Also, the spatial relationships supposed by the crosscutting are confirmed (i.e., we assumed that John was looking at Mary, then that Mary was looking at John, and that thus the two were in spatial proximity; but this is not confirmed until the two-shot). The sequence is the cinematic equivalent of a musical cadence that progresses through alternative dissonances to resolution.

But spatial and kinetic relationships are not separable in Ford from content and emotion. As Frank Nugent said, "he works from the character more than anything else"; and the key to Ford's style is the dialectic between his cutting and his vignette characterization. In our simple example, the discursive content (boy alone, girl alone, the couple united) may, in its formal presentation (each alone, then two together), arouse in an audience emotions rooted first in existential loneliness, then in societal fulfillment. The point here is that this formal presentation is not simply "content": John could have met Mary in a single shot, but the director has chosen to emphasize their solitary stares into space. And what distinguishes Ford's use of this formula is the fervency with which, thanks to Ford's vignette characterization and Murnau-like intensity of mood, each character inhabits his or her separate world and saturates it with the vibrations of his or her soul. In such a case, their eventual union in a two-shot may be eventful indeed.

Since Ford wishes to maintain his strong presence as narrator, his camera's physical point of view is generally *objective*. Only terribly rarely is it *subjective* (i.e., when the camera gazes from the physical position of one of the characters). "Over-the-shoulder" shots—which may be called *conversational* point of view—are, however, common; unlike a shot from a charac-

---

* /=cut. × = crosscut.

ter's subjective perspective, the over-the-shoulder shot retains an objective narrative presence (Ford's) exterior to the action: rather than seeing *Mary* (as seen by John), we see *John looking at Mary.*

The result of Ford's objective camera style is that we do not "identify" with the characters. Instead, we stare *at* them and relate *to* them. There is an instance of a character's (i.e., subjective) point of view during *Stagecoach's* dinner scene, when Mrs. Mallory's piercing dolly-in on Dallas comes *before* the near-180° crosscut identifying the dolly as having been from Mrs. Mallory's point of view. Typically, Ford shows a "reaction" shot before showing what prompts the reaction, thus discouraging identification and securing his own narrative posture. But, subsequently, by varying the intensity of his narrative presence (through camera placement, but also through lighting and all other techniques), Ford intriguingly exploits the tensions between various gradations of identity and distancing.

There is, of course, a difference between "distance" and "distancing." It is an artist's entire aesthetic sensibility rather than simply the long shot that accounts for distancing. Hitchcock's movies contrast violently with Ford's, so intensely subjective and manipulative, literally *plucking* emotion out of the audience, that we may be said to be *participants,* whereas with Ford, no matter how intensely emotional, we are also critical, judging *witnesses.* Ford's cinema, in other words, is presentational; his painterly style suits "comedies of manners" in which a culture's mores are displayed. Style itself becomes a distancing device, because his thorough aestheticism, the Mozart-like importance he accords to beauty for its own sake, strikes up a dialectic with his documentary-like subjects. It is style, rather than an artist's real-life personality, that we refer to in speaking of his personality or presence. The example of Stendhal and Balzac make it clear, as Arnold Hauser has written, "that the service an artist renders to progress depends not so much on his personal convictions and sympathies as on the power with which he portrays the problems and contradictions of social reality."[53] And what is "power," if not style?

Although Ford's presentational style means he avoids setting up identification mechanisms (as Hitchcock does), he does "set up" personality. That is, after getting accustomed to Ford, it is curious how often so many other filmmakers, particularly shop directors like Lloyd, Fleming, or Whale (who rarely controlled their own cutting), seem constantly to be cutting *away* from characters. With Ford, on the other hand, characters are cut *to,* and then they are there for (apparently) leisurely absorption, to be empathized with, but not identified with. (Few dead spots occur midst the kinetic happenings of a Ford film, but each little event occurs with such clarity and proportion that haste never intrudes.)

Antonioni too does everything possible to create forms expressive of mood; but rather than exploiting montage, he prefers to roam with his camera through spaces that, although thus unstructured themselves, are littered with (often cubist) structures. Ford's space, in contrast, is almost always structured; he is obsessed with lines, planes, interior angles, depth-of-field alleys, which take on force in relation to defined space (the frame), and even this he emphasizes, by angling his stage slightly to his focal plane. Ford's highly active montage creates dynamic poetry out of elements that have no existence in Antonioni's movies, and whose exclusion there signifies man's ideological rootlessness and uncertainty. A moving camera tends to deemphasize real space and time; a still camera tends to emphasize them. The moving camera distracts from movement within the frame, whereas the still reinforces it. The moving camera (even gentle follow-pans) tends to separate a character from his milieu, the still to emphasize the milieu.

A pan of 45 degrees, or perhaps much less, is a grandiloquent gesture in Ford. He rejects florid movement not because it threatens the illusion of reality, but because he does not wish to sacrifice the advantages of the autonomous shot, and because (given the quasi-determinist role milieu plays) he does wish to emphasize the rapport between character and milieu. Extended camera movement, as in Ophuls, tends to leave characters adrift in (structured) time but divorced from structured space, and Ford once in a while will employ camera movement for disorienting effect. In contemporary subjects, too, like *When Willie Comes Marching Home* or *Gideon's Day,* he may adopt a fairly mobile "TV style," though even here the hint of disorientation is deliberate. Elaborate trackings are reserved for occasions when the movement is capable of defining space; the track of the priest in *The Fugitive* riding against twilighted arches is a good instance. And even here, as in the track of Denver in *Wagon Master* running away from Travis's marriage proposal, the Godard-like abstractness distances and indicates disorientation.

Sound and Music. Ford welcomed the talking picture with elation, and thirty-five years later declared, "It's still a silent medium. . . . Pictures, not words, should tell the story."[54] Nevertheless, it was only in the talking movie that Ford mastered silent cinema. His silents have so many titles that they are virtually illustrated storybooks. Given spoken dialogue, Ford could become more complex visually; given control over music and sound effects, he could create the powerful, modal cinema Murnau has suggested. In 1928 he called for development of "auditory images," for "the use of sound as well as sight images."[55]

He conceived his pictures while listening to period music; thus his films are modal music-dramas from the moment of their conception. Composer Richard Hageman says Ford directed "with one ear on the music. . . . We didn't have to rescore a scene [of *3 Godfathers*], because he knows in advance what the music is and paces the action to it."[56] Although Ford complained once of "too much music," he generally used a symphony orchestra during wilderness scenes when he was in charge (and, generally, he *was* responsible for his movies' music). Often, as in *Stagecoach*, music is densely expressionistic, shunning realism, like other aspects of his cinema, for the sake of atmosphere. While he never made a "musical," many of his movies have more music than some musicals. Rare indeed is the Ford movie not essentially a choreography to music through most of its duration.

Often, too, music derives from on-camera sources. But the patently anachronistic score of *Wagon Master* interrupts on-camera music in order to serve a narrative and distancing function. Music in *Donovan's Reef* impersonates an unseen character and chorus, as do background sounds in *Mogambo*. Folk songs, folk tunes, and patriotic hymns function, as surely as do manners, costumes, and decor, as symbols of the ethos of an age and culture. Other "auditory images" include sounds for mood and psychology. The latter reached a nadir (but gained an Oscar) in Max Steiner's "Mickey Mousing" scores for *The Informer* and *Mary of Scotland*, where every word or feeling was imitated musically. Far more subtle are Elmer Bernstein's contrapuntal signals in *7 Women*, or Alfred Newman's leitmotifs, which begin by designating characters, in *Young Mr. Lincoln*, and finish by evoking worlds of specific emotions associated with them, and even appear in much later pictures, setting up complex cross-relations.

Ford customarily used only a single microphone. Whenever possible, he showed rather than told: thus the abundance of signs, newspapers, and words themselves.

Preliminaries and Structures. Ford contended that the short story was the perfect form for a motion picture. It provided him with just enough of a trend, a frame, for the character delineation in which he was far more interested than the plot itself. Then, according to Ford, "Usually I take the story, and get every line of printed material I can find on the subject. And then I take the boat and simply cruise until I've read it all. I eat, sleep, and drink whatever picture I'm working on—read nothing else, think of nothing else; which is probably the reason the continuity and mood of my products stay at an exact level."[57]

"Ford," said Frank Nugent, "thinks in terms of a complete story line, a general conception of what he wants to do, and he thinks in the forms of individual scenes, bits, and characters. He works something like a painter, selecting his colors and doing a palette—blues, greens, yellows, he lays them all out in his mind. Then, putting his thumb in here with a broad splash of color, then a little touch on the other side. He goes home at night after a day's talk and reads books, or listens to records. And, listening to the music, pictures, colors, or moods come into his mind. He has a great feeling for characters, some from his own imagination. These series of impressions, images, moods—music moods, character moods, atmosphere—become in effect his raw material."[58] One could go so far as to define Ford's cinema as the "musicalization" of painting.

This attention to shifting moods, reminiscent of Mozart and Chekhov, is a principal hallmark of Ford's style. To structure these moods he preferred fairly definite sequences, optimally about two minutes long. Thus when Dudley Nichols worried that he could write a play but not a script, Ford told him to write a play in fifty or sixty scenes.[59] Such a large number of discrete sequences results in incredible density of mood, detail, and character.

If a movie is to be fundamentally formal, cinematically, its screenplay will outline the structure of its formal movements. As a result of clear structure—each sequence autonomous in mood, tempo, action, theme, setting—one gets a definite feeling of suitelike *progression:* developing movement, in plot, form, and theme. Ford: "I very seldom play a sequence to its full effect, and so my stuff is usually confusing to both cast and producers in its uncut form. Before I make a single set-call I outline the story, as it will appear on the screen, in my mind, and separate details are subordinated to the final complete effect."[60]

Contrast. "Realism," said Brecht, "doesn't consist in reproducing reality, but in showing how things really are." Thus realism is a function of style (and thus differing greatly from one artist to another); but too often the term is used in ways both meaningless and confusing. What critics praised in 1935 as the ultimate word in realism seems today ultimate contrivance. To many casual movie-goers, any film made before 1970 looks artificial and anything made today looks realistic. This state of affairs exists because people are reluctant to engage a movie on a stylistic level.

Among movie artists Ford should be classed with Murnau, Sternberg, Vidor, Renoir, Ophuls, Mizoguchi, and Rossellini, as denoting a cinema of felt expression through aesthetic form. Ford's sort of movie implies complete stylization of every element. All content becomes formalized; every quality of sight or sound is thoroughly aestheticized. This process of stylization was, it seems, prompted by Murnau's demonstration of the artistic potential of cinema: how cinema could formalize feelings, and be "modal." Such stylization, far from being antipathetic to "realism," treats our sense of reality as a feeling to be formalized and intensified.

On the other hand, there was a second vein of theatricality in Ford, already well developed, of vignette characterization ("turns") and intense changefulness. The distinction between the two veins is that this simpler theatricality was concerned mostly with the subject before the camera only, whereas the Murnau process of modification formalized the cinematic medium itself.

The mature Ford was a fusion of these two tendencies. He began to "compose" his movies in terms of mood, dramatic style, and cinematic form (angles, lines, light, gesture, movement, montage). The aspects of contrast resulting from this fusion fall into three modes:

1. Mixture of contrasting styles. Within a single scene Ford will juxtapose elements of naturalness, expressionism, slapstick, impressionism, neorealism, or whatever; e.g., the combination of "theatricality" and "documentary realism" in *She Wore a Yellow Ribbon*.

2. Mixture of contrasting moods. A tragic moment is typically contrasted with a happy one. Comedy is injected whenever possible. In Ford's view of human drama, as Wilmington put it, "what is most noble, poignant and terrifying is frequently a hair's-breadth away from howling absurdity."[61] Most better Fords switch rapidly through a wide gamut of emotional moods.

3. Mixture of contrasting modes. Cinema by its nature is a combining medium. Ford treats shapes, motions, light and dark, colors, sound, music, cutting, and camera movement, each of them expressively and autonomously, and juxtaposes them polyphonically rather than simply combining them toward a single effect.

Thus it may be said Ford exploits every aspect of multimedia cinema. At its ideal, his cinema is "operatic": everything is choreographed. Diverse aspects of cinema are interrelated, sometimes harmonically, sometimes polyphonically. There is a baroque sense of contrast.* Sequence contrasts with sequence, motion with motion. Multiple stories are told simultaneously with multiple classes of society, multiple dramas unfold within the same scene, often reflecting multiple sensitivities. Ford's disposition toward the vignette combined with the Murnau influence to result in swift changes of mood, large casts (ensemble pictures rather than one- or two-character ones), multiple plot lines, coordination of technique and theme into suitelike sequences that build schematically. The style implied its evolution toward increasingly ambiguous characters and structures.

---

*Vsevolod Pudovkin during a conference on Ford held in Moscow in 1946 was also struck by these aspects in Ford's work: "Even in superficial analysis you will find in his pictures a collision of most divergent methods, up to and including the method defining the genre of the work itself. Side by side with sharp grotesque you will find painstaking and minutely detailed realistic elaboration of scenes, at times bordering on naturalism. And suddenly arises a sentimental tale, filled with abstract symbolism, like an illustration to a Sunday bible sermon. Recall the scene showing the pastor in *How Green Was My Valley*, where Christ in a jacket teaches a child to walk on the blossoming and blessed earth as in a valley of paradise. And a second later the factory chimneys are belching smoke, water pours from the dirty roofs, dark crowds are moving through the gloomy, dirty streets, and the tale acquires the epic austerity of an unconcerned and thoughtful onlooker."

Pudovkin also praised Ford because, despite having grown up in the American environment and thus not yet being "able to envisage man of the masses as the historical master of life, still . . . he tries to envisage man not isolated but included within the diversified world." Pudovkin found a "sub-text" or "spirit" in Ford that "in its most general aspect says: 'Everything in our life is not as it should be. There can be dreams of a beautiful world, but how to find the path to this beautiful world I know not.'" (Pudovkin's text along with those of others was sent to Ford and is among the Ford Papers, Lilly Library, Indiana University. Parts of it are also in Philippe Haudiquet, *John Ford* [Paris: Seghers, 1966], pp. 141–142.)

Form and Theme

Chaos (incoherence)	*Order* (stasis, repression)
motion	rest
freedom	determinism
liberty	law
reality (documentary re-creation)	theater (re-created documentary)
parade	house
change	subsistence

Ford's master antinomy is probably chaos/order. Art (and men) labor to exist (and balance) between such extremes, and motion and rest are so much the formal bases of Ford's cinema that they would alone suffice to render *How Green Was My Valley* personal. But Ford liked, also, to philosophize over History (History, he once said, was his "real profession"); and his better movies chronicle change and speculate on man's dubious authority over his own fate. Often, in later years, the *parade* proved a splendid image by which to suggest change, continuity, and man's doubtful ability to control his own fate.

The parade represents life's pilgrimage, in the Augustinian sense, but Ford never lost sight of the void that is faith's *volte face*. The parade— "man's unceasing search for something he can never find"[62] —is often a substitute for reason. And in daily life the parade, without even its elusive goal, may become form without meaning. Thus life is a constant passage without a map, with only immediate purposes, but with the seduction of the moment giving life its validity. For most people, perfect freedom is too precarious and its attendant self-responsibility is too onerous; the surety of order and prescribed duty is more comfortable. Nowhere better than in the military is this opposition between freedom and order exemplified, and for this reason Ford in later years increasingly chose such disciplined social organisms for his subjects. With such societal contexts, commonplace actions become rituals, partake of myth, and are contemplated with awe. But myths may breed myopia.

There is evil of the common sort in Ford—characters who wallow in the intrigues, deceptions, and callow practicalities that distinguish the real world—but, for Ford, lack of commitment, honor, or friendship damn beyond the pale. The evil, the true evil, that haunts his films is the evil of good intentions.

Any effort persisted in becomes corrupt. The sense of duty that sustains Ford's individuals (and also their sense of faith) commonly leads them astray into aberrations or death. Duty-bound, they invade others' privacy, and arrogate knowledge of higher good, right, and judgment: judges, ministers, soldiers, outlaws, priests. Thus racism, war, or any form of intolerance, becomes a function of society.

In tracing Ford's pictures (particularly *Judge Priest, How Green Was My Valley, This Is Korea!, The Man Who Shot Liberty Valance*) we have seen how people (and governments) act from feeling, not from logic. Man is made of dreams as much as of reality. And we have seen how Ford, in awakening around 1927 to cinema's ability to be art through total stylization, awakened simultaneously to his art's high task: to help us free ourselves from determining ideologies. Art, after all, has the capability of making us understand things through emotion that we would be absolutely incapable of understanding through the intellect. Within a determining milieu, particularly when that milieu is challenged, free will, human nature, life's worth, a benign divinity's existence, all must necessarily be posed in question. And so Ford pictures ideally construct in minute detail a social set of apparent homogeneity (thus often military-like) in order to analyze that society within its historic moment, and in order to demonstrate how the garments of society, together with history itself, operate on the individual. It is for these reasons that Jean-Marie Straub has called Ford the most "Brechtian" of all filmmakers.[63] (Footnote 63 elucidates the comparison further.)

Civilization always attempts to impose order in Ford, and repression and chaos always result. Augustine, Hegel, and Marx also envisioned history as a process of dialectical clashes. But where they all saw this dialectic leading toward an ideal state, Ford was always bothered by the possibility that the apparent movement of history may only be the chance by-product of chaos, or merely the cosmos's eternally violent quest for equilibrium. One senses the contest between order and freedom in Ford as early as the 1927–1935 period, although only in his final period is it full and dynamic. In between, after 1935, repression reigns. Feeble heroes occasionally challenge, and suppressed violence once in a while erupts; but, like hurricanes, these interruptions pass. In such an atmosphere, ideological clashes occur on mundane levels—conflicts with Indians and outlaws and gangsters—and otherwise are sublimated into myths.

Pilgrimages and long voyages end where hope does, midst disintegration and defeat, yet they fail to dim the gentle confidences exchanged en route. Bleak indeed are the ways of the world in Ford, save for a congeniality forever contradicting life's essential sadness.

Community and Family

Fordian communities are islands apart, and stress is usually laid, at beginning and end of movie, on the need to traverse the outer world in order to arrive (by train, boat, stagecoach . . .) *here*. Thus a community has a sense of "us and them." "Us" includes, of course, a set of groups, each defined by class, culture, and race, perpetually divisive, and each thinking "us and them." Finally comes the family; the family, almost always depicted as an isolated pocket of existential security, as a refuge from loneliness (but, like "home," it is an ideal rarely attained, and generally imperfect, fragmented, lacking one parent*). The individual's self-identity is, contrary to some current assumptions, constituted far less by his individuality than by his sense of identity within the family unity, thence within his specific class, culture, race, religion, etc.

A Fordian character is always distinctly characterized as representative of a specific culture. There is no confusing a Boston Wasp with an Irish-American or Swede. And people do not rebel consciously against socio-ethical-religious prescriptions of childhood. For Ford's pioneers, virgin land represents opportunity not for innovation but for continuity; even for Ford's blacks, true freedom can be envisioned only within existent structures.

Twin problems arise from this situation. The first of these is that the family is always being threatened from without: members are kidnapped, persecuted, or separated by prejudice. But whatever the variation, the specific threat to the family is always a form of intolerance. Intolerance, whether racial or "moral" (e.g., illegitimate birth), means denial that another shares fully our humanity; in other words, intolerance springs not only from self-identity, from recognition of membership in a unity, but also from basic *misunderstanding* of identity and unity, from well-meaning attempts to pursue virtue. In fact, these threaten the things they seek to preserve.

The second problem occurs when a family member, say, a child grown up, seeks to extend himself into the world outside. As, axiomatically, he cannot leave his family, he must extend it, into marriage, into new lands, into alien cultures. Such fusion will encounter difficulty: intolerance.

When a community falls into intolerance, to restore itself, to mediate between the twin evils of chaos and order, it requires a hero. The hero's specific task is always to restore a missing family member, one fallen victim to intolerance.

The Fordian Hero

$$\frac{\text{Myths}}{\text{Reality}} : \frac{\text{apparent harmony}}{\text{actual disharmony}} : \frac{\text{visions of good}}{\text{fact of evil}} \Big\} \text{Subsist}$$

Ford's tendencies toward stylization match his inclination to treat people as archetypes and quotidian events as sacred ritual. In his art, style so encodes reality that cinema necessarily becomes myth.

---

*Of Ford's fifty-five sound pictures, thirty-seven feature families, of which seven are complete families and thirty either fragmented or (ten times) about to become so. Family structures disintegrate in twenty-one instances, and are threatened but preserved in eighteen others (mostly earlier). Only in one instance, *Rio Grande*, is a family refabricated. In fact, families fare badly under most better American directors. There are none in Chaplin, Lang, Lubitsch, Aldrich, Mankiewicz, DeMille, Edwards, Losey, Mann, Wilder, Huston, Allen, Zimmermann, or Hawks; and only a couple in Ophuls, Sternberg, Wyler, Walsh, Penn, Sturges, or

That myth hides (and preserves) truths about life, often by rendering palatable the unpalatable, suits the Hollywood moviemaker's dual task, to entertain and enlighten, and invites "double-level" narratives. An inevitable, unhappy ending can be hidden (and preserved) under a "false" happy ending or a *deus ex machina;** a disgusting character can be rendered comic; actions wrong, pernicious, suicidal can be justified subjectively and greeted with approbation. Thus is revealed discordancy between myth and reality, which breeds misdirected attempts to act rightly, which is the intolerance from which most human suffering flows. Some would remedy this situation by destroying the myths; others would destroy reality. The Fordian hero, perceiving that myths (even defective) are necessary to sustain us, seeks to mediate between myth (repressive order) and reality (chaos), in order, by purifying myth, to revitalize society.

To this end, he may not be passive, a "sheep" crying for a "shepherd" (like the Mormons in *Wagon Master*), or a passive drifter (like Marty Maher in *The Long Gray Line*). He must, perceiving that life can be hell, strive to keep atop the maelstrom; like Tom Joad, he must climb to critical consciousness of life's contradictions. And then, he must be willing to act, to intervene, to assume authority over others. Such intervention, often entailing immense moral arrogance, even violence (e.g., Mudd, Lincoln, Priest, Doniphon, Cartwright), he justifies by claimed knowledge of transcendent truth: he cites duty, justice, rightness.

Occasionally, a false hero forgets his role as mediator, fixates on myopic truths, and sows chaos in the guise of order (Hannah Jessop, DeLaage, Wyatt Earp, Ransom Stoddard, Colonel Thursday, et al.). The true hero mediates, "balances," encourages subsistence and peace—often symbolized by reunification of a family: Harry Carey, Will Rogers, Lincoln, Priest, Ethan Edwards (oddly), Doniphon, Cartwright.

Emotional vulnerability rather than physical prowess characterizes the Fordian hero, and he acts from the pressure of outer events or inner conscience rather than from free will. (The false hero, indeed, often seems arbitrary.) Sometimes the Fordian hero resembles a Hegelian one: his native prescience leads mankind closer toward the ideal but he himself is placed outside normal, biological history—he is almost always celibate, almost never "gets the girl," seldom reaps life's humble pleasures. He is often a combination of soldier, judge, and priest, symbolizing his intervention, authority, and self-sacrifice. And although he may be a fixture of society, he is yet an outsider, because he is purer than the average man in service of

Mulligan. Others see more to lament than to praise in the family: Ray, McCarey, Welles, Coppola, Sirk, Minnelli, Capra, Hitchcock. Vidor and Ford emphasize families. (See my "Looking Homeward—in Vain: The Family in American Film," *Mosaic* [Winnipeg] 16, no. 1–2 [Winter / Spring 1983], pp. 71–82.)

*E.g., *Air Mail, How Green Was My Valley, Fort Apache;* also many Capras, such as *Mr. Smith Goes to Washington, American Madness, It's a Wonderful Life.*

such accepted values as tolerance, justice, medical duty, preservation of family, and love (whereas the false hero serves racism, vengeance, law, "duty," intolerance, and glory). As shepherd, the hero cannot be sheep; others subsist within contradictions, he must get outside them. He, like Moses, is denied the promised land; he walks away after uniting couples, families, or communities. Interiorly compelled to acquiesce in appointed duty, he is fully conscious that his redemptive acts will, like Christ's, efface, condemn, even destroy him.* Yet always he upholds for humanity, for his community, or merely for a friend, a lantern, a flower, pointing toward a better vision.

Individual Consciousness

> *I remarked, and have often remarked since, how most people do not care for things which are authentic. They prefer mixtures and make-up.*   JEAN RENOIR,
> *Les Cahiers du
> Capitaine Georges*

When all is said and done, in life as in art what counts is the discovery of soul. Yet nothing is more difficult in the dramatic arts than the creation of a true-to-life character. Dramatization by its nature tends to schematize and concentrate, to make things neat and tidy, to present ideas and conflicts in clear patterns. A dramatic character tends also to be schematized: he is very definitely one way and not another; he professes and exhibits one mind and not another; he is consistent with himself from one moment to the next. But generally, as we know, this is not at all the way matters stand in real life with real people. Real people sprawl, they contradict themselves, they behave in ways contrary to their intentions, and their personalities are subject to innumerable momentary distractions.

Audiences contribute to the dramatist's dilemma, for they often prefer conflicts of ideas to conflicts of persons, and, in any case, they tend to try to force characters into molds. A character (like Ethan Edwards, in *The Searchers*) may fascinate by spilling out of his mold, but if he sprawls too much, the audience will reject him as incoherent. The writer too contributes to the dilemma, for his very task is to make solid the things that the director wishes to be ephemeral. Thus most directors devise methods to encourage accidental nuances, and thus Ford rigorously refused to verbalize in preproduction (by script or storyboard) what he would do on set. The problem is to get "life" into a character.

---

*Conventional wisdom is viewed cynically from early on. Arrowsmith, Duke Talbot (*Air Mail*), and Doctor Bull flee their communities loathingly. In later years, heroes grow increasingly desperate and isolated. John Wayne kills for vengeance unquestioningly in *Stagecoach*, but fights only after soul-searching in *The Quiet Man*; his struggle is existential and private in *The Searchers*, is waged against his own body in *The Wings of Eagles*, and, in *Liberty Valance*, he is compelled to heroic action entailing self-destruction.

But there are limits to what a director can do. For all Ford's technical acumen, formal inventiveness, and dialectical philosophy, at a certain level he was dependent upon the actor. Cinema, almost all the time, is a method of manipulating an actor, of using him as a piece of décor, and of injecting life and spontaneity into him. And virtually all respected actors support this effort.

But the quality in an actor Ford most valued was "naturalness." Naturalness cannot be treated like décor, it cannot be created by a director if it is not already latent in the actor (although it may be encouraged), and it is the rarest quality. It is difficult to appreciate, impossible to analyze, and very few stars ever possessed it. One who did was Will Rogers. Rogers, at least in his Ford pictures, did not *play* his roles.

To explain this, contrast him with Katherine Hepburn or John Wayne, both of whom *play* their parts. Hepburn does so at an intellectual level. Both she and Ford made thorough *studies* of Mary Stuart (in this instance), by reading books and researching costumes, and the character as a result is a synthetic product of their studies: the emotions portrayed result from cogitations by actor and director. The intrigue or fascination of any Hepburn character lies in our attempt to get past the "construct" of her character to the person we sense present before us. But such intellectualization can be limiting: it tends to schematization, since it results from analysis, and real people are usually not schematic. Wayne, in comparison, tends to relate emotionally to his character, rather than seeking to understand him intellectually; this method of feeling (rather than thinking) his way into a character allows the possibility of distractions at the intellectual level—of nuances which do not entirely cohere to an intellectual concept of the character—and which thus give an appealing autonomy to fleeting instants of emotion. Nonetheless, in Wayne too one is slightly (and pleasantly) conscious of a distance between player and character.

Other sorts of distance may be found in, say, Cary Grant, under either Hawks or Hitchcock. To a certain extent, both these directors encourage actors not only to *perform*—to exaggerate, to stylize, often to have a good time *playing*—but also, within this performance, to be themselves. Thus, in speaking of characters in many Hawks or Hitchcock movies, we can often talk interchangeably of, say, "Cary Grant" or the specific name of his personage. And, again, we are conscious of acting.

But we are not conscious of acting with Will Rogers, nor with Harry Carey, Ben Johnson, Francis Ford, J. Farrell MacDonald, Wayne (in *Stagecoach* and occasionally elsewhere), Slim Summerville (in *Submarine Patrol*), Jack Pennick, Helen Chandler *(Salute)*, Anna Massey *(Gideon's Day)*, Mae Marsh, Ruth Clifford, nor perhaps with Ward Bond, or Grace Kelly (in *Mogambo*). Naturalness, in these and other cases, means the absence of an apparent distance between character and player. Thus, in discussing John

Ford pictures, it seems more appropriate to designate a character *solely* by the name of his personage, and almost never by the name of the actor. Of course, naturalness is an immeasurable quality, and evaluations of it may differ. But one thing is certain: the sort of performances that generally win plaudits from critics and admiration from audiences are not of this sort at all, but precisely those in which distance is most evident (i.e., in which one senses the actor acting). Ford, for all his exploitation of distancing devices, tried to avoid distance between player and role (with the special-case exception of *The Man Who Shot Liberty Valance*). He resembles, in this respect, Ophuls and Rossellini, and together they might be contrasted to Sternberg, Hawks, Hitchcock, Lang, Griffith, even Murnau, among whom characters are externalizations or representations, at any rate something other than the essences incorporating them.

Many, but not all, of Ford's nonsynthetic, natural performances are of simple-souled characters, yet they invariably emerge as far more complex than such heady types as Arrowsmith or Mary Stuart. They are all not-of-a-piece types; they are individuals but their glances and gestures do not cohere, do not uniformly contribute to a single impression; they always leave us feeling that we are seeing only bits and pieces of who they really are. They do not "satisfy," they just "be," tantalizingly, hidden, but free, self-willed, naturally theatrical, and alive.

"I learned a great deal from Harry Carey," said Ford. "He was a slow moving actor when he was afoot. You could read his mind, peer into his eyes and see him think."[64] "The secret," said Ford of moviemaking, "is people's faces, their eye expression, their movements."[65]

It is because John Ford's movies center contemplatively on the most real qualities of actors that a corrective balance is attained with his synthetic qualities of expressionism, just as emotional instinct balances intellectual analysis.

Notes

Abbreviations

Anderson   Lindsay Anderson, *About John Ford* (London: Plexus, 1981).

Bogdanovich   Peter Bogdanovich, *John Ford*, 2d ed. (Berkeley: University of
                California Press, 1978).

Dan Ford   *Pappy: The Life of John Ford* (Englewood Cliffs, N. J.:
                Prentice-Hall, 1979).

JFP   The John Ford Papers, Lilly Library, Indiana University. Includes
                reminiscences undated, but presumably c. 1973.

Parrish   Robert Parrish, *Growing Up in Hollywood* (New York: Harcourt
                Brace Jovanovich, 1976).

Sinclair   Andrew Sinclair, *John Ford: A Biography* (New York: Dial, 1979).

Wilkinson   James L. Wilkinson, *An Introduction to the Career and Films of
                John Ford*, unpublished M.A. thesis, UCLA, August 1960
                (microfilm copy in Library and Museum of the Performing Arts,
                Lincoln Center, New York).

1   Prologue: Youth and Apprenticeship

1. Biographical information throughout the book derives chiefly from Dan
Ford, Sinclair, Wilkinson (whose family tree I have revised), the John Ford Papers,
and interviews with Cecil McLean de Prida, Harry Carey, Jr., and George O'Brien.

Ford's birth certificate is reproduced in Wilkinson and in the Film Study Center at the Museum of Modern Art, New York. Baptismal information was obtained by Grafton Nunes.

2. Philip Jenkinson, unreleased filmed interview with Ford, 1969.

3. Quoted in Wilkinson, p. 17, from his interview with Francis Ford, January 21, 1951.

4. Ford's reminiscences, JFP.

5. Quoted in Walter Wagner, *You Must Remember This* (New York: Putnam's, 1975), p. 57.

6. Quoted in Sinclair, p. 11, from taped interview by Bogdanovich, JFP.

7. Ford's reminiscences, JFP.

8. Bogdanovich, p. 108.

9. Wilkinson, p. 23, from letter from boyhood friend Joseph D. McDonnell.

10. Josephine Feeney's reminiscences, JFP.

11. Ford's reminiscences, JFP.

12. Quoted in Wagner, *You Must Remember This*, p. 57.

13. Quoted in Eric Leguèbe, *Le Cinéma Americain par ses auteurs* (Paris: Guy Authier, 1977), p. 75. My translation.

14. For Francis Ford, see my "Brother Feeney," *Film Comment*, November 1976, pp. 12–18. For the Melies Company, see runs of *Film Index* and *Moving Picture World;* Madeleine Malthête-Méliès, *Méliès l'enchanteur* (Paris: Hachette, 1973); Patrick McInroy, "Hollywood Ruined S. A. Filming," *San Antonio Light*, May 30, 1976, "To-day" section, p. 1. For Ince, see Ince, "The Early Days at Kay Bee," *Photoplay*, March 1919, pp. 42–46; George Pratt, "See Mr. Ince . . . ," *Image*, 1956, pp. 100–111; George Mitchell, "Thomas Ince," *Films in Review,* October 1960, pp. 464–84; Paul O'Dell, *Griffith and the Rise of Hollywood* (New York: Castle, 1970); David Robinson, *Hollywood in the Twenties* (New York: A. S. Barnes, 1968); Jean Mitry, *Histoire du cinéma*, vol. 1. (Paris: Editions Universitaires, 1968), pp. 332, 342, 437–43, a great improvement over his earlier articles but still a bit fanciful. Jon Tuska, *The Filming of the West* (New York: Doubleday, 1976), pp. 25–30, perhaps overstates somewhat the case for Francis Ford. See also Fred C. Balshofer and Arthur Miller, *One Reel a Week* (Berkeley: University of California Press, 1967), as well as the records of the New York Motion Picture Company from 1913 onward, at the Wisconsin Center for Film Research, Madison, which, however, provide only scant information.

15. *Motion Picture Directory*, 1921, p. 263.

16. "Francis Ford Expresses His Ideas on Serials," *Moving Picture World*, August 16, 1919, p. 998.

17. Bogdanovich, p. 40.

18. Universal's *Moving Picture Weekly*, October 16, 1915, p. 41.

19. Richard Willis, "Francis Ford, of the Gold Seal Company," *Motion Picture Magazine*, June 1915, p. 104.

20. Ibid., pp. 101–2.

21. Ibid., p. 104.

22. Ince, "Early Days," p. 44.

23. Anthony Slide and Robert Gitt, "Frank Baker," unpublished interview, July 30, 1977, unpaginated.

24. Theodore Huff Memorial Film Society, handout, March 23, 1970.

25. "Francis Ford Expresses His Ideas on Serials."

26. *Moving Picture World,* August 27, 1927, p. 588.

27. Slide and Gitt, "Frank Baker."

28. Willis, "Francis Ford," p. 101.

29. Quoted in Frank S. Nugent, "Hollywood's Favorite Rebel," *The Saturday Evening Post,* September 23, 1949, p. 97.

30. Ibid.

31. Quoted in Cecilia Ager, "Then and Now," *The New York Times Magazine,* September 20, 1959, p. 62.

32. Ford's reminiscences, JFP.

33. Quoted in Richard Schickel, "Good Days, Good Years," *Harpers,* October 1970, p. 46.

34. Author's interview with Cecil McLean de Prida, March 1979.

35. April 28, 1917.

36. *Moving Picture Weekly,* May 19, 1917, p. 18.

37. Ibid., June 2, 1917, p. 19.

38. Quoted in Wilkinson, p. 186.

39. Ibid.

40. Quoted in *Moving Picture Weekly,* July 28, 1917, p. 11.

41. *Los Angeles Evening Herald Examiner,* February 28, 1944, p. B4.

42. Bogdanovich, p. 39.

43. *Moving Picture Weekly,* August 18, 1917; also, *Moving Picture World,* September 1, 1917, p. 1433. But the present "happy" ending is given in *Moving Picture Weekly,* January ?, 1925.

44. Bogdanovich, p. 108.

45. Wagner, *You Must Remember This,* p. 59.

46. Author's interview with Olive Carey, March 1979.

47. Author's interview with Harry Carey, Jr., March 1979.

48. Olive Carey's reminiscences, JFP.

49. Author's interview with Olive Carey.

50. *Los Angeles Evening Herald Examiner,* February 28, 1944, p. B4.

51. Arthur H. Lewis, *It Was Fun While It Lasted* (New York: Trident Press, 1973), p. 313.

52. Author's interview with Harry Carey, Jr.

53. *Moving Picture World,* March 29, 1919, p. 1768.

54. Anthony Slide and June Banker, unpublished interview with Mary Ford, 1970, unpaginated.

55. Ibid.

56. Letter begun November 19, 1921, from John to Mary Ford, JFP.

57. Letter, January (?), 1922, from John to Mary Ford, JFP.

58. Dan Ford, p. 24.

59. List from George N. Fenin and William K. Everson, *The Western* (New York: Grossman, 1973), p. 139.

60. Quoted in Bertrand Tavernier, "John Ford à Paris," *Positif* 82 (March 1967), p. 20. My translation.

61. Anderson, p. 20.

62. Quoted in Kevin Brownlow, *The War, the West, and the Wilderness* (New York: Knopf, 1978), p. 392.

63. Author's interview with Frank Baker, March 1979.

64. Author's interview with Cecil McLean de Prida.

65. Bogdanovich, p. 47.

66. Dan Ford, p. 33

67. Many mysteries would clarify, were less early Ford lost.

68. Author's interview with George O'Brien, May 1979.

69. Quoted in notes of Maurice Zolotow, Zolotow Manuscripts, Library of the University of Texas, Austin.

70. Quoted by Dan Ford, JFP.

71. Author's interview with Frank Baker.

72. Ibid.

73. Ibid.

74. Ibid.

75. Ibid.

76. Ibid.

77. Ibid.

78. Quoted by Dan Ford, JFP.

79. Slide and Banker, interview with Mary Ford.

80. Mary Ford's reminiscences, JFP.

81. John Ford's reminiscences, JFP.

82. Author's interview with George O'Brien.

83. Letter from John to Mary Ford, January 1931, JFP.

84. Author's interview with George O'Brien.

85. Ibid.

86. Jon Tuska, interview with H. Bruce Humberstone, in *Close Up: The Contract Director* (Metuchen, N.J.: Scarecrow Press, 1976).

87. Dan Ford, p. 67.

88. Ibid., p. 68.

89. Sinclair, p. 38, and author's interview with Cecil McLean de Prida.

90. Author's interview with Frank Baker.

2   First Period (1927–1935): The Age of Introspection

1. *Moving Picture World*, March 26, 1927, p. 342. Most sources estimate audiences were roughly equally male and female, but no definite information exists.

2. Ibid., March 3, 1927, p. 35.

3. Erich Rohmer, *L'organisation de l'espace dans le "Faust" de Murnau* (Paris: Editions 10/18, 1977), pp. 112, 118. My translation.

4. *Moving Picture World*, April 2, 1927, p. 490.

5. Rohmer, "Faust," p. 32.

6. John Ford, "Veteran Producer Muses," *The New York Times*, June 10, 1928, sec. 8, p. 4.

7. *Moving Picture World*, April 21, 1928, p. 342.

8. *Film Spectator*, May 12, 1928, pp. 5–7.

9. Ibid., November 3, 1928, p. 10, and November 10, 1928, pp. 6–7.

10. *The New York Times*, October 11, 1930, p. 21.

11. Quoted in Juliet Benita Colman, *Ronald Colman: A Very Private Person* (New York: Morrow, 1975), p. 113.

12. Richard Griffith, *Samuel Goldwyn: The Producer and His Film* (New York: Simon & Schuster, 1956), p. 21.

13. John Brosnan, *Movie Magic* (New York: St. Martin's Press, 1974), pp. 68–71.

14. Bogdanovich, p. 57.

15. Ibid.

16. Max Steiner, "Scoring the Film," in Nancy Naumburg, ed., *We Make the Movies* (New York: Norton, 1937), p. 221.

17. Bogdanovich, p. 59.

18. Ibid., p. 47.

19. R. G. Collingwood, *The Idea of History* (New York: Oxford University Press, 1946), p. 44.

20. Ibid., p. 39, quoting Furneaux, ed., *Cornelii Taciti Annalium,* Libri I–IV (Oxford, 1886), pp. 3–4.

21. Jean Mitry, *John Ford* (Paris: Editions Universitaires, 1954), pp. 23, 28–29. My translation.

22. See Carlos Clarens, *Crime Movies* (New York: Norton, 1980), p. 141.

23. Philip Dunne, *Take Two: A Life in Movies and Politics* (New York: McGraw-Hill, 1980), p. 92.

24. Dan Ford, p. 98.

25. Author's interview with Frank Baker.

26. Reminiscences of Katharine Hepburn (with John Ford), c. 1972, JFP.

27. Ibid.

28. Dan Ford, p. 99.

29. Ibid.

30. Letter from Katharine Hepburn to John Ford, April 10, 1937, JFP.

31. Reminiscences of John Ford, JFP. The assertion that his mother had thirteen children is most likely blarney; that he was the last certainly is.

32. Quoted in Howard Sharpe, "The Star Creators of Hollywood," *Photoplay,* October 1936, p. 100. Reprint: see Biliography.

33. Parrish, p. 131.

34. Author's interview with Frank Baker. The story has been told many times, but Baker claims to have witnessed it.

35. Recounted by Dan Ford, JFP.

36. Author's interview with Leon Selditz, April 1979.

37. Reminiscences of Katherine Clifton, JFP.

38. Reminiscences of Katharine Hepburn, JFP.

39. Reminiscences of Nunnally Johnson, JFP.

40. Quoted in Max Wilk, *The Wit and Wisdom of Hollywood* (New York: Atheneum, 1971), pp. 278–79.

41. Reminiscences of Nunnally Johnson, JFP.

3 Second Period (1935–1947): The Age of Idealism

1. Quoted in Anderson, p. 63.

2. Anderson, p. 22.

3. George J. Mitchell, "Ford on Ford," *Films in Review,* June 1964, pp. 324–25.

4. Bogdanovich, p. 59.

5. Anderson, p. 88.

6. Quoted in Anderson, p. 86.

7. Dan Ford, p. 84. Nichols, in Anderson (p. 240), gives a quite different account, claiming the script was essentially his own—and suggesting that Ford may

imagine after a film that his (Ford's) contributions were greater than they were.

8. See, for example, in Lewis Jacobs, *The Rise of the American Film* (New York: Teachers College Press, 1967), pp. 479–84.

9. Author's interview with Frank Baker.

10. John Baxter, *The Cinema of John Ford* (New York: A. S. Barnes, 1971), p. 49.

11. Peter C. Rollins, "Will Rogers and the Relevance of Nostalgia: *Steamboat Round the Bend,*" in John E. O'Connor and Martin A. Jackson, eds., *American History/American Film* (New York: Ungar, 1979), pp. 78–79.

12. Bogdanovich, p. 57.

13. Robert Wilson, ed., *The Film Criticism of Otis Ferguson* (Philadelphia: Temple University Press, 1971), p. 121.

14. Sharpe, "Star Creators," p. 98.

15. Mary Astor, *A Life on Film* (New York: Dell, 1972), p. 134.

16. Mel Gussow, *Don't Say Yes Until I Finish Talking* (New York: Pocket Books, 1972), p. 150.

17. Quoted in Bob Thomas, ed., *Directors in Action* (New York: Bobbs Merrill, 1973), pp. 143–44.

18. Quoted in Paul Jensen, "Dudley Nichols," in Richard Corliss, ed., *The Hollywood Screenwriters* (New York: Avon, 1972), p. 118.

19. Nick Browne, "The Spectator-in-the-Text: The Rhetoric of *Stagecoach,*" *Film Quarterly*, Winter 1975, pp. 26–38.

20. Ibid., pp. 35–37.

21. Ibid., p. 31.

22. Ibid., p. 38.

23. Quoted in Thomas, *Directors in Action*, p. 160.

24. Bogdanovich, p. 20.

25. Quoted in Axel Madsen, interview with Ford, *Cahiers du Cinéma* 183 (October 1966), p. 48. My translation.

26. Quoted by Fonda in Mike Steen, "Henry Fonda," in *Hollywood Speaks! An Oral History* (New York: Putnam's, 1974), p. 40.

27. Editors of *Cahiers du Cinéma*, "John Ford's *Young Mr. Lincoln,*" *Cahiers du Cinéma* 223 (August 1970), pp. 29–47. Translation by Helene Lackner and Diana Matias, in *Screen*, Autumn 1972, pp. 5–28. Reprinted in Gerald Mast and Marshall Cohen, eds., *Film Theory and Criticism*, 2d ed. (New York: Oxford University Press, 1979), pp. 778–831. The *Cahiers* article, although thoroughly meretricious, has spawned a host of admiring commentaries—for which reason I have felt obliged to consider it here. Some of the commentaries are listed in the Bibliography.

28. J. A. Place, *The Non-Western Films of John Ford* (New York: Citadel, 1979), pp. 56–67.

29. Robert Parrish, "Témoignage sur John Ford," *Présence du Cinéma* 21 (March 1965), pp. 18–20. My translation.

30. Andrew Sarris, *The John Ford Movie Mystery* (Bloomington: Indiana University Press, 1976), p. 50.

31. *The New York Times*, January 25, 1940, p. 17; January 28, 1940, sec. 9, p. 5.

32. Mitchell, "Ford on Ford," p. 331.

33. Quoted in Tavernier, "John Ford à Paris," p. 18. My translation.

34. Dan Ford, p. 143.

35. *Cahiers du Cinéma* 165 (April 1965), p. 11.
36. *Friday,* August 9, 1940.
37. Quoted in Anderson, p. 247.
38. David Thomson, "John Ford," in *A Biographical Dictionary of Film* (New York: Morrow, 1979), pp. 185–86. Anderson (p. 71) writes in similar terms, alas.
39. Dunne, *Take Two,* p. 94.
40. Quoted in Gussow, *Don't Say Yes,* p. 87.
41. Ibid., p. 88.
42. Author's interview with Anna Lee, March 1979.
43. Quoted by Dan Ford, p. 158.
44. Jenkinson, interview with Ford.
45. Author's interview with Cecil McLean de Prida. Information about Ford's activities during the war derives from Mrs. de Prida, Dan Ford, Sinclair, Parrish, author's interview with George O'Brien, and materials in JFP.
46. Slide and Banker, interview with Mary Ford.
47. Quoted in *Los Angeles Evening Herald Examiner,* February 28, 1944, p. B4.
48. Slide and Banker, interview with Mary Ford.
49. Parrish (pp. 137–42) describes in detail how Ford sent him and another man to take spy photos of the White House; Parrish was arrested, but Ford presided over his court of inquiry.
50. Author's interview with Harry Carey, Jr.
51. Parrish, p. 142.
52. Nugent, "Hollywood's Favorite Rebel," p. 25.
53. Madsen, interview with Ford, October 1966, pp. 48–51.
54. Photographer Second Class Jack MacKenzie, Jr., tells a slightly different story regarding his activity. See *American Cinematographer,* February 1944.
55. Jenkinson, interview with Ford.
56. Parrish (pp. 144–51) des ribes Ford's machinations in great detail.
57. Ibid., p. 145.
58. Ibid., p. 151.
59. Dan Ford, p. 176.
60. Sinclair, p. 114.
61. Letter, dated 1942, from Ford to Wellman, JFP.
62. Dan Ford, p. 183.
63. Ibid., p. 182.
64. Ibid.
65. Letter, dated June 1, 1943, from Mary to John Ford, JFP.
66. Parrish (p. 152), Sinclair (p. 115), and numerous references in JFP contradict Dan Ford's statement (p. 185) that Ford flew.
67. Dan Ford, p. 188.
68. Sinclair, p. 124.
69. Author's interview with John Stafford.
70. Sinclair, p. 118.
71. Parrish, p. 159.
72. Sinclair, p. 126.
73. Dan Ford, p. 274.
74. Bogdanovich, p. 82.

75. Anderson, pp. 20–21.

76. Ibid., p. 73.

77. Mitchell, "Ford on Ford," p. 331.

78. Dan Ford, p. 199.

79. Letter, October 17, 1946, from Ford to Zanuck, JFP.

80. Anderson, p. 22.

81. Bogdanovich, p. 85.

82. Anderson, p. 90.

83. Author's interview with Harry Carey, Jr.

84. Reminiscences of Olive Carey, JFP.

85. Author's interview with Harry Carey, Jr.

86. Dan Ford, p. 259.

87. Letter, dated 1952, from Mary Ford (Frank's wife) to Mary Ford (John's wife).

88. Author's interview with Frank Baker.

4   Third Period (1948–1961): The Age of Myth

1. Sarris, *John Ford Movie Mystery*, p. 124.

2. "Burt Kennedy Interviews John Ford," *Action*, August 1968. Reprinted in Thomas, *Directors in Action*, p. 134.

3. Anderson, p. 22.

4. Tavernier, "John Ford à Paris," p. 17. My translation.

5. Quoted in Anderson, p. 244.

6. Bogdanovich, p. 86.

7. Jenkinson, interview with Ford.

8. Madsen, interview with Ford, October 1966, p. 51.

9. Quoted in Anderson, p. 244.

10. Bogdanovich, p. 88.

11. Tavernier, "John Ford à Paris," p. 20. My translation.

12. Mitchell, "Ford on Ford," p. 33.

13. Raoul Walsh, *Each Man in His Time* (New York: Farrar Straus Giroux, 1974), p. 186.

14. Jean Mitry, interview with Ford, *Cahiers du Cinéma* 45 (March 1955), p. 5. My translation.

15. Anderson, p. 22.

16. Ibid.

17. Mitchell, "Ford on Ford," p. 332.

18. Anderson, p. 19.

19. Ibid.

20. Mitchell, "Ford on Ford," p. 332.

21. Bogdanovich, p. 19.

22. Anderson, p. 22.

23. Mitchell, "Ford on Ford," p. 332.

24. Joe McInerney, "John Wayne Talks Tough," *Film Comment*, September 1972, p. 53.

25. "Kennedy Interviews Ford," p. 134.

26. Tavernier, "John Ford à Paris," p. 17. My translation.

27. Mitry, interview with Ford, p. 6. My translation.

28. Quoted by Dore Schary, *Heyday* (New York: Berkeley Books, 1979), p. 256.

29. Quoted in Bill Libby, "The Old Wrangler Rides Again," *Cosmopolitan,* March 1964.

30. Quoted in Joseph McBride, *"The Searchers," Sight and Sound,* Spring 1972, p. 212.

31. Ford recounts this story in Mark Haggard, "Ford in Person," *Focus on Film* 6 (Spring 1971), p. 33.

32. Author's interview with Harry Carey, Jr.

33. Author's interview with John Stafford.

34. Haggard, "Ford in Person," p. 32.

35. Author's interview with Harry Carey, Jr.

36. Draft of speech, dated 1933, JFP.

37. Remark to author by Maurice Rapf, 1976.

38. Resolution, dated 1947, JFP.

39. Draft of letter, dated January 1952, from Ford to Department of Defense, JFP.

40. Kenneth L. Geist, *Pictures Will Talk* (New York: Scribner's, 1978), pp. 202–4.

41. Bogdanovich, p. 14.

42. Leguèbe, "John Ford," p. 77. My translation.

43. Letter, dated September 1937, from Ford to Bob Ford, JFP.

44. Tavernier, "John Ford à Paris," pp. 13–14. My translation. On other occasions, Ford made vague allusions to having voted for Goldwater and, later, for Nixon, his reason being that he *knew* them both, rather than for political motives.

45. Anderson, p. 25.

46. Parrish, p. 154.

47. Allan Dwan's reminiscences (with Dan Ford), JFP.

48. Dan Ford, p. 268.

49. Bogdanovich, p. 96.

50. Louis Marcorelles, *Cahiers du Cinéma* 85 (July 1958), p. 54. My translation.

51. Michael Killanin, "Poet in an Iron Mask," *Films and Filming,* February 1958, p. 9.

52. Ibid.

53. Marcorelles, *Cahiers* 85, p. 54. My translation.

54. Bogdanovich, p. 102.

55. Author's interview with Anna Lee.

56. Colin Young, "The Old Dependables," *Film Quarterly,* Fall 1969, pp. 8–9.

57. Louis Marcorelles, *Cahiers du Cinéma* 101 (November 1959), pp. 48–49. My translation.

58. J. A. Place, *The Western Films of John Ford* (New York: Citadel, 1975), p. 179.

59. Quoted in Joseph McBride and Michael Wilmington, *John Ford* (New York: Da Capo, 1975), p. 169.

60. Bogdanovich, p. 97.

61. Madsen, interview with Ford, *Cahiers du Cinéma* 168 (July 1965), p. 79. My translation.

5 Final Period (1962–1965): The Age of Mortality

1. Letter, dated June 20, 1951, from Barbara to John Ford, JFP.

2. Author's interview with Frank Baker.

3. If, however, I read allusions in the correspondence in JFP of this period cor-

rectly, Pat ended up living on a lot in which John had invested money—his sole real estate investment.

4. Bob Thomas, *Selznick* (New York: Pocket Books, 1970), p. 259.

5. Author's interview with Harry Carey, Jr.

6. Author's interview with Frank Baker.

7. Hedda Hopper, unpublished conversation with Ford, April 13, 1962, Library of Motion Picture Arts and Sciences, Beverly Hills.

8. Letter, dated May 19, 1959, from Bea Benjamin to Captain Henry Yeager, JFP.

9. Author's interview with Frank Baker.

10. Slide and Banker, interview with Mary Ford.

11. Scott Eyman, interview with William Clothier, *Take One* 4, no. 8 (November–December 1973 [published March 1975], p. 13. That it was a *toy:* reminiscences of Clothier (with Dan Ford), JFP.

12. Quoted in author's interview with Harry Carey, Jr.

13. Hedda Hopper, conversation with Ford.

14. John Ford, "Veteran Producer Muses," p. 4.

15. Bogdanovich, p. 99.

16. Ibid., p. 16.

17. Remark to author, 1975.

18. See Jean-Louis Comolli, "Signes de piste," *Cahiers du Cinéma* 164 (March 1965), p. 75; Dan Ford, pp. 296–305; Sinclair, pp. 198–200; remarks by scenarist James R. Webb, in Philippe Haudiquet, *John Ford* (Paris: Seghers, 1966), pp. 128–30.

19. François Truffaut, *Hitchcock* (New York: Simon and Schuster, 1966); e.g., on *Paradine Case*, p. 127; on *Strangers on a Train*, p. 146; on *I Confess*, p. 149; et al.

20. Andrew Sarris, "John Ford," in *The American Cinema* (New York: Dutton, 1968), p. 48.

21. Sarris, *John Ford Movie Mystery*, p. 160.

22. Bogdanovich, p. 104.

23. Madsen, interview with Ford, October 1966, p. 42. My translation.

24. Noel Burch, *To the Distant Observer* (Berkeley: University of California Press, 1979). One of Burch's principal theses lies in his attempt to contrast Japan's prewar *presentational* modes of cinema with Hollywood's *representational* (i.e., illusion of realism) modes, but his argument seems to me to reveal prejudices that blind him to the essential features of Western cinema—certainly to auteurist cinema.

25. Leguèbe, "John Ford," pp. 78–79. My translation.

26. Bogdanovich, p. 141.

27. Sarris, *John Ford Movie Mystery*, p. 185.

28. Arthur Knight, a review of 7 *Women, Saturday Review*, January 8, 1966, p. 97.

29. Madsen, interview with Ford, October 1966, p. 51. My translation.

30. Sarris, *John Ford Movie Mystery*, p. 185.

31. Author's interview with Anna Lee.

32. Joyce Haber, "If I Could Film a Dream . . . " *Philadelphia Inquirer*, May 13, 1972.

33. Tavernier, "John Ford à Paris," p. 18.

34. Slide and Banker, interview with Mary Ford.

35. Reminiscences of Bea Benjamin, in JFP.

36. Remark to author, 1974.

37. Author's interview with Frank Baker.

38. Slide and Banker, interview with Mary Ford.

6 Conclusion
1. Sharpe, "Star Creators," p. 98.
2. Slide and Gitt, "Frank Baker."
3. Balshofer and Miller, *One Reel a Week*, p. 186.
4. Quoted in Leonard Maltin, *The Art of the Cinematographer* (New York: Dover, 1978), p. 70.
5. Ibid.
6. Balshofer and Miller, *One Reel a Week*, p. 187.
7. Quoted in Steen, "Henry Fonda," p. 27.
8. Karyn Kay and Gerald Peary, "Talking to Pat O'Brien," *Velvet Light Trap* 15 (Fall 1975), p. 32.
9. Astor, *A Life on Film*, p. 134.
10. Raymond Massey, *A Hundred Different Lives* (Boston: Little Brown, 1979), pp. 212, 215.
11. Quoted in Sinclair, p. 168.
12. Author's interview with Anna Lee.
13. Parrish, p. 149.
14. Author's interview with Ruth Clifford, March 1979.
15. Author's interview with Harry Carey, Jr.
16. Dan Ford, p. 158.
17. *7 Women* pressbook, Free Library of Philadelphia Theater Collection.
18. Author's interview with Harry Carey, Jr.
19. *7 Women* pressbook.
20. Sharpe, "Star Creators," p. 100.
21. Frederick T. Weber, "Portrait Painting," *Encyclopaedia Britannica* (1957).
22. Mitchell, "Ford on Ford," p. 33.
23. Eyman, interview with William Clothier, p. 32.
24. Gabriel Figueroa, letter to author, May 1979.
25. Mitchell, "Ford on Ford," p. 26.
26. "Kennedy Interviews Ford," p. 135.
27. Ibid., p. 136.
28. Robert Parrish, "De Chaplin à Fuller," *Cahiers du Cinéma* 142 (April 1963), p. 11. My translation.
29. Lefty Hough's reminiscences, JFP.
30. Author's interview with Barbara Ford, March 1979.
31. Quoted in William Frough, *The Screenwriter Looks at the Screenwriter* (New York: Macmillan, 1972), p. 240.
32. Dan Ford, p. 284.
33. Anderson, p. 244.
34. Quoted in Wilkinson.
35. Quoted in Sinclair (p. 194), from *Films and Filming*, April 1966.
36. Frank Nugent, "In Remembrance of Hot-Foots Past," *The New York Times*, March 3, 1949, p. 33.
37. Tavernier, "John Ford à Paris," p. 18.
38. Jensen, "Dudley Nichols," p. 111.
39. McBride and Wilmington, *John Ford*, p. 24.
40. Hal Humphrey, "Veteran John Ford Looks Back," *Philadelphia Bulletin*, April 11, 1965.
41. *7 Women* pressbook.

42. Madsen, interview with Ford, July 1965, p. 79. My translation.

43. Mitry, *John Ford*, p. 26. My translation.

44. Stanley Cavell, *The World Viewed* (Cambridge: Harvard University Press, 1979), p. 33.

45. Quoted in Jacques Barzun, *The Energies of Art* (New York: Harper Bros., 1956), p. 257.

46. Ibid., p. 262.

47. Anderson, p. 242.

48. Killanin, "Poet in an Iron Mask," p. 9.

49. Sharpe, "Star Creators," p. 98.

50. Author's interview with Harry Carey, Jr.

51. Sharpe, "Star Creators," p. 99.

52. Author's interview with Anna Lee.

53. Arnold Hauser, *The Social History of Art,* vol. 4 (New York: Random House), p. 30.

54. Mitchell, "Ford on Ford," p. 330.

55. Ford, "Veteran Producer Muses," p. 4.

56. Grady Johnson, "A Paean of Economy," *The New York Times,* June 27, 1944, sec. 2, p. 4.

57. Sharpe, "Star Creators," p. 98.

58. Wilkinson.

59. Anderson, p. 237.

60. Sharpe, "Star Creators," p. 100.

61. McBride and Wilmington, *John Ford*, p. 32.

62. Ford, "Veteran Producer Muses," p. 4.

63. When Straub made this remark to the author in 1975 (after seeing *Pilgrimage* and *Donovan's Reef*) he was referring not so much to Ford's *acting style*—in that sense *no* films are truly Brechtian—as to Ford's manner of stripping naked social ideologies that are elsewhere unacknowledged. To Joseph McBride, Straub said Ford is the most Brechtian of filmmakers, "because he shows things that make people think . . . by [making] the audience collaborate on the film" (McBride and Wilmington, *John Ford*, p. 108). McBride analyzes *Fort Apache* in this light, pointing out how Captain York donning Colonel Thursday's hat at the end is a Brechtian device [like the cardinal donning the pope's robes in Brecht's *Galileo*], and that we see clearly that an insane system needs the dedication of noble men to perpetuate itself.) Less simply, one might call Ford Brechtian because every element in his cinema is engaged dialectically with every other element (whether one speaks of elements of—or between—style, content, myth, ideology, or whatever), with the result that Ford's films are self-reflexive and transparent in their workings.

This notion—essentially the thesis of this book—flies violently in the face of a recent critical tendency to regard the "classical" cinema of Hollywood as a monolithic system that sought to mask its "codes" (e.g., its *montage*) in order to create an apparently unmediated representation of the real world; it sought to entertain passively and left unacknowledged its own governing ideology. (Cf., *Stagecoach:* my argument with Browne ("Spectator-in-the-Text"); also Burch, *Distant Observer;* Robert Phillip Kolker, *The Altering Eye* [New York: Oxford, 1983]; Thomas Schatz, *Hollywood Genres* [New York: Random House, 1981]). "Modernist" (i.e., some post-1960) cinema, on the other hand, subverts our absorption in emotion, story, or character, and exposes its "codes" (e.g., by showing the camera, discordant editing, having an actor speak directly to us), in order to force us to relate intellectually rather than through emotional identification.

In these circles, Straub is admired as epitomizing "modernist" cinema, while Ford is often derided (although not by most of the above-named critics) as a sentimental reactionary. Thus Straub's comparison of Brecht and Ford caused considerable head-shaking. It is, of course, generally agreed that many films cater exclusively to an audience's desire for passive spectacle (e.g., *Star Wars*, some of Hitchcock); and all research shows that audiences generally watch movies in order *not* to think. Nonetheless, the fallacies of "modernist" critics are multitudinous (even including their arrogation of the label "modern"). Firstly, their premise of a monolithic classical system is a pure fantasy that reveals little sensibility for the complexity of pre-1960 cinema and almost no acquaintance with the actual films themselves. Secondly, they naively assume that audiences can be *forced* to think, whereas "modernist" techniques soon lose their initial shock and audiences happily re-immerse themselves into the fictional worlds of even the most determinedly antipathetic movies. Thirdly, because their basis is exclusively materialist, they, like Grierson and Aristarco before them, distrust emotions and aestheticism and would destroy the art of cinema in favor of a cinema of political propaganda.

An examination of Brecht's 1930 table, in which he gave cursory comparison between the (bad) "dramatic" and the (good, Brechtian) "epic" theaters, will, in the light of Straub and this book, show Ford very much on the "epic" side—the "modernist":

Dramatic Theater	*Epic Theater*
plot	narrative
implicates spectator into drama	makes spectator an observer
wears down his capacity for action	arouses his capacity for action
provides him with sensations	forces him to make decisions
provides experience	provides a picture of the world
involves the spectator	confronts the spectator
suggestion	argument
feelings are preserved	feelings are propelled into perceptions
man is assumed known	man is the object of inquiry
man unalterable	man alterable and altering
suspense about the outcome	suspense about the progress
each scene exists for another	each scene for itself
linear development	in curves
evolutionary determinism	evolutionary leaps
the world, as it is	the world, as it becomes
what man ought to do	what man is forced to do
man as a fixed point	man as a process
his instincts	his motivations
thought determines being	social being determines thought

(Brecht did not intend, obviously, that epic theater be absolutely one way and not at all the other way; it is a question more of tendency.)

64. Ford, unpublished, untitled article, supposed to be on "The Man's Story," for a projected book by Bill Hawkes, 1946, JFP. Ford, of course, went out of his way to show that he was not to be categorized as a "man's director."

65. Reminiscences of Barbara Ford, with John Ford, JFP.

Appendix:

Grosses and Earnings

Ford's yearly earnings are taken from working copies of his federal or (when asterisked) state tax forms, supplemented by figures given on film contracts or as noted by Dan Ford. Salary figures for specific films are given when known and are included in the yearly earnings totals (but not necessarily during the year of the film's release). When a salary includes a percentage (e.g., +10%), such additional payment was due only after twice the cost of the negative had been earned, and, usually, after distribution costs were deducted as well. The latter were not inconsiderable. 7 *Women*, for example, cost $2,308,000 to make ("negative cost") and by 1970 had grossed $937,432 worldwide, but distribution costs amounted to $930,000, bringing 7 *Women's* net loss to $2,300,000.

Grosses generally are listed for the first year of release domestically; foreign first year earnings often equalled domestic ones. The figure after a film title is the cost of the negative. Business is rated *Excellent, Good, Fair,* or *Poor,* and for this information I am indebted to Lee Beaupré, who, however, cautions that prewar figures may be extremely untrustworthy. E = Estimate. A = Actual rental figure.

Year	Ford's Earnings Year (total)	Film fees	Title—Negative Cost (when known)	Domestic Gross (first year)
1917	$75 to $100 weekly			
1918	$150 weekly			
1919	$300 weekly			

Year	Ford's Earnings Year (total)	Film fees	Title—Negative Cost (when known)	Domestic Gross (first year)
1920	$300 to $600 weekly			
1921	$13,618			
1922	$27,891			
1923	$44,910			
1924	$30,118		The Iron Horse— $280,000	E: $2 million plus (worldwide)
1925	$73,954			
1926	$82,272		3 Bad Men—$650,000	
1927	$83,114			
1928	$47,112			
1929	$133,977		Strong Boy	Fair to Poor
			The Black Watch— $400,000	Good: E: $800,000
			Salute	Fox's best in 1929
1930	$145,094 minus stock loss	$14,000	Men Without Women	Fair to poor
			Born Reckless	Fair to poor
			Up the River	Fair. E: $650,000
1931	$41,952 minus stock loss	$12,000	Seas Beneath	Fair to poor
			The Brat	Poor
			Arrowsmith	Excellent, among year's top 20. A: $1,250,000
1932	$81,130 minus $50,000 stock loss	$36,000	Air Mail—$305,000	Fair
			Flesh	Good. E: $850,000
1933	$72,903		Pilgrimage	Fair to good. E: $650,000
			Doctor Bull	Fair
1934	$141,355		The Lost Patrol— $254,000	Good. E: $750,000
			The World Moves On	Fair. E: $450,000
			Judge Priest	Very good. E: $900,000
1935	$121,290	$50,000	The Whole Town's Talking	Fair. A: $300,000
			The Informer—$215,000	Fair to poor
			Steamboat Round the Bend	Very good. E: $1,000,000
1936	$192,586		The Prisoner of Shark Island	Fair to good. E: $750,000
			Mary of Scotland	Very good. E: $1,000,000
			The Plough and the Stars	Poor
1937	$159,066		Wee Willie Winkie	Very good. E: $1,250,000
		$100,000 + 12%	The Hurricane	Excellent, among year's top 20. E: $1,400,000

Year	Ford's Earnings Year (total)	Film fees	Title—Negative Cost (when known)	Domestic Gross (first year)
1938	$220,068	$75,000	Four Men and a Prayer	Fair. E: $600,000
		$75,000	Submarine Patrol	Fair to good. E: $750,000
1939	No information	$50,000	Stagecoach	Good. E: $1,000,000
		$75,000	Young Mr. Lincoln	Fair to good. E: $750,000
		$75,000	Drums Along the Mohawk	Very good. E: $1,250,000
1940	$178,000	$75,000	The Grapes of Wrath	Good to very good. E: $1,100,000
			The Long Voyage Home	Fair. E: $600,000
1941	$168,000		Tobacco Road	Fair to good. E: $900,000
			How Green Was My Valley—$1,300,000	2nd biggest of year, after Sergeant York. A: $2,800,000
1942	$27,000			
1943	$14,300			
1944	$22,650			
1945	$115,000	$300,000 (donated)	They Were Expendable	Among year's top 20. A: $3,250,000
1946	$141,000		My Darling Clementine	Very good. A: $2,750,000 domestic $1,750,000 foreign
1947	$199,000		The Fugitive	Poor. E: $750,000
1948	$176,000		Fort Apache—$1,200,000	Among year's top 20. A: $3,000,000 domestic $1,900,000 foreign
			3 Godfathers	Fair to good. A: $2,700,000
1949	No information		She Wore a Yellow Ribbon—$1,600,000	Very good. A: $2,700,000 domestic $2,500,000 foreign
1950	$188,000		When Willie Comes Marching Home	Fair to good. A: $1,700,000
			Wagon Master	Fair to poor. E: $1,000,000
			Rio Grande—$1,238,000	Very good. A: $2,250,000
1951	$133,000			
1952	$258,000		The Quiet Man—$1,750,000	In top 10. A: $3,800,000
			What Price Glory	Good. A: $2,000,000
1953	No information		The Sun Shines Bright	Poor
1954	$84,000		Mogambo	In top 10. A: $5,200,000
1955	$317,000		The Long Gray Line—$1,748,000	Very good. A: $3,450,000 domestic $2,150,000 foreign

Year	Ford's Earnings Year (total)	Film fees	Title—Negative Cost (when known)	Domestic Gross (first year)
1956	No information	$175,000 + 10%	*The Searchers*	In top 20. A: $4,450,000
1957	$144,000	No Salary	*The Rising of the Moon*—$256,016	Very poor. A: $950,000 worldwide
			The Wings of Eagles	Good. A: $2,250,000
1958	No information	No salary	*Gideon of Scotland Yard* (U.S.) $453,600	Poor. E: $400,000
		$125,000 + 25%	*The Last Hurrah*	Poor to fair. A: $950,000
1959	No information	$375,000 + 10%	*The Horse Soldiers*	In top 20. A: $3,600,000
1960	$180,000*		*Sergeant Rutledge*	Poor
		$3,500	*The Colter Craven Story*	(Television)
1961	$267,000*	$225,000 + 25% (includes Pat Ford salary)	*Two Rode Together*	Fair. A: $1,600,000
1962	$189,000*	$150,000 + 25% ownership	*The Man Who Shot Liberty Valance*—$3,200,000	Very good. A: $3,200,000
		$50,000	"The Civil War," *How the West Was Won*	
1963	$184,000*		*Donovan's Reef*—$2,686,585	Very good. A: $3,300,000
1964	$137,000	$200,000 + %	*Cheyenne Autumn*—$4,200,000	Good. A: $3,150,000
1965	No information	$262,00 + %	*7 Women*—$2,308,190	Very poor. A: (by 1966): $204,000 domestic $51,00 foreign $433,000 domestic $504,000 foreign
1966	$102,000			

No information for years after 1966.
Net worth (1965): E: $1,700,000

Filmography

The present filmography is based upon previously published ones but contains many corrections and additions. Plot summaries for the silent period have been drawn from contemporary periodicals and differ from those in Peter Bogdanovich's filmography, where they appear to have been drawn from Universal's records.

Information on John Ford's work prior to *The Tornado* in 1917 is sketchy. His niece speaks of a film co-directed with Edward Laemmle, for example, of which nothing is known. Ford liked to say he got his start as a director with some action sequences for Carl Laemmle's guests in 1916; these were incorporated into a western directed by someone else (not one by Francis Ford), but nothing else is known. Although John participated in some fashion in thirty or more Francis Ford pictures (possibly beginning with *Lucille Love*, a fifteen-chapter serial issued weekly from April 14, 1914) and worked also for other filmmakers (such as Allan Dwan), only those pictures in which he has been definitely identified have been listed. John Stewart's *Filmarama* (Metuchen, N.J.: Scarecrow Press, 1975) lists, without further detail, two *stage* appearances for Ford: in 1901 (!) in *King's Carnival* and in 1919 in *Tumble In*.

*denotes a presumably lost film.

†denotes films in which Ford participated but which he did not direct.

All films prior to 1928 are silent; all those after 1929 are all-talking. Films in the transition years are identified accordingly.

All films are in black and white, unless otherwise described. For silents, quoted reviews are from trade journals from the weekly number closest to the film's issue date.

*†1914 **The Mysterious Rose** (Gold Seal–Universal). 2 reels. November 24. Director: Francis Ford. Writer: Grace Cunard. Filmed August 7–15. With Francis Ford (Phil Kelly), Grace Cunard (Raffles), Jack Ford (Dopey), Harry Schumm (D.A.'s son), Wilbur Higby (ward boss), Eddie Boland (Yeen Kee).

Political wars between ward bosses and D.A. Detective Kelly solves assassination with two roses as clue, and lets Raffles escape. Sixth in the "My Lady Raffles" series.

*†1915 *Smuggler's Island* (Gold Seal–Universal). 2 reels. January 19. Director: Francis Ford. Writer: Grace Cunard. With Ford, Cunard, Jack Ford (smuggler).

Ford saves Grace from smugglers who capture her when she discovers their lair.

†1915 *The Birth of a Nation* (Epoch Producing Corp.). 12 reels. February 8. Director: D. W. Griffith.

Jack Ford supposedly played a Ku Klux Klansman.

*†1915 *Three Bad Men and a Girl* (101 Bison–Universal). 2 reels. February 20. Director: Francis Ford. Writer: Grace Cunard. Filmed December 23–29. With Francis Ford (Joe), Jack Ford (Jim), Major Paleolagus (Shorty), Grace Cunard (girl), Lewis Short (sheriff), F. J. Denecke (his assistant).

Mistaken for badmen, three good men capture real badmen and free girl from Mexican settlement. Satire on fanciful westerns, murders every fifty feet; Ford leaps seventy-nine feet; Grace crosses chasm on laundryline.

*†1915 *The Hidden City* (101 Bison–Universal). 2 reels. March 27. Director: Francis Ford. Writer: Grace Cunard. With Francis Ford (Lt. Johns), Grace Cunard (princess), Jack Ford (Johns's brother), Eddie Polo (Minister Poleau).

Captured after losing a battle, Johns refuses love of a princess of desert city in India, but she helps Jim escape and substitutes herself as sacrifice to fire god.

*†1915 *The Doorway of Destruction* (101 Bison–Universal). 2 reels. April 17. Director: Francis Ford. Writer: Grace Cunard. Assistant: Jack Ford. Filmed February 26–March 4. With Francis Ford (Col. Patrick Feeney), Jack Ford (Edward Feeney), Mina Cunard (Cecille McLain), Harry Schumm (Gen. McLain), Howard Daniels (Frank).

Sent by British on a suicide mission, an Irish regiment assaults a Sepoy citadel waving an Irish flag made by Feeney's mother.

*†1915 *The Broken Coin* (Special Features–Universal). 44-reel serial: 22 two-reelers released weekly from June 21. Director: Francis Ford. Writer: Grace Cunard, novelized by Emerson Hough. Cameramen: R. E. Irish, Harry Maguire. Assistant: Jack Ford. Exteriors: Bisbee, Calif. With Grace Cunard (Kitty Gray), Francis Ford (Count Frederick), Eddie Polo (Roleau), Harry Schumm (King Michael II), Ernest Schields (Count Sacchio), Jack Ford (Sacchio's accomplice), W. C. Canfield (Gorgas the outlaw), Reese Gardiner (the Apache), Doc Crane (pawnbroker), Harry Mann (servant), Vic Goss (servant), Lewis Short (prime minister), Mr. Uttal (henchman), Bert Wilson (confidante), Mina Cunard (king's sweetheart [also doubled for Grace]), Carl Laemmle (editor).

Girl reporter finds half a coin hinting at vast treasure and sets off to Balkan kingdom of Gretzhoffen, where she becomes involved in palace intrigues and daredevil adventures.

*†1915 *The Campbells Are Coming* (Broadway Feature–Universal). 4 reels. October 16. Director: Francis Ford. Writer: Grace Cunard. With portions filmed in late 1914. With Francis Ford (Nana Sahib), Duke Worne (Azimooah), Grace Cunard (Scotch lassie), F. J. Denecke (Campbell), Harry Schumm (lassie's sweetheart), Lewis Short (her father), Jack Ford, 7,000 extras. Working titles: "The Lumber Yard Gang," "The Yellow Streak."

Sepoy, 1857: Nana Sahib ascends throne, sends Azimooah to Queen Victoria to learn father's pension discontinued because Nan is only an adopted son. Returning, Azimooah falls in love with Scotch lassie, whom Nan seizes for harem but who escapes during rebellion. The Campbells attack Lucknow in mammoth battle, and Nan is left prey to jungle beasts without food or water.

*†1916 *The Strong Arm Squad* (Rex-Universal). 1 reel. February 15. Director: Francis Ford. Writer: Grace Cunard. Filmed in Maine, November 26–29, 1915. With Francis Ford (Phil Kelly), Elsie Maison, Cecil McLean, Jack Ford (crook), William White (detective), Dandy Bowen (police chief), John, Abbie, Pat, Eddie, Mary, and Jo Feeney.

Kelly allows sweetheart's brother to escape when proved head of the Lumber Yard Gang.

*†1916 *Chicken-Hearted Jim* (Rex–
Universal). 1 reel. April 23.
Director-writer: Francis Ford. Filmed in
Maine, November 10–17, 1915. With
Francis Ford (Jimmie Endicott), John A.
Feeney (his father), Abbie Feeney (his
mother), Cecil McLean (Jib), Phil Kelly
(her father, captain), Pat Feeney (mate),
Jack Ford, Eddie Feeney (crew), Mary
Feeney, Jo Feeney (Jim's sisters).

Jim worries his parents by his nightly
debauches; fleeing the cops, he joins a
schooner, single-handedly thwarts a mutiny,
and marries the captain's daughter. (Almost
exactly the same plot as Ford-Cunard's
Captain Billie's Mate (2 reels, September
27, 1913).

*†1916 *Peg O' the Ring.* (Universal).
31-reel serial: 15 2-reelers (except chapter
1: 3 reels) released weekly from May 1.
Director: Francis Ford. Writers: Grace
Cunard, with Joe Brandy (Universal
general manager), Walter Hill (circus
publicity man). Photographers: Harry
Grant, Abel Vallet. With Grace Cunard
(Peg; Peg's mother), Francis Ford (Dr.
Lund, Jr.), Mark Fenton (Dr. Lund), Jack
Ford (his accomplice), Pete Gerald (Flip),
Jean Hathaway (Mrs. Lund), Irving
Lippner (Marcus, the Hindoo), Eddie
Boland (his pal), Ruth Stonehouse, Charles
Munn, G. Raymond Nye, Eddie Polo.

Circus girl is subject to spells because
mother clawed by lion.

*†1916 *The Bandit's Wager* (Big U–
Universal). 1 reel. November 15. Director:
Francis Ford. Writer: Grace Cunard. With
Grace Cunard (Nan Jefferson), Francis
Ford (her brother), Jack Ford.

Nan comes west to keep house for
brother. Her car breaks down one day,
and she meets bandits, but it's her
brother testing her courage.

*†1916 *The Purple Mask* (Universal).
33-reel serial: 16 2-reelers (except chapter
1: 3 reels) released weekly from December
25. Director: Francis Ford. Writer: Grace
Cunard. With Francis Ford (Phil Kelly,
"The Sphinx"), Grace Cunard (Patricia
Montez), Jean Hathaway, Peter Gerald,
Jerry Ash, Mario Bianchi, John
Featherstone, John Duffy, Jack Ford.

Parisian society tomboy steals aunt's
jewels to baffle detective who snubbed her;
but jewels are stolen again and she joins
Apache to trace them.

*1917 *The Tornado* (101 Bison–
Universal). 2 reels. March 3. Director-
writer: Jack Ford. With Ford (Jack Dayton,
the No-Gun Man), Jean Hathaway (his
Irish mother), John Duffy (Slick, his
partner), Peter Gerald (Pendleton, banker
of Rock River), Elsie Thornton (his
daughter Bess), Duke Worne (Lesparre,
chief of the Coyote Gang).

Jack Dayton, the No-Gun Man, son of
Old Ireland, wants to send money to his
mother in Ireland to pay for her cottage. In
Rock River, Lesparre, chief of the Coyote
Gang, covets the mayor's daughter; his
gang robs the bank and kidnaps Bess.
$5,000 reward. Jack joins gang to save
Bess, jumps a passing train from his horse
to fight Lesparre, whom he throws off the
train. He gets the girl and the money.

*1917 *The Trail of Hate* (101 Bison
–Universal). 2 reels. April 28.
Director-writer: Jack Ford. With Ford (Lt.
Jack Brewer), Duke Worne (Capt. Dana
Holden), Louise Granville (Madge), Jack
Lawton.

Lt. Brewer, risen from the ranks in the
67th, is adored by his men but hated by
West Pointer Holden. When Madge's
father is killed in a stage holdup, Jack
marries her after an awkward courtship,
but Madge leaves him for Holden. Years
later, in the Philippines, Jack is leading
troops against the Moros. Holden, trapped
in the interior, abandons his men, his post,
and Madge (now his wife) to save himself.
When Jack saves Madge, she begs his
forgiveness but is rejected in disgust.

Bogdanovich, citing a notice in *Motion
Picture News* (April 28, 1917), credits
direction to Francis Ford. But *Universal
Weekly* (April 21, 1917) makes a big fuss
about it being directed by Jack.

*1917 *The Scrapper* (101 Bison–
Universal). 2 reels. June 9.
Director-writer: Jack Ford. Photographer:
Ben Reynolds. With Ford (Buck Logan,
the scrapper), Louise Granville (Helen
Dawson), Duke Worne (Jerry Martin, a
parasite), Jean Hathaway (Martha Hayes).

All the guys on the ranch like the
teacher, Helen, and the pugnacious Buck
saves her life when her team runs away.
But she decides to return to the city. Buck
proposes for the twentieth time, but she
won't promise anything. Meanwhile the
town madam (Martha) and pimp (Martin)
plan to use her to snare Col. Stanton and

fake an attack so that Martin can rescue her and gain her confidence. She is given a new gown and taken to a party to meet the colonel, but Buck and the boys arrive and wreck the brothel, saving Helen. All escort Buck and Helen to board the train west.

*1917 *The Soul Herder* (101 Bison–Universal). 3 reels. August 7. Director: Jack Ford. Writer: George Hively. Photographer: Ben Reynolds. With Harry Carey (Cheyenne Harry), Jean Hersholt (the parson), Elizabeth Jones (his daughter, Mary Ann), Fritzi Ridgeway (June Brown), Vester Pegg (Topeka Jack), Hoot Gibson (Chuck Rafferty), Bill Gettinger (Bill Young), Duke Lee, Molly Malone. Working titles: "Buckhorn Hits the Trail," "The Sky Pilot." Reissued as 2-reeler in 1922.

A badman becomes a minister. For plot, see text, page 17.

*1917 *Cheyenne's Pal* (Universal Star Featurette). 2 reels. August 13. Director: Jack Ford. Scenarist: Charles J. Wilson, Jr., from story by Ford. Photographer: Friend F. Baker. Filmed May 20–23. With Harry Carey (Cheyenne Harry), Jim Corey (Noisy Jim), Gertrude Aster (dancehall girl), Vester Pegg, Steve Pimento, Hoot Gibson, Bill Gettinger, Ed Jones (cowboys), Pete Carey (Cactus, the horse). Working titles: "Cactus My Pal," "A Dumb Friend." Made to promote sales of war bonds.

Cheyenne Harry sells horses to the British Army, but not Cactus My Pal. But he blows his money and, drunk, sells Cactus for $350, which he loses gambling. So Harry gets a horse-tending job on the boat, but at midnight jumps off (with horse) and swims to shore. Jim Corey lets them go.

1917 *Straight Shooting* (Universal Butterfly). 5 reels (music timing: 67 minutes, 55 seconds). August 27. Director: Jack Ford. Writer: George Hively. Photographer: George Scott. With Harry Carey (Cheyenne Harry), Molly Malone (Joan Sims), Duke Lee (Thunder Flint), Vester Pegg (Placer Fremont), Hoot Gibson (Sam Turner), George Berrell (Sweetwater Sims), Ted Brooks (Ted Sims), Milt Brown (Black-Eyed Pete). Working titles: "The Cattle War," "Joan of the Cattle Country." Reissued as 2-reeler, *Straight Shootin'*, January 1925.

Cattlemen vs. homesteaders. For plot, see text, page 19.

*1917 *The Secret Man* (Universal Butterfly). 5 reels. October 1. Director: Jack Ford. Writer: George Hively. Photographer: Ben Reynolds. With Harry Carey (Cheyenne Harry), Morris Foster (Harry Beaufort), Elizabeth Jones (his child), Steve Clemente (Pedro, foreman), Vester Pegg (Bill), Elizabeth Sterling (Molly, his sister), Hoot Gibson (Chuck Fadden), Bill Gettinger. Working titles: "The Round Up," "Up Against It."

Molly gets a note about a sick child and runs away from her brother Bill and lover Chuck. Meanwhile, Cheyenne Harry escapes from prison in a garbage truck and is aided on a train by Harry Beaufort, who gives him a job on his ranch. But when the sheriff starts poking around, Cheyenne leaves, and Beaufort has Pedro take his little girl to another town. When Molly hears Pedro has had an accident and the child is dead, she loses her mind, because she is secretly married to Beaufort. Meanwhile, Cheyenne finds the child and spends the night with her. The posse shoots his horse, and the girl is hurt when they fall down a cliff. They find no water, only bones, so Cheyenne signals for the posse. Back in town, the girl is to be raffled at a church bazaar, but Cheyenne reunites the family and stops Bill from killing Beaufort, who explains that his uncle from whom they had concealed their marriage is now dead. Molly forgives him; Cheyenne and Chuck look at each other, and one after the other they go out into the night.

*1917 *A Marked Man* (Universal Butterfly). 5 reels. October 29. Director: Jack Ford. Scenarist: George Hively, from story by Ford. Photographer: John W. Brown. With Harry Carey (Cheyenne Harry), Molly Malone (Molly Young), Harry Rattenbury (Young, her father, a rancher), Vester Pegg (Kent), Mrs. Townsend (Harry's mother), Bill Gettinger (sheriff), Hoot Gibson.

Hiding in rain in rocks from posse, Harry reads letter from his mother, who thinks he has a ranch and wife. He stumbles into a house, helped by Molly and her father (Harry had held up Molly's train and allowed her to keep her dead mother's brooch), who then lend Harry money to enter the rodeo—to get money to visit his mother back East. But Ben Kent cuts Harry's cinch, so that Harry, losing the rodeo, will help Ben hold up a stage, which they do, in a river, and Harry protests when Ben shoots the driver. They are caught and sentenced to hang, but when news arrives that his mother is coming, Harry is given two weeks' grace and the use of Young's ranch and Molly. After a wonderful visit, Harry gives himself up, but a stagecoach passenger testifies he is innocent.

Remade as *Under Sentence* (1920) by Ford's brother Edward.

*1917 *Bucking Broadway* (Universal Butterfly). 5 reels. December 24. Director: Jack Ford. Producer: Harry Carey. Writer: George Hively. Photographer: John W. Brown. With Harry Carey (Cheyenne Harry), Molly Malone (Helen Clayton), L. M. Wells (Ben Clayton, her father), Vester Pegg (Capt. Thornton, a cattle buyer).

Harry's fiancée, Helen, is seduced away to New York by horse-buyer Thornton. Harry, distraught, follows in pursuit. Sharpshooters try to take his money, but a lady crook befriends him and helps him locate Helen. Thornton, still putting off marriage, holds a party, and Helen sends Harry a little redwood heart he once gave her. The V-Plus Ranch boys show up to help, riding down Broadway, and brawl along the rooftops.

*1918 *The Phantom Riders* (Universal Special). 5 reels. January 28. Director: Jack Ford. Producer: Harry Carey. Scenarist: George Hively, from a story by Henry McRae. Photographer: John W. Brown. Filmed September 8–27, 1917. With Harry Carey (Cheyenne Harry), Molly Malone (Molly), Buck Connor (Pebble, her father), Bill Gettinger (Dave Bland), Vester Pegg (leader of the Phantom Riders), Jim Corey (foreman).

Bland dominates Paradise Creek Valley, open government grazing land, through masked, white-coated riders led by Unknown, and he wants Molly too. Harry brings a small herd into the valley, is warned to leave, replies he will fight Bland single-handed, slaps him for insulting Molly, and is sentenced to hang by Bland. Molly's father goes to his aid, Harry finds him hanging dead from a tree, then is captured again after routing six phantoms in a bar celebrating Bland's marriage to unwilling Molly, who rides for help and rescues Harry with U.S. Rangers.

*1918 *Wild Women* (Universal Special). 5 reels. February 25. Director: Jack Ford. Producer: Harry Carey. Writer: George Hively. Photographer: John W. Brown. With Harry Carey (Cheyenne Harry), Molly Malone (the princess), Martha Maddox (the queen), Vester Pegg, Ed Jones, E. Van Beaver, W. Taylor.

Harry gets drunk celebrating a rodeo victory in San Francisco and passes out. He and his pals are shanghaied, mutiny, and cast onto a desert island with native girls; the possessive queen pursues him as he pursues the princess—till he wakes up with a hangover.

*1918 *Thieves' Gold* (Universal Special Feature). 5 reels. March 18. Director: Jack Ford. Scenarist: George Hively, from story "Back to the Right Train," by Frederick R. Bechdolt. Photographer: John W. Brown. With Harry Carey (Cheyenne Harry), Molly Malone (Alice Norris), L. M. Wells (Savage), Vester Pegg (Simmons, or Padden, an outlaw), Harry Tenbrook, M. K. Wilson, Martha Maddox.

Harry leaves the herds for Mexico with Padden, who, drunk, shoots someone. Next day Harry holds up an auto, is arrested, but will not rat on Padden. When fiancée Alice deserts him, Harry goes to Mexico, beats Padden at cards, Padden wounds Harry and dies, and Alice finds Harry unconscious and forgives him.

Received poor reviews.

*1918 *The Scarlet Drop* (Universal Special). 5 reels. April 22. Director: Jack Ford. Scenarist: George Hively, from story by Ford. Photographer: Ben Reynolds. With Harry Carey (Kaintuck Cass), Molly Malone (Molly Calvert), Vester Pegg (Capt. Marley Calvert), M. K. Wilson (Graham Lyons), Betty Schade, Martha Maddox, Steve Clemente. Working title: "Hill Billy."

Kaintuck Cass hates the Calverts, aristocrats, and they consider Casses trash, unworthy to fight with the Confederacy in the Civil War. So Cass becomes a bandit, holds up a stage, and takes Molly Calvert prisoner, but falls in love with her and sends her home. Later she falls in love with him when he saves her from rape by gentleman Lyons (blackmailing her because her mother was Negro). Calvert hides Cass from cops in attic, while Molly offers them tea, but a falling drop of blood betrays Cass. He eventually escapes back to Molly.

The plot resembles Francis Ford's *War Time Reformation* (1914). Reviewers found it "old hat."

*1918 *Hell Bent* (Universal Special Attraction). 5,700 feet. June 29. Director: Jack Ford. Writers: Ford, Harry Carey. Photographer: Ben Reynolds. With Harry Carey (Cheyenne Harry), Neva Gerber (Bess Thurston, his girl), Duke Lee (Cimarron Bill, his pal), Vester Pegg (Jack Thurston), Joseph Harris (Beau, an outlaw), M. K. Wilson, Steve Clemente.

Escaping to Rawhide after a shooting spree and finding dancehall and hotel full, Harry forces Cimarron to share a room; friendship. Harry meets Bess, whose brother Jack has been fired from Wells Fargo and whose mother is ill, and who has to earn money in dancehall, so Harry gets himself hired as bouncer to protect her. Beau covets Bess, hates Harry, and persuades Jack to join his holdup gang, who kidnap Bess. Harry pursues, corners Beau, but to avoid Bess thinking him cowardly, challenges Beau to race on foot fifty miles across desert to Yaqui waterhole; but the hole is dry, Beau dies, and Cimarron rescues Harry, who marries Bess.

The film begins with author of story rejected for lack of punch admiring Remington picture called "The Misdeal," which comes to life to start the story—which pokes fun at itself.

Exhibitors' Trade Review: "Typical Harry Carey picture, which means that thrills and excitement are plentifully distributed about, and that speed and more speed is the keynote . . . A tickling tone of merriment."

*1918 *A Woman's Fool* (Universal Special Attraction). 60 minutes. August 12. Director: Jack Ford. Scenarist: George Hively, from novel *Lin McLean,* by Owen Wister. Photographer: Ben Reynolds. With Harry Carey (Lin McLean), Betty Schade (Katy), Roy Clark (Tommy Lusk), Molly Malone (Jessamine).

Lin loves Katy, a biscuit shooter in a Denver railroad restaurant, and offers her a home in the West. Then there is a drought and Katy's husband shows up offering to make it rain for six hours for $1,000, and does so, and Katy returns to him. Broken-hearted Lin goes to another town, where he meets a young pal, Tommy, who turns out to be Katy's abandoned child.

Lin adopts him, and falls in love with Jessamine, a station agent; Katy reappears and, after failing to wreck their marriage, kills herself, and Tommy reunites the couple.

*1918 *Three Mounted Men* (Universal Special Attraction). 6 reels. October 7. Director: Jack Ford. Writer: Eugene B. Lewis. Photographer: John W. Brown. With Harry Carey (Cheyenne Harry), Joe Harris (Buck Masters), Neva Gerber (Lola Masters), Harry Carter (the warden's son), Ella Hall.

Harry is put in solitary for fighting with Buck. Buck is a friend of warden's son, a forger, and pardoned. But Buck bribes son for hush money, so Harry, on hard labor, is released to get Buck. Harry arranges a holdup with Buck and Buck is arrested. But then Harry discovers Buck is Lola's brother, and so he rescues him from cops and marries Lola.

Exhibitors' Trade Review (November 21, 1918) complained of too much realism, too much filth and rats in prison. "Carey consistently portrays a rough character throughout the picture. The only wonder of it is that anyone should attempt to heroize such a type. There may be such men in the west, but it is best on the screen to show them up as horrible examples of what a man may be."

*†1919 *The Craving* (Universal-Bluebird). 5 reels. January 6. Directors: Francis and Jack Ford. Story and scenario: Francis Ford. With Francis Ford (Carroll Wayles), Mae Gaston (Beaulah Grey), Peter Gerald (Ala Kasarib), Duke Worne (Dick Wayles), Jean Hathaway (Mrs. Wayles). Working title: "Delirium."

Carroll Wayles, scientist with powerful explosive, has a rival, Ala Kasarib, an East Indian come to America for the formula with Beaulah Grey, under Kasarib's hypnotic control, to seduce Wayles. Wayles refuses to drink, recounting his past deliria (special effects recreate girls poured from bottles into wineglasses, battlefields in Europe, etc. "Everywhere he looked he saw nude women"). In a mental battle in his lab, Kasarib gets the formula, and Wayles takes to drink. Later, he fights Kasarib in the latter's lab, an explosion leaves Kasarib dead, and Wayles and Beaulah fall in love.

Bogdanovich removes *The Craving* from Ford's credit, and even quotes Ford's disclaimer. Yet *Universal Weekly* (January 14, 1919) insists Jack participated. Curiously, *Moving Picture World* (October 12, 1918!) reviews it unfavorably and credits distribution to M. H. Hoffman, a states' rights agent, rather than to Universal. Everything about the picture smells of Francis; if Jack helped, it was just help.

*1919 *Roped* (Universal Special). 6 reels. January 13. Director: Jack Ford. Writer: Eugene B. Lewis. Photographer: John W. Brown. With Harry Carey (Cheyenne Harry), Neva Gerber (Aileen Judson Brown), Molly McConnell (Mrs. Judson Brown), J. Farrell MacDonald (butler), Arthur Shirley (Ferdie Van Duzen).

Harry is a millionaire cattleraiser in Arizona in need of a housekeeper, so his hands put a marry ad in the newspaper and a note arrives from a poor but beautiful girl living at the Ritz in New York City. Harry goes east and marries Aileen, ensnared by her bankrupt society mother who, when a baby is born, will not let him see it and tells him it is dead (preferring alimony and a lounge lizard to marriage). Harry returns from a business trip to find them gone, but the butler tips him off, and Harry and his cowboys find them, knock out the lounge-lizard, and the couple takes a honeymoon to Grand Canyon.

*1919 *Harry Carey Tour Promotional Film* (Universal). ½ reel (500 feet). February. Directors: Harry Carey, and Jack Ford. With Harry Carey.

A compilation of sensational stunts to illustrate Carey's tour talk.

*1919 *The Fighting Brothers* (Universal). 2 reels. March 10. Director: Jack Ford. Scenarist: George Hively, from story by George C. Hull. Photographer: John W. Brown. Filmed February 8–15. With Pete Morrison (Sheriff Pete Larkin), Hoot Gibson (Lonnie Larkin), Yvette Mitchell (Conchita), Jack Woods (Ben Crawley), Duke Lee (Slim). Working title: "His Buddy."

Sheriff Larkin does his duty, arresting for murder his brother, whom he knows to be innocent. Then he takes off his badge and helps him escape.

*1919 *A Fight for Love* (Universal Special Attraction). 6 reels. March 24. Director: Jack Ford. Writer: Eugene B. Lewis. Photographer: John W. Brown. Exteriors

filmed in California's Big Bear region. With Harry Carey (Cheyenne Harry), Joe Harris (Black Michael), Neva Gerber (Kate McDougall), Mark Fenton (Angus McDougall, her father), J. Farrell MacDonald (the priest), Princess Neola Mae (Little Fawn), Chief Big Tree (Swift Deer). Working title: "Hell's Neck."

Harry crosses to Canada and rolls a cigarette gazing at the posse pursuing him. But the Americans call the Mounties and Harry hides with Indians and fights with whiskey-runner Black Michael over an Indian girl. Michael is also Harry's rival for Kate, whom he abducts, killing an Indian boy and confessing to a priest; then, pursued by Harry and falling from a cliff, he confesses again to the law and dies.

Exhibitors' Trade Review commented on its many fights for love, exciting chases, Indians, and spellbinding locations.

*1919 *By Indian Post* (Universal). 2 reels. April 12. Director: Jack Ford. Scenarist: H. Tipton Steck, from story "The Trail of the Billy-Doo," by William Wallace Cook. Filming began February 18. With Pete Morrison (Jode McWilliams), Duke Lee (Pa Owens), Magda Lane (Peg Owens), Ed Jones (Stumpy, the cook), Jack Woods (Dutch), Harley Chambers (Fritz), Hoot Gibson (Chub), Jack Walters (Andy), Otto Myers (Swede), Jim Moore (Two-Horns, an Indian). Working title: "The Love Letter."

Stumpy writes a love letter to Peg for Jode, copying it from "Lothario's Compendium," but other cowboys find the letter and tack it to a door, where Two-Horns, admiring the "paper talk," finds it and shows it to everyone he meets. Before Jode can catch him, Two-Horns shows it to Peg, with happy effect. Working title: "The Love Letter."

*1919 *The Rustlers* (Universal). 2 reels. April 26. Director: Jack Ford. Writer: George Hively. Photographer: John W. Brown. Filmed February 22–March 8. With Pete Morrison (Ben Clayburn), Helen Gibson (Postmistress Nell Wyndham), Jack Woods (Sheriff Buck Farley), Hoot Gibson (his deputy). Working title: "Even Money."

A government ranger infiltrates a rustler gang so effectively that Nell has to save him from a lynch mob.

*1919 *Bare Fists* (Universal Special). 5,500 feet. May 5. Director: Jack Ford. Scenarist: Eugene B. Lewis, from story by

Bernard McConville. Photographer: John W. Brown. Filming began July 20, 1918. With Harry Carey (Cheyenne Harry), Molly McConnell (his mother), Joseph Girard (his father), Howard Ensteadt (his brother, Bud), Betty Schade (Conchita), Vester Pegg (Lopez), Joe Harris (Boone Travis), Anna Mae Walthall (Ruby, a dancehall girl). Working title: "The Man Who Wouldn't Shoot."

Harry's father is marshall of Hays City, a lawless bordertown. His mother begs them not to intervene in a saloon fight, but they do and Pa is killed, Harry killing two of the slayers. So mother makes him swear on the Bible not to carry a gun again. But Harry is framed for Boone's murder of Conchita and sentenced to die, and when his mother makes her last visit, he learns brother Bud has been branded a cattle thief. So Harry escapes and gets the real thieves.

*1919 *Gun Law* (Universal). 2 reels. May 10. Director: Jack Ford. Writer: H. Tipton Steck. Photographer: John W. Brown. Filmed March 11–21. With Peter Morrison (Dick Allen), Hoot Gibson (Bart Stevens, alias Smoke Gublen), Helen Gibson (Letty), Jack Woods (Cayuse Yates), Otto Myers, Ed Jones, H. Chambers (Yates's gang). Working title: "The Posse's Prey."

A government agent infiltrates a mine to prove its owner is a mail robber, but in the process he falls in love with the guy's sister and the guy saves his life, causing a dilemma alleviated by recovery of the intact mailbags.

*1919 *The Gun Packer* (Universal). 2 reels. May 24. Director: Jack Ford. Scenarist: Karl R. Coolidge, from a story by Ford and Harry Carey. Photographer: John W. Brown. Filming began March 25. With Ed Jones (Sandy McLoughlin), Pete Morrison ("Pearl Handle" Wiley), Magda Lane (Rose McLoughlin), Jack Woods (Pecos Smith), Hoot Gibson (outlaw leader), Jack Walters (Brown), Duke Lee (Buck Landers), Howard Ensteadt (Bobby McLoughlin). Working title: "Out Wyoming Way." Reissued August 1924.

A reformed gunman, sheepmen, and a gang of outlaws unite to win water rights from cattle barons.

*1919 *Riders of Vengeance* (Universal Special). 6 reels. June 9. Director: Jack Ford. Producer: P. A. Powers. Writers: Ford, Harry Carey. Photographer: John W. Brown. With Harry Carey (Cheyenne Harry), Seena Owen (the Girl), Joe Harris (Sherriff Gale Thurman), J. Farrell MacDonald (Buell), Jennie Lee (Harry's mother), Glita Lee (Virginia), Alfred Allen, Betty Schade, Vester Pegg, M. K. Wilson.

As Harry and his bride emerge from the church, she and his parents are murdered. Harry reappears a year later to post the names of those he will kill in revenge, which he does, one by one, till Gale Thurman. But Harry rescues Thurman's girl from stage holdup, cares for her in his cave/home after considering harming her, and falls in love. Then, trapped with Thurman in the desert and fighting off Apache, he discovers the man's innocence and tries to save him for the girl's sake, but Thurman dies.

According to W. P. Wooten, Ford, taking over when the original director took ill, only directed portions. *Exhibitors' Trade Review* used phrases like: "sympathetic," "strenuous," "action," "color," "lots of suspense." *Moving Picture World* (May 24, 1919): "scenic," "lots of killings."

*1919 *The Last Outlaw* (Universal). 2 reels. June 14. Director: Jack Ford. Scenarist: H. Tipton Steck, from story by Evelyne Murray Campbell. Photographer: John W. Brown. Filmed April 8–12. With Ed "King Fisher" Jones (Bud Coburn), Richard Cumming (Sheriff Brownlo), Lucille Hutton (Idaleen Coburn), Jack Walters (Chad Allen), Billie Hutton. Working title: "A Man of Peace." Reissued December 1923; remade as feature, 1936.

Bud returns home from ten years in jail to find his town gone "civilized and dry" and his daughter in the clutches of a bootlegger. So the old outlaw kidnaps his daughter and is wounded saving her.

*1919 *The Outcasts of Poker Flat* (Universal Special). 6 reels. July 6. Director: Jack Ford. Producer: P. A. Powers. Scenarist: H. Tipton Steck, from stories "The Outcasts of Poker Flat" and "The Luck of Roaring Camp," by Bret Harte. Photographer: John W. Brown. With Harry Carey (Square Shootin' Lanyon; John Oakhurst), Cullen Landis (Billy Lanyon; Tommy Oakhurst), Gloria Hope (Ruth Watson; Sophy), J. Farrell MacDonald, Charles H. Mailes, Victor Postel, Joe Harris, Duke R. Lee, Vester Pegg.

Square Shootin' Harry Lanyon, owner of Arizona gambling hall, loves ward Ruth but thinks she loves his adopted son Billy and will not interfere. Then he reads Harte's "Outcasts of Poker Flat" and sees in it similarities to his own situation. (John Oakhurst befriends Sophy as she is about to kill herself on a steamboat, deserted by gambler fiancé Stratton. Oakhurst brings Sophy to Poker Flat and encourages her to marry his son Tommy. Then Stratton reappears, coveting Sophy; but vigilantes drive everyone out of the town, where they are caught in a storm and only Sophy and Tommy survive.) Impressed, Lanyon vows not to make similar mistakes and discovers Ruth loves him, not Billy. Remakes by Christy Cabanne, 1937, and Joseph Newman, 1952.

Moving Picture World (June 28, 1919): "Catches admirably the spirit of the early days in California." *Photoplay:* "Two remarkable things are Harry Carey's rise to real acting power, and director Ford's marvelous river locations and absolutely incomparable photography. This photoplay is an optic symphony."

*1919 *The Age of the Saddle* (Universal Special). 6 reels. August 18. Director: Jack Ford. Producer: P. A. Powers. Scenarist: George Hively, from story by B. J. Jackson. Photographer: John W. Brown. Exteriors filmed in the Rio Grande Valley. With Harry Carey (Cheyenne Harry Henderson), Joe Harris (Sheriff "Two Gun" Hildebrand of Yucca County), Duke R. Lee (Sheriff Faulkner of Pinkerton County), Peggy Pearce (Madeline Faulkner, his daughter), Jack Walters (Inky O'Day), Vester Pegg (gambler), Zoe Ray, Howard Ensteadt (the children), Ed "King Fisher" Jones (Home Sweet Holmes), William Cartwright (Humpy Anderson), Andy Devine. Working title: "A Man of Peace."

Yucca's sheriff is in cahoots with rustlers of Harry's steers, and it is outside of Pinkerton sheriff's jurisdiction; but Harry falls in love with latter's daughter, who makes him give up guns. When his water is poisoned, Harry drags his cabin into Pinkerton County with six horses. Rustlers kidnap Madeline, Harry rescues her, and posse captures leaders, who, however, are saved by a raid at their trial, only to be lured by Harry to his cabin, knocked out with the poisoned water, and recaptured.

*1919 *The Rider of the Law* (Universal Special). 5 reels. November 3. Director: Jack Ford. Producer: P. A. Powers. Scenarist: H. Tipton Steck, from story

"Jim of the Rangers" by G. P. Lancaster. Photographer: John W. Brown. With Harry Carey (Jim Kyneton), Gloria Hope (Betty, his girl), Vester Pegg (Nick Kyneton), Theodore Brooks (the Kid), Joe Harris (Buck Souter), Jack Woods (Jack West), Duke R. Lee (Capt. Graham Saltire), Claire Anderson (Roseen), Jennie Lee (mother).

Jim loves mother's ward Betty, but thinks she loves brother Nick. Betty loves Jim, thinks he loves pretty, treacherous Roseen. Saloonman Buck loves Roseen, but vows vengeance on Jim, thinking Roseen loves Jim. Jim is a Texas Ranger after Midas Mine thieves; duty is his middle name and he arrests his own brother Nick and locks all in cabin; but Roseen, repulsed by Jim, lets them out. Jim, accused a traitor, captures them again, but Nick rides off cliff rather than be captured. Jim marries Roseen.

Exhibitors' Trade Review (October 18, 1919): "Typical Harry Carey . . . wild chases, commingling of bathos and humor, realistic."

*1919 *A Gun Fightin' Gentleman* (Universal Special). 5 reels. November 30. Director: Jack Ford. Producer: P. A. Powers. Scenarist: Hal Hoadley, from story by Ford and Harry Carey. Photographer: John W. Brown. With Harry Carey (Cheyenne Harry), J. Barney Sherry (John Merritt), Kathleen O'Conner (Helen Merritt), Lydia Yeamans Titus (her aunt), Harry von Meter (Earl of Jollywell), Duke R. Lee (Buck Regan), Joe Harris (Seymour), Johnny Cooke (the old sheriff), Ted Brooks (the Youngster).

Harry refuses to surrender land to Merritt Packing Co., eludes their hired men, but is dispossessed when a lawyer finds a title flaw. Harry goes to Chicago, but at dinner Merritt mocks his clothes and manners. So Harry becomes an outlaw, robs Merritt's payrolls, finally abducts his daughter Helen, and falls in love. When Merritt comes to save her, she makes him right wrong.

*1919 *Marked Men* (Universal Special). 5 reels. December 21. Director: Jack Ford. Producer: P. A. Powers. Scenarist: H. Tipton Steck, from story "The Three Godfathers," by Peter B. Kyne. Photographer: John W. Brown. Editors: Frank Lawrence, Frank Atkinson. With Harry Carey (Cheyenne Harry), J. Farrell

MacDonald (Tom "Placer" McGraw), Joe Harris (Tom Gibbons), Winifred Westover (Ruby Merrill), Ted Brooks (Tony Garcia), Charles Lemoyne (Sheriff Pete Cushing), David Kirby (Warden "Bruiser" Kelly). Working title: "The Trail of Shadows."

Harry, Bill, and Tom, in state pen for train robbery, escape. Later Harry leaves Ruby to rob bank with Bill and Tom. but they are chased into Mojave Desert, encounter a dying mother and vow to save her baby; only Harry survives, staggering into a dancehall Christmas Eve. Ruby and sheriff learn the baby is his nephew and obtain pardon from governor. Numerous remakes, including Ford's *3 Godfathers*, 1948.

*1920 *The Prince of Avenue A* (Universal Special). 5 reels. February 23. Director: Jack Ford. Scenarist: Charles J. Wilson, Jr., from story by Charles and Frank Dazey. Photographer: John W. Brown. With James J. "Gentleman Jim" Corbett (Barry O'Conner), Mary Warren (Mary Tompkins), Harry Northrup (Edgard Jones), Cora Drew (Mary O'Conner), Richard Cummings (Patrick O'Conner), Frederik Vroom (William Tompkins), Mark Fenton (Father O'Toole), George Vanderlip (Reggie Vanderlip), Johnny Cooke (butler), Lydia Yeamans Titus (housekeeper), George Fisher.

The prince is Barry O'Conner, whose father, Patrick, is district ward boss and supports Tompkins for mayor, whose daughter Mary is pleasant to Barry for political reasons, but Barry falls in love. At her dance, all refuse to dance with him, so he invites a maid to "trip the light fantastic" and Mary, humiliated, orders him out. Patrick, insulted, demands apology, and Tompkins and Mary come to call and Mary consents to be Barry's partner at Grand Ball. There, O'Conner's rival insults Mary, and Barry defends her in a gigantic brawl, winning Mary. *Exhibitors' Trade Review* (January 17, 1920): "Wealth of human interest, good comedy, a bit of pathos . . . atmosphere . . . one can always be sure of clever details when Ford has taken a hand at things." *Moving Picture World* (January 17, 1920): "A triumph among unique character stories . . . a story of genuine life . . . an undercurrent of humor." Ford's first non-western.

*1920 *The Girl in No. 29* (Universal Special). 4,775 feet. April 3. Director: Jack Ford. Scenarist: Philip J. Hurn, from story

"The Girl in the Mirror," by Elizabeth Jordan. Photographer: John W. Brown. With Frank Mayo (Laurie Devon), Harry Hilliard (Rodney Bangs), Claire Anderson (Doris Williams), Elinor Fair (Barbara Devon), Bull Montana (Abdullah, the strangler), Ray Ripley (Ransome Shaw), Robert Bolder (Jacob Epstein).

Laurie Devon wrote a successful play and will not work again. Friends deplore his rut. One day he sees a girl across the way holding a revolver to her head, breaks in to prevent her suicide, begs to be her protector, discovers Shaw is bothering her, follows Shaw, gets dumped into cellar, escapes, learns girl abducted, rescues her from thugs, thinks he has killed Shaw, then learns the whole thing is a joke by his friends, and marries the girl. (Lots of rain and night.)

*†1920 *Under Sentence* (Universal). 2 reels. June 12. Director: Edward Feeney. Scenarist: George Hively, from story by Jack Ford. Shooting started April 12. With Bob Anderson, Ethel Ritchie, Jennie Lee, J. Farrell MacDonald, Cap Anderson, Jack Woods.

Remake of Ford's *A Marked Man*, 1917, by younger brother Edward, who later changed his name to O'Fearna and served as assistant director on many of John's pictures.

*1920 *Hitchin' Posts* (Universal Special). 5 reels. August 29. Director: Jack Ford. Scenarist: George C. Hull, from story by Harold M. Schumate. Photographer: Benjamin Kline. With Frank Mayo (Jefferson Todd), Beatrice Burnham (Ophelia Bereton), Joe Harris (Raoul Castiga), J. Farrell MacDonald (Joe Alabam), Mark Fenton (Col. Carl Bereton), Dagmar Godowsky (octoroon), Duke R. Lee (Col. Lancy), C. E. Anderson (steamboat captain), M. Biddulph (Maj. Gray).

Todd, a Southern gentleman whose lands are confiscated by Yankees, takes to gambling for livelihood and on a Mississippi riverboat wins last possessions of Col. Bereton—four race horses. Bereton commits suicide that night, and the captain asks Todd to inform Bereton's daughter Barbara; but Bereton had already asked Castiga to do this. Todd and Castiga meet on plantation, and Todd dislikes Castiga for his treatment of his wife, Todd's sister. They duel: Castiga fires before allowed, but Todd reserves his shot in accord with promise to Todd's sister. Barbara, penniless, goes West to homestead, Todd and Castiga, too, separately, and unknown to Barbara. Todd and Castiga race for oil claim on Bereton's horses, fight, and Castiga drowns. Todd's sister has died and he marries Barbara.

1920 *Just Pals* (William Fox–20th Century Brand). 5 reels. November 14. Director: Jack Ford. Scenarist: Paul Schofield, from story by John McDermott. Photographer: George Schneiderman. With Buck Jones (Bim), Helen Ferguson (Mary Bruce, schoolteacher), George E. Stone (Bill), Duke R. Lee (sheriff), William Buckley (Harvey Cahill), Edwin Booth Tilton (Dr. Stone), Eunice Murdock Moore (Mrs. Stone), Burt Apling (brakeman), Slim Padgett, Pedro Leone, (outlaws), Ida Tenbrook (maid), John J. Cooke (elder).

Norwalk, a village on the border between Wyoming and Nebraska: Bim, the town bum, befriends a ten-year-old hobo, and together they thwart an express office robbery and win the schoolteacher's heart.

*1921 *The Big Punch* (William Fox–20th Century Brand). 5 reels. January 30. Director: Jack Ford. Scenarists: Ford, Jules Furthman, from story "Fighting Back," by Furthman. Photographer: Frank Good. With Buck Jones (Buck), Barbard Bedford (Hope Standish), George Siegmann (Flash McGraw), Jack Curtis (Jef, Buck's brother), Jennie Lee (Buck's mother), Jack McDonald, Al Fremont (Jed's friends), Edgar Jones (sheriff), Irene Hunt (dancehall girl), Eleanor Gilmore (Salvation Army girl).

Buck is planning to go to theological seminary, his mother a widow alone on ranch. Buck finds brother Jed drunk with pals in saloon listening to McGraw plan new crime. Hope Standish, Salvation Army girl, comes selling *War Crys*, and McGraw will throw her out if she does not kiss him, so she does, coldly, and crowd buys all her papers. Buck forces Jed to come home, McGraw's gang attacks him, but Jed and pals support Buck, and McGraw swears revenge. He has crony sheriff arrest them for sheep rustling and Buck, trying to warn them, is arrested too, getting two years, the others ten. In prison, Buck loves Hope, who visits, and studies for ministry. Ordained after release, he takes over the old circuit rider's route, lives down his "reputation," learns to love work and Hope, and converts Jed when Jed escapes from prison.

Exhibitors' Trade Review: "Action," "full of human touches," "heart tugs."

*1921 *The Freeze Out* (Universal Special). 4,400 feet. April 9. Director: Jack Ford. Writer: George C. Hull. Photographer: Harry C. Fowler. With Harry Carey (Ohio, the Stranger), Helen Ferguson (Zoe Whipple), Joe Harris (Headling Whipple), Charles Lemoyne (Denver Red), J. Farrell MacDonald (Bobtail McGuire), Lydia Yeamans Titus (Mrs. McGuire).

A stranger rides into Broken Buckle to open a gamblinghouse to rival Red and Whipple's. Teacher Zoe, who disapproves of brother Whipple's house, tries to interest the Stranger in reform but is ignored. But the new house turns out to be a school and library.

*1921 *The Wallop* (Universal Special). 4,539 feet. May 7. Director: Jack Ford. Scenarist: George C. Hull, from story "The Girl He Left Behind Him," by Eugene Manlove Rhodes. Photographer: Harry C. Fowler. With Harry Carey (John Wesley Pringle), Joe Harris (Barela), Charles Lemoyne (Matt Lisner), J. Farrell MacDonald (Neuces River), Mignonne Golden (Stella Vorhis), Bill Gettinger (Christopher Foy), Noble Johnson (Espinol), C. E. Anderson (Applegate), Mark Fenton (Major Vorhis). Working title: "The Homeward Trail."

Adventurer Harry Pringle makes his strike and returns home and recognizes his lost love, Stella, in a movie theater. Alas, she loves another, Chris, who is running for sheriff against incumbent Lisner. Foiled by Harry in an attempt to kill Chris, Lisner frames Chris for murder. A posse pursues Chris and Stella, who hide in a cave; Harry finds them, ties up Chris, claims the reward, then frees him, reveals Lisner's corruption and, having reunited Chris and Stella, goes back alone to his mine.

Exhibitors' Trade Review: "Pleasing to all . . . interesting story . . . big outdoors . . . night and rain, with only a campfire for light."

*1921 *Desperate Trails* (Universal Special). 4,577 feet. July 9. Director: Jack

Ford. Scenarist: Elliot J. Clawson, from story "Christmas Eve at Pilot Butte," by Courtney Riley Cooper. Photographers: Harry C. Fowler, Robert DeGrasse. Filmed March 14–April 11. With Harry Carey (Bert Carson), Irene Rich (Mrs. Walker), George E. Stone (Danny Boy), Helen Field (Carrie), Barbara La Marr (Lady Lou), George Siegmann (Sheriff Price), Charles Insley (Dr. Higgins), Ed Coxen (Walter A. Walker). Working title: "Christmas Eve at Pilot Butte."

Loved by Widow Walker, Harry loves Lady Lou, and goes to prison to protect Lou's brother, where, discovering the "brother" is her lover, he escapes and kills him. To give Widow Walker the reward for his capture, he turns himself in to her boy on Christmas eve; but Lou has confessed the frame-up.

Exhibitors' Trade Review: "No padding," "good night scenes." *Motion Picture News:* "The closing reels show the slow change of seasons in the trackless forest."

*1921 *Action* (Universal Special). 4,590 feet. September 12. Director: Jack Ford. Scenarist: Harvey Gates, from "The Mascotte of the Three Star," by J. Allen Dunn. Photographer: John W. Brown. With Hoot Gibson (Sandy Brooke), Francis Ford (Soda Water Manning), J. Farrell MacDonald (Mormon Peters), Buck Conners (Pat Casey), Byron Munson (Henry Meekin), Clara Horton (Molly Casey), William R. Daley (J. Plimsoll), Charles Newton (Sheriff Dipple), Jim Corey (Sam Waters), Ed "King Fisher" Jones (Art Smith), Dorothea Wolbert (Mirandy Meekin). Working title: "Let's Go."

Molly is an orphan, heir to ranch and mine, alone, threatened. Sandy, Soda Water, and Mormon wander in from range and take interest. Sandy falls in love, works mine, fends off conspirators and sends Molly east to school. But conspirators conspire and Molly returns to find all in jail, but she straighten things out.

Hoot Gibson's first feature starring role, and Francis Ford's first appearance under Jack's direction. *Exhibitors' Trade Review:* 'Unusually good," "artistic," "box office," "original."

*1921 *Sure Fire* (Universal Special). 4,481 feet. November 5. Director: Jack Ford. Scenarist: George C. Hull, from story "Bransford of Rainbow Ridge," by Eugene

Manlove Rhodes. Photographer: Virgil G. Miller. With Hoot Gibson (Jeff Bransford), Molly Malone (Marian Hoffman), Reeves "Breezy" Eason, Jr. (Sonny), Harry Carter (Rufus Coulter), Murdock MacQuarrie (Major Parker), Fritzi Brunette (Elinor Parker), George Fisher (Burt Rawlings), Charles Newton (Leo Ballinger), Jack Woods (Brazos Bart), Jack Walters (Overland Kid), Joe Harris (Romero), Steve Clemente (Gomez), Mary Philbin.

Jeff's girl, Marian, is down on him for lack of ambition, and *her* married sister, Elinor, is about to elope with an Eastern lover (who, her child tells Jeff, has just stolen $5,000 mortgage money for Elinor's house). Mr. Parker discovers Jeff there, and Elinor Parker puts the blame on Jeff, who escapes to a cabin. Meanwhile, bandits kill the Easterner, take the money, abduct Marian, and escape to the same cabin, where Jeff saves Marian. Posse arrives, finds loot on a baddy. Elinor's secret is safe, her husband (still complaisantly ignorant) gives Jeff the $5,000 for his marriage to Marian.

*1921 *Jackie* (William Fox). 4,943 feet. November 27. Director: Jack Ford. Scenarist: Dorothy Yost, from story by Countess Helena Barcynska (pseudonym for Marguerite Florence Helene Jervis Evans). Photographer: George Schneiderman. With Shirley Mason (Jackie), William Scott (Mervyn Carter), Harry Carter (Bill Bowman), George E. Stone (Benny), John Cooke (Winter), Elsie Bambrick (Millie).

Jackie, a Russian waif, is apprenticed to a cheap roadshow. But her lustful manager assaults her, and she flees with Benny, a crippled boy, to London, where she dances on the street. Carter, a wealthy American, picks her up, pays for an operation for Benny and lessons for her. Then, after her successful debut, he has to dispose of her former master before marrying her.

Exhibitors' Trade Review: "Wealth of pathos," "colorful." "The production is remarkable for the insistent adherence to accurate and artistic detail which have distinguished director Jack Ford's contributions to the screen in the past."

*1922 *Little Miss Smiles* (William Fox). 4,884 feet. January 15. Director: Jack Ford. Scenarist: Dorothy Yost, from "Little Aliens," by Myra Kelly, adapted by Yost and Jack Strumwasser. Photographer: David Abel. With Shirley Mason (Esther Aaronson), Gaston Glass

(Dr. Jack Washton), George Williams (Papa Aaronson), Martha Franklin (Mama Aaronson), Arthur Rankin (Dave Aaronson), Baby Blumfield (Baby Aaronson), Richard Lapan (Leon Aaronson), Alfred Testa (Louis Aaronson), Sidney D'Albrook (the Spider).

Ups and downs of a Jewish family in New York ghetto tenement. The mother is losing her eyesight, daughter Esther loves young Dr. Jack, and brother Dave's ambitions to become a prizefighter worry his parents. Complications arise when Dave, in bad company, shoots a gangster for insulting Esther. But Dr. Jack restores mother's eyesight and marries Esther.

Exhibitors' Trade Review: "Ghetto stories usually popular, this one is unoriginal, but very good: pathos and comedy, realistic people and places."

*†1922 *Silver Wings* (William Fox). 8,271 feet. August 26. Directors: Jack Ford (the Prologue), Edwin Carewe (the Play). Writer: Paul H. Stone. Photographers: Joseph Ruttenberg, Robert Kurle. With (in the Prologue): Mary Carr (Anna Webb), Lynn Hammond (John Webb), Knox Kincaid (John, their child), Joseph Monahan (Harry, another son), Maybeth Carr (Ruth, their daughter), Claude Brook (Uncle Andrews), Robert Hazelton (the priest), Florence Short (widow), May Kaiser (baby); and (in the Play): Mary Carr (Anna Webb), Percy Halton (John), Joseph Striker (Harry), Jane Thomas (Ruth), Roy Gordon (George), Florence Haas (Little Anna), Claude Brook (Uncle Andrews), Roger Lytton (banker), Ernest Hilliard (Jerry).

The Prologue: John Webb invents an improved sewing machine, enriching his family, then dies. The Play: Eldest son Harry, however, mismanages affairs, John skips town, accused of stealing the money Harry embezzled, Ruth elopes. Mother Abba sells the business to cover Harry's debts and, impoverished, takes a menial factory job. Later, a magazine story of her life helps reunite the family.

The Ford sequence contained an affecting scene of a baby's death.

*†1922 *Nero* (William Fox). c. 11,500 feet. September 17. Director: J. Gordon Edwards. With Jacques Gretillat, Alexander Salvini. Filmed mostly in Italy.

Ford wrote and directed scenes to heighten Edwards's climax. As Edwards's

Christians are being torn apart by lions, Ford, in parallel montage, added scenes of horsemen gathering, like Griffith's klans, while enormous drums beat. These horsemen, spearheading the rebellious army of Galba, assault the city, but are opposed by Nero's soldiers at a bridge over the Tiber; some of them fall into the Tiber spectacularly before they gain the bridge. At this point the film returned to Edwards's shot of the horsemen entering the arena just in time to save the star Christians.

*1922 *The Village Blacksmith* (William Fox). 7,540 feet. November 2. Director: Jack Ford. Scenarist: Paul H. Sloane, from poem by Henry Wadsworth Longfellow. Photographer: George Schneiderman. With William Walling (John Hammond, blacksmith), Virginia True Boardman (his wife), Virginia Valli (Alice Hammond), David Butler (Bill Hammond), Gordon Griffith (Bill, as child), Ida Nan McKenzie (Alice, as child), George Hackthorne (Johnnie), Pat Moore (Johnnie, as child), Tully Marshall (Squire Ezra Brigham), Caroline Rankin (Mrs. Brigham), Ralph Yeardsley (Anson Brigham), Henri de la Garrique (Anson, as child), Francis Ford (Asa Martin), Bessie Love (Rosemary Martin), Helen Field (Rosemary, as child), Mark Fenton (Dr. Brewster), Lon Poff (Gideon Crane, schoolteacher), Cordelia Callahan (Aunt Hattie), Eddie Gribbon (village gossip), Lucille Hutton (flapper).

In a prologue, Johnnie Hammond, one of the blacksmith's two sons, falls crippling himself from a tree young Anson Brigham has dared him to climb. Anson is the son of the squire, who hates the blacksmith for marrying the woman the squire loved. She dies. Years later (around 1923), son Bill Hammond goes off to medical school (for Johnnie), and Anson, back from college, ensnares Hammond's daughter, Alice, arousing gossip. Bill is injured in a train accident, and Alice, accused of stealing church money (actually stolen by Anson), tries suicide in storm; crippled Johnnie pursues Anson. The blacksmith arrives to save Alice and forces Anson and the squire to confess. Bill recovers and operates successfully on Johnnie.

*1923 *The Face on the Barroom Floor* (William Fox). 5,787 feet. January 1. Director: Jack Ford. Scenarists: Eugene B. Lewis, G. Marion Burton, from poem by Hugh Antoine D'Arcy. Photographer:

George Schneiderman. With Henry B. Walthall (Robert Stevens, an artist), Ruth Clifford (Marion Von Vleck), Walter Emerson (Richard Von Vleck), Alma Bennett (Lottie), Norval McGregor (governor), Michael Dark (Henry Drew), Gus Saville (fisherman).

As a derelict paints a girl's face on a barroom floor, flashbacks tell his story: Robert Stevens is a famous artist engaged to socialite Marion. In Maine he paints a charming fisherman's daughter, but Marion's brother dishonors her and she kills herself. Stevens, shielding Marion's brother, is blamed and Marion drops him. He drifts from bad to worse; when thieves plant a stolen wallet on him, he is sent to prison. During a riot he escapes, saves the governor's life, swims to a lighthouse, and when the keeper is too ill to work, signals for him and saves ships. Returning to prison, he is pardoned and eventually reunited with Marion.

*1923 *Three Jumps Ahead* (William Fox). 4,854 feet. March 25. Director-writer: Jack Ford. Photographer: Daniel B. Clark. With Tom Mix (Steve Clancy), Alma Bennett (Annie Darrell), Virginia True Boardman (Mrs. Darrell), Edward Piel (Taggit), Joe E. Girard (Annie's father), Francis Ford (Virgil Clancy), Margaret Joslin (Juliet), Henry Todd (Cicero), Buster Gardner (Brutus).

Steve Clancy and his uncle Virgil are captured by outlaws and imprisoned in their mountain hideout cave, where another prisoner, Darrell, imprisoned there two years, is forced to flog them. Darrell escapes, and the baddies promise Steve they will release his uncle if he recaptures Darrell but will kill him if he fails. Steve, outside, meets Ann, traps Darrell, returns him, discovers he is Ann's father, rescues him.

1923 *Cameo Kirby* (William Fox). 5,910 feet. October 21. Director: John Ford. Scenarist: Robert N. Lee, from play by Harry Leon Wilson and Booth Tarkington. Photographer: George Schneiderman. Released with tinted sequences. With John Gilbert (Cameo Kirby), Gertrude Olmstead (Adele Randall), Alan Hale (Col. Moreau), William E. Lawrence (Col. Randall), Jean Arthur (Ann Playdell), Richard Tucker (Cousin Aaron), Phillips Smalley (Judge Playdell), Jack McDonald (Larkin Bruce), Eugenie Ford (Mme. Dauezac), Frank Baker.

Riverboat gambler Kirby wins Colonel Randall's estate solely to save him from crooked Moreau. But Randall kills himself and Moreau, blaming Kirby, shoots him in the back. Kirby kills Moreau in a second duel, but a Randall brother, deceived by Moreau, pursues Kirby, who, hiding in the Randall house, discovers his secret love Adele is Randall's daughter and proves his innocence. Remade, 1929, by Irving Cummings.

Ford's first billing as "John Ford." *Exhibitors' Trade Review* (October 27, 1923): "As though the men and women of that pre–Civil War period had come to life again in the full vigor and beauty of their joy of living. Ranks with the best of the year." Despite some pretty pictures, it seems overtitled tedium today.

*1923 *North of Hudson Bay* (William Fox). 4,973 feet. November 19. Director: John Ford. Writer: Jules Furthman. Photographer: Daniel B. Clark. Released with tinted sequences. With Tom Mix (Michael Dane, a rancher), Kathleen Kay (Estelle MacDonald), Jennie Lee (Dane's mother), Frank Campeau (Cameron MacDonald), Eugene Pallette (Peter Dane), Will Walling (Angus MacKenzie), Frank Leigh (Jeffrey Clough), Fred Kohler (Armand LeMoir). Working title: "Journey to Death."

Rancher Michael Dane falls in love with Estelle while en route to northern Canada, where his brother Peter has struck gold. But there he finds his brother dead and his partner MacKenzie sentenced to walk the "death trail" until dead. Dane tries to help MacKenzie, earns the same sentence, but both escape, battling wolves, and meet Estelle, pursued by her uncle, the real murderer, who dies after a canoe chase over a waterfall.

Only portions of the film survive—with Czech titles.

*1923 *Hoodman Blind* (William Fox). 5,434 feet. December 20. Director: John Ford. Scenarist: Charles Kenyon, from play by Henry Arthur Jones and Wilson Barrett. Photographer: George Schneiderman. With David Butler (Jack Yeulette), Gladys Hulette (Nance Yeulette; Jessie Walton), Regina Connelly (Jessie Walton, the first), Frank Campeau (Mark Lezzard), Marc MacDermott (John Linden), Trilby Clark (Mrs. John Linden), Eddie Gribbon

(Battling Brown), Jack Walters (Bull Yeaman).

John Linden, a victim of wanderlust, deserts wife and daughter and goes West with a village girl, with whom he has a second daughter, then leaves them as well. In South Africa he finds wealth. Meanwhile, both mothers die. Nancy, the legitimate daughter, marries a fisherman; look-alike Jessie, the illegitimate daughter, becomes a whore. Through their resemblance, crooked lawyer Mark Lezzard arouses the jealousy of Nancy's husband, hoping to gain Nancy for himself and thus the money that Linden sends her through Lezzard. Linden returns and is reunited with his daughters, after Nancy's husband heroically rescues Jessie from a sinking boat.

Exhibitors' Trade Review: Atmospheric, crooked streets, character studies, almost all outside and at night, "with that eerie and striking contrast of flickering light and sharp shadows." "Heavy melodrama that seems to depress instead of entertain," wrote an exhibitor to *Moving Picture World* (August 29, 1925).

1924 *The Iron Horse* (William Fox). 11,335 feet. August 28. Director: John Ford. Scenarist: Charles Kenyon, from story by Kenyon and John Russell. Photographers: George Schneiderman, Burnett Guffey. Titles: Charles Darnton. Music score: Erno Rapee. Assistant director: Edward O'Fearna. Released with tinted sequences. Filmed January–March. With George O'Brien (Davy Brandon), Madge Bellamy (Miriam Marsh), Judge Charles Edward Bull (Abraham Lincoln), William Walling (Thomas Marsh), Fred Kohler (Deroux), Cyril Chadwick (Peter Jesson), Gladys Hulette (Rudy), James Marcus (Judge Haller), Francis Powers (Sgt. Slattery), J. Farrell MacDonald (Cpl. Casey), James Welch (Pvt. Schultz), Colin Chase (Tony), Walter Rogers (Gen. Dodge), Jack O'Brien (Dinny), George Waggner (Col. Buffalo Bill Cody), John Padjan (Wild Bill Hickok), Charles O'Malley (Maj. North), Charles Newton (Collis P. Huntington), Delbert Mann (Charles Crocker), Chief Big Tree (Cheyenne chief), Chief White Spear (Sioux chief), Edward Piel (old Chinaman), James Gordon (David Brandon, Sr.), Winston Miller (Davy, as child), Peggy Cartwright (Miriam, as child), Thomas Durant (Jack Ganzhorn), Stanhope Wheatcroft (John Hay), Frances Teague

(Polka Dot), Dan Borzage, Frank Baker. Working titles: "The TransContinental Railroad," "The Iron Trail."

Building the transcontinental railroad.

Most prints derive from a poorly edited British negative.

*1924 *Hearts of Oak* (William Fox). 5,336 feet. October 5. Director: John Ford. Scenarist: Charles Kenyon, from play by James A. Herne. Photographer: George Schneiderman. With Hobart Bosworth (Terry Dunnivan, a sea captain), Pauline Starke (Chrystal), Theodore von Eltz (Ned Fairweather), James Gordon (John Owen), Francis Powers (Grandpa Dunnivan), Jennie Lee (Grandma Dunnivan), Francis Ford, Frank Baker.

Terry Dunnivan, an elderly sea captain, adopts orphan Chrystal, who grows up and loves Ned. But Ned voyages and is reported missing. Two years pass, the old captain is about to wed his ward, but a steamer is wrecked and Ned is a survivor. The captain marries Nancy, but learns of her love for Ned, follows him, takes him on an Arctic trip and, dying midst frozen wastes, hears the voice of his wife and baby ("Goodby Daddy"). Ned and Chrystal wed.

Exhibitors' Trade Review: "Great Bosworth." "Photos of sea, Arctic, New England"—"a veritable triumph of realism." "Good box-office."

1925 *Lightnin'* (William Fox). 8,050 feet. August 23. Director: John Ford. Scenarist: Frances Marion, from play by Winchell Smith and Frank Bacon. Photographer: Joseph A. August. Assistant director: Edward O'Fearna. With Jay Hunt (Lightnin' Bill Jones), Madge Bellamy (Millie), Edythe Chapman (Mother Jones), Wallace McDonald (John Marvin), J. Farrell MacDonald (Judge Lemuel Townsend), Ethel Clayton (Margaret Davis), Richard Travers (Raymond Thomas), James Marcus (Sheriff Blodgett), Otis Harlan (Zeb), Brandon Hurst (Everett Hammond), Peter Mazutis (Oscar).

Lightnin' Bill Jones is thin, lazy old codger, named in jest, who, with his wife, owns the Calivada Hotel on the California-Nevada border. "Mother" Jones wants to sell the hotel, but a young lawyer, John Marvin convinces Lightnin' that the offer is fraudulent. When Mother persists, Lightnin' exiles himself to the veterans' home, but everything is cleared up in court, and Marvin wins the Joneses' adopted daughter.

A downbeat comedy from a record-running stageplay, the prestige production received excellent distribution and played around for almost two years—unusual for the 1920s. Exhibitors invariably praised it, but said its box-office appeal was mediocre. Today, Madge Bellamy aside, the humor seems ponderous and mostly in the titles. Remade, 1930, by Henry King, with Will Rogers.

1925 *Kentucky Pride* (William Fox). 6,597 feet. September 6. Director: John Ford. Writer: Dorothy Yost. Photographers: George Schneiderman, Edmund Reek. Assistant director: Edward O'Fearna. Filmed in Kentucky. With Henry B. Walthall (Roger Beaumont), J. Farrell MacDonald (Mike Donovan), Gertrude Astor (Mrs. Beaumont), Malcolm Waite (Greve Carter), Belle Stoddard (Mrs. Donovan), Winston Miller (Danny Donovan), George Read (butler), Peaches Jackson (Virginia Beaumont), and the horses Man O'War, Fair Play, The Finn, Confederacy, and Virginia's Future (herself), Negofol (her sire), Morvich (her husband).

A horse story.

*1925 *The Fighting Heart* (William Fox). 6,978 feet. October 18. Director: John Ford. Scenarist: Lillie Hayward, from "Once to Every Man," by Larry Evans. Photographer: Joseph H. August. Released with tinted sequences. With George O'Brien (Danny Bolton), Billie Dove (Doris Anderson), J. Farrell MacDonald (Jerry), Diana Miller (Helen Van Allen), Victor McLaglen (Soapy Williams), Bert Woodruff (Grandfather Bolton), James Marcus (Judge Maynard), Lynn Cowan (Chub Morehouse), Harvey Clark (Dennison), Hank Mann (his assistant), Francis Ford (the town fool), Francis Powers (John Anderson), Hazel Howell (Oklahoma Kate), Edward Piel (Flash Fogarty), Frank Baker (manager).

The townspeople look down on the Boltons, the male members having all succumbed to drink except young Denny, who feels the situation keenly. He gives Soapy Williams a sound thrashing when he discovers him selling bootleg hootch to his grandfather. When grandfather dies and sweetheart Doris turns against him (suspecting he is drinking), Denny follows a reporter's advice to go to New York and become a prizefighter. He gets a tryout at Flash Fogarty's gym and earns a match against Williams (now heavyweight champ), but Williams's fan Helen vamps Denny into breaking training, so he loses the fight. Later Denny meets Williams and Helen outside a nightclub and, taunted, licks him on the street and returns home to Doris.

Moving Picture World (September 26, 1925): George O'Brien a he-man, not a "dude like Mix." Just a good programmer. Too mucn character and atmosphere, slow pace.

*1925 *Thank You* (William Fox). 6,900 feet. November 1. Director: John Ford. Producer: John Golden. Scenarist: Frances Marion, from play by Winchell Smith and Tom Cushing. Photographer: George Schneiderman. Released with tinted sequences. With George O'Brien (Kenneth Jamieson), Jacqueline Logan (Diana Lee, the mother), Alec Francis (David Lee), J. Farrell MacDonald (Andy), Cyril Chadwick (Mr. Jones), Edith Bostwick (Mrs. Jones), Vivian Ogden (Miss Glodgett), James Neill (Dr. Cobb), Billy Rinaldi (Sweet, Jr.), Maurice Murphy (Willie Jones), Robert Milasch (Sweet, Sr.), George Fawcett (Jamieson, Sr.), Marion Harlan (Millie Jones), Ida Moore, Frankie Bailey (gossips).

After a series of escapades, Kenneth Jamieson's millionaire father banishes him to a chicken farm in the slow village of Dedham, where, on the same day, Diane, niece of Rev. David Lee, arrives from Paris with French clothes and delights David. A few days later Kenneth gets drunk and offends Diane, but David talks to him and he reforms. David, underpaid and always having to beg, is refused an increase in pay unless he sends Diane away; busybody Jones notifies Jamieson, Sr., who goes after Diane roughshod, expecting to find a golddigger. But Diane wins him over, particularly after she nurses Kenneth back from an illness, and Jamieson, Sr. gives the townspeople a sound verbal thrashing, calling them hypocrites and pharisees at their treatment of David. Not long after, David and Jamieson, Sr., who were old cronies, are overjoyed at engagement of Diane and Kenneth.

Moving Picture World (October 3, 1925): "sympathetic, but too much characterization slows story."

1926 *The Shamrock Handicap* (William Fox). 5,685 feet. May 2. Director: John Ford. Scenarist: John Stone, from story by Peter B. Kyne. Photographer: George Schneiderman. Titles: Elizabeth Pickett. Assistant director: Edward O'Fearna. Released with tinted sequences. With Leslie Fenton (Neil Ross), J. Farrell MacDonald (Con O'Shea), Janet Gaynor (Sheila O'Hara), Louis Payne (Sir Michael O'Hara), Claire McDowell (Molly O'Shea), Willard Louis (Orville Finch), Andy Clark (Chesty Morgan), George Harris (Benny Ginsburg), Ely Reynolds (Virus Cakes), Thomas Delmar (Michael), Brandon Hurst (the procurer).

Horse racing, Ireland and America.

Some filmographies give different character names; those above correspond to the existing print.

1926 *3 Bad Men* (William Fox). 8,710 feet. August 28. Director: John Ford. Scenarists: Ford, John Stone, from the novel *Over the Border*, by Herman Whitaker. Photographer: George Schneiderman. Filmed at Jackson Hole, Wyoming, and in the Mojave Desert, March–May. Released with tinted sequences. With George O'Brien (Dan O'Malley), Olive Borden (Lee Carlton), J. Farrell MacDonald (Mike Costigan), Tom Santschi (Bull Stanley), Frank Campeau (Spade Allen), Louis Tellegen (Sheriff Layne Hunter), George Harris (Joe Minsk), Jay Hunt (old prospector), Priscilla Bonner (Millie Stanley), Otis Harlan (Zack Leslie), Walter Perry (Pat Monahan), Grace Gordon (Millie's friend), Alec B. Francis (Rev. Calvin Benson), George Irving (Gen. Neville), Phyllis Haver (prairie beauty), Vester Pegg, Bud Osborne.

Dakota land rush, 1876.

1926 *The Blue Eagle* (William Fox). 6,200 feet. September 12. Director: John Ford. Scenarist: L. G. Rigby, from story "The Lord's Referee," by Gerald Beaumont. Photographer: George Schneiderman. Assistant director: Edward O'Fearna. Released with tinted sequences. With George O'Brien (George Darcy), Janet Gaynor (Rose Cooper), William Russell (Big Tim Ryan), Robert Edeson (Father Joe), David Butler (Nick Galvani), Phillip Ford (Limpy Darcy), Ralph Sipperly (Slats Mulligan), Margaret Livingston (Mary Rohan), Jerry Madden (Baby Tom), Harry

Tenbrook (Bascom), Lew Short (Capt. McCarthy), Frank Baker.

On shipboard, a submarine attack interrupts a grudge fight between Darcy and Ryan, who both love Rose Cooper. After the war, their skipper (and pastor of a dock-front parish) unites them momentarily to blow up a submarine used by dope smugglers; then he referees their fight. Darcy wins and gets Rose. But Father Joe finds a widow for Ryan and it all ends with an American Legion parade.

The soldier-priest prefigures Ward Bond's pugnacious roles, and inventive humor redeems a pedestrian film. Janet Gaynor has only a couple of scenes, alas. Rated good entertainment in 1926. The surviving print is missing a number of sequences.

†1926 *What Price Glory?* (William Fox). 12 reels. November 23. Director: Raoul Walsh. With Victor McLaglen, Edmund Lowe, et al.

Ford is said to have directed shots in the going-off-to-the-front sequence.

*1927 *Upstream* (William Fox). 5,510 feet. January 30. Director: John Ford. Scenarist: Randall H. Faye, from story "The Snake's Wife," by Wallace Smith. Photographer: Charles G. Clarke. Assistant director: Edward O'Fearna. With Nancy Nash (Gertie King), Earle Foxe (Eric Brasingham), Grant Withers (Jack LeVelle), Raymond Hitchcock (the star boarder), Lydia Yeamans Titus (Miss Breckenbridge), Emile Chautard (Campbell Mandare), Ted McNamara, Sammy Cohen (a dance team), Francis Ford (juggler), Judy King, Lillian Worth (sister team), Jane Winton (soubrette), Harry Bailey (Gus Hoffman), Ely Reynolds (Deerfoot), Frank Baker.

In a vaudeville boardinghouse, conceited Brasingham is chosen (for his wealthy name) for a West End revival of Hamlet and makes good. But he fails to credit his coach and coming home to a wedding (his sweetheart marrying her knife-throwing partner) assumes it's a part for him, and gets kicked out; but he smiles for photographers.

Derived from Francis Ford's unreleased *Matinee* (1925).

†1927 *7th Heaven* (William Fox). 12 reels. May 6. Director: Frank Borzage. With

Janet Gaynor, Charles Farrell, etc.

Ford directed portions of the taxis-to-the-Marne sequence.

*1928 *Mother Machree* (William Fox). 75 minutes. January 22. Director: John Ford. Scenarist: Gertrude Orr, from lyric and song by Rida Johnson Young. Photographer: Chester Lyons. Editors and title-writers: Katherine Hilliker, H. H. Caldwell. Assistant director: Edward O'Fearna. Released with sequences tinted light amber, lavender, green, and blue. General release: March 5. Synchronized music and sound effects, with the title song sung with voice synch. With Belle Bennett (Ellen McHugh, Mother Machree), Neil Hamilton (Brian McHugh), Philippe de Lacy (Brian, as child), Pat Somerset (Bobby De Puyster), Victor McLaglen (Terence O'Dowd, Giant of Kilkenny), Ted McNamara (Harper of Wexford), William Platt (Pips, Dwarf of Munster), John MacSweeney (Irish priest), Eulalie Jensen (Rachel van Studdiford), Constance Howard (Edith Cutting), Ethel Clayton (Mrs. Cutting), Jacques Rollens (Signor Bellini), Rodney Hildebrand (Brian McHugh, Sr.), Joyce Wirard (Edith Cutting, as child), Robert Parrish (child).

A family is divided in 1899 Ireland, reunited years later in America.

The Story of Mother Machree was announced in Fox publicity in June 1926 and went into production that September. In November its premiere was announced for December 12, 1926, tied in to marketing of music and discs of the title song. But no film appeared. In February, just after completion of *Sunrise*, Ford voyaged to Germany, returning in April. In May 1927, at Fox sales convention in Atlantic City, *Sunrise*, *7th Heaven*, and *Mother Machree* were privately screened (with Movietone scores?), and in April the first Movietone Sound newsreels were shown at the Roxy. In September *Sunrise* opened, with Movietone track, and *Four Sons* was nearing completion. In January 1928 *Mother Machree* was said to have cost $750,000 and its "delay" to have been worthwhile. (It was, however, shown in prerelease at the Astoria Theater, London, in September 1927—presumably a silent version.) Only three reels (one of them mostly entry music) survive.

1928 *Four Sons* (William Fox). 100 minutes. February 13. Director: John Ford.

Scenarist: Philip Klein, from story "Grandma Bernle Learns Her Letters," by I. A. R. Wylie, and from a treatment thereof by Herman Bing (uncredited). Photographers: George Schneiderman, Charles G. Clarke. Music arranger: S. L. Rothafel. Original score: Carli Elinor. Theme song: "Little Mother," by Erno Rapee, Lee Pollack; sung by Harold van Duzee and the Roxy Male Quartette. Editor: Margaret V. Clancey. Title writers: Katherine Hilliker, H. H. Caldwell. Assistant director: Edward O'Fearna. Released with music and synchronized sound effects. With Margaret Mann (Frau Bernle), James Hall (Joseph Bernle), Charles Morton (Johann Bernle), George Meeker (Andres Bernle), Francis X. Bushman, Jr. (Franz Bernle), June Collyer (Annabelle Bernle), Albert Gran (postman), Earle Foxe (Major Von Stomm), Frank Reicher (headmaster), Jack Pennick (Joseph's American friend), Archduke Leopold of Austria (German captain), Hughie Mack (innkeeper), Wendell Franklin (James Henry), Auguste Tollaire (Major), Ruth Mix (Johann's girl), Robert Parrish (child), Michael Mark (Von Stomm's orderly), L. J. O'Conner (aubergiste), Ferdinand Schumann-Heink, Capt. John Porters, Carl Boheme, Constant Franke, Hans Furberg, Tibor von Janny, Stanley Blystone, Lt. George Blagoi (officers), Frank Baker (soldier).

A Bavarian mother loses three sons in World War I and goes to America to join the fourth.

1928 *Hangman's House* (William Fox). 6,518 feet. May 13. Silent. Director: John Ford. Scenarists: Marion Orth, Willard Mack, from novel by Brian Oswald Donn-Byrne, adapted by Philip Klein. Photographer: George Schneiderman. Editor: Margaret V. Clancey. Title-writer: Malcolm Stuart Boylan. Assistant director: Phil Ford. With Victor McLaglen (Citizen Hogan), Hobart Bosworth (James O'Brien, Lord Chief Justice), June Collyer (Connaught O'Brien), Larry Kent (Dermott McDermott), Earle Foxe (John D'Arcy), Eric Mayne (legionnaire colonel), Joseph Burke (Neddy Joe), Belle Stoddard (Anne McDermott), John Wayne (spectator at horse race; hanging man), Frank Baker (English officer).

An exile returns to Ireland to rid it of a scoundrel.

*1928 *Napoleon's Barber* (William Fox–Movietone). 2,980 feet. November 24. All-talking. Director: John Ford. Scenarist: Arthur Caesar, from his own play. Photographer: George Schneiderman. Title-writer: Malcolm Stuart Boylan. Released with talking sound. With Otto Matiesen (Napoleon), Frank Reicher (the barber), Natalie Golitzin (Josephine), Helen Ware (barber's wife), Philippe De Lacy (barber's son), Russell Powell (blacksmith), Buddy Roosevelt, Ervin Renard, Joe Waddell, Youcca-Troubetzkoy (French officers), Henry Herbert (soldier), D'Arcy Corrigan (tailor), Michael Mark (peasant).

A barber brags what he would do to Napoleon, not knowing his customer *is* Napoleon.

Ford recorded Josephine's coach crossing a bridge, against the advice of the sound man, and achieved perfect results. His claim that it was "the first time anyone ever went outside with a sound system" is correct only in dramatic films. Fox Movietone News had frequently recorded outdoors, notably the West Point cadets (shown April 30, 1927 at the Roxy) and the Lindbergh takeoff, May 20, 1927.

Moving Picture World (February 26, 1927), noting a Georges Renavant production of *Napoleon's Barber* at the Grove Street Theater, called it a gem of a "screen laugh-maker that would be almost certain to go big with a star like Buster Keaton or Harry Langdon." Ford began filming September 29, 1928.

1928 *Riley the Cop* (William Fox). 67 minutes. November 25. Director: John Ford. Writers: James Gruen, Fred Stanley. Photographer: Charles G. Clarke. Editor: Alex Troffey. Assistant director: Phil Ford. Released with music and synchronized sound effects. With J. Farrell MacDonald (Aloysius Riley), Louise Fazenda (Lena Krausmeyer), Nancy Drexel (Mary), David Rollins (Davy Collins), Harry Schultz (Hans Krausmeyer), Billy Bevan (Paris cab driver), Mildred Boyd (Caroline), Ferdinand Schumann-Heink (Julius), Del Henderson (judge), Russell Powell (Kuchendorf), Mike Donlin (crook), Robert Parrish.

A kindly New York cop travels to Germany.

?*?1929 *Strong Boy* (William Fox). 63 minutes. March 3. Director: John Ford. Scenarists: James Kevin McGuinness, Andrew Bennison, John McLain, from story by Frederick Hazlett Brennan. Photographer: Joseph H. August. Title-writer: Malcolm Stuart Boyland. Released with music and synchronized sound effects. With Victor McLaglen (William "Strong Boy" Bloss), Leatrice Joy (Mary McGregor), Clyde Cook (Pete), Slim Summerville (Slim), Kent Sanderson (Wilbur Watkins), Tom Wilson (baggage master), Jack Pennick (baggageman), Eulalie Jensen (the queen), David Torrence (railroad president), J. Farrell MacDonald (Angus McGregor), Dolores Johnson (usherette), Douglas Scott (Wobby), Robert Ryan (porter), Frank Baker. Working title: "The Baggage Smasher."

A railroad porter becomes a hero and marries the boss's daughter.

The only print of this film—a 35mm nitrate—was reportedly in a private collection in Australia. Does it still exist?

1929 *The Black Watch* (William Fox). 93 minutes. May 8. All-talking. Director: John Ford. "Staged by": Lumsden Hare. Scenarists: James Kevin McGuinness, John Stone, Frank Barber, from novel *King of the Khyber Rifles*, by Talbot Mundy. Photographer: Joseph H. August. Art director: William Darling. Song: "Flowers of Delight," by William Kernell. Editor: Alex Troffey. Assistant director: Edward O'Fearna. Filmed: January–February. With Victor McLaglen (Capt. Donald King), Myrna Loy (Yasmani), Roy D'Arcy (Rewa Ghunga), Pat Somerset (Highlanders' officer), David Rollins (Lt. Malcolm King), Mitchell Lewis (Mohammed Khan), Walter Long (Harem Bey), Frank Baker, David Percy (Highlanders' officers), Lumsden Hare (colonel), Cyril Chadwick (Maj. Twynes), David Torrence (Marechal), Francis Ford (Maj. MacGregor), Claude King (general in India), Frederick Sullivan (general's aide), Joseph Diskay (muezzin), Richard Travers (adjutant), Joyzelle.

Remade 1954, by Henry King, as *King of the Khyber Rifles*.

1929 *Salute* (William Fox). 86 minutes. September 1. All-talking. Director: John Ford. Scenarist: James K. McGuinness, from story by Tristram Tupper, John Stone. Photographer: Joseph H. August. Editor: Alex Troffey. Title-writer: Wilbur Morse, Jr. Assistant directors: Edward

O'Fearna, R. L. Hough. Filmed at Annapolis, May–July. With William Janney (Midshipman Paul Randall), Helen Chandler (Nancy Wayne), Stepin Fetchit (Smoke Screen), Frank Albertson (Midshipman Albert Edward Price), George O'Brien (Cadet John Randall), Joyce Compton (Marion Wilson), Cliff Dempsey (Maj. Gen. Somers), Lumsden Hare (Rear Adm. Randall), David Butler (navy coach), Rex Bell (cadet), John Breeden, Ward Bond, John Wayne (midshipmen).

A young man enters Annapolis.

*†1929 *Big Time* (William Fox). 83 or 87 minutes. September 7. All-talking. Director: Kenneth Hawks. With Lee Tracy, Mae Clark, Stepin Fetchit, John Ford (as himself).

A melodrama about a vaudeville family drifting to Hollywood.

*1930 *Men Without Women* (William Fox). 77 minutes. January 31. Director: John Ford. "Staged by": Andrew Bennison. Scenarist: Dudley Nichols, from story "Submarine," by Ford, James K. McGuinness. Photographer: Joseph H. August. Art director: William S. Darling. Music: Peter Brunelli, Glen Knight. Editor: Paul Weatherwax. Assistant director: Edward O'Fearna. Technical advisor: Schuyler E. Gray. Filmed at Catalina, fall 1929. With Kenneth MacKenna (Burke), Frank Albertson (Price), Paul Page (Handsome), Pat Somerset (Lt. Digby, R.N.), Walter McGrail (Cobb), Stuart Erwin (Jenkins, radio operator), Warren Hymer (Kaufman), J. Farrell MacDonald (Costello), Roy Stewart (Capt. Carson), Warner Richmond (Lt. Commander Bridewell), Harry Tenbrook (Winkler), Ben Hendricks, Jr. (Murphy), George LeGuere (Pollosk), Charles Gerrard (Weymouth), John Wayne, Robert Parrish, Frank Baker.

A Shanghai nightclub: Weymouth thinks "Burke" is Quartermain, sole survivor of a destroyer torpedoed carrying "England's greated Field Marshall"; there had been scandal about a Lady Patricia, whom Quartermain had visited, but "I voted to clear the woman and damned the memory of my best friend." Later, one man must stay behind in a trapped submarine. Burke tells Price about Quartermain, "a man whose name are dead but who didn't die himself." When Price surfaces he tells

Weymouth, "His name was Burke, he's from my home town."

The only known surviving prints are of a silent edition with intertitles. The talking version seems lost.

1930 *Born Reckless* (William Fox). 82 minutes. May 11. Director: John Ford. "Staged by": Andrew Bennison. Scenarist: Dudley Nichols, from novel *Louis Beretti,* by Donald Henderson Clarke. Photographer: George Schneiderman. Art director: Jack Schulze. Associate producer: James K. McGuinness. Editor: Frank E. Hull. Assistant director: Edward O'Fearna. With Edmond Lowe (Louis Beretti), Catherine Dale Owen (Joan Sheldon), Lee Tracy (Bill O'Brien), Marguerite Churchill (Rosa Beretti), Warren Hymer (Big Shot), Pat Somerset (Duke), William Harrigan (Good News Brophy), Frank Albertson (Frank Sheldon), Ferike Boros (Ma Beretti), J. Farrell MacDonald (district attorney), Paul Porcasi (Pa Beretti), Eddie Gribbon (Bugs), Mike Donlin (Fingy Moscovitz), Ben Bard (Joe Bergman), Paul Page (Ritzy Reilly), Joe Brown (Needle Beer Grogan), Jack Pennick, Ward Bond (soldiers), Roy Stewart (District Attorney Cardigan), Yola D'Avril (French girl).

New York, 1917: For publicity, a D.A. sends three burglars to war instead of "up the river." After France, one, Louie Beretti, swears vengeance on a mobster who shot his sister's husband, but we hear no more of that storyline. He goes to propose to Joan, but meets her fiancé; so much for love. 1920: prospering with a speakeasy, he alibis for Big Shot, who shot a stoolie. 1922: Big Shot kidnaps Joan's child; Louie rescues her and kills Big Shot.

1930 *Up the River* (William Fox). 92 minutes. October 12. Director: John Ford. "Staged by": William Collier, Jr. Writers: Maurine Watkins with Ford, William Collier, Sr. Photographer: Joseph H. August. Set designer: Duncan Cramer. Music and lyrics: Joseph McCarthy, James F. Hanley. Wardrobe: Sophia Wachner. Editor: Frank E. Hull. Assistant directors: Edward O'Fearna, Wingate Smith. Filmed: summer. With Spencer Tracy (St. Louis), Warren Hymer (Dannemora Dan), Humphrey Bogart (Steve), Claire Luce (Judy), Joan Lawes (Jean), Sharon Lynn (Edith La Verne), George McFarlane

(Jessup), Gaylord Pendleton (Morris), Morgan Wallace (Frosby), William Collier, Sr. (Pop), Robert E. O'Connor (warden), Louise MacIntosh (Mrs. Massey), Edythe Chapman (Mrs. Jordan), Johnny Walker (Happy), Noel Francis (Sophie), Mildred Vincent (Annie), Wilbur Mack (Whitelay), Goodee Montgomery (Kit), Althea Henley (Cynthia), Carol Wines (Daisy Elmore), Adele Windsor (Minnie), Richard Keene (Dick), Elizabeth and Helen Keating (May and June), Robert Burns (Slim), John Swor (Clem), Pat Somerset (Beauchamp), Joe Brown (Deputy Warden), Harvey Clark (Nash), Black and Blue (Slim and Klem), Morgan Wallace (Fosby), Robert Parrish.

A comedy set in a prison.

The surviving print is missing numerous shots.

1931 *Seas Beneath* (William Fox). 99 minutes. January 30. Director: John Ford. Scenarist: Dudley Nichols, from story by James Parker, Jr. Photographer: Joseph H. August. Editor: Frank E. Hull. Filmed at Catalina, November. With George O'Brien (Comdr. Bob Kingsley, USN), Marion Lessing (Anna Marie Von Steuben), Warren Hymer (Lug Kaufman), William Collier, Sr. (Mugs O'Flaherty), John Loder (Franz Schilling), Walter C. "Judge" Kelly (Chief Mike "Guns" Costello), Walter McGrail (Joe Cobb), Henry Victor (Ernst Von Steuben, commandant, U-boat 172), Mona Maris (Lolita), Larry Kent (Lt. MacGregor), Gaylord Pendleton (Ens. Richard Cabot), Nat Pendleton (Butch Wagner), Harry Tenbrook (Winkler), Terry Ray (Reilly), Hans Furberg (Fritz Kampf, 2nd officer, U-172), Ferdinand Schumann-Heink (Adolph Brucker, engineer, U-172), Francis Ford (trawler captain), Kurt Furberg (Hoffman), Ben Hall (Harrigan), Harry Weil (Jevinsky), Maurice Murphy (Merkel), Frank Baker.

World War I: A U.S. freighter, disguised, decoys German subs.

1931 *The Brat* (Fox Film). 81 minutes. August 23. Director: John Ford. Scenarists: Sonya Levien, S. N. Behrman, Maud Fulton, from play by Fulton. Photographer: Joseph H. August. Editor: Alex Troffey. With Sally O'Neil (the brat), Alan Dinehart (MacMillan Forester), Frank Albertson (Stephen Forester), Virginia Cherrill (Angela), June Collyer (Jane), J. Farrell MacDonald (Timson, the butler), William Collier, Sr. (judge), Margaret Mann (housekeeper), Albert Gran (bishop), Mary Forbes (Mrs. Forester), Louise MacIntosh (Lena), Ward Bond (policeman).

In court for not paying for spaghetti, a waif is discharged for book research to writer MacMillan and taken to his mother's Long Island estates, where she encounters mother, two courting ladies, a jovial bishop, and a proper butler. MacMillan coldly has his way with her until she chooses drunk brother Steve and goes to his Wyoming ranch (which mother had wished to sell for a two-story yacht for MacMillan).

1931 *Arrowsmith* (Samuel Goldwyn–United Artists). 108 minutes. December 1. Director: John Ford. Producer: Samuel Goldwyn. Scenarist: Sidney Howard, from the novel by Sinclair Lewis. Photographer: Ray June. Art director: Richard Day. Music: Alfred Newman. Editor: Hugh Bennett. With Ronald Colman (Dr. Martin Arrowsmith), Helen Hayes (Leora), A. E. Anson (Prof. Gottlieb), Richard Bennett (Sondelius), Claude King (Dr. Tubbs), Beulah Bondi (Mrs. Tozer), Myrna Loy (Joyce Lanyon), Russell Hopton (Terry Wickett), De Witt Jennings (Mr. Tozer), John Qualen (Henry Novak), Adele Watson (Mrs. Novak), Lumsden Hare (Sir Robert Fairland), Bert Roach (Bert Tozer), Charlotte Henry (a young girl), Clarence Brooks (Oliver Marchand), Walter Downing (city clerk), David Landau, James Marcus, Alec B. Francis, Sidney Grey, Florence Britton, Bobby Watson, Ward Bond (policeman), Frank Baker (ship captain).

Glory, medicine, and his wife compete for a doctor's loyalties. Four Oscar nominations: best picture, best adaptation (Sidney Howard); art direction (Richard Day); photography (Ray June).

† 1932 *Hot Pepper* (Fox Film). 76 minutes. Director: John G. Blystone. With Victor McLaglen, Edmund Lowe, Lupe Velez.

A sequel to *What Price Glory?*

Ford directed some second unit scenes.

1932 *Air Mail* (Universal). 83 minutes. November 3. Director: John Ford. Producer: Carl Laemmle, Jr. Scenarists: Dale Van Every, Lt. Comdr. Frank W. Wead, from story by Wead. Photographer: Karl Freund. Special effects: John P. Fulton.

Aerial stunts: Paul Mantz. With Pat O'Brien (Duke Talbot), Ralph Bellamy (Mike Miller), Gloria Stuart (Ruth Barnes), Lillian Bond (Irene Wilkins), Russell Hopton ("Dizzy" Wilkins), Slim Summerville (Slim McCune), Frank Albertson (Tommy Bogan), Leslie Fenton (Tony Dressel), David Landau (Pop), Tom Corrigan (Sleepy Collins), William Daly (Tex Lane), Hans Furberg (Heinie Kramer), Lew Kelly (drunkard), Frank Beal, Francis Ford, James Donlan, Louise MacIntosh, Katherine Perry (passengers), Beth Milton (place attendant), Edmund Burns (radio announcer), Charles de la Montte, Lt. Pat Davis (passenger plane pilots), Jim Thorpe (Indian), Enrico Caruso, Jr., Billy Thorpe, Alene Carroll, Jack Pennick.

Conflicts and daredevilry punctuate pilots' dreary days.

1932 *Flesh* (Metro-Goldwyn-Mayer). 95 minutes. December 9. Director: John Ford. Scenarists: Leonard Praskins, Edgar Allen Woolf, and (uncredited) William Faulkner, from story by Edmund Goulding. Dialogue: Moss Hart. Photographer: Arthur Edeson. Editor: William S. Gray. With Wallace Beery (Polokai), Karen Morley (Lora Nash), Ricardo Cortez (Nicky), Jean Hersholt (Mr. Herman), John Miljan (Joe Willard), Vince Barnett (waiter), Herman Bing (Pepi), Greta Meyer (Mrs. Herman), Ed Brophy (Dolan), Ward Bond (wrestler), Nat Pendleton.

A female ex-con marries a German wrestler, but sells him out for her boyfriend.

1933 *Pilgrimage* (Fox Film). 90 minutes. July 12. Director: John Ford. Scenarists: Philip Klein, Barry Connors, from story "Gold Star Mother," by I. A. R. Wylie. Dialogue: Dudley Nichols. Photographer: George Schneiderman. Art director: William Darling. Music: R. H. Bassett. Musical direction: Samuel Kaylin. Wardrobe: A. R. Luick. Editor: Louis R. Loeffler. Assistant director: Edward O'Fearna. Dialogue director: William Collier, Sr. Filmed in February. With Henrietta Crosman (Hannah Jessop), Heather Angel (Suzanne), Norman Foster (Jim Jessop), Marian Nixon (Mary Saunders), Maurice Murphy (Gary Worth), Lucille La Verne (Mrs. Tally Hatfield), Charles Grapewin (Dad Saunders), Hedda Hopper (Mrs. Worth), Robert Warwick (Maj. Albertson), Betty Blythe (Janet

Prescot), Francis Ford (Mayor Elmer Briggs), Louise Carter (Mrs. Rogers), Jay Ward (Jim Saunders), Francis Rich (nurse), Adele Watson (Mrs. Simms), Jack Pennick (sergeant).

An Arkansas mother realizes her guilt during a journey to France.

1933 *Doctor Bull* (Fox Film). 76 minutes. September 22. Director: John Ford. Scenarist: Paul Green, from novel *The Last Adam*, by James Gould Cozzens. Dialogue: Jane Storm. Photographer: George Schneiderman. Music: Samuel Kaylin. Filmed in June. With Will Rogers (Dr. Bull), Marian Nixon (May Tripping), Berton Churchill (Herbert Banning), Louise Dresser (Mrs. Banning), Howard Lally (Joe Tripping), Rochelle Hudson (Virginia Banning), Vera Allen (Janet Cardmaker), Tempe Pigotte (Grandma), Elizabeth Patterson (Aunt Patricia), Ralph Morgan (Dr. Verney), Andy Devine (Larry Ward), Nora Cecil (Aunt Emily), Patsy O'Byrne (Susan), Effie Ellsler (Aunt Myra), Veda Buckland (Mary), Helen Freeman (Helen Upjohn), Robert Parrish, Francis Ford (mayor). Working title: "Life's Worth Living."

A folksy doctor tries to help an intolerant community.

1934 *The Lost Patrol* (RKO Radio). 74 minutes. February 16. Director: John Ford. Executive producer: Merian C. Cooper. Associate producer: Cliff Reid. Scenarists: Dudley Nichols, Garrett Fort, and (uncredited) Frank Baker from story "Patrol," by Philip MacDonald. Photographer: Harold Wenstrom. Art directors: Van Nest Polglase, Sidney Ullman. Music: Max Steiner. Editor: Paul Weatherwax. Technical advisor: Frank Baker. Filmed in the Yuma desert. With Victor McLaglen (sergeant), Boris Karloff (Sanders), Wallace Ford (Morelli), Reginald Denny (George Brown), J. M. Kerrigan (Quincannon), Billy Bevan (Herbert Hale), Alan Hale (cook), Brandon Hurst (Bell), Douglas Walton (Pearson), Sammy Stein (Abelson), Howard Wilson (flyer), Neville Clark (Lt. Hawkins), Paul Hanson (Jock Mackay), Francis Ford, Frank Baker (relieving colonel; Arab).

A British patrol is picked off one by one by unseen desert Arabs.

Remake, 1943: *Bataan*, by Tay Garnett.

1934 *The World Moves On* (Fox Film). 90 minutes. June 27. Director: John Ford.

Producer: Winfield Sheehan. Writer: Reginald C. Berkeley. Photographer: George Schneiderman. Art director: William Darling. Set decorator: Thomas Little. Costumes: Rita Kaufman. Music: Max Steiner, Louis De Francesco, R. H. Bassett, David Buttolph, Hugo Friedhofer, George Gershwin. Songs: "Should She Desire Me Not," by De Francesco; "Ave Maria," by Charles Gounod. With Madeleine Carroll (Mrs. Warburton, 1824; Mary Warburton, 1914), Franchot Tone (Richard Girard, 1824 and 1914), Lumsden Hare (Gabriel Warburton, 1824; Sir John Warburton, 1914), Raul Roulien (Carlos Girard, 1824; Henri Gerard, 1914), Reginald Denny (Erik von Gerhardt), Siegfried Rumann (Baron von Gerhardt), Louise Dresser (Baroness von Gerhardt), Stepin Fetchit (Dixie), Dudley Diggs (Mr. Manning), Frank Melton (John Girard, 1824), Brenda Fowler (Mrs. Girard, 1824), Russell Simpson (notary public, 1824), Walter McGrail (French duelist, 1824), Marcelle Corday (Miss Girard, 1824), Charles Bastin (Jacques Girard, 1914), Barry Norton (Jacques Girard, 1929), George Irving (Charles Girard, 1914), Ferdinand Schumann-Heink (Fritz von Gerhardt), Georgette Rhodes (Jeanne Girard, 1914), Claude King (Braithwaite), Ivan Simpson (Clumber), Frank Moran (Culbert), Jack Pennick, Francis Ford (legionnaires), Torbin Mayer (German chamberlain, 1914).

1825, New Orleans: Cotton King Sebastian Girard's will directs his sons to set up branches in France, Prussia, America, and, with Warburton, Manchester; all vow unity. Richard kills Mary's offender in a duel, but, the vow barring love, she sails for England with her husband. 1914: New generations renew the vow. Richard and Mary think they recognize each other. Germany: Jeanne marries Fritz. World War I: Richard and Henri enlist for France, Fritz and Erik for Germany, Fritz's sub sinks a liner carrying Girards, then is sunk itself. Mary runs English firm, marries Richard. Henri is killed, Erik maimed, Richard, wounded in Germany, is cared for by Erik's parents. 1924: Manic Richard tries to corner cotton. 1929: Bankruptcy returns him to Mary.

1934 *Judge Priest* (Fox Film). 81 minutes. October 5. Director: John Ford. Producer: Sol Wurtzel. Scenarists: Dudley Nichols, Lamar Trotti, from stories by Irvin S.

Cobb. Photographer: George Schneiderman. Music: Samuel Kaylin. With Will Rogers (Judge William Priest), Henry B. Walthall (Rev. Ashby Brand), Tom Brown (Jerome Priest), Anita Louise (Ellie May Gillespie), Rochelle Hudson (Virginia Maydew), Berton Churchill (Senator Horace K. Maydew), David Landau (Bob Gillis), Brenda Fowler (Mrs. Caroline Priest), Hattie McDaniel (Aunt Dilsey), Stepin Fetchit (Jeff Poindexter), Frank Melton (Flem Tally), Roger Imhof (Billy Gaynor), Charley Grapewin (Sgt. Jimmy Bagby), Francis Ford (juror no. 12), Paul McAllister (Doc Lake), Matt McHugh (Gabby Rives), Hy Meyer (Herman Feldsburg), Louis Mason (Sheriff Birdsong), Robert Parrish.

1890 Kentucky.

1935 *The Whole Town's Talking* (Columbia). 95 minutes. February 22. Director: John Ford. Producer: Lester Cowan. Scenarist: Jo Swerling, from novel by W. R. Burnett. Dialogue: Robert Riskin. Photographer: Joseph H. August. Editor: Viola Lawrence. Assistant director: Wilbur McGaugh. With Edward G. Robinson (Arthur Ferguson Jones; Killer Mannion), Jean Arthur (Miss "Bill" Clark), Wallace Ford (Mr. Healy), Arthur Byron (Mr. Spencer), Arthur Hohl (Det. Sgt. Michael Boyle), Donald Meek (Mr. Hoyt), Paul Harvey (J. G. Carpenter), Edward Brophy (Slugs Martin), J. Farrell MacDonald (warden), Etienne Girardot (Mr. Seaver), James Donlan (Howe), John Wray (henchman), Effie Ellsler (Aunt Agatha), Robert Emmett O'Connor (police lieutenant), Joseph Sawyer, Francis Ford, Robert Parrish. Working title: "Passport to Fame."

A timid clerk resembles Public Enemy No. 1.

Prison footage from Hawks's *The Criminal Code* (1931).

1935 *The Informer* (RKO Radio). 91 minutes. May 1. Director: John Ford. Associate producer: Cliff Reid. Scenarist: Dudley Nichols, from novel by Liam O'Flaherty. Photographer: Joseph H. August. Art directors: Van Nest Polglase, Charles Kirk. Set decorator: Julia Heron. Costumes: Walter Plunkett. Music: Max Steiner. Editor: George Hively. Assistant directors: Eddie Donahue, Edward O'Fearna. Filmed: February. With Victor McLaglen (Gypo Nolan), Heather Angel (Mary McPhillip), Preston Foster (Dan

Gallagher), Margo Grahame (Katie Madden), Wallace Ford (Frankie McPhillip), Una O'Connor (Mrs. McPhillip), J. M. Kerrigan (Terry), Joseph Sawyer (Bartley Muiholland), Neil Fitzgerald (Tommy Conner), Donald Meek (Pat Mulligan), D'Arcy Corrigan (the blindman), Leo McCabe (Donahue), Gaylord Pendleton (Daley), Francis Ford (Judge Flynn), May Boley (Mrs. Betty), Grizelda Harvey (an obedient girl), Dennis O'Dea (street singer), Jack Mulhall (lookout), Robert Parrish (soldier), Clyde Cook, Barlowe Borland, Frank Moran, Arthur McLaglen, Frank Baker.

1922 Dublin: Gypo Nolan informs on a buddy.

Awards: See main text, page 121.

1935 *Steamboat Round the Bend* (Fox Film—20th Century–Fox). 80 minutes. September 6. Director: John Ford. Producer: Sol M. Wurtzel. Scenarists: Dudley Nichols, Lamar Trotti, from story by Ben Lucian Burman. Photographer: George Schneiderman. Art director: William Darling. Set decorator: Albert Hogsett. Music director: Samuel Kaylin. Title song: Oscar Levant (uncredited). Editor: Alfred De Gaetano. Assistant director: Edward O'Fearna. Casting: Al Smith. Script clerk: Stanley Scheuer. Camera: James Gordon, Paul Lockwood. Location photography on Sacramento River. With Will Rogers (Dr. John Pearly), Anne Shirley (Fleety Belle), Eugene Pallette (Sheriff Rufe Jeffers), John McGuire (Duke), Berton Churchill ("The New Moses"), Stepin Fetchit (George Lincoln Washington), Francis Ford (Efe), Irvin S. Cobb (Capt. Eli), Roger Imhof (Pappy), Raymond Hatton (Matt Abel), Hobart Bosworth (Chaplin), Louis Mason (boat race organizer), Charles B. Middleton (Fleety's father), Si Jenks (a drunk), Jack Pennick (ringleader of boat attack).

Patent medicine and waxworks fuel a riverboat race to save a life.

1936 *The Prisoner of Shark Island* (20th Century–Fox). 95 minutes. February 12. Director: John Ford. Producer: Darryl F. Zanuck. Associate producer–scenarist: Nunnally Johnson, from life of Dr. Samuel A. Mudd. Photographer: Bert Glennon. Art director: William Darling. Set decorator: Thomas Little. Costumes: Gwen Wakeling. Music director: Louis

Silvers. Editor: Jack Murray. Assistant director: Edward O'Fearna. With Warner Baxter (Dr. Samuel A. Mudd), Gloria Stuart (Mrs. Peggy Mudd), Claude Gillingwater (Col. Jeremiah Milford Dyer), Arthur Byron (Mr. Erickson), O. P. Heggie (Dr. McIntyre), Harry Carey (Comdt. of Fort Jefferson, "Shark Island"), Francis Ford (Cpl. O'Toole), John Carradine (Sgt. Rankin), Frank McGlynne, Sr. (Abraham Lincoln), Douglas Wood (Gen. Ewing), Joyce Kay (Martha Mudd), Fred Kohler, Jr. (Sgt. Cooper), Francis McDonald (John Wilkes Booth), John McGuire (Lt. Lovell), Ernest Whitman (Buckingham Montmorency Milford), Paul Fix (David Herold), Frank Shannon (Holt), Leila McIntyre (Mrs. Lincoln), Etta McDaniel (Rosabelle Milford), Arthur Loft (carpetbagger), Paul McVey (Gen. Hunter), Maurice Murphy (orderly), Jack Pennick (soldier who sends flag messages), J.M. Kerrigan (Judge Maiben), Whitney Bourne, Robert Parrish, Frank Baker.

True story of doctor who innocently helped John Wilkes Booth and got condemned to life imprisonment.

†1936 *The Last Outlaw* (RKO Radio). 62 minutes. June 19. Director: Christy Cabane. Associate producer: Robert Sisk. Screenplay: John Twist, Jack Townley, from story by John Ford and Evelyne Murray Campbell. Photographer: Jack MacKenzie. Art director: Van Nest Polglase. Associate: Jack Gray. Musical direction: Alberto Colombo. Song: "My Heart's on the Trail," music by Nathaniel Shilkret, lyrics by Frank Luther. Sound: Denzil A. Cutler. Editor: George Hively. With Harry Carey (Dean Payton), Hoot Gibson (Chuck Wilson), Margaret Callahan (Sally Mason), Tom Tyler (Al Goss), Henry B. Walthall (Bill Yates), Ray Meyer (Joe), Harry Hans (Jess), Frank M. Thomas (Dr. Mason), Russell Hopton (Sheriff Billings), Frank Jenks (Tom), Maxine Jennings (receptionist), Fred Scott (Larry Dixon).

A remake of Ford's 1919 two-reeler.

1936 *Mary of Scotland* (RKO Radio). 123 minutes. July 24. Director: John Ford. Producer: Pandro S. Berman. Scenarist: Dudley Nichols, from play by Maxwell Anderson. Photography: Joseph H. August. Art directors: Van Nest Polglase, Carroll Clark. Set decorator: Darrell Silvera. Costumes: Walter Plunkett. Music: Max Steiner. Editor: Jane Loring.

Assistant editor: Robert Parrish. Special effects: Vernon L. Walker. Filmed in January–March. With Katharine Hepburn (Mary Stuart), Fredric March (Bothwell), Florence Eldridge (Elizabeth), Douglas Walton (Darnley), John Carradine (David Rizzio), Monte Blue (Messager), Jean Fenwick (Mary Seton), Robert Barrat (Morton), Gavin Muir (Leicester), Ian Keith (James Stuart Moray), Moroni Olsen (John Knox), Donald Crisp (Huntley), William Stack (Ruthven), Molly Lamont (Mary Livingston), Walter Byron (Sir Francis Walsingham), Ralph Forbes (Randolph), Alan Mowbray (Trockmorton), Frieda Inescort (Mary Beaton), David Torrence (Lindsay), Anita Colby (Mary Fleming), Lionel Belmore (English fisherman), Doris Lloyd (his wife), Bobby Watson (his son), Lionel Pape (Burghley), Ivan Simpson, Murray Kinnell, Lawrence Grant, Nigel DeBrulier, Barlowe Borland (judges), Alec Craig (Donal), Mary Gordon (nurse), Wilfred Lucas (Lexington), Leonard Mudie (Maitland), Brandon Hurst (Arian), D'Arcy Corrigan (Kirkcaldy), Frank Baker (Douglas), Cyril McLaglen (Faudoncide), Robert Warwick (Sir Francis Knellys), Earle Foxe (Duke of Kent), Wyndham Standing (sergeant), Gaston Glass (Chatelard), Neil Fitzgerald (nobleman), Paul McAllister (Du Croche).

1936 *The Plough and the Stars* (RKO Radio). 67 minutes. December 26. Director: John Ford. Associate producers: Cliff Reid, Robert Sisk. Scenarist: Dudley Nichols, from play by Sean O'Casey. Photography: Joseph H. August. Art director: Van Nest Polglase. Music: Nathaniel Shilkret, Roy Webb. Editor: George Hively. With Barbara Stanwyck (Mora Clitheroe), Preston Foster (Jack Clitheroe), Barry Fitzgerald (Fluther Good), Dennis O'Day (the Young Covey), Eileen Crowe (Bessie Burgess), Arthur Shields (Padraic Pearse), Erin O'Brien Moore (Rosie Redmond), Brandon Hurst (Sgt. Tinley), F. J. McCormick (Capt. Brennon), Una O'Conner (Maggie Corgan), Moroni Olsen (Gen. Connolly), J. M. Kerrigan (Peter Flynn), Neil Fitzgerald (Lt. Kangon), Bonita Granville (Mollser Gogan), Cyril McLaglen (Cpl. Stoddart), Robert Homans (barman), Mary Gordon (first woman), Mary Quinn (second woman), Lionel Pape (Englishman), Michael Fitzmaurice (ICA), Gaylord Pendleton (ICA), Doris Lloyd, D'Arcy

Corrigan, Wesley Barry, Frank Baker (English officer).
Dublin, Easter Rebellion.

1937 *Wee Willie Winkie*. (20th Century–Fox). 99 minutes. July 30. Director: John Ford. Producer: Darryl F. Zanuck. Associate producer: Gene Markey. Scenarists: Ernest Pascal, Julian Josephson, from story by Rudyard Kipling. Photography: Arthur Miller. Art director: William Darling. Set decorator: Thomas Little. Music: Louis Silvers. Editor: Walter Thompson. Released with tinted sequences (sepia for day, blue for night). With Shirley Temple (Priscilla Williams), Victor McLaglen (Sgt. MacDuff), C. Aubrey Smith (Col. Williams), June Lang (Joyce Williams), Michael Whalen (Lt. "Coppy" Brandes), Cesar Romero (Khoda Khan), Constance Collier (Mrs. Allardyce), Douglas Scott (Mott), Gavin Muir (Capt. Bibberbeigh), Willie Fung (Mohammed Dihn), Brandon Hurst (Bagby), Lionel Pape (Major Allardyce), Clyde Cook (Pipe Maj. Sneath), Lauri Beatty (Elsi Allardyce), Lionel Braham (Maj. Gen. Hammond), Mary Forbes (Mrs. MacMonachie), Cyril McLaglen (Cpl. Tummel), Pat Somerset (officer), Hector Sarno (conductor).
A little girl stops a war in 1890s India.
Many prints in circulation have been abridged to about 80 minutes. Oscar nomination: interior decoration (Thomas Little).

1937 *The Hurricane* (Samuel Goldwyn–United Artists). 102 minutes. December 24. Director: John Ford. Producer: Samuel Goldwyn. Associate producer: Merritt Hulburd. Scenarists: Dudley Nichols, Ben Hecht (uncredited), from novel by Charles Nordhoff, James Horman Hall, adapted by Oliver H. P. Garrett. Associate director: Stuart Heisler. Hurricane sequence: James Basevi. Photographer: Bert Glennon, Archie Stout (second unit). Art directors: Richard Day, Alex Golitzen. Set decorator: Julie Heron. Costumes: Omar Kiam. Music: Alfred Newman. Editor: Lloyd Nosler. Sound recording: Thomas Moulton. Assistant director: Wingate Smith. Exterior locations at Samoa, Catalina. Filmed in summer. With Dorothy Lamour (Marama), Jon Hall (Terangi), Mary Astor (Mrs. DeLaage), C. Aubrey Smith (Father Paul), Thomas Mitchell (Dr. Kersaint), Raymond

Massey (Gov. Eugene DeLaage), John Carradine (guard), Jerome Cowan (Capt. Nagle), Al Kikume (Chief Meheir), Kuulei DeClercq (Tita), Layne Tom, Jr. (Mako), Mamo Clark (Hitia), Movita Castenada (Arai), Reri (Reri), Francis Kaai (Tavi), Pauline Steele (Mata), Flora Hayes (Mama Rua), Mary Shaw (Marunga), Spencer Charters (judge), Roger Drake (captain of the guards), Inez Courtney (girl on boat), Paul Strader, *Araner.*

After completion of rough cut, some interiors were reshot with new dialogue by Ben Hecht.

South Sea Island.

Awards: See text, page 137.

†1938 *The Adventures of Marco Polo* (Samuel Goldwyn–United Artists). 100 minutes. April 15. Director: Archie Mayo. Producer: Samuel Goldwyn. Scenarist: Robert E. Sherwood, from story by N.A. Pogson. Photography: Rudolph Maté. Art director: Richard Day. Music: Alfred Newman. Special effects: James Basevi. With Gary Cooper, Sigrid Gurie, Basil Rathbone.

Ford shot scenes for a brief montage in which, in seconds, Polo is shipwrecked by a storm, caught in a desert sandstorm, and crosses a mountain.

1938 *Four Men and a Prayer* (20th Century–Fox). 85 minutes. April 29. Director: John Ford. Producer: Darryl F. Zanuck. Associate producer: Kenneth MacGowan. Scenarists: Richard Sherman, Sonya Levien, Walter Ferris, and (uncredited) William Faulkner, from novel by David Garth. Photographer: Ernest Palmer. Art directors: Bernard Herzbrun, Rudolph Sternad. Set decorator: Thomas Little. Music: Louis Silvers, Ernst Toch. Editor: Louis R. Loeffler. Costumes: Royer. With Loretta Young (Lynn Cherrington), Richard Greene (Geoffrey Leigh), George Sanders (Wyatt Leigh), David Niven (Christopher Leigh), William Henry (Rodney Leigh), C. Aubrey Smith (Col. Loring Leigh), J. Edward Bromberg (Gen. Torres), Alan Hale (Farnoy), John Carradine (Gen. Adolfo Arturo Sebastian), Reginald Denny (Douglas Loveland), Berton Churchill (Martin Cherrington), Claude King (Gen. Bryce), John Sutton (Capt. Drake), Barry Fitzgerald (Mulcahy), Cecil Cunningham (Pyer), Frank Baker (defense attorney), Frank Dawson, Lina Basquette (Ah-nee), Winter Hall (judge), Will Stanton (Cockney), John Spacey, C. Montague Shaw (lawyers), Lionel Pape (coroner), Brandon Hurst (jury foreman).

Four sons roam the world to establish the innocence of their disgraced (and murdered) father.

1938 *Submarine Patrol* (20th Century–Fox). 95 minutes. November 25. Director: John Ford. Producer: Darryl F. Zanuck. Associate producer: Gene Markey. Scenarists: Rian James, Darrell Ware, Jack Yellen and (uncredited) William Faulkner, from novel *The Splinter Fleet,* by John Milholland. Photography: Arthur Miller. Art directors: William Darling, Hans Peters. Costumes: Gwen Wakeling. Set decorator: Thomas Little. Music director: Arthur Lange. Editor: Robert Simpson. With Richard Greene (Perry Townsend III), Nancy Kelly (Susan Leeds), Preston Foster (Lt. John C. Drake), George Bancroft (Capt. Leeds), Slim Summerville (Ellsworth "Spuggs" Ficketts—"Cookie"), Joan Valerie (Anne), John Carradine (Matt McAllison), Warren Hymer (Rocky Haggerty), Henry Armetta (Luigi), Douglas Fowley (Brett), J. Farrell MacDonald (Quincannon), Dick Hogan (Johnny), Maxie Rosenbloom (Sgt. Joe Duffy), Ward Bond (Olaf Swanson), Robert Lowery (Sparks), Charles Tannen (Kelly), George E. Stone (Irving Goldfarb), Moroni Olsen (Capt. Wilson), Jack Pennick (Guns McPeck), Elisha Cook, Jr. ("Professor" Pratt), Harry Strang (Grainger), Charles Trowbridge (Adm. Joseph Maitland), Victor Varconi (chaplain), Murray Alper (sailor), E.E. Clive.

World War I: Citizen sailors on a wooden sub chaser.

1939 *Stagecoach.* (Walter Wanger–United Artists). 97 minutes. March 2. Director: John Ford. Executive producer: Walter Wanger. Scenarist: Dudley Nichols, from story "Stage to Lordsburg," by Ernest Haycox. Photography: Bert Glennon. Art director: Alexander Toluboff (credited; actually, set decorator: Wiard B. Ihnen). Costumes: Walter Plunkett. Music (adapted from seventeen American folk tunes of early 1880s): Richard Hageman, W. Franke Harling, John Leipold, Leo Shuken, Louis Gruenberg. Editorial supervision: Otho Lovering. Editors: Dorothy Spencer, Walter Reynolds. Assistant director: Wingate Smith. Filmed in Monument Valley and other locations in

Arizona, Utah, and California, October–December. With John Wayne (the Ringo Kid), Claire Trevor (Dallas), John Carradine (Hatfield), Thomas Mitchell (Dr. Josiah Boone), Andy Devine (Buck), Donald Meek (Samuel Peacock), Louise Platt (Lucy Mallory), Tim Holt (Lt. Blanchard), George Bancroft (Sheriff Curly Willcox), Berton Churchill (Henry Gatewood), Tom Tyler (Hank Plummer), Chris Pin Martin (Chris), Elvira Rios (Yakima, his wife), Francis Ford (Billy Pickett), Marga Daighton (Mrs. Pickett), Kent Odell (Billy Pickett, Jr.), Yakima Canutt, Chief Big Tree (stuntman), Henry Tenbrook (telegraph operator), Jack Pennick (Jerry, barman), Paul McVey (Express agent), Cornelius Keefe (Capt. Whitney), Florence Lake (Mrs. Nancy Whitney), Louis Mason (sheriff), Brenda Fowler (Mrs. Gatewood), Walter McGrail (Capt. Sickel), Joseph Rickson (Luke Plummer), Vester Pegg (Ike Plummer), William Hoffer (sergeant), Bryant Washburn (Capt. Simmons), Nora Cecil (Dr. Boone's housekeeper), Helen Gibson, Dorothy Annleby (dancing girls), Buddy Roosevelt, Bill Cody (ranchers), Chief White Horse (Indian chief), Duke Lee (sheriff of Lordsburg), Mary Kathleen Walker (Lucy's baby), Many Mules (Geronimo), Ed Brady, Steve Clemente, Theodore Larch, Fritzi Brunette, Leonard Trainor, Chris Phillips, Tex Driscoll, Teddy Billings, John Eckert, Al Lee, Jack Mohr, Patsy Doyle, Wiggie Blowne, Margaret Smith, Frank Baker (scalped corpse).

1884, a stagecoach journey in New Mexico.

Awards: See text, page 146.

1939 *Young Mr. Lincoln* (Cosmopolitan–20th Century–Fox). 101 minutes. June 9. Director: John Ford. Executive producer: Darryl F. Zanuck. Producer: Kenneth Macgowan. Scenarist: Lamar Trotti, based on life of Abraham Lincoln. Photography: Bert Glennon, Arthur Miller (uncredited, river locations). Art directors: Richard Day, Mark Lee Kirk. Set decorator: Thomas Little. Music: Alfred Newman. Editor: Walter Thompson. Costumes: Royer. Sound effects editor: Robert Parrish. Filmed in February. With Henry Fonda (Abraham Lincoln), Alice Brady (Abigail Clay), Marjorie Weaver (Mary Todd), Dorris Bowdon (uncredited) (Carrie Sue Clay),

Eddie Collins (Efe Turner), Pauline Moore (Ann Rutledge), Arleen Whelan (Sarah Clay), Richard Cromwell (Matt Clay), Ward Bond (John Palmer Cass), Donald Meek (John Felder), Spencer Charters (Judge Herbert A. Bell), Eddie Quillan (Adam Clay), Milburn Stone (Stephen Douglas), Cliff Clark (Sheriff Billings), Robert Lowery (juror), Charles Tannen (Ninian Edwards), Francis Ford (Sam Boone), Fred Kohler, Jr. (Scrub White), Kay Linaker (Mrs. Edwards), Russell Simpson (Woolridge), Charles Halton (Hawthorne), Edwin Maxwell (John T. Stuart), Robert Homans (Mr. Clay), Jack Kelly (Matt Clay, as child), Dicky Jones (Adam Clay, as child), Harry Tyler (hairdresser), Louis Mason (court clerk), Jack Pennick (Big Buck), Steven Randall (juror), Clarence Wilson, Elizabeth Jones. Credited as Carrie Sue, but not appearing: Judith Dickens.

Lincoln's discovery of the Law, his love for Ann Rutledge, and his first public victory—in a murder trial.

1939 *Drums Along the Mohawk* (20th Century–Fox). Technicolor. 103 minutes. November 3. Director: John Ford. Executive producer: Darryl F. Zanuck. Producer: Raymond Griffith. Scenarists: Lamar Trotti, Sonya Levien, and (uncredited) William Faulkner, from novel by Walter D. Edmonds. Photography: Bert Glennon, Ray Rennahan. Art directors: Richard Day, Mark Lee Kirk. Color set consultant: Natalie Kalmus, Henri Jaffa. Costumes: Gwen Wakeling. Set decorator: Thomas Little. Music: Alfred Newman. Editor: Robert Simpson. Sound effects editor: Robert Parrish. Filmed in Utah's Wasatch Mountains, summer. With Claudette Colbert (Lana Borst Martin), Henry Fonda (Gilbert Martin), Edna May Oliver (Mrs. McKlennan), Eddie Collins (Christian Reall), John Carradine (Caldwell), Dorris Bowdon (Mary Reall), Jessie Ralph (Mrs. Weaver), Arthur Shields (Fr. Rosenkranz), Robert Lowery (John Weaver), Roger Imhof (Gen. Nicholas Herkimer), Francis Ford (Joe Boleo), Ward Bond (Adam Hartmann), Kay Linaker (Mrs. Demooth), Russell Simpson (Dr. Petry), Chief Big Tree (Blue Back), Spencer Charters (Fisk, innkeeper), Arthur Aylesworth (George), Si Jenks (Jacobs), Jack Pennick (Amos), Charles Tannen (Robert Johnson), Paul McVey (Capt. Mark Demooth), Elizabeth Jones

(Mrs. Reall), Lionel Pape (general), Clarence Wilson (paymaster), Edwin Maxwell (pastor), Clara Blandick (Mrs. Borst), Beulah Hall Jones (Daisy), Robert Greig (Mr. Borst), Mae Marsh, Ruth Clifford, Frank Baker (commander of colonial troops).

Mohawk Valley pioneers during Revolutionary War.

Oscar nominations: Best supporting actress (Edna May Oliver).

1940 *The Grapes of Wrath* (20th Century–Fox). 129 minutes. March 15. Director: John Ford. Producer: Darryl F. Zanuck. Associate producer–scenarist: Nunnally Johnson, from novel by John Steinbeck. Photography: Gregg Toland. Art directors: Richard Day, Mark Lee Kirk. Set decorator: Thomas Little. Music: Alfred Newman. Song "Red River Valley" played on accordion by Dan Borzage. Technical consultant: Tom Collins. Costumes: Gwen Wakeling. Second-unit director: Otto Brower. Editor: Robert Simpson. Sound: George Leverett, Roger Heman. Sound effects editor: Robert Parrish. Assistant editor: Edward O'Fearna. Filmed: September– November. With Henry Fonda (Tom Joad), Jane Darwell (Ma Joad), John Carradine (Casey), Charley Grapewin (Grampa Joad), Dorris Bowdon (Rosasharn), Russell Simpson (Pa Joad), O. Z. Whitehead (Al), John Qualen (Muley), Eddie Quillan (Connie), Zeffie Tilbury (Grandma Joad), Frank Sully (Noah), Frank Darien (Uncle John), Darryl Hickman (Winfield), Shirley Mills (Ruth Joad), Grant Mitchell (guardian), Ward Bond (policeman), Frank Faylen (Tim), Joe Sawyer (accountant), Harry Tyler (Bert), Charles B. Middleton (conductor), John Arledge (Davis), Hollis Jewell (Muley's son), Paul Guilfoyle (Floyd), Charles D. Brown (Wilkie), Roger Imhof (Thomas), William Pawley (Bill), Arthur Aysleworth (father), Charles Tannen (Joe), Selmar Jackson (inspector), Eddie C. Waller (proprietor), David Hughes (Frank), Cliff Clark (townsman), Adrian Morris (agent), Robert Homans (Spencer), Irving Bacon (conductor), Kitty McHugh (Mae), Mae Marsh, Francis Ford, Jack Pennick.

An evicted Oakie family seeks a new home during the 1930s.

Awards: See text, page 176.

1940 *The Long Voyage Home* (Argosy Pictures–Wanger–United Artists). 105

minutes. October 8. Director: John Ford. Producer: Walter Wanger. Scenarist: Dudley Nichols, from one-act plays "The Moon of the Caribbees," "In the Zone," "Bound East for Cardiff," "The Long Voyage Home," by Eugene O'Neill. Photography: Gregg Toland. Art director: James Basevi. Set decorator: Julia Heron. Music: Richard Hageman. Editor: Sherman Todd. Sound editor: Robert Parrish. Special effects: Ray Binger, R. T. Layton. Filmed in summer. With Thomas Mitchell (Aloysius Driscoll), John Wayne (Ole Olsen), Ian Hunter (Thomas Fenwick, "Smitty"), Barry Fitzgerald (Cocky), Wilfred Lawson (captain), Mildred Natwick (Freda), John Qualen (Axel Swanson), Ward Bond (Yank), Joe Sawyer (Davis), Arthur Shields (Donkeyman), J.M. Kerrigan (Crimp), David Hughes (Scotty), Billy Bevan (Joe), Cyril McLaglen (mate), Robert E. Perry (Paddy), Jack Pennick, (Johnny Bergman), Constantin Frenke (Narvey), Constantin Romanoff (Big Frank), Dan Borzage (Tim), Harry Tenbrook (Max), Douglas Walton (second lieutenant), Raphaela Ottiano (Daughter of the Tropics), Carmen Morales, Carmen d'Antonio (girls in canoe), Harry Woods (the admiral's sailor), Edgar "Blue" Washington, Lionel Pape, Jane Crowley, Maureen Roden-Ryan.

The Glencairn's crew dream of land, but always return to the sea.

Awards: See text, page 182.

1941 *Tobacco Road* (20th Century Fox). 84 minutes. February 20. Director: John Ford. Producer: Darryl F. Zanuck. Associate producers: Jack Kirkland, Harry H. Oshrin. Scenarist: Nunnally Johnson, from play by Kirkland and novel by Erskine Caldwell. Photography: Arthur C. Miller. Art directors: Richard Day, James Basevi. Set decorator: Thomas Little. Music: David Buttolph. Editor: Barbara McLean. Sound effects editor: Robert Parrish. With Charley Grapewin (Jeeter Lester), Marjorie Rambeau (Sister Bessie), Gene Tierney (Ellie May Lester), William Tracy (Dude Lester), Elizabeth Patterson (Ada Lester), Dana Andrews (Dr. Tim), Slim Summerville (Henry Peabody), Ward Bond (Lov Bensey), Grant Mitchell (George Payne), Zeffie Tilbury (Grandma Lester), Russell Simpson (sherriff), Spencer Charters (employee), Irving Bacon (teller), Harry Tyler (auto salesman), George Chandler (employee), Charles Halton (mayor), Jack Pennick (deputy sheriff), Dorothy Adams (Payne's secretary), Francis Ford (vagabond).

Life among decadent rural whites in Georgia.

1941 *Sex Hygiene* (Audio Productions— U.S. Army). 30 minutes. Director: John Ford. Producer: Darryl F. Zanuck. Photographer: George Barnes. Editor: Gene Fowler, Jr. With Charles Trowbridge, Robert Lowery, George Reeves.

An army training film on venereal disease.

1941 *How Green Was My Valley* (20th Century–Fox). 118 minutes. December. Director: John Ford. Producer: Darryl F. Zanuck. Scenarist: Philip Dunne, from novel by Richard Llewellyn. Photography: Arthur Miller. Art directors: Richard Day, Nathan Juran. Set decorator: Thomas Little. Costumes: Gwen Wakeling. Music: Alfred Newman. Choral effects: Eisteddfod Singers of Wales. Editor: James B. Clark. Narrator: Irving Pichel. U.K. version narrator: Rhys Williams. Filmed in June–August. With Walter Pidgeon (Mr. Gruffydd), Maureen O'Hara (Angharad Morgan), Donald Crisp (Gwilym Morgan), Sara Allgood (Mrs. Beth Morgan), Anna Lee (Bronwyn Morgan), Roddy McDowall (Huw Morgan), John Loder (Ianto Morgan), Patrick Knowles (Ivor Morgan), Richard Fraser (Davy Morgan), James Monks (Owen Morgan), Barry Fitzgerald (Cyfartha), The Welsh Singers (singers), Morton Lowery (Mr. Jonas), Arthur Shields (Mr. Parry), Ann Todd (Ceiwen), Frederick Worlock (Dr. Richards), Evan E. Evans (Gwinlyn), Rhys Williams (Dai Bando), Lionel Pape (Old Evans), Ethel Griffies (Mrs. Nicholas), Marten Lamont (Jestyn Evans), Mae Marsh (miner's wife), Louis Jean Heydt (miner), Denis Hoey (Motschell), Tudor Williams (singer), Clifford Severn, Eva March, Frank Baker.

A Welsh mining family in the 1890s.

Awards: See Text, Page 184.

†1941–46 Field Photo films for OSS: Many training films and documentaries for restricted use made by Ford's crews under his general supervision (amounting to zero or greater?), including: *How to Operate Behind Enemy Lines* (with Dana Andrews?); *How to Interrogate Enemy Prisoners; Living Off the Land; Nazi Industrial Manpower; Dunkirk in Reverse; Inside Tibet* (Kodachrome, in National Archives), etc.

Report, November 1941: Condition of Atlantic Fleet (by Ford, Ray Kellogg). *Canal Report:* on Panama defenses, December–January 1942 (Ford directed, photographed, edited, wrote, and spoke narration; also by Al Jolkes, Al Ziegler, Robert Parrish).
Report: Doolittle raid on Tokyo, April 1942 (Ford, et al.).
Coverage: Allied landings at Oran, Algiers, Casablanca, November 1942.

1942 *The Battle of Midway* (U.S. Navy–20th Century–Fox). Kodachrome / Technicolor. 17 minutes. September. Director: Lt. Comdr. John Ford, USNR. Narration: Ford, Dudley Nichols, James Kevin McGuinness. Photography: Ford, Jack McKenzie, Lt. Kenneth M. Pier, Gregg Toland. Music: Alfred Newman. Editors: Ford, Robert Parrish. Sound effects editor: Phil Scott. With voices of Henry Fonda, Jane Darwell, Donald Crisp, Irving Pichel.

A report on the actual battle.

Oscar: Best documentary.

1942 *Torpedo Squadron* (U.S. Navy). Kodachrome. 8 minutes (8mm). Director: Lt. Comdr. John Ford, USNR.

According to Bogdanovich, Ford's unit took some footage of life on a PT-boat (Torpedo Squadron 8) in 16mm color shortly before the Battle of Midway. All but one of the squadron were killed, and the edited footage was delivered by personal envoys (such as Joe August) to the dead sailors' families.

1943 *December 7th* (U.S. Navy). 85 and 34 minutes. Directors: Lt. Gregg Toland, USNR, Lt. Comdr. John Ford, USNR. Photography: Toland. Second-unit directors: Ray Kellogg, James C. Havens, USMC. Music: Alfred Newman. Editor: Robert Parrish. Additional narration: James K. McGuinness. With Harry Davenport, Walter Huston.

A study of life in Hawaii, before and after Pearl Harbor. Mostly Toland's work.

Originally made 85 minutes long, but unreleased; nontheatrically distributed in a 34-minute version.

Oscar: Best documentary.

1943 *Victory in Burma:* On Mountbatten and Father Stuart; (directed by Irving Asner, assisted by Jack Swain, Bob Rhea, Arthur Meehan).

etc. (Mark Armistead, supervisor; Ford shot some China portions).
Coverage: Allied landings at Normandy, June 1944.
Research: documentary footage for use at Nuremberg trials (by Ray Kellogg, Budd and Stewart Schulberg, Joe Ziegler, Bob Webb), later released as *Nuremberg* (War Dept.: 1946, 76 minutes); compiled by Pare Lorentz and Stuart Schulberg. Prints available from National Archives).

†1943 *We Sail at Midnight* (Crown Film Unity–U.S. Navy), 20 minutes. July. Director: Ford (?). Narration written by Clifford Odets. Music: Richard Addinsell.

Hazards of merchant shipping in combat zones.

An extant fragment shows cargo handling in New York City and trucks on Broadway. Attribution to Ford is *very* dubious.

1945 *They Were Expendable* (Metro-Goldwyn-Mayer). 136 minutes. December 20. Director-producer: John Ford. Associate producer: Cliff Reid. Scenarist: Frank W. Wead, from book by William L. White. Photography: Joseph H. August. Art directors: Cedric Gibbons, Malcolm F. Brown. Set decorators: Edwin B. Willis, Ralph S. Hurst. Music: Herbert Stothert. Editors: Frank E. Hull, Douglas Biggs. Second-unit director: James C. Havens (rear projection plates by Robert Montgomery). Assistant director: Edward O'Fearna. Filmed in Florida, February–April. With Robert Montgomery (Lt. John Brickley), John Wayne (Lt. Rusty Ryan), Donna Reed (Lt. Sandy Davis), Jack Holt (Gen. Martin), Ward Bond (Boots Mulcahey), Louis Jean Heydt (Ohio, flyer in hospital), Marshall Thompson (Snake Gardner), Russell Simpson (Dad, chief of shipyard), Leon Ames (Maj. Morton), Paul Langton (Andy Andrews), Arthur Walsh (Jones), Donald Curtis (Shorty Long), Cameron Mitchell (George Cross), Jeff York (Tony Aiken), Murray Alper (Slug Mahan), Harry Tenbrook (Larsen), Jack Pennick (Doc Charlie), Charles Trowbridge (Adm. Blackwell), Robert Barrat (Gen. Douglas MacArthur), Bruce Kellogg (Tomkins), Tim Murdock (Ens. Brown), Vernon Steele (doctor), Trina Lowe (Gardner's girlfriend), Alex Havier (Benny), Eva March (nurse), Pedro de Cordoba (priest), Pacita Tod-Tod (nightclub singer), William B. Davidson

(hotel manager), Robert Emmett O'Conner (Silver Dollar bartender), Max Ong (mayor of Cebu), Bill Wilkerson (Sgt. Smith), John Carlyre (Lt. James), Philip Ahn (orderly), Betty Blythe (officer's wife), Kermit Maynard (airport officer), Stubby Kruger, Sammu Steon, Michael Kirby, Blake Edwards (boat crew), Wallace Ford, Tom Tyler, Frank Baker.

Brickley and Ryan pioneer PT-boats in combat during America's defeat in the Philippines.

1946? *In Memoriam Manuel Quezon.* c. 20 minutes. A print of this film, 16 mm Kodachrome, is among the John Ford Papers, Lilly Library, Indiana University, but it was not permitted that it be examined. Dan Ford thinks John Ford is responsible for it. Manuel Quezon was the first president of the Philippines, in 1935.

1946 *My Darling Clementine* (20th Century–Fox). 97 minutes. November. Director: John Ford. Producer: Samuel G. Engel. Scenarists: Engel, Winston Miller, from story by Sam Hellman, based on book *Wyatt Earp, Frontier Marshall*, by Stuart N. Lake. Photography: Joseph P. McDonald. Art directors: James Basevi, Lyle R. Wheeler. Set decorators: Thomas Little, Fred J. Rode. Costumes: René Hubert. Music: Cyril J. Mockridge. Editors: Dorothy Spencer, (uncredited) Darryl F. Zanuck. Special effects: Fred Sersen. Assistant director: William Eckhardt. Exteriors filmed in Monument Valley, May–June. With Henry Fonda (Wyatt Earp), Linda Darnell (Chihuahua), Victor Mature (Doc John Holliday), Walter Brennan (Old Man Clanton), Tim Holt (Virgil Earp), Ward Bond (Morgan Earp), Cathy Downs (Clementine Carter), Alan Mowbray (Granville Thorndyke), John Ireland (Billy Clanton), Grant Withers (Ike Clanton), Roy Roberts (Mayor), Jane Darwell (Kate Nelson), Russell Simpson (John Simpson), Francis Ford (Dad, old soldier), J. Farrell MacDonald (Mac, barman), Don Garner (James Earp), Ben Hall (barber), Arthur Walsh (hotel clerk), Jack Pennick, Robert Adler (stagecoach drivers), Louis Mercier (François), Mickey Simpson (Sam Clanton), Fred Libby (Phin Clanton), Harry Woods (Luke), Charles Stevens (Indian troublemaker), William B. Davidson (Oriental saloon owner), Earle Foxe (gambler), Aleth "Speed" Hansen (guitarist), Danny Borzage (accordionist),

Frank Conlan (pianist), Don Barclay (opera house owner), Mae Marsh (old lady going to church).

Based on myths of Wyatt Earp, Doc Holliday, and the Battle of the O. K. Corral. A remake of *Frontier Marshall* (Allan Dwan, 1939): remade as *Wichita* (Jacques Tourneur, 1955), *Gunfight at the O. K. Corral* (John Sturges, 1957), and others.

1947 *The Fugitive* (Argosy Pictures–RKO Radio). 104 minutes. November 3. Director: John Ford. Producers: Ford, Merian C. Cooper. Associate producer: Emilio Fernandez. Scenarist: Dudley Nichols, from novel *The Labyrinthine Ways* (or *The Power and the Glory*), by Graham Greene. Photography: Gabriel Figueroa. Art director: Alfred Ybarra. Set decorator: Manuel Parra. Music: Richard Hageman. Orchestration: Lucien. Editor: Jack Murray. Executive assistant: Jack Pennick. Directorial assistant: Melchor Ferrer. Assistant director: Jesse Hibbs. Filmed in forty-seven days on locations in Mexico and at Churubusco Studios, Mexico City. With Henry Fonda (A Fugitive), Dolores Del Rio (An Indian Woman), Pedro Armendariz (A Lieutenant of Police), Ward Bond (El Gringo), Leo Carrillo (A Chief of Police), John Qualen (A Refugee Doctor), Fortunio Bonanova (The Governor's Cousin), Chris-Pin Martin (An Organ Player), Miguel Inclan (A Hostage), Fernando Fernandez (A Singer), Jose I. Torvay (A Mexican), Melchor Ferrer.

A hunted priest struggles with his conscience.

1948 *Fort Apache* (Argosy Pictures–RKO Radio). 127 minutes. March 9. Director: John Ford. Producers: Ford, Merian C. Cooper. Scenarist: Frank S. Nugent, from story "Massacre," by James Warner Bellah. Photography: Archie Stout, William Clothier (second unit). Art director: James Basevi. Set decorator: Joe Kish. Music: Richard Hageman. Editor: Jack Murray. Special effects: Dave Koehler. Costumes: Michael Meyers, Ann Peck. Camera: Eddie Fitzgerald. Script supervisor: Meta Sterne. Choreography: Kenny Williams. Technical consultants: Maj. Philip Kieffer, Katharine Spaatz. Research editor: Katharine Clifton. Costume research: D. R. O. Hatswell. Second-unit director: Cliff Lyons. Production manager: Bernard McEveety. Assistant directors: Lowell

Farrell, Jack Pennick. Filmed in forty-five days on locations in Utah and Monument Valley, June 1947. With John Wayne (Capt. Kirby York), Henry Fonda (Lt. Col. Owen Thursday), Shirley Temple (Philadelphia Thursday), John Agar (Lt. Michael O'Rourke), Ward Bond (Sgt. Maj. O'Rourke), George O'Brien (Capt. Sam Collingwood), Victor McLaglen (Sgt. Mulcahy), Pedro Armendariz (Sgt. Beaufort), Anna Lee (Mrs. Collingwood), Irene Rich (Mrs. O'Rourke), Guy Kibbee (Dr. Wilkens), Grant Withers (Silas Meachum), Miguel Inclan (Cochise), Jack Pennick (Sgt. Shattuck), Mae Marsh (Mrs. Gates), Dick Foran (Sgt. Quincannon), Frank Ferguson (newspaperman), Francis Ford (bartender), Ray Hyke (Gates), Movita Castenada (Guadalupe), Hank Worden (Southern recruit), Harry Tenbrook (courier), Mary Gordon (woman in stagecoach), Frank Baker, Ben Johnson (stunt riders).

Life on a calvalry post, 1876.

†1948 *Red River* (Monterey Productions–United Artists). Director: Howard Hawks. With John Wayne, Montgomery Clift, Joanne Dru.

Hawks was having great difficulties getting the footage he had shot worked into a coherent film. Ford made numerous editing suggestions, including the use of a narrator.

1948 *3 Godfathers* (Argosy Pictures–Metro-Goldwyn-Mayer). Technicolor. 106 minutes. December 1. Director: John Ford. Producers: Ford, Merian C. Cooper. Scenarists: Laurence Stallings, Frank S. Nugent, from story by Peter B. Kyne. Photography: Winton C. Hoch, Charles P. Boyle (second unit). Art director: James Basevi. Set decorator: Joe Kish. Music: Richard Hageman. Editor: Jack Murray. Color consultants: Natalie Kalmus, Morgan Padelford. Camera: Harvey Gould, Edward Fitzgerald (second unit). Production manager: Lowell Farrell. Assistant directors: Wingate Smith, Edward O'Fearna. Filmed in thirty-two days on locations in the Mojave Desert. With John Wayne (Robert Marmaduke Sangster Hightower), Pedro Armendariz (Pedro Roca Fuerte), Harry Carey, Jr. (William Kearney, "the Abilene Kid"), Ward Bond (Perley "Buck" Sweet), Mildred Natwick (mother), Charles Halton (Mr. Latham), Jane Darwell (Miss Florie),

Mae Marsh (Mrs. Perley Sweet), Guy Kibbee (judge), Dorothy Ford (Ruby Latham), Ben Johnson, Michael Dugan, Don Summers (patrolman), Fred Libby (deputy sheriff), Hank Worden (deputy sheriff), Jack Pennick (Luke, train conductor), Francis Ford (drunk), Ruth Clifford (woman in bar).

Three bandits fleeing across a desert adopt a baby.

Remake of Ford's *Marked Men* (1919), G. M. Anderson's *Bronco Billy and the Baby* (1915), Wyler's *Hell's Heroes* (1929), and Boleslawski's *Three Godfathers* (1936).

†1949 *What Price Glory* Stage production. Supervisor: John Ford. Assistant supervisor: George O'Brien. Directed by: Ralph Murphy. Produced by the Masquers Club of Hollywood for the Military Order of the Purple Heart. Producer: Harry Joe Brown. Assistant: Eddie Oxford. Management: Jacques Pierre. Stage manager: G. Pat Collins. Performed: February 22, 1949, Long Beach; February 24, 1949, San Jose; February 25, 1949, Oakland; February 27, 1949, San Francisco; March 1, 1949, Pasadena; March 2, 1949, Los Angeles. With Ward Bond (Flagg), Pat O'Brien (Quirt), George O'Brien, Alan Hale, Sr., Robert Armstrong, Wallace Ford, Oliver (Babe) Hardy, Charles Kemper, Henry O'Neill, Jimmy Lydon, Herbert Rawlinson, Louis Alberni, Harry Carey, Jr., Forrest Tucker, Fred Graham, Larry Blake, Michael J. Dugan, Don Summers, G. Pat Collins, Gregory Peck, John Wayne, Maureen O'Hara.

Pat O'Brien: "It was always Ford's wish to do a stage play because he loved actors for the theater. . . . It was all for charity. None of us got a quarter." (Karyn Kay and Gerald Peary, "Talking to Pat O'Brien," *Velvet Light Trap*, Fall 1975.) The proceeds, $30,000, went to build a clubhouse for paraplegic veterans. Ford was then president of the Purple Heart organization.

†1949 *Mighty Joe Young* (Argosy Pictures–RKO Radio). 94 minutes. Director: Ernest B. Schoedsack. Producers: John Ford, Merian C. Cooper. Scenarist: Ruth Rose, from story by Cooper. Photography: J. Roy Hunt. Art director: James Basevi. With Terry Moore, Ben Johnson, Robert Armstrong, Frank McHugh, Regis Toomey.

"I had nothing to do with it," said Ford to Bogdanovich.

1949 *She Wore a Yellow Ribbon* (Argosy Pictures–RKO Radio). Technicolor. 103 minutes. October 22. Director: John Ford. Producers: Ford, Merian C. Cooper. Associate producer: Lowell Farrell. Scenarists: Frank S. Nugent, Laurence Stallings, from story "War Party," by James Warner Bellah. Photography: Winton C. Hoch, Charles P. Boyle (second unit). Art director: James Basevi. Set decorator: Joe Kish. Music: Richard Hageman. Conductor: Constantin Bakaleinikoff. Editor: Jack Murray. Assistant editor: Barbara Ford. Second-unit director: Cliff Lyons. Assistant directors: Wingate Smith, Edward O'Fearna. Technical consultants: Cliff Lyons, Maj. Philip Kieffer. Color consultants: Natalie Kalmus, Morgan Padelford. Special effects: Jack Caffee. Costumes: Michael Meyers, Ann Peck. Camera: Harvey Gould. Historical technical advisor: D. R. O. Hatswell. Filmed in thirty-two days on locations in Monument Valley, October 1948. With John Wayne (Capt. Nathan Brittles), Joanne Dru (Olivia), John Agar (Lt. Flint Cohill), Ben Johnson (Sgt. Tyree), Harry Carey, Jr. (Lt. Pennell), Victor McLaglen (Sgt. Quincannon), Mildred Natwick (Mrs. Abbey Allshard), George O'Brien (Maj. Mack Allshard), Arthur Shields (Dr. O'Laughlin), Francis Ford (barman, Irish), Harry Woods (Karl Rynders), Chief Big Tree (Pony That Walks), Noble Johnson (Red Shirt), Cliff Lyons (Trooper Cliff), Tom Tyler (Quayne), Michael Dugan (Hochbauer), Mickey Simpson (Wagner), Fred Graham (Hench), Frank McGrath (trumpeter), Don Summers (Jenkins), Fred Libby (Cpl. Krumrein), Jack Pennick (Sgt. Major), Billy Jones (courier), Bill Gettinger (officer), Fred Kennedy (Badger), Rudy Bowman (Pvt. Smith), Post Park (officer), Ray Hyke (McCarthy), Lee Bradley (interpreter), Chief Sky Eagle, Dan White, Frank Baker.

An aging captain leads a final cavalry patrol, 1876.

Oscar: Photography—Winton C. Hoch.

†1949 *Pinky* (20th Century–Fox). 102 minutes. November. Director: Elia Kazan. Producer: Darryl F. Zanuck. Scenarists: Philip Dunne, Dudley Nichols, from novel *Quality*, by Cid Ricketts Summer.

Photography: Joseph MacDonald. Music: Alfred Newman. Assistant director: Wingate Smith. With Jeanne Crain, Ethel Barrymore, Ethel Waters, William Lundigan, Basil Ruysdael.

A Negro girl passes for white.

Ford prepared the production and worked a day on it before taking ill, although illness was apparently a pretext for his withdrawal, desired both by himself and Zanuck. Nothing in the finished film seems Fordian.

1950 *When Willie Comes Marching Home* (20th Century–Fox). 82 minutes. February. Director: John Ford. Producer: Fred Kohlmar. Scenarists: Mary Loos, Richard Sale, from story "When Leo Comes Marching Home," by Sy Gomberg. Photography: Leo Tover. Art directors: Lyle R. Wheeler, Chester Gore. Set decorators: Thomas Little, Bruce MacDonald. Music: Alfred Newman. Editor: James B. Clark. Assistant director: Wingate Smith. Production manager: Joe Behm. Special effects: James B. Clarke. Choreography: Kenny Williams. Camera: Till Gabbani. Costumes: Charles LeMaire, Travilla. Script supervisor: Meta Sterne. With Dan Dailey (Bill Kluggs), Corinne Calvet (Yvonne), Colleen Townsend (Marge Fettles), Lloyd Corrigan (Major Adams), William Demarest (Herman Kluggs), James Lydon (Charles Fettles), Evelyn Varden (Gertrude Kluggs), Kenny Williams (musician), Lee Clark (musician), Charles Halton (Mr. Fettles), Mae Marsh (Mrs. Fettles), Jack Pennick (sergeant), Mickey Simpson (MP Kerrigan), Frank Pershing (Maj. Bickford), Don Summers (MP Sherve), Gil Herman (Lt. Comdr. Crown), Peter Ortiz (Pierre), Luis Alberni (barman), John Shulick (pilot), Clarke Gordon, Robin Hughes (marine officers), Cecil Weston (Mrs. Barnes), Harry Tenbrook (Joe, taxi driver), Russ Clark (Sgt. Wilson), George Spaulding (Judge Tate), James Eagle (reporter), Harry Strang (sergeant), George Magrill (chief petty officer), Hank Worden (choir leader), John McKee (pilot), Larry Keating (Gen. G. Reeding), Dan Riss (Gen. Adams), Robert Einer (Lt. Bagley), Russ Conway (Maj. J. A. White), Whit Bissell (Lt. Handley), Ann Codee (French instructor), Ray Hyke (Maj. Crawford), Gene Collins (Andy), James Flavin (Gen. Brevort), David McMahon (Col. Ainsley), Charles Trowbridge (Gen.

Merrill), Kenneth Tobey (Lt. K. Geiger), Maj. Sam Harris (hospital patient), Alberto Morin, Louis Mercier (resistance fighters), Paul Harvey (officer), James Waters, Ken Lynch, Frank Baker, J. Farrell MacDonald, Vera Miles.

Comedy about small-town war fever.

1950 *Wagon Master* (Argosy Pictures–RKO Radio). 86 minutes. April 19. Director: John Ford. Producers: Ford, Merian C. Cooper. Associate producer: Lowell Farrell. Writers: Frank S. Nugent, Patrick Ford. Photography: Bert Glennon, Archie Stout (second unit). Art director: James Basevi. Set decorator: Joe Kish. Music: Richard Hageman. Songs: "Wagons West," "Rollin' Shadows in the Dust," "Song of the Wagon Master," "Chuck A-Walla-Swing," by Stan Jones, sung by the Sons of the Pioneers. Editor: Jack Murray. Assistant editor: Barbara Ford. Second-unit director: Cliff Lyons. Assistant director: Wingate Smith. Costumes: Wes Jeffries, Adele Parmenter. Special effects: Jack Caffee. Technical consultant: D. R. O. Hatswell. Filmed in Monument Valley and in Professor Valley, Utah. With Ben Johnson (Travis Blue), Harry Carey, Jr. (Sandy Owens), Joanne Dru (Denver), Ward Bond (Elder Wiggs), Charles Kemper (Uncle Shiloh Clegg), Alan Mowbray (Dr. A. Locksley Hall), Jane Darwell (Sister Ledeyard), Ruth Clifford (Fleuretty Phyffe), Russell Simpson (Adam Perkins), Kathleen O'Malley (Prudence Perkins), James Arness (Floyd Clegg), Fred Libby (Reese Clegg), Hank Worden (Luke Clegg), Mickey Simpson (Jesse Clegg), Francis Ford (Mr. Peachtree), Cliff Lyons (sheriff of Crystal City), Don Summers (Sam Jenkins), Movita Castenada (young Navajo girl), Jim Thorpe (Navajo), Chuck Haywood (Jackson).

A Mormon wagon train, 1849.

1950 *Rio Grande* (Argosy Pictures–Republic). 105 minutes. November 15. Director: John Ford. Producers: Ford, Merian C. Cooper. Scenarist: James Kevin McGuinness, from story "Mission with No Record," by James Warner Bellah. Photography: Bert Glennon, Archie Stout (second unit). Art director: Frank Hotaling. Set decorators: John McCarthy, Jr., Charles Thompson. Music: Victor Young. Songs, sung by the Sons of the

Pioneers: "My Gal Is Purple," "Footsore Cavalry," "Yellow Stripes," by Stan Jones; "Aha, San Antone," by Dale Evans; "Cattle Call," by Tex Owens; and "Down by the Glen Side," "You're in the Army Now." Editor: Jack Murray. Assistant editor: Barbara Ford. Second-unit director: Cliff Lyons. Costumes: Adele Palmer. Special effects: Howard and Theodore Lydecker. Filmed in Monument Valley, June–July. With John Wayne (Lt. Col. Kirby Yorke), Maureen O'Hara (Mrs. Yorke), Ben Johnson (Trooper Tyree), Claude Jarman, Jr. (Trooper Jeff Yorke), Harry Carey, Jr. (Trooper Daniel Boone), Chill Wills (Dr. Wilkins), J. Carroll Naish (Gen. Philip Sheridan), Victor McLaglen (Sgt. Quincannon), Grant Withers (deputy marshall), Peter Ortiz (Capt. St. Jacques), Steve Pendleton (Capt. Prescott), Karolyn Grimes (Margaret Mary), Alberto Morin (lieutenant), Stan Jones (sergeant), Fred Kennedy (Heinze), Jack Pennick, Pat Wayne, Chuck Roberson, The Sons of the Pioneers (regimental singers): Ken Curtis, Hugh Farr, Karl Farr, Lloyd Perryman, Shug Fisher, Tom Doss.

A family reunites on a cavalry post.

†1950 *The Bullfighter and the Lady* (Republic). 87 minutes. Director: Budd Boetticher. With Robert Stack.

Ford assisted Boetticher in editing the picture.

1951 *This Is Korea!* (U.S. Navy–Republic). 3-Strip Trucolor. 50 minutes. August 10. Director: Rear Adm. John Ford, USNR. Narration: James Warner Bellah, Frank Nugent, Ford. Photography: Charles Bohuy, Bob Rhea, Mark Armistead. With the voices of John Ireland, Irving Pichel, George O'Brien.

An on-the-spot documentary of the marines in Korea.

1952 *The Quiet Man* (Argosy Pictures–Republic). Technicolor. 129 minutes. September 14. Director: John Ford. Producers: Ford, Merian C. Cooper, and (uncredited, Michael Killanin). Scenarists: Frank S. Nugent, from story by Maurice Walsh (*The Saturday Evening Post*, February 11, 1933), adapted by Richard Llewellyn (uncredited). Photography: Winton C. Hoch, Archie Stout (second unit). Art director: Frank Hotaling. Set decorators: John McCarthy, Jr., Charles Tompson. Music: Victor

Young. Songs: "The Isle of Innisfree," by Richard Farrelly; "Galway Bay," by Dr. Arthur Colahan, Michael Donovan; "The Humour Is on Me Now," by Richard Haywood; "The Young May Moon," by Thomas Moore; and "The Wild Colonial Boy," "Mush-Mush-Mush." Editor: Jack Murray. Assistant editor: Barbara Ford. Second-unit directors (uncredited): John Wayne, Patrick Ford. Assistant director: Andrew McLaglen. Color consultant: Francis Cugat. Costumes: Adele Palmer. Exteriors filmed in Ireland, June–July. With John Wayne (Sean Thornton), Maureen O'Hara (Mary Kate Danaher), Barry Fitzgerald (Michaeleen Og Flynn), Ward Bond (Fr. Peter Lonergan), Victor McLaglen (Red Will Danaher), Mildred Natwick (Mrs. Sarah Tillane), Francis Ford (Dan Tobin), Eileen Crowe (Mrs. Elizabeth Playfair), May Craig (woman at railroad station), Arthur Shields (Rev. Cyril Playfair), Charles FitzSimmons (Forbes), Sean McClory (Owen Glynn), James Lilburn (Fr. Paul), Jack McGowran (Feeney), Ken Curtis (Dermot Fahy), Mae Marsh (Fr. Paul's mother), Harry Tenbrook (policeman), Maj. Sam Harris (general), Joseph O'Dea (guard), Eric Gorman (railroad conductor), Kevin Lawless (fireman), Paddy O'Donnell (porter), Webb Overlander (railroad station chief), Hank Worden (trainer in flashback), Harry Tyler (Pat Cohen), Don Hatswell (Guppy), David H. Hughes (constable), Douglas Evans (physician), Jack Roper (boxer), Al Murphy (referee), Patrick Wayne, Antonia Wayne, Melinda Wayne, Michael Wayne (children at race), Pat O'Malley, Bob Perry, Frank Baker.

A Yank returns to his birthland in Ireland.

Awards: See text, page 278–279.

1952 *What Price Glory* (20th Century–Fox). Technicolor. 111 minutes. August. Director: John Ford. Producer: Sol C. Siegel. Scenarists: Phoebe and Henry Ephron, from play by Maxwell Anderson, Laurence Stallings. Photography: Joseph MacDonald. Art directors: Lyle R. Wheeler, George W. Davis. Set decorators: Thomas Little, Stuart A. Reiss. Music: Alfred Newman. Song: "My Love, My Life," by Jay Livingston, Roy Evans. Editor: Dorothy Spencer. Color consultant: Leonard Doss. Costumes: Charles LeMaire, Edward Stevenson. Special effects: Ray Kellogg. Choreography: Billy

Daniel. With James Cagney (Capt. Flagg), Corinne Calvet (Charmaine), Dan Dailey (Sgt. Quirt), William Demarest (Cpl. Kiper), Craig Hill (Lt. Aldrich), Robert Wagner (Lewisohn), Marisa Pavan (Nichole Bouchard), Casey Adams (Lt. Moore), James Gleason (Gen. Cokely), Wally Vernon (Lipinsky), Henry Letondal (Cognac Pete), Fred Libby (Lt. Schmidt), Ray Hyke (Mulcahy), Paul Fix (Gowdy), James Lilburn (young soldier), Henry Morgan (Morgan), Dan Borzage (Gilbert), Bill Henry (Holsen), Henry "Bomber" Kulkovich (company cook), Jack Pennick (Ferguson), Ann Codee (nun), Stanley Johnson (Lt. Cunningham), Tom Tyler (Capt. Davis), Olga André (Sister Clotilde), Barry Norton (priest), Luis Alberni (the great uncle), Torben Meyer (mayor), Alfred Zeisler (English colonel), George Bruggeman (English lieutenant), Scott Forbes (Lt. Bennett), Sean McClory (Lt. Austin), Charles FitzSimmons (Capt. Wickham), Louis Mercier (Bouchard), Mickey Simpson (MP), Peter Ortiz, Paul Guilfoyle.

World War I in France.

1953 *The Sun Shines Bright* (Argosy Pictures–Republic). 90 minutes. May 2. Director: John Ford. Producers: Ford, Merian C. Cooper. Scenarist: Laurence Stallings, from stories "The Sun Shines Bright," "The Mob from Massac," "The Lord Provides," by Irvin S. Cobb. Photography: Archie Stout. Art director: Frank Hotaling. Set decorators: John McCarthy, Jr., George Milo. Costumes: Adele Palmer. Music: Victor Young. Editor: Jack Murray. Assistant editor: Barbara Ford. Assistant director: Wingate Smith. Filmed in 1952. With Charles Winninger (Judge William Pittman Priest), Arleen Whelan (Lucy Lee Lake), John Russell (Ashby Corwin), Stepin Fetchit (Jeff Poindexter), Russell Simpson (Dr. Lewt Lake), Ludwig Stossel (Herman Felsburg), Francis Ford (Brother Finney), Paul Hurst (Sgt. Jimmy Bagby), Mitchell Lewis (Andy Radcliffe), Grant Withers (Buck), Milburn Stone (Horace K. Maydew), Dorothy Jordan (Lucy's mother), Elzie Emanuel (U. S. Grant Woodford), Henry O'Neill (Jody Habersham), Slim Pickens (Sterling), James Kirkwood (Gen. Fairfield), Mae Marsh (Amora's companion), Jane Darwell (Amora Ratchitt), Ernest Whitman (Uncle Pleasant Woodford), Trevor Bardette (Rufe, leader of lynch

mob), Hal Baylor (his son), Eva March (Mallie Cramp), Clarence Muse (Uncle Zack), Jack Pennick (Beaker), Ken Williams, Patrick Wayne (cadet).

Portrait of a 1905 Kentucky town.

1953 *Mogambo* (Metro-Goldwyn-Mayer). Technicolor. 116 minutes. October 9. Director: John Ford. Producer: Sam Zimbalist. Scenarist: John Lee Mahin, from play "Red Dust," by Wilson Collison. Photography: Robert Surtees, Fredrick A. Young. Art director: Alfred Junge. Costumes: Helen Rose. Editor: Frank Clarke. Second-unit directors: Richard Rossen, Yakima Canutt, James C. Havens. Assistant directors: Wingate Smith, Cecil Ford. Color consultant: Joan Bridge. Special effects: Tom Howard. Safari director: Carr Hartley, superintendent of Mount Kenya reserve. Interiors filmed in London. Exteriors filmed in Tanganyika, Kenya, Uganda, French Equatorial Africa, October–February. With Clark Gable (Victor Marswell), Ava Gardner (Eloise Y. Kelly), Grace Kelly (Linda Nordley), Donald Sinden (Donald Nordley), Philip Stainton (John Brown Pryce), Erick Pohlmann (Leon Boltchak), Laurence Naismith (Skipper John), Dennis O'Dea (Fr. Joseph), Asa Etula (native male), Wagenia Tribe of Belgian Congo, Smuru Tribe of Kenya Colony, Bahaya Tribe of Tanganyika, M'Beti Tribe of French Equatorial Africa.

A game hunter, a playgirl, and a sheltered English couple on safari in Africa.

Remake of Victor Fleming's *Red Dust* (1932). In Vincente Minnelli's *The Courtship of Eddie's Father* (1963), Glenn Ford sees a scene from *Mogambo* on TV (Gable and Kelly by a waterfall.)

†1954 *Hondo* (Wayne-Fellows–Warner Brothers). Warnercolor /3-D. 83 minutes. December. Director: John Farrow. Producer: Robert Fellows. Scenarist: James Edward Grant, from story by Louis L'Amour. Photography: Robert Burks, Archie Stout. With John Wayne, Geraldine Page, Ward Bond.

Two shots, only, were directed by Ford—of a troop of cavalry that Wayne sees when he visits an army post—but they stand out in this film like Delacroixes in a gallery of *TV Guide* covers.

1955 *The Long Gray Line* (Rota Productions–Columbia). Technicolor /

Cinemascope. 138 minutes. February 9. Director: John Ford. Producer: Robert Arthur. Scenarist: Edward Hope, from autobiography *Bringing up the Brass*, by Marty Maher with Nardi Reeder Champion. Photography: Charles Lawton, Jr. Art director: Robert Peterson. Set decorator: Frank Tuttle. Music adaptation: George Duning. Music conductor: Morris Stoloff. Editor: William Lyon. Assistant directors: Wingate Smith, Jack Corrick. Costumes: Jean Louis. Color consultant: Francis Cugat. Filmed at West Point, March–May 1954. With Tyrone Power (Martin Maher), Maureen O'Hara (Mary O'Donnell), Robert Francis (James Sunstrom, Jr.), Donald Crisp (Old Martin), Ward Bond (Capt. Herman J. Koehler), Betsy Palmer (Kitty Carter), Phil Carey (Charles Dotson), William Leslie (Red Sundstrom), Harry Carey, Jr. (Dwight Eisenhower), Patrick Wayne (Cherub Overton), Sean McClory (Dinny Maher), Peter Graves (Sgt. Rudolph Heinz), Milburn Stone (Capt. John Pershing), Erin O'Brien-Moore (Mrs. Koehler), Walter D. Ehlers (Mike Shannon), Don Barclay (Maj. Thomas), Martin Milner (Jom O'Carberry), Chuck Courtney (Whitey Larson), Willis Bouchey (doctor), Jack Pennick (Tommy, sergeant).

Fifty years of an Irish immigrant at West Point.

1955 *The Red, White and Blue Line* (U.S. Treasury Dept.–Columbia). Technicolor / Cinemascope. 10 minutes. Director: John Ford (?). Writer: Edward Hope. Photography: Charles Lawton, Jr. Narrator: Ward Bond.

A savings bond promotional made on set of *The Long Gray Line* and featuring, according to Joseph McBride, about seven minutes from that picture, plus scenes on set of cast at supper table, discussing bonds, during which Donald Crisp serves stew.

†1955 *Mister Roberts* (Orange Productions–Warner Brothers). Warnercolor / Cinemascope. 123 minutes. July 30. Directors: John Ford, Mervyn LeRoy, and (uncredited) Joshua Logan. Producer: Leland Hayward. Scenarists: Frank Nugent, Joshua Logan, from play by Logan, Thomas Heggen, and novel by Heggen. Photography: Winton C. Hoch. Art director: Art Loel. Set decorator: William L. Kuehl. Music: Franz Waxman.

Editor: Jack Murray. Assistant director: Wingate Smith. Costumes: Moss Mabry. Production manager: Norman Cook. Technical consultants: Adm. John Dale Price, USN, Ret., Comdr. Merle MacBain, USN. Exteriors filmed in the Pacific, Midway Island, September 1954. With Henry Fonda (Lt. (jg) Roberts), James Cagney (captain), Jack Lemmon (Ens. Frank Thurlowe Pulver), William Powell (Doc), Ward Bond (CPO Dowdy), Betsey Palmer (Lt. Ann Girard), Phil Carey (Mannion), Nick Adams (Reber), Harry Carey, Jr. (Stefanowski), Ken Curtis (Dolan), Frank Aletter (Gerhart), Fritz Ford (Lidstrom), Buck Kartalian (Mason), William Henry (Lt. Billings), William Hudson (Olson), Studdy Kruger (Schlemmer), Harry Tenbrook (Cookie), Perry Lopez (Rodriguez), Robert Roark (Insigna), Pat Wayne (Bookser), Tige Andrews (Wiley), Jim Maloney (Kennedy), Denny Niles (Gilbert), Francis Conner (Johnson), Shug Fisher (Cochran), Danny Borzage (Jonesey), Jim Murphy (Taylor), Kathleen O'Malley, Maura Murphy, Mimi Doyle, Jeanne Murray-Vanderbilt, Lonnie Pierce (nurses), Martin Milner (shore patrol officer), Gregory Walcott (shore patrolman), James Flavin (MP), Jack Pennick (marine sergeant), Duke Kahanamoko (native chief).

Life on a backwater cargo boat, World War II.

1955 *Rookie of the Year* (Hal Roach Studios, episode for the *Screen Directors Playhouse* TV series). 29 minutes. December. Director: John Ford. Scenarist: Frank S. Nugent. Photography: Hal Mohr. Filmed in summer 1955. With John Wayne (Mike Cronin), Vera Miles (Ruth Delbert), Pat Wayne (Lyn Goodhue), Ward Bond (Larry Goodhue, alias Buck Garrison), James Gleason (Ed Shaeffer), Willis Bouchey (Mr. Cully, newspaper editor), Henry Tyler (Wright), William Forrest (Walker), Robert Leyden (Willie). John Ford appears in the introduction, spotlit on a director's chair, with baseball gear.

A cynical newsman thinks he has discovered a great story, one that will liberate him from ten years with the "Emeryville Post-Gazette": the Rookie of the Year is the son of Buck Garrison, a great player who took a bribe. But he withholds the story, out of decency to Buck, and lands a tour of the Orient.

Rapidly paced, loaded with invention, fantastic dialogue, and great caricatures.

1955 *The Bamboo Cross* (Lewman Ltd.–Revue; episode for the *Fireside Theatre* TV series). 27 minutes. December 6. Director: John Ford. Producer: William Asher. Scenarist: Laurence Stallings, from play by Theophane Lee. Photographer: John MacBurnie. Art director: Martin Obzina. Set decorator: James S. Redd. Music supervisor: Stanley Wilson. Supervising editor: Richard G. Wray. Assistant director: Wingate Smith. Filmed November 7–11. With Jane Wyman (Sister Regina), Betty Lynn (Sister Anne), Soo Yong (Sichi Sao), Jim Hong (Mark Chu), Judy Wong (Tanya), Don Summers (Ho Kwong), Kurt Katch (King Fat), Pat O'Malley (priest), Frank Baker.

Maryknoll nuns are captured by Chinese Communists eager to prove the "unmarried ladies" kill babies with "poisoned cakes" (i.e., Communion wafers). Sister Regina oozes pietism, the commissar is rarely less than apoplectic—until a servant, who had joined the Communists to learn "the truth of the poverty and ignorance of my people," leaps into the frame brandishing a long knife. The commissar dies gurgling percussively off-camera, and the nuns are saved.

The low point of Ford's career.

1956 *The Searchers* (C. V. Whitney Pictures–Warner Brothers). Technicolor / Vista Vision. 119 minutes. May 26. Director: John Ford. Producers: Merian C. Cooper, C. V. Whitney. Scenarist: Frank S. Nugent, from novel by Alan LeMay. Associate producer: Patrick Ford. Photography: Winton C. Hoch, Alfred Gilks (second unit). Art directors: Frank Hotaling, James Basevi. Set decorator: Victor Gangelin. Music: Max Steiner. Title song: Stan Jones. Editor: Jack Murray. Production supervisor: Lowell Farrell. Assistant director: Wingate Smith. Color consultant: James Gooch. Costumes: Frank Beetson (M), Ann Peck (F). Special effects: George Brown. Script supervisor: Robert Gary. Filmed in Colorado and Monument Valley, summer and fall 1955. With John Wayne (Ethan Edwards), Jeffrey Hunter (Martin Pawley), Vera Miles (Laurie Jorgensen), Ward Bond (Capt. Rev. Samuel Clayton), Natalie Wood (Debbie Edwards), John Qualen (Lars Jorgensen),

Olive Carey (Mrs. Jorgensen), Henry Brandon (Chief Scar), Ken Curtis (Charlie McCorry), Harry Carey, Jr. (Brad Jorgensen), Antonio Moreno (Emilio Figueroa), Hank Worden (Mose Harper), Lana Wood (Debbie as child), Walter Coy (Aaron Edwards), Dorothy Jordan (Martha Edwards), Pippa Scott (Lucy Edwards), Pat Wayne (Lt. Greenhill), Beulah Archuletta (Look), Jack Pennick (private), Peter Mamokos (Futterman), Bill Steele (Nesby), Cliff Lyons (Col. Greenhill), Chuck Roberson (man at wedding), Ruth Clifford (deranged woman at fort), Mae Marsh (woman at fort), Dan Borzage (accordionist at funeral), Billy Cartledge, Chuck Hayward, Slim Hightower, Fred Kennedy, Frank McGrath, Dale van Sickle, Henry Wills, Terry Wilson (stuntman), Away Luna, Billy Yellow, Bob Many Mules, Exactly Sonnie Betsuie, Feather Hat, Jr., Harry Black Horse, Jack Tin Horn, Many Mules Son, Percy Shooting Star, Pete Grey Eyes, Pipe Line Begishe, Smile White Sheep (Comanche).

Seven years roaming the West in search of a girl kidnapped by Comanche.

1957 *The Rising of the Moon* (Four Province Productions–Warner Brothers). 81 minutes. May 16 (Dublin); June (G.B.); August 10 (U.S.). Director: John Ford. Producer: Michael Killanin. Scenarist: Frank S. Nugent, from stories. Photography: Robert Krasker. Art director: Ray Simm. Costumes: Jimmy Bourke. Music: Eamonn O'Gallagher. Editor: Michael Gordon. Assistant editor: Dennies Bertera. Continuity: Angela Martell. Production manager: Teddy Joseph. Camera: Dennys Coop. Technical consultants: Earnon O'Malley, Lennox Robinson, Patrick Scott. Filmed in Ireland, spring 1956. Introduced by Tyrone Power.

"The Majesty of the Law," from story by Frank O'Connor. 23 minutes, 24 seconds. Noel Purcell (Dan O'Flaherty), Cyril Cusack (Inspector Michael Dillon), Jack McGowran (the poteen maker: Mickey J.), Eric Gorman, Paul Farrell (neighbors), John Cowley (the Gombeen Man).

An old farmer goes to jail to defend his honor.

"A Minute's Wait," from play by Michael J. McHugh. 23 minutes, 43 seconds. Jimmy O'Dea (porter), Tony Quinn (railroad station chief), Paul Farrell (chauffeur), J. G. Devlin (guard), Michael Trubshawe (Col. Frobisher), Anita Sharp

Bolster (Mrs. Frobisher), Maureen Porter (barmaid), Maureen O'Connell (May Ann McMahon), May Craig (May's aunt), Michael O'Duffy (singer), Ann Dalton (fisherman's wife), Kevin Casey (Mr. McTigue).

A train stops at a station.

"1921," from play "The Rising of the Moon," by Lady Gregory. 27 minutes, 53 seconds. Dennis O'Dea (police sergeant), Eileen Crowe (his wife), Maurice Good (P. C. O'Grady), Frank Lawton (major), Edward Lexy (RQMS), Donal Donnelly (Sean Curran), Joseph O'Dea (chief of guards), Dennis Bennan, David Marlowe, Dennis Franks (English officers), Doreen Madden, Maureen Cusack (false nuns), Maureen Delaney (old woman), Martin Thornton (sergeant), John Horan (bill poster), Joe Hone, John Comeford, Mafra McDonagh (IRA men), and members of the Abbey Theatre Company.

A patriot escapes during 1921 rebellion. (This episode resembles Francis Ford's 1916 *The Cry of Erin*.)

Ford did not personally direct the framing scenes with Tyrone Power.

1957 *The Wings of Eagles* (Metro-Goldwyn-Mayer). Metrocolor. 110 minutes. February 22. Director: John Ford. Producer: Charles Schnee. Associate producer: James E. Newcom. Scenarists: Frank Fenton, William Wister Haines, based on life and writings of Comdr. Frank W. Wead, USN. Photography: Paul C. Vogel. Art directors: William A. Horning, Malcolm Brown. Set decorators: Edwin B. Willis, Keogh Gleason. Maureen O'Hara's wardrobe: Walter Plunkett. Music: Jeff Alexander. Editor: Gene Ruggiero. Aerial stunts: Paul Mantz. Recording supervisor: Dr. Wesley G. Miller. Makeup: William Tuttle. Assistant director: Wingate Smith. Color consultant: Charles K. Hagedon. Technical advisors: Adm. John Dale Price, USN, Ret., Dr. John Keye. Special effects: A. Arnold Gillespie, Warren Newcombe. Filmed in August 1956. With John Wayne (Frank W. "Spig" Wead), Maureen O'Hara (Minne Wead), Dan Dailey (Carson), Ward Bond (John Dodge), Ken Curtis (John Dale Price), Edmund Lowe (Adm. Moffett), Kenneth Tobey (Herbert Allen Hazard), James Todd (Jack Travis), Barry Kelley (Capt. Jock Clark), Sig Ruman (manager), Henry O'Neill (Capt. Spear), Willis Bouchey (Barton), Dorothy Jordan (Rose

Brentmann), Peter Ortiz (Lt. Charles Dexter), Louis Jean Heydt (Dr. John Keye), Tige Andrews (Arizona Pincus), Dan Borzage (Pete), William Tracy (air force officer), Harlan Warde (executive officer), Jack Pennick (Joe), Bill Henry (naval aide), Alberto Morin (second manager), Mimi Gibson (Lila Wead), Evelyn Rudie (Doris Wead), Charles Trowbridge (Adm. Crown), Mae Marsh (Nurse Crumley), Janet Lake (nurse), Fred Graham (officer in brawl), Stuart Holmes (producer), Olive Carey (Bridy O'Faolain), Maj. Sam Harris (patient), May McEvoy (nurse), William Paul Lowery (Wead's baby, Commodore), Chuck Roberson (officer), Cliff Lyons, Veda Ann Borg, Christopher James.

Story of a navy man between the wars who became a screenwriter after being paralyzed.

1957 *The Growler Story* (U.S. Navy). Eastmancolor. 22 minutes. Director: John Ford. Producer: Mark Armistead. Photography: Pacific Fleet Combat Camera Group. Editor: Jack Murray. Assistant editor: Barbara Ford. Narrator: Dan Dailey. Filmed in the Pacific, November 1956 (Navy Film No. MN 8679). With Ward Bond (Quincannon), Ken Curtis (Capt. Howard W. Gilmore), and navy personnel, wives, and children.

Made for navy personnel. An actual World War II incident. Capt. Gilmore bids farewell to his tearful wife and two children; Quincannon leaves his wife and eight children. A dockside band plays "Far Away Places," wives wave anxiously, flower wreaths are thrown into the water as the submarine sails out of Pearl Harbor. At sea the log records the sinking of a freighter, the rescue of downed flyers, until one day an enemy vessel emerges from the fog: Gilmore is wounded but gives the order to submerge, saving the ship at the cost of his life. Back at Pearl his wife receives his Medal of Honor and a wreath floats from *The Growler*'s prow. Gilmore is a background character, as Ford lavishes cornball sentimentality on Ward Bond's Quincannon, whose eight kids stand in line from tallest to shortest to salute goodbye, who hears of a ninth child coming while giving blood, and who grins broadly when *The Growler* gets her first kill. Such (inhumane?) exuberance is typical of Ford's documentaries, in contrast to his usual moral responsiveness. The picture employs open forms and a zoom lens, and spends half its length poeticizing the farewell.

1958 *Gideon's Day* (Columbia British Productions). Technicolor. 91 minutes. March 1958 (G.B.); February 1959 (U.S.). U.S. title: *Gideon of Scotland Yard.* Director: John Ford. Producer: Michael Killanin. Associate producer: Wingate Smith. Scenarist: T. E. B. Clarke, from novel by J. J. Marric (pseudonym for John Creasey). Photography: Frederick A. Young. Art director: Ken Adam. Music: Douglas Gamley. Editor: Raymond Poulton. Assistant director: Tom Pevsner. Costumes: Jack Dalmayne. Production manager: Bill Kuly. Filmed in London, September 1957. With Jack Hawkins (Inspector George Gideon), Dianne Foster (Joanna Delafield), Anna Massey (Sally Gideon), Anna Lee (Mrs. Kate Gideon), Cyril Cusack (Herbert "Birdie" Sparrow), Andrew Ray (P. C. Simon Farnaby-Green), James Hayter (Robert Mason), Ronald Howard (Paul Delafield), Howard Marion-Crawford (chief of Scotland Yard), Laurence Naismith (Arthur Sayer), Derek Bond (Det. Sgt. Eric Kirby), Griselda Harvey (Mrs. Kirby), Frank Lawton (Det. Sgt. Liggott), John Loder (Ponsford, the Duke), Doreen Madden (Miss Courtney), Miles Malleson (judge at Old Bailey), Marjorie Rhodes (Mrs. Rosie Saparelli), Michael Shepley (Sir Rupert Bellamy), Michael Trubshawe (Sgt. Golightly), Jack Watling (Rev. Julian Small), Hermione Bell (Dolly Saparelli), Donal Donnelly (Feeney), Billie Whitelaw (Christine), Malcolm Ranson (Ronnie Gideon), Mavis Ranson (Jane Gideon), Francis Crowdy (Fitzhubert), David Aylmer and Brian Smith (Manners and White-Douglas, Fitzhubert's acolytes), Barry Keegan (Riley, chauffeur), Maureen Potter (Ethel Sparrow), Henry Longhurst (Rev. Mr. Courtney), Charles Maunsell (Walker), Stuart Saunders (Chancery Lane policeman), Dervis Ward (Simmo), Joan Ingram (Lady Bellamy), Nigel Fitzgerald (Insp. Cameron), Robert Raglan (Dawson), John Warwick (Insp. Gillick), John LeMesurier (prosecuting attorney), Peter Godsell (Jimmy), Robert Bruce (defending attorney), Alan Rolfe (CID man at hospital), Derek Prentice (first employer), Alastair Hunter (second employer), Helen Goss (woman employer), Susan Richmond

(Aunt May), Raymond Rollett (Uncle Dick), Lucy Griffiths (cashier), Mary Donevan (usherette), O'Donovan Shiell, Bart Allison, Michael O'Duffy (policemen), Diana Chesney (barmaid), David Storm (court clerk), Gordon Harris (CID man).

A day in the life of a Scotland Yard detective.

1958 *The Last Hurrah* (Columbia). 121 minutes. November. Director-producer: John Ford. Scenarist: Frank Nugent, from novel by Edwin O'Connor. Photographer: Charles Lawton, Jr. Art Director: Robert Peterson. Set decorator: William Kiernan. Editor: Jack Murray. Assistant directors: Wingate Smith, Sam Nelson. With Spencer Tracy (Frank Skeffington), Jeffrey Hunter (Adam Caulfield), Dianne Foster (Maeve Caulfield), Pat O'Brien (John Gorman), Basil Rathbone (Norman Cass, Sr.), Donald Crisp (the cardinal), James Gleason (Cuke Gillen), Edward Brophy (Ditto Boland), John Carradine (Amos Force), Willis Bouchey (Roger Sugrue), Basil Ruysdael (Bishop Gardner), Ricardo Cortez (Sam Weinberg), Wallace Force (Charles J. Hennessey), Frank McHugh (Festus Garvey), Anna Lee (Gert Minihan), Jane Darwell (Delia Boylan), Frank Albertson (Jack Mangan), Charles FitzSimmons (Kevin McCluskey), Carleton Young (Mr. Winslow), Bob Sweeney (Johnny Degnan), Edmund Lowe (Johnny Byrne), William Leslie (Dan Herlihy), Ken Curtis (Monseigneur Killian), O. Z. Whitehead (Norman Cass, Jr.), Arthur Walsh (Frank Skeffington, Jr.), Helen Westcott (Mrs. McCluskey), Ruth Warren (Ellen Davin), Mimi Doyle (Mamie Burns), Dan Borzage (Pete), James Flavin (police captain), William Forrest (doctor), Frank Sully (fire chief), Charlie Sullivan (chauffeur), Ruth Clifford (nurse), Jack Pennick (policeman), Richard Deacon (Plymouth Club director), Harry Tenbrook, Eve March, Bill Henry, James Waters, Frank Baker.

An old-style politician's last campaign.

1959 *Korea: Battleground for Liberty* (U.S. Dept. of Defense). Eastmancolor. c. 40 minutes. Director: Rear Adm. John Ford, USNR. Producers: Ford, Capt. George O'Brien, USN, Ret. Filmed in and around Seoul, fall 1958. With O'Brien, Kim-Chi Mi, Choi My Ryonk.

An orientation film for American

soldiers being stationed in Korea. Cameos trace life and culture as Sgt. Cliff Walker, at first terrified, befriends a Korean family, serves on a community council, and combats prostitution with a 4H club. Speeches by Eisenhower and Rhee conclude, dissolving into bathers at a rock pool; pop musicians; Walker and Korean picnicking; DMZ lookout post. The film encourages fraternization between U.S. soldiers and Korean civilians. Ford had planned to direct additional such films on Taiwan and Vietnam, and may have consulted on their scripts.

1959 *The Horse Soldiers* (Mirisch Company–United Artists). Deluxe Color. 119 minutes. June. Director: John Ford. Producers-scenarists: John Lee Mahin, Martin Rackin, from novel by Harold Sinclair. Photography: William H. Clothier. Art director: Frank Hotaling. Set decorator: Victor Gangelin. Music: David Buttolph. Song: "I Left My Love," by Stan Jones. Editor: Jack Murray. Special effects: Augie Lohman. Costumes: Frank Beetson (M), Ann Peck (F). Assistant directors: Wingate Smith, Ray Gosnell, Jr. Filmed in Louisiana and Mississippi, October–December 1958. With John Wayne (Col. John Marlowe), William Holden (Maj. Hank Kendall), Constance Towers (Hannah Hunter), Althea Gibson (Lukey), Hoot Gibson (Brown), Anna Lee (Mrs. Buford), Russell Simpson (Sheriff Capt. Henry Goodboy), Stan Jones (Gen. U.S. Grant), Carleton Young (Col. Jonathan Miles), Basil Ruysdael (commandant, Jefferson Military Academy), Willis Bouchey (Col. Phil Secord), Ken Curtis (Wiklie), O. Z. Whitehead (Hoppy Hopkins), Judson Pratt (Sgt. Major Kirby), Denver Pyle (Jagger Jo), Strother Martin (Virgil), Hank Worden (Deacon), Walter Reed (Union officer), Jack Pennick (Sgt. Maj. Mitchell), Fred Graham (Union soldier), Chuck Hayward (Union captain), Charles Seel (Newton Station bartender), Stuart Holmes, Maj. Sam Harris (passengers to Newton Station), Richard Cutting (Gen. Sherman), Bing Russell, William Forrest, William Leslie, Bill Henry, Ron Hagherty, Dan Borzage, Fred Kennedy.

Civil War: Union cavalry raids deep within Confederate lines.

1960 *Sergeant Rutledge* (Ford Productions–Warner Brothers). Technicolor. 111 minutes.

May. Director: John Ford. Producers: Patrick Ford, Willis Goldbeck. Writers: Goldbeck, James Warner Bellah. Photography: Bert Glennon. Art director: Edie Imazu. Set decorator: Frank M. Miller. Music: Howard Jackson. Song: "Captain Buffalo," by Mark David, Jerry Livingston. Editor: Jack Murray. Assistant directors: Russ Saunders, Wingate Smith. Costumes: Marjorie Best. Filmed in Monument Valley, May–June 1959. With Jeffrey Hunter (Lt. Tom Cantrell), Constance Towers (Mary Beecher), Woody Strode (Sgt. Braxton Rutledge), Billie Burke (Mrs. Cordelia Fosgate), Juano Hernandez (Sgt. Matthew Luke Skidmore), Willis Bouchey (Col. Otis Fosgate), Carleton Young (Capt. Shattuck), Judson Pratt (Lt. Mulqueen), Bill Henry (Capt. Dwyer), Walter Reed (Capt. MacAfee), Chuck Hayward (Capt. Dickinson), Mae Marsh (Nellie), Fred Libby (Chandler Hubble), Toby Richards (Lucy Dabney), Jan Styne (Chris Hubble), Cliff Lyons (Sam Beecher), Charles Seel (Dr. Eckner), Jack Pennick (sergeant), Hank Worden (Laredo), Chuck Roberson (juror), Eva Novak, Estelle Winwood (spectators), Shug Fisher (Mr. Owens).

1880s: The trial of a Negro cavalry sergeant for rape and murder of a white girl.

1960 *The Colter Craven Story* (Revue Productions–MCA; episode for the *Wagon Train* series.) 53 minutes. May. Director: John Ford. Producer: Howard Christie. Writer: Tony Paulson. Photographer: Benjamin N. Kline. Art director: Martin Obzina. Music: Stanley Wilson. Theme tune: Jerome Morros. Set decorator: Ralph Sylos. Editors: Marston Fay, David O'Connell. Costumes: Vincent Dee. Assistant director: James H. Brown. With Ward Bond (Maj. Seth Adams), Carleton Young (Colter Craven), Frank McGrath (Chuck Wooster), Terry Wilson (Bill Hawks), John Carradine (Park), Chuck Hayward (Quentin), Ken Curtis (Kyle), Anna Lee (Alarice Craven), Cliff Lyons (Weatherby), Paul Birch (Sam Grant), Annelle Hayes (Mrs. Grant), Willis Bouchey (Jesse Grant), Mae March (Mrs. Jesse Grant), Jack Pennick (drill sergeant), Hank Worden (Shelley), Charles Seel (Mort), Bill Henry (Krindle), Chuck Roberson (Junior), Dennis Rush (Jamie), Harry Tenbrook (Shelley's friend), Beulah Blaze, Lon Chaney,' Jr., John Wayne (billed as Michael Morris) (Gen. Sherman).

The wagon train picks up Craven and

his wife. Craven is a doctor who worked through med school in a slaughter house, then graduated to Shiloh, where 500 of his patients died. Now, taken to drink, he is afraid to perform a caesarian. But Adams tells him the story of his friend Sam, who was a failure back in Wilmette, but whom he met again at Shiloh, after losing all but 19 of his 223 townsmen. But Sam (Grant) had 30,000 casualties and still overcame "defeat." Craven delivers the baby.

The episode uses footage from Ford's *Wagon Master* (on which the series was based). Only the wonderful nine-minute Wilmette flashback looks strongly Fordian, within an otherwise shoddy film.

† 1960 *The Alamo* (Batjac–United Artists). Technicolor/Todd-A.O. 192/161 minutes. October. Director-producer: John Wayne.

Ford was present for most of the shoot. His dance scene was deleted before release; then most of his dramatic scenes for the 161-min. version. Various shots remain: artillery fords a river; Harvey welcomes Wayne; Wayne meets Blind Nell; Harvey shoots Mexican as gate shuts; Santa Anna's army parades past; chapel blows up; and, perhaps, Avalon and Boone's riverbank scene.

1961 *Two Rode Together* (Ford-Sheptner Productions—Columbia). Pathecolor. 109 minutes. July. Director: John Ford. Producer: Stan Sheptner. Scenarist: Frank Nugent, from novel *Comanche Captives*, by Will Cook. Photography: Charles Lawton, Jr. Art director: Robert Peterson. Set decorator: James M. Crowe. Music: George Duning. Editor: Jack Murray. Assistant director: Wingate Smith. Costumes: Frank Beetsson. Filmed in southwest Texas, November 1960. With James Stewart (Guthrie McCabe), Richard Widmark (Lt. Jim Gary), Shirley Jones (Marty Purcell), Linda Cristal (Elena de la Madriaga), Andy Devine (Sgt. Darius P. Posey), John McIntire (Maj. Frazer), Paul Birch (Edward Purcell), Willis Bouchey (Harry J. Wringle), Henry Brandon (Quanah Parker), Harry Carey, Jr. (Ortho Clegg), Ken Curtis (Greely Clegg), Olive Carey (Abby Frazer), Chet Douglas (Ward Corbey), Annelle Hayes (Belle Aragon), David Kent (Running Wolf), Anna Lee (Mrs. Malaprop), Jeanette Nolan (Mrs. McCandless), John Qualen (Ole Knudsen), Ford Rainey (Henry Clegg),

Woody Strode (Stone Calf), O. Z. Whitehead (Lt. Chase), Cliff Lyons (William McCandless), Mae Marsh (Hannah Clegg), Frank Baker (Capt. Malaprop), Ruth Clifford (woman), Ted Knight (Lt. Upton), Maj. Sam Harris (post doctor), Jack Pennick (sergeant), Chuck Roberson (Comanche), Dan Borzage, Bill Henry, Chuck Hayward, Edward Brophy.

A cynical sheriff and a cavalry officer ride into Comanche territory to ransom white captives.

1962 *The Man Who Shot Liberty Valance* (Ford Productions– Paramount). 122 minutes. April. Director: John Ford. Producer: Willis Goldbeck. Scenarists: Goldbeck, James Warner Bellah, from story by Dorothy M. Johnson. Photography: William H. Clothier. Art directors: Hal Pereira, Eddie Imazu. Set decorators: Sam Comer, Darrell Silvera. Costumes: Edith Head. Music: Cyril J. Mockridge; theme from *Young Mr. Lincoln*, by Alfred Newman. Editor: Otho Lovering. Assistant director: Wingate Smith. Filmed in September 1961. With James Stewart (Ransom Stoddard), John Wayne (Tom Doniphon), Vera Miles (Hallie Stoddard), Lee Marvin (Liberty Valance), Edmond O'Brien (Dutton Peabody), Andy Devine (Link Appleyard), Ken Murray (Doc Willoughby), John Carradine (Starbuckle), Jeanette Nolan (Nora Ericson), John Qualen (Peter Ericson), Willis Bouchey (Jason Tully), Carleton Young (Maxwell Scott), Woody Strode (Pompey), Denver Pyle (Amos Carruthers), Strother Martin (Floyd), Lee Van Cleef (Reese), Robert F. Simon (Handy Strong), O. Z. Whitehead (Ben Carruthers), Paul Birch (Mayor Winder), Joseph Hoover (Hasbrouck), Jack Pennick (barman), Anna Lee (passenger), Charles Seel (president, election council), Shug Fisher (drunk), Earle Hodgins, Stuart Holmes, Dorothy Phillips, Buddy Roosevelt, Gertrude Astor, Eva Novak, Slim Talbot, Monty Montana, Bill Henry (credited, but not appearing, as a poker player), Frank Baker (uncredited, replacing Henry), John B. Whiteford, Helen Gibson, Maj. Sam Harris.

A senator returns to Shinbone for a pauper's funeral and tells the true story of his youth.

1962 *Flashing Spikes* (Avista Productions– Revue–MCA; episode for the *Alcoa Premiere* TV series). 53 minutes. October 4. Director: John Ford. Associate producer: Frank Baur. Scenarist: Jameson Brewer, from novel by Frank O'Rourke. Photographer: William H. Clothier. Art director: Martin Obzina. Set decorators: John McCarthy, Martin C. Bradfield. Music: Johnny Williams, Stanley Wilson. Costumes: Vincent Dee. Editors: Richard Belding, Tony Martinelli. Titles: Saul Bass. Sound editor: David J. O'Connell. Technical consultant: Cy Malis. Series host: Fred Astaire. With James Stewart (Slim Conway), Jack Warden (commissioner), Pat Wayne (Bill Riley), Edgar Buchanan (Crab Holcomb), Tige Andrews (Gaby Lasalle), Carleton Young (Rex Short), Willis Bouchey (mayor), Don Drysdale (Gomer), Stephanie Hill (Mary Riley), Charles Seel (judge), Bing Russell (Hogan), Harry Carey, Jr. (man in dugout), Vin Scully (announcer), Walter Reed (second reporter), Sally Hughes (nurse), Larry Blake (first reporter), Charles Morton (umpire), Cy Malis (the bit man), Bill Henry (commissioner's assistant), John Wayne (umpire in Korea), Art Passarella (umpire), Vern Stephens, Ralph Volkie, Earl Gilpin, Bud Harden, Whitey Campbell (baseball players).

At a hearing, columnist Short charges rookie sensation Riley took a bribe from blacklisted Slim Conway to throw a series game. In flashback, Conway recounts a semipro game in which, midst myriad wondrous cameos, a riot nearly breaks out over Conway, and Conway is spiked by Riley—who, however, apologizes. So Conway gets old pal Lasalle to give Riley a tryout; but Riley is drafted and has to go to Korea first. Then, at spring training, Conway intervenes to prevent a fight when Short insults Riley's wife. Barred from the Series stadium, he listens in the parking lot, where Short sees him hand Riley an envelope, presumably a bribe. Actually, it was a brochure of Conway's fishing place. Riley is cleared, and it turns out Conway was framed, years ago.

First rate Ford.

1962 *How the West Was Won* (Cinerama–Metro-Goldwyn-Mayer). Technicolor / Cinerama / Ultra Panavision. 162 minutes. November. Directors: John Ford ("The Civil War"), George Marshall ("The Railroad"), Henry Hathaway ("The Rivers," "The Plains," "The Outlaws"). Producer: Bernard Smith. Scenarist: James

R. Webb, suggested by series in *Life*. Art directors: George W. Davis, William Ferrari, Addison Hehr. Set decorators: Henry Grace, Don Greenwood, Jr., Jack Mills. Music: Alfred Newman, Ken Darby. Editor: Harold F. Kress. Costumes: Walter Plunkett. Cinerama supervisors: Thomas Conroy, Walter Gibbons-Fly. Historical consultant: David Miller. Special effects: A. Arnold Gillespie, Robert R. Hoag. Color consultant: Charles K. Hagedon. Narrator: Spencer Tracy.

Ford sequence ("The Civil War"): 25 minutes, 13 seconds. Photography: Joseph La Shelle. Assistant director: Wingate Smith. With George Peppard (Zeb Rawlings), Carroll Baker (Eve Prescott Rawlings), Russ Tamblyn (Confederate deserter), Claude Johnson (Jeremiah Rawlings), Andy Devine (Cpl. Peterson), Willis Bouchey (surgeon), Henry (Harry) Morgan (Gen. U. S. Grant), John Wayne (Gen. Sherman), Raymond Massey (Abraham Lincoln).

A farm boy leaves home to go to war.

1963 *Donovan's Reef* (Ford Productions–Paramount). Technicolor. 109 minutes. July. Director-producer: John Ford. Scenarists: Frank Nugent, James Edward Grant, from story by Edmond Beloin, adapted by James Michener. Photography: William Clothier. Art directors: Hal Pereira, Eddie Imazu. Set decorators: Sam Comer, Darrell Silvera. Costumes: Edith Head. Music: Cyril J. Mockridge. Editor: Otho Lovering. Assistant director: Wingate Smith. Special effects: Paul K. Lerpae, Farciot Edouart. Color consultant: Richard Mueller. Filmed on the island of Kauai (Hawaii) in the South Pacific. With John Wayne (Michael Patrick "Guns" Donovan), Lee Marvin (Thomas Aloysius "Boats" Gilhooley), Elizabeth Allen (Amelia Sarah Dedham), Jack Warden (Dr. William Dedham), Cesar Romero (Marquis André de Lage), Dorothy Lamour (Miss Lafleur), Jacqueline Malouf (Lelani Dedham), Mike Mazurki (Sgt. Menkowicz), Marcel Dalio (Fr. Cluzeot), Jon Fong (Mister Eu), Cheryline Lee (Sally Dedham), Tim Stafford (Luki Dedham), Carmen Estrabeau (Sister Gabrielle), Yvonne Peattie (Sister Matthew), Frank Baker (Captain Martin), Edgar Buchanan (Boston notary), Pat Wayne (navy lieutenant), Dan Ford, John Stafford (children), Charles Seel (Grand Uncle

Sedley Atterbury), Chuck Roberson
(Festus), Mae Marsh, Maj. Sam Harris
(members of family council), Dick
Foran, Cliff Lyons (officers), and Ford's
ketch, *Araner*.

A comedy of manners—and racism—
on a South Pacific isle.

1964 *Cheyenne Autumn* (Ford-Smith
Productions–Warner Brothers).
Technicolor / Panavision 70. 159 minutes.
October. Director: John Ford. Producer:
Bernard Smith. Scenarists: James R. Webb
and (uncredited) Patrick Ford, from book
by Mari Sandoz. Photography: William
Clothier. Art director: Richard Day. Set
decorator: Darrell Silvera. Associate
director: Ray Kellogg. Music: Alex North.
Editor: Otho Lovering. Sound editor:
Francis E. Stahl. Assistant directors:
Wingate Smith, Russ Saunders. Technical
consultant: David H. Miller. Filmed in
Monument Valley; Moab, Utah; Gunnison,
Colorado, October–December 1963. With
Richard Widmark (Capt. Thomas Archer),
Carroll Baker (Deborah Wright), James
Stewart (Wyatt Earp), Edward G.
Robinson (Secretary of the Interior Carl
Schurz), Karl Malden (Capt. Wessels), Sal
Mineo (Red Shirt), Dolores Del Rio
(Spanish woman), Ricardo Montalban
(Little Wolf), Gilbert Roland (Dull Knife),
Arthur Kennedy (Doc Holliday), Patrick
Wayne (2nd Lt. Scott), Elizabeth Allen
(Guinevere Plantagenet), John Carradine
(Maj. Jeff Blair), Victor Jory (Tall Tree),
Mike Mazurki (Top Sgt. Stanislaw
Wichowsky), George O'Brien (Maj.
Braden), Sean McClory (Dr. O'Carberry),
Judson Pratt (Maj. "Dog" Kelly), Carmen
D'Antonio (Pawnee woman), Ken Curtis
(Joe), Walter Baldwin (Jeremy Wright),
Shug Fisher (Skinny), Nancy Hsueh (Little
Bird), Chuck Roberson (platoon sergeant),
Harry Carey, Jr. (Trooper Smith), Ben
Johnson (Trooper Plumtree), Jimmy
O'Hara (trooper), Chuck Hayward
(trooper), Lee Bradley (Cheyenne), Walter
Reed (Lt. Peterson), Willis Bouchey
(colonel), Carleton Young (aide to Carl
Schurz), Denver Pyle (Senator Henry),
John Qualen (Svenson), Nanomba
"Moonbeam" Morton (Running Deer),
Dan Borzage, Dean Smith, David H.
Miller, Bing Russell (troopers). Narrators:
Spencer Tracy, Richard Widmark.
Working title: "The Long Flight."

Two-hundred-eighty-five Cheyenne
flee a reservation to go back home.

†1965 *Young Cassidy* (Sextant Films–
Metro-Goldwyn-Mayer). Technicolor. 110
minutes. March. Directors: Jack Cardiff,
John Ford. "A John Ford Film." Producers:
Robert D. Graff, Robert Emmett Ginna.
Associate producer: Michael Killanin.
Scenarist: John Whiting, from autobio-
graphy *Mirror in My House*, by Sean
O'Casey. Photography: Ted Scaife. Art
director: Michael Stringer. Costumes:
Margaret Furse. Music: Sean O'Riada.
Editor: Anne V. Coates. Production
manager: Teddy Joseph. Assistant director:
John Quested. Titles: Maurice Binder.
Casting: Miriam Brickman. Technical
consultant (for teaching Rod Taylor a
Dublin accent): Jack McGowan. Camera:
Jack Atchelor. Filmed in Ireland in July.
With Rod Taylor (Sean Cassidy), Maggie
Smith (Nora), Julie Christie (Daisy
Battles), Flora Robson (Mrs. Cassidy), Sian
Phillips (Ella), Michael Redgrave (William
Butler Yeats), Dame Edith Evans (Lady
Gregory), Jack McGowan (Archie), T. P.
McKenna (Tom), Julie Ross (Sara), Robin
Sumner (Michael), Philip O'Flynn
(Mick Mullen), Pauline Delaney (Bessie
Ballynoy), Arthur O'Sullivan (foreman),
Tom Irwin (constable), John Cowley
(barman), William Foley (publisher's clerk),
John Franklyn (bank teller), Harry Brogan
(Murphy), James Fitzgerlad (Charlie
Ballynoy), Donald Donnelly (undertaker's
man), Harold Goldblatt (director of Abbey
Theatre), Ronald Ibbs (theatre employee),
May Craig, May Cluskey (women in the
hall), Tom Irwin, Shivaun O'Casey, and
members of the Abbey Theatre.

Young Sean O'Casey in Dublin: his
romances, his mother's death, his first
production.

Ford prepared script, cast, and locations, but fell sick after two weeks'
shooting, which included the scene with
Daisy Battles (but the close-ups were
added later by Cardiff); the opening scene
when Cassidy becomes a laborer; the inn
scene with the three sons and football
players; some scenes with Mrs. Cassidy; a
scene with Rod Taylor and the tree in
bloom after his mother's death—about ten
minutes in total. The script seems poor,
but Ford scripts rely for sense on his direction. The key Nora-Cassidy relationship
lacks motivation, and boring monotonality
has replaced Ford's intense changefulness.
Only the inn scene has spontaneity and
economy.

1965 *7 Women* (Ford-Smith Productions–
Metro-Goldwyn-Mayer). Metrocolor /
anamorphic Panavision. 86 minutes.
November. Director: John Ford. Producer:
Bernard Smith. Scenarists: Janet Green,
John McCormick, from story "Chinese
Finale," by Norah Lofts. Photography:
Joseph LaShelle. Art directors: George W.
Davis, Eddie Imazu. Set directors: Henry
Grace, Jack Mills. Costumes: Walter
Plunkett. Music: Elmer Bernstein. Editor:
Otho S. Lovering. Assistant director:
Wingate Smith. Production manager: Rex
Bailey. Special effects: J. McMillan
Johnson. Filmed in February–April. With
Anne Bancroft (Dr. D. R. Cartwright),
Margaret Leighton (Agatha Andrews),
Flora Robson (Miss Binns), Sue Lyon
(Emma Clark), Mildred Dunnock (Jane
Argent), Betty Field (Florrie Pether), Anna
Lee (Mrs. Russell), Eddie Albert (Charles
Pether), Mike Mazurki (Tunga Khan),
Woody Strode (Lean Warrior), Jane Chang
(Miss Ling), Hans William Lee (Kim),
H. W. Gim (coolie), Irene Tsu (Chinese
girl).

1935 China: women missionaries
encounter plague and bandits.

Anne Bancroft replaced Patricia Neal
when the latter became ill after three days'
shooting. Prints released for television
include additional scenes.

† 1972 *Vietnam! Vietnam!* (Ford
Production–USIA). Eastmancolor. 58
minutes. September 1971. Director:
Sherman Beck. Executive producer: John
Ford. Producer: Bruce Herschensohn.
Scenario: Thomas Duggan, Ford. Editor:
Leon Selditz. Location photography:
Vietnam, October–December 1968.
Narrator: Charlton Heston.

Although Ford went to Vietnam, he did
not participate in production, nor does the
zoom work, rack-focusing, or light texture
suggest Ford. But subsequently Ford
supervised the editing and rewrote the
scenario. Although longer and costlier
($252,751) than any other USIA production,
its interpretation of the war had become

embarrassing by the time of its release,
and, after a few overseas showings in U.S.
Information Agency libraries and cultural
offices, it was withdrawn from circulation.

Its prologue is a montage of stills of
some fifty 1960s headliners (Koufax, the
Beatles, the pill, etc.), ending with
Vietnam. Part 1 explores the country's
background, culture, and the war. Shots of
refugees, mutilated children, burnt bodies
of babies, sobbing women, mass graves.
"To those in command of North Vietnam
and the Vietcong the pursuit was a united
Vietnam under Hanoi with a Communist
government. To those in South Vietnam
the pursuit was to be left alone." POW
wives describe their efforts for information; the USSR's involvement is shown;
American "End the War" demonstrators
parade with North Vietnamese flags. In
Part 2, cameos of a couple of dozen people
debate the war: Rush, Reagan, Johnson,
McCarthy, U.S. soldiers, Fulbright, Sam
Brown, hippies, a Hungarian freedom
fighter. Vietnamese parade at night with
7-Up–can torches, people singing hymns.
"The flames were still bright on December
31, 1969, but if that fire would be a permanent light of freedom or would be
extinguished was not to be known within
the decade."

1976 *Chesty* (James Ellsworth Productions).
28 minutes. April 4. Director: John Ford.
Producer: James Ellsworth. Writer: Jay
Simms. Photography: Brick Marquard.
Music: Jack Marshall. Editor–associate
producer: Leon Selditz. Assistant to
producer: Charles C. Townsend. Filmed
August 1968–April 1970. First public
showing at Filmex, Los Angeles.
Unreleased. Host: John Wayne.

A documentary about Lt. Gen. Lewis
"Chesty" Puller, USMC. Made for TV,
but never sold or released. Originally
sixty minutes, but shortened to encourage
sale. Ford is said to have preferred the
shorter version.

Unrealized Projects (among many)

1926 *Corncob Kelly's Romance,* story by
Peter B. Kyne.

1928 *Blockade,* story by Berthold Viertel.

1928 *Captain Lash.* A Mississippi
riverboat story to star Victor McLaglen.

1928 *Frozen Justice,* an Alaskan saga
which Murnau lost to Ford and neither
made.

1940 *Four Sons.* A remake.

1941 *The African Queen.*

1943 *The Last Outlaw.* A remake of Ford's 1919 two-reeler and Cabanne's 1936 feature, to star Harry Carey, for Republic Pictures.

1947 *The Family.* A White Russian family exiled to China after the revolution, from Nina Federova's 1940 novel, with John Wayne and Ethel Barrymore, for Argosy.

1947 *Janitzio.* To be made in Mexico, after *The Fugitive,* by Argosy.

1952 *Famine,* story by Liam O'Flaherty, for Four Provinces in Ireland.

1952 *Demi-Gods,* story by James Stephen, for Four Provinces in Ireland.

1952 *Seven Pillars of Wisdom,* by T. E. Lawrence.

1952 *Two-Headed Spy,* to be filmed in Germany with Kirk Douglas; at Douglas's initiation. Filmed in 1958 in England by André de Toth with Jack Hawkins.

1952 "Ghost Story," an episode for *The Rising of the Moon,* with Katharine Hepburn.

1956 *The Judge and the Hangman,* a mystery, to be filmed in Munich and ski country in the Alps, with Spencer Tracy or John Wayne.

1956 *Drama of Inish,* aka *Is Life Worth Living,* story by Lennox Robinson, for Four Provinces, in Ireland, with Katharine Hepburn.

1956 *The Valiant Virginians,* by James Warner Bellah, to be made for C. V. Whitney, at first as a trilogy of three features, then as a single film; with John Wayne.

1960 *The White Company,* by Sir Arthur Conan Doyle. A youth goes to fight in France during the Hundred Years War. John Wayne, Laurence Olivier, Alec Guinness, Susan Hampshire. Negotiations were carried on for nearly ten years and filming almost took place in Spain, for Samuel Bronston Productions, but Doyle's estate demanded colossally unreasonable sums for the literary rights: $100,000 plus 25 percent of producer's net at one point; $200,000 flat at another. Ford was still talking about doing it in the 1970s.

1962 *A Scout for Custer,* by Willis Goldbeck and John Ford. The story, both comic and tragic, of General Custer's younger brother Tom's stubborn and repeated attempts to bring common sense into the general's reckless campaigning. A story of gallant failure of a man who was brave without conviction in what he was attempting.

1964 *Rupert of Hentzau,* a project promoted by David Selznick for Jennifer Jones.

1965 *The Miracle of Merriford,* aka *Trumpets over Merriford.* A small English town's church is damaged during World War II by Americans, who then try to raise money for repairs. A comedy in the vein of *The Quiet Man,* from a novel by Reginald Arkell. Ford had signed with Metro, Dan Dailey had been cast, and the script by Willis Goldbeck and James Warner Bellah was completed, when Metro shelved the project barely a week before filming was to begin in Utah.

1967 *April Morning.* A boy's family during the battles of Lexington and Concord. From novel by Howard Fast. Scripted by Michael Wilson, to have been produced by Samuel Goldwyn, Jr.

1967 *OSS.* The story of Maj. Gen. William J. "Wild Bill" Donovan and the intelligence agency during World War II. With John Wayne.

1969 *Valley Forge.* To have been co-produced with Frank Capra.

1970? *Comanche Stallion.* A stallion, stolen from Apache and believed by them to be a god who will restore their greatness, tramples to death the son of a drunk cavalry officer, who vows to capture and torture it, but fails.

1973 *The Josh Clayton Story.* About the first black to graduate from West Point. With Fred Williamson. Alternate title: "Appointment with Precedence."

Radio and Television Appearances

1957 *This Is Your Life.* Appeared on Ralph Edwards's television show devoted to Maureen O'Hara.

1958 *Wide Wide World.* Appeared on television June 8, to promote *Horse Soldiers.*

1962 *The Unreal West.* CBC Radio (Toronto). Producer: Jack Vance. Scenarist-narrator: Tony Thomas. Broadcast: July 25. 60 minutes. Interviews with Richard Boone, John Wayne, Olive Stokes Mix (a Cherokee, and Tom Mix's widow), Randolph Scott, Tom McCoy, Johnny Mack Brown, Yakima Canutt, John Ford.

1966 *John Ford,* in the ORTF (Paris) *Cinéastes de notre temps* series. A lengthy interview broadcast June 16.

1973 *American Film Institute First Annual Life Achievement Award* (CBS). Producer: George Stevens, Jr. Taped March 31, broadcast April 2. President Richard Nixon presented Ford with the Civilian Medal of Honor and promoted him to admiral. John Wayne, Maureen O'Hara, Danny Kae, Jack Lemmon, and others.

Films about Ford

1971 *Directed by John Ford* (California Arts Commission–AFI). Color. Director-writer-interviewer: Peter Bogdanovich. Producers: George Stevens, Jr., James R. Silke. Interview photography: Laszlo Kovacs, Gregory Sandor, Brick Marquard, Eric Sherman. Editor: Richard Patterson. Assistant: Mae Woods. Associate producer: David Shepard. Narrator: Orson Welles. First shown: Thirty-second Venice Film Festival, September 15, Ford present to receive festival award. With Ford, John Wayne, Henry Fonda, James Stewart.

Interviews with actors and brief glimpses of Ford; most of the picture consumes excerpts from twenty-seven Ford films.

1971 *The American West of John Ford* (Group One–Timex–CBX). Director: Denis Sanders. Executive producer: Bob Banner. Producers: Tom Egan, Britt Lomond, Dan Ford. Writer: David H. Vowell. Photographer: Bob Collins.

Editor: Keith Olson. Broadcast December 5. With Ford, John Wayne, James Stewart, Henry Fonda.

According to Bogdanovich, this documentary includes clips from Ford westerns, interviews with Stewart and Fonda at Ford's home, with Wayne in Monument Valley directing a stunt, and material with Fonda overlooking the old Fox lot in Century City.

1974 *John Ford: Memorial Day 1970.* Director-writer-editor: Mark Haggard. Producers: Haggard, Paul Magwood, Lowell Peterson. Photographer: Douglas Knapp. Narrator: Linda Strawn. 12 minutes. First shown: April. With John Ford, Walter Pidgeon, Anna Lee, Harry Carey, Jr., Olive Carey, Dan Borzage, Dick Amador, Meta Sterne, George Bagnall, Ray Kellogg, Mary Ford, Wingate Smith.

Members of Ford's field unit at twenty-fourth Annual Memorial Day Service at the Motion Picture Country Home in Woodland Hills, California.

Selected Bibliography

Titles preceded by an asterisk have been found particularly valuable.

BOOKS AND ARTICLES

Ager, Cecilia. "Then and Now." *The New York Times Magazine*, September 20, 1959, p. 62. An interview with Ford and Hoot Gibson.
*Anderson, Lindsay. *About John Ford*. London: Plexus, 1981. Contains reprints of interviews, letters, and articles previously published in *Sequence* and *Cinema*, plus new material.
Astor, Mary. *A Life on Film*. New York: Dell, 1972.
Baby, Yvonne. "John Ford à Paris." *Le Monde*, September 16, 1966.
*Balshofer, Fred C., and Arthur Miller. *One Reel a Week*. Berkeley: University of California Press, 1967.
Baroncelli, Jean de. "Avec Alfred Hitchcock et John Ford." *Le Monde*, January 7, 1955.
Baxter, John. *The Cinema of John Ford*. New York: A. S. Barnes, 1971.
Behlmer, Rudy. "Merian C. Cooper." *Films in Review*, January 1966, pp. 17–35.
Berggen, Noel. "Arsenic and Old Directors." *Esquire*, April 1972, p. 135.

Bogdanovich, Peter. "The Autumn of John Ford." *Esquire*, April 1964, pp. 102–7, 144–45. Expanded version in Bogdanovich, *Pieces of Time*. New York: Arbor House, 1973, pp. 172–93.

*———. *John Ford*. 2d ed. Berkeley: University of California Press, 1978.

Browne, Nick. "The Spectator-in-the-Text: The Rhetoric of Stagecoach." *Film Quarterly*, Winter 1975, pp. 26–38.

Calum, Per, ed. *John Ford: En Dokumentation*. Copenhagen: Dankse Filmmuseum, 1968.

Capozzi, George, Jr. *The John Wayne Story*. New Rochelle, N. Y.: Arlington, 1972.

Comolli, Jean-Louis. "Ford et forme." *Cahiers du Cinéma* 183 (October 1966), p. 54.

Corliss, Richard. "Dudley Nichols" and "Frank Nugent." In *Talking Pictures*. Woodstock, Conn.: Overlook, 1974, pp. 225–35, 330–35.

Delahaye, Michel. "De John Ford à Sean O'Feeney, jalons et repères." *Cahiers du Cinéma* 183 (October 1966), pp. 55–59.

Dempsey, Michael. "John Ford: A Reassessment." *Film Quarterly*, Summer 1975, pp. 2–15. An anti-Ford diatribe.

Dunne, Philip. *Take Two: A Life in Movies and Politics*. New York: McGraw-Hill, 1980.

Eisenburg, Emanuel. Interview with Ford. *New Theater*, April 1936, p. 18.

Ericson, Peter. "Recent Works of John Ford." *Sequence* 2 (Winter 1947), pp. 18–25.

Everett, Eldon K. "The Great Grace Cunard—Francis Ford Mystery." *Classic Film Collector*, Summer 1973, pp. 22–25.

Everson, William K. "Forgotten Ford." *Focus on Film*, Spring 1971, pp. 13–19.

Eyman, Scott. Interview with William Clothier. *Take One* 4, no. 8, (November–December 1973 [published March 1975]), pp. 8–14.

Ferrini, Franco. *John Ford*. Florence: La Nuova Italia, 1974.

*Ford, Dan. *Pappy: The Life of John Ford*. Englewood Cliffs, N. J.: Prentice-Hall, 1979.

*Ford, John. "Veteran Producer Muses." *The New York Times*, June 10, 1928, sec. 8, p. 4. Reprinted in *Hollywood Directors 1914–1940*, by Richard Koszarski, New York: Oxford University Press, 1976, p. 198–201.

———. "Forward." In *The Name Above the Title*, by Frank Capra, New York: Macmillan, 1971. Actually ghost-written, but with Ford's collaboration, by Katherine Clifton.

———. John Ford Presents: *Cowboy Kings of Western Fame: John Ford Series of Famous Western Stars*. Western Series, 1973. $120 collection of 11 × 16 reproductions of templates by artist Will Williams.

———. "Il mio amico John Wayne," *Bis* 4, no. 33, August 18, 1951, p. 15. (No English language source is known for this 1500 word Italian article, lacking detail, in praise of John Wayne.)

"Francis Ford." *Universal Weekly*, December 20, 1913, p. 4.

"Francis Ford Expresses His Ideas on Serials." *Moving Picture World*, August 16, 1919, p. 998.

Gallagher, Tag. "Brother Feeney." *Film Comment*, November 1976, pp. 12–18. Reprinted with changes and a Francis Ford filmography, in *Griffithiana*, edited by Paolo Cherchi Usai and Livio Iacob, "Thomas Ince: Il Profeta del Western," special edition (Genoa, Italy), year 7, nos. 18–21, October 1984, pp. 59–72 and (filmography) 205–20.

Gussow, Mel. *Don't Say Yes Until I Finish Talking.* New York: Pocket Books, 1972.

Haber, Joyce. "If I Could Film a Dream . . . ." *Philadelphia Inquirer*, May 13, 1972. Ford muses about the White Company.

Haggard, Mark. "Ford in Person." *Focus on Film* 6 (Spring 1971), pp. 31–37. Ford at the University of Southern California, March 1969 and February 1970.

Haudiquet, Philippe. "En bavardant avec John Ford." *Les lettres françaises*, July 21, 1966.

———. *John Ford.* Paris: Seghers, 1966.

Hopper, Hedda. Unpublished conversation with Ford, April 13, 1962. Library of Academy of Motion Picture Arts and Sciences, Beverly Hills.

Humphrey, Hal. "Veteran John Ford Looks Back." *Philadelphia Bulletin*, April 11, 1965.

"An Interview with John Ford." *Focus!*, October 1969, pp. 3–4. Ford at the University of Chicago.

*Jenkinson, Philip. Unreleased filmed interview with Ford, 1969.

———. "John Ford Talks to Philip Jenkinson About Not Being Interested in Movies." *The Listener*, February 12, 1970, pp. 217–18. Excerpts from the filmed interview.

Jensen, Paul. "Dudley Nichols." In *The Hollywood Screenwriters*, edited by Richard Corliss. New York: Avon, 1972, pp. 107–24.

Johnson, Grady. "A Paean of Economy." *The New York Times*, June 27, 1948, sec. 2, p. 4.

Kay, Karyn, and Gerald Peary. "Talking to Pat O'Brien." *Velvet Light Trap* 15 (Fall 1975), pp. 29–32.

Kennedy, Burt. "Burt Kennedy Interviews John Ford." *Action*, August 1968. Reprinted in *Directors in Action*, edited by Bob Thomas. New York: Bobbs Merrill, 1973, pp. 133–37.

Kezich, Tullio. *John Ford.* Parma: Guanda, 1958.

Killanin, Michael. "Poet in an Iron Mask." *Films and Filming*, February 1958, pp. 9–10. A conversation with Ford.

Lachize, Samuel. "Brève rencontre avec John Ford." *Cinéma 61* (February 1961).

Lahue, Kalton C. *Continued Next Week: A History of the Moving Picture Serial.* Oklahoma City: University of Oklahoma, 1964.

———. "Grace Cunard," In *Ladies in Distress.* New York: A. S. Barnes, 1973, pp. 52–61.

Leguèbe, Eric, "John Ford." In *Le Cinéma Americain par ses auteurs.* Paris: Guy Authier, 1977 , pp. 71–81.

Libby, Bill. "The Old Wrangler Rides Again." *Cosmopolitan*, March 1964, pp. 12–21. Ford on the western.

McBride, Joseph. "County Mayo Go Bragh." *Sight and Sound*, Winter 1970–71, pp. 43–44, 52. Interview with Ford.

———. "Bringing in the Sheaves." *Sight and Sound*, Winter 1973–74, pp. 9–11. Ford's funeral.

McBride, Joseph, and Gerald Peary. Interview with Howard Hawks. *Film Comment*, May 1974, pp. 44–53.

McBride, Joseph, and Michael Wilmington. *John Ford.* New York: Da Capo, 1975.

McHenry, William. "Her Grace and Francis I: The Royal Pair of Photo-Melodrama." *Motion Picture Photoplay*, January 1916.

McInerney, Joe. "John Wayne Talks Tough." *Film Comment*, September 1972, pp. 52–55.

McInroy, Patrick. "Hollywood Ruined S. A. Filming." *San Antonio Light*, May 30, 1976, Today section, pp. 1–2.

Madsen, Axel. Interview with Ford. *Cahiers du Cinéma* 168 (July 1965), p. 79.

*———. Interview with Ford. *Cahiers du Cinéma* 183 (October 1966), pp. 38–53.

Malthête-Méliès, Madeleine. *Méliès l'enchanteur*. Paris: Hachette, 1973.

Maltin, Leonard. *The Art of the Cinematographer*. New York: Dover, 1978.

*Mitchell, George J. "Ford on Ford." *Films in Review*, June 1964, pp. 321–32. Ford at a University of California, Los Angeles, tribute.

Mitry, Jean. *John Ford*. Paris: Editions Universitaires, 1954.

———. Interview with Ford. *Cahiers du Cinéma* 45 (March 1955), pp. 3–9. Abridged translation in *Interviews with Film Directors*, edited by Andrew Sarris. New York: Avon, 1969, pp. 193–201.

———. *Histoire du cinéma*. vols. 1–3. Paris: Editions Universitaires, n.d. (c. 1968).

Motte, Michele. "Le Vieux John Ford parle du western." *Paris-Presse*, July 12, 1966.

Murphy, William T. "John Ford and the Wartime Documentary." *Film and History*, February 1976, pp. 1–8.

Nichols, Dudley. "The Writer and the Film." In *Film: A Montage of Theories*, edited by Richard Dyer McCann. New York: Dutton, 1966, pp. 73–87.

Nugent, Frank S. "In Remembrance of Hot-Foots Past." *The New York Times*, March 3, 1949, p. 33.

*———. "Hollywood's Favorite Rebel." *The Saturday Evening Post*, September 23, 1949, pp. 26, 96–98.

———. "Eire Happily Revisited." *The New York Times*, July 14, 1957, sec. 2, p. 5.

Parrish, Robert. "De Chaplin à Fuller." *Cahiers du Cinéma* 142 (April 1963), pp. 1–16.

———. "Témoignage sur John Ford." *Présence du Cinéma* 21 (March 1965), pp. 18–20.

*———. *Growing Up in Hollywood*. New York: Harcourt Brace Jovanovich, 1976.

Philippe, Claude-Jean. "John Ford en chair et en os." *Télérama*, July 31, 1966.

Place, J. A. *The Western Films of John Ford*. New York: Citadel, 1975.

———. *The Non-Western Films of John Ford*. New York: Citadel, 1979.

Reed, Joseph W. *Three American Originals: John Ford, William Faulkner, and Charles Ives*. Middletown, Conn.: Wesleyan University Press, 1984. Excellent critical treatment of Ford's later films.

Rieupeyront, Jean-Louis. "Rencontre avec John Ford." *Cinéma 61* (February 1961).

Roy, Jean. *Pour John Ford*. Paris: Editions du Cerf, 1977.

Sarris, Andrew. "John Ford." In *The American Cinema*. New York: Dutton, 1968, pp. 43–49.

———. *The John Ford Movie Mystery*. Bloomington: Indiana University Press, 1976.

Schickel, Richard. "Good Days, Good Years." *Harper's*, October 1970, p. 46.

*Sharpe, Howard. "The Star Creators of Hollywood." *Photoplay*, October 1936, pp. 15, 98–100. Reprinted in *The Talkies*, edited by Richard Griffith. New York: Dover, 1971; pp. 116, 167, 333–37.

*Sinclair, Andrew. *John Ford: A Biography*. New York: Dial, 1979.

"Six Pioneers." *Action*, November 1972; pp. 17–18. John Ford at Directors Guild theater.

*Slide, Anthony, and June Banker. Unpublished interview with Mary Ford, 1970.

*Slide, Anthony, and Robert Gitt. "Frank Baker." Unpublished interview, July 30, 1977. Sponsored by the Archival Acquisitions Program of the Los Angeles Film and Television Study Group.

Tavernier, Bertrand. "La Chevauchée de Sganarelle." *Présence du Cinéma* 21 (March 1965), pp. 1–6.

*_____. "John Ford à Paris." *Positif* 82 (March 1967), pp. 7–22. An interview.

Tavernier, Claudine. "Le 4ème dimension de la vieillesse." *Cinéma* 69. (June 1969).

Wagner, Walter. "John Ford." In *You Must Remember This*. New York: Putnam's, 1975, pp. 55–65.

*Wilkinson, James L. *An Introduction to the Career and Films of John Ford*. Unpublished M.A. thesis, University of California, Los Angeles, August 1960. Microfilm copy, Library and Museum of the Performing Arts, Lincoln Center, New York.

Willis, Richard. "Francis Ford: A Director with a Heart." *Motion Picture Magazine*, February 1915, p. 112.

_____. "Francis Ford of the Gold Seal Company." *Motion Picture Magazine*, June 1915, pp. 101–4.

Young, Colin. "The Old Dependables." *Film Quarterly*, Fall 1969, pp. 2–17.

Zolotow, Maurice. *Shooting Star: A Biography of John Wayne*. New York: Simon & Schuster, 1974.

REVIEWS AND ARTICLES ON PARTICULAR PICTURES

In order of film chronology.

Hangman's House (1928)
Beaton, Cecil. *Film Spectator*, May 12, 1928, pp. 5–7.

Riley the Cop (1928)
Beaton, Cecil. *Film Spectator*, November 3, 1928, p. 10; November 10, 1928, pp. 6–7.

Doctor Bull (1933), *Judge Priest* (1934), and *Steamboat Round the Bend* (1935)
Rollins, Peter C. "Will Rogers and the Relevance of Nostalgia: *Steamboat Round the Bend*." In John E. O'Connor and Martin Jackson, eds., *American History / American Film*. New York: Ungar, 1979, pp. 77–96.

Rubin, Martin. *Film Comment*, January 1974, pp. 54–57.

Submarine Patrol (1938)
Nugent, Frank S. *The New York Times*, November 19, 1938, p. 9.

Stagecoach (1939)
Anobile, Richard, ed. *Stagecoach*. New York: Avon, 1974. A shot-by-shot series of frame blow-ups.

Interviews with Ford, Wayne, Trevor, Canutt, Smith, Reynolds, Spencer, Devine, Plunkett, Carradine. Articles by A. Sarris and A. Knight. In *Directors in Action*, edited by Bob Thomas. New York: Bobbs Merrill, 1973, pp. 140–73.

Young Mr. Lincoln (1939)

Brewster, Ben. "Notes on the Text 'John Ford's *Young Mr. Lincoln.*'" *Screen,*
Autumn 1972, pp. 29–41. A critique of the *Cahiers* article below.

Editors of *Cahiers du Cinéma*. "John Ford's *Young Mr. Lincoln.*" *Cahiers du
Cinéma* 223 (August 1970), pp. 29–47. Translation by Helene Lackner and Diana
Matias in *Screen,* Autumn 1972, pp. 5–28. Reprinted in *Film Theory and
Criticism,* edited by Gerald Mast and Marshall Cohen. 2d ed. New York: Oxford
University Press, 1979, pp. 778–831.

Eisenstein, Sergei. "Mister Lincoln par Mister Ford." *Positif* 74 (March 1966), pp.
74–83. French translation of article written in 1945.

Fluck, von Winfried, ed. *Young Mr. Lincoln —der Text der Cahiers du Cinéma und
der Film von John Ford: Ergebnisse und Materialien eines Seminars.* Berlin: J. F.
Kennedy-Institut für Nordamerikastudien, Freie Universität Berlin, 1978.

The Grapes of Wrath (1940)

Bluestone, George. *Novels into Film.* Baltimore: Johns Hopkins Press, 1957.

French, Warren. *Filmguide to "The Grapes of Wrath."* Bloomington: Indiana
University Press, 1973.

Semple, Tom. *Screenwriter: The Life and Times of Nunnally Johnson.* New York:
A. S. Barnes, 1980.

The Long Voyage Home (1940)

Friday, August 9, 1940. Ford on the film.

My Darling Clementine (1946)

Lyons, Robert, ed. *My Darling Clementine* [script]. New Brunswick, NJ: Rutgers
University Press, 1984.

The Searchers (1956)

Arizona Highways, April 1956. Feature story on production.

Cahiers du Cinéma 63 (November 1956), p. 61. Anonymous unfavorable three-line
review.

The Searchers: Materials and Approaches," special number of *Screen Educator,* 17
(Winter 1975–76). (Contents: John Caughie, "Teaching through Authorship," pp.
3–13; David Lusted, "*The Searchers* and the Study of the Image," pp. 14–26;
Tom Ryall, "Teaching Through Genre," pp. 27–33; Douglas Pye, "*The Searchers*
and Teaching the Industry," pp. 34–48; Edward Buscombe, "Critics and *The
Searchers,*" pp. 49–51; Alan Lovell, "*The Searchers* and the Pleasure Principle,"
pp. 52–57.) Brian Henderson, *Film Quarterly* (Winter, 1980–81).

Gideon's Day (1958)

Marcorelles, Louis. *Cahiers du Cinéma* 85 (September 1958), p. 54.

The Horse Soldiers (1959)

Marcorelles, Louis. *Cahiers du Cinéma* 101 (November 1959), pp. 46–49.

Robinson, David. *Sight and Sound,* Winter 1959–60, p. 36.

Sergeant Rutledge (1960)

Givray, Claude de. *Cahiers du Cinéma* 114 (December 1960), pp. 63–64.

How the West Was Won (1962)

Fieschi, Jean-André. *Cahiers du Cinéma* 148 (October 1963), pp. 58–60.

Cheyenne Autumn (**1964**)
Comolli, Jean-Louis, *Cahiers du Cinéma* 164 (March 1965), p. 75.

7 Women (**1965**)
Aprà, Adriano. *Cinema e Film* (Rome) 1 (Winter 1966–67), pp. 139–43.
Clipping from *New York Morning Telegraph*, 1966. *7 Women* file, Library and
  Museum of the Performing Arts, Lincoln Center, New York.
Comolli, Jean-Louis. *Cahiers du Cinéma* 182 (September 1966), pp. 14–20.
Knight, Arthur. *Saturday Review*, January 8, 1966, p. 97.
Narboni, Jean. *Cahiers du Cinéma* 182 (September 1966), pp. 20–24.
Pressbook. Theater collection, Free Library of Philadelphia.

Vietnam! Vietnam! (**1972**)
McBride, Joseph. "Drums Along the Mekong." *Sight and Sound*, Autumn 1972,
  pp. 213–16.
Morgenstern, Joseph. *Newsweek*, May 15, 1972, p. 38.

Chesty (**1976**)
McBride, Joseph. *Variety*, December 26, 1974, p. 13.

FILMOGRAPHIES

Bogdanovich, Peter. In *John Ford*. 2d ed. Berkeley: University of California Press,
  1976, pp. 113–49.
Brion, Patrick. In *Cahiers du Cinéma* 183 (October 1966), pp. 60–70.
Mitchell, George J. In *Films in Review*, March 1963, pp. 129–45.

COLLECTIONS

John Ford issues

Cahiers du Cinéma 183 (October 1966). John Ford issue.
Cinema & Cinema (Florence) 31 (April–June, 1982). John Ford issue.
Cult Movie (Florence) 9/10 (April–July 1982). John Ford issue.
Filmkritik 181 (January 1972). John Ford issue.
Focus on Film 6 (Spring 1971). John Ford issue.
Presénce du Cinéma 21 (March 1965). John Ford issue.
Velvet Light Trap 2 (August 1971). John Ford issue.
Wide Angle 2, no. 4 (1978). John Ford issue.

Journal runs

Exhibitors' Trade Review (*Motion Picture Daily*), 1916– .
Film Index, 1907–11.
Motion Picture (*Story*) *Magazine*, 1911– .
Motion Picture News, 1909– .
Motography, 1909– .
Moving Picture World (Herald), 1907– .
Photoplay, 1913– .
Universal Weekly (*Moving Picture Weekly*), 1913– .

Library collections

Clipping collections. Free Library of Philadelphia Theater Collection.
Clipping collections. Library of the Academy of Motion Picture Arts and Sciences, Beverly Hills.
Clipping collections. Library and Museum of the Performing Arts, Lincoln Center, New York.
John Ford Papers. Lilly Library, Indiana University.

Author's interviews

Interviews with Frank Baker, Olive Carey, Harry Carey, Jr., Ruth Clifford, Cecil McLean de Prida, Barbara Ford, Anna Lee, George O'Brien, Leon Selditz, John Stafford. March–May, 1979.

Index

An asterisk after a subject entry indicates a character from a film.
Boldface type used for a subject entry indicates a theme or motif in Ford's pictures.
Boldface type used for a page reference indicates the principal discussion.